THIRD EDITION

World Politics

Interests, Interactions, Institutions

THIRD EDITION

World Politics

Interests, Interactions, Institutions

Jeffry A. Frieden

Harvard University

David A. Lake

University of California, San Diego

Kenneth A. Schultz

Stanford University

W. W. Norton & Company

New York • London

W. W. Norton & Company has been independent since its founding in 1923, when William Warder Norton and Mary D. Herter Norton first published lectures delivered at the People's Institute, the adult education division of New York City's Cooper Union. The firm soon expanded its program beyond the Institute, publishing books by celebrated academics from America and abroad. By midcentury, the two major pillars of Norton's publishing program—trade books and college texts—were firmly established. In the 1950s, the Norton family transferred control of the company to its employees, and today—with a staff of four hundred and a comparable number of trade, college, and professional titles published each year—W. W. Norton & Company stands as the largest and oldest publishing house owned wholly by its employees.

Editor: Ann Shin

Associate Editor: Emily Stuart

Assistant Editor: Samantha Held

Editorial Assistant: Tomas Unger

Project Editor: Sujin Hong

Managing Editor, College Digital Media: Kim Yi

Media Editor: Spencer Richardson-Jones

Associate Media Editor: Michael Jaoui

Marketing Manager, Political Science: Erin Brown

Production Manager: Eric Pier-Hocking

Photo Editor: Stephanie Romeo

Permissions Manager: Megan Jackson

Design Director: Rubina Yeh

Composition: Graphic World

Manufacturing: Transcontinental

Library of Congress Cataloging-in-Publication Data.

ISBN: 978-0-393-93809-8 (pbk.)

W. W. Norton & Company, Inc., 500 Fifth Avenue, New York, NY 10110

wwnorton.com

W. W. Norton & Company Ltd., Castle House, 75/76 Wells Street, London W1T 3QT

1 2 3 4 5 6 7 8 9 0

Contents in Brief

Contents

Part One: Foundations

Chapter 1: What Shaped Our World? A Historical Introduction   2

Chapter 2: Understanding Interests, Interactions, and Institutions 42

Part Two: War and Peace

Chapter 3: Why Are There Wars? 88

Chapter 10: Development: Causes of the Wealth and Poverty of Nations

420

Part Four: Transnational Politics

Chapter 11: International Law and Norms

456

Part Five: Looking Ahead

Preface

As this textbook has evolved over the course of three editions, we have been guided throughout by two principles that spurred our enthusiasm for the project and that, we believe, make this textbook special. First, this text is organized around substantive puzzles that draw scholars and students alike to the study of world politics. This is a field that grapples with some of the most interesting and important questions in political science: Why are there wars? Why do countries have a hard time cooperating to prevent genocides or global environmental problems? Why are some countries rich while others are poor? This book gives students the tools they need to start thinking analytically about the answers to such questions. Second, we have sought to bridge the gap between how scholars of international relations conduct their research and how they teach their students. The text draws from the insights and findings of contemporary international relations scholarship, and presents them in a way that is accessible to undergraduates who are just starting out in this field. Our ambition is to provide students with a "toolbox" of analytic concepts common to many theories of world politics that can be applied to a wide variety of topics. We hope to lay a solid foundation on which students can build their own understanding of the continually evolving world of international politics.

The core concepts in this toolbox are interests, interactions, and institutions. Chapter 2 presents the framework, and the remaining chapters apply it. The book is organized around the principle that problems in world politics can be analyzed using these key concepts:

- Who are the relevant actors and what are their interests?

- What is the nature of their interactions? What strategies can they be expected to pursue? When are their choices likely to bring about cooperation or conflict?

- How do institutions constrain and affect interactions? How might they impede or facilitate cooperation? When and how do institutions favor different actors and their interests?

Different problems and issues will emphasize interests, interactions, or institutions to varying degrees. There is no single model of world politics that applies equally to war, trade and international financial relations, and the struggles for improved human rights and a cleaner global environment. Nonetheless, any complete understanding must include all three concepts. Although we do not refer extensively to the traditional paradigms based on realism, liberalism, and constructivism in the book, we show briefly in the Introduction how each of these major "-isms" of international relations theory can be understood as a different set of assumptions about interests, interactions, and institutions in world politics.

Pedagogical Features

Our approach to the study of international relations is problem-oriented. Each chapter begins with a puzzle about world politics: a question or set of questions that lack obvious answers. We then use the concepts of interests, interactions, and institutions—along with known empirical regularities, current research results, and illustrative cases—to "solve" the puzzle and lead students to a deeper understanding of world politics. Each chapter includes numerous pedagogical features intended to facilitate student learning.

- **"Thinking Analytically"** sections at the start of each chapter preview how the concepts of interests, interactions, and institutions are used in the chapter's analysis.

- **"What Shaped Our World?"** boxes apply the interests, interactions, and institutions framework to explain historical events that continue to shape contemporary world politics and illustrate the analytic theme of the chapter.

- **"Controversy"** boxes probe ethical issues to stimulate classroom discussion and show how interests, interactions, and institutions can help us understand—if not necessarily resolve—the difficult normative trade-offs involved.

- **"How Do We Know?"** boxes survey published research findings and describe empirical facts or regularities that are important for understanding the larger puzzle discussed in the chapter.

- Expanded **"Study Tool Kit"** sections at the end of each chapter include key terms, further readings, and new "Interests, Interactions, and Institutions in Context" sections that review key analytic insights in the chapter.

An extensive set of ancillary materials for instructors and students supports this book's goal of making an analytical approach to world politics accessible to introductory-level students. The free online Coursepack offers chapter-based assignments, quizzes, and test banks, as well as assessments tied to "What Shaped Our World?" exercises and unique Bargaining Tutorials and Interactives. For instructors, Norton offers a Test Bank, an Instructor's Manual, and a PowerPoint set—all of which have been developed specifically to accompany *World Politics*.

Acknowledgments

We owe many debts in preparing this text. Roby Harrington at Norton brought us together and encouraged us to write this book. His vision, judgment, and steady editorial hand are reflected throughout. Ann Shin at Norton expertly guided the project from first draft to finished product and educated us in the art of writing and revising a textbook. The final form and content of this book reflect her efforts to keep three sometimes over-committed academics on track, on theme, and on time. We are grateful also to the rest of the Norton team that worked on this Third Edition, including Lisa McKay, for her thoughtful editorial suggestions; Sujin Hong, for her work as project editor; and Jude Grant, for her thorough copyediting. Assistant editor Samantha Held and editorial assistant Tomas Unger helped keep the many pieces of the manuscript moving throughout the process, and production manager Eric Pier-Hocking kept a close eye on the quality of the printed book as all those pieces came together. Spencer Richardson-Jones and Michael Jaoui brought creativity and order to the development of the ancillary resources. We owe thanks to all of them.

We are enormously grateful to the many reviewers and class-testers who provided guidance and helpful comments at many different stages of this project. For their advice on the First Edition, we would like to thank

Rodwan Abouharb, *Louisiana State University*

Karen Adams, *University of Montana*

Todd Allee, *University of Illinois, Urbana-Champaign*

Juliann Allison, *University of California, Riverside*

Claire Apodaca, *Florida International University*

Alan Arwine, *Texas Tech University*

Robert Brown, *Temple University*

Renato Corbetta, *University of Alabama, Birmingham*

Andrew Cortell, *Lewis & Clark College*

Benjamin Fordham, *Binghamton University*

Giovanna Gismondi, *Ohio University*

Darren Hawkins, *Brigham Young University*

Paul Hensel, *Florida State University*

Uk Heo, *University of Wisconsin, Marathon*

Tobias Hofmann, *College of William & Mary*

Elizabeth Hurd, *Northwestern University*

Michael Kanner, *University of Colorado, Boulder*

Scott Kastner, *University of Maryland*

Jonathan Keller, *James Madison University*

Alan Kessler, *University of Texas*

Andy Konitzer, *Samford University*

David Leblang, *University of Virginia*

Ashley Leeds, *Rice University*

Lisa Martin, *University of Wisconsin*

Ronald Mitchell, *University of Oregon*

Layna Mosely, *University of North Carolina*

Will H. Moore, *Florida State University*

Robert Packer, *Pennsylvania State University*

Robert Pahre, *University of Illinois, Urbana-Champaign*

Glenn Palmer, *Pennsylvania State University*

Leanne Powner, *College of Wooster*

Tonya Putnam, *Columbia University*

Stephen Quackenbush, *University of Missouri*

John Quinn, *Truman State University*

Robert Rauchhaus, *University of California, Santa Barbara*

Chad Rector, *George Washington University*

Dan Reiter, *Emory University*

Stephen Saideman, *McGill University*

Idean Salehyan, *University of North Texas*

Todd Sechser, *University of Virginia*

Megan Shannon, *University of Mississippi*

Randolph Siverson, *University of California, Davis*

Oleg Smirnov, *Stony Brook University*

Mark Souva, *Florida State University*

Patricia Sullivan, *University of Georgia*

Hiroki Takeuchi, *Southern Methodist University*

Aleksandra Thurman, *University of Michigan*

Kelly Wurtz, *Trinity College*

For the Second Edition, we received helpful advice from the following reviewers:

David Andersen, *CSU Sacramento*

Philip Barker, *Austin College*

Marijke Breuning, *University of North Texas*

Tom Brister, *Wake Forest University*

Terry Chapman, *University of Texas Austin*

John Conybeare, *University of Iowa*

Michaelene Cox, *Illinois State University*

Monti Datta, *University of Richmond*

David Dreyer, *Lenoir-Rhyne University*

Sean Ehrlich, *Florida State University*

Traci Fahimi, *Irvine Valley College*

David Grondin, *University of Ottawa*

Surupa Gupta, *University of Mary Washington*

Tamar Gutner, *American University*

Yoram Haftel, *University of Illinois at Chicago*

Phil Kelly, *Emporia State University*

Robert S. Kravchuk, *University of North Carolina-Charlotte*

Ashley Leeds, *Rice University*

Anika Leithner, *California Polytechnic State University*

Doug Lemke, *Pennsylvania State University*

Lisa Martin, *University of Wisconsin-Madison*

Molly Melin, *Loyola University Chicago*

Amanda Murdie, *Kansas State University*

Rusty Nichols, *Southwestern College*

Richard Nolan, *University of Florida*

Ausra Park, *Davidson College*

Mark Pollack, *Temple University*

Kathy Powers, *University of New Mexico*

Melanie Ram, *California State University, Fresno*

Dan Reiter, *Emory University*

Kirsten Rodine Hardy, *Northeastern University*

Stephen Saideman, *McGill University*

Chris Saladino, *Virginia Commonwealth University*

Susan Sell, *George Washington University*

Megan Shannon, *University of Mississippi*

Nicole Simonelli, *Purdue University*

Oleg Smirnov, *Stony Brook University*

Mark Souva, *Florida State University*

Allan Stam, *University of Michigan*

Richard Stoll, *Rice University*

Jelena Subotic, *Georgia State University*

Joel Trachtman, *Tufts University*

James Walsh, *University of North Carolina Charlotte*

Jesse Wasson, *Rochester Institute of Technology*

Jeremy Youde, *University of Minnesota Duluth*

For their valuable suggestions for this Third Edition, we thank

Klint Alexander, *Vanderbilt University*

Sarah Bush, *Temple University*

Jennifer De Maio, *California State University, Northridge*

Erik Gartzke, *University of California, San Diego*

Amy Gurowitz, *University of California, Berkeley*

Marcus Holmes, *Fordham University*

Jesse Johnson, *Kansas State University*

Joon Kil, *Irvine Valley College*

Jenn Larson, *New York University*

Kyle M. Lascurettes, *Lewis & Clark College*

Brooke Miller, *Middle Georgia State College*

Paul Musgrave, *Georgetown University*

Simon Nicholson, *American University*

Dave Ohls, *American University, School of International Service*

Andy Owsiak, *University of Georgia*

Tonya Putnam, *Columbia University*

Ryan Salzman, *Northern Kentucky University*

Randolph Siverson, *University of California, Davis*

Adam Van Liere, *University of Wisconsin, La Crosse*

Byungwon Woo, *Oakland University*

For research assistance, we thank Cynthia Mei Balloch, Eric Belz, Jeffrey Bengel, Charles Frentz, Lonjezo Hamisi, Oliver Kaplan, Aila Matanock, Brandon Merrell, Alexander Noonan, Priya Rajdev, and Stephanie Young. We also thank Helena de Bres of Wellesley College for her thoughtful ideas and hard work on the "Controversy" boxes in the First Edition, some of which carry over into this Third

Edition; and David Singer of MIT for his work on the figures and boxes in the international political economy chapters. Nancy Frieden graciously hosted an authors' meeting. Robert Trager of the University of California, Los Angeles, developed simulations and interactive bargaining models to accompany the text. Noah Zerbe of Humboldt State University created content for the online Coursepack. Susan Soll of George Washington University revised the PowerPoint set that accompanies the book. Daniel Fuerstman of the State College of Florida spent many hours working on the Test Bank for the Third Edition. Gregory Dixon of the University of West Georgia brought his experience as a teacher to the Instructor's Manual for the Third Edition. We are grateful for their contributions to the project.

Introduction

What Is World Politics and Why Do We Study It?

In the spring of 1921, Arabs and Jews living in Palestine came to the brink of war.[1] Angered by the influx of Jewish settlers, a group of Arabs set out to attack Jewish homes near their settlement at Tel Aviv. The Jews rushed out to confront them, and shots were exchanged. But the two parties did not go to war that day. A rabbi named Ben Zion Uziel donned his rabbinical robes, walked out between the two sides, and implored them to go back to their homes. Uziel reminded both sides how the land over which they fought was once a barren desert plagued with disease and famine. By working together, he observed, Jews and Arabs had created a rich and fertile land whose natural resources were only starting to be enjoyed. The rabbi urged both sides to forswear war and instead focus on creating prosperity that all could enjoy: "We have the entire land in front of us, let us work shoulder to shoulder to cultivate her, uncover her treasures, and live together in brotherhood." The appeal worked. Both sides put down their arms and returned home.

We know now, of course, that the peace forged that day would not last. Fighting between Arabs and Jews would begin anew only eight years later. In 1948, the state of Israel was created on that land, and that state has since seen frequent clashes with neighboring Arab states and with the stateless Palestinian people who once lived there. The Arab-Israeli conflict is one of the most intractable and dangerous rivalries in the world today. Still, as one scholar notes, "on that day in 1921, some men who otherwise would have died went home to enjoy life with their families."[2]

Though little more than a footnote in history, this anecdote illustrates what we study when we study world politics, and why we study it. The field of world politics—also called international relations—seeks to understand how the peoples and countries of the world get along. As the account suggests, international relations can span the continuum from open warfare to peaceful cooperation. Some countries fight wars against one another and, when they are not fighting, spend significant resources preparing to fight; while other countries have managed to live in peace for long periods. Sometimes countries engage in lucrative economic dealings,

---

1. This story is told in Abraham Joshua Heschel, *Israel: An Echo of Eternity* (New York: Farrar, Strauss, and Giroux, 1969), 175–78. We are grateful to Arthur Stein for making us aware of this anecdote. See Arthur A. Stein, *Why Nations Cooperate* (Ithaca, NY: Cornell University Press, 1990), 210.

2. Stein, *Why Nations Cooperate*, 210.

selling each other goods and services and investing in one another's economies. These interactions can make some people and nations very rich, while others stay mired in poverty. Like the people in the anecdote, the countries of the world are also increasingly aware of the natural resources they share and depend on: the atmosphere, the water, the land. The common threat of environmental degradation creates a need for international cooperation; in some cases, governments have responded to this need, and in other cases, they have not. And, as the story of Rabbi Uziel suggests, small groups—even individuals—can sometimes make a difference, whether through the work of a mediator, the lobbying of human rights groups, or more ominously, the activities of terrorist organizations. Understanding this varied landscape of conflict and cooperation is the task of those who study world politics. Getting students to start down this path is the task of this book.

Why study world politics? The nineteenth-century Scottish historian Thomas Carlyle once wrote of economics that it was not a happy science but rather a "dreary, desolate, and, indeed, quite abject and distressing one; what we might call. . . . the dismal science." Those who study world politics often think that Carlyle's criticism applies equally well to the field of international relations. The history of world politics, in fact, offers its fair share of distressing observations: international wars have claimed millions of lives, and civil wars and genocides have claimed millions more, and in most cases, outsiders who might have prevented these deaths have chosen not to get involved. Since 1945, international politics have taken place under the threat of nuclear war, which could destroy the planet, and fears about the potential use of these weapons have intensified since the terrorist attacks of September 11, 2001. International economic relations have in some cases been harmonious and generated great wealth for some countries. And yet, as one looks around the globe today, the inequality in living standards is stark. About one third of the world's population— more than 2 billion people—live on less than two dollars a day.[3] Most countries have signed treaties promising to protect the basic human rights of their citizens, but some governments still kill, arrest, and torture their people, and outsiders usually do little to stop these violations. And despite the increasing awareness of threats to the global environment, international efforts to do something about it often fail.

Still, the picture is not entirely bleak. One can point to a number of examples in which the world has changed for the better. For hundreds of years, the continent of Europe experienced horrific warfare, culminating in the first half of the twentieth century in two world wars that claimed tens of millions of lives. Today, the countries of Europe are at peace, and a war between, say, Germany and France in the foreseeable future is inconceivable. After World War II, many countries emerged economically shattered, or destitute after decades of colonial rule, but some have experienced extraordinary prosperity in the decades since. For example, in the 1950s, South Korea had one of the world's poorest economies, with a per capita national income of less than $150 a year. Today, South Korea boasts the fourteenth largest economy in the world, with a per capita national income of over $35,000 a

---

3. World Bank, "Poverty Overview," www.worldbank.org/en/topic/poverty/overview (accessed 07/15/15).

year.[4] At the beginning of the twentieth century, only a handful of countries world-wide had political systems that guaranteed the civil rights of their citizens and gave people a say in their government through free and fair elections. By the beginning of the twenty-first century, more than half of the world's population lived in democratic countries. And despite the uneven track record of efforts to protect the global environment, cooperation in this area was virtually unknown a few decades ago. In recent years, the number of international environmental treaties and organizations has grown dramatically, as has awareness of the common challenges we face.

We study world politics because the bad things that happen in the world distress us and because the good things give us hope that, through understanding and effort, the world could be a better place.

Twelve Puzzles in Search of Explanations

This book is organized around what we consider to be the most compelling and pressing puzzles in the study of world politics. Puzzles are observations about the world that demand an explanation. In some cases, they arise because the world does not work the way that we might expect. Some things that happen seem like they should not, and other things that don't happen seem like they should. War, for example, is a puzzling phenomenon. Given the enormous human and material costs that wars impose on the countries that fight them, one might wonder why countries do not settle their conflicts in other, more reasonable ways. The difficulty of achieving international cooperation to end genocides or to protect the environment presents another such puzzle: Given the widespread agreement that genocide is horrific and that the environment needs protecting, why is it so hard for countries to do something about these issues? Other puzzles arise because of variations that need to be explained. Some countries today are enormously wealthy, with living standards more opulent than ever experienced in world history; in many other countries, people scrape by on meager incomes and suffer from malnutrition, poor health, and inadequate schooling. What accounts for these vastly different outcomes? The study of world politics is the effort to make sense of these puzzles.

After a historical overview in Chapter 1, and the introduction of analytical tools in Chapter 2, this book seeks to understand twelve puzzles:

- Given the human and material costs of military conflict, why do countries sometimes wage war rather than resolve their disputes through negotiations? (Chapter 3)

- What if there are actors within a country who see war as beneficial and who expect to pay few or none of its costs? Do countries fight wars to satisfy influential domestic interests? (Chapter 4)

---

4. Figures are 2014 estimates from U.S. Central Intelligence Agency, *The World Factbook*, www.cia.gov/library/publications/the-world-factbook/ (accessed 07/13/15).

- Why is it so hard for the international community to prevent and punish acts of aggression among and within states? (Chapter 5)

- Why is so much political violence in the contemporary world conducted by or against nonstate actors, including rebel groups and terrorist organizations? Why do people sometimes use violence against their own governments or unarmed civilians? (Chapter 6)

- Why are trade barriers so common despite the universal advice of economists? Why do trade policies vary so widely? (Chapter 7)

- Why is international finance so controversial? Why are international financial institutions like the International Monetary Fund so strong? (Chapter 8)

- Why do countries pursue different currency policies, from dollarizing or joining the euro, to letting their currency's value float freely? (Chapter 9)

- Why are some countries rich and some countries poor? (Chapter 10)

- How can the international community constrain a sovereign state's actions? When and why do states do what is "right"? (Chapter 11)

- Why do countries sometimes try to protect the human rights of people outside their borders? In light of widespread support for the principle of human rights, why has the movement to protect those rights not been more successful? (Chapter 12)

- Given that nearly everyone wants a cleaner and healthier environment, why is it so hard to cooperate internationally to protect the environment? (Chapter 13)

- Why are some periods marked by extensive global conflict while other periods experience robust efforts at cooperation? Which of these patterns will hold in the future? (Chapter 14)

After laying out one of these puzzles, each chapter shows how we can build theories to make sense of them. A **theory** is a logically consistent set of statements that explains a phenomenon of interest. When we confront the puzzle "Why did this happen?" theories provide an answer. They specify the factors that play a role in causing the events we are trying to understand, and they show how these pieces fit together to make sense of the puzzle. A theory of war explains why wars happen and identifies the conditions that make war between countries more or less likely. A theory of trade explains why countries sometimes choose to trade with each other and identifies what factors increase or decrease the amount of that trade. A theory of international environmental policy identifies the factors that foster or impede cooperation in this area.

In addition to this primary role of explanation, theories also help us to describe, predict, and prescribe. They help us to *describe* events by identifying which factors are important and which are not. Since it would be impossible to catalog all of the events that precede, say, the outbreak of a war, we need theories to filter the events that are worth including from those that are not. Theories help us to *predict* by offering a sense of how the world works, and how a change in one factor will lead to

theory
A logically consistent set of statements that explains a phenomenon of interest.

changes in behavior and outcomes. And theories may help *prescribe* policy responses by identifying what has to be changed to foster better outcomes. Once a good understanding has been established of why wars happen, it might be possible to take steps to prevent them. Knowing what factors help countries emerge from poverty makes it possible to advocate policies that have a chance of helping. Just as an understanding of how the human body works is important for curing diseases, developing theories of how the world works is the first step in the quest to make it better.

Theories also provide manageable explanations for complex phenomena. Given how complicated the world is, simplifying it in this way may seem like a misguided pursuit. Whereas the movement of a falling object may be characterized by mathematical equations dictated by the laws of physics, the decisions of individuals and groups are influenced by factors too innumerable to list, let alone predict. Any theory, therefore, is doomed to oversimplify. But this is precisely the point of theorizing. We do not build theories because we believe the world is simple or mechanical. Rather, we build them because we know the world is extraordinarily complex, and the only way to understand important phenomena is to cut away some of the complexity and identify the most important factors. As a result, any general explanation will not be right in every single case.

Given this outlook, we generally aspire for probabilistic claims. A probabilistic claim is an argument about the factors that increase or decrease the likelihood that some outcome will occur. For example, while we cannot predict with certainty whether a given conflict will end in war or peace, we can identify conditions that increase or decrease the danger of war. Similarly, we use theories to identify factors that make trade protection, or international investment, or cooperation to protect human rights or the environment more or less likely. Given the world's complexity, developing a compelling probabilistic argument is no small feat.

The Framework: Interests, Interactions, and Institutions

No single theory adequately answers all the puzzles posed in this book. Instead, we offer a framework—a way of thinking about world politics that will be useful in building theories that shed light on these puzzles. The framework rests on three core concepts: interests, interactions, and institutions. **Interests** are the goals that actors have, the outcomes they hope to obtain through political action. A state may have an interest in protecting its citizens or acquiring more territory; businesses *Capitalism* generally have an interest in maximizing profits; an environmental activist has an interest in protecting the atmosphere, the oceans, or whales. **Interactions** are the ways in which two or more actors' choices combine to produce political outcomes.

The outcomes that we observe—wars, or trade and financial exchanges, or cooperation to protect human rights or the environment—reflect the choices of many actors, each looking out for their own interests, but also taking into account

interests

What actors want to achieve through political action; their preferences over the outcomes that might result from their political choices.

interactions

The ways in which the choices of two or more actors combine to produce political outcomes.

the interests and likely actions of others. War is the product of an interaction because it requires at least two sides: one side must attack, and the other must decide to resist. Similarly, efforts at international cooperation require multiple states to coordinate their policy choices toward a common goal. An **institution** is a set of rules, known and shared by the relevant community, that structure political interactions. Institutions define the "rules of the game," often embodied in formal treaties and laws or in organizations like the United Nations. Institutions create procedures for making joint decisions, such as voting rules; they also lay out standards of acceptable behavior, and often include provisions for monitoring compliance and punishing those that violate the rules.

Applying this framework to any particular puzzle is straightforward. We first think about who the relevant political actors are and what interests they may have. We think about the choices, or strategies, available to each actor; how those choices interact to produce outcomes; and how the strategic interaction influences what the actors actually decide to do. And we think about what institutions, if any, might exist to govern their behavior.

The framework is intentionally flexible, pragmatic, and open to a variety of assumptions about which interests, interactions, and institutions matter. A theory emerges when we identify the specific interests, interactions, and institutions that work together to account for the events, or pattern of events, we hope to explain.

In building explanations, we do not precommit to any one set of actors or interests as being the most important, regardless of issue area. Sometimes, it is useful to think about states as actors pursuing goals such as power, security, or territorial aggrandizement. In other situations, we get more leverage thinking about politicians concerned with holding on to their office, or businesses interested in maximizing profits, or labor unions interested in protecting their members' jobs, or groups of like-minded individuals with strong ideological interests in, say, protecting human rights or extending the dominion of a particular religion. We cannot judge whether any particular assumption about actors and interests is right or wrong; rather, we judge whether or not that assumption is useful in explaining the puzzle. Indeed, assumptions are simplifying devices, which means that, strictly speaking, none captures the exact, entire truth. Since not all decisions are made by individuals, it is not precisely accurate to say that a state or an interest group or an institution is an actor; and yet, sometimes, it is quite useful to assume precisely that. Similarly, when we ascribe interests to individuals—such as assuming that politicians care primarily about holding on to office—this is a sweeping generalization that cannot be right 100 percent of the time; and yet, very powerful insights can be drawn from this assumption.

We focus on two broad types of interactions that arise, to one degree or another, in all aspects of politics: bargaining and cooperation. **Bargaining** describes situations in which two or more actors try to divide something they both want. States may bargain over the allocation of a disputed territory; finance ministers may bargain over how high or low to set the exchange rate between their currencies; rich countries may bargain with poor countries over how much aid the former will give and what the recipients will do in return; governments may bargain over how

institution
A set of rules (known and shared by the community) that structure interactions in specific ways.

bargaining
An interaction in which actors must choose outcomes that make one better off at the expense of another. Bargaining is redistributive; it involves allocating a fixed sum of value between different actors.

cooperation

An interaction in which two or more actors adopt policies that make at least one actor better off relative to the status quo, without making the others worse off.

much each will pay to alleviate some environmental harm. **Cooperation** occurs when actors have common interests and need to act in a coordinated way to achieve those interests. Governments that want to stop one country from invading another may try to act collectively to impose military or economic sanctions on the aggressor. Governments that share an interest in preventing climate change or degradation of the ozone layer need to cooperate in restraining their countries' emissions of the offending pollutants. Individuals who want to lobby for a particular trade policy or an environmental regulation have to pool their time, money, and effort to achieve their common aim. In short, bargaining and cooperation are everywhere in political life.

The institutional setting can vary considerably depending on the issues at stake. In some areas of world politics, there are well-established rules and mechanisms for enforcing them. International trade, for example, is governed by the World Trade Organization (WTO), which sets out rules that determine what kinds of trade policies member countries can and cannot have, and provides a dispute resolution mechanism that allows countries to challenge one another's policies. Other areas of world politics have weaker institutions. As we will see in Chapter 5, the United Nations (UN) theoretically governs the use of military force by states, but in practice, it has had a hard time enforcing these rules on its strongest members. As we will see in Chapter 12, there is an extensive body of international human rights law setting out standards for how governments should treat their citizens; unfortunately, noncompliance is common, and offenders are rarely punished. We will also at times focus on institutions at the domestic level—that is, the rules that govern who rules within countries and how they make decisions. Domestic political institutions determine which actors have access to and influence on the policy-making process. In some cases, differences in domestic political institutions can have profound effects on world politics. In Chapter 4, for example, we will encounter a phenomenon known as the "democratic peace": the observation that mature democratic states have rarely, if ever, engaged in a war against one another.

Levels of Analysis

The variety of actors and institutions that play a role in world politics means that we will see important interactions at three levels:

- At the **international level**, the representatives of states with different interests interact with one another, sometimes in the context of international institutions, such as the UN or WTO.

- At the **domestic level**, subnational actors with different interests—politicians, bureaucrats, business and labor groups, voters—interact within domestic institutions to determine the country's foreign policy choices.

- At the **transnational level**, groups whose members span borders—such as multinational corporations, transnational advocacy networks, terrorist organizations—pursue their interests by trying to influence both domestic and international politics.

These levels are interconnected. The interests that states pursue at the international level often emerge from their domestic politics. For example, whether or not a country's representatives push for liberalizing trade agreements with other countries depends on whether the interests within that country that support freer trade prevail over those that oppose it. Similarly, the relative influence of actors within domestic politics may depend on international conditions. Leaders may be able to use militarized conflict with other states to enhance their hold on power at home. International institutions that promote trade liberalization enhance the power of domestic interests that benefit from trade. Finally, transnational actors operate at all levels. Transnational networks like Amnesty International or Greenpeace try to change national policies by lobbying governments or mobilizing public opinion within key countries, and they try to change international outcomes by working with (or against) international institutions.

Because of these interconnections, we do not automatically privilege one level of analysis over others. Although international relations scholarship has experienced vigorous debates over which level of analysis is the "right" or the "best" one,[5] we find that no single level is always superior to others in making sense of the puzzles. In some cases, it is possible to build useful explanations from the bottom up, in a two-step process: (1) domestic interests, interactions, and institutions determine the interests that state representatives bring to the international level, and then (2) these interests combine in international interactions and institutions to determine the final outcome. The chapters on international political economy in Part Three generally rely on this two-step logic. In other cases, however, it is more useful to start elsewhere. In Part Two, we start the analysis of war on the international level. Given that states have conflicting interests over things like territory or one another's policies or regime composition, why does the bargaining interaction sometimes lead to war? Only after laying out this basic logic do we turn to some of the domestic factors that push states toward more or less belligerent policies. In Part Four, transnational actors play a central role, and we show how they pursue their goals by altering domestic interests and changing the prospects for international cooperation.

Integrating Insights from Realism, Liberalism, and Constructivism

In adopting a flexible framework based on interests, interactions, and institutions, we depart from the way the field of world politics is often organized. Many textbooks and courses on world politics emphasize the contrast between three schools of thought: realism, liberalism, and constructivism. Unlike our framework, which holds few preconceptions about how the world works, these three "-isms" represent different worldviews about the nature of international politics. Much ink has been spilled over the years by proponents arguing for the superiority of their preferred approach.

---

5. For a classic statement of this debate, see J. David Singer, "The Levels-of-Analysis Problem in International Relations," *World Politics* 14, no. 1 (October 1961): 77–92.

TABLE A *Realism, Liberalism, and Constructivism*

	INTERESTS	INTERACTIONS	INSTITUTIONS
Realism	The state is the dominant actor. States seek security and/or power. States' interests are generally in conflict.	International politics is primarily about bargaining, in which coercion always remains a possibility.	The international system is anarchic, and institutions exert little independent effect. International institutions reflect the interests of powerful states.
Liberalism	Many types of actors are important, and no single interest dominates. Wealth is a common goal for many actors. Actors often have common interests, which can serve as the basis for cooperation.	International politics has an extensive scope for cooperation. Conflict is not inevitable but occurs when actors fail to recognize or act on common interests.	International institutions facilitate cooperation by setting out rules, providing information, and creating procedures for collective decision making. Democratic political institutions increase the scope for international politics to reflect the common interests of individuals.
Constructivism	Many types of actors are important. Actors' interests are influenced by culture, identity, and prevailing ideas. Actors' choices often reflect norms of appropriate behavior, rather than interests.	Interactions socialize actors to hold particular interests, but transformations can occur, caused by alternative understandings of those interests.	International institutions define identities and shape action through norms of just and appropriate behavior.

We can understand the differences among realism, liberalism, and constructivism by mapping them into our framework (see Table A). Each school of thought is defined by a cluster of assumptions about what interests, interactions, and institutions are most important to understanding world politics.

Realism Realist ideas can be found in the writings of Thucydides (ca. 460–400 B.C.E.), Niccolò Machiavelli (1469–1527), Thomas Hobbes (1588–1679), and Jean-Jacques Rousseau (1712–1778). Realism was most forcefully introduced to Americans by Hans Morgenthau, a German expatriate whose 1948 book *Politics among Nations* remains a classic statement of the realist approach. Realism was given its modern and scientific guise by the contemporary scholar Kenneth Waltz.[6]

Realism starts with two key assumptions: that states are the dominant actors—indeed, some would say the only relevant actors—on the international stage, and

---

6. Hans Morgenthau, *Politics among Nations: The Struggle for Power and Peace* (New York: Alfred A. Knopf). First published in 1948, this book has been released in many editions since then. Kenneth N. Waltz, *Theory of International Politics* (Reading, MA: Addison-Wesley, 1979).

that the institutional setting of world politics is characterized by anarchy. **Anarchy**, a term we will revisit in Chapter 2, refers in this context to the absence of a central authority in the international system, the fact that there is no world government ruling over states the way that countries have governments that rule over their citizens.

anarchy

The absence of a central authority with the ability to make and enforce laws that bind all actors.

Realists assume that anarchy profoundly shapes the interests and interactions that matter in world politics. Because there is no central government and no international police force, states must live in constant fear of one another. With no external restraint on the use of military force, every state must first and foremost look out for its own survival and security. Hence, all states have an interest in security, and this interest dominates other possible interests because no other goal can be realized unless the state is secure. In practice, the interest in security leads to an interest in acquiring power—primarily, military capabilities. By accumulating power and ensuring that potential enemies do not become more powerful, states can ensure that they are not vulnerable to attack and conquest. Unfortunately, the quest for power inevitably brings states' interests into conflict with one another: when one state improves its military capabilities to enhance its own security, it typically undermines the security of its now comparatively weaker neighbors, a problem known as the "security dilemma." For realists, then, international politics is as Hobbes described, the "state of nature": a war of "every man, against every man" in which life is "nasty, brutish, and short."

Because states are concerned with security and power, nearly all interactions involve bargaining and coercion. Each state tries to get a bigger share for itself; one state's gain is another state's loss; and the threat of war looms over everything. Even when the potential gains from cooperation are large, realists argue, states worry more about the division of the benefits than about the overall gain. Each must fear that the state gaining the most will be able to exploit its gains for some future advantage. As a result, states may forgo mutually beneficial exchanges if they expect to be left at a disadvantage. Cooperation, realists conclude, is difficult and rare.

Finally, realists assert that because of the anarchic nature of the international system, international institutions are weak and exert little independent effect on world politics. Institutions like the UN and the WTO merely reflect the interests and power of the dominant countries, which had the most say in their creation and design. Although realists may recognize that institutions can matter at the margin, they conclude that rules are unlikely to be followed and that states will always bow to interests and power in the end.

In short, realism sees a rather bleak world of states jockeying for power under the shadow of war, and many of the unpleasant features of world politics mentioned above flow from this understanding. War is a permanent fixture of international relations because there is nothing to stop states from waging war when it is in their interests to do so. The risk of war can be managed by careful diplomacy and temporary alliances between states that face common threats, but neither domestic nor international institutions can deliver lasting peace. Even the realm of international economic relations is colored by the struggle for power. Economists tell us that unfettered commerce makes all countries collectively better off, but realists understand that restrictions on trade and capital flows oftentimes as sensible measures to increase or preserve a state's relative power. Finally, cooperation is hard because states look out for themselves, and international institutions are generally too weak to compel desirable behaviors. As a result, realists are not surprised that many of the world's collective needs, such as the protection of human rights and the global environment, go unmet.

Liberalism An equally venerable tradition, liberalism is rooted in the writings of philosophers John Locke (1632–1704) and Immanuel Kant (1724–1804), and economists Adam Smith (1723–1790) and David Ricardo (1772–1823). Contemporary advocates include Bruce Russett and John R. Oneal, who make the modern case for the pacifying effects of democracy, international commerce, and international law; and Robert O. Keohane and Joseph S. Nye, whose work helped bring the study of international institutions to the fore.[7]

Analytically, liberalism is the school of thought that most closely resembles the approach taken in this book. Liberal theorists accept many different types of actors as important in world politics: individuals, firms, nongovernmental organizations, and states. Unlike realism, liberalism does not require that any one interest dominate all others. Instead, liberal theory, like the framework presented here, is quite flexible in ascribing goals to actors. While realism assumes that states' interests in security and power derive from external imperatives (i.e., the need to survive in an anarchic world), liberals are more likely to see governments' interests as coming from within (i.e., from the interplay of different domestic actors operating within domestic political institutions). Moreover, since wealth can be used to purchase the means to accommodate many different desires, liberals assume that, for many practical purposes, actors can be treated as if they desire to maximize wealth.

Liberals are generally optimistic about the possibilities for cooperation in world politics. Whereas realists see most situations as involving conflicting interests over relative power, liberals see many areas in which actors have common interests that can serve as the basis for cooperation. The costs of war mean that states have common interests in avoiding conflict. The potential for profitable exchanges creates a common interest in lowering barriers to allow the flow of goods and money across borders and in creating institutions to facilitate international transactions. The common interest in clean air and clean water creates a basis for cooperating to protect these shared resources. Although liberals acknowledge that world politics is often wracked by conflict, they do not believe that conflict is inevitable; rather, conflict arises when actors fail to recognize or act on common interests.

Whether or not actors can cooperate to further their common interests depends a great deal on institutions, both domestic and international. At the

---

7. Bruce Russett and John R. Oneal, *Triangulating Peace: Democracy, Interdependence, and International Organizations* (New York: Norton, 2001). Robert O. Keohane and Joseph S. Nye, *Power and Interdependence: World Politics in Transition* (New York: Longman). First published in 1977, this volume is now available in Third Edition, published in 2000. Robert O. Keohane, *After Hegemony: Cooperation and Discord in the World Political Economy* (Princeton, NJ: Princeton University Press, 1984).

domestic level, liberals believe that democracy is the best way to ensure that governments' foreign policies reflect the underlying harmony of interests among individuals. In this view, which we will revisit in Chapter 4, conflict and war are the fault of selfish politicians, voracious militaries, and greedy interest groups, whose influence can be tamed only by empowering the people through democratic institutions. At the international level, the scope for cooperation gives rise to a demand for institutions. Liberals posit that international institutions facilitate cooperation by resolving a host of dilemmas that arise in strategic interactions and by making it easier for states to make collective decisions. In Chapter 2, we will consider these dilemmas and the ways in which institutions might resolve them.

Thus, while liberalism does not see a perfect world, it envisions a world in which progress is possible. The danger of war can be reduced by spreading democracy, strengthening global institutions, and fostering economic interdependence so that every country's welfare will be linked to that of others. Economic activity also has the potential to create great wealth, making it possible to lift countries and people out of poverty. And global challenges can give rise to international institutions that can make cooperation possible. While this optimistic view makes liberalism a more appealing theory than realism, theories must be judged by how closely they describe the world in which we actually live, not the world in which we would like to live.

Constructivism A relatively new approach, constructivism has roots in critical theory and sociology, and its most forceful proponents in world politics have been Peter J. Katzenstein, John G. Ruggie, and Alexander Wendt.[8] Like liberals, constructivists focus on a wide variety of actors and interests in world politics, and believe that international institutions can be effective, even transformative. They depart from liberals, however, by de-emphasizing the material sources of interests (e.g., wealth) and instead focusing on the role of nonmaterial factors, such as ideas, culture, and norms. What actors want is not fixed and predetermined, but a function of their culture, prevailing ideas, and identity, or the conception of who they are. Whether states perceive common or conflicting interests depends not only on their relative military power or economic ties, but also on whether they share a common political or cultural identity (e.g., "we are all democracies" or "we are all Western") or identify each other as foes (e.g., "you are not like us").

One prominent strand of constructivist thought emphasizes the role of norms, or standards of behavior defined in terms of rights and obligations (see Chapter 11). Whereas the other schools of thought assume that actors are purposive, selecting among possible alternatives according to their anticipated effects, constructivists assume that social actors pursue what they believe is right and proper based

---

8. Peter J. Katzenstein, ed., *The Culture of National Security: Norms and Identity in World Politics* (New York: Columbia University Press, 1996). John G. Ruggie, *Constructing the World Polity: Essays on International Institutionalization* (New York: Routledge, 1998). Alexander Wendt, *Social Theory of International Politics* (New York: Cambridge University Press, 1999).

on their conceptions of who they are and how they wish others to view them. So, for example, if a large number of countries decide that using a certain kind of weapon is barbaric, then states that wish to be seen as civilized may decide to forgo those weapons—even if using those weapons would enhance their security. Thus, a desire to conform to certain standards of behavior can trump other interests. Institutions, in turn, embody the rules appropriate for behavior, and thereby exert a profound effect on actions and observed outcomes. For example, once an international agreement or institution proscribes a behavior as illegal or illegitimate, states that care about how others view them will have incentive to conform. Thus, compliance with international institutions depends not only on their ability to monitor and enforce their terms, but also on the members' desire to be seen as compliant.

Because ideas about right or appropriate behaviors can change, constructivists see significant potential for change, even fundamental transformation, in world politics. The rough-and-tumble international system described by realists is not, according to this view, foreordained by the condition of anarchy. If actors come to understand their interests differently, their conception of appropriate behavior could change dramatically. More concretely, state behavior can be altered by the conscious efforts of activists to promote new norms, such as norms against the use of certain weapons (Chapter 11), norms promoting intervention in genocidal conflicts (Chapters 5 and 11), and norms favoring the protection of human rights (Chapter 12). For this reason, constructivists place particular emphasis on the role of transnational actors, such as advocacy networks of human rights or environmental activists, who try to spread norms around the world.

All three approaches offer insights into important problems of world politics. Nonetheless, each tends to emphasize particular aspects of our framework at the expense of others, and all make strong assumptions about which interests, interactions, and institutions matter the most. As a result, each sacrifices explanatory power and flexibility for the sake of intellectual purity. Not surprisingly, most international relations scholarship in recent years has moved away from arguments based on a single approach, instead borrowing insights from more than one. Indeed, as the field progresses, it has become harder to pigeonhole scholars and their work into any one category. For example, many contemporary scholars believe that coercive power plays a fundamental role in international politics (realism) but that power is often used in pursuit of goals that arise from the interplay of domestic interests (liberalism) and ideas (constructivism).[9] Hence, rather than trying to promote one school of thought over others, our goal is to answer important puzzles of international politics and, in the process, use the tools developed in this book to help us understand today's complex world.

---

9. See, for example, Jeffrey W. Legro and Andrew Moravcsik, "Is Anybody Still a Realist?" *International Security* 24, no. 2 (Autumn 1999): 5–55.

The Plan of the Book

This book has five parts. The first part (Chapters 1 and 2) introduces the broad patterns of conflict and cooperation in international history and lays out the text's framework. Part Two (Chapters 3 through 6) deals with the central puzzles in the study of war: why wars happen and whether they serve the interests of actors within the state, why the international community has such a hard time cooperating to prevent wars, and why nonstate actors such as rebel groups and terrorist organizations account for much of the political violence in the contemporary world. Part Three (Chapters 7 through 10) discusses the main puzzles in international economic relations: why countries trade with one another, why financial investments flow across borders, why some countries have separate national currencies, and why some countries are rich while others are poor. Part Four (Chapters 11 through 13) considers relatively new issues associated with global governance, including the development of international law and norms, the promotion of human rights, and the efforts to protect the global environment. Part Five presents the concluding chapter (Chapter 14), which reviews the broad historical trends in world politics, and considers what that knowledge, together with our theories, can tell us about the future.

By the end of the course, students should not only know a lot about international politics, they should also know how to *think* about international politics. When bad or puzzling things happen, they should be able to ask: "Whose interests did that outcome serve? Why were the people or countries involved not able to cooperate to achieve something better? How might new institutions be created, or existing institutions reformed, so that this does not happen again?"

Ultimately, we study world politics because doing so lets us grapple with important and interesting questions about ourselves and our world. This book cannot provide definitive answers to all the questions. After all, while we are confident that we understand certain things, in other cases, our understanding is still evolving and our theories are tentative—perhaps waiting to be overturned by the next generation. Instead, this book seeks to equip students with the tools they need to develop their own understanding. In the "information age," in which facts (and assertions masquerading as facts) are cheap and plentiful, the most valuable skill is the ability to think critically and analytically about what shapes our world.

THIRD EDITION

World Politics

Interests, Interactions, Institutions

1

What Shaped Our World?
A Historical Introduction

THE PUZZLE *How has conflict among nations ebbed and flowed over the centuries? When and how have war or peace, prosperity or stagnation, prevailed?*

Above: During the nineteenth century, global trade grew at a rapid rate. While the increase in international trade was most pronounced in the advanced economies of Europe, many people in Asia also found themselves integrated into the global economy in new ways during this period. By the time this painting was done, around 1840, Canton, China (present-day Guangzhou), had become a significant international trading port.

Most western Europeans and North Americans born around 1800 spent their adult lives in an atmosphere of peace and economic growth. So too did their children, and their children's children, and their children's children's children. Between the end of the Napoleonic Wars in 1815 and the start of World War I in 1914, peace and prosperity by and large reigned in western Europe and North America. There were periodic wars among the European great powers, but they were relatively short; there were brutal conflicts with the indigenous peoples of the Americas, but they were on sparsely inhabited frontiers; there was a bloody civil war in the United States, but it was confined to one country. There were occasional financial panics and recessions, but between 1815 and 1914 the advanced economies of western Europe and North America grew more than eightfold while output per person quadrupled.[1] This was the fastest growth in world history by a very long shot—it roughly equaled in a hundred years what had been achieved in the previous thousand.

1. Angus Maddison, *The World Economy: A Millennial Perspective* (Paris: Development Centre of the Organisation for Economic Co-operation and Development, 2001).

Europeans and North Americans born around 1900 had a very different experience. While they were in their teens, the world plunged into a horrific, protracted war that wiped out the better part of a generation of young men. If those born around 1900 were fortunate enough to survive World War I, they and their children spent the next 10 years being subjected to postwar violence, economic uncertainty, fragile democracy, financial boom, and ethnic conflict. In 1929, the world spiraled even further downward into economic depression, mass unemployment, dictatorship, trade wars, and eventually another global war. If they, and their children and their children's children, were again lucky and survived World War II, their world was divided into two hostile camps, one led by the United States and the other led by the Soviet Union. These two contending alliances carried on a cold war that included the deployment of enough nuclear weapons to annihilate life on earth several times over.

International relations profoundly affected these many generations of Europeans and North Americans—as they did, in different ways, generations of people in Africa, Asia, and Latin America. During the nineteenth century, the inhabitants of many poor countries found

3

themselves absorbed into a world economy for the first time; some prospered, others struggled. Latin Americans achieved independence from their colonial masters while much of Africa and Asia were subjected to new colonial rule and domination by Europeans. The twentieth century brought industrialization and urbanization to much of the developing world and eventually saw the end of colonialism. For people north and south, east and west, global events beyond their control—great-power war, international financial crises, colonial expansion, the division of the world into warring camps—changed their lives profoundly, as they continue to change ours, and as they have changed lives for centuries.

Thinking Analytically about What Shaped Our World

Whether in the military realm or in that of international economics, the world's experiences range from deadly conflict to fruitful cooperation. At times, when national interests have clashed, countries have engaged in bitter armed battles over everything from territory to theology, and in equally bitter commercial conflicts over markets and money. At other times, the same countries have found common ground upon which to base harmonious interactions on everything from geopolitics to trade, investment, and finance.

What will the future bring for those born around 2000? Will they experience general peace and prosperity, or war and deprivation? Will those born in the world's poor nations come closer to the living standards of the rich or fall further behind? Will governments cooperate or clash? Whose interests and which institutions will shape these interactions? These are the kinds of questions that the study of international politics hopes to illuminate. We do not aspire to predict the future, but we do seek to gain a fuller understanding of the past and present by providing guidelines for analyzing the choices available to people and governments and how they decide among those choices.

Much of the rest of this book provides and applies analytical tools to understand international relations. This chapter sets the stage for what follows by reviewing the course of international political and economic relations in modern times, since about 1500. On this basis, we move in subsequent chapters to providing theoretical principles with which to understand international relations and then to applying them to a wide variety of contemporary topics.

The Emergence of International Relations: The Mercantilist Era

The world as a meaningful political and economic unit only emerged after 1500. Before then, most major societies existed in practical or complete isolation from all but those on their immediate borders. To be sure, there was some trade among societies: China to Constantinople, Central Africa to North Africa, Constantinople to Europe. But this trade was extraordinarily difficult and expensive, and therefore it involved only the most valuable and easily transported goods.

All that changed after 1492, as wave upon wave of explorers, conquerors, traders, and settlers went forth from Europe's Atlantic nations. First Spain and Portugal, then England, France, and the Netherlands sent soldiers and traders all over the New World, Africa, and Asia in search of possessions and profit. By 1700, the world was unquestionably controlled by western Europeans. They exercised direct rule over vast colonial possessions in the Western Hemisphere, India, Southeast Asia, and elsewhere; and their military might allowed them to assert their will on local rulers even where they did not establish colonial domain. European influence was rarely welcomed by local populations, and its effects were often disastrous for local societies. Nonetheless, western Europe's economic influence was global, and it dictated the character and direction of economic activity on every continent.

The centuries of European expansion after 1492 meant that world politics was dominated by European politics. In fact, the Europeans used their military prowess to control much of the rest of the world, with formal empires or without them. The European economies were the world center of economic activity. Important as developments outside Europe may have been for the people living there, the analysis of world politics after 1492 necessarily has Europe at its core. This would only change in the twentieth century, with the rise of militarily and economically important non-European powers: the United States, Japan, the Soviet Union, and eventually China.

For several hundred years beginning in the 1500s, however, it was the rulers of western Europe who held sway over the rest of the world. These governments, almost all of them absolute monarchies, had two main interests. First, they wanted to ensure their own political and military power. These interests led them to desire control over ever greater territories and ever greater resources. Second, the European governments wanted access to markets and resources in other parts of the world. The European societies had thriving commercial classes, typically strongly allied with their respective monarchies, and each crown was hungry for revenue. There were rich natural treasures to be had abroad—precious metals, spices, tropical crops—and customers for the products of Europe's growing industries.

Western Europeans' economic and military interests were closely related and were reflected in the colonial order they established, known as mercantilism.

mercantilism

An economic doctrine based on a belief that military power and economic influence complemented each other; applied especially to colonial empires in the sixteenth through eighteenth centuries. Mercantilist policies favored the mother country over its colonies and over its competitors.

Mercantilism was a system by which imperial governments used military power to enrich themselves and their supporters, then used those riches to enhance their military power. Mercantilism's principal mechanism was the establishment of monopolies that controlled trade and other economic activities, manipulating them so as to direct money into the coffers of the government and its business supporters.

Some mercantilist monopolies were held by a government itself, such as the Spanish crown's control over many of its colonies' gold and silver mines. Other mercantilist monopolies were granted by a government to private businesses, such as the Dutch East Indies Company and the Hudson's Bay Company. These private enterprises held exclusive rights to economic activities in vast areas of the colonial world.

Mercantilist powers' most important controls were those applied to trade. These controls typically served to manipulate the terms of trade, the prices paid for imports and received for exports. In the case of mercantilist policies, the goal was to turn the terms of trade against the colonies and in favor of the mother country—to reduce the prices that the mother country paid its colonists for what it bought and to raise the prices the mother country charged its colonists for what it sold. One common way of achieving this effect was to require colonies only to buy and sell certain goods from and to the colonial power. In colonial Virginia, for example, farmers could only sell their tobacco to England, which artificially reduced demand for their tobacco and therefore its price; and Virginians could buy many manufactured goods only from England, which artificially reduced the supply of manufactures and therefore raised their price. Subjects received less for what they produced and paid more for what they consumed, but in return they obtained the protection of a powerful empire. Supporters of mercantilism argued that it benefited both the empire, which got richer and more powerful, and its subjects, who got protected. Not all colonial subjects agreed, as "How Do We Know?" on page 7 explains.

The mercantilist powers' international political and economic interests were closely intertwined. For mercantilism's proponents, this was one of its great attractions. The English philosopher Thomas Hobbes wrote, "Wealth is power, and power is wealth." One of his fellow mercantilist thinkers drew out the connections: "Foreign trade produces riches, riches power, power preserves our trade and religion." And a French mercantilist was even more explicit: "Our colonies depend on our navy, our trade depends on our colonies, and our trade allows the state to maintain armies, increase the population, and provide for ever more glorious and useful functions."[2]

The British imposed mercantilist policies on their colonies in North America. For example, the tobacco being loaded onto these ships in the Virginia Colony could be exported only to Britain, where the American producers received a lower price for their crops than they would on world markets.

---

2. All cited in Jacob Viner, "Power versus Plenty as Objectives of Foreign Policy in the Seventeenth and Eighteenth Centuries," *World Politics* 1, no. 1 (October 1948): 15-16.

Mercantilism and the 13 Colonies

British colonialism in North America followed the patterns of mercantilism, the system adopted by European colonial powers after about 1500. How did mercantilism work? Whom did it help and hurt? Why did many colonies come to oppose it? Economic historian Robert Paul Thomas has estimated the cost to the colonies of mercantilist economic restrictions in 1770, a representative year in the decade leading up to the outbreak of the American Revolution (Table A).

The most costly restriction was the "enumeration" of certain goods, which meant they could only be exported to Britain. This measure artificially increased the supply of the enumerated goods to the British market, which caused their price to drop, and it kept American producers from selling in markets with higher prices. There were also restrictions on what could be imported in the colonies, and certain goods were only available if they were bought from Britain—at a higher price than available elsewhere.

The principal cost to the 13 colonies was the lower price received for enumerated goods, especially the tobacco and

rice that made up most of the colonies' exports. Thomas calculated that without enumeration the colonists would have been able to sell their tobacco at a price 49 percent higher than what they actually received and their rice for more than double. If prices had been higher, we can also assume that the colonists would have produced more of the goods, so the forgone production is factored in as well. In 1770, the total cost of these export controls, almost all due to tobacco and rice, was $2.4 million. Thomas further estimated that the restrictions on imports raised the price of goods that the colonists bought from abroad by more than one-third, a total burden of $560,000. Thomas then took into account rewards ("bounties") the colonists earned for producing favored goods. The total net cost in 1770 was about $2.7 million, approximately $1.24 per person.

However, the 13 colonies received benefits from being in the British Empire. Most important was the protection of the British army and navy. Thomas calculated these benefits in two ways. First, he estimated the cost to the British government of stationing its troops in the region, along with how much American shippers would have had to pay for private insurance if they had not had the protection of the world's greatest navy. Second, Thomas calculated how much the American government spent to provide these services itself after independence. The lower of the two estimates was $1,775,000 in 1770. Subtracting the benefits from the costs, Thomas figured that the colonies' net burden from imperial rule in 1770 was about $885,000—or 42 cents per person, less than 0.5 percent of a colonist's average annual income. (When he calculated the average from 1763 to 1772, the net burden on the colonists was even lower: 26 cents per person per year.)

It hardly seems worth fighting a revolution over 42 cents a year. Even in today's money, the net burden (costs minus benefits) would come to about $200. It is important to note that the burden of mercantilism did not fall evenly on all colonists. The principal losers were the tobacco and rice planters of Virginia and South Carolina, as well as the merchants and craftsmen of New England. The former lost owing to export controls, the latter owing to restrictions on shipping and manufacturing. Thus, it is perhaps not surprising that the principal supporters of independence were in these regions where the costs of colonialism were highest.

TABLE A ***Mercantilism: Costs and Benefits***

	1770	1763–72 (AVERAGE/YEAR)
Burdens		
Burden on colonial foreign commerce	$2,660,000	$2,255,000
Burden per capita	$1.24	$1.20
Benefits		
Benefit of British protection	$1,775,000	$1,775,000
Benefit per capita	$.82	$.94
Balance	$–.42	$–.26

Source: Robert Paul Thomas, "A Quantitative Approach to the Study of the Effects of British Imperial Policy on Colonial Welfare," *Journal of Economic History* 25, no. 4 (December 1965).

As the European powers took control of ever-larger portions of the world, they also battled with one another over wealth and power. The struggle for supremacy in Europe was inextricably linked to the battle for possessions elsewhere, and the search for military advantage was closely tied to economic competition. International politics and markets were battlegrounds on which the major powers contended.

First the Spanish and Portuguese fought for predominance in the New World and elsewhere. After the Spaniards emerged victorious, they faced new contenders. Beginning in the 1560s, the Spanish possessions in the Netherlands revolted and eventually formed the new Dutch Republic. The British challenged Spain continually from the 1580s onward, defeating the Spanish Armada in 1588. Finally, in the Thirty Years' War (1618–48), the French, Dutch, and other allies sealed the decline of Spain. This war ended with the **Peace of Westphalia**, which stabilized the borders of the belligerents and attempted to resolve some of the religious conflicts that had complicated their relations. Because the peace treaties called on governments not to interfere in the internal affairs of other countries, some scholars regard this as the beginning of the modern system of states, which are expected to respect one another's **sovereignty** within their borders.

Once the anti-Spanish alliance had defeated Spain, its members turned on one another. The English and the Dutch fought each other in a series of wars, and both the wars and rapid English commercial growth meant that by the 1660s the English had surpassed the Dutch as the world's leading trading and maritime power. This launched a 150-year conflict between England and its allies, on the one hand, and France and its allies, on the other. Anglo-French rivalry culminated with the Seven Years' War (1756–63, also called the French and Indian War in North America), which effectively ended the French presence in the New World and established British predominance. The French challenge to Britain resurged during the French Revolution, which began in 1789 and led to the Napoleonic Wars (1804–15). The British and their supporters finally defeated Napoleon at Waterloo in 1815, sealing British international **hegemony**.

For three centuries after 1492, world politics was dominated by the efforts of the principal European states to overpower one another and to control the non-European parts of the world (see "What Shaped Our World?" on p. 9). They pursued their economic and military interests by creating formal mercantilist colonial empires in some areas, by exercising less formal military and economic dominion elsewhere. Meanwhile, the principal European powers battled one another for their possessions and for global predominance. The rulers of western Europe fought on two fronts—to subdue the populations of their empires and to expand at the expense of other European rulers.

By the end of the Napoleonic Wars in 1815, however, both central organizing principles of the mercantilist eras were being challenged. With the defeat of France by the anti-Napoleon coalition, conflict among the principal powers in Europe subsided and their security interests evolved. Meanwhile, the Industrial Revolution gathered force in Britain and in continental Europe, and this started to alter the economic interests of the industrializing nations.

Peace of Westphalia

The settlement that ended the Thirty Years' War in 1648; often said to have created the modern state system because it included a general recognition of the principles of sovereignty and nonintervention.

sovereignty

The expectation that states have legal and political supremacy—or ultimate authority—within their territorial boundaries.

hegemony

The predominance of one nation-state over others.

Colonialists and the Colonized

Most of the Europeans who came to dominate the world after 1500 viewed Africa, Asia, and Latin America as full of primitive peoples who were centuries behind the civilizations of Europe. The reality was quite different. In 1500, as the first European colonial surge began, only one of the world's 10 largest cities was in Europe: the world's most populous city, Beijing, was more than three times the size of Europe's largest city, Paris. When Spanish explorers arrived in Tenochtitlán, the capital city of the Aztecs—what is now Mexico City—they were amazed. One of the Spaniards wrote: "These great towns and temple-pyramids and buildings rising from the water, all made of stone, seemed like an enchanted vision."[a] The gap between Europe and the regions the Europeans colonized was often small; most of these regions had well-developed economies, social systems, and governments. How, then, did Europe come to rule the world so quickly and so completely?

Spanish invaders in Tenochtitlán, 1520.

Interests The causes of European imperialism remain hotly contested. At a minimum, European states were interested in securing access to the precious metals and trade of the lands they had newly "discovered." Rulers sponsoring the transoceanic expeditions wanted to enhance their own wealth and that of their merchants. They also wanted to strengthen their economies and societies against other European states, which they feared might gain riches abroad that would give them an advantage within Europe. These political interests overlapped with a religious motive, pushed by a still-powerful church and missionaries who sought new converts and to "uplift" supposedly primitive peoples to the standards of Christian civilization.

Interactions Imperialism was facilitated by industrialization in Europe, which quickly widened the wealth gap between it and the rest of the world: by 1870, income per person in the United Kingdom was five or six times what it was in Africa and Asia.[b] As this happened, technological developments in transportation and communications gave Europeans tremendous advantages: the steamship, the railroad, and the telegraph were crucial to imperial expansion. The Europeans' technological advantages meant that they largely controlled the result of their interactions with people elsewhere. Perhaps the most important European technological advances were the development of new weapons—such as long-distance artillery, accurate rifles, and the Maxim self-powered machine gun—that allowed relatively small numbers of Europeans to defeat large military forces in the rest of the world.

Institutions The institutional arrangements that resulted from these increasingly one-sided and violent interactions were colonial empires. Empire was an institution that transferred political authority from the local ruler to the imperialist home country. The European colonial powers typically ruled their colonies so as to further their own interests. Valuable resources were controlled by the colonialists, while the imperial powers usually gave the colonies only as much authority as was in the interests of the imperial center. Although local elites often retained some measure of autonomy, this existed only at the discretion of the imperial state. It was the lack of political rights and self-rule that eventually gave rise to demands for independence, starting with the American Revolution of 1776 against the British, the revolts against Spain and Portugal by Latin American states in the early eighteenth century, and finally the collapse of nearly all remaining European empires after World War II.

---

a. Quoted in Michael E. Smith, *The Aztecs* (Oxford: Blackwell, 1996), 2.

b. Maddison, *The World Economy: A Millennial Perspective* (Paris: Development Centre of the Organisation for Economic Co-operation and Development, 2001), 264.

The Pax Britannica

The century from 1815 to 1914 was remarkably different from those that preceded it and the one that followed. The major powers were far more interested than they had been in trading and investing worldwide, including with one another. Instead of imposing strict restraints on the movement of goods and money around the world, most governments welcomed ever-greater links among their economies. Their economic interactions became more cooperative as they pursued a common interest in global economic integration. This contributed to the accelerated economic growth that much of the world experienced during this period (Figure 1.1). On the military front, global conflicts among the major powers gave way to generally peaceful ties among the countries of Europe (and, eventually, to North America and Japan). To be sure, Europeans continued to use military and economic means to tighten and expand their control over people in their colonies and other poor countries. But interactions among the industrialized nations were generally pacific, and the world economy became very tightly integrated.

Figure sources: Angus Maddison, *The World Economy: Historical Statistics* (Paris: OECD, 2004); 2010 data from www.ggdc.net/maddison/maddison-project/data/mpd_2013-01.xlsx (accessed 10/10/14).

*1990 International Geary-Khamis dollars (internationally comparable dollars of 1990).

The Hundred Years' Peace

Between 1815 and 1914, relations among the European powers—and such rising non-European powers as the United States and Japan—were far calmer than they had been for 300 years. While powerful nations certainly continued to care about their security interests, their relations became much more stable and cooperative.

FIGURE 1.1 *Gross Domestic Product per Capita, 1500–2010**

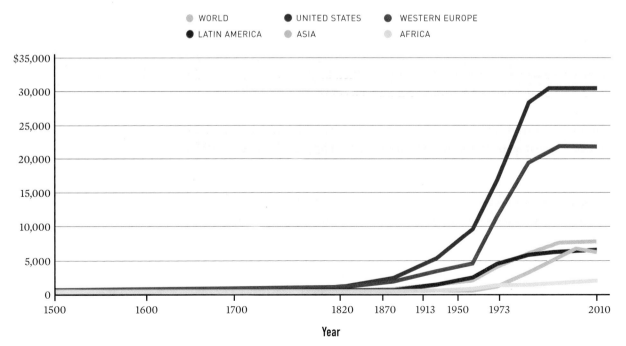

There were several sources of the greater cooperation among European powers. The first was a common interest in protecting their ruling regimes from new political pressures. The French Revolution and the ensuing wars had, among other things, pitted democratic revolutionaries against absolutist and autocratic governments, and the autocrats had won. Few European nations were at all democratic, and those that were democratic were very partially so—in 1830, barely 2 percent of the British population was permitted to vote, and even then the disproportionate allocation of seats meant that those city dwellers who could vote were unlikely to have much influence. All through the nineteenth century, however, movements for greater representation of the middle classes, farmers, and the working classes grew in strength. Sometimes rulers gave in to these demands. But throughout Europe there was a common fear of revolution—by democratic forces originally, and eventually by the growing Socialist and Communist movements.

The common interest of the European rulers in suppressing revolution helped overcome their political differences. The monarchies that ruled Prussia, Russia, and Austria, in fact, established a formal Holy Alliance in 1815 that was largely aimed at facing the revolutionary threat. Eventually, this was extended to most of Europe, in what came to be called the Concert of Europe, a system under which the major powers consulted on important diplomatic affairs. At the same time, the growing integration of the markets of the European powers gave them some common economic interests as well, as we will discuss in the next section.

In addition to the convergence of interests among the principal powers, their interactions were also stabilized by the reality of British diplomatic, military, and economic predominance. In fact, the period is sometimes called the **Pax Britannica** (Latin for "British peace," by analogy with the Pax Romana that Rome was said to have created within its classical empire). British hegemony proved a stabilizing force among European nations. British military power was important—the British navy "ruled the waves" with few challengers—but the country's significance rested also on its role in affecting interactions among European countries that had long been in conflict. Britain tried to prevent the supremacy of any one country on the European continent, acting to maintain a balance of power. (As we will see in Chapter 5, countries may form alliances in an effort to balance the power of a stronger country.) If one country or coalition seemed too strong, Britain would ally itself with an opposing country or coalition. This rough balance, which was the general goal of British foreign policy throughout the century, helped deter military conflict among the European powers.

Conflicts among the powers were muted, and there were few periods of open military strife. The age of massive intra-European war appeared to be over. To be sure, the power balance did not always serve to keep interactions peaceful, and European (and non-European) powers continued to compete with one another for military advantage and influence. The decline of one empire and the rise of another led to the century's biggest conflicts. The Ottoman Empire, which ruled much of the Middle East, North Africa, and southeastern Europe, weakened continually

Pax Britannica

"British Peace," a century-long period beginning with Napoleon's defeat at Waterloo in 1815 and ending with the outbreak of World War I in 1914 during which Britain's economic and diplomatic influence contributed to economic openness and relative peace.

over the course of the nineteenth century. As the Ottoman state tottered, Russia attempted to expand its influence in the Middle East; and when other European countries sought to restrain Russia, the Crimean War (1853–56) and Russian defeat were the result. Meanwhile, Prussia gradually unified a new German empire under its control. The French tried to discourage this process, but Prussia's victory in the Franco-Prussian War (1870–71) settled the matter. The finalization of German unification indicated the arrival of a new power in Europe. Despite these conflicts, the century from 1815 to 1914 was one of relative peace among the world's principal diplomatic and military powers.

Free Trade

Just as the absolutist European rulers—monarchs or others—could agree on a common opposition to democratic and other revolutionaries, they could also agree on the desirability of ending the mercantilist economic controls of the earlier imperial period. To some extent, the reduction of barriers to trade among nations reflected the more peaceful nature of relations among the principal powers. But the reversal of mercantilism also came from changes in the economic interests of the major powers themselves.

British desires for more open trade first displaced mercantilist interests. In the late eighteenth century, British inventors and industrialists introduced a flurry of technological innovations that revolutionized production. Employers brought workers together in large factories to use new machinery, new energy sources, and new forms of organization. Power looms and mechanical spinners transformed the textile industry. Improvements in the use of water power, and eventually the development of steam power, made the machinery more powerful still. By the 1820s, British industry was producing cotton and other textiles, iron, chemicals, and machinery at an unprecedented rate and at extremely low prices.

The economic interests created by Britain's Industrial Revolution saw mercantilist barriers to trade as irrelevant or harmful. Allowing foreigners to sell their products freely to Britain promised several positive effects. British manufacturers could lower their costs directly by importing cheaper raw materials and indirectly because cheaper imported food would allow factory owners to pay lower wages without reducing workers' standard of living. And if foreigners earned more by selling to Britain, they would be able to buy more British goods. For these reasons, Britain's manufacturing classes and regions developed a dislike of mercantilism and a desire for free trade. The City of London, which had become the world's financial center, added its influence to that of other free-trade interests. After all, Britain's international bankers had a powerful reason to open up the British market to foreigners: the foreigners were their customers. American or Argentine access to the thriving British market would make it easier for the Americans and Argentines to pay their debts to London. Of course, there were supporters of mercantilism and of barriers to trade more generally. Foremost among them were British farmers, who were protected by the Corn Laws. These were taxes, or tariffs, on imported grain. For 20 years, protectionist British farmers squared off against industrialists and other city dwellers. Eventually, over the course of the 1840s, Parliament repealed most of the previous British mercantile controls on foreign trade.

After Britain, the world's most important economy, discarded mercantilism, many of the nation's customers and suppliers followed suit. In 1860, France joined Great Britain in a sweeping commercial treaty that freed trade between them and subsequently drew most of the rest of Europe in this direction. As the German states moved toward unification in 1871, they created a free-trade area among themselves and then opened trade with the rest of the world. Many New World governments also reduced trade barriers, as did the remaining colonial possessions of the free-trading European powers. Mercantilism was dead, and integration into world markets—trade liberalization—was the order of the day. Over the course of the 1800s, the trade of the advanced countries grew two to three times as fast as their economies; by the end of the century, trade was seven or eight times as large a share of the world's economy as it had been at the beginning of the century.[3]

The opening of world trade was encouraged by, and itself encouraged, major advances in transportation and communications. The railroad fundamentally changed the speed and cost of carrying cargo overland. The steamship revolutionized oceangoing shipping, reducing the Atlantic crossing from over a month in 1816 to less than a week in 1896. By the late 1800s, telegraphs, telephones, steamships, and railroads had replaced horses, carrier pigeons, couriers, and sails. The transportation revolution led to a 20-fold increase in the world's shipping capacity during the nineteenth century.[4]

The Gold Standard

The **gold standard** organized monetary relations in this global economic order. When a country's government went "on gold," it promised to exchange its currency for gold at a preestablished rate. The country's currency became equivalent to gold, interchangeable at a fixed rate with the money of any other gold-standard country. Britain had had a gold-backed currency since 1717. As international trade and investment grew, more countries were drawn away from silver and other monetary metals and toward gold, the traditional international medium of exchange. Great Britain's status as the global market leader attracted other countries to use the same monetary system.

By the 1870s, most of the industrial world had adopted the gold standard. With all major currencies directly convertible into gold at fixed rates, the industrial world essentially shared one international currency. The predictability of the gold standard facilitated world trade, lending, investment, migration, and

gold standard
The monetary system that prevailed between about 1870 and 1914, in which countries tied their currencies to gold at a legally fixed price.

---

3. Angus Maddison, *Monitoring the World Economy, 1820-1992* (Paris: Development Centre of the Organisation for Economic Co-operation and Development, 1995), 38. For an excellent survey of the period, see Peter T. Marsh, *Bargaining on Europe: Britain and the First Common Market, 1860-1892* (New Haven, CT: Yale University Press, 1999).

4. Peter Mathias and Sidney Pollard, *The Industrial Economics: The Development of Economic and Social Policies. The Cambridge Economic History of Europe*, vol. 8 (Cambridge: Cambridge University Press, 1989), 56; and Maddison, *The World Economy*, 95.

payments (which we will examine in more detail in Chapter 8 on international monetary relations).

International trade, investment, and immigration grew dramatically. Citizens of rich countries invested huge portions of their savings abroad. In the 75 years before 1914, 50 million people left Europe for other continents, and another 50 million more left their homelands in Asia to live elsewhere. World markets for goods, labor, and capital were linked more tightly than they had ever been by free trade, the gold standard, and the new technologies of transportation and communications. In short, the world entered its first era of what we now call globalization.

Colonial Imperialism

However peaceful their diplomatic and economic relations may have been in Europe, the principal powers continued to use military force and economic controls on countries in the rest of the world. After a lull in the early part of the century, there was a burst of territorial expansion after 1870 that left most of Africa and Asia part of colonial empires.

The European powers, and eventually non-European powers such as the United States and Japan, were interested in the poor countries of Latin America, Africa, and Asia, for both security and economic reasons. The rich nations were interested in the resources and markets of the poor countries, in many cases wanting to secure them for themselves (rather than sharing them with others). The major powers also saw the rest of the world as a sort of chessboard on which they could fight battles among themselves in their quest for military supremacy. The European (and American and Japanese) presence in the rest of the world expanded, contracted, and adjusted in accordance with the changing goals of the major powers and changes in the interactions among them.

The colonies had been central to the mercantilist system, but as mercantilism declined, the economic interests in colonialism faded. For a hundred years after 1760, in fact, the European empires shrunk dramatically. Many previous supporters of colonialism in the colonies began to favor independence, and many people in Europe (such as the father of modern economics, Adam Smith, along with other free traders in Britain) came to see the colonies as unnecessarily burdensome. Eventually, Britain, France, Spain, and Portugal lost almost all their New World colonies, and by 1850 the only major colonial possessions remaining were British India, the Dutch East Indies (now Indonesia), and French Algeria.[5]

In the 1870s, however, colonial expansion started anew. The new powers that arose in and outside Europe—Germany, Italy, Japan, the United States—saw colonial possessions as a way of improving their military position. The established powers, especially Britain and France, did not want their newer rivals accumulating colonial power and wealth at their expense. At the same time, the growth

---

5. Britain's Canadian and Australian possessions had obtained effective autonomy by the 1850s, although they were still formally colonies. Within the British Empire, certain colonial areas were given extensive grants of self-government; for all intents and purposes, by the late nineteenth century, Canada, Australia, and New Zealand acted as if they were independent.

of industry in the developed world increased the desire for overseas markets and resources. And there was an upsurge in nationalist sentiment, especially in such newly important nations as Germany, Italy, and Japan, which spurred governments to satisfy nationalistic demands for expansion.

The result was a scramble for new colonies. From a few scattered outposts in Africa, Europeans quickly spread out to occupy and rule the entire continent, leaving only Ethiopia and Liberia independent by 1890. Britain consolidated and extended its control of South Asia, while it, France, the Netherlands, Germany, Japan, and the United States took over almost all the rest of Southeast and East Asia (Map 1.1). Within the space of a few decades, the industrialized nations had subjected most of the poor regions of the world to direct colonial control. The only major exceptions were Latin America, Persia (Iran), Siam (Thailand), and China, and even they had their sovereignty restricted by military and economic constraints imposed by the European nations, Japan, and the United States.

The Thirty Years' Crisis

A century of relative peace and prosperity in Europe ended with the most devastating military and economic conflicts in modern history. Generations of people in the advanced industrial world had their expectations of stability and security shattered by two terrible world wars and a catastrophic worldwide economic depression. The collapse of Europe's diplomatic balance led to three decades of global conflicts on the military, diplomatic, economic, and political fronts.

Tension in Europe

Contention among the principal powers had grown after 1900. One source of renewed conflict was the changing European power balance. On the one hand, the Ottoman, Austro-Hungarian, and Russian empires were weakening under the weight of socio-economic stagnation, political instability, and ethnic conflict. On the other hand, new economic and political actors were joining the world stage: the United States, after decades of avoiding foreign entanglements, was becoming more engaged with the rest of the world both politically and economically, and Japan had become a serious international force, as reflected in its decisive victory in the Russo-Japanese War of 1904–5.

The most striking change in the European power balance was the rise of Germany. In 1870, the French and German populations and economies were of roughly similar size, and their economies were substantially smaller than Britain's, but by 1900 Germany's population and economy were the largest in Europe, larger even than those of Britain. This created frictions among European nations. The Germans, who had come late onto the world scene, felt that they had fallen behind in the race for colonies. Frustrated with their meager colonial possessions, Germany focused on Europe and appeared to have designs on neighboring lands with large German populations. These neighbors feared German expansionism and domination. For decades, the major European nations had been able to expect cooperative

MAP 1.1 *The Colonial Empires, 1914*

After 1870, European countries, Japan, and the United States dramatically expanded their colonial possessions. By 1914, almost all of Asia and Africa had been taken over by the colonial powers. In the poorer regions of the world, only Latin America, China, and a handful of countries in Africa and Asia remained independent.

Pacific Ocean

Atlantic Ocean

Imperial Powers

- AUSTRIA-HUNGARY
- BELGIUM
- BRITAIN
- CHINA
- DENMARK
- FRANCE
- GERMANY
- ITALY
- JAPAN
- NETHERLANDS
- OTTOMAN EMPIRE
- PORTUGAL
- RUSSIA
- SPAIN
- UNITED STATES

Arctic Ocean

NORWAY
SWEDEN
BRITAIN
IRELAND
NETH.
DENMARK
BEL.
GER.
FRANCE
AUSTRIA-
HUNGARY
RUSSIAN EMPIRE
MONGOLIA
KOREA
JAPAN
SPAIN
ITALY
PORTUGAL
GREECE
OTTOMAN
EMPIRE
AFGHANISTAN
CHINA
SPANISH
MOROCCO
PERSIA
TIBET
FRENCH
MOROCCO
CYRENAICA
QATAR
NEPAL
TAIWAN
ALGERIA
EGYPT
TRUCIAL
INDIA
RIO DE ORO
ERITREA
OMAN
BURMA
Pacific Ocean
GAMBIA
FRENCH
WEST AFRICA
SUDAN
OMAN
ADEN
FRENCH
SOMALILAND
SIAM
FRENCH
INDOCHINA
PHILIPPINES
FR.
EQUATORIAL
AFRICA
ETHIOPIA
CEYLON
MALAY STATES
GHANA
NIGERIA
CAMEROON
BRITISH
SOMALILAND
TOGO
UGANDA
ITALIAN SOMALILAND
LIBERIA
RIO MUNI
BELGIAN
CONGO
GERMAN
EAST
AFRICA
BRITISH EAST AFRICA
GERMAN
NEW GUINEA
SIERRA
LEONE
DUTCH EAST INDIES
PAPUA
FR.
EQUATORIAL
GUINEA
ANGOLA
MOZAMBIQUE
N. RHODESIA
NYASALAND
Indian Ocean
PORTUGUESE
GUINEA
S. RHODESIA
GER.
SW.
AFR.
BECHUANA-
LAND
MADAGASCAR
SWAZILAND
BASUTOLAND
UNION OF
SOUTH
AFRICA
AUSTRALIA

NEW ZEALAND

political and economic relations, largely under British hegemony; now, the prospect of a challenge to the previous arrangements made governments wary and suspicious.

Eventually, Europe divided into two hostile camps. On the one side were the central and southern European powers of Germany, Austria-Hungary, and the Ottoman Empire; on the other were Britain and France to the west and Russia to the east. Crises, whether in Morocco or the Caribbean, the Balkans or Africa, aggravated tensions until war erupted in the summer of 1914. The Central powers—Germany, Austria-Hungary, the Ottoman Empire, and Bulgaria—were arrayed against most of the rest of Europe (Map 1.2).

MAP 1.2 *Europe, 1914*

World War I and Its Effects

Although all participants expected the war to be short and decisive, it turned out to be long and largely inconclusive—but extraordinarily bloody. Especially on the western front, in Belgium and northern France, huge armies settled into entrenched positions. Trench warfare was punctuated by attempts to break through enemy lines that typically led only to massive losses in dead, wounded, and captured troops on both sides. The first battle of the Marne, in September 1916, cost each side about a quarter million dead and wounded in the course of a week. The eventual entry of the United States in April 1917 on the side of the Allies, and the failure of German submarine warfare to cut Britain off from its supplies, guaranteed the defeat of the Central powers, but the victors had little to show for their success. The war was far longer and far costlier than anyone had imagined it would be; it took the lives of at least 15 million people, including about 7 million civilians.

Despite its immense cost, World War I did little to resolve the underlying political and military tensions that had unsettled Europe and, indeed, exacerbated them. The war utterly disrupted European politics both among and within nations. It led to the collapse of the four great empires of central, eastern, and southern Europe. In the territory from Finland to Yugoslavia, the Austro-Hungarian and Russian empires shattered into pieces, and central and eastern Europe suddenly had a dozen new "successor states." The Ottoman Empire, which before the war had stretched from the Persian Gulf to Libya, and from Albania to Yemen, was reduced to the far smaller country of Turkey. The German Empire lost what few colonies it had had, along with large portions of its European territory and population (Map 1.3).

In addition to changing the political map of Europe, the war fundamentally altered domestic social and economic conditions. For most of Europe, economic recovery was slow and partial; many central and eastern European countries went through debilitating bouts of hyperinflation, with prices rising by thousands or millions of percentages. In the most dramatic case, that of Germany, prices rose to a level *1 million million times*—that is, a trillion times—their immediate post-war level. The German mark, previously traded at 4.2 to the dollar, was eventually valued at 4,200,000,000,000—that is, 4.2 trillion—to the dollar. In the final months of the German hyperinflation, the central bank had to print so much currency that it used more than 30 dedicated paper mills, 29 plate manufacturers, and 132 printing plants.[6] This terrible experience bankrupted much of the central European middle classes and helped alienate them from the new democratic systems. Along with farmers, the dissatisfied middle classes grew to be an important base for extreme right-wing movements, such as the Fascists in Italy and the Nazis in Germany. At the same time, the war and its aftermath increased the power and organization of European labor movements and the Socialist parties they supported. In Russia, a radical Socialist movement took power, and soon there were Communist parties

---

6. Gerald D. Feldman, *The Great Disorder: Politics, Economics, and Society in the German Inflation, 1914–1924* (New York: Oxford University Press, 1993), 782–85.

MAP 1.3 *Europe after World War I, 1920*

everywhere, representing a revolutionary left-wing challenge to capitalism. The Communists favored government ownership of the means of production rather than capitalist private property, and a planned economy rather than a market system. Politics was polarized and nationalist sentiments inflamed, which promoted tensions among European nations.

While it further weakened the bases of peace in Europe, the war demonstrated the international economic and military predominance of the United States. The entry of the United States into the war in 1917 effectively guaranteed the Allied victory, both with its millions of troops and with its billions of dollars in loans to the Allies. President Woodrow Wilson guided the negotiations that led to the **Treaty of Versailles**, which ended the war. Economically, while the Europeans were engulfed in war, the United States rushed into the vacuum they left in the rest

Treaty of Versailles

The peace treaty between the Allies and Germany that formally ended World War I on June 28, 1919.

of the world and seized a dramatically increased share of global trade and investment. In fact, the United States became the principal source of war loans to the Allies, such that between 1914 and 1919 America changed from being the world's biggest debtor to its biggest lender. The European powers were dependent on the United States for financial, commercial, and diplomatic leadership to rebuild from the most destructive war the world had ever known.

However, after this flurry of involvement in European politics and economics, the United States drew back. President Wilson could not convince the U.S. Senate to approve American entry into the **League of Nations**. Ironically, this was an international institution created, largely along lines defined by Wilson at Versailles, to bring the world's nations together to increase cooperation and guarantee the peace. In 1920, the Republican Party swept the presidency and both houses of Congress on a platform opposed to Wilson's internationalism and committed to an isolationist foreign policy that would insulate the United States from the uncertainties of intra-European conflict.

Interwar Instability

Europe was left to its own devices, without even the semblance of the pre-1914 balance. The French and British were weak in victory, Germany was bitter in defeat, Russia was isolated in its Communist experiment, and the Ottoman and Austro-Hungarian empires had dissolved into a series of small states beset by constant diplomatic and economic tensions. Economic conditions were unsettled, political systems were unstable, and diplomatic relations were tense when they were not downright hostile.

The French and Germans, in particular, continued to clash diplomatically over issues left unsettled on the battlefield. These included control of the border regions of Alsace, Lorraine, and the Saar—the former two of which went to France, the latter to Germany. Another issue was Germany's commitment not to militarize the Rhineland, a region of Germany bordering on France. Germany objected to this restriction on its sovereignty while France regarded the movement of troops into a border region as a threat.

French and German interests also conflicted over the so-called war debts–reparations tangle. The Treaty of Versailles imposed payments of reparations, a fine levied on the losers for having started the war. This created great resentment in Germany, especially given the country's troubled economic conditions. The French argued, among other things, that they needed reparations to pay their debts to the United States. They would, they said, reduce demands on Germany if the United States would forgive some or all of these war debts—after all, the European Allies had paid a high price in lives and property. But the Americans were in no mood to give away billions of dollars to further their involvement with Europe. And so all throughout the 1920s and 1930s, the principals in World War I continued their battles in the diplomatic and economic realm.

The worst was yet to come: in 1929, the world spiraled downward toward further conflict. The global Great Depression that began in that year was more

League of Nations

A collective security organization founded in 1919 after World War I. The League ended in 1946 and was replaced by the UN.

After World War I ended, continuing tensions prevented cooperation on economic issues. Germany suffered hyperinflation that made its currency, the mark, virtually worthless. Here, children play with bundles of useless marks in the street.

severe, lasted longer, and caused more hardship than any economic downturn in modern history. Industrial production dropped by half in the United States, and by 1932 one-quarter of the country's workers were unemployed. In Germany, unemployment topped one-third of the labor force. No country was untouched. The economic catastrophe deepened political polarization within nations, in many cases bringing extreme right-wing, highly nationalistic, often militaristic governments to power. By the late 1930s, the Nazis and their Fascist allies controlled all of central, eastern, and southern Europe, as well as Japan. All these countries were hostile to the international economy and to the rich nations of western Europe and North America. In Latin America and in the colonial world, the collapse of the world economy drove nations to turn inward, strengthening the hand of nationalist and anticolonial forces.

World War II

Europe descended once again into war. World War II largely pitted the Fascist governments that had turned against the global economy, on the one hand, against the democratic powers that remained committed to some form of international economic cooperation (along with the Soviet Union), on the other. In 1940, the three major Fascist powers—Germany, Italy, and Japan—aimed at restoring and increasing their military might and territory, and in 1940 they formed a formal alliance, the Axis. By invasion, coercion, and persuasion, they built a network of followers, protectorates, and colonies—Japan in East Asia, Italy and Germany in Europe and North Africa.

An expansionist Nazi Germany annexed Austria in 1938 and occupied Czechoslovakia in 1939. In 1939, Germany attacked Poland and quickly overpowered it, leading Britain and France to declare war on Germany in support of their Polish ally. But in May 1940, Germany invaded France, which it defeated and occupied within six weeks. The Axis powers thus controlled virtually all of Europe and Asia except for Britain and the Soviet Union; the democratic Allies were restricted to Britain, North America, Australia, and New Zealand. In June 1941, Germany invaded the Soviet Union, and soon German troops were on the outskirts of Moscow. In December, Japan—which had already occupied most of China and Indochina—attacked the American naval base at Pearl Harbor.

The United States had been supporting the British with supplies, but the Japanese attack on Pearl Harbor in 1941 overcame any lingering American reluctance to get involved in another world war. From then on, the war pitted the Axis against the three major Allies—the United States, Britain, and the Soviet Union. The bulk of the war in Europe was fought along the eastern front, between the Germans and the Soviets, where millions of troops faced each other over thousands of miles of territory. After an initial frenzied retreat, the Soviets battled back and turned the tide at Stalingrad in early 1943. Meanwhile, the British and Americans carried out operations in North Africa before invading Italy in 1943 and France in 1944 while American forces advanced against Japan in the Pacific. In May 1945, Germany surrendered unconditionally. In August, in an attempt to force a Japanese surrender, the United States dropped nuclear weapons on the Japanese cities of Hiroshima and Nagasaki; the Japanese surrendered several days later.

The human and economic costs of World War II were unimaginably large. About 110 million people served in the combined armed forces, of whom 25 million were killed. Approximately 30 million civilians were killed by the war directly, and this does not include the 7 million or more people, mostly Jews, whom the Germans and their allies murdered in a planned genocide. Four-fifths of the dead were from Allied nations, including some 20 million from the Soviet Union (13 million military, 7 million civilian). Most of Europe and Japan was left in ruins.

The Cold War

Collective action
Diversionary incentive

The impact of World War II on international politics was profound. Unlike in 1918, the results of the world war were conclusive, and they fundamentally altered international power relations. Germany, Japan, Italy, France, and Britain, which had defined great-power politics before the war, were effectively finished as world powers; the only two nations with the ability to project significant military power were the United States and the Soviet Union. The question that remained was how this two-power world would be ordered. On the one hand, the two principal wartime allies had cooperated in defeating the Axis powers. On the other hand, they represented fundamentally different socioeconomic systems and had divergent interests in the organization of the postwar world.

The Superpowers Emerge

At war's end, the United States, the Soviet Union, Great Britain, and France were united in victory. The Allies defined the terms of the peace, carved up Germany into zones of occupation, and divided Europe into spheres of influence. Many people, including in the United States, felt that the four principal victors could, should, and would cooperate under the auspices of the new United Nations (UN) to manage international relations peacefully.

But within months, conflicts grew between the United States and the Soviet Union. Perhaps disagreements were inevitable between a capitalist democracy and a Communist one-party system. It may be that the two superpowers were driven toward discord by the very structure of their power relations, as they struggled for influence in Europe. Scholars continue to debate whether the source of the division was the inherently different economic or military interests of the two superpowers or rather some failure in their attempts to interact productively.

By 1949, the two superpowers were consolidating control over their respective blocs. The United States drew together its new allies—including the defeated Axis nations—into a Western system. The Americans worked to solidify their coalition as a common military alliance, the **North Atlantic Treaty Organization (NATO),** and as a collaborative economic order, the **Bretton Woods System.** The Soviet Union, for its part, now led a Communist alliance that stretched from central Europe to the Pacific, as China, North Korea, and North Vietnam had joined. The international order divided into Communist and capitalist parts, and the Cold War between them was the defining characteristic of international politics from the late 1940s until the late 1980s.

The Blocs Consolidate

The Cold War pitted the two superpowers against each other. Their military and economic interests were almost diametrically opposed. The United States favored market-based, capitalist economic activities while the Soviet Union rejected markets and capitalism in favor of a centrally planned socialism. In the geopolitical sphere, the Soviets regarded a pro-American Western Europe as a threat to their western borders, and a pro-American Japan as a threat to their east; the Americans saw the Soviets and their Communist allies as a military menace to their European and Asian allies. In an atmosphere of trust and stability, it might have been possible for the two superpowers to work out an amicable understanding; but as it turned out, interactions between them quickly turned hostile and suspicious, and they devoted their efforts to fortifying themselves one against the other.

Each superpower went about building up its respective coalition. In the 20 years after World War II, the two major world alliances strengthened their internal ties, added members, and fortified themselves against the rival bloc. The United States provided $14 billion in Marshall Plan and other aid to Western Europe and Japan in order to speed postwar reconstruction. It also led the Western world in creating a system of military alliances in the North Atlantic, Southeast Asia, Latin America, and elsewhere. The most important of these, NATO, brought together North America and most of Western Europe in a collective military institution united against the Soviet Union and its allies (see Chapter 5 for more details on NATO and other military alliances).

The United States also guided its allies toward a newly integrated and strongly institutionalized Western economic order. The Bretton Woods System, so called because its founding documents were negotiated at the Bretton Woods resort in New Hampshire, included institutions intended to encourage the freer

North Atlantic Treaty Organization (NATO)
An alliance formed in 1949 among United States, Canada, and most of the states of Western Europe in response to the threat posed by the Soviet Union. The alliance requires the members to consider an attack on any one of them as an attack on all.

Bretton Woods System
The economic order negotiated among allied nations at Bretton Woods, New Hampshire, in 1944, which led to a series of cooperative arrangements involving a commitment to relatively low barriers to international trade and investment.

movement of goods and capital around the world. In trade relations, the General Agreement on Tariffs and Trade (GATT) oversaw a substantial reduction in trade barriers.[7] In monetary affairs, the International Monetary Fund (IMF) supervised a restored but reformed gold-dollar standard, in which the U.S. dollar was tied to gold and all currencies were tied to the dollar. The International Bank for Reconstruction and Development (also called the World Bank) worked to encourage a resumption of private investment, especially in the developing nations (these economic institutions are discussed in more detail in Part 3). By the early 1960s, the Western world had rebuilt an integrated international economy—not a copy of the pre-1914 age of free trade and the gold standard, but something new. The commitment to economic integration was now combined with social welfare programs such as unemployment insurance and the widespread public provision of health care, pensions, housing, and other social benefits. This extensive social safety net helped cushion workers from the harshest effects of global competition, and the Bretton Woods System thus represented a compromise between economic integration and national commitments to social reform and the welfare state.

The Soviet Union also consolidated its bloc. It created a military alliance with its European allies, the **Warsaw Pact**. It strengthened military ties with the Communist government that took power in China in 1949. In the economic realm, the Soviet bloc developed a Socialist variant of economic integration in which different nations specialized in different products. This economic cooperation was overseen by an institution called the Council for Mutual Economic Assistance, which brought together the Communist nations and some of their supporters in the developing world. The Cold War, indeed, extended to competition over the support of many newly independent countries in Africa, Asia, and the Caribbean. Eventually, there was a rough division of the world between countries that tended to ally with the United States and those that tended to ally with the Soviet Union (Map 1.4).

The defining feature of military relations between the two superpowers was the development of nuclear weapons. By 1954, both the United States and the Soviet Union had atomic and hydrogen bombs, possessing a destructive power far beyond anything previously possible. With the development of long-distance bombers and missiles, eventually both superpowers had the ability to destroy each other (and their allies) many times over. This led to a real fear that war between the two superpowers might be unimaginably devastating and might threaten all humanity.

However, the roughly equal arsenals of nuclear weapons created something of a stand-off: each side's destructive capacity was sufficient to deter an attack on its homeland or its close allies. Since neither the United States nor the Soviet Union could really hope to conquer the other or its principal friends, their competition was limited to other regions of the globe.

Warsaw Pact

A military alliance formed in 1955 to bring together the Soviet Union and its Cold War allies in Eastern Europe and elsewhere; dissolved on March 31, 1991, as the Cold War ended.

---

7. The original institution was to be the International Trade Organization, but it encountered opposition in the United States. As a result, an "interim" institution, the GATT, took its place.

MAP 1.4 *The Cold War and Its Alliances, 1980*

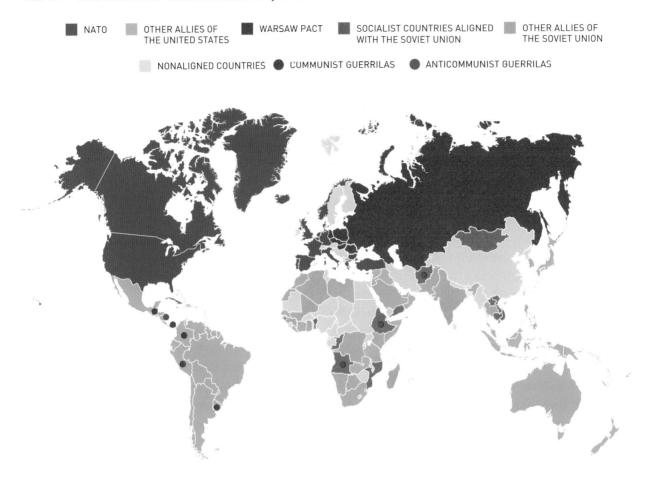

Indeed, despite the absence of direct warfare between the superpowers, the Cold War was by no means a peaceful time for people in much of the world. On several occasions, crises between the two came to the brink of war, such as the 1949 Berlin airlift and the 1962 Cuban missile crisis. In the aftermath of the German surrender, Germany was divided into four zones, controlled respectively by the Americans, British, French, and Soviets. The country's traditional capital, Berlin, which was located deep inside the Soviet zone, was also divided in four. Over time, the Western allies worked together in their zones, but there was constant friction between them and the Soviets. In June 1948, the Soviet Union blockaded land and rail routes into Berlin from the Western zones. This cut West Berlin (the American, British, and French portion) off from supplies of everything from food to coal. The Soviets clearly expected the Western allies to either withdraw or give in to several Soviet demands about the occupation. But the allies quickly organized a massive airlift that lasted nearly a year and involved almost 300,000 flights, providing millions of tons of supplies to the residents of

West Berlin. In May 1949, the Soviets finally backed down and once again permitted transport between the Western occupation zones and West Berlin. But the level of tension between East and West had been raised substantially. Indeed, some scholars regard the Berlin blockade and airlift as the opening salvo in the Cold War.

Perhaps the most dramatic confrontation of the Cold War took place almost 15 years later in Cuba. In 1959, a left-wing nationalist movement headed by Fidel Castro succeeded in ousting pro-American dictator Fulgencio Batista. Over the next several years, the new revolutionary government of Cuba moved quickly leftward and allied itself with the Soviet Union. An American-sponsored invasion in April 1961 failed, but the Cuban government was deeply fearful of American attempts to undermine it. Meanwhile, the Soviet government under Nikita Khrushchev was concerned that it was losing the nuclear arms race to the United States. In the summer of 1962, the Soviets secretly began installing nuclear missiles in Cuba; these were intended both to help protect the pro-Soviet Cuban government and, more important, to help even out the nuclear balance by putting Soviet missiles within easy striking distance of the United States. In October 1962, American spy planes spotted the missile installations, which the U.S. government regarded as a clear and present danger to American national security. American ships encircled the island, prepared to prevent Soviet naval vessels from reaching it, and plans for an American invasion were developed, even though many of the participants realized that this might lead to a nuclear war between the two sides. For about a week, the U.S. and Soviet governments bargained over the missiles in an atmosphere of extraordinary tension and widespread expectation that war would break out. Finally, the two sides agreed to a deal: the Soviets would dismantle their missiles in Cuba if the United States withdrew its nuclear missiles from Turkey. This represented a major concession by the Soviets, especially as the Turkish withdrawal was secret at the time; it appeared to most observers that Khrushchev had backed down. As Secretary of State Dean Rusk told President John F. Kennedy at the time, "We were eyeball to eyeball, and the other fellow just blinked."[8]

In addition to the threat of war between the two nations, each superpower routinely used military force in order to prevent other countries from falling into the sphere of its rival. The United States had its military and intelligence services undermine governments that were Communist or seen as likely to come under Communist influence: Iran in 1953, Guatemala in 1954, the Congo in 1961, Cuba in 1961, the Dominican Republic in 1962, Chile in 1971, and Nicaragua from 1979 to 1988. The Soviet Union similarly used military power to extend or preserve its own influence. Its forces invaded Hungary in 1956 and Czechoslovakia in 1968 when these allies seemed likely to leave the Soviet orbit. The Soviet Union also invaded

8. One recent addition to the enormous literature on the crisis is Michael Dobbs, *One Minute to Midnight: Kennedy, Khrushchev, and Castro on the Brink of Nuclear War* (New York: Knopf, 2008). The tense showdown during the crisis is an example of brinksmanship, which we will discuss in Chapter 3.

Afghanistan in 1979, leading to a decade-long war that sapped the Soviets' military might.

In the colonial and postcolonial world, especially, the two superpowers constantly jockeyed for influence. Wars in Korea and Vietnam were the most obvious instances. In both cases, the Soviets supported one side of a civil conflict while the Americans supported another side. The United States and some of its allies sent troops to both South Korea and South Vietnam; the Soviet Union and some of its allies sent supplies to both North Korea and North Vietnam. The same sort of "proxy war" was fought in many regions and over many decades. Much of the developing world became a Cold War battleground between pro-American and pro-Soviet forces.

Decolonization

The involvement of the two superpowers in the affairs of Africa, Asia, and Latin America was part of a broader emergence of these regions to a prominent place in world politics. This was a relatively new phenomenon in the modern era: between 1914 and the mid-1950s, the developing world was largely at the margins of world politics. Europe, North America, and Japan were preoccupied with two world wars, the Great Depression, postwar reconstruction, and the Cold War. Under these conditions, relations with the colonies and the independent developing nations were of less importance. The economic implications were particularly striking. For decades, Africa, Asia, and Latin America had supported themselves by exporting agricultural products and raw materials to the industrial world and importing manufactured products. But for much of the time between 1914 and 1955, the rich nations were unwilling or unable to continue normal trade relations—they were absorbed in war, devastated by economic crisis, or rebuilding after war.

The developing world thus was forced to rely less on its economic ties with the industrial nations and more on its own markets and products. While in the early stages it was external events—depression and war—that cut the developing world off, eventually governments encouraged the process. Many countries, and even some colonies, undertook substantial efforts at industrial development, providing at home what had previously been imported from Europe or North America. For example, by the early 1960s Brazil's industries supplied 99 percent of the country's consumer goods, 91 percent of its intermediate inputs (such as steel and chemicals), and 87 percent of its capital goods (such as machinery and equipment).[9] At that point the Brazilian economy, which was roughly the size of the Dutch economy, was close to self-sufficient in manufactured goods.

This economic turn inward was accompanied by an upsurge in nationalist sentiment. In Latin America, China, and Turkey, this brought to power governments that were unfavorable—even hostile—to foreign trade, foreign investment, and foreign finance. In many colonies, the rise in nationalism fed into dissatisfaction with continued colonial rule.

---

9. Werner Baer, *The Brazilian Economy: Growth and Development*, 3rd ed. (New York: Praeger, 1989), 70.

After World War II ended, the colonial clamor for greater autonomy, and even independence, increased. The European empires had been weakened by the war, and their ability to sustain colonialism by force had diminished. Meanwhile, many of the nationalist movements had grown in strength and resolve, and they demanded autonomy and even independence more insistently. **Decolonization** was on the agenda for the first time in years, as colonial subjects fought to leave the colonial empires. In some instances, such as British India, the colonial powers gave in to these demands, albeit reluctantly, recognizing that they had little alternative. But in other instances, such as British Kenya, French Algeria, and the Dutch East Indies (Indonesia), independence came only after violent conflict between the colonialists and the colonized.

Pressure on the colonial powers did not only come from the nationalist independence movements. In many instances, the United States encouraged its European allies to release their subjects. American anticolonialism had moral sources but also more material origins. For example, American businesses welcomed a decolonization that would allow them fuller access to the markets of the developing world. And in the context of the Cold War, the United States was particularly concerned that colonialism would undermine American influence in the developing world. With so much of the world under European colonial control, it was hard for the United States to make a case for the evils of Soviet domination. The Soviet Union and China had good anticolonial credentials, and the Americans feared that colonialism would push Africans and Asians toward the Communists in the search for allies.

Developments within the colonies, within the imperial nations, and in international politics brought the end of colonialism more quickly than anyone had

decolonization

The process of shedding colonial possessions, especially the rapid end of the European empires in Africa, Asia, and the Caribbean between the 1940s and the 1960s.

During the Cold War, both superpowers sought the support of newly independent African countries. This Soviet poster calls for "Death to Colonialism!" and the liberation of Antoine Gizenga, a political prisoner in the Congo.

imagined possible. Within a few years of the end of World War II, almost all of colonial Asia and the Middle East was independent; North Africa gained its independence over the course of the 1950s, and by 1965 almost all of Africa was free. Colonialism was finished, and the world was made up of sovereign states.

The Rise of the Third World

Many of the newly independent nations of Africa, Asia, and the Caribbean resisted involvement in the battle between the American and Soviet blocs. They concentrated on problems in the relationship between the rich industrialized nations and the poor developing countries—the divide between North and South rather than East and West. In the late 1950s and early 1960s, leaders of such countries as India, Egypt, Ghana, and the Philippines came together to form a nonaligned movement of nations that professed independence from either bloc. These members of the third world, so called to distinguish them from the capitalist first and Communist second worlds, aimed to redress perceived inequities in their relationship with the advanced industrial world, especially in the nature of their economic ties.

Most third-world attempts to reform the international economy were ineffectual, as they lacked the power to make their points any more than rhetorically. But in 1973, the success of the major oil-producing developing nations in manipulating world oil markets and dramatically increasing oil prices held out hope for more balance in North-South economic relations. The developing nations had raw materials that the industrialized world wanted, and if they could organize themselves as effectively as had the members of the Organization of Petroleum Exporting Countries (OPEC), they might be able to extract more resources from the rich nations. Some producers of raw materials followed OPEC in organizing cartels to try to raise prices (copper, bauxite, and bananas, for example), with mixed success. But the third world also agitated more generally for what they called the New International Economic Order, which would be more favorable to developing nations.

The Cold War Thaws

Even as the developing world organized itself in ways that did not fit the East-West dimension, by the middle 1960s the two superpower alliances were themselves beginning to show signs of strain. France withdrew from NATO, and the United States got bogged down in a war in Vietnam that was unpopular both abroad and at home. The Soviet Union lost its most important ally when China broke with the rest of the Soviet bloc while dissatisfaction in Eastern Europe and at home put pressure on the Soviet government to provide greater political and economic freedoms.

Although conflict persisted in relations between the United States and the Soviet Union, in the 1970s both sides warily attempted a relaxation of tensions. The two blocs built more political, economic, and cultural ties, and they negotiated a series of agreements to limit the arms race between them. This reduction in hostility, or détente, was set back by continued competition in the third world and Europe, but the threat of armed conflict seemed to recede.

The Age of Globalization

The relaxation of U.S.-Soviet tensions reduced the threat of superpower war. But the postwar patterns of international political and economic relations were soon disrupted by two decades of upheavals. Even as the world economy became more globalized, states faced new diplomatic and security challenges.

The Cold War Ends

In 1979, relations between the United States and the Soviet Union, which had been improving for over 15 years, took a turn toward much greater hostility. In December of that year, Soviet troops entered Afghanistan to support a fragile pro-Soviet government. The United States and its allies responded vigorously to this first direct use of Soviet troops outside of the Warsaw Pact, imposing trade sanctions, financing Afghan insurgents, and boycotting the 1980 Olympic Games in Moscow. Soviet troops were soon bogged down in a guerrilla war that many observers compared to the American experience in Vietnam.

In 1981, Ronald Reagan took office as U.S. president, committed to a strongly anti-Soviet stance. The Reagan administration substantially increased military spending, especially spending connected to U.S.-Soviet rivalry. The United States made plans to deploy a new generation of missiles in Western Europe, within a few minutes' striking distance of major Soviet cities. It also began work on its Strategic Defense Initiative, a "defensive shield" against potential missile attacks. These

The fall of the Berlin Wall in 1989 provided a powerful symbol of the end of the Cold War. During the Cold War, the Berlin Wall divided West Berlin from Communist East Berlin.

measures threatened to upset the rough balance between the United States and the Soviet Union; in reaction, the Soviets attempted to increase their own military spending.

The renewed tension put great strains both on international relations and the Soviet economic and political order. The Soviet economy was falling increasingly behind that of the West, and the faltering Soviet system was finding it more difficult to keep up militarily. Eventually, after Mikhail Gorbachev took power in the Soviet Union in 1985, he moved quickly to improve relations with the United States and to encourage greater political openness (glasnost) and economic reconstruction (perestroika) in the troubled Soviet system. In 1988, the Soviets relaxed their control over their Eastern European allies; in 1989, Soviet troops withdrew from Afghanistan, the Berlin Wall came down, and Communists began loosening their grip on governments all over central and eastern Europe. By 1991, the Soviet Union had dissolved into 15 new independent non-Communist countries, and the Communist governments of the Soviet Union's European allies were out of power. The Cold War was over, and only one superpower was left standing.

Worldwide Economic Developments

It was not just in the world of East-West diplomacy that the 1970s and 1980s led to great change. After the OPEC oil shocks of 1973–74, the industrialized capitalist world entered a decade of recession, high unemployment, and high inflation. In the early 1980s, austerity measures to cut government spending and restrain wages helped bring inflation under control, but many economies remained stagnant. The developing nations too ran into trouble as a global debt crisis erupted in 1982 and drove many heavily indebted poor nations into crisis. As mentioned, economic growth in the Soviet bloc slowed dramatically, and social unrest exploded into open protest.

Over the course of the 1980s, supporters and opponents of increasing the role of market forces in economic activity faced off in developed, developing, and Communist countries. In almost all instances, the crisis eventually led to a turn toward the market. The fact that international trade, finance, and investment were at very high levels probably increased the attractiveness of this evolution, as it held out the promise of access to lucrative global economic opportunities.

In the West, cross-border trade and investment increased very substantially. Regional trade agreements (RTAs) were strengthened. The European Union, first created as the European Coal and Steel Community by Belgium, France, West Germany, Italy, the Netherlands, and Luxembourg in 1951, grew to include almost all of western Europe by 1995 (only Norway, Iceland, and Switzerland refrained from joining), removed all barriers to the movement of goods and capital among member states in 1991, and eventually replaced most of their national currencies, such as the French franc and the German mark, with a common currency, the euro, in 2002. The United States, Canada, and Mexico created the North American Free Trade Agreement (NAFTA) in 1994, which similarly removed many economic barriers among themselves. Figure 1.2 provides an overview of RTAs established during the 1948–2014 period.

FIGURE 1.2 *Regional Trade Agreements (RTAs), 1948–2014*

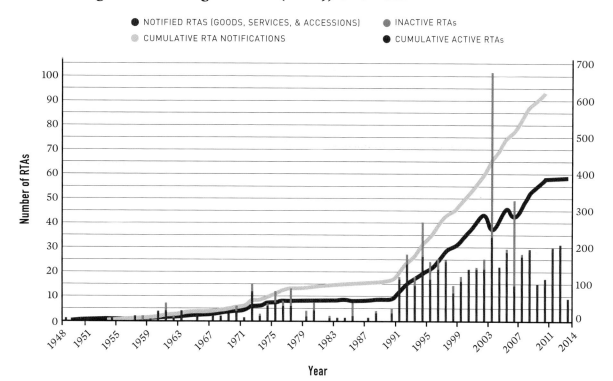

● NOTIFIED RTAS (GOODS, SERVICES, & ACCESSIONS)   ● INACTIVE RTAs
○ CUMULATIVE RTA NOTIFICATIONS   ● CUMULATIVE ACTIVE RTAs

Most developing countries responded to the difficulties of the 1980s by removing previous barriers to international economic involvement, welcoming foreign trade and investment. The watchword of the 1990s and early 2000s was *globalization,* with a level of international economic integration that had not been seen since 1914.

The most stunning changes took place in the Communist world. China and Vietnam embraced capitalist economic reform in the early 1980s but maintained their one-party systems. The Soviet Union under Gorbachev embarked on a program of economic reform, but the reforms were rapidly overtaken by events as the country fragmented into 15 separate independent states. Some of them, and most of the Soviet Union's former allies in central and eastern Europe, quickly moved to integrate with the European Union. Russia remained somewhat aloof from Europe, and tensions with the United States continued.

Despite differences among regions and countries, by the turn of the millennium it was clear that the world economy was globalized and likely to remain so for the foreseeable future. Unlike in the interwar period or the Cold War era, every major country was committed to substantial involvement in world trade, investment, and finance. Although many aspects of globalization remained controversial, most people in most countries seemed to accept the general principle that national economies should, and would, be quite integrated with the rest of the world economy.

Figure source: World Trade Organization, www.wto.org/english/tratop_e/region_e/regfac_e.htm (accessed 04/24/15).

New Diplomatic Challenges

The end of the Cold War was not the end of military and diplomatic conflict in world politics. Even as the Soviet Union was disintegrating, a new crisis erupted in the Persian Gulf. In August 1990, Iraq, led by President Saddam Hussein, invaded its small neighbor Kuwait. The two countries had been embroiled in disputes over Iraqi debts to Kuwait, over oil policy, and over a contested border, but the invasion took almost everyone by surprise (for more on these events, see the discussion in Chapter 3). The international response to the Iraqi invasion was widely seen as an indication of how world politics might evolve in the new post–Cold War environment.

Almost immediately, the UN Security Council and the Arab League condemned the invasion. The UN eventually established a deadline of January 15, 1991, for Iraq to withdraw from Kuwait while the United States assembled a coalition of 34 countries willing to participate in military action to expel Iraqi troops from Kuwait. Two days after the deadline passed, the American-led coalition began a month of massive air attacks on Iraq, followed by a ground assault that defeated Iraqi forces within three days.

The overwhelming defeat of the Iraqi invasion seemed to presage an era in which the world community, acting through the UN, might act collectively to resolve diplomatic problems of general concern. This trend was visible in the expansion of UN involvement in a series of difficult military, diplomatic, and humanitarian issues over the course of the 1990s. In 1992, a UN mission went to Somalia to try to ensure that humanitarian supplies would reach the civilian population as the country descended into a state of lawlessness; the mission was a qualified success. In 1993, another UN mission went to Rwanda to try to mediate a resolution of that country's civil war. But a year later, the mission was powerless to halt a horrific genocide in which the Rwandan government orchestrated the murder of as many as 1 million Rwandan citizens, most of them from the minority Tutsi ethnic group. Meanwhile, UN peacekeeping forces were deployed in the former Yugoslavia to try to moderate continuing conflicts among the new governments, and diverse ethnic groups, in the region. These forces had some successes and some failures, including a very visible inability to keep Serbian forces from massacring some 8,000 Bosnian boys and men in Srebrenica, which the UN had declared a "safe area." Despite a mixed record, UN involvement in these and other conflicts held out the hope of further international collaboration to resolve difficult diplomatic and military problems.

At the same time, more traditional unilateral and alliance military actions continued. In 1995 and again in 1999, NATO launched air strikes in the former Yugoslavia to try to achieve diplomatic goals. In the first instance, the strikes were on Bosnian Serbian forces in the former Yugoslav province of Bosnia-Herzegovina; the strikes had the goal of ending ethnic fighting there. In the second instance, the attacks were on Yugoslav military forces, with the purpose of forcing the Yugoslav government to withdraw its troops from the contested, majority-Albanian, province of Kosovo. Both NATO undertakings were essentially successful: the Bosnian war ended with a peace agreement, and Yugoslav troops were withdrawn from Kosovo.

The world was awakened to a new kind of international conflict by the terror attacks of September 11, 2001. On that day, 19 members of the Islamic extremist network Al Qaeda hijacked four passenger airplanes from Boston, New York, and Washington, D.C. The terrorists flew two of the planes into the World Trade Center in New York City and one into the Pentagon outside Washington; the fourth crashed in rural Pennsylvania. Some 3,000 people were killed in the attacks. Within a month, the United States and its NATO allies launched an invasion of Afghanistan, whose extremist government harbored Al Qaeda's leader Osama bin Laden and refused to hand him over to American authorities. The regime fell quickly, but conflict continued between Islamic extremists and the new American-backed government. Demonstrating the new geopolitical environment, the Security Council eventually provided a UN security force to help enforce peace in the country in the face of a continued extremist insurgency.

The tension between traditional and newer diplomatic approaches was highlighted in 2002–2003 as the major powers debated how to deal with the Iraqi government of Saddam Hussein. As we will see in Chapters 2 and 5, some policy makers wanted the UN to formulate a common response to Iraq's flouting of previous UN decisions. But the United States was dissatisfied with the speed and character of UN actions, and it and the United Kingdom organized an independent "coalition of the willing," which launched an invasion and occupation of Iraq in March 2003.

As it turned out, the second Iraq war was only the beginning of a period of international and domestic turmoil in the Middle and Near East, much of which

The Arab Spring uprisings that spread through much of the Muslim world in 2011 promised greater democracy but also uncertainty. In Syria, anti-regime protests were met with a prompt government crackdown, resulting in a brutal civil war that has drawn in the United States and other foreign countries.

led to military conflict. The war in Iraq dragged on for years, continuing even after American and other coalition troops left the country. Meanwhile, a series of anti-authoritarian uprisings began late in 2010 in Tunisia, and soon spread throughout North Africa and much of the rest of the Muslim world. The so-called Arab Spring held out the prospect of greater democracy in that region, but the unrest also created uncertainty about the nature of the regimes that would emerge and what kinds of policies they would pursue. Democracy appears consolidated in some countries; in others, there has been a return to authoritarian rule; in still others, the movement never got far. Some of the more dramatic events took place in Syria, where opposition to the regime turned into outright civil war, and eventually spilled into a region-wide conflict that appeared to pit, variously, Sunni against Shiite, Kurds against Arabs, Islamists against secularists, and extremists against moderates.

The Middle and Near Eastern conflicts frequently flared into armed battles. NATO forces provided military support for the rebels that overthrew Libyan leader Mu'ammar Qaddafi in 2011. The civil war in Syria soon drew in supporters of the various sides, both governments and radical movements. NATO and other foreign troops reduced their numbers in Afghanistan, but armed conflict continued and a NATO presence remained. The United States even returned to Iraq in August 2014, carrying out air strikes against the Islamic State of Iraq and Syria, an extremist group that grew in the civil war in Syria and then conquered much of northern Iraq that summer. Throughout the region, political, ethnic, geopolitical, and other rivalries continually threatened to erupt into violence—and often did.

Even as turmoil in the Middle and Near East captured the world's attention, new conflicts brewed elsewhere in Asia. An economically and politically resurgent China confronted several of its neighbors, especially Japan and Vietnam, over long-standing territorial disputes. North Korea continued to threaten to develop nuclear weapons.

Perhaps most important, Russia and the West found themselves locked in the most serious disagreement since the end of the Cold War. These tensions erupted into military confrontation over the course of 2014. The pro-Russian government of Ukraine was forced out of office by popular demonstrations in February of that year and was replaced by a pro-European coalition. The Russian government, furious at losing an important ally on its border, responded by annexing the Crimean Peninsula, a largely Russian-speaking region that had been ceded to Ukraine under Soviet rule in the 1950s. Even as the United States and its allies protested, Russian-backed separatists in the largely Russian-speaking eastern Ukraine launched military operations aimed either at achieving great autonomy or at joining Russia. The West responded with escalating economic sanctions against Russia as the Ukrainian government gradually battled to recover the secessionist region. The conflict over Ukraine was reminiscent of Cold War–era "proxy wars," with the Ukrainian government backed by the West and the separatists backed by Russia.

While the 25 or so years since the end of the Cold War have certainly seen a reduction in geopolitical tension, these events made it clear that disputes among the major powers had not disappeared and could erupt into military conflict.

This raises questions about how world politics might evolve over the coming decades. On the one hand, there has been a gradual growth of UN involvement in military and diplomatic conflicts. This may signal a new trend in world politics, especially in military affairs, toward greater use of the UN and other international institutions and less reliance on unilateral action. On the other hand, recent conflicts resemble more traditional power politics, which is unlikely to disappear.

What Will Shape Our World in the Future?

Today, the two overriding realities of international affairs are America's leading role in world politics and globalization. On the military and diplomatic front, the United States remains predominant: its military spending is roughly equal to that of the rest of the world combined. However, there are other powers on the horizon, and it is not clear how the relationship between them and the United States will develop. At the same time, over a decade of fighting in Iraq and Afghanistan has demonstrated that U.S. military power faces severe limits in confronting determined militant groups or piecing together war-torn societies. Economically, the world is more tightly linked than it has been since 1914, and international trade and investment continue to grow rapidly. However, there remain important uncertainties about both the security and the economic dimensions of world politics. To understand where the world is likely to head we need to identify the interests of the major actors in contemporary world politics and to analyze how these interests interact as they play themselves out on the world stage.

American Predominance and Challenges to It

For the foreseeable future, the United States and its allies will dominate the international political order. There is no realistic prospect of armed hostilities among the world's major nations. The European Union and Japan remain strongly allied with the United States. Russia and China do not particularly like America's predominance, but open conflicts among these powers remain muted and direct military conflict seems highly unlikely. America's military superiority raises several questions about the future. The first question has to do with American interests: What are the security and economic goals it will attempt to further with its leading position?

The second set of questions has to do with the ways in which the United States and other major countries interact in the international arena: Will such other countries (or groups of countries) as the European Union, Russia, and China focus on collaborating with the United States in pursuit of common goals, or will they attempt to challenge its position in particular regions or issue areas? How will the United States react to the rise of new powers, such as China, or the resurgence of old ones, such as Russia, that may challenge American policies in some regions or issue areas? And how will the United States, its allies, and its potential rivals deal with the continuing challenges they all face from Islamic extremists whose influence in the Muslim world seems to remain strong and whose resources—including military might—appear substantial?

Globalization

Whatever disagreements there may be among the world's major nations, they all seem to agree on the general desirability of continued international economic integration—that is, globalization. Nonetheless, the world economy faces continuing problems and enduring issues.

The most immediate problems surfaced with the economic crisis that began in 2007 (for details, see Chapter 8). That crisis led to major upheavals on global financial markets, a serious drop in world trade, and costly debt crises in a succession of countries. The world economy entered its deepest economic downturn since the 1930s, and many observers feared a 1930s-style turn toward protectionism and economic nationalism. Despite major problems and continuing economic stagnation in many countries, the general structure of international economic institutions and interactions was strong enough to survive the crisis and its aftermath.

Nevertheless, the crisis raised many questions about the extent to which some countries see their interests tied to closer integration with the global economy. While almost all governments continue to profess an interest in economic openness, ongoing disputes may indicate that these interests are not so clear-cut. Up to now, for example, neither Russia nor China has been willing to open its borders fully to international trade, finance, and investment. Some developing countries, after enacting a flurry of economic reforms, appear to be pulling back as the changes prove less effective, and more costly, than anticipated. There are Americans who worry that the European Union is turning in on itself, and Europeans who fear that the United States (and its close neighbors in the Americas) is also turning inward. Did enthusiasm for international economic engagement peak in the 1990s? Are countries (and regional groupings such as the European Union and NAFTA) now more concerned with their own affairs than with global cooperation?

At the same time, globalization has brought challenges to the patterns of international interaction that have characterized the Western world since World War II. As in the geopolitical and military realms, newer or resurgent powers express dissatisfaction with Western dominance of both the international economy and international economic institutions. This dissatisfaction has led to a common effort by the "BRICS"—Brazil, Russia, India, China, and South Africa—to obtain reforms favorable to their interests in international economic negotiations. Their first major institutional measure in 2014 was to create a BRICS development bank as an alternative to the World Bank and the IMF, which they see as dominated by the United States, Europe, and Japan. It is still unclear whether these initiatives constitute a meaningful challenge to Western economic predominance. Will interactions among the world's major economies remain generally cooperative, or will they become more conflictual?

There is also growing concern that international economic trends may pose a threat to social and environmental goals. Certainly, rapid growth in the developing world challenges the planet's ability to support more industry, more cities, more automobiles—more of the features of modern life to which billions of poor people aspire but that may not be compatible with environmental sustainability. Is there enough interest among governments to deal with the problem? Is there an ability to work together to address the issues?

Looking Ahead

What will the lives of those born around 2000 be like in the future? Will there be serious military threats, and will these threats come from such new powers as China or from religiously motivated terrorists? Will the industrialized world collaborate in confronting such challenges, or will it splinter into contending blocs? For those born in the poor nations of Asia, Africa, and Latin America, will the next 50 years bring prosperity and a hope of catching up with the West, or will poverty persist and spread? Can the international economic order remain open and relations among the major economic centers remain collaborative, or will countries and regions turn toward self-sufficiency?

Our best hope for understanding the future of world politics is to develop analytical tools that accurately reflect the basic forces at play. This brief overview of the historical processes and events that created today's world shows how the interests of people and countries affect the way they interact with one another, as well as how their interactions influence and are influenced by the institutions of international politics. The chapters that follow suggest ways of thinking about the interests, interactions, and institutions that have shaped the world we live in and that will continue to shape it for us, our children, and our children's children.

Study Tool Kit

Interests, Interactions, and Institutions in Context

- Conflict and cooperation among nations have ebbed and flowed over time. Individual countries have also varied in their own relations with other nations. Explaining the ebbs and flows, and the differences among countries, is the principal purpose of the study of international relations.

- Our explanations focus on understanding how the interests of the world's countries, and of the people in them, lead the world's nations to interact with one another and to what effect.

- We also study the kinds of international institutions that arise from and mediate these interactions.

Key Terms

mercantilism, p. 6

Peace of Westphalia, p. 8

sovereignty, p. 8

hegemony, p. 8

Pax Britannica, p. 11

gold standard, p. 13

Treaty of Versailles, p. 20

League of Nations, p. 21

North Atlantic Treaty
Organization (NATO), p. 24

Bretton Woods System,
p. 24

Warsaw Pact, p. 25

decolonization, p. 29

For Further Reading

Burbank, Jane, and Frederick Cooper. *Empires in World History: Power and the Politics of Difference.* **Princeton, NJ: Princeton University Press, 2011.** Surveys the role of empires and imperialism from Roman times to the present.

Carr, E. H. *The Twenty Years' Crisis, 1919–1939.* **New York: Harper & Row, 1964.** Originally published in 1939, serves as a classic analysis of how and why the world collapsed into conflict over the decades after World War I.

Craig, Gordon, and Alexander George. *Force and Statecraft: Diplomatic Problems of Our Time, 4th ed.* **New York: Oxford University Press, 2007.** Gives an overview of modern diplomatic history, with an analysis of basic concepts in diplomacy.

Findlay, Ronald, and Kevin O'Rourke. *Power and Plenty: Trade, War, and the World Economy in the Second Millennium.* **Princeton, NJ: Princeton University Press, 2007.** Surveys the interrelated development of international trade and international power politics since early medieval times.

Frieden, Jeffry A. *Global Capitalism: Its Fall and Rise in the Twentieth Century.* **New York: Norton, 2006.** Presents an overview of the development of the modern world economy from the 1890s to the present.

O'Rourke, Kevin, and Jeffrey Williamson. *Globalization and History: The Evolution of a Nineteenth-Century Atlantic Economy.* **Cambridge, MA: MIT Press, 1999.** Analyzes the development of the classical world economy of the nineteenth and early twentieth centuries.

2

Understanding Interests, Interactions, and Institutions

THE PUZZLE *What explains the patterns of world politics? Why do interests, interactions, and institutions matter in international relations?*

Above: Fighters for the Islamic State (IS), an insurgent group that seized nearly one-fourth of Iraq in the summer of 2014, celebrate their victories. After U.S. forces withdrew from Iraq at the end of 2011, sectarian rule and continuing violence created the political opening for the IS to challenge the regime in Baghdad.

On March 19, 2003, the United States launched a preventive war against Iraq. Thus began one of the longest wars in U.S. history. Between 2003 and 2011, when U.S. forces first withdrew, 4,487 American soldiers died and 32,226 were wounded; U.S. allies suffered 318 deaths. More than 10,000 Iraqi soldiers were killed in the war and subsequent insurgency, and up to 500,000 Iraqis may have died as a result of the fighting.[1]

Tensions between the United States and Iraq had been high since August 1990, when Iraq invaded Kuwait—its small, oil-rich neighbor—and the United States led a multinational coalition to war in early 1991 to restore sovereignty to Kuwait. As a condition of the cease-fire that ended the 1991 war, Iraq agreed to eliminate its programs to develop nuclear, chemical, and biological weapons and to permit United Nations (UN) inspectors to monitor its compliance. For most of the next decade, the UN and Iraq played a game of hide-and-seek as the

weapons inspectors sought to enforce the ban on weapons of mass destruction (WMD) and the Iraqi government attempted to undermine the inspections regime and its economic sanctions. In 2002, the administration of U.S. president George W. Bush argued that Iraq's WMD programs were rapidly reaching fruition. Concerned that Iraq might use its new weapons to act aggressively in the region, the Bush administration decided to remove Iraq's dictator, Saddam Hussein, from power—by force if necessary. President Bush may also have been seeking to assert American power to demonstrate a new, more forceful foreign policy, to secure supplies of oil from the Persian Gulf, and to transform the Middle East by building an effective democracy in an important country.

The United States turned to the UN Security Council to support its policy of regime change in Iraq, threatening that the organization would become irrelevant if it failed to enforce its own resolutions on Iraq's weapons programs. However, the United States faced determined opposition from France, Russia, and China, each of which can veto any substantive resolution within the Security Council. Although these states shared concerns about the Iraqi regime and its suspected weapons programs,

1. Estimates of Iraqi casualties vary widely. Amy Hagopian et al., "Mortality in Iraq Associated with the 2003–2011 War and Occupation: Findings from a National Cluster Sample Survey by the University Collaborative Iraq Mortality Study," *PLOS Medicine* 10, no. 10 (October 15, 2013): e1001533, derive the estimate of 461,000.

shared
interest

43

they were reluctant to endorse military action. As a result, the United States ultimately failed to obtain authorization from the Security Council for the war. Nonetheless, the United States claimed sufficient authority under past UN resolutions on Iraq and under the right of self-defense in the UN Charter. After Hussein rejected an ultimatum to step down, the United States led a "coalition of the willing" to a rapid military victory.

To the surprise of many, including the U.S. intelligence services, the United States did not find the stockpiles of chemical and biological weapons it had claimed existed. This embarrassment helped turn sentiment at home against the war, contributing to a stark decline in the president's popularity during his second term. The Bush administration also did not consider adequately the extent to which Saddam Hussein had brutalized Iraqi society and gutted any social institutions not loyal to the regime, nor did it anticipate the damage that the decade of sanctions had wrecked on Iraq's social and physical infrastructure. Planning on a rapid turnover of political power to Iraqi exiles and other insurgent groups, the Bush administration soon found itself leading a "failed state" and embroiled in a broad-based insurgency. With a surge in U.S. forces beginning in early 2007 and a new counter insurgency strategy, the United States eventually tamped down the violence but tensions between the Shiite majority and the Sunni minority remained high, and the Kurds established essentially an autonomous enclave in the north of the country.

By the summer of 2014, Sunni extremists calling themselves the Islamic State (IS)[2] seized large sections of territory in northern and northwestern Iraq. The Iraqi central government in Baghdad had long been hesitant to cooperate with Kurdish defense forces, but officials were eventually compelled to combine their efforts as the IS continued to gain ground in the interior of the country. The international community also responded to the escalation of violence. President Barack Obama ordered the delivery of humanitarian assistance to tens of thousands of Kurdish refugees, deployed 3,000 American military advisers to Iraq, and finally authorized a series of airstrikes against IS forces. These moves reestablished a significant U.S. military role in Iraq for the first time since American soldiers withdrew in 2011.

The facts of the Iraq War and its aftermath lead us to consider several questions. Why did the United States seek regime change in Iraq in 2003? Was the U.S. government motivated by concerns about American security, an economic interest in Middle East oil, the president's own political fortunes, or something else? Why did Saddam Hussein resist demands to cooperate fully with weapons inspectors and, later, to step down from power peacefully? The invasion shattered his country and led to his eventual execution in 2006. Certainly Hussein would have been better off accepting the U.S. ultimatum and slinking into a comfortable retirement in exile. Why did the Bush administration attempt to pursue its policy through the UN, and why did it eventually abandon those efforts? Would the war in Iraq, and its aftermath, have unfolded differently if it had been carried out under the auspices of the UN?

Thinking Analytically about Interests, Interactions, and Institutions

We study international relations in order to gain insight into such questions of conflict and cooperation. We seek to understand why states and their leaders make certain choices and why we observe certain outcomes. To help in our task, this chapter takes a closer look at three core concepts that enable us to think analytically about world politics: interests, interactions, and institutions.

As we will see, interests are the fundamental building blocks of politics. Explanations of international political events begin by specifying the relevant actors (such as the United States or Saddam Hussein) and their interests (such as power or security). As actors pursue their interests, they interact with other actors; the nature of these interactions affects the outcomes and whether actors can get what they want. Institutions (such as the UN) may also influence the outcomes of interactions by providing rules that facilitate cooperation. This framework can be used to analyze and understand not only the Iraq War but also the puzzles described in the chapters that follow and, equally important, others that will arise in the future.

---

2. Variants of this title include the Islamic State of Iraq and Syria (ISIS) and the Islamic State of Iraq and the Levant (ISIL).

Interests: What Do Actors Want from Politics?

Interests are what actors want to achieve through political action. For example, in international relations we often assume that states have an interest in security— that is, in preventing attacks on their territories and citizens. This interest prompts states to take steps to confront potential enemies and to protect friends whose security is linked to their own. In the showdown with Iraq, an interest in security might explain the U.S. government's desire to remove a regime that threatened American allies in the region and was suspected of developing WMD. As the primary motivations behind actors' choices, interests are the fundamental building blocks of any political analysis.[3]

More precisely, interests are the preferences of actors over the possible outcomes that might result from their political choices. Interests determine how actors rank the desirability of different outcomes, from most to least preferred. An actor motivated by an interest in money prefers outcomes in which it receives more money to those in which it receives less. A state interested in security prefers outcomes that strengthen it and weaken its adversaries over outcomes that have the opposite effect. For example, given the United States' general interest in security, it might prefer a democratic Iraq that is friendly toward American allies and encourages the democratization of other states in the Middle East (Map 2.1). If this best outcome were to prove impossible, the United States' second-best result might be a pro-Western dictator in Iraq. This outcome would be preferable to an anti-American Islamist government, which, in turn, would be preferable to widespread instability and chaos in Iraq and the region more generally. Between each of these broad alternatives, of course, are many intermediate outcomes that can be similarly rank-ordered.

Interests can be many and varied depending on the specific policy or event under examination. In identifying the interests of an actor, analysts sometimes draw on prior theories of human nature or behavior; at other times, they rely on the statements or actions of the actors themselves; and at other times still, they simply assume that actors have a particular interest. At the most general level, analysts often group interests into three categories: power or security, economic or material welfare, and ideological goals. In the first category, all political actors are understood to require a degree of security as a prerequisite to all other goals or, at an extreme, to desire power and the ability to dominate others either as part of human nature or as essential to survival in a competitive international environment. In the second category, political actors are presumed

interests

What actors want to achieve through political action; their preferences over the outcomes that might result from their political choices.

---

3. For a more extensive treatment of the theoretical and methodological issues in studying interests, see Jeffry A. Frieden, "Actors and Preferences in International Relations," in *Strategic Choice and International Relations*, ed. David A. Lake and Robert Powell, 39-76 (Princeton, NJ: Princeton University Press, 1999).

MAP 2.1 *The Middle East*

to desire a higher standard of living or quality of life, defined largely in terms of greater income, more consumable goods and services, or more leisure time (less work). This second set of interests is not incompatible with the first if we think of economic welfare as the long-term goal and security or power as a means to this end. Finally, political actors may also desire moral, religious, or other ideological goals, including democracy, human equality and dignity, the glory of a particular god, and so on. In this category, ideas often play a key role in shaping what actors want or believe to be good and desirable, including even what it means to be secure or wealthy. Again, there is not necessarily a conflict between these interests and others, as power or wealth may be a means toward ideological ends.

Scholars have long debated whether one conception of interest is more universal, true, or useful than others. Indeed, the three sets of general interests roughly divide the three schools of realism, liberalism, and constructivism identified in this book's Introduction. In turn, various debates over what the interests of actors *should be* are often tied to debates over what policies should be pursued in specific contexts. For example, the Iraq War tapped into a long-standing debate in the United States over whether foreign policy should be narrowly defined to meet security threats or should also seek to undermine repressive regimes and promote the spread of democracy. Our approach in this book is agnostic—that is, we do not assume that one set of interests is always better in helping unravel puzzles of world politics. Rather, for some puzzles it may be sufficient to specify a general interest in security, increased international trade, or protecting the environment. For other puzzles, it may be necessary to move beyond general assumptions and specify interests over narrow sets of outcomes—say, between deploying 100,000 versus 200,000 troops or between negotiating a multilateral international environmental treaty versus following a unilateral policy. Whichever level of detail is relevant depends on the purpose of the analysis, the questions being asked, and the puzzle under consideration.

Actors and Interests

There are many different types of actors in international relations. In the story of the Iraq War, we have already encountered *states* (the United States and Iraq), *governments* (the Bush administration and the regime of Saddam Hussein), *groups* within countries (the Sunni and Shiite religious groups in Iraq), and *international organizations* (the UN Security Council). Individuals are always the most basic political actors, as they cannot be divided into smaller political units. And in some cases, particular individuals, such as Bush and Hussein, are crucial actors in their own right. But it is often convenient to group individuals into larger categories of people who share common interests (the Sunnis in Iraq, for instance) or who somehow combine their conflicting desires into a joint or collective interest (the election of a government, for example). We call both individuals and these composite groups of individuals **actors.**

Of these composite actors, one that has particular prominence in international relations is the state. A **state** is a central authority that has the ability to make and enforce laws, rules, and decisions within its territory. Most countries are governed by states, though some may experience a breakdown of central authority and become what are sometimes called failed states.[4] The concept of sovereignty is a key part of the definition of the state. **Sovereignty** refers to the expectation that states have legal and political supremacy within their boundaries. To say that states are sovereign means that they have ultimate authority over their own policies and political processes, such as the maintenance of domestic order and the provision of governance (see "What Shaped Our World?" on p. 48). In theory, state sovereignty is

actors

The basic unit for the analysis of international politics; can be individuals or groups of people with common interests.

state

A central authority with the ability to make and enforce laws, rules, and decisions within a specified territory.

sovereignty

The expectation that states have legal and political supremacy—or ultimate authority—within their territorial boundaries.

---

4. On failed states and state building, see Timothy Sisk, *Statebuilding: War and Conflict in the Modern World* (Malden, MA: Polity, 2013).

The Rise of the State

We currently live in a world of nearly 200 states. States are some of the most important actors in world politics. So how did an international system of states come to be?

Interests All political systems involve a relationship between the rulers and the ruled. The rulers aim to satisfy their interests in wealth and power, whereas the ruled hope to obtain physical security, basic needs, and public amenities such as education and roads. Thus, the rulers and the ruled make an exchange: the rulers are supposed to provide the goods that their citizens want, and the ruled provide military manpower, money (usually in the form of taxes), and perhaps other kinds of service. The nature of the bargain is not always fair, and one of the core dilemmas of politics is how to structure the relationship so that the rulers actually act in the interests of the ruled.

Institutions The modern state is just one, relatively recent, way of organizing politics. Sociologist Max Weber (1864–1920) defined the state as "a human community that (successfully) claims the monopoly of the legitimate use of physical force within a given territory." This means that states are territorially bounded political units in which a central governing authority is the only actor that can legitimately use force, both against its own citizens and against other states.

Yet things were not always this way. In 1000 C.E., Europe was fractured into an uncounted number of political units, all enmeshed in often cross-cutting lines of authority. Under feudalism, kings granted landholdings to the aristocracy, who in turn owed obligations to the king, including supplying military manpower. Nobles in one realm could acquire lands in another, thereby owing obligations to two or more kings. There were also self-governing "free cities," which owed allegiance to no king. The Catholic Church wielded political authority through entities like the Holy Roman Empire (962–1806). Prior to the emergence of the state, many rulers shared and competed for authority over any particular area.

Over time, an informal international institution emerged to ensure the state's exclusive control within its boundaries: sovereignty. Sovereignty is composed of four core elements: (1) the sovereign possesses ultimate authority over the people and territory of a given realm, (2) other states and religious bodies are excluded from exercising political authority over a sovereign people or territory, (3) sovereignty is indivisible, and (4) all sovereign units are formally equal or have the same legal status. The core principles of sovereignty are often violated in practice, but the concept has profound impact on world politics.

Interactions So how did a system of sovereign states come about? One prominent argument comes from Charles Tilly, who argued that "states make wars, and wars make the state." As they bargained and fought over territory and wealth, small units either merged or were absorbed by larger ones. Polities that managed to raise money and manpower effectively outcompeted those that did not.

The institution of sovereignty also emerged out of competitive interactions. The Thirty Years' War (1618–48) was a bloody, European-wide affair that stemmed in part from emerging states' efforts to meddle in one another's internal affairs. The Peace of Westphalia, which ended that conflict, enshrined (even if it did not invent) the concept of sovereignty as a way to restrain this destructive behavior.

As we will see in later chapters, new actors and interactions have challenged the nature of sovereignty. Although the future remains uncertain, what is clear is that states as political units will continue to evolve.

The signing of the Peace of Westphalia.

often assumed to be a defining feature of the modern international system, creating a condition of **anarchy** in which there is no legal authority higher than or above the state to make and enforce laws that bind international actors.[5]

When discussing states as actors, we may use the term in two different ways that are important to distinguish. Scholars sometimes assume that states are motivated by an interest in security—that is, safety from external and internal threats—and in accumulating power as a means to ensure security. These goals are said to be **national interests**, or interests that belong to the state itself. In this usage, the states-as-actors assumption sees international politics as driven by states' quest for security and power.

Alternatively, the states-as-actors concept serves as convenient shorthand for sets of national leaders acting in the name of their countries. This use of the term reflects the fact that many actions in international politics are taken by individuals who represent the state: political leaders, diplomats, members of the armed forces, or others acting in an official capacity. Hence, we often lapse into language like "the United States threatened Iraq" when in fact it was certain representatives of the United States who threatened representatives of Iraq. In this case, we make no prior assumption about where the interests pursued by those agents originate. Sometimes the state's representatives might act on behalf of a particular domestic interest group—for example, when negotiating a trade agreement that is in the interest of exporting industries. Alternatively, state leaders might act to further their own personal or political agendas. In such cases, the interests that matter are those of the interest group or politician, but when those interests play out at the international level, they are pursued by people acting in the name of the state.

As this discussion suggests, there is no fixed or permanent set of actors in international relations. Like the concept of interest, an actor is an analytic concept that is imposed on explanations by observers seeking to understand why events happen in a certain way. Selecting the set of individuals who are identified as the actors in any explanation is a choice we make to help account for observed outcomes. There is no right or wrong way to specify the actors in any event or set of events. As with the concept of interests, we judge different conceptualizations only by whether they are useful in helping us understand world politics.

For example, we know that President Bush made the decision to invade Iraq, but how should we interpret his choice? We could think of him as the head of a state seeking to further the state's interest in security or access to a key natural resource; in this case, the state is the actor whose interests are driving choices. We could also understand Bush as a politician pursuing his personal interest in getting reelected to the presidency; in this case, the individual

anarchy
The absence of a central authority with the ability to make and enforce laws that bind all actors.

national interests
Interests attributed to the state itself, usually security and power.

---

5. The most forceful statement of the importance of anarchy in international relations is Kenneth N. Waltz, *Theory of International Politics* (Reading, MA: Addison-Wesley, 1979). For a critique, see Helen V. Milner, "The Assumption of Anarchy in International Relations: A Critique," *Review of International Studies* 17 (1991): 67-85.

politician is the actor whose political interests are driving the choices. We might also focus on the interests of groups that helped support President Bush's reelection bid, such as oil companies or defense contractors that benefited from war. Alternatively, we could think of Bush as an individual motivated by personal ideology about democracy. For any given policy choice, it may be difficult to know for sure which interests are being pursued; indeed, a single decision may further more than one interest. In these cases, we judge any assumption about actors by how useful it is in explaining the overall pattern of events we observe.

Table 2.1 presents a list of key categories of actors in world politics, the interests commonly ascribed to these actors by analysts, and specific examples. The list, of course, is not exhaustive. Any of the actors can be broken down into smaller sets of individuals for explanatory purposes. But we will encounter these actors again and again throughout this book. In the following chapters, we specify different sets of actors and their interests as needed to explain the puzzles being addressed.

TABLE 2.1 *Key Categories of Actors and Interests in World Politics*

ACTOR	COMMONLY ASCRIBED INTERESTS	EXAMPLES
States	Security, power, wealth, ideology	United States, Canada, China, Switzerland, India, Uruguay
Politicians	Reelection/retention of office, ideology, policy goals	President of the United States, Prime Minister of Great Britain, Speaker of the U.S. House of Representatives
Firms, industries, or business associations	Wealth, profit	General Motors, Sony, the pharmaceutical industry, National Association of Manufacturers, Business Roundtable
Classes or factors of production	Material well-being, wealth	Capital, labor, land, human capital
Bureaucracies	Budget maximization, influence, policy preferences; often summarized by the adage of "where you stand depends on where you sit"	Department of Defense, Department of Commerce, National Security Council, Ministry of Foreign Affairs
International organizations	As composites of states, they reflect the interests of member states according to their voting power. As organizations, they are assumed to be similar to domestic bureaucracies.	United Nations, International Monetary Fund, International Postal Union, Organisation for Economic Co-operation and Development
Nongovernmental organizations, often transnational or international in scope and membership	Moral, ideological, or policy goals; human rights, the environment, religion	Red Cross, Amnesty International, Greenpeace, the Catholic Church

Interactions: Why Can't Actors Always Get What They Want?

Actors make choices in order to further their interests. Yet political outcomes depend not just on the choices of one actor but on the choices of others as well. The United States might have preferred that Saddam Hussein step down peacefully, but the Iraqi dictator refused to yield, and it ultimately took a war to drive him from power. Interests are essential in analyzing any event in international relations because they represent how actors rank alternative outcomes. But to account for outcomes, we must examine the choices of all the relevant actors and how their choices interact to produce a particular result. As we use the term here, **interactions** refers to the ways in which the choices of two or more actors combine to produce political outcomes.

When outcomes result from an interaction, actors have to anticipate the likely choices of others and take those choices into account when making their own decisions. In March 2003, Saddam Hussein's interests in his personal well-being might have led to the following ordering of possible outcomes: (1) stay in power and continue present policies, (2) go into exile in some friendly state, (3) fight and lose a war with the United States. Hussein's only chance at getting his best possible outcome required that he resist U.S. demands to step down. But this risked bringing about his worst possible outcome: war. Whether resisting would lead to his best or worst outcome depended on what the United States would do in response. Would Bush carry out his threat to attack, or would he back down? Whether it made sense for Hussein to resist or step down depended crucially on the answer to this question. If he expected Bush to back down, then resisting U.S. demands would get him his best outcome; if Hussein expected Bush to carry out his threat, then resistance would lead to his worst outcome, and it would have been better to step down. Hence, in making his choice, Hussein had to consider not only what he himself wanted but also what he expected Bush to do. In this case, there is evidence suggesting that Hussein expected opposition on the part of other states, especially Russia and France, to prevent Bush from carrying out his threat—an erroneous expectation that led him to resist.[6] When combined with Bush's determination to invade, this choice ensured a war. Had Hussein been certain that Bush would act as he did, bringing about his eventual execution, he might have chosen differently even though his underlying interests would have been the same. We call such situations *strategic* interactions because each actor's strategy, or plan of action, depends on the anticipated strategy of others. Many of the most intriguing puzzles of international politics derive from such interactions.

interactions
The ways in which the choices of two or more actors combine to produce political outcomes.

[handwritten margin note: Hussein failed to see that American people would disrespect Bush stepping down—hurt chance of reelection.]

---

6. Kevin Woods, Lacey James, and Williamson Murray, "Saddam's Delusions: The View from Inside," *Foreign Affairs* 75 (May–June 2006): 2–26.

The demolition of this large statue of Saddam Hussein in Baghdad in April 2003 symbolized the dictator's fall from power. How can we understand Hussein's decision to risk war with a much more powerful country?

We make two assumptions in studying interactions. First, we assume that actors behave with the intention of producing a desired result. That is, actors are assumed to choose among available options with due regard for their consequences and with the aim of bringing about outcomes they prefer. Second, in cases of strategic interaction, we assume that actors adopt strategies based on what they believe to be the interests and likely actions of others. That is, actors develop strategies that they believe are a best response to the anticipated strategies of others. In the example above, if Hussein believed that Bush would back down from his threat, the best response was to resist American demands; if he believed that Bush would carry out his threat, then the best response was to step down even though doing so would have meant accepting his second-best outcome. A best-response strategy is the actor's plan to do as well as possible in light of the interests and likely strategies of the other relevant actors. Together, these assumptions link interests to choices and, through the interaction of choices, to outcomes.

Formulating a strategy as a best response, of course, does not guarantee that the actor will obtain its most preferred or even a desirable outcome. Sometimes the choices made by others leave actors facing a highly unwelcome outcome, one that may leave them far worse off than the status quo. If one state chooses to initiate a war, for instance, the other state must respond by either giving in to its demands or fighting back, and both options may leave the second state less well off than before the attack. Saddam Hussein was clearly better off before the U.S. attack in March 2003; but once the fighting began, the prewar status quo was no longer an option. A strategy is a plan to do as well as possible given one's expectations about the interests and actions of others. It is not a guarantee that one will obtain one's most preferred result.

Understanding the outcomes produced by the often complex interplay of the strategies of two or more actors can be difficult. A specialized form of theory, called game theory, has been invented to study strategic interactions. We offer a brief introduction to game theory in the "Special Topic" appendix to this chapter, focusing on relatively simple games to communicate the core ideas behind strategic interaction.

Cooperation and Bargaining

Interactions can take various forms, but most can be grouped into two broad categories: cooperation and bargaining. Political interactions usually involve both forms in varying degrees.

Interactions are cooperative when actors have a shared interest in achieving an outcome and must work together to do so. **Cooperation** occurs when two or more actors adopt policies that make at least one actor better off without making any other actor worse off. Opportunities for cooperation arise all the time in social and political life. A group of friends may want to throw a party, but none of them can spare the time or money to do so alone. If they all contribute a little, then they can each enjoy the benefits of throwing the party. The members of a community would all benefit if there were good roads to drive on and clean water to drink, but again, no individual may be able to provide these on his or her own. If they all agree to pay taxes to some central agency that will provide roads and water, then they can all be better off. A group of firms may share an interest in lobbying Congress for trade protection from foreign imports. By pooling their resources and acting together, they may be more effective at getting their way than they would be on their own. In the international system, states may have opportunities to cooperate to defend one another from attack, to further a shared interest in free trade or stable monetary relations, to protect the global environment, or to uphold human rights. We will look more closely at each of these types of situations in the following chapters. In the case of Iraq, a number of states in the international community loathed or feared Saddam Hussein's regime, and they may have seen his removal as preferable to the status quo. Some of these—especially the United States and Great Britain—chose to cooperate in a military effort to oust Hussein's regime. Both contributed significant military forces and other resources in the expectation that joint action would make them better off relative to either maintaining the status quo or acting alone.

Cooperation is defined from the perspectives of the two or more actors who are interacting. Even though their cooperation may make those actors better off, it may hurt other parties. The friends agreeing to throw a party together may disrupt their neighbors by making noise late into the night. Firms that cooperate to lobby Congress for trade protection may impose higher prices on consumers. The countries that cooperated to oust Saddam Hussein clearly made the

cooperation
An interaction in which two or more actors adopt policies that make at least one actor better off relative to the status quo without making others worse off.

dictator worse off. Indeed, cooperation is not always an unmitigated good; its benefits exist only for those who adjust their policies to bring about an outcome they prefer.

Figure 2.1 presents a simple depiction of the problem of cooperation between two actors. Imagine that two actors can enact policies that have the potential to increase their overall income or welfare. The income of the actors is depicted along two dimensions, with Actor A's income increasing along the horizontal axis and Actor B's income increasing along the vertical axis. All points within the graph represent possible outcomes produced by different combinations of policies chosen by the two actors.

Assume that by cooperating the two actors can make as much as $1,000, a limit determined in this case by the available technology and resources. This limit is depicted by the downward-sloping line in Figure 2.1, which shows all the different ways $1,000 can be divided between the two actors. The point at which the line touches the horizontal axis depicts a situation in which Actor A gets $1,000 and Actor B gets nothing; the point at which the line touches the vertical axis depicts a situation in which Actor B gets all the money; and every point in between represents different divisions of the maximum feasible income. For example, if the two actors cooperate to make the maximum income in such a way that State A gets $600, then State B would get $400; if State A gets $200, then State B gets $800. This line representing the possible divisions of the maximum feasible benefit is called the *Pareto frontier*, after the Italian economist Vilfredo Pareto (1848–1923), who developed these ideas.

FIGURE 2.1   *Cooperation*

In this world, there is $1000 worth of a good that can be captured by State A and State B. In the status quo, State A gets $200 and State B gets $200. Through cooperation, both states can improve their outcomes by capturing and sharing the remaining $600. The green shaded triangle—defined by the points *q*, *a*, and *b*—outlines all possible superior outcomes.

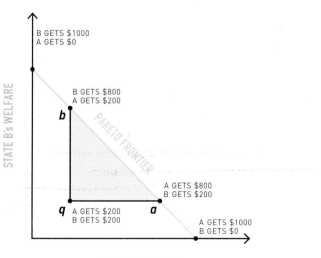

However, the actors may have chosen policies that do not result in the maximum possible benefit. Let us assume that past policy combinations have produced an outcome referred to as the status quo (q). As q is depicted here, the actors are not doing as well as they could, with each making, say, $200, for a total of $400 rather than $1,000. This means that they could potentially benefit by changing their policies to get closer to the Pareto frontier line and thus to the maximum feasible income. Any policy combination that leads to an outcome in the shaded area *qba* would make both actors better off than they are under the status quo. Moving outward from q, into the shaded area, represents cooperation, or an improvement in the welfare of at least one actor.

We can see that policies along the line segment between q and a improve A's welfare at no loss to B, while policies along the line segment between q and b improve B's welfare at no loss to A. Any movement into the shaded area between points q, b, and a represents an improvement in the welfare of both actors, and any policy combination on the Pareto frontier between b and a makes the actors as well off as possible given available resources and technology. Cooperation consists of mutual policy adjustments that move actors toward or onto the Pareto frontier, increasing the welfare of some or all partners without diminishing the welfare of any one actor. Because it makes at least one party better off than otherwise, we refer to cooperation as a *positive-sum game*.

Whereas cooperative interactions involve the potential for mutual gain, **bargaining** describes an interaction in which actors must choose outcomes that make one better off at the expense of another. For example, two states may want the same piece of territory. Bargaining describes the process by which they come to divide the territory. They may negotiate, impose sanctions on one another, or fight. All these tactics are different forms of bargaining. Given the nature of the situation, the more territory one side gets, the less the other gets. Bargaining is represented in Figure 2.2. When actors bargain, they move along the Pareto frontier, as represented by the green arrow. On the frontier line, any improvement in A's welfare comes strictly at the expense of B's welfare. For this reason, bargaining is sometimes called a *zero-sum game* because the gains for one side perfectly match the losses of the other. For example, if Actor A gains 100 percent of a contested piece of territory under a given bargain, that means Actor B gets 0 percent of the territory; if Actor A gives up 20 percent of the territory through bargaining, Actor B gains that 20 percent of the territory. Bargaining is purely redistributive; that is, rather than creating additional value, as in the case of cooperation, it only allocates a fixed sum of value between different actors. We typically represent war as a bargaining interaction. In the case of the Iraq War, the United States and Iraq were not cooperating but bargaining over the latter's WMD programs and, ultimately, its regime. We will take a closer look at bargaining in war in Chapter 3.

Most interactions in international relations combine elements of both cooperation and bargaining (Figure 2.3). Although both may gain by moving to the frontier, A prefers bargains that leave it closer to a, whereas B prefers bargains that leave it closer to b. Movement toward the frontier makes at least one actor better off, but where on the frontier they end up makes an important difference.

bargaining
An interaction in which actors must choose outcomes that make one better off at the expense of another. Bargaining is redistributive: it involves allocating a fixed sum of value between different actors.

FIGURE 2.2 *Bargaining*

State A and State B are bargaining over the division of $1000. Each point along the line is a possible division. For every $1 that State A gains, State B loses $1, and vice versa.

The horizontal bar below is a different representation of the same concept as the diagonal bar above. The bar represents a good that both State A and State B want. The more State A gets, the less State B gets (possible deal 1); the more State B gets, the less State A gets (possible deal 2).

For example, even as the United States, Britain, and other states had interests in cooperating to defeat Iraq, they bargained over how much each would contribute to the effort. In many interactions, actors are cooperating and bargaining simultaneously, and the outcomes of both interactions are linked. Successful cooperation generates gains worth bargaining over. And if the actors cannot reach a bargain over the division of gains, they may end up failing to cooperate.[7]

---

7. On bargaining and cooperating simultaneously, see James D. Fearon, "Bargaining, Enforcement, and International Cooperation," *International Organization* 52 (1998): 269–305.

FIGURE 2.3 ***Cooperation and Bargaining***

Through cooperation, State A and State B can improve their joint outcome from the starting point—the status quo—to capture an additional $600. But they have to bargain over exactly how that $600 will be divided between them.

Cooperation and bargaining can succeed or fail for many reasons. Just because actors might benefit from cooperation does not mean they will actually change their policies to realize the possible gains. And even though bargaining might seem doomed to fail—after all, why would one actor agree to reduce its welfare?—actors often do succeed in redistributing valuable goods between themselves. We now turn to some of the primary factors that influence the success or failure of cooperation and, later, bargaining.

When Can Actors Cooperate?

If cooperation makes actors better off, why do they sometimes fail to cooperate? By far the most important factor lies in each actor's interests. Even when actors have a collective interest in cooperating, there are situations in which their individual interests lead them to "defect"—that is, to adopt an uncooperative strategy that undermines the collective goal. How strong the incentives are to defect goes a long way toward determining the prospects for cooperation.[8]

Consider the easiest kind of cooperative interaction, what we call a problem of **coordination**. This kind of situation arises when actors need only coordinate their actions with one another, and once their actions are coordinated, none receives any benefit from defecting. A classic example is deciding which side of the road

coordination

A type of cooperative interaction in which actors benefit from all making the same choices and subsequently have no incentive to not comply.

---

8. On the general forms of cooperation reviewed here, see Arthur A. Stein, "Coordination and Collaboration Regimes in an Anarchic World," *International Organization* 36 (1982): 299–324; Duncan Snidal, "Coordination versus Prisoner's Dilemma: Implications for International Cooperation and Regimes," *American Political Science Review* 79 (December 1985): 923-42; and Lisa L. Martin, "Interests, Power, and Multilateralism," *International Organization* 46 (1992): 765–92.

cars should drive on. Drivers have a shared interest in avoiding crashes, so they are always better off if all drive on the right or the left rather than some driving on each side of the road. It does not matter which side of the road is selected; indeed, different countries have different rules: cars drive on the right side of the road in the United States and continental Europe and on the left side in Great Britain and Japan. What matters is that all drivers in the region make the same choice. Moreover, no driver would intentionally deviate from that choice, since doing so would be very dangerous. In short, there is no incentive to defect from the coordinated arrangement. In the international economy, firms, industries, and even governments face coordination problems all the time, as suggested by the numerous agreements on international standards. There are many ways to encode information to be sent over the Internet, for instance, but all firms producing devices connected to the Internet—computers, smartphones, gaming devices and the like—are better off coordinating on a single format. Similarly, it is more important for international airline pilots to speak a single language so as to communicate effectively with one another and with air traffic controllers worldwide than which language they choose. In coordination situations, cooperation is self-sustaining because once coordination is achieved, no one can benefit by unilaterally defecting.

A more serious barrier to cooperation arises if the actors have an individual incentive to defect from cooperation, even though cooperation could make everyone better off. Cooperative interactions in which actors have a unilateral incentive to defect are called problems of **collaboration**. This kind of problem is often illustrated by a simple game called the Prisoner's Dilemma. Imagine that two criminals have been detained by the police. The district attorney does not have enough evidence to convict them on felony charges but can convict each suspect for a misdemeanor. She confines the prisoners separately and presents each with the following offer: "If neither of you are willing to testify, I will charge both of you with a misdemeanor and sentence you each to one year in prison. If you defect on your accomplice by providing evidence against him, I will let you go free and will put him in prison for ten years. However, he has been offered the same deal. If he provides evidence against you, you'll be the one behind bars. Finally, if you both squeal on one another, you'll each be charged with a felony, but your sentences will be reduced to five years in exchange for testifying."

Collectively, the prisoners would do best by cooperating with each other and refusing to testify–they would, together, only serve a total of only two years behind bars. However, the prisoners are motivated not by the collective outcome but rather by the desire to shorten their own individual sentences. Thus, they have an incentive to rat out the other. Each prisoner reasons as follows: "Suppose my partner stays quiet. In that case, I should defect on him so that I will be released immediately rather than remain quiet and spend a year behind bars. On the other hand, suppose that my accomplice plans to defect on me. In that case, I should also defect on him, because giving testimony will reduce my sentence to five years rather than the ten I will face if I stay quiet."

Because both prisoners reason the same way, both will end up providing evidence against the other and both will be imprisoned for five years. This outcome, of

collaboration

A type of cooperative interaction in which actors gain from working together but nonetheless have incentives to not comply with any agreement.

FIGURE 2.4 *U.S. and USSR/Russian Strategic Nuclear Weapons Inventories, 1945–2013*

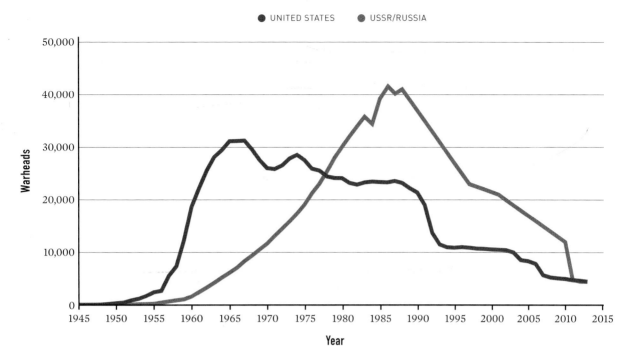

course, is worse for each of them than the outcome they could have achieved if they cooperated with one another and remained silent; the dilemma is that each individual's incentive to defect against the other undermines their collective interest in cooperation. This dilemma is explored further using game theory in the chapter appendix.

Although the dilemma of fictional prisoners may seem remote from the subject matter of this book, analogous situations often arise in international relations. Consider the nuclear arms race between the United States and the Soviet Union during the Cold War. Both countries built costly nuclear weapons at a furious pace, such that by the late 1980s the United States had about 23,000 nuclear weapons while the Soviet Union had around 36,000 (Figure 2.4). One might ask, Why not agree to stop building when the United States had 2,300 warheads and the Soviet Union had 3,600? That would have kept the same ratio of forces but at much lower cost. Both states might have been better off with such an agreement. The problem, however, is that each state had an incentive to cheat on such a deal in order to attain superiority over the other. If one stopped building, the other would be tempted to keep going. Therefore, each feared that its own restraint in building weapons would be exploited, leaving it vulnerable. Given these incentives and fears, the best strategy for each state was to go on amassing weapons. This left both countries worse off than if they could have cooperated to limit their arms competition.[9]

Figure source: Hans M. Kristensen and Robert S. Norris, "Global Nuclear Weapons Inventories, 1945–2013," *Bulletin of the Atomic Scientists* 69 (2013): 75–81.

---

9. In fact, the United States and the Soviet Union did sign several arms control agreements, which may have prevented the arms race from being even worse. It was not until the collapse of the Soviet Union in 1991 that serious reductions in nuclear armaments took place.

public goods

Products that are nonexcludable and nonrival in consumption, such as national defense.

collective action problems

Obstacles to cooperation that occur when actors have incentives to collaborate but each acts in anticipation that others will pay the costs of cooperation.

free ride

To fail to contribute to a public good while benefiting from the contributions of others.

A specific type of collaboration problem arises in providing **public goods**, which are products such as national defense, clean air and water, and the eradication of communicable diseases. Public goods are defined by two qualities. First, if the good is provided to one person, others cannot be excluded from enjoying it as well (formally, the good is *nonexcludable*). If one person in a country is protected from foreign invasion, for instance, all other citizens are also protected. Second, if one person consumes or benefits from the public good, this does not diminish the quantity available to others (formally, the good is *nonrival in consumption*). Again using an example from national defense, one person's enjoyment of protection from foreign invasion does not diminish the quantity of security available to others. Many global environmental issues, such as ozone depletion and climate change, are also public goods (as we will discuss in more detail in Chapter 13). Public goods are contrasted with purely private goods, which are products that only one person can possess and consume. Your sandwich for lunch is a private good—that is, if it's available to you, it is not automatically available to all others; and if you eat it, it is not available to be eaten by others.

Efforts to produce public goods always face **collective action problems**, which we will encounter many times in this book. Given that actors can enjoy public goods whether or not they contribute to the provision of those goods, each acts in anticipation that others will pay to produce the good while it gets to enjoy the good for free. That is, each actor aims to benefit from the contributions of others without bearing the costs itself. For example, individuals would prefer to benefit from national security without paying taxes or volunteering for military service. Alternatively, all states might want a genocide to be stopped, but each would prefer that others assume the risks of the necessary military intervention. In the case of Iraq, it is quite possible that some countries publicly opposed the U.S.-led invasion *not* because they opposed ousting Hussein, but because they wanted to benefit from the regime change without paying the military, political, or diplomatic costs of backing the invasion. In such situations, even though everyone wants the public good to be provided, each individual has an incentive to **free ride** by not contributing while benefiting from the efforts of others. When contributions are voluntary, free riding leads public goods to be provided at a lower level than that desired by the actors.

This is why public goods are often provided by governments, which have the power to tax citizens or otherwise mandate their contributions. Free riding is no longer so attractive if, say, the failure to contribute taxes can lead to steep fines or imprisonment. This is also why collaboration among governments on global issues can prove so difficult, as there is no international authority that can mandate their contributions to global public goods.

As this discussion suggests, some of the problems associated with cooperation are addressed by institutions, which might be able to alter actors' incentives so that their individual interests line up with the collective interest. The role of institutions in promoting cooperation is discussed later in this chapter. Even in the absence of institutions, though, we can identify several factors that facilitate cooperation.

Factors that facilitate cooperation

Numbers and Relative Sizes of the Actors

It is easier for a smaller number of actors to cooperate and, if necessary, to monitor each other's behavior than for a larger number of actors to do so. Two actors can communicate more readily and observe the other's actions better than a thousand actors can. Thus, the smaller the number of actors, the more likely they are to cooperate successfully. As we shall see in Chapter 7, firms can organize more easily to lobby their governments for trade protection than can consumers, who are typically more numerous. Environmental agreements are easier to monitor and enforce—thus, more likely to be agreed upon—among small groups of countries.

In the case of public goods, moreover, there may be groups in which a single member or a small coalition of members is willing to pay for the entire public good. This would happen if these members receive benefits from the public good sufficient to offset the entire costs of providing it. In such *privileged groups*, the single member or small coalition of members provides the public good despite free riding by others.[10] As we will see in Chapter 5, international efforts to enforce agreements in civil conflicts generally require that a very powerful state, such as the United States, be motivated to conduct a peacekeeping operation largely on its own. Similarly, success in limiting ozone emissions (see Chapter 13) stemmed in part from the disproportionately large role of the United States, Russia, and Japan in the industries responsible for the emissions. Some analysts attribute the economic openness of the international economy in the mid-nineteenth and mid-twentieth centuries to public goods like the international monetary regime provided unilaterally by Britain and the United States, which were the largest powers in those eras, respectively.

Iteration, Linkage, and Strategies of Reciprocal Punishment

Cooperation is more likely to occur when actors have opportunities to cooperate over time and across issues. The incentive to defect or free ride in any given interaction can be overcome if actors expect to be involved in multiple, repeated interactions with the same partners.[11] In this situation—commonly known as **iteration**—actors can prevent one another from cheating by threatening to withhold cooperation in the future. Even when actors have incentives to defect in the current interaction, knowing that the other actor will refuse to cooperate with it in the future can offset those temptations. Thus, "good behavior" can be induced today by the fear of losing the benefits from cooperation tomorrow. The threat of reciprocal punishment can be a powerful tool for enforcing cooperation even when actors are tempted to cheat.[12] You are more likely to leave a generous tip for the waiter at a local restaurant you are likely to

iteration
Repeated interactions with the same partners.

---

10. On privileged groups, see Mancur Olson, *The Logic of Collective Action: Public Goods and the Theory of Groups* (Cambridge, MA: Harvard University Press, 1965).

11. On iteration and international cooperation, see Robert Axelrod, *The Evolution of Cooperation* (New York: Basic Books, 1984).

12. For the expectation of future punishment to induce current cooperation, however, actors must value the future enough that future gains matter. Everyone discounts the future—that is, they value it somewhat less than the present. A dollar today is worth more to us than a dollar next year and much more than a dollar received in 20 years. The more actors discount the future, the less likely the threat of future punishment is to encourage them to cooperate today. Conversely, the more actors value the future, the more likely the threat of future punishment is to encourage cooperation now.

Interactions: Why Can't Actors Always Get What They Want?   **61**

For decades, the United States and Great Britain have cooperated closely. In 2012, U.S. President Barack Obama met with British Prime Minister David Cameron to coordinate troop withdrawals from Afghanistan. Even though the two leaders come from opposite ends of the political spectrum, the repeated interactions between the countries have sustained a history of deep cooperation.

linkage

The linking of cooperation on one issue to interactions on a second issue.

frequent in the future—lest you get poor service on another visit—than you are in a restaurant you will never visit again. Countries are less likely to cheat on a trade agreement with a country they trade with more often and expect to trade with again in the future (see Chapter 7).

Closely related to iteration is the concept of **linkage**, which ties cooperation on one policy dimension to cooperation on other dimensions. Whereas iteration allows victims to punish cheaters by withholding the gains from future cooperation, linkage allows victims to retaliate by withholding cooperation on other issues. Defection on military affairs, for instance, might be punished by withdrawing cooperation on economic matters. One of the reasons the United States and Great Britain have been able to sustain their "special relationship" of deep cooperation, including on Iraq, is that they are bound together on so many different issues. The failure of cooperation on one dimension puts cooperation on other issues at risk and reinforces cooperation on all.

Information Finally, the availability of information affects the likelihood of cooperation. In some cases, it is easy to observe whether a partner has cooperated or defected, such as when cooperation entails a public act like participating in a military operation. In other cases, however, cooperative and uncooperative acts may be hard to observe or distinguish from one another. If cooperation involves reducing armaments, for example, the fact that states can build weapons in secret means that defection may not be observed.

When actors lack information about the actions taken by another party, cooperation may fail due to uncertainty and misperception.[13] A state might defect under the mistaken belief that it can get away with it, or because it doubts other parties will abide by its terms. Alternatively, cooperation might unravel if cooperative acts are mistaken for defection. Suppose one party mistakenly believes that the other has defected and cuts off cooperation as punishment; the other party, which has been cooperating all along, then perceives the first actor's punishment as a new defection and then cuts off cooperation in retaliation. Simple misperceptions can lead to hostile punishments and the

---

13. On the consequences of misperception, see Robert Jervis, *Perception and Misperception in International Relations* (Princeton, NJ: Princeton University Press, 1976).

breakdown of cooperation even though all actors thought they were acting cooperatively.[14] In the years leading up to the Iraq War, Saddam Hussein really had dismantled his WMD programs as required by the UN, but he was reluctant to reveal this information because he wanted to use the possibility of such weapons to deter domestic insurgents and other regional powers, especially Iran.[15] Had Iraq's disarmament been more easily confirmed, the main rationale for the war would have been eliminated.

Who Wins and Who Loses in Bargaining?

Whereas cooperation has the potential to make actors collectively better off, bargaining creates winners and losers: each actor's gains come at the expense of someone else. When two or more actors desire the same good—for example, a sum of money or a piece of territory—it is impossible for all of them to get their best possible outcome at the same time. Why, then, are bargains ever reached? Why do actors consent to losses? What determines who wins and who loses?

Considering these questions introduces a core concept in international politics: power. In the standard definition, which we owe to the political scientist Robert Dahl, **power** is the ability of Actor A to get Actor B to do something that B would otherwise not do.[16] In the context of bargaining, power is most usefully seen as the ability to get the other side to make concessions and to avoid having to make concessions oneself. The more power an actor has, the more it can expect to get from others in the final outcome of bargaining.

Power is one of the most frequently used, yet ambiguous terms in the study of international relations. Sometimes it is understood as an end in itself—an interest, as we have defined that concept above—and sometimes as a means toward other ends. Other times, it is conceived as a structure or constraint created by past interactions that limit the choices currently available to actors. Their large economies, past investments in military forces, and large stockpiles of nuclear weapons, for instance, gave the United States and Soviet Union enormous political advantages over other countries during the Cold War, deterring other states from even contemplating challenging the core interests of either superpower.

Our focus here, in the context of explaining bargaining outcomes, is on what is sometimes called compulsory power, or the ability of one actor to compel another to act in certain ways.[17] Understood in this way, the outcome of any bargaining interaction is fundamentally influenced by what would happen in the event that no bargain is reached. The outcome that occurs when no bargain is achieved is often

power

The ability of Actor A to get Actor B to do something that B would otherwise not do; the ability to get the other side to make concessions and to avoid having to make concessions oneself.

---

14. George W. Downs, David M. Rocke, and Randolph M. Siverson, "Arms Race and Cooperation," in *Cooperation under Anarchy*, ed. Kenneth Oye, 118–46 (Princeton, NJ: Princeton University Press, 1986).

15. This is the conclusion reached by the Iraq Survey Group, which examined Iraq's WMD program after the regime fell. See U.S. Central Intelligence Agency, "Comprehensive Report of the Special Advisor to the DCI on Iraq's WMD," September 30, 2004, www.cia.gov/library/reports/general-reports-1/iraq_wmd_2004/index.html (accessed 05/09/08).

16. Robert A. Dahl, "The Concept of Power," *Behavioral Scientist* 2 (July 1957).

17. See Michael Barnett and Raymond Duvall, eds., *Power in Global Governance* (New York: Cambridge University Press, 2005).

nothing is achieved

called the *reversion outcome*. In some cases, the reversion outcome is the same as the status quo. For example, if a car buyer and a prospective seller cannot agree on a price, then the seller is left with his car and the buyer keeps her money. What is lost is a chance to make a potentially profitable deal. When actors bargain over the terms of cooperation, a failure to agree can prevent the collective benefits from being enjoyed. For example, if states contemplating intervention in a civil war or negotiating an environmental treaty cannot agree on how to divide the costs, then the civil conflict will rage on or the environmental harm will continue. In other cases, the consequences of disagreement are more severe: the reversion outcome may be a war or some other kind of conflict, such as economic sanctions, that leaves one or even both actors worse off than before the dispute began.

The actor that would be more satisfied with the reversion outcome generally has less incentive to make concessions in order to reach a successful bargain. Conversely, the actor that would be less satisfied with the reversion outcome becomes desperate to reach an agreement and thus offers relatively bigger concessions in the hopes of inducing the more satisfied actor to agree. In short, bargaining power belongs to those actors who would be most satisfied with, or most willing to endure, the reversion outcome. In the car-buying example, if the seller needs money and is anxious to sell the car quickly, a more patient buyer can extract a better deal. Internationally, in negotiations over global climate change, the United States has been less willing to go along with other countries in part because the expected costs of climate change to the United States are lower. Given its geography and economic resources, the United States is better equipped than many other states to weather the effects of a warming planet and rising sea levels. As a result, the United States has, so far, successfully shifted the burden of cutting greenhouse gas emissions onto others (see Chapter 13). In the case of Iraq, the United States had a great stake in rebuilding that country and ending the violence that killed thousands of U.S. troops. Despite its enormous power in most respects, the United States had a hard time convincing other countries, which were less directly hurt by the status quo, to share the costs of Iraq's reconstruction. Those most in need of agreement are likely to get worse bargains than those who can better tolerate the reversion outcome.

Because bargaining outcomes are largely determined by how each actor evaluates the reversion outcome, power derives from the ability to make the reversion outcome better for oneself and/or worse for the other side. To shift the reversion outcome in their favor, actors have three basic ways of exercising power: coercion, outside options, and agenda setting.

coercion

A strategy of imposing or threatening to impose costs on other actors in order to induce a change in their behavior.

Coercion   The most obvious strategy for exercising power is coercion. **Coercion** is the threat or imposition of costs on others to reduce the value of the reversion outcome (no agreement) and change their behavior. Thus, states can use their ability to impose costs on others to demand a more favorable bargain than they would otherwise receive. The demand of the United States that Saddam Hussein step down or be removed by force is an example of coercive bargaining that left the Iraqi dictator worse off than before the threat was made. The target, of course, can itself try to impose costs on the challenger. What matters is the net ability to impose costs on the other—that is, the difference between the coercion employed by one side and that employed by the other. If the costs each side can impose on the other are equal, neither party has power. The reversion outcome for both parties will be worse than the status quo and both will be more desperate to reach agreement, but neither will have any greater power over the other. It is the ability to impose greater costs on the other actor than that actor can impose on the first that creates power through coercion.

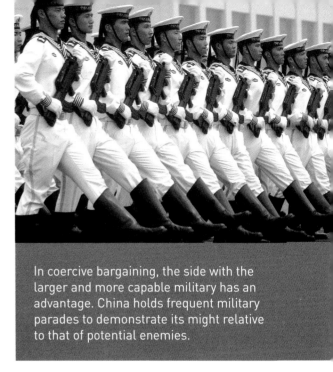

In coercive bargaining, the side with the larger and more capable military has an advantage. China holds frequent military parades to demonstrate its might relative to that of potential enemies.

Means of international coercion include military force and economic sanctions. The ability to impose costs on others and to defend against others' efforts to impose costs on oneself, derives in large part from material capabilities: the physical resources that allow an actor to inflict harm and/or withstand the infliction of harm. In coercive interactions among states, these capabilities are often measured in terms of military resources—such as the number of military personnel or level of military spending—as well as measures of economic strength, since economic resources can be converted into military power. The balance of such capabilities among states is a strong predictor (though not the only one) of who wins and who loses in warfare.[18] Similarly, the size of a country's economy has an impact on its ability to impose and/or withstand economic sanctions, which cut off a country's access to international trade.

Although material capabilities such as guns and money are important components of power, we will see in Chapter 3 that other factors can also be sources of power in coercive bargaining. Since the use of force is costly and risky, an actor's willingness to absorb costs and take risks can also generate an advantage. The economist Thomas Schelling famously described international crises as competitions in risk taking likely to be "won" by the side that blinks second (see the game of Chicken described in this chapter's appendix).[19] This helps explain why weak states can at times defeat great powers. When France tried to reassert colonial control over Vietnam after World War II, the leader of the Vietnamese resistance, Ho Chi Minh, warned the French that their superior military power would not matter: "You will kill 10 of our men, and we will kill 1 of yours, and in the end it will be you who tire of it."[20] The Vietnamese leader's optimism sprang from the belief that his people were more willing to bear the costs of war. His power stemmed not from military capabilities but from what we will refer to in Chapter 3 as resolve.

Outside Options Actors can also get a better deal when they have attractive **outside options**, or alternatives to reaching a bargain with a particular partner that are more

outside options
The alternatives to bargaining with a specific actor.

---

18. See, for example, Dan Reiter and Allan C. Stam, *Democracies at War* (Princeton, NJ: Princeton University Press, 2002).

19. Thomas C. Schelling, *The Strategy of Conflict* (Cambridge, MA: Harvard University Press, 1960).

20. This quotation is often cited, and the exact wording sometimes varies. The original source is Jean Sainteny, *L'histoire d'une paix manquée: Indochine, 1945–47* (Paris: Amiot-Dumont, 1953), 231.

attractive than the status quo. In this case, the reversion outcome is the next-best alternative for the party with the outside option. The actor with an attractive alternative can walk away from the bargaining table more easily than an actor without such an option.

The actor with the better outside option can use its leverage, the threat to leave negotiations, to get a better deal. For example, even though the United States might have preferred to work through the UN to remove Saddam Hussein from power in Iraq in 2003, the U.S. government felt that it had an attractive outside option: acting unilaterally. The United States' military capabilities meant that even though it might benefit from international support, it did not feel that such support was necessary to prevail. Thus, while other countries on the Security Council tried to influence U.S. policy in the dispute, their bargaining power was greatly diminished by the fact that the United States felt that it could "go it alone."

Like coercion, however, it is the relative attractiveness of each actor's outside option that matters. Both actors may have alternatives, but the one with the more attractive outside option can more credibly threaten to walk away and, therefore, can get the better deal. In competitive economic markets with many buyers and sellers, for instance, there is little power exercised by any actor, as every buyer or seller has equally attractive outside options. In the case of the UN, again, the United States had an ability to act unilaterally that was not available to the Security Council, which had only the very unattractive alternatives of fielding a military force of its own to stop the United States from invading Iraq or perhaps imposing sanctions on the United States for ignoring its wishes. The Security Council could not, therefore, exercise any significant power over the United States.

Agenda Setting

agenda-setting power

A "first mover" advantage that helps an actor to secure a more favorable bargain.

Agenda Setting Similarly, actors might gain leverage in bargaining through **agenda-setting power.** Whereas an outside option is exercised in the event bargaining fails, agenda setting involves actions taken prior to or during bargaining that make the reversion outcome more favorable for one party. A party that can act first to set the agenda transforms the choices available to others. For example, by sponsoring legislative proposals, calling public attention to issues, and cajoling individual legislators, the president of the United States has important agenda-setting power in Congress. Faced with a presidential proposal or a presidentially inspired public outcry, legislators often have little choice but to respond to the president's initiative; they do not necessarily have to agree with the president's proposal, but they must respond to an issue they might have otherwise preferred to avoid.[21] The same agenda-setting power exists between countries. When the United States deregulated its airline industry to capitalize on its market position and benefit its domestic consumers, other countries were forced to deregulate their industries as well in order to remain competitive, often over the opposition of their national air carriers. In the Iraq War, the United States exercised its agenda-setting power both by bringing the inspections issue before the UN Security Council and by unilaterally initiating a war against Iraq, to which other countries were then forced to respond.

---

21. John W. Kingdon, *Agendas, Alternatives, and Public Policies,* 2nd ed. (New York: HarperCollins, 1995).

Even though bargaining creates winners and losers, bargains can be made as long as they give all parties more than (or at least as much as) they can expect to get in the reversion outcome. In other words, actors consent to painful concessions when the consequences of not agreeing are even more painful. As we will see in Chapter 3, the fact that there exist bargains that all sides prefer over war does not guarantee that those bargains will always be reached. There are a host of problems that can prevent actors from finding or agreeing to mutually beneficial deals. For example, uncertainty about how each side evaluates its prospects in a war can make it hard to know which bargains are preferable to war. There may also be situations in which states cannot credibly promise to abide by an agreement that has already been made. Bargaining may also be complicated if the good being bargained over is hard to divide. (Since this is a broad topic, we leave fuller consideration of these issues for Chapter 3.)

In sum, both interests and interactions matter in politics. Political outcomes depend on the choices of two or more actors. Since political outcomes are contingent on the choices of two or more actors, any given actor does not always or even most of the time get its most preferred interest. Indeed, in bargaining, an actor may be worse off afterward than if it had not entered the interaction at all. Interactions are often quite complex, but they are critical to understanding how interests are transformed into outcomes—often in paradoxical ways.

Institutions: Do Rules Matter in World Politics?

Institutions play a major role in social and political life, domestically and internationally. We typically define **institutions** as sets of rules, known and shared by the relevant community, that structure interactions in specific ways. Many political institutions are embodied in laws or organizations. The U.S. Congress has rules that determine who gets elected to it and how it passes laws. Further rules determine how Congress deals with other American political institutions, such as the presidency and the courts. The UN is an institution in which states make collective decisions about military actions or economic sanctions; the UN has rules that determine which states have a say over these matters and how their votes are counted. International economic institutions include the International Monetary Fund (IMF), the World Trade Organization (WTO), and the World Bank. Other institutions are more informal and exist only as shared understandings of principles and norms. These informal institutions, such as the widespread international norm against slavery, can also be important (see Chapter 11).

Institutions vary in their goals and rules, but they generally serve to facilitate cooperation among their members.[22] As discussed in the previous section, even

institution

A set of rules (known and shared by the community) that structure interactions in specific ways.

---

22. See Robert O. Keohane, *After Hegemony: Cooperation and Discord in the World Political Economy* (Princeton, NJ: Princeton University Press, 1984).

when actors have common interests, there may be factors that make cooperation more difficult. Cooperation can flounder if the problems identified above—incentives to defect, large numbers of actors, nonrepeated interactions, and imperfect information—are not successfully resolved. Institutions can provide solutions to these problems. Indeed, it is precisely to facilitate cooperation that actors first create and subsequently comply with the rules embodied in institutions.

How Do Institutions Affect Cooperation?

In much of political and social life, the primary way that institutions promote cooperation is through enforcement, or the imposing of punishments on actors who fail to cooperate. Imagine, for example, that the prisoners in the Prisoner's Dilemma game were both members of an organized crime group, and it was understood that members who rat each other out will find themselves at the bottom of a river wearing cement shoes. In that case, the prisoners no longer have an individual incentive to defect on each other; the external enforcement by the organization changes the way they rank-order the possible outcomes, and cooperation between them now makes sense both individually as well as collectively. Similarly, governments provide public goods by compelling individuals to pay for them in the form of taxes; the threat of fines or jail time for failing to pay weakens the incentive to free ride on the contributions of others. Cooperation among private actors within a country may also be enforced by institutions. For example, a sales contract between a customer and a firm can be enforced by courts, whose rulings are backed by the police powers of the state. In short, when institutions have means of imposing punishments for defection, they can effectively enforce cooperation.

Institutions at the international level generally lack the capacity to impose punishments on states. The international system is characterized by anarchy as explained above. Whereas most countries are governed by states—a central authority with the ability to make and enforce laws within its boundaries—there is no such central authority at the global level. Some people think the UN is a world government, but as we will see in Chapters 5 and 11, this is not the case. Even poor, weak states have more enforcement power over their citizens than the UN has over actors in the international system. It cannot tax, raise its own military, or field its own police force.

The condition of anarchy means that international institutions do not generally enforce cooperation among their members. Instead, cooperation at the international level has to be self-enforcing: that is, the members have to police themselves and assume responsibility for punishing defectors. The fact that countries are largely dependent on self-help does not mean that international institutions are useless, but it does shape our understanding of the role they play. In general, international institutions, even informal ones, facilitate cooperation by making self-enforcement easier. They do so in at least four ways: by setting standards of behavior, verifying compliance, reducing the costs of joint decision making, and resolving disputes. Different institutions may emphasize one or another of these tasks, but all are important.

Setting Standards of Behavior
Clear standards of behavior reduce ambiguity and enhance cooperation. For example, parents who tell a teenager, "Don't stay out too late or else," invite continuing conflict. What does "too late" mean? "Or else" is also ambiguous. If the parent grounds the teenager for a week, is this "unfair," as the aggrieved youth will likely claim, or "letting her off easy," as the parent will likely retort? The costs of this conflict could have been avoided by making clear that the teenager should "be home by midnight, or you'll be grounded for a week." The teenager might still choose to stay out later, but the standard for evaluating lateness and the consequences would no longer be in dispute.

International institutions set standards of behavior in similar ways. The North American Free Trade Agreement (NAFTA) among the United States, Mexico, and Canada contains 22 chapters and seven annexes of detailed rules governing trade and investment among the three countries, as well as exceptions to general rules for particular practices and industries. Arms control agreements between the United States and the Soviet Union during the Cold War often ran to hundreds of pages detailing precise numbers for different types of weapons systems and limits on their capabilities. Following the 1991 Persian Gulf War, the UN Security Council passed Resolution 661 prohibiting Iraq from possessing or developing all chemical, biological, and nuclear weapons and any ballistic missile with a range greater than 150 kilometers; it also banned all facilities for the development, support, or manufacture of such weapons, their precursors, or their sub-components. This resolution defined carefully what weapons Iraq was and was not allowed to possess.

Clear standards of behavior allow others to determine whether or not an actor is violating an agreement. The aggrieved parties can call violators to account and if violations are not corrected, such parties can withdraw from cooperation entirely or impose sanctions. Clear standards are especially important for international agreements, which must be enforced by participants (as opposed to third parties, as in domestic affairs). Without an authoritative third-party enforcement mechanism, such as the courts or the police, there is a real potential for disputes to escalate on account of incomplete or inaccurate information. International institutions can help defuse potentially costly cycles of reciprocal punishments set off by misperceived violations by accurately identifying violations and violators.

Clear standards of behavior cannot eliminate all disputes. Rules can never address all possible circumstances, and there may well be ambiguous situations that those looking to evade the rules can exploit. Saddam Hussein skirted his obligations under UN Security Council Resolution 661 and played on divisions among the permanent members of the Security Council to avoid complying with restrictions, especially in reporting and inspections. But the resolution was nonetheless important in setting the standard against which his behavior was ultimately judged. Although disputes occur, clear standards help support cooperation by identifying violations and allowing enforcement procedures to function.

Verifying Compliance
In addition to standards against which actors can judge compliance, institutions often provide ways to acquire information on compliance.

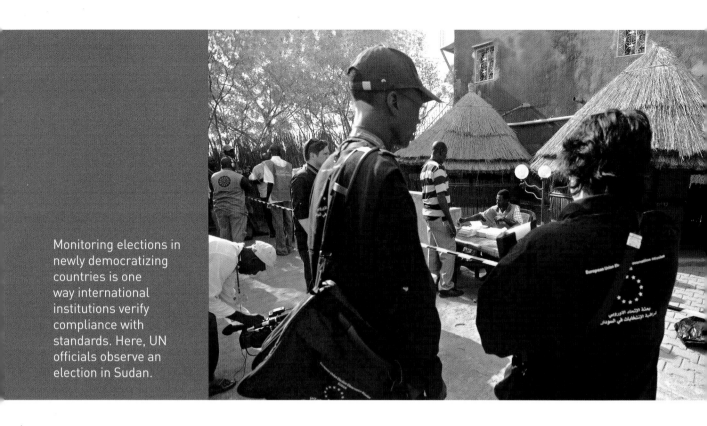

Monitoring elections in newly democratizing countries is one way international institutions verify compliance with standards. Here, UN officials observe an election in Sudan.

President Ronald Reagan famously said about arms control agreements with the Soviet Union, "Trust, but verify"—a rough translation of an old Russian proverb.

In many international institutions, self-reporting is common practice: countries are required to submit reports documenting their compliance. Such a procedure might appear weak, but it allows other parties to the agreement to inspect the self-reporting of others, assess those reports against their private knowledge of others' compliance, and publicize and criticize any inconsistencies. Discrepancies between self-reports and later verified accounts open the country to further disrepute and possible sanctions. In the fall of 2002, for example, the United States asked the UN Security Council to demand of Iraq a detailed accounting of its WMD programs, and then the United States highlighted inconsistencies not only within the hundreds of thousands of pages of documents but also among the documents, past inspection reports, and its own intelligence estimates.

At the other extreme, some international agreements permit on-site inspections. The International Atomic Energy Agency (IAEA), for instance, inspects declared nuclear material facilities in over 70 countries under the Treaty on the Non-Proliferation of Nuclear Weapons (NPT). This treaty, adopted in 1968, prohibits most countries from diverting fissionable material from civilian nuclear reactors for use in making nuclear weapons. The IAEA inspectors help to monitor compliance with this prohibition. UN Security Council Resolution 661 also provided for the IAEA to lead inspection teams in Iraq to search for possible nuclear weapons and development sites. Today, the international monitoring of elections in newly democratizing countries has become an international norm (see "How Do We Know?" on p. 71).

The International Diffusion of Election Monitoring

Before 1962, no national election was ever monitored by international observers. Today, nearly 80 percent of all elections are observed by a variety of organizations, including other national governments, international organizations, and private entities. This growing trend is illustrated in Figure A. International election monitoring challenges the norm of international sovereignty, which posits that states may not interfere in the domestic affairs of other states. Incumbent governments must invite international monitors, and most now do so seemingly voluntarily. How did this new international institution of election monitoring get established?

In original research, Susan Hyde theorizes that election monitoring grew from the need for "true" democrats to signal their commitment to free and fair elections in the face of international skepticism and from the desire of established democratic states to promote new democracies. Hyde begins from the supposition that some leaders—like the first U.S. president George Washington, who intentionally stepped down after two terms in office to set a precedent of limited executive rule—are sincere in their commitment to democracy. Other leaders, she argues, are pseudo-democrats who will cheat to obtain or remain in office. In elections in countries that have reestablished democracy after periods of authoritarian rule or that have recently gained independence, true democrats must find some way of identifying

themselves to voters at home and supporters abroad as sincerely committed to democracy. Inviting observers to monitor the election and certify the result as "free and fair" is one way of doing this. Thus, the first leaders to invite international monitors were trying to distinguish themselves from the potentially larger set of leaders who were not necessarily committed to democracy. It was in the interests of these true democrats to invite election monitors, and as the figure demonstrates, few early cases of monitoring were criticized for significant electoral fraud. True democrats do not cheat.

As the practice of monitoring began to spread, established democracies in North American and Europe started to reward leaders that both invited monitors and held honest elections. Greater foreign aid was one of a range of benefits provided. This change in their interactions with donor states reinforced the desire of true democrats to invite election monitors. Yet this same interaction prompted some pseudo-democrats also to invite international election monitors in the hopes that (1) their cheating would go undetected and (2) they could receive the benefits provided by the international community as well. In short, the pseudo-democrats had an interest in mimicking the behavior of true democrats. The result of this now broader set of interactions, however, was to spread the institution of election monitoring to nearly all countries. At present, any new democracy that does not invite election monitors is immediately suspected of engaging in election fraud.

Ironically, as the practice of election monitoring spread, more and more cases of electoral fraud were discovered. Pseudo-democrats both invite monitors and cheat, and their efforts to manipulate elections are sometimes uncovered. Hyde finds that true democrats respond by inviting larger and more professional observer missions, further institutionalizing the practice of election monitoring. In turn, pseudo-democrats once again copy their true democratic cousins and invite larger missions as well. The effect has been to expand and institutionalize the practice of election monitoring. Whether or not total electoral fraud has gone down as a result of this increase in monitoring remains an open and very difficult to answer question.

FIGURE A   *International Election Monitoring, 1960–2006*

Source: Susan D. Hyde, *The Pseudo-Democrat's Dilemma: Why Election Observation Became an International Norm* (Ithaca, NY: Cornell University Press, 2011).

Finally, institutions protect the ability of countries to verify compliance independently. Rules specifying the status of embassies and the treatment of embassy personnel allow for diplomatic representation of one country on the territory of another, but they also permit embassy officials on-site access to collect information and track developments in the foreign state. Similarly, the Treaty on Open Skies, signed in 1992 and ratified by the United States and 34 other countries, formally permits states to use "national technical means," including satellites and high-flying spy planes, to observe developments on the ground below in foreign territories. Such tools were important in verifying the arms control agreements between the United States and the Soviet Union during the Cold War. The treaty, which was negotiated just as the Cold War was ending, formally acknowledged and ratified what had been long-standing practice. National technical means were important—even if misleading and incomplete—in monitoring Iraq's WMD programs in the 1990s.

Reducing the Costs of Joint Decision Making

Institutions make it easier for actors to make decisions collectively. Recall the example of the "rules of the road" from the discussion of coordination earlier in this chapter. In a society in which the side-of-the-road rule has not been established, each driver would have to negotiate with each oncoming car over who would drive on the left and who would drive on the right. Stops would be frequent, and crashes would be inevitable. The time lost in arriving at a destination as a result of negotiating these individual encounters, as well as the crashes, would be the costs of joint decision making. Given the huge costs, societies establish institutions—rules of the road—to routinize decision making, avoid conflicts, and reduce the costs of driving. The smooth flow of traffic and faster commutes are the benefits of the institution.

Domestic political institutions similarly operate to reduce the costs of joint decision making. Imagine that a society needed to decide collectively on all matters of policy in the absence of any agreed-upon rules. Every time someone wanted to propose a new policy, he or she would have to get all citizens to figure out how they would decide. Should the policy be enacted by popular referendum? If so, who could vote? Would it pass by a simple majority (50 percent plus one vote), by a supermajority (greater than 50 percent, usually two-thirds), or by unanimous consent? Alternatively, would policy be decided by some subgroup of society? Would this subgroup be a representative body, only the most highly affected individuals, or a single individual? What powers would this subgroup have? Would it be able to not only establish the policy but also tax others if necessary to implement the policy? The list of possible decision-making rules and the alternatives to be considered for each policy are virtually endless. In the absence of some agreed-upon rules on collective decision making, the costs of any policy initiative would be enormous. These might be so large, in fact, that no policy would ever generate sufficient benefits to offset the costs of enacting that policy. Nothing would ever get done. As a result, societies create political institutions—rules of the political game—that define how joint political decisions will be made. These institutions are useful because they reduce the costs of joint decision making.

International institutions serve to reduce the costs of joint decision making among nations in the same way. The UN was created as a permanent forum in which countries could come together to deliberate and attempt to resolve disagreements. Since its founding, the UN and its associated agencies have undertaken 69 peacekeeping operations, fought the Korean War, authorized the 1991 Persian Gulf War, rewritten the law of the sea, managed refugee problems worldwide, fed people displaced by conflict or famine, helped eliminate smallpox worldwide, and undertaken a host of other activities. There is a relatively clear set of rules on which issues get referred to the General Assembly and which to the Security Council, as well as specific voting rules for each body. These rules reduce the costs of joint decision making among member states just as they do in other social settings. A large number of other international institutions help reduce the costs of joint decision making on a broad range of issues.

Resolving Disputes International institutions also facilitate cooperation by providing mechanisms for resolving disputes. When parties disagree about whether one or more of them have violated an agreement or how to interpret the terms of an agreement, it can be helpful to have prior agreement on how to handle such differences. Domestically, disputes are routinely referred to courts for authoritative resolution; in fact, courts are the default forum for dispute resolution unless the parties to an agreement have specifically agreed to other provisions, such as arbitration. Most international agreements, however, do not contain explicit dispute resolution procedures, and each party may seek to interpret the agreement according to its own interests and be limited only by its desire for a reputation as a "good partner."

Nonetheless, many international economic transactions regularly delegate dispute resolution to national courts—for instance, agreeing in advance that disputes will be decided according to the laws of the state of New York—or to one of many international arbitration boards. In a limited number of cases, states will create new dispute settlement procedures as part of an agreement, as in the WTO and regional economic blocs such as NAFTA. By creating mechanisms to resolve disputes, actors increase their expectations that others will uphold their commitments, prevent retaliation from escalating out of control, resolve ambiguities in their agreements, and allow mutually beneficial cooperation to occur. This does not, it should be noted, hinge on the dispute resolution body itself enforcing the rules by punishing violators. Rather, by interpreting rules when they are ambiguous or subject to conflicting interpretations, dispute settlement bodies help identify violator and victim, permit actors to employ self-help sanctions more efficiently, and potentially keep disputes from escalating.

In sum, institutions facilitate international cooperation in important ways. International institutions do not, however, directly enforce cooperation, except in extremely rare cases when they are empowered to punish defectors directly. Rather, despite a well-developed infrastructure of institutions, international politics remains largely a realm of self-help in which states alone must choose whether and how to penalize those who fail to cooperate. What international institutions do, however, is make compliance more likely by clarifying the terms of cooperation, providing information, and lowering the costs of joint decision making—including the costs of deciding when to punish those states that choose not to follow the rules.

Whom Do Institutions Benefit?

Institutions may help states cooperate, and in that sense they can make all their members better off. But institutions rarely benefit everyone equally. Institutions are themselves a product of the cooperation and bargaining that brought them into being. They reflect past political bargains, with the winners getting to write the rules or, at least, having a disproportionate say over the rules. As a result, rules are never neutral; instead, they embody the bargaining strength of the actors at the time the rules were written or amended. Thus, all institutions contain what we describe as a policy bias.[23]

Institutions bias outcomes in many ways. In the United States, for instance, citizens' interests are represented at the national level through different electoral institutions. These institutions themselves are a reflection of bargaining within the constitutional convention of 1787. The more populous states at the time sought a legislature in which representatives were allocated by population, which would give them a larger voice. The less populous states, knowing they would be routinely outvoted, wanted some form of guaranteed representation. The result was a compromise, with seats in the House of Representatives being determined by population and seats in the Senate being reserved two for each state. The larger states were forced to compromise by the unwillingness of the smaller states to agree to the Constitution without this provision.

These rules matter. Being elected by and responsive to different subsets of the national population, it is hardly surprising that the majority of the House of Representatives, the majority of the Senate, and the president—with the largest constituency—often differ in their interests. Indeed, the framers of the Constitution explicitly intended to create competing branches of government with different constituencies and policy preferences. Institutions that represent many smaller constituencies are likely to produce policies that favor particular groups in society through large, omnibus "log rolls" that contain something for everyone. Institutions that represent larger constituencies are more likely to enact policies that benefit society as a whole. For this reason, Congress is often thought to be more beholden to "special interests," whereas the president is expected to act more in the national interest. One manifestation of this difference is that members of the House of Representatives are typically more responsive to industries in their districts that compete with foreign imports and thus are more protectionist in trade policy. The president, on the other hand, is more likely to support freer trade, which promotes the interests of consumers as a whole.

---

23. For a review of the effects of institutions, including policy bias, see Ronald Rogowski, "Institutions as Constraints on Strategic Choice," in Lake and Powell, *Strategic Choice*, 115-36.

International institutions differ widely in their rules and in their policy bias. Many institutions, including the General Assembly of the UN, have a one country–one vote rule. China, with a population of over 1.3 billion, has the same official weight as Tuvalu, whose population is under 11,000. This gives each citizen of Tuvalu the same voice in the General Assembly as about 125,000 Chinese. The Security Council, by contrast, has voting rules that privilege five particular states—the United States, Great Britain, France, Russia, and China—by giving them a veto over any action the Security Council might take. This means that even if a majority of states on the Security Council, or around the world, want the UN to enact a particular policy, it can nevertheless be blocked by any one of these five states. Why these particular states? They were the five major victors of

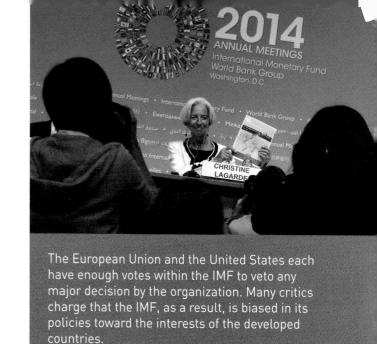

The European Union and the United States each have enough votes within the IMF to veto any major decision by the organization. Many critics charge that the IMF, as a result, is biased in its policies toward the interests of the developed countries.

World War II, and hence they were in a position to write the rules when the UN was created in the aftermath of that war. The privileged position of these states helps explain why French and Russian opposition to the U.S.-led invasion of Iraq was so consequential—without their support, the Security Council could not authorize the use of force.

Other organizations have weighted voting rules, which give the largest contributors the most influence. In the IMF, for example, the United States contributes about 17 percent of the fund's resources, and consequently it gets 17 percent of the votes on the organization's Board of Governors—by far the largest vote share of any individual country. The weights have been periodically renegotiated to reflect changes in the contributions and bargaining power of states, but the United States and the European Union still retain large enough shares of the votes to each block any important decision within the organization. Still other institutions operate by unanimous consent, permitting any member to veto an action. In its early decades, the Council of Ministers of the European Economic Community (later the European Community, now the European Union) used a unanimity rule. As the policy-making demands of deeper economic integration became more intense, the council made a historic decision to adopt a qualified majority voting rule in the Single European Act signed in 1986. This was understood to be a major transfer of power away from member states, who could previously veto any initiative they found objectionable, to the European Community as a whole. As in domestic institutions, rules matter in international institutions.

Because institutions matter and bias policy in consequential ways, states struggle over their rules. Institutions are both the shapers of politics (by facilitating cooperation) and the products of political action. Given the relative consistency in the basic institutions of government in the United States and many other countries, we often attribute a "taken for granted" or natural quality to political institutions. But it is important to understand that all institutions reflect particular policy biases and, as a result, are always the object of continuing political debate and struggle.

Why Follow the Rules?

Why do actors follow rules? If they have incentives to defect from rules and ignore institutions, why do they not always do so? If the rules are biased against them, why would they go along with them anyway? These have been key questions for many scholars of international relations. Some analysts argue that states ignore institutions whenever they do not serve their interests, so the institutions we see merely reflect the current bargaining strength of states and do not affect policy.[24] Others argue that if institutions did not matter, states would not devote so much energy to writing the extensive rules we observe. In this view, rates of compliance in international politics are surprisingly high. Indeed, although this finding remains contested, international lawyers argue that when states do violate international rules it is more often from a lack of capacity to live up to their obligations than from an attempt to seize an advantage over others.[25]

Actors comply with institutions for two reasons. First, since many problems in international relations combine both cooperation and bargaining, actors may agree to comply with rules for the broader cooperation they facilitate even though the outcome of those particular rules is biased against them. In these situations, the value of the cooperation created by the institution outweighs the costs of a relatively disadvantageous bargain. States observe the rules of the WTO not just because other countries might be authorized to punish them for violations but also because the wider system of free trade that the WTO supports and promotes is of great benefit to them. They fear that defiance of its mandates would place at risk the whole system of trade rules and the gains from trade. Thus, even the United States, the world's largest trader, complies with the findings of the WTO dispute settlement process. In 1995, the small country of Costa Rica brought suit against the United States in the WTO, for instance, for restrictions on cotton and synthetic-fiber underwear exported from that country. The United States tried to defend its restrictions as necessary to prevent serious damage to its domestic industry, but it was repeatedly found to be in violation of the WTO rules. Washington eventually complied, to the protests of domestic producers, even though retaliation from Costa Rica itself would have been but a minor irritant. Similarly, countries abide by the NPT not just because the inspections of the IAEA may

---

24. For a skeptical view of international institutions, see John J. Mearsheimer, "The False Promise of International Institutions," *International Security* 19 (1994): 5–49.

25. See Abram Chayes and Antonia Handler Chayes, "On Compliance," *International Organization* 47, no. 2 (1993): 175–205. This view is criticized by George W. Downs, David M. Rocke, and Peter N. Barsoom, "Is the Good News about Compliance Good News about Cooperation?" *International Organization* 50, no. 3 (1996): 397–406.

reveal cheating that could then be referred to the UN Security Council for possible sanctioning but also because the restraints on all countries make the world a safer place. In such cases, the prospect of continued, mutually beneficial cooperation restrains the short-run temptation for countries to ignore rules they do not like.

Second, actors comply with institutions because they are already in place and often cheaper to use, even if they are biased, than are the costs of creating a brand-new institution that might more fully reflect their interests. Creating new institutions is not easy. As discussed above, actors must agree on the members, voting rules, and many other procedures that comprise the institution. Since those rules will affect the cooperation and bargains reached, actors will struggle over which rules should be adopted. In the negotiations that eventually led to the end of the Vietnam War, the parties spent over six months just wrangling over the shape of the table at which they would sit. The time and effort spent negotiating new rules can be considerable. In the case of an existing institution, the costs of creating a set of rules have already been paid. The costs of any new institution, however better suited to the matter now under discussion, would have to be paid anew. If the policy bias of an institution is not too large, actors may choose to work within the existing rules rather than create new ones from scratch. If the policy bias is too large, of course, actors will choose to disband the institution, ignore it, or reform it.[26] In many circumstances, however, they recognize that maintaining the institution is far from ideal but less costly than creating a new one.

The benefits of an established forum and set of rules for joint decision making are substantial. Indeed, the United States continues to work through the UN even though the other member states have failed to approve policies it supports. Despite failing to get UN approval for its invasion of Iraq, by 2006 the United States was once again working vigorously through the Security Council to condemn Iran's past violation of IAEA safeguards and to prevent its progress toward acquiring a nuclear weapon. In this case, the cooperation of all major powers is required for effective sanctions should Iran not halt its uranium enrichment program. The UN remains the most effective forum for negotiating a common position with other states. Even though the United States has not gotten its way in the past and may not ultimately sway others to its position on Iran's nuclear weapons program, the institution remains sufficiently valuable that the United States often prefers to work within rather than outside its rules or to create yet another organization.

Institutions are the rules of the political game. Valued and respected for the cooperation they facilitate, institutions are not, however, a panacea for problems of international cooperation. When the temptation to defect becomes too large, or

---

26. Joseph Jupille, Walter Mattle, and Duncan Snidal, *Institutional Choice and Global Commerce* (New York: Cambridge University Press, 2013).

the fear of being taken advantage of grows too severe, countries will violate the rules—just as individuals, firms, and other actors within countries choose at times to disobey the law. Yet institutions do make international cooperation more likely, and countries that desire cooperation follow the rules more often than we might otherwise expect.

Conclusion: Explaining World Politics

This chapter has outlined the basic concepts of interests, interactions, and institutions that serve throughout the book to unravel a variety of puzzles of international politics.

To illustrate how this analytic framework can be used in concrete ways, we return to the example that opened this chapter. In the Iraq War of 2003, the interests of the United States and Iraq were diametrically opposed, thus throwing the two countries into an interaction of pure bargaining. The United States wanted, at a minimum, to eliminate Iraq's ability to deploy weapons of mass destruction and, at a maximum, to eliminate the regime of Saddam Hussein. The maximum demand of the United States was rooted in a belief that even though he might be successfully contained today, Hussein could not be trusted not to develop or use WMD in the future. These interests were reinforced by (1) the personal interests of the U.S. president and others in his administration to stand tough in international politics and promote democracy abroad, especially in the Middle East, (2) the desire for stable and cheap oil from Middle East suppliers, and (3) a general sense of insecurity on the part of many Americans after the terrorist attacks of 9/11. This confluence of interests combined to justify taking a hard-line stance against Iraq's purported weapons programs. The Iraqi ruler, in turn, wanted to remain in power and perhaps build Iraq into a regional power. Given these opposing interests, the United States and Iraq were bargaining over the extent of international controls on the latter's weapons programs and the nature of its government. With its coercive power and ability to set the agenda by increasing pressure on Iraq and, ultimately, initiating war, the United States was unwilling to accept anything less than Iraq's complete capitulation.

As we shall see more fully in Chapter 3, war is a bargaining failure in which the parties are unable to reach an agreement on acceptable terms. In this case, the United States and Iraq were unable to devise a set of institutions, or to use existing ones, that would set agreed-upon standards for Iraq's weapons programs or effectively monitor and enforce the restrictions desired by the United States. In retrospect, it also became clear that the United States suffered from a serious lack of information—not only about Iraq's weapons program and military capabilities but also about the costs of rebuilding the country and ensuring internal political stability after the war. Despite facing almost certain defeat, in turn, Saddam Hussein gambled that he would be no worse off after the war than if he voluntarily left power and went into exile. In either case, he would lose office and likely be killed either in battle or in retribution for his crimes against the Iraqi people—as he eventually was in December 2006. He had little to lose by choosing to stand and fight. He also misjudged the United States' willingness to fight a war to remove him from power.

The great tragedy of the Iraq War of 2003 is that the previous inspection and disarmament efforts after the 1991 Gulf War conducted through the UN had effectively disarmed Iraq. The inspection regime—an international institution— had worked. But for a variety of reasons, Iraq could not allow the UN open access to all possible weapons sites. For Saddam Hussein to admit that he did not have stockpiles of WMD might have emboldened domestic insurgents and other regional powers, especially Iran. In turn, the United States, after a decade of failed Iraqi promises and thwarted inspections, did not believe it could trust Hussein to honor any agreement. As a result, there was no way Iraq could credibly demonstrate to the United States that it had, in fact, dismantled its weapons programs. The United States only discovered the truth for itself after it had begun what turned out to be a long and costly war.

Study Tool Kit

Interests, Interactions, and Institutions In Context

- Interests are the fundamental building blocks of politics. Explanations of international political events begin by specifying the relevant actors and their interests.

- Cooperation is a type of interaction involving two or more actors working together to achieve a preferred outcome. Successful cooperation depends on the number and relative sizes of actors involved, the number of interactions among the actors, and the accuracy of the information they possess.

- Bargaining is a type of interaction involving the distribution of a fixed value. That is, if one actor gets "more," someone else necessarily gets "less." In bargaining, outcomes depend on what will happen in the event that no agreement is reached. Actors derive power from their ability to make the consequences of no agreement less attractive for the other side.

- Institutions are sets of rules. Actors comply with institutions because they facilitate cooperation and lower the cost of joint decision making in the pursuit of valued goals.

- Institutions also bias policy outcomes. Rules restrain what actors can and cannot do, and thus they make some outcomes more or less likely. Actors struggle over institutions in efforts to shift policy toward outcomes they prefer.

Key Terms

For Further Reading

Bueno de Mesquita, Bruce, Alastair Smith, Randolph M. Siverson, and James D. Morrow. *The Logic of Political Survival. Cambridge,* MA: MIT Press, **2003.** Integrates interests, interactions, and institutions to explain a wide range of behaviors in domestic and international politics.

Glaser, Charles L. *Rational Theory of International Politics: The Logic of Competition and Cooperation.* Princeton, NJ: Princeton University Press, **2010.** Focuses on how interests and information interact with material capabilities to shape world politics.

Gordon, Michael R., and General Bernard E. Trainor. *The Endgame: The Inside Story of the Struggle for Iraq, from George W. Bush to Barack Obama.* New York: Vintage, 2013. Offers a good contemporary history and analysis of the Iraq War.

Keohane, Robert O. *After Hegemony: Cooperation and Discord in the World Political Economy.* Princeton, NJ: Princeton University Press, 1984. Presents a classic statement on the role and importance of international institutions.

Kydd, Andrew H. *International Relations Theory:* The Game Theoretic Approach. New York: Cambridge University Press, 2015. Provides an introduction to game theory with applications to world politics.

Lake, David A. "Two Cheers for Bargaining Theory: Rationalist Explanations of the Iraq War." *International Security 35* (2010/11): 7–52. Examines the strengths and weaknesses of bargaining theory through the Iraq War of 2003.

Lake, David A., and Robert Powell, eds. *Strategic Choice and International Relations.* Princeton, NJ: Princeton University Press, 1999. Examines interests, interactions, and institutions in more detail within the context of international relations theory.

Milner, Helen V. *Interests, Institutions, and Information: Domestic Politics and International Relations.* Princeton, NJ: Princeton University Press, 1997. Explores the effects of interests, domestic institutions, and information asymmetries on international cooperation.

Monteiro, Nuno P. *Theory of Unipolar Politics.* New York: Cambridge University Press, 2014. Presents an analytic framework in understanding world politics since 1989.

SPECIAL TOPIC

A Primer on Game Theory

Game theory is a tool for analyzing strategic interactions. Over the last 50 years, it has been developed and applied broadly in nearly all the social sciences as well as in biology and other physical sciences—and it is even making inroads in the humanities. Among its earliest and most useful applications is to international politics. We provide here a brief overview of game theory to introduce strategic thinking and illustrate concepts discussed in the text.

Imagine two actors, Actor 1 (A1) and Actor 2 (A2), with only two choices, which we call cooperation (C) and defection (D). Since each actor has two choices, there are four possible outcomes to this "game": both might cooperate (CC), both might defect (DD), A1 might cooperate while A2 defects (CD), and A1 might defect while A2 cooperates (DC). The mapping of choices into outcomes is best depicted using a 2 × 2 matrix, as shown in Figure A.1.[a] As defined in the text, the actors' interests determine how they rank the four possible outcomes from best (4) to worst (1), with higher "payoffs" representing more preferred outcomes. A1's payoffs are given first in each cell, A2's second.

Both actors choose simultaneously without knowledge of the other's choices but with knowledge of their own preferences and those of the other actor.[b] The outcome we observe is a function of the interaction—that is, the choices of both actors. Each actor can choose only C or D, but their payoffs differ across all four possible outcomes. A1 may desire or rank CC (mutual cooperation) over CD and decide to choose C, but in doing so it only partially controls which outcome arises. Having chosen C, A1's actual payoff depends crucially on whether A2 chooses C (creating CC) or D (creating CD). This highlights a key point: that *strategic interaction depends on the choices of all relevant actors*, and it is most important in explaining situations in which outcomes are contingent on the choices of all parties.

In such a setting, purposive actors—that is, actors who seek their highest expected payoff—choose strategies, or plans of action, that are a best response to the anticipated actions of the other. In some cases, it makes sense for an actor to make the same choice (C or D) regardless of what the opponent does; in this case, the actor is said to have a *dominant strategy*. In other cases, each player's best choice depends on what the opponent does. For example, it might be a best response to cooperate when the other side cooperates and defect when the other side defects. Since each player is trying to play a best response, and since each

---

a. The same games can be represented in extensive form as a "game tree." Both are common in the larger literature.

b. In some of the games discussed here, the outcome does not depend on the assumption that the actors move simultaneously.

A Game Matrix

expects the other to play a best response, the outcome of the game is given by two strategies, each of which is a best response to the other. An outcome that arises from each side playing best response strategies is called an *equilibrium*. An equilibrium outcome is stable because the actors have no incentive to alter their choices; since in equilibrium both are playing their best responses, by definition they cannot do better by changing their choice. In all the games below, the equilibrium (or *equilibria*, when there is more than one) is denoted by an asterisk (*) in the appropriate cell.

The Prisoner's Dilemma

As we saw in the text (pp. 58–59), the Prisoner's Dilemma is a commonly cited game in international relations because it captures problems of collaboration, including arms races and public goods provision. Reread the full text on pages 58–59, and keep in mind that each prisoner can either *cooperate with his accomplice* and refuse to provide evidence to the district attorney or *defect on his accomplice* by ratting him out. As a result, there are four possible outcomes for each player, ranked from worst to best as follows: (1) the prisoner cooperates while his partner defects (CD), meaning that he goes to prison for 10 years while his partner goes free; (2) the prisoner and his partner both defect (DD) and are each imprisoned for 5 years; (3) the prisoner and his partner both cooperate (CC) and therefore each spend only 1 year in prison; (4) the prisoner defects while his partner cooperates (DC), meaning that he is freed immediately while his partner is jailed for 10 years. In short, each prisoner has identical interests and ranks the four possible outcomes as DC > CC > DD > CD, as depicted in Figure A.2 (the "greater than" symbol should be read as meaning that the first outcome is "preferred to" the second).

What each prisoner should do is unclear at this point, but here is where the techniques of game theory help. As is evident once the matrix is examined carefully, each criminal has a dominant strategy of defecting regardless of his partner's

FIGURE A.2 *The Prisoner's Dilemma*

		A2	
		C	D
A1	C	Both prisoners get out and split the loot.	A1 goes to jail; A2 goes free and keeps all the loot.
	D	A1 goes free and keeps all the loot; A2 goes to jail.	Both go to jail and split the loot later.

		A2	
		C	D
A1	C	3, 3	1, 4
	D	4, 1	2, 2*

actions. If his partner cooperates (that is, stays quiet), he is better off defecting (that is, talking to the district attorney) (DC > CC). If his partner defects, he is also better off defecting (DD > CD). The equilibrium that results from each prisoner playing his best response is DD, or mutual defection. The paradox, or dilemma, arises because both criminals would be better off remaining silent and getting released relatively quickly than both providing evidence and going to jail (CC > DD). But despite knowing this, each still has incentives to defect in order to get off easy (DC) or at least safeguard against his partner's defection (DD). The only actor who wins in this contrived situation is the district attorney, who sends both criminals to jail.

Although it is a considerable simplification, many analysts have used the Prisoner's Dilemma to capture the essential strategic dilemma at the core of the collective action problem. Each individual prefers to free ride while others contribute to the public good of, say, national defense, rather than contributing if everyone else does and receiving the good, to not contributing if no one else does, and finally to contributing if no one else contributes (DC > CC > DD > CD). As with the prisoners, each individual has a dominant strategy of not contributing (that is, defecting); thus, the public good of national defense is not provided voluntarily. The dilemma is solved only by the imposition of taxes by an authoritative state.

Chicken

The game of Chicken represents a second strategic dilemma. The animating story here is the game played by teenagers in the 1950s (and perhaps today by teenagers not yet familiar with game theory!). Two drivers speed down the middle of the road toward one another. The first to turn aside, the "chicken," earns the derision of his or her peers. The other driver wins. If both swerve simultaneously, neither is humiliated. If neither turns aside, both risk death in a serious wreck. If turning aside is understood as cooperation and continuing down the middle of the road as defection, the actors' interests are DC > CC > CD > DD,

		A2	A2

		C	D
A1	C	Both drivers swerve; neither is humiliated or harmed.	A1 is "chicken"; A2 "wins."
	D	A1 "wins"; A2 is "chicken."	Both drivers are killed in a serious wreck.

		C	D
A1	C	3, 3	2, 4*
	D	4, 2*	1, 1

as shown in Figure A.3 (note that this is the same preference ordering as in the Prisoner's Dilemma, except for the reversal of the last two outcomes).

Lacking a dominant strategy, the key to one's strategy in Chicken is to do the opposite of what you think the other driver is likely to do. If you think your opponent will stand tough (D), you should turn aside (C). If you think your opponent will turn aside (C), you should stand tough (D). Two equilibria exist (DC and CD). The winner is the driver who by bluster, swagger, or past reputation convinces the other that she is more willing to risk a crash.

Chicken is often taken as a metaphor for coercive bargaining (pp. 64–65). Nuclear crises are usually thought of as Chicken games. Both sides want to avoid nuclear disaster (DD), but each has incentives to stand tough and get the other to back down (DC). The state willing to take the greatest risk of nuclear war is therefore likely to force the other to capitulate. The danger, of course, is that if both sides are willing to run high risks of nuclear war to win, small mistakes in judgment or calculation can have horrific consequences.

The Stag Hunt

A final game, which is often taken as a metaphor for problems of coordination in international relations (p. 57), is the Stag Hunt. This is one of a larger class of what are known as assurance games.[c] The motivating parable was told by political philosopher Jean-Jacques Rousseau. Only by working together can two hunters kill a stag and feed their families well. One must flush the deer from the forest, and the other must be ready to fire his arrow as the animal emerges. In the midst of the hunt, a

---

c. Another common assurance game is Battle of the Sexes. In this game, a couple desires to spend the evening together, but one partner wants to attend a sporting event and the other a movie. The worst outcome for each is to spend the evening alone. Interested readers should model this game and describe its dynamics in terms similar to those for the Stag Hunt and the other games in this appendix.

lone rabbit wanders by. Each hunter now faces a decision: he could capture the rabbit alone, but to do so he must abandon the stag, ensuring that it will get away. A rabbit is good sustenance but not as fine as the hunter's expected share of the stag. In this game, both hunters are best off cooperating (CC) and sharing the stag. The next best outcome is to get a rabbit while the other tries for the stag (DC); however, if both go for the rabbit (DD), they then split the rabbit. The worst outcome for each hunter is to spend time and energy hunting the stag while the other hunts the rabbit (CD), leaving him and his family with nothing. Thus, each hunter's interests create the ranking CC > DC > DD > CD, as depicted in Figure A.4.

Despite the clear superiority of mutual cooperation, a coordination dilemma nonetheless arises. If each hunter expects that the other will cooperate and help bring down the stag, each is best off cooperating in the hunt. But if each expects that the other will be tempted to defect and grab the rabbit, thereby letting the stag get away, he will also defect and grab the rabbit. Lacking a dominant strategy, each can do no better than what he expects the other to do—creating two equilibria (CC and DD).

The Stag Hunt resembles the problem of setting international standards (p. 69). If a firm expects all others to use one format (C) for encoding DVDs, it should also use that format; if it expects others to use a different format (D), even if that format is inferior, it should use the second format as well. The worst outcome is for it to manufacture a product using the opposite format, leaving it with no compatible users. The Stag Hunt also captures situations in which the primary barrier to cooperation is not an individual incentive to defect but a lack of trust. If we define trust in this context as an expectation that the partner will cooperate, then trust leads to mutual cooperation while a lack of trust leads to mutual defection. (By contrast, in the Prisoner's Dilemma, it never makes sense to trust an accomplice, and if one accomplice expects the other accomplice to cooperate, the best response is to defect.)

As this brief survey suggests, game theory helps clarify the core dilemmas in certain types of strategic situations. Many games are far more complex than the

---

FIGURE A.4 *The Stag Hunt*

| | | A2 | A2 |
		C	D
A1	C	Both hunters split the stag.	A1 goes hungry; A2 eats the rabbit.
A1	D	A1 eats the rabbit; A2 goes hungry.	Both hunters split the rabbit.

| | | A2 | A2 |
		C	D
A1	C	4, 4*	1, 3
A1	D	3, 1	2, 2*

examples noted here, with more possible actions than "cooperate" or "defect," information asymmetries, random chance, and many more devices to capture elements of real-world strategic situations. The games presented here are more like metaphors than accurate representations of actual situations in international relations. But they illustrate how thinking systematically about strategic interaction helps us understand why actors cannot always get what they want—and, in fact, often get rather disappointing outcomes even though all actors might prefer other results. In both the Prisoner's Dilemma and the Stag Hunt, for instance, all actors prefer CC to DD, and this is known in advance. Nonetheless, in the Prisoner's Dilemma mutual defection is the equilibrium result, and in the Stag Hunt it is one of two expected outcomes. In all three games, outcomes are the result of the choices not of one actor but of all.

3

Why Are There Wars?

THE PUZZLE *War is an extremely costly way for states to settle their disputes. Given the human and material costs of military conflict, why do states sometimes wage war rather than resolving their disputes through negotiations?*

Above: States may use military force to seize territory belonging to another country. In March 2014, Russian soldiers, here shown riding in armored personnel carriers, took control of Crimea, a Ukrainian region. Days later, Russia officially annexed Crimea, an act that has not been recognized by the international community.

In August 1914, the major countries of Europe embarked on a war the likes of which the world had never before seen. Convinced that the war would be over by Christmas, European leaders sent a generation of young men into a fight that would last four years and claim more than 15 million lives. The fighting was so intense that in one battle the British army lost 20,000 soldiers in a single day, as wave after wave of attacking infantrymen were cut down by German machine guns. At the time, it was called the Great War. Those who could never imagine another such horrific event dubbed it the "war to end all wars." Today, we know this event as the First World War, or World War I, because 20 years later the countries of Europe were at it once again. World War II (1939–45) claimed 30 million to 50 million lives.

There is no puzzle in the study of international politics more pressing and important than the question of why states go to war. It is the most tragic and costly phenomenon that we observe in social and political life. The costs of war can be counted on a number of dimensions. The most obvious cost is the loss of human life. By one estimate, wars among states in the twentieth century led to 40 million deaths directly from combat plus tens of millions more

deaths owing to war-related hardships. In addition, wars have left untold millions injured, displaced from their homes and countries, impoverished, and diseased. There are economic and material costs associated with war as well. Between 2001 and 2014, the United States spent almost $1.6 trillion fighting wars in Iraq and Afghanistan.[2] Large sums of money are also spent every year to prepare for the possibility of war. In 2014, military expenditures by all countries amounted to about $1.78 trillion—a sum that represented about $250 per person.[3] Wars can also disrupt the international economy. Conflicts in the oil-rich Middle East, including the Iran-Iraq War (1980–88), the Persian Gulf War (1990–91), the Iraq War (2003–10), the

---

1. Bethany Ann Lacina and Nils Petter Gleditsch, "Monitoring Trends in Global Combat: A New Dataset of Battle Deaths," *European Journal of Population* 21 (2005): 145–66.

2. Amy Belasco, "The Cost of Iraq, Afghanistan, and Other Global War on Terror Operations Since 9/11," Congressional Research Service Report for Congress, December 8, 2014, www.fas.org/sgp/crs/natsec/RL33110.pdf (accessed 01/19/15).

3. Sam Perlo-Freeman et al., "Trends in Word Military Expenditure, 2014," Stockholm International Peace Research Institute, April 13, 2015, http://books.sipri.org/files/FS/SIPRIFS1504.pdf (accessed 04/20/15).

intervention in Libya by the United States and its western allies (2011), and the threat of U.S. air strikes against Syria (2013) all contributed to spikes in world oil prices (see Figure 4.1 on p. 141). In short, as U.S. Civil War general William Sherman famously declared, "War is hell."

But if everyone recognizes that war is hell, why do wars happen? The very costs that make the puzzle of war so pressing also make the phenomenon so puzzling. Given the enormous costs associated with war, why would states sometimes choose this course?

At first glance, the answer might seem straightforward: states fight wars because they have conflicting interests over important issues. Often, two states desire the same piece of territory. Nazi Germany wanted to expand into central Europe; World War II started when the Poles, who did not want to give up their territory, fought back. In 1980, Iraq invaded Iran in part to seize the latter's southern oil fields, leading to the Iran-Iraq War. Alternatively, one state might object to the policies or ideology of another. World War I grew out of Austria-Hungary's demand that Serbia end nationalist agitation that threatened to tear the multiethnic empire apart. The war between the United States and Afghanistan in 2001 occurred because the United States wanted Afghanistan to hand over Osama bin Laden and disman-tle terrorist training camps on its territory, something that the Afghans refused to do. Clearly, part of the expla-nation for any war requires that we identify the conflict-ing interests that motivated the combatants.

Although such explanations are correct, they are also incomplete. By identifying the object or issue over which a war was fought, they neglect the key question of why war was the strategy that states resorted to in order to resolve their dispute. In each case, the conflicts were disastrously costly to at least one and, in some cases, all the states involved. In addition to the millions of dead mentioned earlier, World War I led to the ouster of three of the lead-ers that brought their countries into to the war, and it hastened the breakup of the Austro-Hungarian, Russian, and Ottoman empires. World War II brought about the defeat and occupation of its main instigators, Germany and Japan. The Nazi leader Adolf Hitler committed sui-cide, and his Italian ally, Benito Mussolini, was hung by his own people. Iran and Iraq fought to a stalemate for eight years, causing 1 million to 2 million casualties and leav-ing Iraq on the brink of economic collapse. The Afghan government's refusal to hand over bin Laden led to its removal from power. Given these grave consequences, it makes sense to wonder whether all participants would have been better off if they could have come to some set-tlement that would have allowed them to avoid the costs of war. Explaining war thus requires us to explain why the participants failed to reach such an agreement.

Thinking Analytically about Why Wars Happen

Most disputes between states are settled without resort to war. Although wars tend to capture our attention, it is important to remember that war is an exceedingly rare phenomenon: most countries are at peace with each other most of the time. Figure 3.1 shows the number of states involved in interstate wars in each year from 1820 to 2014 expressed as a percentage of the total number of states in existence at the time. As the figure indicates, war is a recurrent feature of international politics in the sense that its frequency fluctuates up and down but never disap-pears completely. And yet war is the exception rather than the rule: in most years, the percentage of states involved in war is quite low. All this peace cannot be explained by an absence of issues to fight over.

Hence, when seeking to explain war, we need to ask not only "What are they fighting over?" but also "Why are they fighting?"[4] In terms of the framework laid out in Chapter 2, answering the first question requires that we understand how states' interests can give rise to conflicts over things like territory, policies, and the com-position or character of each other's government. The answer to the second question lies in the strategic inter-actions that determine whether or how these conflicts are resolved. As we saw, the international system lacks institutions—such as legislatures, courts, or interna-tional police forces—that can resolve conflicts between states through legal, judicial, or electoral mechanisms. As a result, interstate conflicts have to be settled through bargaining. Understanding why wars occur requires that we identify the factors that sometimes prevent states from settling their conflicts through peaceful bargains that would permit them to avoid the costs of war.

---

4. The theory of war developed in this chapter relies exten-sively on James Fearon, "Rationalist Explanations for War," *International Organization* 49 (Summer 1995): 379–414.

FIGURE 3.1 *The Percentage of States Involved in Interstate War per Year, 1820–2014*

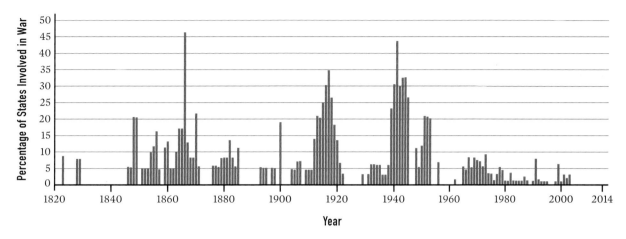

What Is the Purpose of War?

A **war** is an event involving the organized use of military force by at least two parties that reaches a minimum threshold of severity.[5] All the components of this definition are important. The requirement that force be organized rules out spontaneous, disorganized violence, such as large-scale rioting. The requirement that force be used by at least two sides distinguishes war from mass killings perpetrated by a government against some group that does not fight back. The minimum threshold—scholars often require that a war cause at least 1,000 battle deaths—excludes cases in which military force is used at low levels, such as brief skirmishes or minor clashes. If the main parties to the conflict are both states, then we refer to the event as an **interstate war**; if the main parties to the conflict are actors within a state—such as a government and a rebel group—then the event is a **civil war**.[6] In this chapter, the discussion will focus on understanding interstate wars. Chapter 6 covers conflicts involving nonstate actors, including civil wars.

Given that scholars have been trying to understand war for millennia, the number of theories and explanations that have been proposed over the years is naturally quite large, and the bargaining model that we lay out in this chapter is only one approach. At least three other broad schools of thought have been influential in modern scholarship. While these approaches contribute important insights, they also have gaps that are filled by the bargaining approach. The first, described in the introduction as realism, argues that war is the inevitable result of international

Figure source: Meredith Reid Sarkees and Frank Wayman, *Resort to War: 1816–2007* (Washington, DC: CQ Press, 2010). Updated to 2014 by author.

war

An event involving the organized use of military force by at least two parties that reaches a minimum threshold of severity.

interstate war

A war in which the main participants are states.

civil war

A war in which the main participants are within the same state, such as the government and a rebel group.

---

5. See, for example, J. David Singer and Melvin Small, *The Wages of War, 1816–1965: A Statistical Handbook* (New York: Wiley, 1972).

6. There are also cases that have elements of both kinds of wars. In the Vietnam War, South Vietnam, with the support of the United States, fought a civil war against a Communist insurgency while at the same time it was fighting an interstate war against Communist North Vietnam, which was supporting the rebellion. See Chapter 6 for more on the international dimensions of civil wars.

anarchy (pp. xxviii–xxx). The absence of a central authority capable of policing interstate relations means that wars can happen because there is nothing to stop states from using force to get their way.[7] Moreover, anarchy creates insecurity and a competition for power. In this view, states fight wars either to increase their own power—such as by enlarging their territory—or to counter the power of others—such as by destroying adversaries and their allies. For this reason, realism emphasizes two primary dynamics that can lead to war. One is a preventive motive: the desire to fight in order to prevent an enemy from becoming relatively more powerful.[8] The second is a phenomenon known as the **security dilemma**. This dilemma arises when efforts that states make to defend themselves, such as acquiring a bigger military, make other states fear that they will be attacked. If threatened states arm themselves in response, the result is a spiral of fear and insecurity that may end in war.[9] As we will see, the bargaining model of war shares realism's presumption that anarchy leads to a world in which military force is often threatened or used to further state interests, and conflicts are addressed through bargaining rather than institutions like courts. The bargaining model also anticipates prevention and the fear of attack as two of several mechanisms that can lead to war. The main departure from realism is in recognizing that the use of military power imposes costs on states, so even if it is useful to threaten force to get a better deal, states are generally better off if they do not have to actually use force—creating the puzzle that is at the heart of this chapter.

A second alternative approach emphasizes the role of misperceptions or mistakes. Starting from the observation that the costs of war often far exceed any potential benefits, scholars in this tradition conclude that wars must occur because decision makers inaccurately estimate their chances of winning or the costs that will have to be paid. When European leaders sent their armies to war in August 1914, most were convinced that the troops would be home by Christmas, a prediction that turned out to be off by four years. Both sides also expected to win the war, meaning that at least one side was being overly optimistic. This kind of argument rests either on research in cognitive psychology showing that people are bad at weighing risks and often fall prey to wishful thinking or on organizational approaches that emphasize how the ideology and interests of political and military elites can lead to incorrect and overly optimistic assessments of war.[10] A concern about such theories is that while perceptual pitfalls are universal, war is quite rare, and these theories have a hard time explaining why wars happen at some points in time but not others. As we will see, uncertainty about the likely outcome and costs

security dilemma

A dilemma that arises when efforts that states make to defend themselves cause other states to feel less secure. This dilemma can lead to arms races and war due to fear of being attacked.

---

7. Kenneth N. Waltz, *Theory of International Politics* (Reading, MA: Addison-Wesley, 1979).

8. See, for example, Dale C. Copeland, *The Origins of Major War* (Ithaca, NY: Cornell University Press, 2000); and Stephen Van Evera, *Causes of War* (Ithaca, NY: Cornell University Press, 2001).

9. Robert Jervis, "Cooperation under the Security Dilemma," *World Politics* 30 (January 1978): 167–214.

10. The classic work applying cognitive psychology to international relations is Robert Jervis, *Perception and Misperception in International Politics* (Princeton, NJ: Princeton University Press, 1976). For an argument that military ideologies can lead to incorrect and overly optimistic assessments, see Stephen Van Evera, "The Cult of the Offensive and the Origins of the First World War," *International Security* 9 (1984): 58–107. The effect of military biases may depend on domestic institutions that influence how much civilians control the military; this argument is taken up in Chapter 4.

of war plays an important role in the approach developed here, but we emphasize not the psychological or organizational origins of potential mistakes but rather the difficulties of gathering the necessary information in the strategic context of bargaining.

Finally, a long tradition of scholarship argues that wars are fought not because they serve the interests of states but because they serve the interests of influential groups within the state, such as corporations, arms merchants, and the military.[11] In this view, the puzzle of war has an easy answer: wars are fought in spite of their costs because those costs do not fall on the actors who call the shots. Although this chapter introduces the bargaining model by treating states as the main actors, without internal politics, we will see in Chapter 4 that the potential role of domestic interests can be incorporated quite easily.

What Do States Fight Over?

At the root of every war lies a conflict over something that states value. The purpose of warfare is not to fight but rather to obtain, through fighting or the threat of fighting, something the state wants. Hence, we should think about the problem of war as a problem of bargaining over objects or issues that are of value to more than one state. Using the framework developed in the previous chapter, we focus on situations in which states' interests conflict, giving rise to a strategic interaction that involves bargaining over the distribution of whatever is in dispute. The analysis thus starts by assuming that there is some object of value—what we will sometimes refer to as a "good"—and that each state prefers more of the good to less.

What kinds of goods do states fight over? *Territory* has historically been the most common source of trouble. Indeed, a study of 155 wars over the last three centuries found that over half (83) involved conflicts over territory—more than any other single issue.[12] States come into conflict if more than one wants the same piece of territory. There are a number of reasons why a piece of territory may be valuable to more than one state. First, it might contribute to the wealth of the state, particularly if it contains valuable resources such as oil, natural gas, or minerals. Iran and Iraq fought a lengthy war from 1980 to 1988 in part because Iraq coveted Iran's southern oil fields. Territory can also be economically valuable simply by adding to the industrial or agricultural resources at the state's disposal. A second reason that territory can cause conflict between two states is if it has military or strategic value. For example, the Golan Heights, on the border between Israel and Syria, has a commanding position over northern Israel from which it is possible to launch devastating attacks on the towns below. Israel seized the Golan Heights from Syria in the 1967 Six Day War, and this territory has been a source of conflict between the two states ever since. Finally, a piece of territory might be valuable for ethnic, cultural, or

---

11. See citations to this literature in Chapter 4.

12. Kalevi J. Holsti, *Peace and War: Armed Conflicts and International Order, 1648–1989* (Cambridge: Cambridge University Press, 1991).

MAP 3.1 *Territorial Claims in the Kashmir Region*

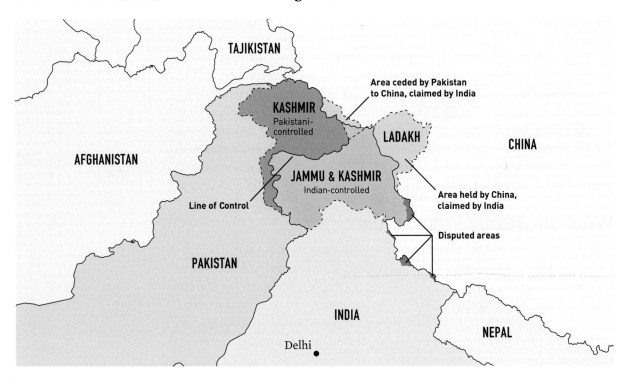

Map note: The Line of Control, which originated as a cease-fire line after the First Kashmir War (1947–48), divides the region into Indian- and Pakistani-administered areas.

historical reasons. The long-standing conflict between Israel and its Arab neighbors stems from the latter's resistance to the creation of a Jewish state on a land where many Arabs lived. In this case, the dispute goes beyond simply the location of a border, as some Arab states have refused to recognize Israel's right to exist.[13] Similarly, the long-running conflict between India and Pakistan is driven by the fact that both have historical and ethnic claims to the region of Kashmir. When the two countries gained their independence from Britain in 1947, India pressured Kashmir's Hindu leader to join with India, which is predominantly Hindu; however, because the people of Kashmir, like the people of Pakistan, are predominantly Muslim, Pakistan has claimed the territory on the basis of religious ties. Map 3.1 illustrates the current boundaries of the disputed area, which is further complicated by China's claims to neighboring portions of Tibet. In territorial disputes, states threaten or use military force to compel concessions and/or to seize and hold disputed land.

Wars can also arise out of conflicts over states' *policies*. Such conflicts come about when one state enacts a policy that benefits it but harms the interests of another. The conflict that led to the Iraq War centered on Iraq's alleged pursuit of weapons of mass destruction (WMD), which the United States saw as threatening

---

13. Egypt recognized Israel in 1979, and Jordan did likewise in 1994.

to its broader interests in the region. Ongoing U.S. conflicts with North Korea and Iran have similar sources. The conflict between Russia and Ukraine that started in 2014 revolved around the latter's decision to pursue closer economic ties to the West and policies that were alleged to harm the interests of ethnic Russians living there. A state's mistreatment of its own citizens can also spark international conflict. For example, the United States and its NATO allies waged war against Serbia in 1999 for its repressive treatment of civilians in the Kosovo region and against the Libyan government in 2011 for its attacks on civilians during the suppression of an armed uprising. Similarly, the United States threatened to bomb Syria in 2013 for using chemical weapons against its own people. When states have policy disputes, war, or the threat of war, may be a mechanism for compelling policy change. In the case of Kosovo, two months of bombing by the United States and its allies led the Serb government to end its military campaign against the Kosovars; in the case of Syria, U.S. threats led to a deal whereby that regime gave up its chemical arsenal. Alternatively, war may be used to replace the offending regime with a friendlier one that will pursue different policies. This was the U.S. plan in Iraq and Afghanistan, though the effort to install more pliant regimes in those countries embroiled American forces in civil wars that lasted much longer than the initial operations to oust the former, hostile regimes (see Chapter 6).

The possibility of using military force to change regimes suggests a third kind of conflict between states: conflicts over *regime type*, or the composition of another country's government. In its conflict with Ukraine, Russia sought reforms of the Ukrainian political system that would give the Russian minority there greater

States sometimes make threats or use military force to influence the policies of foreign governments. In August 2013, the Syrian government attacked a rebel-held village with chemical weapons, killing hundreds. In response, the United States threatened to use air strikes, and the Syrian government subsequently agreed to give up its chemical arsenal.

autonomy and influence. During the Cold War, the United States saw Communist regimes as natural allies of the Soviet Union, and hence it sought to prevent the establishment of such regimes. U.S. involvement in the Vietnam War was driven by the desire to protect the pro-American South Vietnamese government from internal and external enemies bent on overthrowing it. During this period both superpowers intervened regularly in other states to prop up friendly governments or to remove unfriendly ones. The role of outside powers in civil wars, such as in Vietnam, will be addressed in Chapter 6.

As this last example suggests, conflicts over territory, policy, and/or regime may spring from deeper conflicts that give rise to concerns about relative power. The specific conflict that started World War II was a territorial dispute between Germany and Poland over a small strip of territory that lay between them. However, Britain and France were concerned that a victory over Poland would further strengthen and embolden Germany, making it a more formidable foe in their ongoing struggle for influence and territory in Europe. Hence, the German-Polish territorial dispute impinged on the interests of other states because of its potential impact on their relative power vis-à-vis Germany. The Cold War rivalry between the United States and the Soviet Union similarly imbued many local conflicts with global importance because of their perceived impact on the relative strength of the superpowers.

Bargaining and War

Conflicting interests are clearly necessary for wars to happen, but they are not sufficient to explain why wars actually do happen. To understand why some conflicts become wars and others do not, we have to think about the strategic interactions that states engage in when they seek to settle their disputes. In a well-functioning domestic political system, the kinds of disputes that lead to wars are often settled through institutional mechanisms. Property disputes can be resolved by courts backed by effective police powers. If one person engages in actions that harm another, the latter may turn to the legal system to solve the problem. Within states, policy disagreements and conflicting ideas over who should govern can be settled by elections. As noted in Chapter 2, however, the international system lacks reliable legal, judicial, and electoral institutions. As a result, states must generally try to settle their conflicts through bargaining.[14]

Bargaining describes interactions in which actors try to resolve disputes over the allocation of a good. They may bargain over the distribution of a disputed territory to determine whether there is a division that is acceptable to both sides. Or they may bargain over each other's policies so that objectionable ones might be modified or eliminated. Although we often think of bargaining as entailing compromise or give-and-take, the bargaining process does not always imply that differences will

---

14. Although some interstate disputes have been adjudicated through institutions like the International Court of Justice (ICJ), these institutions lack strong enforcement mechanisms to guarantee compliance with their rulings, and disputants often engage in bargaining after an ICJ ruling to determine whether and how its terms will be implemented. Hence, these rulings are a part of, rather than a substitute for, the bargaining process. See, for example, Cole Paulson, "Compliance with Final Judgments of the International Court of Justice since 1987," *American Journal of International Law* 98 (2004): 434–61.

be split. Indeed, in many cases, states assume "all or nothing" bargaining positions. For example, when President Bush demanded in October 2001 that the Afghan government hand over Al Qaeda leaders responsible for the 9/11 terrorist attacks, he declared that "these demands are not open to negotiation or discussion."[15]

A crisis occurs when at least one state seeks to influence the outcome of bargaining by threatening to use military force in the event that it does not get what it wants. At this point, we enter the domain of coercive bargaining, in which the consequences of not reaching an agreement can involve the use of force, including war. We sometimes refer to bargaining under the threat of war as **crisis bargaining** or **coercive diplomacy**. In all such interactions, at least one state sends the message "Satisfy my demands, or else"—where the "or else" involves imposing costs on the other side through military action. In some cases, this message takes the form of an explicit ultimatum, such as Bush's March 2003 ultimatum giving Iraqi leader Saddam Hussein 48 hours to leave the country or face an invasion. In other cases, the threat is conveyed implicitly, through menacing actions such as mobilization of troops or military maneuvers. The Russian military incursion into Ukraine in August 2014 was preceded by the massing of troops on the border and military exercises, but not by an explicit ultimatum or set of demands (at least not publicly). Whether explicit or implicit, the purpose of such actions is clear: they seek to wrest concessions from the other side by making the alternative seem unacceptably costly.

The costs and likely outcome of a war determine which deals each side will consider acceptable in crisis bargaining. We can generally assume that the best possible outcome for a state in a crisis is to get the entire good without having to fight. If the other side gives in, the state gets its most preferred settlement of the underlying issue and avoids the need to pay the costs associated with war. It is quite likely, though, that a state would also accept something less than its most preferred settlement, given that the alternative of fighting is costly. For example, imagine a conflict over a piece of territory worth $100 million. Assume that a state believes that in the event of a war, it is certain to win the territory; however, the costs of war, if put in monetary terms, would amount to $30 million. In that case, the expected value of going to war for that state is $100 million – $30 million = $70 million. Hence, the state should be willing to accept any deal that gives it at least $70 million worth of the territory. Since a state has the option to wage war if it determines that it is in its interests to do so, a state will only accept a bargain that gives it at least as much as it can expect to get from war. And for any deal to prevent a war, it must satisfy all sides in this way: each state must decide that it prefers the deal to fighting a war. Hence, in our simple example, war can only be averted if the other state is willing to settle for the remaining $30 million worth of territory or less.

The discussion at the outset of this chapter implies a very simple proposition: because war is costly, a settlement that all sides prefer to war generally exists.[16] The graphic on page 98 illustrates the simple idea behind this

crisis bargaining

A bargaining interaction in which at least one actor threatens to use force in the event that its demands are not met.

coercive diplomacy

The use of threats to influence the outcome of a bargaining interaction.

---

15. Elizabeth Bumiller, "Bush Pledges Attack on Afghanistan Unless It Surrenders bin Laden Now," *New York Times*, September 21, 2001, A1.

16. See Fearon, "Rationalist Explanations for War."

The Model: Bargaining and War

1. A possible deal: Two states, A and B, have conflicting interests over a good (represented by the green bar). Both states want as much of the good as possible. The dotted line represents the distribution of the good based on *one* possible deal. Any deal determines A's and B's shares.

STATE B's IDEAL OUTCOME

STATE B's SHARE

A

B

STATE A's SHARE

POSSIBLE DEAL

STATE A's IDEAL OUTCOME

2. The expected outcome of war: As they bargain, each state evaluates how much it can expect to get as a result of war. The dotted line shows the expected outcome of war. Here, A would get more by going to war than by accepting the above deal.

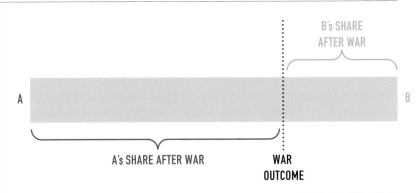

B's SHARE AFTER WAR

A

B

A's SHARE AFTER WAR

WAR OUTCOME

3. Costs of war: However, war also involves costs, and these costs must be subtracted from what each state hopes to gain. So, although war would give A more of the good than it would get under the deal in the first figure, the costs incurred reduce the value of war to A.

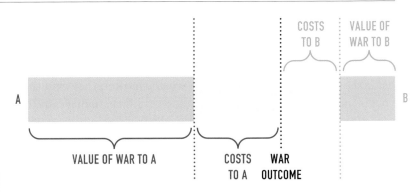

COSTS TO B

VALUE OF WAR TO B

A

B

VALUE OF WAR TO A

COSTS TO A

WAR OUTCOME

4. The bargaining range: Each state prefers any deal that gives it more than its expected value of war once costs are subtracted. Because war inflicts costs on both sides, there is a range of possible deals that both sides would prefer over war.

DEALS B PREFERS TO WAR

WAR OUTCOME

VALUE OF WAR TO B

A

BARGAINING RANGE

B

VALUE OF WAR TO A

DEALS A PREFERS TO WAR

An Example: Bargaining Over Territory

POSSIBLE DEAL

1. A conflict over territory:
Imagine two states have a conflict of interest over a piece of territory. State A would like to have the whole territory, as would State B. A deal is proposed to divide the territory at the dotted line.

WAR OUTCOME

2. The expected outcome of war:
Based on the strength of their respective armies and other resources, a war over the territory is expected to result in State A winning the portion of the territory to the left of the dotted line.

WAR OUTCOME

COSTS OF WAR

3. Costs of war: Each side also considers the costs of war. Imagine that State A values the territory it would win as a result of war at $100 million but values the costs of war (both financial and human) at $30 million. These costs would reduce the value of war to A by 30 percent.

WAR OUTCOME

BARGAINING RANGE

4. The bargaining range: Each side should prefer any deal that gives it more territory than what it expects from war, once the costs of war are subtracted from the territory it wins. Any border drawn through the shaded range divides the territory into shares that both sides prefer over war.

proposition. Assume that two states, call them State A and State B, have conflicting interests over the division of some good, represented by the green bar on the left-hand page. To make this concrete, think of this good as a piece of territory, as in the example on the right-hand page. Any line dividing the bar, such as the dotted line labeled *Possible Deal* in panel 1, represents a possible division of the good, such as a border drawn through the territory. State A receives the share of the good to the left of that line, and State B receives the share of the good to the right. Since both states prefer more of the good to less, State A wants to get a deal as far to the right as possible, and State B wants to get a deal as far to the left as possible. Put another way, State A's most preferred outcome, or ideal point, is at the far right of the bar, which would mean State A gets all the good, and State B's ideal point is on the far left, which would mean State B gets all the good. (Hence, this horizontal bar is identical to the diagonal line used to illustrate bargaining in Figure 2.2 on p. 56). Now consider what happens if the two states go to war. Moving to panel 2, the line labeled *War Outcome* indicates the actual, or expected, outcome of a violent conflict. In the case of a conflict over territory, we can think of this line as indicating how much territory each state would control after a war. The farther that line is to the right, the better State A is expected to fare in the event of war; the farther it is to the left, the better State B is expected to fare.

Crucially, fighting entails costs. These costs diminish the value of the expected war outcome to each state. As shown in panel 3, the value of war to each state is the share of the good that it expects to win minus the costs that it expects to incur. Notice that the value of war to State A (which corresponds to the portion of the bar to the left of the dotted red line) is smaller than the share of the good that it expects to get from war (the portion of the bar to the left of the *War Outcome*). Indeed, as the figure is constructed, State A expects to win more of the good in a war than it would get from the *Possible Deal* in the first panel, but once the costs of war are taken into account, the *Possible Deal* is actually preferable to war. To understand how the costs affect the value of war for each state, we have to think about those costs as they relate to the value of the good. Looking at the example in the right-hand side of the page, imagine that State A expects to win 70 percent of the territory at the cost of 5,000 lives. State A's war value hinges on how much State A values those lost lives relative to the value of the territory. If State A thinks that losing those soldiers is equivalent to losing 20 percent of the territory, then its value for war is 70 – 20 = 50 percent of the value of the territory. State B would make a similar calculation. For both states, the costs of war would effectively go up if either the number of lives lost went up or the value attached to the territory went down.

As panel 4 shows, State A prefers any deal over war that gives it more than its value for war (deals that fall to right of the dotted red line). Deals in this range give State A more than it expects to get through war once the costs are taken into account. Similarly, State B prefers any deal over war that gives it more than its value for war (deals that fall to the left of the dotted blue line). Notice that the set of deals that both State A and State B prefer over war overlap, creating a region called the **bargaining range**. Any division of the good in this bargaining range gives both states more than they expect to get from fighting a war. As this exercise demonstrates, the fact that war imposes costs on both sides means that such a range of deals always exists. Hence, in theory, there are bargains that both sides would prefer over war.

Although this exercise treated the good in dispute as a piece of territory, the general framework and insight can be applied to any kind of issue over which states have conflicting interests. For example, consider the conflict between North Korea and the United States over the former's nuclear program. In this case, the United States' ideal outcome, which we could put at one end of the bar, is for North Korea to disarm completely and become a democratic state. North Korea's ideal outcome, which would be located at the opposite end of the bar, would be for the United States to accept North Korea's status as a nuclear power and recognize its existing regime. In between are various compromise alternatives that neither considers ideal, including the current status quo, in which North Korea has a small number of nuclear devices but the United States refuses to recognize its right to them. This point is close to North Korea's ideal point. Another point on the bar, closer to the U.S. ideal point than to the status quo, would be for North Korea to freeze its nuclear program and admit international inspectors. Though the substantive meaning of any location on the bar depends on the exact issue in dispute, the basic argument for the existence of a bargaining range holds across issues. (See the "Controversy" on p. 102 for an extended discussion of negotiations between United States and North Korea.)

This simple model is useful not because it is right in the sense that it correctly describes the complexity of real-world bargaining interactions. Rather, the model is useful because it forces us to think about all the ways in which it could go wrong. Understanding why wars happen even though a peaceful bargain theoretically exists in virtually any conflict is the main purpose of this chapter.

(See the "Controversy" on p. 102 for an extended discussion of negotiations between United States and North Korea.)

Compellence and Deterrence: Varieties of Coercive Bargaining

The model is also useful for thinking about the conditions under which states might have an interest in initiating a crisis in the first place. The pre-crisis distribution, or status quo, can be represented as a line dividing the bar. Where the status quo is located relative to the states' values for war determines which state, if any, might have an interest in changing the status quo through a threat of force. If a state is already getting from the status quo at least as much as it expects to get through war, then it generally cannot gain by threatening war to change the status quo. However, if a state expects to get more through war than it has in the status quo, then it has an interest in making a challenge. The top panel of

bargaining range
The set of deals that both parties in a bargaining interaction prefer to the reversion outcome. When the reversion outcome is war, the bargaining range is the set of deals that both sides prefer to war.

Should We Negotiate with Rogue Regimes?

North Korea has one of the most oppressive regimes on the planet. It has been governed by a draconian dictatorship passed down across three generations: from Kim Il-Sung, who ruled for 46 years (1948–94), to his son Kim Jong-Il (1994–2011), who was then succeeded by his own son, Kim Jong-Un (pictured on the next page). The regime has murdered, tortured, and starved its people into submission. It has sealed them off from the outside world, denying virtually all contact with foreign visitors and media and keeping them separated from relatives in South Korea. In foreign affairs, North Korea has waged war on its southern neighbor, spewed threats at others in the region, sold ballistic missile technology to other "rogue" regimes, and kidnapped Japanese citizens. North Korea has also been developing nuclear weapons, and the United States and other countries have worked for more than two decades to prevent this regime from acquiring the world's most destructive weapons.

These efforts have had discouraging results. After going to the brink of war in 1994, the United States and North Korea signed an Agreed Framework, under which North Korea pledged to freeze construction and operation of all nuclear reactors. In return, the United States promised oil, two proliferation-resistant nuclear reactors, and a normalization of trade and diplomatic relations, which have been suspended since the Korean War (1950–53). While this agreement initially appeared to work, neither party fully carried out its obligations. North Korea engaged in provocative acts, including a missile test over Japan in 1998, and the United States dragged its feet on the promised reactors and diplomatic normalization. In 2002, the deal collapsed completely after the United States accused North Korea of circumventing the agreement by engaging in uranium enrichment. In 2006, North Korea tested a nuclear device, signaling its entry into the nuclear club. Renewed negotiations led to a deal in 2007, which provided for North Korea to dismantle its nuclear reactors. Although this deal seemed promising at first, it too unraveled in the spring of 2009, when North Korea test-launched a long-range missile. North Korea responded to international criticism by expelling inspectors, restarting plutonium production, and then testing a second nuclear device. Yet another deal was signed in 2012, providing for North Korea to freeze its program in exchange for food aid. But this deal threatened to unravel before the ink was dry, when North Korea conducted a (failed) missile test only weeks later. In February 2013, the country detonated a third nuclear device. Today, North Korea is believed to possess 10 to 20 nuclear weapons, and it is hard to be optimistic about prospects for freezing or reversing North Korea's nuclear program.

The strategy of bargaining with North Korea is clearly fraught with problems. North Korea has repeatedly demonstrated its willingness to break agreements, and the regime's secretive nature fuels mistrust. At the same time, North Korea fears the consequences of disarmament. Wracked by an insecurity that is largely of its own making, the regime seems to have decided that its very survival depends on fears abroad that it both has and is willing to use nuclear weapons. Given the long-standing conflict with the United States, North Korean leaders likely worry that losing the nuclear option will leave their regime vulnerable to subsequent American pressure. To ease these concerns, Washington would have to credibly commit to not seek regime change if North Korea lowers its defenses. Such a commitment would involve economic and energy assistance to help bolster the regime and promote development. North Korea has also sought security guarantees, including a formal promise that the United States will not attack it and a reduction of the U.S. military presence in South Korea and Japan.

Should the United States and its allies pursue such a bargain? Detractors of this strategy raise several objections. First, some argue that negotiating with dictators like Kim Jong-Il is like "making deals with the devil," rewarding the regime for its odious behavior. The package of aid and security guarantees that might entice North Korea to disarm would, by propping up this regime, make outsiders complicit in the suffering of its people. Such a policy could also encourage other tyrants to aspire to a similar deal. Critics also argue that North Korea's closed, aggressive regime presents a fundamental impediment to bargaining, since Pyongyang cannot be trusted to honor any agreement. A nuclear program can be advanced in secrecy, away from the prying eyes of satellites and inspectors, creating the danger that North Korea could cheat on the deal and escape detection. In this view, regime change is a *precondition* for successful negotiations, not a bargaining chip to be given away.

Those who support negotiations acknowledge these concerns but argue that there is no feasible alternative to bargaining and that regime change, however desirable, is not a workable strategy. Prior to the 1994 Agreed Framework, some policy makers considered a preventive strike against North Korea. But even without nuclear weapons, North Korea has a strong military that is capable of retaliating against South Korea (a close ally of the United States) with devastating effect. At the time, the U.S. military estimated that in the first three months of a war, there would be 50,000 U.S. casualties, nearly a half-million casualties from the South Korean military, and untold numbers of civilian casualties, not to mention property losses in the tens of billions of dollars.[a] Attacks on nuclear sites also risk the release of radioactive material, which would threaten people throughout the region. Regime change might be hastened by imposing comprehensive economic sanctions, but this strategy also has drawbacks. Not only would sanctions result in further catastrophe for North Korea's already desperate population but, to be successful they would

require international cooperation that is currently elusive. China, North Korea's largest trading partner, has at times tried to rein in Pyongyang, but it has no interest in seeing its neighbor collapse. Finally, while refusing to bargain with North Korea may let the United States avoid a moral compromise, it does nothing to prevent the building of weapons. Indeed, Kim Jong-Il used the period of start-and-stop talks from 2003 to 2006 to build and test a weapon. For all their faults and eventual failures, the 1994 and 2007 deals succeeded in slowing North Korea's nuclear progress while they were in effect. In early 2015, Kim Jong-Un proposed a resumption of talks, but whether negotiations would even start, much less lead to a new deal, remained uncertain at the time of this writing. Despite the bleak track record of negotiating with North Korea, continued efforts to seek a bargain may be the best of a very bad set of options for the United States and its partners.

---

a. William M. Drennan, "Nuclear Weapons and North Korea: Who's Coercing Whom?" in *The United States and Coercive Diplomacy*, ed. Robert J. Art and Patrick M. Cronin, 157–224 (Washington, DC: U.S. Institute of Peace Press, 2003).

Figure 3.2 depicts such a situation: in the status quo, State A's share of the good is less than its value for war, even when the costs of war are taken into account. This does not mean that there will be a war since, after all, a bargaining range still exists. But in this situation, the dissatisfied state can profit by threatening war in order to get a better deal. As the lower panel in Figure 3.2 shows, this logic divides the bar into three segments. If the status quo is to the left of the red dotted line, indicating State A's value for war, then States A has an interest in threatening war to try to get a better outcome. Similarly, if the status quo is to the right of the blue dotted line, indicating State B's value for war, then State B prefers war over the status quo and thus has an interest in sparking a crisis. Finally, if the status quo is in the bargaining range, then both prefer the current situation to war, and neither can expect to gain by waging war.

We often classify threats according to whether they are intended to preserve or change the existing relationship between states. An effort to change the status quo through the threat of force is called **compellence**. A compellent threat is intended

compellence

An effort to change the status quo through the threat of force.

FIGURE 3.2   *Bargaining and the Status Quo*

Here, the status quo clearly gives State A less than its value of war (the war outcome minus costs).

State A has an incentive to challenge any status quo that gives it less than its value of war, because it could do better by going to war. The same holds for State B. If the status quo is within the bargaining range, however, neither State A nor State B could improve its outcome by going to war, so neither state will challenge the status quo.

to coerce the target state into making a concession or changing a current policy. Compellent threats take the form of "Give me *y*, or else" (where *y* is something that the threatener values) or "Stop doing *x*, or else" (where *x* is an objectionable policy). The U.S. demand that Afghanistan hand over Osama bin Laden and stop harboring the Al Qaeda terrorist network after the 9/11 attacks is an example of compellence.

Deterrence, by contrast, is used to preserve the status quo by threatening the other side with unacceptable costs if it seeks to alter the current relationship. A deterrent threat takes the form of "Don't do *x*, or else" (where *x* is some possible future action that the threatener finds objectionable). The most common deterrent threat is one that all states make implicitly all the time: "Don't attack me, or I'll fight back." The effort to deter attack on one's own country is referred to as *general deterrence,* and it is an activity that states are constantly engaged in. Another form of deterrence occurs when a state seeks to protect a friend. In this case, the deterrent message takes the form of "Don't attack my ally *x*, or else." This kind of threat is generally referred to as *extended deterrence* because in this case the threatener attempts to extend protection to another state. Extended deterrence is crucial in the context of alliances, a subject that we will consider in Chapter 5.

In a 2012 speech to the United Nations, Israeli prime minister Benjamin Netanyahu declared that Israel would not permit Iran to reach the final stage of acquiring a nuclear weapon. He argued that a credible threat of military action was needed to deter Iran from crossing that "red line."

deterrence

An effort to preserve the status quo through the threat of force.

In general, crises may involve a combination of deterrent and compellent threats. When one side tries to compel another, the target may issue deterrent threats, or some third state may issue a deterrent threat on its behalf. Crises often involve such threats and counterthreats, as each side tries to improve its bargaining position by bringing to bear its capability to harm the other. In many cases, threats alone will succeed in bringing about an outcome that both sides find acceptable. Indeed, the most effective threats never need to be carried out, since they coerce the target into making the desired concessions or refraining from objectionable actions. It is when this contest of threats fails to generate an outcome that both sides prefer to fighting that we observe the descent into war.

Do Wars Happen by Mistake? War from Incomplete Information

In July 1990, Iraq was engaged in coercive diplomacy with its small neighbor to the south, Kuwait. Two years earlier, Iraq had emerged from a disastrous, eight-year war with Iran, and Iraqi leader Saddam Hussein desperately needed to rebuild his shattered economy. Given that Iraq was sitting on oil deposits containing an estimated 112 billion barrels of oil, it was not hard to imagine where money for reconstruction would come from. But Hussein was not content simply to pump and sell Iraq's own oil, and he quickly turned his gun sights on Kuwait. Kuwait's 95 billion barrels of recoverable oil reserves made a tempting target, and, moreover, Hussein felt that his neighbor was standing in the way of his plans for economic recovery. For one thing, Kuwait was pumping more oil than it had previously agreed to. This extra supply meant that the price of oil was lower than it would otherwise be, depriving Iraq of needed revenue. Iraq also charged that Kuwait was stealing oil from oil fields that straddled the countries' shared border. Finally, Kuwait had loaned Iraq substantial sums of money during the war, and Saddam Hussein hoped to get this debt forgiven. When Kuwait refused these demands, Iraq flexed its military muscle. Beginning in mid-July, Iraq started moving its forces closer to the border with Kuwait, at one point moving an entire division per day. By the end of the month, 100,000 Iraqi troops, supported by thousands of tanks, were in position near the border.

With the help of spy satellites, American officials watched the buildup, and they passed on their intelligence to the Kuwaitis. Despite their concern, most officials in the U.S. government did not anticipate that Iraq would invade, nor did the Kuwaitis bow to Hussein's demands. To many observers, the Iraqi moves looked like an effort to intimidate, not a prelude to invasion. According to reporter Bob Woodward's account, "Everything Saddam had to do to prepare for an invasion was exactly what he also had to do if his intention was simply to scare the Kuwaitis. There was no way to distinguish the two."[17] On August 2, with Kuwait still holding out, Hussein revealed that he had not simply been bluffing: Iraqi forces swept into Kuwait and fully occupied the country in a matter of hours.

In retrospect, it is clear that Iraq was willing and able to wage war against Kuwait if its demands were not met. At the time, however, key decision makers in Kuwait and Washington were not sure of Hussein's intentions. Would he really risk the wrath of the world by gobbling up his small neighbor? Would he be willing to put his military and his country through another war so soon after the last one? The invasion of Kuwait happened in part because, unsure of the answers to these questions, the Kuwaitis decided that calling Hussein's bluff was preferable to giving in to his demands. When it became apparent that the threat was not in fact a bluff, war was already upon them.

This episode illustrates one reason that bargaining can fail to resolve disputes and avert war. When states have poor and incomplete information about one another's willingness and ability to wage war, two mistakes are possible, both of which can lead to war. First, a state confronted by demands may mistakenly yield too little or not at all—just as Kuwait failed to budge in the face of Hussein's threats. In these cases, bargaining can break down because at least one state feels that it can achieve more through fighting (in this case, Iraq) than the other is willing to offer in the negotiations (Kuwait). The second, related danger is that a state may demand too

---

17. Bob Woodward, *The Commanders* (New York: Pocket Star Books, 1991), 200.

much (Iraq) under the mistaken belief that the other side will cave in (Kuwait, and its protector, the United States). In this event, the state may not realize its mistake until war is already upon it. In either case, even though there might be a settlement of the issue that both sides would prefer to war, uncertainty about one another's willingness to wage war can prevent such a settlement from being reached.

Where does this uncertainty come from? Recall that the main issue in crisis bargaining is how each state evaluates its prospects in a war. How likely is it that the state will be able to win the war? What will the human, financial, and political costs be? These assessments are important because each state's value for war determines what bargains it prefers to fighting. If one state is uncertain of how much its adversary values war, then it is also uncertain of how much it must concede in order to prevent a war. This uncertainty will arise whenever a state lacks information about any of the myriad factors that determine its adversary's evaluation of war.

A poker analogy is useful here. In poker, the fact that at least some cards are hidden from view means that each player knows more about the strength of her own hand than do her opponents. The hidden cards are what might be called private information: important facts that are known only to the player who observes those cards. Because no player sees all the cards, the game is played under a condition known as **incomplete information**. Every player lacks information about his or her opponents' hands and has private access to information about his or her own hand.

Incomplete information arises in crisis bargaining when states cannot readily observe or measure the key political and military factors that determine their adversaries' expected value for war. The hidden cards in this context can be many and varied, and we typically differentiate between two broad classes of unknowns: capabilities and resolve. *Capabilities* refers to the state's physical ability to prevail in war: the number of troops it can mobilize, the number and quality of its armaments, the economic resources it has to sustain the war effort. We might also include in this list the quality of the country's military leadership and military strategies. In addition, since third parties sometimes join wars on one or both sides, any uncertainty about what those third parties will do can lead to uncertainty about the capabilities each side will bring to bear in the event of war (see Chapter 5).

Resolve, a more abstract concept, refers to a state's willingness to bear the costs of fighting and how much the state values the object of the dispute relative to those costs. How many people is the country willing to lose in order to obtain, say, a given piece of territory? How much is it willing to pay in blood and money in order to win policy concessions or change another country's regime? Resolve has a direct impact on how much of the state's potential capabilities are actually mobilized in the event of war. We often make the distinction between *total wars* (in which states mobilize their entire military and economic resources) and *limited wars* (in which states fight with something less than their full potential), often because their aims are limited or of relatively low value. How a state evaluates the stakes of conflict determines where on this continuum its effort will be. World War II, for example, was seen as a war of national survival, and during those years (1942–45) the United States spent more than one-third of its gross domestic product (GDP) on defense;

incomplete information
A situation in which actors in a strategic interaction lack information about other actors' interests and/or capabilities.

resolve
The willingness of an actor to endure costs in order to acquire some good.

U.S. soldiers made significant sacrifices fighting in Afghanistan, but as a country, the United States devoted only a small fraction of its resources to this limited war. How much of a country's capabilities it is willing to mobilize for war can be a source of uncertainty in bargaining.

risk-return trade-off

In crisis bargaining, the trade-off between trying to get a better deal and trying to avoid a war.

by contrast, total U.S. defense spending in 2008 amounted to about 4 percent of GDP, and only a portion of that paid for the wars in Iraq and Afghanistan. Resolve is obviously a difficult quality to measure, as it hinges on a variety of political, ideological, and psychological factors. Indeed, it may be difficult for a leader to accurately assess his own country's resolve, much less the resolve of its adversary.

How could such uncertainty lead to war? When states have incomplete information about the capabilities and/or resolve of their opponents, bargaining over goods that they both desire may fail to achieve peaceful settlements. A central dynamic of bargaining under this kind of uncertainty is a phenomenon known as a **risk-return trade-off**: essentially, there is a trade-off between trying to get a good deal and trying to minimize the possibility that war will break out. On the one hand, a state can generally ensure peace by capitulating to all of its adversary's demands. "Peace at any price" might not be a very attractive outcome, however. Kuwait, for example, could have given in to all of Iraq's demands and would likely have avoided war. On the other hand, a state can hold firm and yield nothing to its adversary. This strategy promises a good deal if it works, but doing so runs a risk that the adversary will decide to fight rather than settle for nothing—as Iraq did when Kuwait refused to give in. Between these extremes, a state will generally find that it can reduce the risk of war only by making more generous offers, moving farther from its ideal outcome. Put another way, a state can improve the bargaining outcome for itself only by embracing a higher risk of war. Although war is costly and regrettable in retrospect, bargaining strategies that entail a risk of war can be perfectly rational given the uncertainty states face.

Incentives to Misrepresent and the Problem of Credibility

Given that incomplete information can lead to war, why can states not simply tell each other how capable and resolved they are and thereby avoid war? Actually, a large part of what goes on in a crisis consists precisely of such efforts at communication. Crises are generally characterized by diplomatic exchanges, threats and counterthreats, mobilization of forces, movement of troops, and weaponry. These actions in part have a military purpose: one cannot wage war, after all, without first mobilizing the necessary forces and putting them in place. But these actions also have a political purpose: they are the language of coercive diplomacy, the vocabulary that states use to convince one another that they are willing to back their bargaining positions with the threat of force.

The problem that arises in this context is that as much as states may have an interest in communicating their hidden information, they may not always be able to do so effectively. A crucial question that arises in crisis bargaining is whether the messages a state sends have **credibility**. A credible threat is a threat that the target believes will be carried out. We say a threat lacks credibility if its target has reason to doubt that the threat will be carried out. The credibility of a threat refers not only to the belief that the threatener will start a war; the target also has to believe that the threatener is willing to fight long and hard enough that it would be better to give in to its demands. In the case of the U.S. war against Afghanistan, the Taliban government probably had little doubt that President Bush would implement his threat to invade, but it may have doubted that the United States would be willing and able to bear the costs of a long war. In other words, the threat to start a war was credible, but the threat to remove Taliban leaders from power was, in their eyes, not. Though the Taliban were removed from power in December 2001 after two short months of combat, the fact that they were able to regroup and mount a serious threat to the U.S.-installed government over the next decade suggests that they may not have been entirely wrong.

Note that the credibility of the threat refers to the target's beliefs, not the actual intentions of the state issuing the threat. A state may fully intend to carry through on a threat, but it may have a hard time conveying that fact in a credible manner. Saddam Hussein genuinely intended to invade Kuwait if his demands were not met; observers in the United States and Kuwait, however, did not see the threat conveyed by his mobilization as credible. Similarly, a state may have no intention of carrying out its threat, but the target may mistakenly believe otherwise. In such cases, the bluff can succeed.

Why is credibility hard to achieve? There are two interrelated reasons. First, carrying through on threats is costly. A state may say that it will wage war if its demands are not met, but the costs of war might be such that it would not make sense to fulfill this threat if called on to do so. This concern about credibility was particularly pronounced during the Cold War between the United States and the Soviet Union. With both sides in possession of large arsenals of nuclear weapons,

credibility

Believability. A credible threat is a threat that the recipient believes will be carried out. A credible commitment is a commitment or promise that the recipient believes will be honored.

it was well understood that war could quickly escalate into total annihilation. Given this situation, officials in the United States worried about how they could deter the Soviet Union from attacking Western Europe. Would the United States really risk New York to save London or Paris? If the Soviets believed the answer to this question was no, then the U.S. commitment to defend Western Europe would lack credibility. It was precisely these kinds of concerns that led Great Britain and France to develop their own nuclear capabilities in order to deter the Soviets; after all, it was much more credible that France would risk Paris to save Paris.

Even without the prospect of nuclear annihilation, threats may lack credibility because their targets appreciate the costs of carrying them out. In the midst of the crisis between Iraq and Kuwait in 1990, the United States announced joint naval exercises with the United Arab Emirates. On the same day, the State Department spokesperson issued an extended deterrent threat by reaffirming the U.S. commitment to protect its friends in the Persian Gulf. Iraq's response was contemptuous. Hussein called the U.S. ambassador to his office the next day and told her that he was not scared by American threats. After all, he reportedly said, "Yours is a society which cannot accept 10,000 dead in one battle."[18] Thus, the U.S. deterrent threat had little credibility in Hussein's eyes because he believed that the United States would be unwilling to bear the costs of war.

The second reason that credibility is hard to achieve stems from the conflicting interests at the heart of the bargaining interaction. Even though states have a common interest in avoiding war, each also wants the best possible deal for itself, and this means that they have incentives to hide or misrepresent their information.

In some cases, this incentive means that states will conceal information about their true strength. After Iraq invaded Kuwait, the United States massed a large force in Saudi Arabia and threatened war unless Iraq retreated. It was widely assumed that if war came, U.S. forces would attack Iraqi positions in Kuwait head-on. Such a strategy would have provided the most direct route to the objective, but there were clear costs involved: the Iraqi forces in Kuwait were dug in behind strong defenses, including trenches filled with oil that could be lit on fire as soon as U.S. troops tried to cross. Saddam Hussein's resistance to U.S. pressure stemmed in part from his belief that his defenses would make the liberation of Kuwait very costly. In fact, war planners in the United States decided early on that they would not attack directly into the strength of the Iraqi positions. Instead, they secretly shifted the bulk of the U.S. force into the desert west of the Kuwaiti border. The military plan called for a "left hook": U.S. tanks would enter Iraq on the western flank of Iraqi forces in Kuwait and then swoop around behind them, thereby outflanking the enemy's fortifications. This tactical decision meant that

18. A transcript of this meeting was published in the *New York Times*, September 22, 1990. Hussein may also have been encouraged to ignore U.S. threats because American ambassador April Glaspie seemed to indicate that the United States had no strong interest in the outcome of the Iraq–Kuwait dispute.

the United States expected to incur lower casualties than Iraq expected to be able to inflict.[19]

Theoretically, if the United States could have communicated these expectations to Iraq, its threat would have been more credible and perhaps Hussein would have decided to back down. But it is easy to see why the United States could not say to Hussein: "You think that war will be too costly for us, but you are mistaken. Rather than attack your forces head-on, we will go around them on the western flank." Had the United States sent such a message, Iraq could have taken measures to counter the tactic, such as by repositioning its forces to the west. Hence, any bargaining advantage the United States might have reaped by revealing its strength would have been nullified. In the strategic context of the crisis, it made sense for the United States to hide its strongest cards.

In other cases, states misrepresent in order to hide their weakest cards. Anyone who has played poker knows that it sometimes makes sense to bluff—that is, to act as if one has a strong hand in the hopes that others will fold. A similar incentive exists in international crises. In this context, a bluff is a threat to use force that the sender does not intend to carry out. In a crisis, a successful bluff could reap large rewards. In 1936, German military forces marched into a region on its border with France known as the Rhineland—a region that, by the 1919 treaty that ended World War I, Germany was required to keep demilitarized. Hitler sent his forces in anyway, daring the Western powers to stop him. Though alarmed by this move, both France and Great Britain chose not to risk a full-scale war over the issue, and the remilitarization of the Rhineland took place unopposed. Interestingly, there is good reason to believe that Hitler's move was a bluff. Although there is some controversy on this point, there is evidence that German troops were under orders to retreat if confronted.[20] If so, then one of the key moments in the lead-up to World War II was a well-executed bluff.

This observation raises a dilemma: how can states credibly convey their information in order to diminish the risk of war due to uncertainty? Given a strategic environment that sometimes rewards misrepresentation, how can a genuine threat be made believable?

Communicating Resolve: The Language of Coercion

To help us answer these questions, another example will be helpful. On June 25, 1950, without any warning, North Korea invaded South Korea. Korea had been split in two after World War II, divided at the 38th parallel between the Communist North and the non-Communist and pro-Western South. North Korea's attack was a bold attempt to reunify the country under Communist rule, and the United States quickly joined the South in repelling the attack. After three months, the U.S. efforts

---

19. For a discussion of Persian Gulf War strategy, see Lawrence Freedman and Efraim Karsh, "How Kuwait Was Won: Strategy in the Gulf War," *International Security* 16 (Autumn 1991): 5–41.

20. James Thomas Emmerson, *The Rhineland Crisis, 7 March 1936* (Ames: Iowa State University Press, 1977), 98–100.

were largely successful, and North Korean forces began to retreat to their side of the 38th parallel. At this point, the United States decided to press the attack, cross into North Korea, and topple the Communist regime there. This possibility raised grave concerns in neighboring China, which had only the previous year been taken over by a Communist government. On October 3, 1950, Chinese diplomats conveyed a message through the Indian ambassador that a move across the 38th parallel would trigger Chinese intervention.[21] Nonetheless, the threat went unheeded. The U.S. operation had been planned and authorized under the assumption that the Chinese would not intervene, and the October 3 warning did nothing to change any minds.[22] U.S. forces crossed into North Korea on October 7 and advanced rapidly. In response, 600,000 Chinese troops poured into the Korean peninsula, leading to three more years of fighting and a costly stalemate.

Why was the Chinese threat dismissed, in the words of Secretary of State Dean Acheson, as "a Chinese Communist bluff"? An October 4 memorandum describes Acheson's rationale:

> The Secretary pointed out that the Chinese Communists were themselves taking no risk in as much as their private talks to the Indian Ambassador could be disavowed. . . . [I]f they wanted to take part in the "poker game" they would have to put more on the table than they had up to the present.[23]

Acheson's reasoning for downplaying the Chinese threat is instructive. The Chinese government was making an extended deterrent threat: "Don't invade North Korea, or we will intervene to defend it." From the U.S. perspective, it was possible that China would actually make good on this threat, but it was also possible that China was simply trying to bluff the United States into staying out of North Korea. Regardless of which of these possibilities was true, the message conveyed through the Indian ambassador was cheap and easy to send. There was nothing in the message or the way it was sent that would give American decision makers reasons to think that China was not simply bluffing. Unless the Chinese were willing to pay some costs—"to put more on the table"—there was little reason to take their threat seriously.

This example suggests a more general insight: for threats to be credible, they have to be costly in such a way that the sender would only make the threat if it really intended to carry the threat out. Consider the problem that the United States faced in October 1950 in these, admittedly oversimplified, terms:

> It is possible that the Chinese government is resolved to intervene if we attack North Korea, and it is possible that it is not so resolved. How can we know if we are facing a

---

21. The United States did not recognize the People's Republic of China as a legitimate government, so the two countries did not have direct diplomatic contacts.

22. See, for example, William Stueck, *Rethinking the Korean War* (Princeton, NJ: Princeton University Press, 2002), chap. 4.

23. U.S. Department of State, *Foreign Relations of the United States, 1950*, vol. 7: Korea (Washington, DC: U.S. Government Printing Office, 1976), 868–69.

"resolute" China or an "irresolute" China? What would we look for to distinguish these two "types" of adversary? The answer is: we would want to look for actions that a resolute China would be willing to take but an irresolute China would be unwilling (or, at least, less likely) to take. If we see such actions, then we are more likely to be facing a resolute China, and we have to take its threat seriously. If we do not see such actions, then there may be reason to doubt China's resolve.

The message that the Chinese actually sent did not have much credibility because an irresolute China could just as easily have made the same claim.

What kinds of actions would help an opponent to distinguish whether its adversary is resolved or not? In general, the literature has identified three mechanisms that states use to make their threats credible: brinksmanship, tying hands, and paying for power.

Brinksmanship: The "Slippery Slope"

Some of the earliest scholarship on the question of how to make threats credible took place in the 1950s, when policy makers and academics were preoccupied by the credibility of threats in the nuclear age. If everyone understood that nuclear war would bring total annihilation to each side, then under what conditions could threats between nuclear powers ever be credible? Since no state would ever intentionally "pull the trigger" and bring about Armageddon, the threat to do so was not credible. This observation raised the question of whether nuclear weapons had any utility at all in the emerging Cold War between the United States and the Soviet Union.

The most important insight into this issue came from Thomas Schelling, an early theorist of the strategy of crisis bargaining. In Schelling's view, although it was understood that no state would intentionally bring about its own destruction by starting a total nuclear war, these weapons could nonetheless be wielded for diplomatic effect through a strategy known as **brinksmanship**. The basic idea was that states could signal their resolve in the crisis by approaching the "brink" of war through provocative actions. Schelling describes this concept:

> The brink is not, in this view, the sharp edge of a cliff where one can stand firmly, look down, and decide whether or not to plunge. The brink is a curved slope that one can stand on with some risk of slipping, the slope gets steeper and the risk of slipping greater as one moves toward the chasm.[24]

The costs of war are such that if faced with a simple choice of whether to jump or not, no sane decision maker would jump. But rational leaders might decide to step out onto the "slippery slope" and thereby increase the risk that war would start inadvertently. Schelling famously referred to such an act as a "threat that leaves something to chance."[25] The willingness to take such a chance separates resolute

brinksmanship
A strategy in which adversaries take actions that increase the risk of accidental war, with the hope that the other will "blink," or lose its nerve, first and make concessions.

---

24. Thomas Schelling, *The Strategy of Conflict* (Cambridge, MA: Harvard University Press, 1960), 199.
25. Schelling, *The Strategy of Conflict*, p.187.

Leaders may use brinksmanship to make the threat of nuclear war credible. In the 1962 Cuban missile crisis, American president John F. Kennedy took steps toward nuclear war—for example, putting missile crews on alert—in order to pressure the Soviets to dismantle nuclear missile sites in Cuba.

from irresolute adversaries. After all, the less the state values the good in dispute, and the more it fears a war over that issue, the less willing it would be to step onto the slope and embrace a risk of war.

In a brinksmanship crisis, each side bids up the risk of war—moving further and further down the slippery slope—until either one side decides to give in or they fall together into the precipice (as in the game of Chicken discussed in the "Special Topic" appendix to Chapter 2). Exactly how a war might start "inadvertently" is not always clear; fortunately, in the case of nuclear war, we do not know the answer to that question. Absent a computer glitch, it still takes a human hand to pull the trigger. The general idea was that as tensions rose in an international crisis, the risk of accidents would increase. A limited skirmish between forces could inadvertently escalate if a nervous local commander thought his position was about to be overrun and decided to launch his tactical nuclear weapons in order not to lose them to the enemy. Or, in the midst of a tense crisis, a flock of geese might be mistaken on the radar for incoming bombers (as actually happened in the 1950s), leading to a decision to launch rather than risk being disarmed by a first strike (which, fortunately, did not happen in this incident). Alternatively, the tension of a nerve-wracking crisis might cause leaders to give in to passion and fury and lose their cool, rational heads. In any event, it was precisely the willingness to court this risk that would credibly separate the genuinely resolved opponents from the bluffers.

Tying Hands A second way in which states can send credible signals of their willingness to fight is by making threats in ways that would make backing down difficult. For example, after Iraq invaded Kuwait in August 1990, President Bush repeatedly and publicly stated that the conquest "will not stand." He made this commitment first on August 5, 1990, and reiterated it throughout the crisis, including during his State of the Union address on January 29, 1991. These words were also matched by deeds, particularly the deployment of over 500,000 U.S. troops to the region and an extensive diplomatic effort to build international consensus for an attack. Unlike the Chinese threat, which Acheson felt could be disavowed, Bush was clearly on record as asserting that the policy of his administration was to reverse the Iraqi invasion. By taking such clear, public statements and actions, Bush put his reputation, and that of the country, on the line. It was not unreasonable to expect that in doing so he had made it quite costly to retreat from this position—to decide, in the face of Iraqi resistance, that the invasion would be allowed to stand after all. Doing so would have been embarrassing for him as a leader and for the country as a whole; it would have called into question the credibility of future U.S. threats, and Bush could expect his political opponents to use such a retreat against him at the next election.

The general insight here is that under some conditions, threats can generate what are known as **audience costs**—that is, negative repercussions that arise in the event that the leader does not follow through on the threat.[26] Two audiences might impose these costs. The first is the international audience—other states that might doubt future threats made by the president or by the country. Such international audience costs could be felt through an inability to convince future adversaries of one's resolve. For example, one of the reasons that U.S. decision makers were skeptical of the Chinese threat to intervene in the Korean War was that it came in the wake of a series of unfulfilled threats over a different issue: Taiwan. As early as March 1949, the Chinese Communist government began issuing threats to "liberate" Taiwan from the Nationalist Chinese forces that had fled there. These threats, repeated several times over the course of the next year and a half, combined with China's failure to carry them out, led some analysts in the United States to discount the threats over Korea as similarly empty bluster.[27] International audience costs might also arise if allies come to doubt the trustworthiness of the country's threats, which may lead them to seek other protectors (see Chapter 5). A second audience that might punish a leader for backing down from a threat is in the leader's own country: voters and political opponents who might seek to punish a president who has tarnished the country's honor and reputation by making empty threats.

In either event, if threats expose state leaders to audience costs, they can have the effect of "tying their hands." This phrase comes from a famous scene in Homer's *Odyssey* in which the main character, Odysseus, asks to have his hands tied to the mast of his ship as they sail past the sirens. The call of the sirens is so beautiful that sailors who hear it are bewitched into steering their ship into the rocks. By tying his

audience costs

Negative repercussions for failing to follow through on a threat or to honor a commitment.

---

26. James D. Fearon, "Domestic Political Audience Costs and the Escalation of International Disputes," *American Political Science Review* 88 (September 1994): 577–92. For recent arguments that audience costs do not play a major role in crises, see Marc Trachtenberg, "Audience Costs: An Historical Analysis," *Security Studies* 21 (2012): 3–42; and Jack Snyder and Erica D. Borghard, "The Cost of Empty Threats: A Penny, Not a Pound," *American Political Science Review* 105 (2011): 437–56.

27. Anne Sartori, *Deterrence by Diplomacy* (Princeton, NJ: Princeton University Press, 2005), 33–39.

hands to the mast, Odysseus hoped to experience the sirens' call without succumbing to this enchantment. State leaders in a crisis tie their hands for similar reasons: because threats are costly to carry out, they know that they might choose not to follow through if faced with that decision. By exposing themselves to audience costs, they blunt the temptation to back down from their threats and thereby tie their own hands.

In the process of tying their hands, of course, state leaders also send a powerful message to their opponents: "I cannot back down; hence, my threat is completely credible." As with acts of brinksmanship, engaging in actions that generate audience costs separates the resolute from the irresolute. Those most likely to back down from a threat are less willing to take steps that will make backing down costly.

Paying for Power A final mechanism that states use to signal their resolve in a crisis involves taking costly steps to increase their capabilities, such as by mobilizing and deploying a large military force, increasing military manpower, and/or spending large sums of money. For example, during a 1961 crisis between the United States and the Soviet Union over Berlin, President Kennedy asked Congress to increase the army's strength by 350,000, with much of the growth coming from an increase in the number of people drafted and a call-up of reserve forces. This last step was particularly costly, in a political sense, because reservists are people who have finished their military service and have families and regular jobs. As a result, calling up 150,000 reservists led to political resistance. There was also a concrete monetary cost to these actions.

As already noted, military mobilizations play an important role in crises because they give the states the material capabilities needed to back up their threats. The most credible threat is not going to be effective unless the action threatened is very costly to the adversary. Thus, one purpose of military mobilization is to put force behind diplomatic maneuvers. At the same time, costly actions of this sort can also affect the opponent's estimate of the state's resolve, through several mechanisms.[28] First, by increasing the state's military capabilities, these actions may decrease the costs associated with carrying out the threat. Since the costs of carrying out a threat are what call credibility into question in the first place, visible steps taken to reduce those costs can make it more believable that the threatener will do what it says. Second, the willingness to pay the costs associated with these actions can signal that this is an issue that the threatening state cares a great deal about. By calling up the reserves, Kennedy was trying to send the message that he cared so much about the fate of Berlin that he was willing to pay the political costs associated with this action.

We started this section by noting that a condition of incomplete information is dangerous because states might miscalculate in bargaining, such as by mistakenly resisting threats that turn out to be genuine. Such mistakes played a role in the Iraqi

---

28. Branislav Slantchev, *Military Threats: The Costs of Coercion and the Price of Peace* (Cambridge: Cambridge University Press, 2011).

invasion of Kuwait in 1990 and in the onset of war between the United States and China in 1950. Brinksmanship, tying hands, and paying for power are strategies for communicating a willingness to fight: they are mechanisms that help states to figure out which threats are genuine and which are not. Interestingly, though, these cures for incomplete information entail risks that can be just as dangerous as the underlying problem they address. This is clearest in the case of brinksmanship strategies, through which states bid up the risk of accidental war in order to prove their resolve. The hope in doing so is that the adversary will blink, and thus war will be averted. But there is no guarantee that the states will not lose control and fall into the precipice. Ironically, then, to avoid a war driven by uncertainty, states have to embrace some risk of accidental war. Hand-tying strategies can have similar risks. In this case, states take actions that make it costly to back down from their threats. Although these actions can convince the other side to give in, there is also a risk that both sides will tie their hands in a contest of threats and counterthreats. Both sides can then become locked into intransigent and incompatible bargaining positions from which it is too costly to retreat. Once each side has eliminated its ability to compromise, war may be inevitable—even if the initial uncertainty that led to the crisis has been removed.

In the case of the Persian Gulf War, it is quite possible that President Bush's hand-tying actions between August 1990 and January 1991 eventually convinced Saddam Hussein that the United States was willing to fight, in spite of his original belief to the contrary. He may have resisted nonetheless because his own pattern of defiance and counterthreats in those months had served to tie his own hands as well. Hussein may have feared domestic repercussions for a retreat in the face of American threats, or he may have been concerned that such a retreat would embolden Iraq's neighbor and long-standing enemy, Iran. By January 15, 1991, neither side was willing to compromise, and the U.S.-led war to liberate Kuwait began. We thus see that incomplete information can cause war both directly, through miscalculation, and indirectly, by forcing states to communicate their resolve in ways that can foreclose successful bargaining.

This discussion generates several predictions about the conditions that make war more or less likely. In general, the harder it is for states to learn about each other's capabilities and resolve, the more severe the problem of incomplete information will be. When states are relatively opaque, in the sense that it is hard for outsiders to observe their military capabilities or their political decision-making processes, there is likely to be greater scope for uncertainties of this kind to arise and bedevil the quest for negotiated settlements. The strategic situation might also influence the degree of uncertainty that states face. For example, as the number of states that might potentially get involved in a particular crisis increases, the number and importance of the "hidden cards" increases dramatically: in the event of a war, who will join and who will not? Finally, this discussion sensitizes us to the question of whether states can find ways to signal their intentions in a credible manner. Problems of incomplete information are more likely to be overcome when states can find costly ways to signal their intentions and thereby convince their adversaries to make concessions.

Can an Adversary Be Trusted to Honor a Deal? War from Commitment Problems

Incomplete information can cause bargaining failures by making it difficult for states to agree on a settlement that all sides prefer to war. The ability to identify such a settlement, however, does not always guarantee that war will be avoided. What happens if the states do not trust one another to abide by that settlement in the future? The sources of bargaining failure considered in this section all arise from a common underlying challenge: the difficulty that states can have making credible promises *not* to use force to revise the settlement at a later date. In this context, credibility has the same meaning as before, but we use it here to describe not a threat to use force but rather a promise not to. A credible commitment to abide by a deal is a commitment that assures the other side that the state will not threaten force to revise the terms of the deal. A commitment problem arises when a state cannot make such a promise in a credible manner.

The Prisoner's Dilemma introduced in Chapter 2 is a quintessential example of such a problem. Although the prisoners in this game would like to commit to cooperating with each other, their incentives are such that a commitment to do so is not credible: when given the choice, they will prefer to defect. Commitment problems are particularly common in the absence of any enforcement mechanism, such as a court, that can hold people to their commitments. In the international system, external enforcement of commitments can be difficult to arrange (though not impossible, as we will see in the concluding section to this chapter). We now consider three ways in which an inability to make credible commitments to a bargain might undermine the search for a peaceful settlement of international disputes.[29]

Bargaining Over Goods That Are a Source of Future Bargaining Power

The clearest place to see the role of commitment problems is in disputes over goods that can serve as a source of future bargaining power. The best examples of such goods are strategically important pieces of territory and weapons programs. States bargain over territory all the time, but in some cases the piece of territory in question has military significance, perhaps because it contains high ground from which one would be able to launch an effective attack or islands that sit astride strategically important sea routes. For example, China and Japan have in recent years been locked in dispute over eight uninhabited islands in the East China Sea, known as the Senkaku to Japan and the Diaoyu to China. Not only

---

29. The ideas are introduced in Fearon, "Rationalist Explanations for War," and are further elaborated by Robert Powell, "War as a Commitment Problem," *International Organization* 60 (2006): 169–203.

are the surrounding waters rich in fish and oil and gas deposits, but the islands are also close to strategically important sea routes that are vital for naval movements in the region. As a result, control over the islands potentially impacts the countries' relative military power.

Bargaining over weapons programs has a similar quality. In recent years, the United States has sought to pressure several states—including Iraq (prior to 2003), Libya, Iran, and North Korea—into abandoning the development of WMD. These efforts have met with varying levels of success. Libya agreed to dismantle its weapons programs in December 2003. North Korea has several times agreed to freeze its nuclear program, but these deals unraveled, and North Korea effectively entered the nuclear club in 2006. As this edition was going to press, the United States and its partners announced the outlines of a deal with Iran to freeze its nuclear program for at least a decade. As with strategically important territory, a deal on this matter does not simply resolve a dispute—it also directly affects the military capabilities of the participants. A country that agrees to give up a weapons program makes itself weaker by doing so.

Territory with military-strategic value can be hard to bargain over because control over the good affects the states' relative military power. The uninhabited Senkaku/Diaoyu Islands have been a source of conflict between China and Japan partly because they sit astride strategically important sea routes.

The difficulty in bargaining over such objects is that a state will be reluctant to render itself more vulnerable to attack without credible promises that the other side will not exploit that vulnerability in the future. The state may be able to avoid war now by making concessions, but doing so entails a risk that its adversary, made stronger by the deal, will then press new claims. Unless there is some way for the other side to credibly commit not to use its newfound power, a threatened state may decide that it would rather fight today than face a future in which it is considerably weaker. Thus, even if there is some deal that is preferable to war now, if this deal will lead to a change in capabilities that can be exploited later on, the state that would be rendered weaker may decide to forgo that deal and gamble on a war.

This strategic dilemma has presented an important obstacle in U.S. efforts to convince countries like North Korea and Iran to give up their nuclear programs peacefully. It is important to remember that the United States had hostile relations with these countries prior to their seeking nuclear weapons. As we already saw, the United States fought a war against North Korea from 1950 to 1953. That war ended with a cease-fire but not a peace treaty, and ever since, more than 30,000 U.S. troops have been stationed in South Korea. U.S. hostility toward the North is driven not only by the lingering issue of Korea's division but also by the nature of its regime, which is one of the most repressive systems in the world. Similarly, hostility between the United States and Iran dates back to the 1979 revolution, which toppled Iran's pro-American leader and installed an Islamic fundamentalist government. To the extent that these states see their nuclear programs as a counterweight against American (and, in the case of Iran, Israeli) power, they would be reluctant to give up those programs if by doing so they would render themselves more vulnerable to U.S. demands on other issues. The experience of Libya is instructive in this respect. As noted earlier, Libya agreed in December 2003 to end its chemical and nuclear weapons programs and to submit to international inspections. In return, the United States and Britain promised to normalize relations with the country and not to press for fundamental changes in the regime of Libyan leader Mu'ammar Qaddafi—even though he ran a brutal dictatorship. In March 2011, however, Qaddafi faced a rebellion against his rule, and his attacks on civilians triggered military action by the United States, Britain, and other European countries. Qaddafi was ousted and then killed by rebel forces seven months later. Whether or not this intervention would have been deterred if Libya had continued its weapons programs, the lesson was clear: a promise by the United States to forswear regime change is not necessarily a credible or lasting guarantee. The success of any effort to end these programs peacefully requires the United States to find a way to commit credibly not to exploit the power shift brought about by disarmament.

Prevention: War in Response to Changing Power

A second, related problem arises if the balance of military capabilities is anticipated to change because of factors external to the bargaining process. A common source of this kind of power shift is different rates of economic growth. As noted in Chapter 1, uneven economic development has led to the relative rise and decline of states over time. The growth of Germany's power in the late nineteenth and early twentieth centuries had a dramatic impact on that country's ability to challenge its neighbors. Similarly, as we will discuss in Chapter 14, China's impressive economic growth since 1980 has greatly increased its influence in international politics. If a state is growing much more rapidly than its adversary, then the military capabilities that it can bring to bear in future disputes will be greater than those it can bring to bear today. A second important source of large shifts in military capabilities is the development and acquisition of new technologies, such as nuclear weapons. The acquisition of nuclear weapons can cause an abrupt and profound shift in a state's capacity to impose costs on its adversaries.

Regardless of their exact source, anticipated changes in military capabilities can present an insurmountable dilemma in crisis bargaining. To see this, we revisit the bargaining model introduced earlier. Figure 3.3 illustrates what happens to the bargaining interaction when the power of one state, in this case State A, is expected to increase. In the top panel, the expected outcome of the war is initially close to State B's ideal point. Let's assume, however, that State A's power is expected to grow, so that, at some time in the future, the new war outcome will be closer to State A's ideal point, as in the lower panel. In the initial period, the states could agree to some distribution inside the bargaining range. But both sides can anticipate

FIGURE 3.3   *Bargaining and Shifting Power*

Initial power distribution: Today, State B is more powerful than State A, thus fighting a war favors State B, as indicated by the fact that the war outcome is close to State B's ideal point.

Future power distribution: Tomorrow, after State A's power increases, fighting a war will favor State A. The war outcome is now close to State A's ideal point. The best deal that State B can get is smaller than its value for war in the top panel. Thus, State B may have an incentive to wage war today to prevent the power shift.

that in the future State A will no longer be satisfied with this deal and will demand a new deal in the new bargaining range. Therefore, as this example is constructed, State B prefers the war outcome it could obtain under the initial power distribution (labeled in blue in the top panel) over any outcome that falls in the future bargaining range. Even the best deal that State B can hope to get in the future (the red dotted line in the lower panel), gives State B less than it expects to get from war today. Hence, State B would rather fight a war now than face worse terms in the future. Notice that this logic is only compelling if it is believed that war will halt, or significantly delay, the anticipated change in power, as might happen if war could successfully disarm the other state or cripple its economic growth. If the shift in power from the upper to the lower panel will happen anyway, then there is nothing to be gained by fighting now only to have the outcome revised later in State A's favor.

Thus, even if the states can locate a deal that they prefer to war today, the state that is getting stronger will face a strong temptation to use its future power to try to revise the deal at some later date. Unless there is some way for the growing state to make a credible commitment not to do that, then its adversary may decide that it is better to gamble on war today in order to stop or slow the anticipated shift. A war that is fought with the intention of preventing an adversary from becoming relatively stronger in the future is a **preventive war**.

The U.S. war against Iraq in 2003 had a preventive logic, even if much of the motivating intelligence turned out to be flawed. Saddam Hussein's regime was believed to have some minimal capability—and a demonstrated intention—to develop WMD. The preventive argument for attacking was that it would be easier to oust Hussein before he had fully developed these capabilities than to do so after he had succeeded in deploying them in his arsenal. Of course, the uncertainties surrounding Iraq's weapons program illustrate a major risk of engaging in preventive war, since the rationale for doing so is only as strong as the evidence that a disadvantageous shift in relative capabilities is coming.

Preemption: War in Response to Fear of Attack

A final commitment problem that can prevent states from reaching negotiated settlements of their disputes arises due to fear of attack by an opponent with a first-strike advantage. A **first-strike advantage** exists when there is a considerable benefit to being the first to launch an attack. It arises when military technology, strategies, and/or geography give an advantage to offensive actions over defensive ones. When defense is relatively effective, a state can afford to wait to see if its opponent is going to attack because a first strike can be defeated or absorbed. When offense is relatively effective, a first strike is potentially devastating, and fear of attack creates incentives to abandon the bargaining table and rush to the battlefield.[30] For example, if one state could launch its nuclear missiles and destroy all of its adversary's missiles on the ground before they could be launched, then that state would enjoy a first-strike advantage. A state that can land a disarming blow may be tempted to do so, and a state that is vulnerable to such a blow may feel a "use it or lose it" imperative to strike first rather than be disarmed.

First-strike advantages can create a potentially insurmountable commitment problem: unless each state can credibly promise the other not to attack first, there is a danger that bargaining will break down as each side hurries to get in the first blow. Each side may be confident that if it manages to strike first, it can do better in war than by accepting the deal that is currently on offer. Indeed, there may be no deal that both sides prefer to a war that they start. An example of this situation

---

preventive war

A war fought with the intention of preventing an adversary from becoming stronger in the future. Preventive wars arise because states whose power is increasing cannot commit not to exploit that power in future bargaining interactions.

first-strike advantage

The situation that arises when military technology, military strategies, and/or geography give a significant advantage to whichever state attacks first in a war.

---

30. There is a considerable literature on the "offense-defense balance" and its effect on the likelihood of war; see, for example, Keir Lieber, "Grasping the Technological Peace: The Offense-Defense Balance and International Security," *International Security* 25 (Summer 2000): 71–104. A related literature emphasizes that what matters is not the actual offense-defense balance but rather the balance that is perceived by military and political leaders; see Van Evera, "The Cult of the Offensive."

Bargaining and the Duration of War

There is a good deal of variation in the duration of interstate wars. Figure A shows the distribution of war durations for 125 interstate wars over the last two centuries. About 10 wars have lasted three years or more, and account for most of the combat deaths from wars in this period. However, most wars are relatively brief.

What determines how long a war will last? A number of factors might explain why some wars are longer than others, including the power of the adversaries and what they are fighting over. But, at a more general level, how long a war lasts is related to the strategic problem that caused the war in the first place. Once the adversaries go to war, the incentive to reach a deal that spares each side the costs of fighting does not disappear. Indeed, relatively few wars are fought until one of the states is completely occupied or unable to mount further operations; most end with some kind of bargain. This observation raises a puzzle: How does war make it possible for states to reach a settlement when they could not do so beforehand?

In a recent book, Alex Weisiger argues that if bargaining failed due to incomplete information about relative capabilities and resolve, then war can bring about a deal by revealing the hidden information.[a] As states compete on the battlefield, features that were hard to observe beforehand—the power of each state, the effectiveness of military technologies and strategies, the willingness of the populace to bear the burdens of war—become observable. In this case, war lasts as long as is necessary for uncertainties to be resolved.

Alternatively, if the war came about due to a commitment problem, then the war can only end when the source of that problem is removed. A preventive war fought in response to the rising power of an opponent can end when either the declining power is unable to keep fighting or the rising power is crippled to the point that its rise has been forestalled.

To test these propositions, Weisiger collected data on 103 cases of interstate war since 1816 and estimated the effect of different factors on how long each war lasted. He found that one of the strongest predictors of long and severe wars was whether the war was preceded by a large shift in the adversaries' relative military capabilities, as measured by not only the size of their militaries but also their population and level of economic development. In particular, the typical duration of a war preceded by a large power shift is three times that of war preceded by little or no such shift. Thus, as expected, the longest wars tend to be those fought between declining and rising states, when preventive motivations loom largest. On the other hand, among wars that were not preceded by a shift in power—and are therefore more likely to be rooted in an information problem—those that experienced relatively frequent and intense battles tended to end more quickly. This finding is consistent with the idea that battles serve to resolve uncertainty, permitting the adversaries to find a settlement that both prefer to continued bloodshed.

FIGURE A   **The Duration of Interstate Wars, 1816–2014**

Source: Meredith Reid Sarkees and Frank Wayman, *Resort to War: 1816–2007* (Washington, DC: Congressional Quarterly Press, 2010).

a.   Alex Weisiger, *Logics of War: Explanations for Limited and Unlimited Conflicts*. Ithaca, NY: Cornell University Press, 2013. For another important study along these lines, see Branislav Slantchev, "How Initiators End Their Wars: The Duration of Warfare and the Terms of Peace," *American Political Science Review* 48 (September 2004): 813–29.

FIGURE 3.4 *Bargaining and First-Strike Advantages*

State A attacks first: State A enjoys a significant advantage in war if it attacks first, and the war outcome will be close to its ideal point.

State B attacks first: Here, the war outcome heavily favors State B. Because the bargaining ranges in the top and lower panels do not overlap, there is no deal that both sides prefer to a war that it initiates.

is depicted in Figure 3.4. Here, we assume that there are two different war outcomes depending on which state lands the first blow: the expected outcome of a war started by State A is depicted in the top bar, and the expected outcome of a war started by State B is depicted in the lower bar. The first-strike advantage is captured by the assumption that each side expects to do better in a war that it starts than in a war started by the adversary (that is, the war outcome in the top panel is closer to State A's ideal point than the war outcome in the lower panel; the opposite is true for State B). As a result, while there exists a set of deals that both states prefer to a war started by either State A or State B, there is no deal that is preferable to both of these possible wars. A deal within the lower bargaining range would satisfy State B but give State A less than it expects to get by attacking first (the area labeled in red on the top bar). Similarly, a deal within the upper bargaining range would satisfy State A, but give State B less than it expects to get by striking first (the area labeled in blue on the lower bar). Under these conditions, neither state will make concessions to the other at the bargaining table; instead, both will likely rush to the exits, each trying to beat the other to the punch. Negotiations in this context may be seen as nothing more than a ploy to delay the other side from mobilizing. A war that arises in this way is a **preemptive war**.[31]

The 1967 Six Day War between Israel and four Arab states (Egypt, Syria, Jordan, and Iraq) is a classic case of a war that started this way. In May 1967, Egypt responded to border skirmishes between Israel and Syria by massing troops on the Israeli border and imposing a partial blockade. On June 5, fearing that war was likely, Israel launched a surprise, preemptive attack on the Egyptian air force, destroying 300 aircraft while they were still on the ground. With Egypt's main offensive threat crippled, the ensuing war lasted six days and left Israel in control of large swaths of formerly Arab-held territory.

This dynamic forms an important component of what we referred to earlier as the security dilemma. When military technology favors offensive action, a state that builds arms, even out of purely defensive motives, inevitably makes other states worry about a possible attack. If threatened states arm in response, the original state will in turn feel less secure, feeding a self-reinforcing cycle of fear. In addition to causing arms races and hampering international cooperation, the commitment problem created by this fear fuels a risk of war.

Both preemption and prevention arise from the difficulty states can have in making credible commitments not to use their military power. The difference between the two concepts revolves around timing. Preemption is a response to an imminent threat when there is an existing first-strike advantage. Prevention is a response to anticipated changes in the distribution of power that might result in an increased threat sometime in the future. (For a discussion of how such considerations contributed to the outbreak of World War I, see "What Shaped Our World?" on p. 126.)

We have seen, then, that even if states can locate a deal that both prefer to war at the moment, concerns about their willingness to abide by the deal in the future can cause bargaining failure and war. Although these concerns can arise for different reasons, all the paths to war discussed in this section have at their root a common commitment problem: the difficulty of committing not to use one's power to one's advantage in the future. In addition to shedding light on the general problem of war, this discussion generates a number of predictions about the conditions under which war is more or less likely to occur. First, war is more likely to occur when the good in dispute is a source of power to those who possess it. For example, it is harder to strike bargains over strategically important territory than over territory that is valuable for other reasons. Second, preventive incentives arise when there are relatively rapid and dramatic changes in the military balance between two countries. Hence, war is more likely when such changes are anticipated or under way. Finally, bargaining failures are more common when the military-strategic situation creates

preemptive war
A war fought with the anticipation that an attack by the other side is imminent.

---

31. It should be emphasized that this example assumes a very large first-strike advantage relative to the costs of war, so it is possible that this kind of situation arises only rarely. For a historical overview of preemptive war, which finds that very few wars start this way, see Dan Reiter, "Exploding the Powder Keg Myth: Preemptive Wars Almost Never Happen," *International Security* 20, no. 2 (Autumn 1995): 5–34.

Prevention and Preemption in World War I

World War I redrew the maps of Europe, the Middle East, and Africa. It decimated a generation of young people, and the postwar settlement contributed to World War II 20 years later, as well as more recent conflicts.

For all its far-reaching consequences, the war had relatively modest origins. On June 28, 1914, Archduke Franz Ferdinand, heir to the throne of the Austro-Hungarian Empire, was assassinated during a visit to neighboring Serbia. How could this event lead to a war that would ultimately involve 32 states fighting on three continents?

Interests Europe in 1914 was rife with conflicting interests. Growing German power brought it into competition with Britain and provoked fear in its neighbors. France hoped to reclaim territory from Germany, which in turn had designs on territory in Russia and overseas. Austria-Hungary and Russia were competing for influence in the Balkan region. The Ottoman Empire was in decline, and outsiders sought to expand at its expense.

Institutions States with compatible interests often form alliances, institutions that help them to cooperate militarily (see Chapter 5). By 1914, the major powers were divided into two hostile camps: Germany, Austria-Hungary, and Italy formed the Triple Alliance against Great Britain, France, and Russia in the Triple Entente. This alliance system meant that any conflict had the potential to expand throughout Europe. It also posed a problem for German military planners, who knew that, in the event of a war, they would face foes to the east and west.

Interactions In this combustible atmosphere, the assassination of the archduke by Serb terrorists created a dangerous spark. Austria-Hungary had a substantial Serb minority, and agitation by Serb nationalists threatened to tear the multiethnic empire apart. Austria-Hungary sought to compel Serbia to end its support for these militants and threatened war. This threat brought a deterrent response from the Russians. Germany then promised to protect the Austrians. Though in principle the conflict could have been defused by a negotiated bargain, preventive and preemptive considerations loomed large.

Although German leaders did not relish a war with Russia, they feared Russia's growing power. In the decades prior to the war, Russia had made great economic strides, building its heavy industries and railroad network. Germany's leaders watched these developments with concern and came to believe that they had a short "window of opportunity" in which to prevent future Russian domination.

In contemplating war with Russia, however, there was a significant obstacle: France. To deal with the possibility of a two-front war, the Germans came up with an audacious solution. The Schlieffen Plan took advantage of the fact that Russia's vast size made its military machine very slow. After the Russians started mobilizing, it would take six weeks before their forces could join the fight. The Germans hoped to exploit this delay to invade and quickly defeat France. German troops could then be shifted to the east, in time to meet the Russian advance.

Planners believed that the strategic situation gave an advantage to whoever struck first. By acting quickly, Germany could seize key bridges and tunnels in Belgium, roll on into Paris, and then turn their attention to Russia. If they waited, the Belgians could fortify or destroy the bridges, causing the German army to bog down in the west, while the Russian "steamroller" bore down from the east. Under these conditions, negotiations threatened an intolerable delay. Preemptive incentives also meant that military mobilizations were not a useful instrument of crisis diplomacy. When the Russians mobilized on July 30, they hoped that signaling their resolve would lead the Austrians to reduce their demands. Instead, Russia's mobilization spurred the adversaries to the battlefield.

By August 3, Europe was at war. When the Russian army mobilized, Germany invaded Belgium and France. Great Britain joined the fray. Other states were tempted by one side or the other to pile on, and the battlefield expanded across and beyond Europe.

substantial advantages for striking first. These advantages generally arise from the nature of military technology, which sometimes imparts large advantages to the actor who goes on the offensive first—although, as we saw in the case of World War I, particular military strategies can also create pressure to act preemptively.

Is Compromise Always Possible? War from Indivisibility

A final problem that can prevent states from reaching mutually beneficial settlements of their disputes arises when the disputed good cannot be divided. A good is divisible if there are ways to split it into smaller shares; an **indivisible good** cannot be divided without destroying its value. Imagine, for example, the difference between having 100 pennies and having one dollar bill. Although the amount of money available is the same in both cases, the pennies can be divided up between two people in many different ways while the dollar bill cannot be split without ruining it. When the good in question is indivisible, compromise solutions are impossible to reach, and the bargaining becomes "all or nothing." It is easy to see how indivisible goods could create an insurmountable obstacle in crisis bargaining. Consider a situation in which each state would prefer to fight a war rather than get none of the good. Even though there might be deals that both sides prefer to war—such as, say, a fifty-fifty split—an inability to divide the good into the necessary shares renders such a deal unattainable. In an all-or-nothing bargaining situation, one state must get nothing. And if both states prefer war to getting nothing, then war becomes inevitable.

Although the logic of indivisibility is quite clear, what is less clear is whether or how often indivisibility is actually a problem in international politics. What goods are truly indivisible? A key point is that indivisibility is not a physical property of a good but rather of the way in which it is valued. This point is made most dramatically by the biblical story in which King Solomon, confronted by two women claiming to be the mother of the same baby, decides that the only fair solution in the face of these incompatible claims is to "cut the baby in half." This solution strikes us as odd not because it cannot be physically implemented but because the process of doing so will kill the baby. (Fortunately, in King Solomon's case, the decision did not have to be carried out, since one woman insisted that she would rather let the other woman have her child than see it killed—whereupon Solomon decided that this woman must be the true mother.) Similarly, in a dispute over a valuable painting, one could slice the painting in two, but doing so would presumably destroy the object's value. Hence, when we say that a good cannot be divided, we generally do not mean this literally. Rather, we mean that the good loses much, if not all, of its value when it is divided.[32] This can be the case with core values that cannot be compromised or with divisible goods that are closely linked to such core values.

indivisible good
A good that cannot be divided without diminishing its value.

---

32. H. Peyton Young, "Dividing the Indivisible," *American Behavioral Scientist* 38, no. 6 (1995): 904–20.

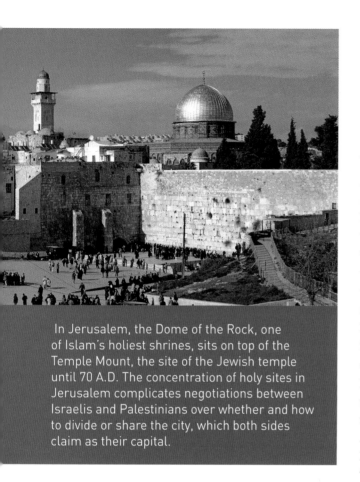

In Jerusalem, the Dome of the Rock, one of Islam's holiest shrines, sits on top of the Temple Mount, the site of the Jewish temple until 70 A.D. The concentration of holy sites in Jerusalem complicates negotiations between Israelis and Palestinians over whether and how to divide or share the city, which both sides claim as their capital.

A commonly cited example of an indivisible good in international relations is the city of Jerusalem.[33] It is a city that contains some of the holiest sites of Christianity, Islam, and Judaism and has historical, cultural, and religious significance unlike any other piece of territory in the world. As a result, the status of Jerusalem is a major stumbling block in efforts to bring about peace in the Middle East. For many Jews, Jerusalem is the focal point of the desire—sometimes symbolic, sometimes literal—to return to the promised land of Zion. Every year at Passover, Jews all over the world utter the words "Next year in Jerusalem," which underscores the role of that city in forging a connection between the land of Israel and the Jewish identity. The centrality of this city has been given political expression as well: a Basic Law passed by Israel in 1980 declares that "Jerusalem, complete and united, is the capital of Israel." For Muslims, East Jerusalem, or Al-Quds, is the third-holiest city (after Mecca and Medina in Saudi Arabia) and the site of the Dome of the Rock, where the prophet Mohammed is believed to have ascended to Paradise. Palestinians claim East Jerusalem, which Israel annexed after the 1967 Six Day War, as the capital of an eventual Palestinian state. This claim clearly clashes with the Israeli position that the city is indivisible and the capital of the Jewish state. Moreover, the holiest sites for both faiths sit literally on top of one another. The Dome of the Rock and Al-Aqsa Mosque were built (1,300 years ago) directly on the Temple Mount—the site of the original Jewish temple—whose Western Wall is an important place of worship for Jews. The question of whether or how to divide the city, and how to ensure that people of all faiths have access to their holy sites, is one that has so far defied resolution.

It is important, however, not to place undue emphasis on indivisibility as a source of bargaining failures. First, some of the difficulty of dealing with indivisible goods arises not from indivisibility per se but because of weak enforcement mechanisms. King Solomon's quandary is one that divorcing parents routinely face when each wants custody of their children. These disputes are settled not by dividing the children physically but by dividing the time they spend with each parent. This kind of alternating possession would generally fail in international politics, however, because a state would not trust its adversary to hand over the good when the time came to do so. In child-custody cases, the deal is enforced by courts and police, which are generally lacking in the international context. Thus, the main obstacle to

---

33. See, for example, Cecilia Albin, "Negotiating Indivisible Goods: The Case of Jerusalem," *Jerusalem Journal of International Relations* 13, no. 1 (1991): 45–76.

striking such a deal lies not in the nature of the good but in the difficulty of making a credible commitment to share it over time.[34]

A second reason to be skeptical of claims of indivisibility is that states may have strategic incentives to claim that they cannot compromise on a particular issue, even if they actually could. Recall that one of the strategies that states employ in crisis bargaining is to tie their hands through public pronouncements from which it would be costly to back down. It is quite possible that claims of indivisibility—such as the Israeli Basic Law mentioned above—have a strategic quality: they represent an effort to tie the government's hands so that it will find compromise difficult, if not impossible. In doing so, the hope is that the other side will realize that it has no choice but to give in entirely. In this sense, objects may take on the appearance of indivisibility in the course of the bargaining process, through the public positions that states take.[35]

The point of this discussion is not to suggest that indivisible goods do not exist in international politics. Rather, it is to suggest that we be appropriately skeptical when the participants in a dispute claim that the good in question is indivisible and hence no compromise is possible. Such a claim may reflect a bargaining position adopted for strategic reasons rather than a true description of the fundamental nature of the good in question.

How Can We Make War Less Likely?

War arises from a variety of factors that can prevent states from reaching peaceful settlements of their disputes. Of course, the reason we study war is not just to understand why it happens; we also study war in the hope that understanding is the first step toward reducing or eliminating its occurrence. What, then, have we learned that might be useful in managing international disputes so that they are less likely to escalate into wars? The following discussion identifies four sets of mechanisms that can facilitate conflict management.

Raising the Costs of War

One of the main disincentives for engaging in war is the human, economic, material, and psychological costs it imposes. Indeed, the costs of war generally ensure that states can do better by finding a negotiated settlement of their disputes. As war becomes less attractive, states will be more willing to make compromises in order to avoid it. Hence, raising the costs of war can expand the set of settlements that all sides prefer to fighting. Perhaps the best illustration of this effect is the apparently pacifying effect of nuclear weapons, a topic to which we will return in Chapter 14. It is striking that despite five decades of intense hostility between the United States and the Soviet Union during the Cold War, the two superpowers never waged war

---

34. See Powell, "War as a Commitment Problem," for a discussion of how indivisibility leads to commitment problems.

35. See Stacie E. Goddard, "Uncommon Ground: Indivisible Territory and the Politics of Legitimacy," *International Organization* 60 (2006): 35–68.

directly against one another. Although there are many theories about the cause of this so-called long peace, it is certain that nuclear weapons and the threat of "mutually assured destruction" induced a dose of caution that helped the superpowers defuse numerous crises without resorting to war.[36] Another argument along these lines holds that trade and financial relations between states can promote peace by increasing the economic costs of going to war. The more two countries value one another as trading partners, the more incentive they will have to avoid conflicts that will disrupt those profitable exchanges. The argument and evidence in favor of this proposition are considered in Chapter 4.

Increasing Transparency

Although uncertainty is commonplace in world politics, mechanisms that increase the transparency of states can reduce some of the dangers of miscalculation. Transparency refers to the ability of outsiders to peer into a state and learn about the factors that influence its decision making about war and peace. A state's military capabilities are probably the easiest factor to make transparent. The advent of satellite technology, for example, has made it possible for advanced states to learn a great deal about one another's weapons systems and force levels. States may also agree to send military officials to each other's country in order to observe one another's activities. International organizations may also enhance transparency by providing neutral observers of a state's military activities. The International Atomic Energy Agency, for example, conducts inspections of members' nuclear energy programs in order to determine whether nuclear fuel has been diverted to produce weapons. None of these mechanisms is foolproof, of course, as the U.S. experience with Iraq from the 1991 Gulf War to the 2003 invasion clearly showed. Weapons can be hidden from view, satellite images can be ambiguous, international observers can be obstructed or misled, and bureaucratic failures can lead to misinterpretation, whether deliberate or not.

Even so, generating information about capabilities is easy relative to the task of creating transparency about the many and complex factors that determine a state's resolve. Trying to observe how much an adversary values the object in dispute, what costs it is willing to pay to obtain the good, and what risks it is willing to run constitutes a much more daunting task than counting the other side's soldiers, tanks, and airplanes. Since resolve can emerge from the political factors within the state, transparency on this dimension often depends on the political systems within states. Some political systems are by nature very transparent, allowing outsiders ample opportunity to observe the internal debate about what values are at stake and whether they are worth fighting for. Other states are relatively opaque, with decisions made by a small number of individuals who operate with little or no public accountability. We will revisit this line of reasoning in Chapter 4, when we consider the possible effects of domestic political institutions on international conflict.

---

36. See, for example, John Lewis Gaddis, "The Long Peace: Elements of Stability in the Postwar International System," *International Security* 10 (Spring 1986): 99–142.

Providing Outside Enforcement of Commitments

A promise not to use one's power to one's advantage is a very difficult commitment to make in a credible fashion. A major part of the problem lies in the fact that states cannot generally rely on repeated interaction to hold one another to such a promise, as they can in the case of compliance with World Trade Organization rulings (see Chapter 2). Repeated interaction can help make promises credible if the prospect of future dealings leads a state to forgo the temptation to break a promise today because it fears retaliation by the other state tomorrow. Under conditions of shifting power, however, the state that is becoming more powerful has less to fear from the other side's retaliation. Furthermore, if a state can use its increased power to destroy the other state, then there may be no "shadow of the future" to stay the growing state's hand. The same holds in situations involving first-strike advantages: the temptation to deliver a crippling blow is hard to blunt if the other side's retaliatory capability will be rendered ineffective in the process.

Because adversaries generally cannot solve this commitment problem on their own, any solutions are most likely to come from third parties—that is, a state or group of states, including international organizations, that are not directly involved in the bargaining game between the opponents. In some cases, such outsiders may be able to help build credibility for the opposing states' commitments not to exploit power or first-strike advantages. Third parties can play this role by monitoring and enforcing agreements, by providing security guarantees to one or both sides, and sometimes by interposing their forces directly between two potential combatants.

For example, after World War II, security guarantees extended by the United States played a large role in reassuring the Western European countries that they had little to fear from the postwar reconstruction of West Germany. Although the war had left Germany devastated and divided, France in particular feared that it was only a matter of time before Germany would recover and once again be in a position to threaten its neighbors. What made a final settlement between the two states possible was an extensive American commitment to station troops in West Germany and to guarantee the security of both states. With a sizable American troop presence monitoring Germany's reconstruction and remilitarization, France could undertake improved relations with its neighbor without fear of Germany's postwar recovery. The U.S. presence and the alliance system it built made credible Germany's commitment to live

Security guarantees and a sizable troop presence from the United States helped reassure Western European countries that were nervous about the reconstruction and rearmament of West Germany after World War II. Here, U.S. Secretary of State John Foster Dulles looks on as French, West German, and British leaders celebrate the signing of an agreement in 1954 that paved the way for West Germany to become a fully sovereign state.

peacefully with its western neighbors. Third-party guarantees worked in this case because the United States had an interest in ensuring peace between its allies in the context of the Cold War with the Soviet Union. Outside actors do not always have such strong interest in getting involved, so this option is not always available. We will revisit this issue in Chapter 5, when we examine the role of international institutions in preventing the outbreak of war.

Dividing Apparently Indivisible Goods

As suggested earlier, there may be ways to allocate apparently indivisible goods that do not involve physical division. One possible mechanism is joint or shared control. It has been proposed, for example, that Israelis and Palestinians jointly control certain portions of Jerusalem to ensure that all people have access to the sacred sites. Indeed, this already happens to some degree at the Temple Mount: though it falls under Israeli sovereignty, the area on top, including the Dome of the Rock and Al Aqsa Mosque, is administered by Islamic authorities. A second mechanism for dealing with indivisible goods is through compensation on another issue. Although a rare painting cannot be physically divided, a dispute over it can be resolved by having one party compensate the other in exchange for the good. In this case, the object is made divisible by adding a new dimension to the deal: rather than arguing about who gets the painting, the issue becomes how much money one is willing to pay to the other to get it. Since money is generally divisible, adding this new dimension creates the possibility for compromise where none previously existed. Hence, disputants may be able to find a second issue dimension on which the loser in the main issue can be compensated. The strategy of making one dispute easier to solve by bringing in a second issue is known as linkage, as we saw in Chapter 2.

Conclusion: Why War?

This chapter posed the puzzle of why states fight wars in spite of the enormous costs associated with fighting. The answer involves two ingredients: a conflict in states' interests, and some factor or factors that prevent states from reaching a peaceful solution to that conflict. States' underlying interests in power, security, wealth, and/or national identities can give rise to disputes over territories, policies, and the composition of one another's governments. In the absence of authoritative institutions that resolve interstate disputes, states engage in a bargaining interaction over these issues, sometimes invoking the threat of military force to enhance their leverage. War occurs when features of this strategic interaction prevent states from reaching a settlement that both prefer to war, with all its uncertainties and costs.

Three kinds of problems can prevent states from settling their disputes in ways that allow them to avoid the costs of war: problems arising from incomplete information, those arising from the difficulty of committing to honor a deal, and those arising from goods that are hard to divide. Since these obstacles occur in different degrees and in different combinations from one crisis to the next, there is no single answer to the puzzle at the heart of this chapter. Instead, the discussion has sought to identify and explore a set of mechanisms that can bedevil the effort to resolve disputes peacefully. Having done so, we are in a better position to understand and interpret behavior and outcomes in international crises. The concepts introduced here highlight some of the key factors that determine whether a dispute can be settled without resort to war.

In particular, we need to pay attention to (1) what the adversaries in a dispute believe about one another's willingness and ability to wage war and how uncertain those beliefs are; (2) how each side seeks to communicate its resolve, whether those efforts are credible, and to what extent they either entail a danger of accidental war or "lock in" incompatible bargaining positions; (3) whether the good in the dispute is a source of future bargaining power; (4) whether the distribution of power between the adversaries is expected to change as a result of different economic growth rates or technological progress; (5) whether the military technologies and strategies of the adversaries generate sizable first-strike advantages; and (6) whether the good in question is indivisible because of its close connection to core values, such as religious identity.

[margin note: Predicting/Preventing War]

In spite of the many things that can go wrong and prevent a peaceful solution, it is important to remember a point we made early in this chapter: wars are rare. Even though information is often incomplete, credible commitments are hard to make, and core values are hard to compromise, most states most of the time are at peace with one another. The costs of war mean that not every disagreement is worth fighting over or even threatening to fight over. Hence, the very costs that make war hell also ensure that war is not the most common way that states settle their disputes.

Study Tool Kit

Interests, Interactions, and Institutions in Context

- States may have conflicting interests over goods like territory, policies, or the composition of one another's governments. However, because war is costly, a peaceful settlement that all sides would prefer to war generally exists. War occurs when the bargaining interaction fails to reach such a deal.

- In the bargaining interaction, states may be unable to reach negotiated settlements when they are uncertain about one another's willingness and ability to wage war.

- Even if states can find a mutually acceptable bargain, peace can break down if they cannot credibly commit to abide by the terms of the agreement.

- Bargaining may also fail if there are features of the disputed good that make it hard to divide, which makes compromise agreements impossible to reach.

- Given this logic, promoting peaceful conflict resolution requires efforts to increase the costs of conflict, to promote transparency and communication between disputants, to bring in third parties to enforce states' commitments to one another, and to find creative ways of sharing apparently indivisible goods.

Key Terms

war, p. 91

interstate war, p. 91

civil war, p. 91

security dilemma, p. 92

crisis bargaining, p. 97

coercive diplomacy, p. 97

bargaining range, p. 101

compellence, p. 104

deterrence, p. 105

incomplete information, p. 107

resolve, p. 107

risk-return trade-off, p. 108

credibility, p. 109

brinksmanship, p. 113

audience costs, p. 115

preventive war, p. 122

first-strike advantage, p. 122

preemptive war, p. 125

indivisible good, p. 127

For Further Reading

Blainey, Geoffrey. *The Causes of War,* 3rd ed. New York: Free Press, 1988. Presents a historical examination of war informed by bargaining theory.

Fearon, James. "Rationalist Explanations of War." *International Organization* 49 (1995): 379–414. Serves as the seminal statement of the theory of war developed in this chapter.

George, Alexander, and Richard Smoke. *Deterrence in American Foreign Policy.* New York: Columbia University Press, 1974. Offers a theoretical and historical overview of deterrence and its use in major U.S. foreign policy crises.

Goddard, Stacie E. *Indivisible Territory and the Politics of Legitimacy: Jerusalem and Northern Ireland.* Cambridge: Cambridge University Press, 2009. Argues that territories can become indivisible because of the way states try to legitimize their claims.

Levy, Jack S., and William R. Thompson. *Causes of War.* Chichester, West Sussex, UK: Wiley-Blackwell, 2010. Systematically reviews contemporary theories on the causes of war, including some alternative approaches not covered in this text.

Powell, Robert. *In the Shadow of Power: States and Strategies in International Politics.* Princeton, NJ: Princeton University Press, 1999. Presents a formal analysis of shifting power and its effects on the potential for war.

Reiter, Dan. "Exploring the Bargaining Model of War." *Perspectives on Politics* 1 (2003): 27–43. Evaluates the argument that war is a product of, as well as a continuation of, interstate bargaining.

Schelling, Thomas. *Arms and Influence.* New Haven, CT: Yale University Press, 1966. Serves as an accessible introduction to the strategic problems that arise in coercive interactions, including problems of credibility and commitment.

Van Evera, Stephen. *Causes of War.* Ithaca, NY: Cornell University Press, 2001. Explores how power shifts and first-strike advantages contributed to major wars throughout history.

4

Domestic Politics and War

THE PUZZLE *War is costly for states, but what if there are actors within the state—such as politicians, businesses, or the military—who see war as beneficial and who expect to pay few or none of its costs? Do states fight wars to satisfy influential domestic interests?*

Above: In democratic systems, voters can influence foreign policy by removing (or threatening to remove) leaders who make unpopular decisions. In 2014, thousands of protesters in London let their government know how they felt about renewing military engagement in Iraq.

On March 30, 1982, thousands of demonstrators marched in the streets of Buenos Aires, the capital of Argentina, denouncing the country's military government for its harsh economic policies and oppressive rule. Riot police used tear gas, rubber bullets, and water cannons to break up the protests, and over 2,000 people were arrested. A week later, the streets of Buenos Aires filled with demonstrators once more, but this time the demonstrations voiced enthusiastic support for the military regime, as many of those who had earlier called for the government's ouster now joined in the outpouring of praise. What had changed in the course of a week? On April 2, Argentine naval forces invaded a small group of islands 300 miles off the Argentine coast that were the subject of a long-standing dispute between Argentina and Britain. Is there any connection between these events? Could the Argentine government have provoked a war with Britain in order to revive its popularity with its people?

In 1954, representatives of the United Fruit Company went to Washington, D.C., to voice concerns about the leader of Guatemala, a man named Jacobo Arbenz. Arbenz had pushed a land reform program that led to the seizure of almost 400,000 acres that belonged to the company. Arbenz offered to compensate United Fruit to the tune of $1.2 million, the value of the land that the company claimed for tax purposes. The U.S. government insisted on behalf of United Fruit that the company be paid almost $16 million. In June of that year, rebels armed and trained by the U.S. Central Intelligence Agency (CIA) invaded Guatemala. Fearing a full-scale American invasion, parts of the Guatemalan military revolted, Arbenz resigned from office and fled the country, and a pro-American leader was installed. The operation cost the CIA just under $3 million.[1] Did the United States overthrow a foreign leader to benefit a single company at the expense of American taxpayers?

Our first look at the puzzle of war in Chapter 3 considered this problem from the perspective of states. We assumed two states in conflict over some good, such as a piece of territory, and trying to arrive at a settlement that avoids the costs of war. This kind of analysis is very common in international relations scholarship, where it is

---

1. The cost information is from U.S. Central Intelligence Agency, "CIA's Role in the Overthrow of Arbenz," Job 79-01025A, Box 153, Folder 3, www.state.gov/r/pa/ho/frus/ike/guat/20181.htm (accessed 11/07/07).

often referred to as the *unitary state assumption*: the treatment of states as coherent actors with a set of interests that belong to the state. While this assumption can be a useful starting place for analysis, we must remember that states are legal and political constructs, not beings capable of taking actions. The choices and actions of states are made by people. Decisions about waging war are made by a state's political leaders. Military plans are drawn up by military officials and carried out by soldiers. Others within the country may also be able to influence foreign policy choices, even if they have no direct say over them. There may be interest groups such as business or ethnic lobbies that influence decision making through their organizational and financial resources. In democratic systems, voters influence policy decisions because of their ability to remove leaders who make unpopular choices. Looking inside the state reveals new actors with varied interests as well as variation across states in the political institutions that determine who affects decision making.

How does our understanding of the causes of war change when we look inside the state and consider the interests, interactions, and institutions within it? In Chapter 3, we argued that to understand why wars happen, we need to understand why states at times cannot solve their conflicts peacefully, in a way that avoids the costs associated with fighting. This argument rested on the assumption that war is costly to those engaged in the interaction. These costs create a bargaining range, or a set of deals that both states prefer to fighting. The assumption that war is costly makes sense when we think of the state as a unitary actor, but once we look inside the state, it is clear that the costs and benefits of war are not distributed equally within the country.

Different actors within the state may place more or less value on the issue in dispute. A disputed territory might represent a source of livelihood, profit, or national pride to some, a tract of worthless land to others. The persecution of a minority group in a foreign country might arouse outrage in some, perhaps owing to ethnic attachment to the victims, while others greet it with indifference. Most Americans in 1954 had little or no stake in the land reform policies of the Guatemalan government; to the United Fruit Company, on the other hand, millions of dollars worth of land were at risk.

The costs of war are also distributed unevenly. Some people, such as those who might be drafted to serve in the military, can expect to pay very high and direct costs from war. Others may see the costs of war in economic terms, if the need to finance the conflict leads to higher taxes. In contrast, there are some groups within a country that may profit from war financially or professionally: arms manufacturers benefit from increased purchases of their products; for military officers, combat experience leads to opportunities for medals and promotions; and for unpopular governments, such as the Argentine junta in 1982, war can build support domestically and solidify their hold on power.

These observations raise a number of questions: To what extent is war rooted not in the information and commitment problems discussed in Chapter 3 but rather in the interests of domestic actors who see personal benefit and little or no cost to war? Do wars serve the national interest or the narrow interests of office-hungry politicians, multinational companies, and/or a "military-industrial complex" composed of glory-seeking militaries and profit-seeking arms merchants? How do domestic institutions, such as democracy, influence a government's decisions and the likelihood of war between states?

Thinking Analytically about Domestic Politics and War

To answer the questions above, we must consider the different interests that domestic actors have in terms of war and peace. Simply identifying these interests is not enough, however, since not all actors within the state have equal say over foreign policy choices and hence not all interests are represented equally. Which domestic interests drive foreign policy choices depends on two factors: the strategic interactions between actors, which determine which individuals and groups can exert effective influence and which cannot, and the institutions within the state, which determine how different actors have access to the decision-making process. Further, we have to recall that war is not the choice of a single state but rather an outcome of the interaction between or among multiple states. Hence, as we consider domestic influences on foreign policy, we need to examine how these factors shape bargaining at the international level.

Whose Interests Count in Matters of War and Peace?

In the previous chapter, we observed that international disputes generally arise over territory, policies, and the characteristics of countries' domestic regimes. Why these conflicts of interest arise in the first place is a complicated question with no single answer. One view, referred to in this book's Introduction as realism, is that states' interests are largely, if not entirely, dictated by external factors. States want to preserve their sovereignty and territorial integrity. To do so, they need power—primarily, military power. Hence, they seek opportunities to expand their own power and/or to diminish the power of those that threaten them. In this view, states' interests are fixed, determined largely by their material resources and geographical position, and they are not shaped by domestic factors.

Although this argument is sometimes useful in understanding sources of conflict in the world, it is also overly simplistic. Conflicts between states often arise from the interests of domestic actors within them, and these interests include more than the basic need for physical security. For example, some conflicts cannot be understood without reference to the ethnic identities and religious beliefs that prevail within states. In early modern Europe, wars often pitted Catholic countries against Protestant countries. A change in the official religion of a country could radically alter who its friends and enemies were. In the present day, ongoing rivalries between India and Pakistan or between Israel and its Arab neighbors are similarly fueled by religious differences. If, say, the majority of citizens in India were Muslim rather than Hindu, its relations with Pakistan would certainly be different. This observation suggests that the interests that states bring to international bargaining cannot be considered in isolation from the interests of actors within the states.

National versus Particularistic Interests

In considering the kinds of domestic interests that can influence foreign policy, it is useful to distinguish between general interests and narrow or particularistic interests. A general interest is something that most, if not all, actors within the country share. For example, virtually everyone has an interest in their country's physical security and economic well-being. If most people within the state share a common religious or ethnic identity, then the state's foreign policy interests likely reflect those identities. It makes sense to refer to such interests as national interests, or interests that are so widely shared that they can be attributed to the state as a whole. Narrow or particularistic interests are those held only by a relatively small number of actors within the country, such as a particular business, an ethnic minority group, or individuals within government.

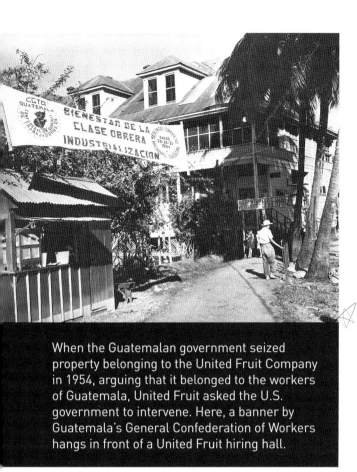

When the Guatemalan government seized property belonging to the United Fruit Company in 1954, arguing that it belonged to the workers of Guatemala, United Fruit asked the U.S. government to intervene. Here, a banner by Guatemala's General Confederation of Workers hangs in front of a United Fruit hiring hall.

To make this distinction concrete, consider the case of oil. The United States has long professed, and acted on, an interest in ensuring a steady supply of oil, particularly from the oil-rich countries in the Middle East. In 1943, President Franklin Roosevelt declared that the defense of Saudi Arabia was vital to the defense of the United States, and an American company, the Arabian-American Oil Company (Aramco), became the main player in developing and exploiting the oil fields there. The commitment to defend Saudi Arabia was reinforced on a number of occasions. In 1979, the Soviet Union invaded Afghanistan, putting Soviet forces on the doorstep of the Middle East and American allies in the Persian Gulf. President Jimmy Carter responded by articulating what became known as the Carter Doctrine: "Any attempt by an outside force to gain control of the Persian Gulf region will be regarded as an assault on the vital interests of the United States of America, and such an assault will be repelled by any means necessary, including military force." And, of course, the need to preserve stability and American influence in this region was cited to justify both the 1991 Persian Gulf War and the 2003 Iraq War.[2]

Why has the United States had such a consistent interest in oil and the Middle East? A national interest–based argument hinges on the observation that oil is vital to U.S. power because a modern military of tanks and airplanes consumes large quantities of fuel. It is no coincidence that Roosevelt's concern for Saudi Arabia arose during World War II, at a time when American war planners were worried about running out of gas. The Cold War that followed did nothing to alleviate concerns about maintaining access to this strategically valuable material that was crucial to the economic and military might of the United States and its allies. In this view, the U.S. interest in oil stems from a national interest in ensuring its military power and security.

An alternative argument, also based on general interests, revolves around the U.S. economy's dependence on stable and plentiful oil supplies. The U.S. economy runs on oil—to fuel cars, to transport goods around the country, to heat homes and power businesses. Shocks to the price of oil can thus have substantial effects on the economic welfare of U.S. citizens, influencing inflation, unemployment, and disposable income. As Figure 4.1 shows, the price of oil over time has been highly sensitive to events in the Middle East, with major spikes occurring during times of war and revolution. Such dramatic price increases can affect people in a variety of ways,

---

2. For a comprehensive history of the role of oil in international politics, see Daniel Yergin, *The Prize: The Epic Quest for Oil, Money, and Power* (New York: Free Press, 1991).

FIGURE 4.1 *The Price of Oil, 1960–2014*

sparking inflation and unemployment and eating into consumers' pocketbooks. Hence, American citizens have a general interest in ensuring stability in the Middle East in order to prevent oil price shocks that would hurt the economy.

Set against these views of the United States' national interest is one that sees the pursuit of oil as benefiting a small group of businesses: oil companies. After World War II, U.S. companies like Aramco played a direct role in pumping and selling Middle Eastern oil, making huge profits. Since the 1960s and 1970s, producer countries have generally nationalized their oil industries, meaning that oil companies have to negotiate deals with these governments. U.S. firms like ExxonMobil profit from their participation in the exploration, drilling, refining, and marketing of oil, but their access to these activities depends on the willingness of foreign governments to do business with them. It is possible, then, that U.S. foreign policy toward the Middle East is driven by these companies' desire to expand and protect their profits. In this view, firms use their influence over policy makers to ensure that the United States defends friendly regimes (like that of Saudi Arabia) and undermines hostile regimes (like that of Iraq under Saddam Hussein) that are bad for business. Because these policies can impose costs on American soldiers and taxpayers, this view sees U.S. foreign policy in the Middle East as benefiting a narrow set of interests within the country at the expense of everyone else.

As this discussion suggests, the distinction between national and particularistic interests is easy to make in the abstract but harder to observe in practice. While oil clearly influences U.S. policy in the Middle East, it is difficult to say with confidence whether the general or narrow interests are more important. Nonetheless, the distinction is crucial for thinking about what causes war. Recall from Chapter 2 that an actor is a group of individuals with similar interests. To the extent that groups or individuals within the state have different interests over the outcomes of international bargaining, the analytical utility of assuming that the state is an actor diminishes—and we have to start looking within the state for new actors. This quest is important because, as discussed in Chapter 3, the analysis of the war assumed that

Figure source: International Monetary Fund, International Financial Statistics, elibrary-data.imf.org (accessed 01/20/15).

*2010 U.S. dollars.

Spoiler Alert: It's this one.

evil

Whose Interests Count in Matters of War and Peace? **141**

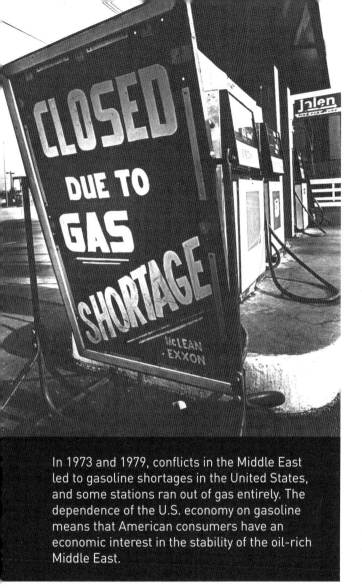

In 1973 and 1979, conflicts in the Middle East led to gasoline shortages in the United States, and some stations ran out of gas entirely. The dependence of the U.S. economy on gasoline means that American consumers have an economic interest in the stability of the oil-rich Middle East.

war is a costly outcome for the actors engaged in international bargaining. These costs ensure the existence of deals that all sides prefer to war, and they underpin an understanding of war that focuses on the information, commitment, and divisibility problems that can prevent such deals from being reached. If, however, the benefits of war are enjoyed by a different set of actors from those that pay the costs, then this view may need to be revised. Does war arise not because of obstacles to the bargaining interaction but because war furthers the interests of particular actors within the country?

Interactions, Institutions, and Influence

When we drop the unitary actor assumption and look within states, an enormous number of individuals and groups, with a variety of interests, come into focus. Which actors matter and which interests are likely to influence foreign policy decisions? The answer lies in institutions and interactions. Recall from Chapter 2 that institutions are sets of rules and decision making procedures. Within each country, domestic institutions help determine who runs the government, how decisions are made, and how disputes are resolved. In a monarchy, for example, the ruler is determined through a system of succession often determined by birth order. In other systems, the leader is the person who commands the greatest support within the military and therefore can repress challengers with force. In democratic political systems, leaders are selected through regular elections in which the winner is decided by the amount of popular support they can muster. Domestic institutions also determine how much power an individual leader has to make decisions. In some political systems, the ruler can dictate the state's policies on his own or with the support of a relatively small number of key actors. In other systems, the institutions of government may distribute decision-making power among more than one body, such as a president and a legislature.

By shaping how leaders obtain power and make decisions, domestic institutions determine which actors' interests are taken into account. Leaders whose hold on power is unchallenged may not have to consider the interests of anyone else, and they can act on the basis of their personal interests or whims. More commonly, a ruler may only have to worry about maintaining the loyalty of the military by catering to that organization's interests. In democratic political institutions, by contrast, the need to win elections forces leaders to think about how the voting public will respond to their policy choices. It also makes them dependent on organized groups that are willing to donate money and time to election campaigns. Although voters and organized interest groups are not literally in the room when decisions are made, democratic institutions force those who *are* in the room to take those actors' interests into account. Thus, institutions determine which actors and interests have a (figurative) seat at the table.

Some domestic actors may also have strategic advantages that magnify their influence. In Chapter 2, we introduced a strategic dilemma known as the collective action problem. This problem arises when a group of individuals with common interests seeks to act collectively to further that interest. As we saw, such efforts can fall short if each individual prefers to free ride on the efforts of others. One implication of this insight is that relatively small groups can be more effective at cooperating to further common interests than large groups. Indeed, small groups of highly motivated and informed individuals are better able to organize and coordinate their activities and prevent others from free riding. By contrast, large, dispersed groups in which each individual has only a small stake in or knowledge about the policy decision are generally very hard to organize. For example, whereas United Fruit stood to lose millions of dollars of property in Guatemala, the intervention cost each U.S. taxpayer only a few pennies. Had taxpayers been opposed to having their money spent this way, they would have had a hard time cooperating, since no individual had any incentive to spend time and money on such an effort. To the extent that a group's political influence depends on the ability of its members to cooperate, this strategic problem favors the few over the many. Thus, a relatively narrow interest group can successfully demand a policy that benefits that group at the expense of everyone else.

Appreciating the role of institutions and interactions, we can organize a discussion of domestic interests around four different kinds of actors, depicted in Figure 4.2.

FIGURE 4.2 *Key Domestic Actors in Foreign Policy*

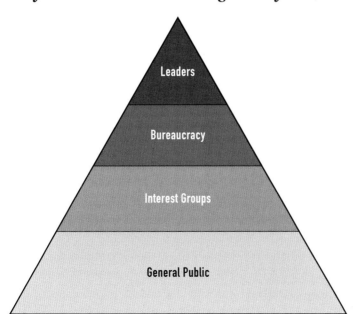

bureaucracy

The collection of organizations—including the military, the diplomatic corps, and the intelligence agencies—that carry out most tasks of governance within the state.

interest groups

Groups of individuals with common interests that organize to influence public policy in a manner that benefits their members.

The first type consists of the leaders who make foreign policy decisions. State leaders decide when to make threats, what demands to issue, and ultimately, whether to wage war. These individuals matter the most because, by whatever rules of politics operate in their country, they have the authority to make these decisions. The next type comprises organized groups that have sufficient resources and information to influence the decisions made by the political leaders. Two such groups are of particular relevance: bureaucratic actors and interest groups. The state apparatus is made up of a variety of different organizations collectively known as the **bureaucracy**. These organizations—which include the military, the diplomatic corps, and the intelligence agencies—may wield considerable influence owing to their institutional resources and knowledge. The military in particular, by virtue of its coercive power, organizational discipline, and expertise in war fighting, can shape decisions about the use of force both through its role in implementation and through its influence over political leaders. **Interest groups** are groups of individuals with common interests that have organized in order to push for policies that benefit their members. Of particular importance in the present context are economic interest groups, such as companies or groups of companies, and ethnic lobbies comprising people with similar policy interests owing to their common ethnic background. In later chapters, when we turn to issues like human rights (Chapter 12) and the environment (Chapter 13), interest groups that organize around other principles will come to the fore.

The final type of actor to consider is the most numerous but rarely the most powerful: the general public. As already suggested, the influence of ordinary citizens varies considerably with domestic institutions. In democratic countries, free and fair elections provide individuals with a low-cost way to participate in deciding who governs. In other kinds of countries, it is harder for individual citizens to have much influence, since political leaders do not depend on their support. As long as the regime can count on the repressive power of the police and military, then general public interests can be ignored. Given this situation, the question of how the general public matters is largely a question of how democracy matters.

As we proceed through this chapter, we walk down the pyramid in Figure 4.2 and consider arguments and evidence about the behavior of actors at each level.

Do Politicians Spark Wars Abroad in Order to Hold On to Power at Home?

As noted earlier in this chapter, Argentina sparked a war with Great Britain in 1982 when it invaded a set of nearby islands that had been in dispute for a century and a half: the Falkland Islands to the British, the Malvinas to Argentines. This war was surprising in a number of respects. First, the islands were not particularly valuable pieces of territory. At the time of the war, the islands' population was under 2,000, and their primary source of income was sheep farming. Indeed, just prior to the war Britain had taken steps to weaken its hold over the islands. In 1981, Britain readied plans to withdraw the last of its naval vessels in the region and passed an act that stripped the islanders of full British citizenship. Second, the war was surprising given the imbalance in military power between the two states. Though separated from the islands by a larger distance, Britain had a far superior naval force. After Argentina invaded and occupied the Falklands on April 2, 1982, it took only 74 days for British forces to retake the islands. There were 255 dead on the British side, 635 on the Argentine side. So why did Argentina pick a fight with such a formidable foe, and why did Britain react so strongly to defend its right to islands that seemed to be of diminishing importance?

A large part of the answer to this puzzle lies not in international considerations but in the domestic political interests of the countries' governments. At the time, leaders in both countries had pressing domestic problems to which military conflict may have seemed the perfect solution. The Argentine government—a group of military officers known as a junta—had seized power in 1976, and its rule became increasingly repressive and unpopular over time. In the early 1980s, Argentina suffered a severe economic downturn, which led to civil unrest and splits within the ruling group. Facing a dire threat to its rule, the junta decided that an attack on the Malvinas might help solve its problem. Knowing that most Argentines resented British control of the islands, the junta leaders hoped that a bold move to seize the islands would stir up nationalist sentiment, distract people from their economic hardships, and give the military government a popular achievement that would bolster its prestige and legitimacy. Indeed, the invasion of the Malvinas had precisely this effect. Hence, the Argentine junta was seeking more than just territory when it seized the islands—it was also looking to solidify its hold on power.[3]

On the British side, Prime Minister Margaret Thatcher also had to worry about her political survival. Like Argentina, Britain in 1982 was in the midst of a severe recession. With unemployment soaring, Thatcher's popularity dropped precipitously. In February 1982, the month before the invasion, only 29 percent of Britons said that they approved of the job she was doing. Thatcher's firm response caused her poll numbers to soar. By May, with British operations to retake the Falklands under way, Thatcher's approval rating jumped to 44 percent. By the end of the war, her approval stood at 51 percent. The British prime minister rode this wave of popularity to electoral victory a year later. Hence, Thatcher's unexpectedly strong response to the Argentine invasion not only restored British control over the Falklands, but it also revived her political fortunes.[4]

---

3. Jack Levy and Lily Vakily, "External Scapegoating in Authoritarian Regimes: Argentina in the Falklands/Malvinas Case," in *The Internationalization of Communal Strife,* ed. Manus Midlarski, 118–46 (London: Routledge, 1992).

4. Approval figures are from David Butler and Gareth Butler, eds., *British Political Fact 1900–1994,* 7th ed. (London: Macmillan, 1994), 256. There is some controversy over how much the Falklands War contributed to the Conservative victory in 1983. See Harold D. Clarke, William Mishler, and Paul Whiteley, "Recapturing the Falklands: Models of Conservative Popularity, 1979–83," *British Journal of Political Science* 20, no 1. (January 1990): 63–81.

What Do Leaders Want?

The leaders of states are not solely, if at all, statesmen or stateswomen looking out for the best interests of the nation; they are also individuals with many varied interests of their own. Some may have very strong ideological beliefs that increase their willingness to pay costs or run risks in foreign policy. It is hard to understand World War II, for example, without reference to German leader Adolf Hitler's extreme ideology, which motivated him to seek out *Lebensraum* ("living space") for the German people by attacking Poland and then the Soviet Union.[5]

Even in the absence of such extreme ideological interests, state leaders may have more prosaic personal motivations. As the story of the Falklands War reminds us, leaders are also politicians, people who benefit from holding political office. Being in office confers all manner of benefits: the ego boost of having power, opportunities to enrich oneself and one's friends, the ability to shape policy in desired ways. As a result, politicians think a lot about how to obtain office and, once in power, how to secure their hold on it. This means that political leaders make choices with an eye toward how those choices will influence their chances of staying in power.

How could these motivations affect leaders' decisions about war and peace? At the most general level, the desire to stay in power means that leaders have to be responsive to the interests of those who control their political fate, whether they be voters, organized interest groups, the military, or some other groups. As a result, the assumption that political leaders want to remain in office plays a key role in almost every aspect of this chapter, since it helps account for the influence of special interest groups that can provide resources that are useful for maintaining power; it contributes to an understanding of the role of the military, whose support is often necessary for a government to stay in power; and it is a necessary element in arguments about the effects of accountability in democratic political systems. In short, the desire to hold office explains how the interests of actors within the country can matter at the level of policy making.

British prime minister Margaret Thatcher benefited politically from the Falklands War. Before the war, poor economic conditions in Britain had helped bring Thatcher's public approval rating down to just 29 percent. Once the war began, the British public rallied behind their leader, sending her approval rating up to 51 percent.

---

5. There is a debate among historians about how much of Hitler's foreign policy is explained by his personal ideology. For a balanced view on this, which ultimately concludes that ideology played an important role, see Allan Bullock, "Hitler and the Origins of the Second World War," in *The Origins of the Second World War: A. J. P. Taylor and His Critics,* ed. William Roger Louis, 117–45 (New York: Wiley, 1972).

But an interest in holding on to power does not turn political leaders into mere instruments of other actors. Strategic politicians can use their control of policy to shape their political environment, rather than just respond to it. In the case of war and peace, a common argument is that leaders sometimes use force abroad not to further any national interest but rather to enhance their hold on power at home.

The Rally Effect and the Diversionary Incentive

The idea that leaders can further their own political interest by fighting a war flows from the rally-round-the-flag effect, or rally effect for short. The **rally effect** refers to people's tendency to become more supportive of their country's government when it experiences dramatic international events, such as wars. This effect is most apparent in countries in which public opinion polling regularly measures the level of support for a leader. Often, approval ratings jump up at the onset of a war or some other international crisis, as in the case of Thatcher's approval ratings at the outset of the Falklands War. The most dramatic rally event ever recorded followed the terrorist attacks of September 11, 2001, which caused President George W. Bush's approval rating to jump immediately from 51 to 86 percent, eventually reaching as high as 90 percent. Even in countries without opinion polls and approval ratings, we see cases in which the start of war caused an upsurge of national unity and support for the government. As we saw at the outset of this chapter, in 1982, Argentina's military government reversed a tide of public discontent by invading the Falkland Islands.

Why do people rally around the flag at times of international crisis? There are a number of explanations. Social psychologists have shown that members of a group often feel greater attachment and loyalty to the group when they experience conflict with outsiders. Hence, international conflict can cause an upwelling of patriotism, and the leader derives increased support as the protector of the group's interests. At the same time, political opponents may decide to dampen their criticism of the government at a time of national crisis, and the government may use the emergency to crack down on dissent. This means that the government dominates the political discourse and can frame the public's evaluation of its policies without fear that opposing voices will split public opinion.[7] International conflict can also create a diversion from problems that might otherwise drag down a leader's popularity, such as economic troubles or scandals. Foreign policy crises tend to drive other issues out of the news headlines, redirecting people's attention away from the domestic issues that divide and disappoint them and toward the more unifying challenge of meeting a foreign threat. Finally, international conflict may give embattled leaders an opportunity to blame foreigners for the country's problems, a phenomenon known as scapegoating.

rally effect
The tendency for people to become more supportive of their country's government in response to dramatic international events, such as crises or wars.

---

6. See, for example, Lewis A. Coser, *The Functions of Social Conflict* (New York: Free Press, 1956). The pioneering work of the rally effect in the United States is John E. Mueller, *War, Presidents, and Public Opinion* (New York: Wiley, 1973).

7. Richard A. Brody and Catherine R. Shapiro, "A Reconsideration of the Rally Phenomenon in Public Opinion," in *Political Behavior Annual,* ed. S. Long, 77–102 (Boulder, CO: Westview Press, 1989).

Just a few days before invading the Falkland Islands, the Argentine government faced massive protests and calls for the overthrow of the ruling junta. Rioters confronted police, and thousands were arrested. The war with Britain provided the Argentine junta a (temporary) reprieve from these problems by shifting the public's attention away from domestic issues.

diversionary incentive

The incentive that state leaders have to start international crises in order to rally public support at home.

The existence of rally effects suggests that political leaders may at times face a **diversionary incentive**: a temptation to spark an international crisis in order to rally public support at home. This idea was popularized in the 1997 movie *Wag the Dog,* in which a scandal-plagued national leader hires a movie director to produce news footage of a fake war in order to boost his approval ratings. The logic, however, long precedes Hollywood. In William Shakespeare's *Henry IV, Part II*, a dying King Henry advises his son, Prince Hal, that to prevent plots against him he needs to "busy giddy minds / With foreign quarrels." This advice echoes in the words of a Russian minister who, during a 1904 dispute with Japan, reportedly told the tsar, "What this country needs is a short, victorious war to stem the tide of revolution."[8] Whether the tsar found this argument persuasive or not, Russia and Japan declared war on each other on February 10, 1904.

The danger posed by the rally effect should be clear from the discussion in Chapter 3. There, it was assumed that a state's first-best outcome in a crisis is to get its way without having to fight. Fighting, after all, imposes costs that the state should prefer to avoid. A diversionary temptation could alter the balance of costs and benefits. If those who control the state's foreign policy think that using force abroad would greatly improve their chances of staying in power, then they may prefer war to a negotiated settlement, even one that gives them most of what they want.

---

8. This quotation is attributed to Russian interior minister Vladimir Plehve. However, the authenticity of the quotation is unclear, and it has been suggested that it was attributed to Plehve only later by his political enemies.

These benefits may be particularly tempting to leaders who are insecure domestically, because of discontent with their policies or hard economic times. Such a leader may decide that she will surely lose office if she does nothing, so waging war and invoking the rally effect may be an appealing gamble. This phenomenon has been called gambling for resurrection: taking a risky action, such as starting a war, when the alternative is certain to be very bad. A sports analogy is useful here. Hockey teams trailing in the final minutes of a game sometimes pull their goalie in order to replace him with an additional attacker. Doing so increases the chances that they can even the score, but it also makes it easier for the other team to score against their undefended net. The gamble makes sense because a loss is a loss regardless of whether a team loses by one goal or many. Consequently, the downside risk of pulling the goalie is small compared to the upside potential of tying the game. Political leaders who are certain they will lose office because of poor economic conditions, such as the Argentine junta in 1982, might similarly see a large upside to starting a war and gambling that the outcome will turn out well.

Do Leaders "Wag the Dog"?

Do leaders routinely gamble for resurrection by starting wars abroad at times of political need? Given the intuitive nature of this argument, it may come as a surprise to learn that scholars have found little consistent support for the hypothesis that leaders systematically resort to force when they are in trouble domestically. Numerous studies have sought to determine whether the likelihood that a state will get involved in military conflict increases when the leader is unpopular or the country is in a recession or facing high unemployment or inflation or, in the case of democratic countries, when a well-timed rally shortly before an election could be particularly useful. Although some studies have shown such effects, the results have been neither consistent nor particularly strong. Rather than a straightforward relationship between, say, economic problems and international conflict, effects tend to be dependent on a number of factors—that is, some kinds of governments may be sensitive to certain kinds of economic conditions at some times.[9] In addition, some research suggests that the relationship between international conflict and the leaders' political security is the opposite of what diversionary theory suggests: international conflict is more likely to be initiated by leaders whose hold on office is relatively strong.[10] For example, in democratic systems, leaders are more likely to start wars right *after* elections, not right before them as diversionary theory would suggest. A democratic leader is most secure just after an election, since the next election is at that point several years away.[11]

---

9. See, for example, Philip Arena and Glenn Palmer, "Politics or the Economy? Domestic Correlates of Dispute Involvement in Developed Democracies," *International Studies Quarterly* 53 (December 2009): 955–75; and Sara McLaughlin Mitchell and Brandon C. Prins, "Rivalry and Diversionary Uses of Force," *Journal of Conflict Resolution* 48 (December 2004): 937–61.

10. See Giacomo Chiozza and Hein E. Goemans, "Peace through Insecurity: Tenure and International Conflict," *Journal of Conflict Resolution* 47 (August 2003): 443–67.

11. Kurt Taylor Gaubatz, "Election Cycles and War," *Journal of Conflict Resolution* 35, no. 2 (June 1991): 212–44.

This is not to say that diversionary incentives never play a role in particular cases; in fact, historians cite many examples in which such logic contributed to the onset of war. What these results do suggest, however, is that leaders do not *systematically* use international conflict for diversionary purposes or to gamble for resurrection. In other words, even if diversionary incentives have contributed to war in some cases, they account for only a small portion of the conflict behavior we observe.

Why might this be the case? If sparking international conflict serves leaders' political interests, why do we not see stronger evidence of this effect? One possible answer is that most political leaders are not as cynical as we assumed and that they would not actually start a war simply to maintain their hold on power. Although we cannot rule out this possibility, there are other possible explanations for why even a cynical leader would not start a war to further his or her own political interests.

The first explanation is that the domestic political benefits of war relative to peace have to be large—perhaps unrealistically large—in order to eliminate the possibility of a peaceful bargain. Recall the simple bargaining framework we illustrated in the previous chapter, now depicted in Figure 4.3. As shown in the top panel, the size of the bargaining range is determined by the sum of the war costs to both sides. Now imagine that the leader of State A expects to reap political

---

FIGURE 4.3 *Rally Effects and the Bargaining Range*

The top panel shows the expected outcome of a war between State A and State B, as well as the resulting bargaining range. The lower panel shows how the bargaining range shrinks if the leader of State A expects political benefits, in the form of a rally, as a result of war. This benefit increases the value of war to A, offsetting some or all of its costs, but as long as the benefit does not exceed the costs of war to *both* states, a bargaining range still exists.

benefits from waging war. This benefit increases the value of war to the leader as indicated in the lower panel. This added benefit shrinks the bargaining range, but even if this benefit is greater than the costs to State A—so that the leader sees a net benefit rather than a net cost to war—a bargaining range could still exist, as shown. The size of this new bargaining range is given by the sum of the net costs (the total costs to both states minus the additional political benefit). Only if this benefit exceeds the sum of the war costs to both states does the bargaining range vanish, making war inevitable. Hence, even if the leader of one state expected large political benefits from waging war, these benefits would be sufficient to cause war only if they outweighed the war costs to *both* sides. This condition becomes more likely if the leaders of both states expect political benefits from war, as was the case in the Falklands War. Notice also that the political benefits from war mean that State A can demand a better deal from State B than it otherwise could. Knowing this, potential targets might avoid picking fights with politically vulnerable leaders, thereby depriving them the opportunity to use force opportunistically.[12] These observations remind us that war is the product of an interaction between at least two actors and not the choice of a single actor.

The Political Costs of War

A second reason why diversionary effects might be weak is that war can impose domestic political costs in addition to promising benefits. This is evident from the Falklands case as well. While Thatcher rode her postwar wave of support to a resounding electoral victory in Britain, the Argentine junta that lost the war met a very different fate. Following Argentina's defeat, angry protesters once again filled the streets, and members of the junta resigned or were stripped of their posts and several went to prison. The story of the Russo-Japanese War has a similar ending. Far from the short, victorious war the Russians hoped for, the war actually lasted almost two years, and the Russians suffered a humiliating defeat at the hands of the Japanese. Rather than stemming the tide of revolution, successive defeats on the battlefield increased unhappiness with the tsar's regime and helped usher in the revolution of 1905, when the tsar was forced to make political concessions to his opponents. Full-scale revolution would hit Russia in 1917, in the midst of yet more battlefield defeats in World War I. Indeed, the initial surge of patriotism that generally accompanies the onset of war can quickly give way to discontent and rebellion if the war goes badly.

One way to see the relationship between the costs of war and its domestic political repercussions is to consider how public support for war changes as the costs mount. Figure 4.4 shows the relationship between public support and battle deaths for major U.S. military operations since and including World War II. As the graph shows, most operations started with very high levels of public support, but

---

12. See, for example, Benjamin O. Fordham, "Strategic Conflict Avoidance and the Diversionary Use of Force," *Journal of Politics* 67 (February 2005): 132–53; and Brett Ashley Leeds and David R. Davis, "Domestic Political Vulnerability and International Disputes," *Journal of Conflict Resolution* 41 (December 1997): 814–34.

FIGURE 4.4 *U.S. Battle Deaths and Public Support for War*

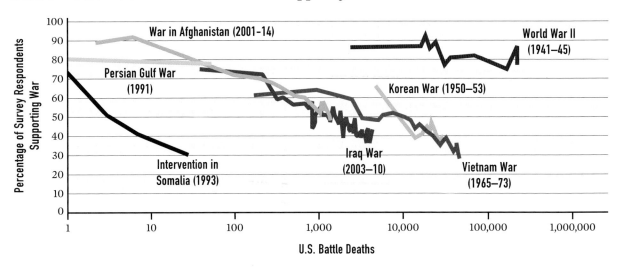

Figure sources: World War II, Korea, Vietnam, Gulf War, and Somalia from Eric V. Larson, *Casualties and Consensus* (Santa Monica, CA: RAND, 1996). Other poll numbers from Gallup, www.gallup.com/poll/1633/Iraq.aspx and www.gallup.com/poll/116233/Afghanistan.aspx (accessed 01/20/15). Casualty figures for Iraq and Afghanistan from www.icasualties.org (accessed 01/20/15).

this support generally fell off as the number of U.S. battle deaths mounted. The only wars that remained popular throughout were World War II—a war of national survival that followed the Japanese attack on the U.S. homeland—and the Persian Gulf War, which caused relatively few deaths on the American side. Moreover, in cases in which support for the war collapsed, the presidents' approval ratings also suffered. During the Korean War, President Truman saw his approval rating fall to as low as 22 percent, and he declined to run for reelection in 1952. The unpopularity of the Vietnam War similarly doomed the presidency of Lyndon Johnson, who dropped his bid for reelection in March 1968. The Iraq War dragged down President Bush's approval ratings, causing his Republican Party to lose control of Congress in 2006 and contributing to the election of Democrat Barack Obama in 2008. More generally, research has shown that leaders who fight losing or costly wars are more likely to be removed from office than those who win wars, as "How Do We Know?" on page 153 explains.

The evidence suggests that in terms of their political interests, leaders should see war not as a pure opportunity but as a gamble—and one that has a downside risk. Hence, in thinking about how reelection incentives influence how leaders think about war and peace, we need to set the costs of losing a war against the potential benefits of the rally effect. These costs may explain why we do not see strong or systematic evidence that politically insecure politicians engage in diversionary conflict.

In light of this observation, it is worth recalling that the scandal-plagued leader in the movie *Wag the Dog* does not start an actual war; instead, he hires a movie producer to stage a fake war for public consumption. The attraction of doing this is clear: when you script the war yourself, you can make sure the right side wins. In the real world, war is a risky gamble—not just for the state but also for the political interests of its leaders.

War and the Fate of Political Leaders

Agamemnon

It is very rare in the modern world <u>for state leaders to fight alongside their militaries and face the direct costs of war—that is, threat to life and limb.</u> Instead, leaders <u>feel the costs of war politically,</u> through its effect on their survival in office. Does winning or losing abroad affect whether leaders win or lose at home?

One systematic study of almost 200 leaders who took their countries to war in the last two centuries shows that losing a war can be very costly indeed.[a] War outcomes were classified into three categories: victories, small losses, and big losses, with small and big losses distinguished by how costly the war was in terms of dead soldiers. For each war, the study examined the fate of the wartime leader within one year of the war's termination. Figure A summarizes the main results. There is a large difference between the political fate of leaders who win wars and those who lose, especially if the loss is very costly. About 85 percent of leaders who lost costly wars also lost office. By contrast, more than two-thirds of war victors were still in office a year after the war ended.

The type of political system makes a difference in this regard. As Figure B shows, democratic leaders who took their countries to war were more likely to lose office within a year of the war's end, regardless of whether or not they won or lost. This difference was particularly pronounced among leaders who lost the war: while a majority (52 percent) of nondemocratic losers managed to stay in office, just over a tenth of democratic losers did.

Losing office, however, is not the worst thing that can happen, as ousted leaders may often suffer additional punishment. For example, of the 48 percent of nondemocratic leaders who lost power after losing a war, almost 90 percent were killed, exiled, and imprisoned as well. By contrast, only 43 percent of democratic leaders who lost office after losing a war suffered additional punishment. Thus, nondemocratic leaders often find themselves, quite literally, fighting for their lives.

FIGURE A   *War and the Fate of Leaders*

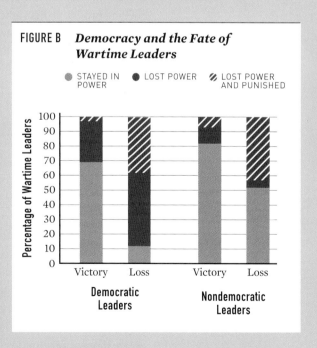

FIGURE B   *Democracy and the Fate of Wartime Leaders*

a. Hein Goemans, *War and Punishment* (Princeton, NJ: Princeton University Press, 2001); Figures A and B are derived from the data on p. 63 of this text.

Do Countries Fight Wars to Satisfy the Military or Special Interest Groups?

From 1898 to 1902, Great Britain engaged in a costly and divisive war with the Boer states in South Africa. The Boer War, which lasted three years and claimed about 50,000 lives, was a climactic episode of a larger process in which the European states carved up and colonized the continent of Africa, as described in Chapter 1. To the British economist J. A. Hobson, this scramble for colonies and the bloody war that it gave rise to presented a puzzle. Why had Britain expended so many young lives and so much money to acquire and defend an empire in Africa, as well as in Asia and the Americas?

The answer that Hobson arrived at was unsettling. He calculated that although imperialism did not benefit the British nation as a whole, it was extremely profitable for a few small groups within the country. The primary beneficiaries, he argued, were rich people with the ability to invest overseas. With colonial possessions came many opportunities for profitable investments. Rich people could invest in railroads, mines, and other properties and receive very high rates of return. They could loan money to colonial governments at favorable interest rates. In pushing for colonial possessions, Hobson argued, financial interests found allies in powerful places: military leaders seeking glory and larger budgets, and arms manufacturers seeking profits. In his view, these groups used their power and influence to force British governments to pursue a policy that benefited them at the expense of the greater good.[13] Hobson's theory of imperialism is not without critics, but the general thesis—that wars are fought to benefit military and business interests—is a familiar one. It echoes famously in the words of U.S. president Dwight Eisenhower, who warned of the influence of a **military-industrial complex**: an alliance of military leaders and arms manufacturers who presumably have an interest in an aggressive foreign policy.

In this section, we consider the influence of the military and interest groups with respect to questions of war and peace. As we will see, there are times when these actors might be expected to have hawkish interests, because they anticipate benefits from war and/or pay few of the costs. These two sets of actors also have strategic advantages that they can exploit in their interaction with political leaders and others within the country. That said, we will see that the primary effect of hawkish actors is not to cause wars per se—that is, by eliminating the bargaining range—but rather to expand the scope of the state's ambitions and to increase the conditions under which the state would consider fighting a war. Hence, hawkish domestic interests do not lead directly to the breakdown of bargaining, but they do create more opportunities for such failures to occur.

military-industrial complex

An alliance between military leaders and the industries that benefit from international conflict, such as arms manufacturers.

---

13. J. A. Hobson, *Imperialism: A Study* (London: James Nisbet & Co., 1902).

Bureaucratic Politics and the Military

Although the ultimate decision to wage war may lie in the hands of a few individuals, the actual machinery of government that deals with matters of war and peace is much larger and more complex. The leader of a modern state sits atop a large bureaucratic apparatus: a collection of organizations that manage many of the details of governance. Wars are planned and implemented by the state's military—usually a massive organization with thousands and, in some cases, millions of individuals. Negotiations with other countries are conducted by a host of diplomats around the world, typically overseen by a ministry of foreign affairs (known, in the United States, as the State Department). Information about other countries' military capabilities and intentions are collected and analyzed by intelligence organizations, like the United States' CIA, Britain's MI6 (Military Intelligence, Section 6), or Russia's SVR (Foreign Intelligence Service). Given all the tasks that governments have to perform and all the individuals that are needed to carry out those tasks, such organizations are a necessary part of any modern state.

This observation opens up the possibility that decisions about war and peace are shaped not only by state leaders but also by the interests of the bureaucratic organizations involved in the decision-making process.[14] While such organizations care about what is best for the country, they may also care about the resources and influence that they wield themselves. They generally seek bigger budgets, more input into policy making, and opportunities for personal promotion. As a result, they may press for policies that boost their own status or fit their own worldview. For example, prior to the 2003 Iraq War there were serious disagreements within the U.S. government between the Defense Department and the State Department. Civilian leaders at the Pentagon generally expected war to be easy, while those at the State Department were more cautious and emphasized the need for international diplomacy. There were also disagreements over which agency should take the lead role in rebuilding Iraq politically and economically in the aftermath of the conflict. These debates reflect a common aphorism about bureaucratic politics that "where you stand depends on where you sit"—that is, the leaders of bureaucratic agencies often take policy stands that reflect their own organizations' needs. In the end, the Defense Department won these scuffles.[15]

As this example suggests, the military is usually the most influential bureaucratic actor in matters of war and peace. To this point, our discussion has treated the military as an instrument of the state—a tool that states use to increase their leverage in international bargaining. What happens when we think about the military as an actor in its own right?

---

14. The classic investigation of bureaucratic politics is Graham Allison and Philip Zelikow, *Essence of Decision: Explaining the Cuban Missile Crisis,* 2nd ed. (New York: Longman, 1999).

15. See, for example, Bob Woodward, *Plan of Attack* (New York: Simon & Schuster, 2004).

There is a compelling—although, as we will see, incomplete—argument to be made that the more influence the military has over foreign policy decision making, the more aggressive the state will be. This argument rests on the assumption that members of the military have ideological, organizational, and professional interests in policies that make war more likely. Ideologically, leaders in the armed forces may be predisposed to seeing military solutions to foreign policy problems, overestimating the effectiveness of force relative to other alternatives. As an organization, the military can demand larger budgets and more personnel when the state is frequently engaged in international conflict than when it is at peace. And professionally, military officers find that combat experience is crucial to being promoted to the highest ranks. All these considerations suggest that the military sees benefits to war that other actors may not.

Perhaps the most dramatic example of how military influence can lead to aggressive foreign policy is the case of Japan in the 1930s. Japan in this period pursued a relentless campaign of expansion against its neighbors, ultimately bringing the country into war with China, France, Britain, the Netherlands, and the United States. This aggressive turn in foreign policy coincided with a creeping takeover by the military, which undermined the democratic system that had been developing in the country. In 1931, elements of the Japanese military provoked a war with China and seized a region known as Manchuria, which military leaders prized for its coal and iron. A year later, the prime minister of Japan was assassinated by a group of naval officers, an event that ushered in the end of civilian control of Japanese politics. The Japanese military became the main instigator of that country's expansionist policies. This case is an extreme example, but there is broader evidence to suggest that countries in which civilian leadership has weak control of the military are more likely to initiate militarized conflicts.[16] (See "What Shaped Our World?" on p. 157 for another example.)

Having said this, it is important not to automatically equate the military with militarism. One study examined the advice that military leaders gave U.S. decision makers in about 20 key crises during the Cold War, comparing how aggressive the officers were relative to the president's civilian advisers. The study found that military advisers were no more likely than civilians to advocate the use of force in a crisis; rather, the main difference between the two groups was over the level of force that should be used in the event of an operation, with military advisers consistently preferring larger deployments. The author concluded that the "stereotype of a belligerent chorus of generals and admirals intimidating a pacific civilian establishment is not supported by the

---

16. Todd S. Sechser, "Are Soldiers Less War-Prone Than Statesmen?" *Journal of Conflict Resolution* 48, no. 5 (2004): 746–74. The idea that civilians can lose control of the military also plays a large role. In explanations of World War I, see Stephen Van Evera, "The Cult of the Offensive and the Origins of World War I," *International Security* 9 (1984): 58–107; and Samuel R. Williamson, Jr., and Russel Van Wyk, *July 1914: Soldiers, Statesmen, and the Coming of the Great War* (Boston: Bedford/St. Martin's, 2003).

The Kargil War and Military Influence in War

One of the more dangerous episodes in modern history started rather quietly in April 1999, when Pakistani military forces secretly infiltrated across the Line of Control (LoC) that separates the Pakistani- and Indian-controlled areas of the disputed Kashmir region. When the incursion was discovered, India mobilized to repel the attack. Over the next several weeks, the two countries fought a war in the high mountains near the town of Kargil. This was neither the first nor the bloodiest war between the two countries, but it was the first that took place under the specter of nuclear war. Only a year earlier, the two countries had openly tested nuclear devices. It was also a rare example of war between two democratic countries. How can we explain this episode?

Interests At the root of the conflict is a long-standing territorial dispute over the region of Kashmir, which both India and Pakistan claim on historical and religious grounds (see Map 3.1 on p. 94). But even while both states want to possess the entire region, actors within each country place different values on it and are willing to pay different costs to obtain it. In particular, the military in Pakistan has generally been more willing than the country's civilian leaders to run a risk of war with India.

Interactions The conflict over Kashmir has led to repeated episodes of bargaining in which force has been threatened and used, including full-scale wars in 1947, 1965, and 1971. Even so, only weeks before the Kargil War broke out, the countries' leaders had met to affirm their desire for a peaceful resolution. The infiltration of Pakistani forces across the LoC thus represented an unexpected escalation, designed to bolster Pakistan's bargaining power. Once India responded, the subsequent fighting took place in the shadow of deterrent threats. Pakistan put its nuclear forces on alert and threatened to use every weapon in its arsenal if India invaded; India responded by putting its own missiles on alert. With the risks so high and foreign pressure mounting, Pakistan had little choice but to pull its forces back behind the LoC. So why did Pakistan initiate such a dangerous gamble?

Institutions The answer lies in the country's domestic political institutions. Even though Pakistan had a democratically elected government, its military is very powerful and has on several occasions ousted civilian leaders that it did not like. Indeed, shortly after the Kargil War, the prime minister, Nawaz Sharif, was deposed and replaced by the army's chief of staff, General Pervez Musharraf. The danger of removal by the military has led to weak civilian control and oversight of that organization.

Although there are many unknowns about Pakistan's decision making in the lead-up to the war, there is good reason to believe that the military command manipulated Sharif into starting a conflict he did not fully understand.[a] When India accused Pakistan of crossing the LoC in May 1999, Sharif claimed that the invaders were local Kashmiri insurgents operating on their own initiative. Sharif and others claim that when he was briefed on the plan to support the insurgency, he was not told that Pakistani military forces would cross the LoC in large numbers. In addition, U.S. officials reportedly believed that the move to put Pakistani nuclear forces on alert during the war was done without Sharif's knowledge.

As this episode suggests, military organizations may sometimes be willing to run greater risks than are the civilian authorities whom they are supposed to serve. When the military wields enormous influence and civilian control is weak, this behavior can have dangerous consequences for the country, its neighbors, and the world.

---

a. This discussion is based on Owen Bennett Jones, *Pakistan: Eye of the Storm* (New Haven, CT: Yale University Press, 2003), 87–109.

evidence."[17] Similarly, a study of elite opinion in the United States shows that military leaders are inclined to advocate the use of force in a narrower set of cases than are civilian leaders without any military experience.[18] Indeed, by all accounts, U.S. military officers were much more reluctant to go to war against Iraq in 2003 than was the civilian leadership at the Pentagon and White House. Many top commanders thought that war with Iraq would be costly and that conducting it successfully would require larger commitments of manpower and money than the civilian leadership was willing to make.[19] Such observations suggest that in some contexts at least, the military's interests push in a conservative direction: more appreciative of the limits of what can be achieved through force and more sensitive to the human costs of war, which are, after all, borne by its personnel.

Interest Groups: Economic and Ethnic Lobbies

The possibility that special interest groups can influence foreign policy in a manner that furthers their particular interests is familiar to most people. In the wake of the 2003 U.S. invasion of Iraq, Vice President Richard Cheney's former company, Halliburton, was awarded contracts worth billions of dollars to rebuild Iraq's infrastructure and supply American troops. By the end of 2006, the company's stock was worth four times its value when the war started. Considering also that President Bush himself was once an oil industry executive, observations such as these led to speculation that the Iraq War was fought at the behest of oil companies interested in Iraq's oil and military contractors interested in taxpayer dollars. Such charges are not new. U.S. interventions in Latin American countries have often been ascribed to the influence of American businesses whose properties in those countries were at risk. The previously mentioned case of Guatemala, where United Fruit feared a major loss at the hands of an unfriendly government, was by no means unique. The United States also intervened in Cuba (1961), the Dominican Republic (1965), and Chile (1973)—all places where American investors had substantial assets.

Although economic actors such as companies and industries figure most prominently in such stories, not all interest groups organize around economic motives. Interest groups that organize around ethnic ties are another influence on foreign policy, particularly in the United States. There is, for example, a very sizable and influential pro-Israel lobby in the United States: a collection of individuals and groups who want the U.S. government to support and defend the state of Israel—a stance that often brings the United States into conflict with Israel's adversaries in the region. The main lobbying arm of this group is the American-Israel

---

17. Richard K. Betts, *Soldiers, Statesmen, and Cold War Crises* (New York: Columbia University Press, 1991), 4.

18. See Peter D. Feaver and Christopher Gelpi, *Choosing Your Battles: American Civil-Military Relations and the Use of Force* (Princeton, NJ: Princeton University Press, 2004).

19. See, for example, Michael R. Gordon and General Bernard E. Trainor, *Cobra II: The Inside Story of the Invasion and Occupation of Iraq* (New York: Pantheon, 2006).

Public Affairs Committee (AIPAC), which is considered one of the most effective lobbying groups in Washington.[20] Other influential lobbying groups represent Cuban Americans opposed to the Communist regime in Cuba. A large number of Cubans fled after Fidel Castro took over in 1959 and seized their property. Cuban American groups have lobbied the U.S. government to take strong actions to contain and undermine the Castro regime, including supporting a failed invasion by exiles in 1961 and imposing a strict economic embargo on the country. In 2014, President Barack Obama announced that he would restore some diplomatic and economic ties with Cuba, arguing that more than five decades of isolation had failed to change the regime. Nonetheless, any effort to lift the embargo is likely to face resistance from the Cuban American lobby and their supporters in the U.S. Congress.

Why do interest groups care about the state's foreign policy? In cases like the pro-Israel and anti-Castro lobbies, group members are motivated by ethnic attachment or ideological interests to support or oppose a particular country or regime. In the case of economic actors, preferences over foreign policy arise whenever an actor's income depends on events in other countries or on the relationship between countries. A multinational company, like United Fruit, may have production facilities in numerous countries. If those countries experience political instability that threatens to disrupt the company's business, or if they have unfriendly regimes that might confiscate the company's property, then the company might lobby for some form of intervention to protect its interests. Similarly, an investor who owns stocks in a foreign company or a bank that has loaned money to a foreign government might lobby its own government to use military force to ensure the return on its investment or the repayment of its loan. Such lobbying could lead to intervention against unstable or unfriendly regimes. In the extreme case that Hobson considered, economic actors with international investments might even lobby their governments to extend direct imperial control over other countries. Although establishing and maintaining such control was costly, imperialism made it safer to invest overseas, since there was less danger that investments would be wiped out by instability or hostile governments. A smaller set of economic actors, primarily those that make and sell military armaments, also have a direct interest in their country's foreign policy, since a belligerent foreign policy keeps them in business.

However, the interests of economic actors need not always lead to a preference for aggressive policies. Indeed, economic actors who depend on peaceful relations with other countries in order to do business could press their governments to pursue friendly relations or even formal alliances with profitable partners. For example, American banks and companies that had important trade, financial, and

---

20. For a recent study arguing that the pro-Israel lobby wields a great deal of influence on U.S. foreign policy, see John J. Mearsheimer and Stephen M. Walt, *The Israel Lobby and U.S. Foreign Policy* (New York: Farrar, Straus & Giroux, 2007). This book generated a great deal of controversy not only because of the content of the claims but also because of concerns about the quality of the evidence. For a careful critique, see Robert C. Lieberman, "The 'Israel Lobby' and American Politics," *Perspectives on Politics* 7 (2009): 235–57.

investment interests in Western Europe played a significant role in lobbying for a strong U.S. commitment to defend Western Europe at the outset of the Cold War. Similarly, banks that depended heavily on loans to Asia lobbied for strong alliance commitments to Japan and South Korea.[21] More recently, U.S. corporations interested in selling goods to China have been a potent political force lobbying for more cooperative relations with that country. In fact, an extensive literature suggests that trade between countries decreases the likelihood of war between them, in part because businesses that profit from the trade lobby against policies that could lead to conflict.[22] In sum, depending on where and how they do business, economic actors can have an interest in peaceful relations with some countries and/or hostile relations with others.

How Can Small Groups Have a Big Influence on Policy?

We have seen that militaries seeking budgets and prestige, businesses seeking profits, and ethnic groups looking out for their kin may all, at times, see particular benefits to war. What is remarkable about each of these actors is how small they are relative to those who pay the costs of war. The generals and admirals who run military organizations are greatly outnumbered by the enlisted personnel who bear the brunt of the fighting, as well as by the rest of the population. Multinational companies and ethnic lobbies tend to make up a small fraction of society. Given how extensively they are outnumbered, when and how can these narrow interests prevail? The answer lies in the nature of the interactions between these different actors and the institutions that regulate their relations.

The military's influence on foreign policy decision making derives from the fact that it controls a large number of guns and people trained to use them. While militaries are generally created in order to defend a state from foreign threats, their capabilities inevitably make them key players domestically as well. In many states, the military plays a direct role in ensuring the continuation of the government. This role can either be very explicit (as with military dictatorships, in which military officers take direct control of executive power) or more subtle but no less potent. In many countries, the military is able and willing to intervene in politics to ensure that the government is to its liking; as a result, a civilian government may have to cater to the military's interests in order to avoid being ousted in a coup d'état. A number of countries in Latin America, Africa, the Middle East, and Asia have experienced frequent alternations between direct military rule and civilian governments that lived under the constant threat of a coup. Moreover, authoritarian regimes that actively suppress popular dissent may rely heavily on the military to put down challenges to their rule. In such systems, the regime's dependence on the armed forces for its continued survival gives military leaders a prominent role in decision making.

---

21. Benjamin Fordham, *Building the Cold War Consensus* (Ann Arbor: University of Michigan Press, 1998).

22. For a review of this argument and supporting evidence, see Bruce Russett and James Oneal, *Triangulating Peace: Democracy, Interdependence, and International Organizations* (New York: Norton, 2001), chap. 4.

In May 2014, the military in Thailand ousted the government in a coup d'état, arresting civilian politicians, banning protests, and imposing media censorship. The ability to topple a government gives military organizations significant influence over foreign and domestic policies.

Even when the government does not depend so heavily on the military to stay in power, the military can have strong influence over foreign policy decision making. All political leaders rely on the information and expertise of bureaucratic actors within the state. No political leader is an expert in every policy area; even if she were, there would not be enough time for her to focus on every task the government has to do. Instead, the job of making policy proposals and analyzing the implications of different decisions rests with the specialists who staff the bureaucratic agencies. When making decisions about war, a leader has to rely on experts within the military and other agencies (such as those dealing with intelligence and diplomacy) to provide key pieces of information: what the country's capabilities are, what the capabilities of potential adversaries are, what plans there are to wage war with a given country and deal with any contingencies that might arise. The political leader's dependence on the military for this kind of information gives the military leadership the ability to shape decisions to their liking. A military bent on war could, for example, give the leader skewed advice about how easily the war could be won and how low the costs would be. Conversely, military officials opposed to war could give conservative estimates of the likelihood of success and magnify the potential costs. In this way, the military would shape the outcome by manipulating the information that the leader uses to calculate the expected value of war and its alternatives.

Organized interest groups also rely on their superior resources and access to information in order to exert influence over policy. Consider an intervention like the one in Guatemala mentioned at the outset of this chapter. In that case, intervention cost U.S. taxpayers about $3 million, and it protected property for which United Fruit Company demanded $16 million. Given that the taxpayers who footed the bill vastly outnumbered the stockholders of the company that benefited, it is useful to think about why the latter would get their way at the expense of the former. How could economic interest groups "hijack" a state's foreign policy for their own narrow interests?

As suggested earlier, much of the answer lies in how the costs and benefits of international conflict are distributed in such situations. Precisely because taxpayers are more numerous, the costs of intervention to any individual are quite low. As a result, no individual citizen has much incentive to become informed about the situation, to call his member of Congress to weigh in on the policy, to go to Washington to bang on the doors of the State Department, and so on. Indeed, in the case of Guatemala and United Fruit Company, most U.S. citizens were likely unaware of what the CIA was up to (in arming and training Guatemalan rebels) and how much taxpayer money was being spent. By contrast, the company that stands to benefit from intervention has a very large stake in the outcome. Company representatives have every incentive to become informed, to lobby representatives, and to exploit contacts within the government. Hence, in the interaction between the many who pay the costs and the few who stand to benefit, the latter have a significant advantage.

Organized interest groups can prevail because they can provide political leaders with things they need and want in exchange for favored policies. Sometimes what interest groups provide is money, which leaders can use to line their pockets or, if that is prohibited, to finance political campaigns. Concerns about the military-industrial complex center around the flow of money: industries give money to elected officials, who then allocate taxpayer money to the military, which then spends the money in ways that benefit the industries, such as by purchasing their arms or intervening to protect their foreign assets.[23]

In democracies, interest groups also gain influence by promising the support of motivated voters. For example, the Cuban American lobby does not give large sums of money relative to big economic interest groups like companies, labor unions, and professional organizations. When representatives of this lobby go to Washington, they primarily remind politicians that 1 million Cuban Americans care enough about U.S. policy toward Cuba that they vote on the basis of that issue. Moreover, these voters are concentrated in Florida—a crucial state in U.S. presidential elections, where a margin of only 500 votes swung the 2000 election to George W. Bush. By contrast, most other voters pay little attention to this issue and do not base their votes on it. Hence, when representatives of the Cuban American or pro-Israel lobby say, "This is an issue our voters care about," politicians tend to listen.

In principle, then, interest groups can wield considerable influence over government policy, even if those policies come at the expense of broader national

---

23. This is an example of a larger phenomenon known in the American politics literature as an "iron triangle": the mutual dependence that arises among members of Congress, interest groups, and government agencies.

interests. So to what extent does this mechanism explain foreign policy choices? Can the puzzle of war be resolved by finding some group within the state that actually benefits from the conflict? Though it can be tempting to see causal connections between policies and the groups those policies benefit, there are at least three reasons why we need to be cautious in jumping too hastily to interest-group explanations for wars.

The first reason has to do with evidence: How can we know that a particular policy was caused by interest-group lobbying? To put it another way, how can we be sure that government would have behaved differently if the interest group did not exist? The challenge here is significant. Just because Halliburton benefited from the invasion of Iraq, we cannot automatically infer that the company actively lobbied for the invasion or that President Bush chose to invade in order to benefit the company. For most foreign policy decisions that bestow benefits on narrow groups, there are alternative justifications based on national interests. Hobson's theory of nineteenth-century imperialism has been disputed by other scholars who argue that imperialism was a product of military-strategic competition among the principal powers.[24] U.S. interventions in Latin America during the Cold War were part of a larger pattern in which the United States sought to prevent the spread of Communism, sometimes in countries in which U.S. investors had no significant assets. Thus, even though United Fruit benefited from the ouster of Arbenz, fears about his association with Communism might have provoked U.S. intervention even without that company's lobbying efforts.[25] And even if oil helps explain the United States' intense interest in removing Iraq's regime in 2003, we have seen that exerting influence over oil-producing regions serves a variety of interests, not all of them unique to oil companies.

A second consideration to keep in mind is that in many issue areas there are multiple groups pushing in different directions. We already saw that economic considerations can just as readily create groups with an interest in peace as those with an interest in war or intervention. Arms manufacturers spend a great deal of political effort competing with each other for government contracts rather than banding together to promote general foreign policy objectives. In the case of U.S. policy toward the Middle East, pro-Israel sentiments sometimes compete with oil interests that favor closer relations with oil-rich Arab states. The United States has regularly sold advanced military technology to Saudi Arabia, even over the objections of the pro-Israel lobby. The existence of opposing groups and demands can make it much harder for any one group to "capture" the state's foreign policy.

The final important consideration is to recall, as before, that war is the product of a bargaining interaction between or among multiple states, not a choice made by a single leader or group. Thus, to evaluate the potential influence of groups that have hawkish interests, we need to revisit the bargaining model.

---

24. See, for example, Benjamin J. Cohen, *The Question of Imperialism* (London: Macmillan, 1974).

25. For an argument against the interest-group interpretation of these cases, see Stephen D. Krasner, *Defending the National Interest* (Princeton, NJ: Princeton University Press, 1978), esp. chap. 8.

How Do Domestic Interests Affect International Bargaining?

How could hawkish actors within a state affect the likelihood of war? The general answer is that domestic interests affect the likelihood of international conflict primarily by determining the extent of the state's ambitions. By influencing the costs and benefits of conflict, such interests can widen or narrow the scope of goods over which the state's leaders might be willing to wage war; they affect when and how often the state's foreign policy interests will come into conflict with those of other states; they determine the size of the demands that the state will make and the risks that it is willing to run. In short, variation in the nature of domestic interests that influence policy making will increase or decrease the opportunities for conflict. Except in rare circumstances, however, these interests will not be sufficient to cause war in any given interaction. Thus, the influence of hawkish interests gives states more things to consider worth fighting over, but they are generally not sufficient to explain why bargaining over those goods fails in some cases but not in others.

To illustrate this point, we return in Figure 4.5 to the bargaining model introduced in Chapter 3 and ask what would happen if the interests of State A changed in response to the influence of hawkish actors. For example, imagine that the object in dispute is a piece of territory with oil in it. In the interaction depicted in the top panel, the government in State A is led by a party whose core supporters are pacifists and environmentalists. As a result, the government considers the costs of war over this territory to be rather high, as shown by the fact that State A's value for war (the portion of the bar to the left of the red dotted line) is far smaller than the share of territory it expects from the outcome of the war. Recall that the costs of war are measured relative to the value of the good in dispute, so they are large when the human and economic costs of war loom large and/or when the benefit associated with possessing the territory is low. Because the dovish interests that control the state see war as very unattractive, they are highly unlikely to start a crisis over this territory. Only if the status quo distribution of the territory is located at the far left of the line—very far from State A's ideal point—would the government in State A see any potential benefit from sparking a crisis.

What happens to the international interaction if the dovish leader in State A is replaced by a leader of a party that draws support from oil companies who would profit from State A's control of the territory? Because of the influence of these actors, the new leader places more weight on the value of the land and less on the costs of war. In terms of our model, the costs of war relative to the value of the good are smaller. The lower panel shows how the value of war changes in the eyes of this hawkish government. Since the costs of war have gone down, State A's value for war shifts to the right. Notice two things about this panel. First, status quo distributions that would have been tolerated by the dovish leader are unacceptable to the hawk. As a result, State A becomes more likely to initiate a crisis, and it will make larger demands on its adversary. Second, even after this shift, a bargaining range, shown in light green, still exists. As before, the costs of war ensure the existence of a set of mutually acceptable bargains.

FIGURE 4.5 *Domestic Interests and International Bargaining*

In the top panel, State A is led by a dovish government and considers the costs of war to be high relative to the value of the good in dispute. In the lower panel, State A is led by a hawkish government and sees the costs of war as less significant, placing more value on the good in dispute. Under hawkish leaders, State A is more likely to challenge the status quo, but a bargaining range still exists.

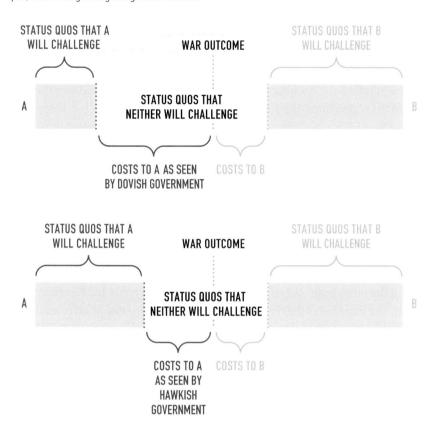

This means that absent the information, commitment, or divisibility problems discussed in Chapter 3, there is no reason why the shift from a dovish to a hawkish government should, on its own, lead to a war. However, the shift does create a danger of war that did not exist before. The new government in State A is more willing to threaten force to change the status quo. The change in governance increases the state's demands and creates a risk of conflict where none previously existed. Whether or not this potential conflict will lead to an actual war depends on features of the bargaining interaction, such as how information is distributed and whether the states can credibly commit to live by any deal they reach.

The one exception to this claim would arise if there are actors who derive benefits from war that cannot be part of a negotiated settlement, as in the case of diversionary conflict. For example, assume that the leader of State A represents arms manufacturers. If there is a war, they get paid to build weapons and to replace those that are destroyed. Since they get these profits only if there is a war, then it is peace rather than war that these actors find costly. Would the influence of such interests change the above logic? As we saw when considering the diversionary incentive, the answer is yes—but only if the net benefits from war are high enough to offset *both* states' costs of war.

Hence, except in rare circumstances, the influence of groups within the state that place high value on the goods that can be acquired through force and/or see little cost to war does not itself ensure that war will happen. When such interests hold sway, they will make the state's foreign policy more belligerent, in the sense that it will make larger demands and come into conflict with more states, but such interests alone are not sufficient to cause war in the absence of the strategic dilemmas discussed in Chapter 3. Thus, when we think about how oil interests influence U.S. policy in the Middle East, it is reasonable to say that oil interests explain why there are issues in the region that American leaders are willing to fight over. It is harder to argue that these interests alone explain why crises over these issues sometimes become wars.

Why Don't Democracies Fight One Another?

For much of the nineteenth and early twentieth centuries, France and Germany were bitter rivals. France resisted the creation of a unified German state in 1870, and the two countries fought three major wars over the next century: the Franco-Prussian War (1870–71), World War I (1914–18), and World War II (1939–45). Millions died in these wars, and cemeteries in both countries are filled with those who fell in this rivalry. Today, however, France and Germany are close allies, and while they have differences of interest and opinion on important issues, it is almost inconceivable that there could be another war between them. The turnaround in this relationship coincided with changes in the countries' political systems, which made them more democratic. France went into the Franco-Prussian War a monarchy, but it emerged with a more democratic system that has become stronger over time. The change in Germany was even more dramatic. Ruled by a hereditary emperor in the nineteenth century, Germany devolved into a murderous dictatorship under Adolf Hitler in the 1930s. After World War II, however, Germany was divided and occupied by the victorious Allies, and what became West Germany was remade into a democratic country. When East and West Germany were reunified in the 1990s, the reborn German state inherited this democratic constitution. There were, of course, a number of factors that helped solidify the relationship between these former adversaries after 1945, including the existence of a shared enemy in the Soviet Union, the reassuring presence of a common ally, the United States, and growing economic and financial ties that would make these two states central partners in a European Union (see Chapter 14). Nevertheless, the emergence of shared democracy helped pave the way for a dramatic shift in how these countries dealt with each other, to the point that war between the two is now unthinkable.

Far from being an isolated example, this case is part of a larger phenomenon that scholars and policy makers call the **democratic peace**. The term refers to a well-established observation that there are few, if any, clear cases of war between mature democratic states. Our choice of words reflects some caveats about this observation. We say "few, if any, clear cases of war" because the strength of the claim depends in part on how one defines democracy and what events one considers wars. Since there are some ambiguous cases, there is not a universal consensus on whether wars between democratic states are nonexistent or simply rare.[26] We say "mature democracy" because some studies have suggested that countries in the process of becoming democracies do not fit this overall pattern.[27] Even taking these qualifications into account, this is still a remarkable observation: over the 200 or so years in which democracies have existed in their modern form, they seem not to have engaged in war with one another—or, at least, they have done so less frequently than we might expect given the overall frequency of war.

Another noteworthy aspect of this observation is that democracies are not, overall, less war prone than other kinds of states. That is, while they rarely, if ever, fight wars against other democratic states, their overall rate of war participation is roughly the same as that of nondemocratic states.[28] This means that although democracies seldom find themselves at war with one another, they are more frequently at war with nondemocratic states. Hence, there is something special about the relationship among democracies that does not carry over to their relationships with other kinds of states.

This observation is so striking and important that it has entered into policy discussions in the United States and elsewhere. In his 1994 State of the Union address, President Bill Clinton cited the democratic peace in arguing for a foreign policy of promoting democracy abroad: "Ultimately, the best strategy to ensure our security and to build a durable peace is to support the advance of democracy elsewhere. Democracies don't attack each other."[29] Similarly, President George W. Bush argued that democracy promotion should be a central aspect of American policy in the Middle East because "democracies don't go to war with each other."[30] This interest in democratic peace has been particularly salient in recent decades, which have seen a remarkable growth in the number of democracies worldwide, as shown in Figure 4.6.

Is this absence of wars among democracies a coincidence, or is there something about democratic institutions that facilitates peaceful relations among states that have them? In what ways might shared democracy influence interstate bargaining?

democratic peace

The observation that there are few, if any, clear cases of war between mature democratic states.

26. For a discussion of the democratic peace finding, definitional issues, and some cases that raise questions, see Bruce Russett, *Grasping the Democratic Peace* (Princeton, NJ: Princeton University Press, 1993), chap. 1.

27. Edward D. Mansfield and Jack Snyder, *Electing to Fight: Why Emerging Democracies Go to War* (Cambridge, MA: MIT Press, 2005).

28. Although there has been some controversy over the issue, this statement reflects the general consensus in the literature. See, for example, Nils Peter Gleditsch and Havard Hegre, "Peace and Democracy: Three Levels of Analysis," *Journal of Conflict Resolution* 41 (1997): 283–310.

29. William J. Clinton, "Address before a Joint Session of the Congress on the State of the Union," *The American Presidency Project*, January 25, 1994, www.presidency.ucsb.edu/ws/index.php?pid=50409 (accessed 1/19/15).

30. Office of the Press Secretary, "President and Prime Minister Blair Discussed Iraq, Middle East," White House Press Conference, November 12, 2004, www.whitehouse.gov/news/releases/2004/11/20041112-5 .html (accessed 11/19/07).

FIGURE 4.6 *The Spread of Democracy, 1800–2013*

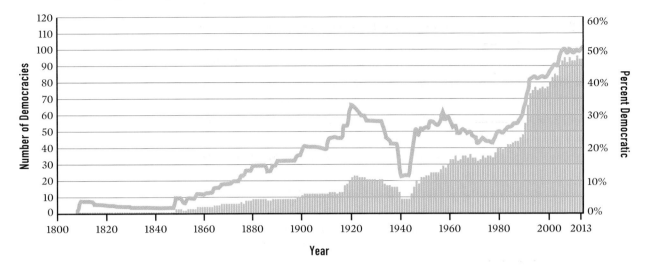

Figure source: Monty G. Marshall, Keith Jaggers, and Ted Robert Gurr, "Polity IV Project: Political Regime Characteristics and Transitions, 1800–2013," www.systemicpeace .org/polity/polity4.htm (accessed 01/20/15).

democracy

A political system in which candidates compete for political office through frequent, fair elections in which a sizable portion of the adult population can vote.

autocracy

A political systems in which an individual or small group exercises power with few constraints and no meaningful competition or participation by the general public.

What Is Democracy?

To answer these questions, we turn to the third leg of our framework: institutions. Domestic institutions determine the rules of political decision making within the state. They govern the relationship between the leadership and the people, and they help determine the extent to which citizens' interests matter when it comes to war and peace. Although there are many different kinds of political systems, the distinction that has attracted the most attention is that between democratic and nondemocratic systems. A **democracy** is a political system in which candidates compete for political office through frequent, fair elections in which a sizable portion of the adult population can vote. This definition encompasses two major aspects of democracy: the ability of different individuals and groups to compete for political office and the ability of a large portion of the people to participate in the selection process through voting. Nondemocratic countries, also known as **autocracies**, fall short of this definition in a variety of ways.[31] In some, leaders obtained office through hereditary succession, as in Saudi Arabia, or on the back of a military coup, as happened in Egypt in 2012. In others, such as China, only one political party is permitted to hold power, and competition from other parties is outlawed. Still others might hold elections among multiple parties but restrict competition so that the ruling party is all but certain to win. Such multiparty or electoral authoritarianism is the most common form of nondemocratic system in the world today; examples include Venezuela, Russia, Ethiopia, and Myanmar.[32] Map 4.1 on page 170 shows the type of regime in each country at the beginning of 2013.

---

31. Indeed, recent research in international relations has explored the effects of different kinds of nondemocratic governments; see, for example, Jessica L. P. Weeks, *Dictators at War and Peace* (Ithaca, NY: Cornell University Press, 2014).

32. There is an extensive literature on the nature and role of elections in authoritarian countries; see, for example, Jennifer Gandhi and Ellen Lust-Okar, "Elections under Authoritarianism," *Annual Review of Political Science* 12 (June 2009): 403–22.

Another term that often accompanies democracy is *liberal*, which we use here in its classic sense to refer to a philosophy that emphasizes the value of individual liberty. Most modern democracies are also liberal democracies, because in addition to allowing competition and voting, they have numerous protections of individuals' civil liberties and political rights, such as rights to free speech, religion, political association, and a free press. Hence, liberal democracies not only choose their leaders by democratic means, but they also impose restrictions on what those elected governments can do by giving citizens rights that cannot be transgressed. We should note that not all democratic countries are liberal, as some have restrictions on religious or press freedoms, or they give rights to ethnic or religious groups at the expense of individual rights. Indonesia, for example, has competitive and free elections, but it recently passed laws restricting the activities of civic and religious organizations, including a ban on the advocacy of certain ideas.[33]

With these definitions in place, we turn to the central question: How could democracies—especially mature, liberal democracies—be different when it comes to war and peace? Not surprisingly, the democratic peace observation has generated a great deal of scholarly interest in this question, and there is no single, settled answer. But the framework of this book suggests two broad ways in which domestic institutions can affect the likelihood of war: either by influencing the interests of states and their leaders or by influencing the bargaining interaction between and among countries.

Representation, Accountability, and Interests in War and Peace

A common argument for the distinctiveness of democracy is rooted in the idea that domestic institutions shape leaders' interests in war and peace. This argument starts with the observation that the costs of war are paid by society at large but generally not by the leader who makes the decision to wage war. It is the people who lose lives or loved ones on the battlefield, who suffer the economic hardship of wars, and who may have to pay higher taxes to support a war effort. The leader, by contrast, rarely has such direct exposure to the costs of war. This disjuncture between the ruler and the ruled was humorously illustrated in the 2001 movie *Shrek*, when evil Lord Far-quaad tells his knights that he is going to send them on a mission to rescue from a fire-breathing dragon a princess whom he wants to marry. Exhorting his men to combat, the prince declares, "Some of you may die, but it's a sacrifice I am willing to make."

Over 200 years before this scene was digitally animated, the German philosopher Immanuel Kant noted a similar dilemma. Kant wrote in the late eighteenth century, when most countries were ruled by monarchs. For such rulers, he noted, "The easiest thing in the world to do is to declare war." Kant reasoned:

> War does not affect [the ruler's] table, his hunt, his places of pleasure, his court festivals, and so on. Thus, he can decide to go to war for the most meaningless of reasons, as if it

---

33. For an assessment of political and civil rights in Indonesia, see Freedom House, Freedom in the World 2014, http://freedomhouse.org/report/freedom-world/2014/indonesia-0#.VCHKsRbTXpA (accessed 09/23/14).

MAP 4.1 *Regime Types*

This map shows the type of government in each country at the start of 2013. While democracy can be found on every continent, it is widespread in the Americas and Europe, present in parts of Asia, and scarce in Africa and the Middle East. Monarchies and military regimes are quite rare, while most autocratic regimes have limited multiparty competition.

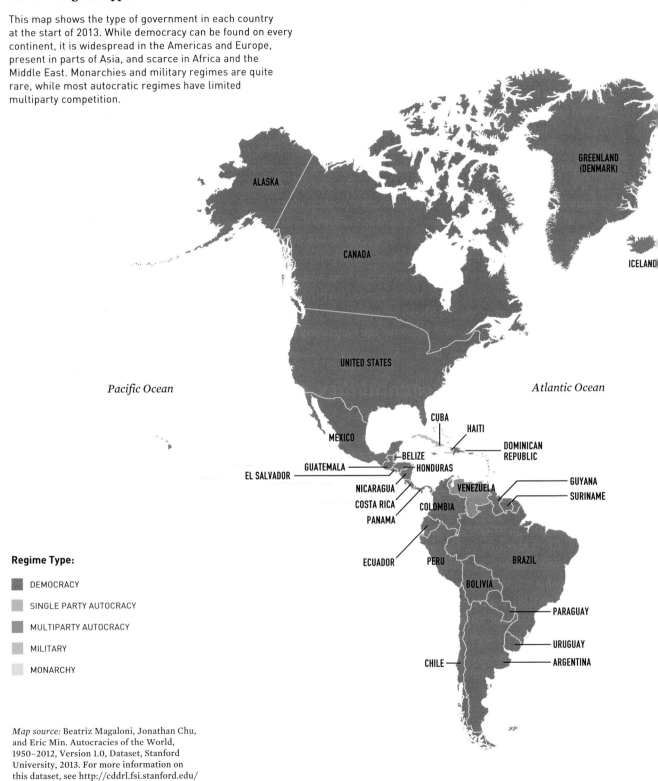

Regime Type:

- DEMOCRACY
- SINGLE PARTY AUTOCRACY
- MULTIPARTY AUTOCRACY
- MILITARY
- MONARCHY

Map source: Beatriz Magaloni, Jonathan Chu, and Eric Min. Autocracies of the World, 1950–2012, Version 1.0, Dataset, Stanford University, 2013. For more information on this dataset, see http://cddrl.fsi.stanford.edu/povgov/research/autocracies_of_the_world_dataset (accessed 01/20/15).

Arctic Ocean

RUSSIA

SWEDEN
FINLAND
NORWAY
UNITED
KINGDOM
GERMANY
BELARUS
IRELAND
UKRAINE
KAZAKHSTAN
MONGOLIA
FRANCE
SWITZERLAND
GEORGIA
N. KOREA
S. KOREA
UZBEKISTAN
KYRGYZSTAN
BOSNIA
JAPAN
ITALY
TURKMENISTAN
TAJIKISTAN
SPAIN
GREECE
TURKEY
CHINA
SYRIA
MOROCCO
ISRAEL
LEB.
IRAQ
IRAN
NEPAL
TAIWAN
JORDAN
KUWAIT
MYANMAR (BURMA)
Pacific Ocean
ALGERIA
LIBYA
EGYPT
SAUDI
ARABIA
INDIA
AURITANIA
UAE
VIETNAM
PHILIPPINES
GAL
MALI
NIGER
CHAD
SUDAN
ERITREA
OMAN
PAKISTAN
THAILAND
GUINEA
YEMEN
LAOS
NIGERIA
AFGHANISTAN
BANGLADESH
CAMBODIA
CAMEROON
CEN.
AFR.
REP.
S.SUDAN
ETHIOPIA
SRI LANKA
MALAYSIA
GHANA
UGANDA
KENYA
IVORY COAST
D.R.
CONGO
PAPUA NEW GUINEA
TANZANIA
Indian Ocean
INDONESIA
ANGOLA
MALAWI
FIJI
ZAMBIA
MADAGASCAR
NAMIBIA
MOZAMBIQUE
AUSTRALIA
ZIMBABWE
SOUTH
AFRICA
SWAZILAND
BOTSWANA
NEW
ZEALAND

were a kind of pleasure party, and he can blithely leave its justification (which decency requires) to his diplomatic corps, who are always prepared for such exercises.[34]

In other words, a basic problem in such political systems was that the interests of the ruler and the ruled were not aligned: the ruler enjoyed the benefit of war, while the people paid its costs. In Kant's view, the solution to this problem was to establish a representative government, one in which the ruler would be accountable to the people: if "the consent of the citizenry is required in order to determine whether or not there will be war, it is natural that they consider all its calamities before committing themselves to so risky a game."[35] In this view, political institutions that foster broad representation would serve to align the interests of the ruler and the ruled, making those with the power to decide on war sensitive to the costs their decisions impose on others.

The primary mechanism through which political institutions influence decisions about war and peace is **accountability**: the ability to punish or reward leaders for their decisions. Even if political leaders do not directly bear the costs of war, they can be punished politically if they make decisions that harm the people or groups on whom they rely to stay in power. In a democratic system, elections and other practices provide a way for citizens to punish leaders for unpopular policies. Democratic leaders thus have to take into account the possibility that failed or costly wars can undermine their political support, jeopardizing their hold on office, as we saw in Figure 4.4. At the same time, by making it easier for voters to make their collective voice heard, electoral institutions weaken the potential influence of small groups who may see concentrated benefits but few costs from waging war. Thus, accountability to voters can raise the political risks of war to an elected leader and ensure representation of broader rather than particularistic interests.

Autocratic leaders may also be held accountable for their actions, but the key actors are different, so the interests that are represented in decision making are different. Though they do not face an electorate with real power to replace them, they may still be subject to removal by a "selectorate": the set of individuals and groups whose support is necessary for a leader to retain office. In nondemocratic systems, this selectorate can be quite small, often involving military, economic, or ethnic elites. Staying in power requires that autocrats prioritize policies that keep these actors satisfied, privileging particularistic interests over the public good. Autocrats are also protected by the fact that the actions needed to remove them, such as a revolution or coup, are risky to undertake. Thus, as long as members of the selectorate are sufficiently protected, paid off, or afraid, the leader can be politically insulated from the costs of war.[36] For example, after losing the first Persian Gulf War in 1991, Saddam Hussein was able to hold on to power, even in the face of popular revolts, because he was able to retain the loyalty of his elite military units and core supporters.

accountability

The ability to punish or reward leaders for the decisions they make, as when frequent fair elections enable voters to hold elected officials responsible for their actions by granting or withholding access to political office.

---

34. Immanuel Kant, "To Perpetual Peace: A Philosophical Sketch," in *Perpetual Peace and Other Essays on Politics, History, and Morals*, trans. Ted Humphrey (Indianapolis, IN: Hackett, 1983), 113.

35. Kant, "To Perpetual Peace," 113.

36. See Bruce Bueno de Mesquita, Alastair Smith, Randolph M. Siverson, and James D. Morrow, *The Logic of Political Survival* (Cambridge, MA: MIT Press, 2003).

In this view, then, democracies are different because their leaders face systematically higher costs from war than do nondemocratic leaders. Holding equal the probability of victory in war, a democratic leader values war less than the nondemocratic leader because the political implications of losing are worse. Holding equal the human and material costs of war, a democratic leader values war less because that leader is more likely to be held accountable for those costs.

Although this logic is compelling, we must point out that losing office is not the worst or only consequence of losing a war. When democratic leaders lose an election, they can generally retire in good comfort, collect their pension, perhaps go on the lecture circuit, and even continue to participate in politics if they want. Nondemocratic leaders, by contrast, often find that life after losing office is not so pleasant. Because their removal often occurs through violent means, such as a coup or revolution, nondemocratic leaders often suffer additional punishment above and beyond simply losing office. For the Russian tsar in 1917, the disastrous showing in World War I not only contributed to his removal from office, but he and his family were executed at the hands of the revolutionaries. The German emperor similarly faced popular uprisings in the wake of his country's defeat in that war, prompting him to abdicate his throne and flee into exile. And the leader of the military junta that led Argentina into the Falklands War was later tried for mishandling the war and spent five years in prison. Indeed, death, exile, and imprisonment are common punishments meted out to autocratic leaders who run afoul of their people. This suggests that the relationship between the political institutions and the costs of losing a war may not be as straightforward as the Kantian logic suggests. (See "How Do We Know?" on p. 153 for more on this point.)

How would this argument about accountability explain the democratic peace? If in fact war is costlier for democratic leaders, this could influence the likelihood of war in several ways. As we saw, an increase in the costs of war diminishes a state's willingness to contest the status quo, reducing the opportunities for conflict. If there are fewer things that a state is willing to fight for, the scope for it to come into violent conflict with other states decreases. Moreover, the logic of political accountability suggests that democratic leaders should be more selective about starting wars—that is, they should be willing to wage war when their chances of victory are sufficiently high. Leaders in nondemocratic political systems may be more willing to gamble on wars in which they have a low chance of winning. This logic would lower the probability of war between two democratic states

In nondemocratic states, like Zimbabwe, a small group of leaders typically makes foreign policy behind closed doors, often limiting what can be reported to the media and the public. This lack of transparency can make it harder for foreign states to gauge the state's capabilities and resolve.

because in such interactions it is unlikely that both leaders would simultaneously judge their chances in war to be high enough.[37]

But how could this argument explain the fact that, overall, democratic states are just as war prone as other states, meaning that they are particularly likely to fight wars against nondemocracies? A possible answer lies in the observation that constraints on the use of force can make democratic states appear to be tempting targets to their nondemocratic foes. Recall how Saddam Hussein dismissed U.S. deterrent threats prior to the Persian Gulf War: "Yours is a society which cannot accept 10,000 dead in one battle."[38] Although he does not say so explicitly, this statement seems to reflect a sense that American leaders would find war politically too costly to fight. This belief made Hussein more likely to resist U.S. efforts to coerce him out of Kuwait. Similarly, Japanese leaders who decided to bomb Pearl Harbor in 1941 did so in part under the mistaken impression that the American public would respond by opposing a war and would therefore constrain President Franklin Roosevelt's ability to respond. In this view, the constraints that make democracies peaceful in their relations with one another can have the opposite effect when democracies square off against less constrained adversaries, who may seek to exploit democracies by making larger demands and discounting their threats, thereby increasing the risk of war.

Democracy and the Bargaining Interaction

Another view of democracy focuses on how institutions influence bargaining interactions between states and, particularly, their ability to solve the information and commitment problems that can cause war. Recall from Chapter 3 that states may fail to find mutually beneficial bargains if they have incomplete information about the military and political factors that determine their value for war. Resolving this informational problem is challenging because states have an incentive to conceal or misrepresent their information in the hopes of getting a better deal. Could domestic institutions help solve this problem and thereby lessen the danger of war?

There are several reasons to think that democratic institutions and processes do make it easier to overcome informational problems. First, democratic political systems are much more transparent than nondemocratic systems because democratic processes are more open and observable. For example, major policy decisions are frequently subject to public and/or legislative debate. A relatively free press can disseminate information about what decision makers are thinking, the level of popular support for war, and even details about the state's military capabilities. Opposition parties can freely voice approval or dissent from the government's actions, thereby revealing the strength (or weakness) of the government's political support within the country. Such practices exist primarily to ensure that the public can scrutinize what its leaders are doing—an essential element of democratic accountability. An inevitable by-product of such openness is that foreign states can

---

37. See Bruce Bueno de Mesquita, James D. Morrow, Randolph M. Siverson, and Alastair Smith, "An Institutional Explanation for the Democratic Peace," *American Political Science Review* 93 (December 1999): 791–807.

38. See Chapter 3, footnote 19.

also glean relevant information about a democratic state's capabilities and resolve. This is not to suggest that democratic states hide nothing—either from their own people or from outside eyes. Rather, the point is that democratic states are *relatively* more transparent than most nondemocratic systems, in which decision making occurs without broad participation, there are restrictions on what can be reported in the media, opposition groups are actively suppressed, and disagreements within the governing group are rarely aired in public. Thus, it is reasonable to expect that all other things being equal, there is less uncertainty about the capabilities and resolve of democratic states.[39]

Another argument about the informational effects of democracy addresses the ability of states to send credible signals in crises. Recall from Chapter 3 that when states have private information, communicating their resolve in a credible manner often requires that they take costly actions—actions that a resolute state would be willing to take but an irresolute one would not. One way in which they can do so is by making statements or taking actions from which it would be difficult to back down. As we saw, such threats are costly if leaders expect to lose domestic political support for failing to follow through on them. A recent study of U.S. public opinion demonstrates this effect. One group of survey respondents was presented with a hypothetical scenario in which a president threatened to defend another country from invasion and then failed to do so. Another group was presented with a similar scenario in which the president failed to defend another country but had never threatened to do so. When asked to assess the president's actions, respondents in the first group gave the president a lower approval rating than those in the second—a result that is consistent with the idea that it is politically costly to back down from a threat.[40]

Policy making in democratic states, like Germany, often involves public and legislative debate, resulting in a more open and observable process. This greater transparency makes it easier for other states to accurately assess the democratic state's capabilities and resolve.

If backing down creates public disapproval, then there is reason to think that democracy magnifies the political importance of this effect. Mechanisms of

39. Kenneth A. Schultz, *Democracy and Coercive Diplomacy* (Cambridge: Cambridge University Press, 2001). For a dissenting view on the effects of democratic transparency, see Bernard I. Finel and Kristin M. Lord, "The Surprising Logic of Transparency," *International Studies Quarterly* 43 (1999): 315–39.

40. Michael Tomz, "Domestic Audience Costs in International Relations: An Experimental Approach," *International Organization* 61, no. 4 (Fall 2007): 821–40.

accountability mean that public disapproval is more likely to result in some kind of punishment for the democratic leader, in the form of either diminished support for his agenda or a greater chance of losing office at the next election. Nondemocratic leaders, by contrast, are more politically insulated from whatever disapproval their actions might engender. If so, then public threats of democratic leaders are more informative because they are costlier to make. This suggests that institutions of accountability make it easier for democratic leaders to credibly communicate their resolve with lower levels of escalation.[41]

A related argument holds that transparency can reduce the risk of preemptive wars between democracies. As we saw in Chapter 3, preemptive wars occur when each side fears that the other can deliver a potent first strike. While first-strike advantages are partly a product of military technology, they can also arise when states have the ability to prepare for attack in secret, so as to gain strategic surprise. However, if each state knows that the other faces large costs from attacking, and neither can mobilize its forces in secret, then each may be sufficiently reassured that there is no need to act preemptively. If so, the commitment to refrain from attacking is made credible by the knowledge that neither state can effectively break that promise.[42]

Domestic Institutions or Strategic Interests?

The preceding arguments all suggest that democratic institutions are the reason for the peace that has prevailed among states that possess them. It is possible, however, that democracy is not responsible for the democratic peace. For example, perhaps some other factor both causes states to become democratic and causes them not to fight. In this case, the relationship between democracy and peace could be a product of the fact that both democracy and peace share a common cause. What could this common cause be? One possibility is economic development. Democracy does tend to go hand in hand with economic development: it generally emerges and endures only in countries that are relatively wealthy. In poorer countries, by contrast, democratic institutions are more likely to break down. There is, however, no general tendency for wealth alone to promote peace between countries, though there is evidence consistent with a "capitalist peace" among countries with free-market economies.[43]

41. James D. Fearon, "Domestic Political Audiences and the Escalation of International Disputes," *American Political Science Review* 88 (September 1994): 577–92. There is some controversy over whether democracies are really special in this respect or whether some kinds of autocrats may also be able to tie their hands by invoking audience costs. For example, Jessica Weiss argues that China manipulates nationalist protests as a way to signal its resolve in crises with Japan and the United States; see Jessica Weiss, *Powerful Patriots: Nationalist Protest in China's Foreign Relations* (Oxford: Oxford University Press, 2014). There is also a robust debate on whether domestic audience costs play an important role in the outcomes of international crises. For a critical view, see Jack Snyder and Erica D. Borghard, "The Cost of Empty Threats: A Penny, Not a Pound," *American Political Science Review* 105 (August 2011): 437–56.

42. Russett, *Grasping the Democratic Peace*, 38–40. See also Bruce Bueno de Mesquita and David Lalman, *War and Reason: Domestic and International Imperatives* (New Haven, CT: Yale University Press, 1992), chap. 4.

43. Erik Gartzke, "The Capitalist Peace," *American Journal of Political Science* 51 (2007): 166–91.

Another alternative argument is that historically the main democratic states have had relatively similar interests. From the late nineteenth century on, the main democratic countries were united against common threats, first against Germany and then against the Soviet Union. During the Cold War, most democracies had similar strategic interests owing to a common perceived threat from the Soviet Union and the Communist bloc (see Chapter 5). Such common interests reduced the opportunities for conflict between democratic states and provided a strong incentive to resolve peacefully any conflicts that did arise. In addition to fighting with each other less often, democratic states in these periods also tended to form alliances with each other—an indication that they perceived common strategic interests.[44]

Could such common interests, and not shared democracy, account for the democratic peace? The verdict is mixed. On the one hand, as we look over the past two centuries, the evidence of a democratic peace gets less conclusive as we go back in time. This is largely due to the fact that there were very few democratic states in the nineteenth century. Given that war is a relatively rare event, there are limits to what we can confidently conclude from the absence of wars between democracies in this period. Moreover, democratic states in the nineteenth century experienced a relatively high number of militarized crises short of war, as the main democratic countries—Great Britain, France, and the United States—clashed frequently over colonial holdings. This has led some scholars to suggest either that the democratic peace emerged only in the twentieth century, with the rise of common enemies or, at least, that the effect grew stronger over time.

On the other hand, was it purely coincidence that the democratic states found themselves united first against Germany and then against the Soviet Union? Did these common threat perceptions arise by chance, or did something about these countries' political systems lead them to see each other as natural allies rather than as threats? One could argue that the constraints operating on these states, as well as their relative transparency, made them less threatening to one another, particularly when compared to the closed and relatively unconstrained autocratic rivals.[45] Recent research shows that people in the United States and United Kingdom are significantly less likely to support military strikes against a state pursuing nuclear weapons if they are told that the target state is democratic. Much of this effect appears to be driven by the fact that people in these countries view other democracies to be less threatening.[46]

In short, the democratic peace raises tantalizing questions for both scholars and policy makers, and we are likely to be debating this issue for some time. (See "Controversy" on p. 178.)

---

44. Joanne Gowa, *Ballots and Bullets: The Elusive Democratic Peace* (Princeton, NJ: Princeton University Press, 1999).

45. David Lake, "Powerful Pacifists: Democratic States and War," *American Political Science Review* 86 (March 1992): 24–37. For a similar argument that hinges on democratic identity, see Thomas Risse-Kappen, "Democratic Peace—Warlike Democracies? A Social Constructivist Interpretation of the Liberal Argument," *European Journal of International Relations* 1 (1995): 491–517.

46. Michael R. Tomz and Jessica L. P. Weeks, "Public Opinion and the Democratic Peace," *American Political Science Review* 107 (November 2013): 849–65.

Should We Prefer a Friendly Dictator or a Hostile Democracy?

On June 30, 2012, Mohamed Morsi (right) was sworn in as the first democratically elected leader in Egypt's 5,000-year history. The emergence of a democratic government in Egypt seemed at the time to be a bright spot for a region undergoing a tumultuous wave of political unrest. Demonstrations throughout the Middle East starting in January 2011 had brought down long-serving authoritarian governments not only in Egypt—where President Hosni Mubarak was forced to step down after 30 years of rule—but also in Tunisia, Libya, and Yemen. Protest movements in other states, including Syria, Jordan, and Bahrain, stepped up their calls for change. But hopes that this so-called Arab Spring would lead to more democratic and less repressive governments in the region were disappointed, as fundamental political reform largely failed to materialize; in Syria, the government crackdown on protesters unleashed a horrific civil war that has claimed hundreds of thousands of lives.

As it turned out, hopes for democracy in Egypt were similarly short-lived. After a year in power, Morsi faced a renewed wave of popular protest, and the Egyptian military took over in a coup d'état in July 2013. A year later, the general who led that coup was elected president in an election lacking real competition, and his government has clamped down on dissent, jailing political opponents and journalists. In May 2015, a court sentenced Morsi to death for his alleged role in a prison break that took place during the initial uprisings. As of this writing, the sentence had not been carried out.

For the United States and other Western powers, the swing in Egypt from authoritarianism to democracy and back to authoritarianism created a foreign policy dilemma. On the one hand, American and other Western policy makers often stress the importance of promoting democracy around the world because it leads to governments that are responsive to their citizens' interests and respectful of their human rights. Moreover, the democratic peace observation suggests that expanding the number of democratic states can lead to a more peaceful

world. On the other hand, the majority of people in a country may have interests that are hostile to or incompatible with those of the United States and its allies. In such cases, it can be easier to deal with an autocratic leader who is free to ignore those views. In other words, policy makers can be torn between liking democratic institutions but not the interests of those empowered by such institutions.

In the case of Egypt, this tension arises from the fact that many Egyptians do not like the United States and are hostile to Israel, a key U.S. ally. Under Mubarak, Egypt had good relations with both countries on the basis of a 1979 peace treaty with Israel that had been brokered by Washington. In the ensuing years, Egypt became a strategic partner of the United States and a major recipient of U.S. military and economic aid. But the treaty was never popular among Egyptians—Mubarak's predecessor, who signed the

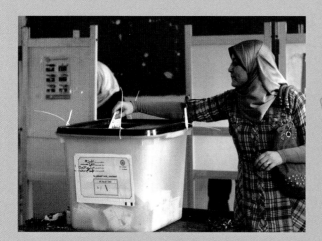

they empower people with very different interests and ideas. While this is not an ethically appealing argument, it is the position that has historically shaped U.S. policy. In the case of Egypt, the United States initially held back aid and military sales after the coup but later released them. President Obama even refused to label Morsi's ouster a coup, since doing so would have triggered a U.S. law barring aid to regimes that came to power that way.

The decision to prioritize security interests over democracy in this case was not new. During the Cold War, the United States feared that elections would empower Communist parties that would then become allies of the Soviet Union; military dictatorships, though brutal to their own people, made more reliable partners. Thus, in several countries—Iran (1953), Guatemala (1954), Chile (1973)—the United States conspired in the overthrow of democratic governments by military dictators. Supporters of this position also argue that the elected leaders who were overthrown were likely to become dictators themselves. Morsi's opponents, for example, questioned whether the Muslim Brotherhood was committed to democracy or human rights. In fact, the military coup enjoyed a great deal of popular support because of dissatisfaction with the Morsi government and constitutional reforms that it had pushed.

The most common argument against placing security interests above democracy is based on moral considerations: people have a right to have a government that is responsive to their interests and respects their civil liberties. By installing or supporting dictators, the United States is complicit in the human rights abuses committed by those regimes. In addition, one could argue that, in the long run, U.S. interests are best served by promoting democracy, even where it is inconvenient to do so in the short run. By supporting authoritarian regimes like Egypt under Mubarak, the United States has stoked anti-American sentiment and contributed to the hostility of Egypt's people. In some cases, this hostility has fed the ranks of terrorist organizations that have targeted the United States and its interests. Ayman al-Zawahiri, the current leader of the Al Qaeda terrorist organization who was second in command when that group attacked the United States on September 11, 2001, is an Egyptian who was radicalized by the repression of Islamists by the Mubarak regime. In this view, the United States would be safer in the long run if it did not prop up autocratic regimes in the region and gave more support to the self-determination of people there.

treaty, was assassinated by extremists—and American aid was seen as propping up a repressive government. Under the autocratic Mubarak, this popular opposition could be ignored or suppressed. The transition to democracy and the election of Morsi threatened this arrangement.

A poll taken in May 2013 showed that 63 percent of Egyptians wanted to annul the treaty with Israel and only 16 percent had a positive view of the United States.[a] Not only was there a danger that a more responsive government would be more hostile to Israel, but Morsi was also the leader of a party, the Muslim Brotherhood, that advocates adherence to Islamic law and seeks to eliminate Western influences from the Arab world. During the Muslim Brotherhood's brief period of rule, Egyptian relations with Israel were strained. By contrast, the military government that ousted Morsi has largely restored the strategic partnership.

How should countries that espouse democratic values manage this dilemma between institutions that are attractive but interests that are hostile? Should the United States continue to send military and economic aid to Egypt's military government, or should it push for the restoration of democracy?

One view is that a country's security interests are the most important consideration and outweigh any commitment to democracy. From the perspective of U.S. policy makers, democratic institutions are desirable in parts of the world where people have similar interests to America's, as in Europe, but they are dangerous where

a. Pew Research Global Attitudes Project, "Egyptians Increasingly Glum," May 16, 2013, www.pewglobal.org/2013/05/16/egyptians-increasingly-glum/ (accessed 09/25/2014).

Conclusion: What If All the World Were Democratic?

When diplomats and state leaders come to the bargaining table with one another, they inevitably bring a great deal of baggage from their home countries. The interests that state representatives advance in international negotiations are themselves a function of interests, interactions, and institutions within the state. Political leaders may care about what is best for their country, but they also care about staying in office. As a result, they must think about how their foreign policy choices will impact the interests of important domestic constituents such as the military, organized interest groups, and in some cases, the general public. When these actors have a stake in the outcome of international bargaining, and when they have the strategic and/or institutional resources to punish or reward the leader, then their interests will be represented at the bargaining table. In particular, when groups with hawkish interests have superior organization and resources, they can push the state toward greater international ambition and thus a greater risk of war. As we have seen, there are times when military organizations and economic or ethnic interest groups have both the interests and the ability to push foreign policy in such a direction.

In contrast, when interactions and institutions empower those who bear the costs of war, they can exert a pacifying effect at the international level. Economic actors who benefit from international commerce and investment may lobby for peaceful relations with profitable partners. Representative institutions give voice to the people who bear the costs of war, thereby weakening the influence of concentrated interests who might promote conflict for their own reasons. Free, fair, and frequent elections provide a relatively low-cost mechanism for people to punish leaders who engage in failed or costly wars. The relative openness and transparency of democratic political processes can reduce informational and commitment problems that can cause bargaining to fail. Although these features may make democracies tempting targets for autocratic foes, they also help account for the relative rarity of war among democratic states.

Does this mean that a world full of democratic states would be a world without war? Certainly, the evidence to date is encouraging, although not definitive. There are at least two reasons to be cautious. First, although the number of democracies in the world has generally increased over time, the spread of democracy has experienced reversals. There have been several periods in which democracy has broken down, particularly in the 1930s (leading to the low point in 1940) and the 1970s. During these periods, economic and international upheaval caused some democratic systems to fail. It is worth remembering that Adolf Hitler came to power in Germany through relatively democratic institutions—which he then subverted before embarking on his campaign of foreign expansion. Hence, democratic systems have given birth to forces that undermined democracy and engaged in aggressive foreign policies. Even if there are no cases of war between two democratic states, there have been wars between democracies and states that were once democratic.

A second reason for caution centers on the interests that will come to be represented by the spread of democracy. Recall that democratic institutions make leaders more sensitive to the interests of the citizenry. Kant, and those who follow in his tradition, assumed that citizens are generally cautious, since it is they who bear the costs of war. But what if the public is motivated by nationalist, ethnocentric, or even genocidal ideas? If fear and hatred of a rival is intense, accountability may induce belligerence rather than caution, and leaders may fear domestic political retribution for being overly "soft" toward the nation's ethnic or religious enemies.[47] The costs of war might, as a result, be offset by the political costs of compromise. We already saw in the case of India and Pakistan that the fact that both were democracies in the spring of 1999 did not prevent a war from breaking out between them. (See "What Shaped Our World?" on p. 157.) A history of conflict and bloodshed, fueled by religious differences, has created a great deal of enmity between not just the governments but also the people in these states. Indeed, the Kargil War was popular on both sides; in Pakistan, people were disappointed only that their country did not prevail.

Hence, the international effects of democracy's spread may very well depend not only on the institutions that take root but also on the interests of those they empower.

---

47. For evidence that leaders may be punished for making concessions to a rival, see Michael Colaresi, "When Doves Cry: International Rivalry, Unreciprocated Cooperation, and Leadership Turnover," *American Journal of Political Science* 48 (2004): 555–70.

Study Tool Kit

Interests, Interactions, and Institutions in Context

- There may be actors within a state who perceive high benefits from war and expect to pay little or none of its costs. In particular, there are conditions under which political leaders, business and ethnic lobbies, and the military will see conflict as furthering their narrow interests.

- These actors have a variety of institutional and organizational advantages that make it possible for them to exert more influence than the general population.

- Except in rare circumstances, these hawkish interests are not sufficient to cause war on their own. Rather, their main effect is to increase the aggressiveness of the state's foreign policy and the scope of its ambitions, thereby creating more opportunities for conflict.

- Democratic political institutions—in particular, free and fair elections, party competition, and free media—can diminish the influence of hawkish interests and help states overcome the strategic problems that can cause the bargaining interaction to end in war.

Key Terms

bureaucracy, p. 144

interest groups, p. 144

rally effect, p. 147

diversionary incentive, p. 148

military-industrial complex, p. 154

democratic peace, p. 167

democracy, p. 168

autocracy, p. 168

accountability, p. 172

For Further Reading

Allison, Graham, and Philip Zelikow. *Essence of Decision: Explaining the Cuban Missile Crisis,* **2nd ed. New York: Longman, 1999.** Presents a classic study of the effects of bureaucratic politics on foreign policy making in one of the most dramatic crises of the Cold War.

Chiozza, Giacomo, and H. E. Goemans. *Leaders and International Conflict.* **Cambridge: Cambridge University Press, 2011.** Explores how democratic and autocratic leaders make decisions about international conflict with an eye toward staying in office and staying alive.

Doyle, Michael. "Liberalism and World Politics." *American Political Science Review* **80 (December 1986): 1151–69.** Offers an influential discussion of how liberal political systems might affect foreign policy choices; this analysis brought the study of the democratic peace to the forefront of political science.

Feaver, Peter D., and Christopher Gelpi. *Choosing Your Battles: American Civil-Military Relations and the Use of Force.* **Princeton, NJ: Princeton University Press, 2004.** Presents a systematic study of how civilians and military officers differ in their views about the use of force.

Fordham, Benjamin. *Building the Cold War Consensus.* **Ann Arbor: University of Michigan Press, 1998.** Examines how different economic interests came together to underpin the United States' international commitments during the Cold War.

Reiter, Dani, and Allan Stam. *Democracies at War.* **Princeton, NJ: Princeton University Press, 2002.** Carefully examines an unanticipated finding that grew out of the study of democracy and war: democracies tend to win the wars they fight.

Russett, Bruce, and James Oneal. *Triangulating Peace: Democracy, Interdependence, and International Organizations.* **New York: Norton, 2001.** Gives a comprehensive review and analysis of the effects of democracy, trade, and international institutions on violent conflict between states.

Snyder, Jack. *Myths of Empire: Domestic Politics and International Ambition.* **Ithaca, NY: Cornell University Press, 1991.** Explores how domestic interest groups and military organizations can push great powers to adopt expansionist foreign policies—often with disastrous consequences for the state as a whole.

Weeks, Jessica L. P. *Dictators at War and Peace.* **Ithaca, NY: Cornell University Press, 2014.** Explores the variation among autocratic governments and how different kinds of nondemocratic leaders weigh decisions about war and peace.

5

International Institutions and War

THE PUZZLE *In a well-governed country, the police prevent and punish acts of violence between individuals. Where are the police in international politics? Why is it so hard for the international community to prevent and punish acts of aggression?*

Above: Collective security organizations like the United Nations can influence interactions between adversaries in ways that promote peaceful outcomes. However, these institutions face significant challenges in achieving their goals.

When North Korea invaded South Korea in June 1950, the United Nations (UN) responded by authorizing member states to use military force to resist this act of aggression. Although North Korea had some influential supporters, including the Soviet Union and China, a coalition of 20 nations led by the United States successfully expelled the North Koreans from South Korea by October 1950. At that point, the UN expanded the forces' mandate and pushed into North Korea. This act provoked China to intervene in order to save its ally, and the Korean War dragged on for another three years.

Around the same time, Chinese forces also invaded Tibet, which neighbors China on the west. China long claimed sovereignty over this vast, mountainous region, but Tibet had declared independence from China in 1911. Although China never recognized this declaration, Tibet was in practice an independent state for the next several decades as China, distracted by civil war and the Japanese invasion in the 1930s, was unable to resist. Not long after the Communists gained control of mainland China in 1949, they sought to reassert the country's historic claim over Tibet. Units of the People's Liberation Army swept into the region in October 1950, quickly defeating the Tibetan army and forcing Tibet's leaders to accept Chinese rule. Tibet's political and religious leader, the Dalai Lama, appealed to the UN to meet the Chinese attack on Tibet with the same kind of response that it had mustered against North Korea. But, in this case, the UN took no action, and the Chinese conquest of Tibet was allowed to stand.

In our everyday lives, we generally count on the police to protect us from acts of aggression by other people. If someone breaks into your house, you can call the police. Assuming you live in a place with an effective police force, the police may come in time to stop the person from harming you or your property. Even if the police cannot always stop a crime in progress, they can investigate and try to bring the perpetrator to justice. This has a deterrent effect on would-be criminals, who can be dissuaded from committing aggression by the expectation that they might be caught and punished. Although total security is rarely possible, people who live in societies with well-functioning police and judicial systems rarely experience acts of violence, and they rarely have to commit acts of violence to defend themselves. Unfortunately, the same cannot be said of actors in the international system.

Where are the police in world politics? The short answer is that the international system has no police force analogous to what exists in most countries. Each state possesses its own police and its own military, but there is no authoritative institution above states with an independent force that can police relations among them. As the examples above suggest, this condition of anarchy means that there is variation in the ways the international community responds to acts of aggression. And this variation has real consequences for people living in the states where such aggression occurs. Thanks to the international efforts that kept it independent, South Korea is today a thriving and prosperous country, with a living standard that far exceeds that of the impoverished North. Tibet, on the other hand, remains a part of China in spite of the fact that many Tibetans want their independence and an active movement for independence continues to this day.

Understanding this variation in international responses requires that we explore the institutions that govern whether and how outside actors respond to acts of violence in the international system. The most obvious of these outside actors are bodies like the UN or its predecessor, the League of Nations (1919–46). Formally known as collective security organizations, these institutions are the closest approximation to a world government that we have. Collective security organizations try to govern relations among their members, providing them with tools for peaceful conflict resolution and a mechanism for organizing collective responses to acts of aggression. To answer the question "Where are the police in international politics?" collective security organizations are a natural first place to look.

For much longer than such organizations have existed, however, states have used an alternative institution to arrange for help from others: alliances. If collective security organizations are like governments, alliances more closely resemble neighborhood associations: relatively small groups of actors who work together to meet common threats or address common needs. Alliances are institutions that help states cooperate militarily, such as by coming to one another's defense in the event of war. In the absence of an effective world police, alliances represent attempts by small numbers of like-minded states to look out for one another.

This chapter continues our inquiry into the puzzle of war by examining how international institutions affect interactions between states as they try to cooperate to prevent or stop international and civil conflict.

Thinking Analytically about International Institutions and War

Alliances and collective security organizations both influence whether or not outsiders will intervene in the event that war breaks out. As a result, they play a role in the bargaining that precedes a war, the bargaining that seeks to end an ongoing war, and the bargaining that takes place in the aftermath of fighting. But, despite these common features, these two kinds of institutions also differ greatly in how they operate. They form in response to different kinds of interests that third parties have in international disputes. And while both kinds of institutions try to facilitate cooperation among states, they address different aspects of the strategic interactions that surround third-party involvement in international disputes. Hence, the factors that predict their success or failure are quite different.

Alliances form when states have compatible interests that motivate them to cooperate militarily. They often seek to influence bargaining interactions with some third party by influencing that adversary's beliefs about the allies' willingness to fight together in the event of war. A core function of these institutions is to strengthen the commitment that allies make to one another and to signal that commitment to others in a credible manner. By contrast, collective security organizations like the UN form around a common interest, which all states are presumed to share, in reducing violence within and between countries. Their primary challenge is to facilitate collective action by the international community to deter, end, and prevent the recurrence of international and civil wars. The task is a daunting one, and international efforts can be stymied either by the opposition of leading states or by their unwillingness to pay the costs of intervention. As a result, collective efforts to keep the peace are uneven, but certainly better than if these organizations did not exist at all.

Alliances: Why Promise to Fight Someone Else's War?

World War II in Europe started as a territorial dispute between Germany and Poland but quickly grew into something much larger. After Germany invaded Poland on September 1, 1939, Britain and France responded two days later by declaring war on Germany. On September 17, the Soviet Union joined the fray, invading Poland from the east, and Poland was quickly swallowed up by its larger neighbors. Several months later, in June 1940, Italy joined the war on the German side and launched an invasion of southern France as German forces attacked France in the north. In each case, states that joined the war were carrying out the terms of alliance treaties that they had signed earlier. France and Poland had long-standing promises, codified in treaties from 1921 and 1925, to help each other in the event of war with Germany. Britain made a similar commitment to Poland in March 1939. Italy and the Soviet Union, for their parts, had each signed treaties pledging support for German military activities. Italy and Germany forged the so-called Pact of Steel in May 1939. Germany and the Soviet Union unveiled the Molotov-Ribbentrop Pact (so named for the two countries' foreign ministers) only days before the invasion of Poland. In that treaty, the two countries pledged not to attack each other and agreed to divide Poland between them; additionally, Germany promised the Soviets control over Finland, Estonia, Latvia, and Lithuania.

Alliances are institutions that help their members cooperate militarily in the event of a war. Like all institutions, alliances specify standards of behavior, or expectations about how states are to behave under certain conditions. They may include provisions for monitoring and verifying each member's compliance and procedures for joint decision making. Alliances also codify bargains between their members that settle distributional issues, such as resolving conflicts that might get in the way of cooperation or specifying how much each member will contribute to the common cause.[1]

These provisions vary depending on the interests of the allies. Some alliances are offensive while others are defensive. An offensive alliance is an agreement between states to join one another in attacking a third state. The Molotov-Ribbentrop Pact is a classic example of such an agreement. It not only specified the nature of Soviet-German military cooperation, but it also spelled out how the spoils of conquest would be divided. More commonly, alliances are defensive: states pledge to come to one another's defense in the event that either is attacked. The British and French pledges to Poland had this character. Defensive alliances may be open-ended in the sense that allies pledge to defend one another

alliances

Institutions that help their members cooperate militarily in the event of a war.

---

1. The role of alliances in settling territorial conflicts among allies is noted by Douglas M. Gibler, "Control the Issues, Control the Conflict: The Effects of Alliances That Settle Territorial Issues on Interstate Rivalries," *International Interactions* 22 (1997): 341–68.

against any and all attackers, or they may be targeted only at specific countries. Alliances may also differ in what the member states are required to do in the event of attack. A typical defensive alliance requires states to come to one another's aid militarily—that is, to treat an attack on the ally as an attack on oneself. Other alliance agreements specify merely that the states will consult one another in the event of war.

The most comprehensive effort to collect and code information on alliances through history, the Alliance Treaty Obligation and Provision (ATOP) project, provides us with a sense of how common these different kinds of provisions are. ATOP researchers identified 538 alliance treaties between states in the period from 1815 to 2003.[2] Of these, just over half (277) involved promises of active military support in the event that one of the allies became involved in a conflict. The vast majority of these alliances (71 percent) were purely defensive in character, only 5 percent were purely offensive, and the rest (24 percent) had both offensive and defensive provisions. Of those agreements that did not provide for active military assistance, most (217) provided for consultation between the allies if either member became involved in military conflict. About a fifth of all alliances include a neutrality clause, which requires that each member promise not to join in any attack against an ally.

The United States currently has defensive alliances with a number of countries: South Korea, Japan, and—through the North Atlantic Treaty Organization (NATO)—Canada and many states in western and central Europe. If any of these states should come under attack, they could invoke the U.S. alliance commitment and ask Americans to come to their aid. In turn, the United States can appeal to others if it is attacked. NATO invoked its mutual defense provision for the first time in the alliance's history after the terrorist attack on the United States in September 2001. European NATO members assisted in flying airborne warning and control systems (better known as AWACS) over U.S. skies from October 2001 to May 2002.

In addition to spelling out their offensive or defensive character, alliances may codify bargains over how much and what each state will contribute to the common defense. Some alliances are symmetric, meaning that the members have similar responsibilities and contribute in roughly equal amounts. Other alliances are highly asymmetric, typically because one of the members is much more powerful than the others. For example, while the United States has pledged to defend South Korea, there is little expectation that South Korea would be in a position to return the favor if the U.S. homeland were attacked. In exchange for protection, South Korea provides bases for American troops in East Asia, has contributed to U.S. military efforts in the region, and generally supports U.S. foreign policy diplomatically and economically.

---

2. A description of the data collection effort is reported in Brett Ashley Leeds, Jeffrey M. Ritter, Sara McLaughlin Mitchell, and Andrew G. Long, "Alliance Treaty Obligations and Provisions, 1815–1944," *International Interactions* 28 (2002): 237–60. The data and codebook are available at http://atop.rice.edu (accessed 07/26/11). The figures reported here do not include nonaggression pacts (that is, agreements to refrain from using force) since these do not meet the definition of an alliance.

The United States maintains numerous military bases in Japan, including this one in Fussa, west of Tokyo, as part of a defensive alliance between the two countries. Countries form alliances when they have compatible interests that motivate them to cooperate.

Interests and Alliances

Given that alliances can drag a country into other countries' wars, why do states sign them? Alliances form when states have compatible interests that provide the basis for cooperation. In some cases, states share a common interest in achieving the same outcome. In the lead-up to World War II, the leaders of Britain and France did not agree to defend Poland out of the goodness of their hearts; they did so because they feared that a German conquest of Poland would make Germany militarily stronger, economically more self-sufficient, and therefore a greater threat to their own security. Thus, Britain and France shared Poland's interest in its own survival. Similarly, the United States formed the NATO alliance after World War II because it believed that securing countries like Britain, France, and West Germany from Soviet domination was crucial to its own security. In other cases, alliance partners might have complementary interests that serve as the basis for a deal. The alliance between the United States and South Korea rests on the fact that South Korea wants protection from North Korea and China, while the United States wants military bases and partners in projecting its power in East Asia. Thus, each partner can provide something that the other values.

Whatever the specific interests are that bring states together into alliances, allies generally have aligned interests in the context of bargaining with third-party states. Figure 5.1 shows how we can depict such an alignment in our bargaining framework. As before, the disputed good is shown as a horizontal bar, and any possible deal separates this good into shares enjoyed by States A and B. We now assume that there is some third state, State C, that also has a stake in the outcome

FIGURE 5.1 *Alignment of Interests*

If State C has common interests with State A, then both State A and State C prefer a deal as far to the right as possible. The more of the good State A gets, the happier State C is.

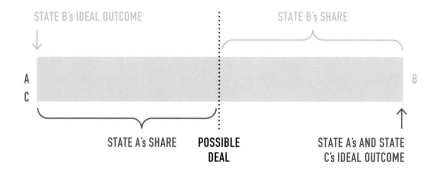

of bargaining between States A and B. If, say, State C has aligned interests with State A, then State C's ideal point is, like State A's ideal point, at the far right end of the bar. This means that the more of the good State A gets, the happier State C is. Thus, their interests are aligned, at least when it comes to this dispute with State B.

How these alignments arise is a complicated question without a single answer. A long tradition in the study of international relations holds that alliances form to create or preserve a **balance of power**—that is, a situation in which the military capabilities of two states or groups of states are roughly equal.[3] When a balance of power exists, no state or bloc has a clear military advantage over the other. A power imbalance, in contrast, is considered threatening to the weaker side's interests. According to this view, alliances form when two or more states need to combine their capabilities in order to match the capabilities of another state and thereby counter the threat to their security. Common interests thus arise from a common threat posed by the power of a stronger state or bloc. In the late nineteenth century, both France and Russia feared the growing power and ambition of imperial Germany. Not only did each state want help in defending itself against a possible German attack, but each also feared that if Germany managed to conquer the other, then it would face an even more formidable foe in the future. As a result, each believed that its own survival depended in part on the survival of the other. The 1894 alliance between these states was formed on basis of this common interest.

balance of power

A situation in which the military capabilities of two states or groups of states are roughly equal.

---

3. See, for example, Edward Gulick, *Europe's Classical Balance of Power* (New York: Norton, 1955). For an influential statement of the theory, see Kenneth Waltz, *Theory of International Politics* (Long Grove, IL: Waveland Press, 2010). For a historical analysis of balancing and its alternatives, see Paul Schroeder, "Alliances, 1815–1945: Weapons of Power and Tools of Management," in *Historical Dimensions of National Security Problems*, ed. Klaus Knorr, 247–86 (Lawrence: University Press of Kansas, 1976).

Although this dynamic can explain some aspects of alliance formation, the balance of power theory does not fully account for all alliance decisions. First, not all alliances form with the intent of balancing a stronger state. When the Soviet Union allied with Nazi Germany against Poland, it joined the stronger state, exacerbating rather than alleviating the imbalance of power in Central Europe. We refer to such behavior as bandwagoning.[4] **Bandwagoning** occurs when states team up with the more powerful side in a dispute in order to share the spoils of conquest. Bandwagoning alliances are often offensive, as the shared interests that underlie them arise not from a common fear but from a desire to cooperate for a common gain.

A second limitation of the balance of power theory is that states can often choose many potential partners in order to balance the capabilities of a stronger state. The arithmetic of balancing capabilities does not explain why some partners are more desirable than others. For example, when Saudi Arabia sought allies against Egypt in 1957, why did it choose to ally with fellow Arab monarchies Jordan and Iraq, rather than with Israel, a state with much more impressive military capabilities and which also had reason to fear Egypt? The answer lies not in the balance of power but rather in the ideological and religious incompatibility between Saudi Arabia and the Jewish state, which made an alliance between the two unthinkable.[5] Conversely, shared cultural or religious identity can help explain why some pairs of states see each other as particularly attractive allies. Strategic cooperation between the United States and Israel, for example, is rooted in part in the perception that Israel is an outpost of Western cultural and democratic values in the Middle East and hence more "like" the United States than other states in the region.[6]

A final problem for the balance of power theory is that not all strong powers provoke similar balancing responses. For example, the United States today has unparalleled military power, accounting for almost 40 percent of all world military spending. And yet, despite some tensions associated with the Iraq War, there has not been a significant tendency toward creating balancing alliances in response. Indeed, the U.S.-led NATO alliance, rather than falling apart after the collapse of the Soviet bloc, has expanded both its membership and the scope of its missions (see "What Shaped Our World?" on p. 204). A likely explanation is that while states sometimes complain about American arrogance and bullying, very few see the United States as an actual threat to their interests. Whatever differences the United States has had with France, for example, there is virtually no danger of war between them. Commercial, cultural, and ideological ties between the countries are strong, and there are no disputed goods in their relationship

4. Randall Schweller, "Bandwagoning for Profit: Bringing the Revisionist State Back In," *International Security* 19 (1994): 72–107.

5. Stephen M. Walt, *The Origins of Alliances* (Ithaca, NY: Cornell University Press, 1987), 204–6.

6. See, for example, Michael N. Barnett, "Identity and Alliances in the Middle East," in *The Culture of National Security*, ed. Peter J. Katzenstein, 400–47 (Ithaca, NY: Cornell University Press, 1996).

that are valuable enough to risk war over. In short, whether or not two states share a common interest vis-à-vis a third state depends on much more than whether or not the third state has an advantage in military capabilities. Other factors such as geographic proximity, ideological and cultural similarity, and the existence (or not) of high-value disputes play a large role in determining which states are considered threatening, and hence worth allying against, and which are not.[7]

Alliances and Interstate Bargaining

The possibility of intervention by an ally influences international bargaining by changing the likely outcome and costs of war for each side. Returning to the three-state example introduced in Figure 5.1, imagine that if States A and B were to fight a war, the expected outcome would be as shown in the top panel of Figure 5.2. In this interaction, State B is assumed to be more powerful, so the war outcome is close to its ideal point. This means that State B can extract a favorable bargain from State A and is likely to challenge State A to try to realize that bargain (in other words, there is a large range of status quo outcomes in which State B will make a demand of State A). If State C were expected to join State A in this war, however, the outcome and costs would be quite different, as shown in the lower panel. With State C's power added to that of State A, the expected outcome shifts to the right, in State A's favor. Moreover, State B is likely to suffer higher costs in a war against two adversaries, whereas State A is likely to incur lower costs now that State C is carrying some of the burden.

As before, the bargaining range is the set of deals that are preferred to war by both sides. Because of the change in the likely war outcome, the bargaining range has shifted to the right in the lower panel, benefiting States A and C. War is less attractive to State B, and it can no longer extract a lopsided deal. State B's incentive to challenge State A also declines. By shrinking the range of status quos that State B can profitably challenge, the prospect of State C's participation deters State B from initiating crises in the first place. Hence, State C's willingness to intervene influences the bargaining interaction between States A and B by shifting each side's evaluation of war.

In addition, the possibility of intervention can affect whether or not the opposing sides reach a bargain. In the example just given, the shift in the bargaining range was based on the assumption that both States A and B believe that State C would intervene in the event of war. In other words, it assumed that the two sides form their expectations on the basis of the same information about State C's intentions. What would happen if this were not the case? For example, what if State A expected State C to join a war, but State B did not?

When the parties to a dispute have different information about what third parties will do, this uncertainty can heighten the probability of a bargaining failure leading to war, for reasons discussed in Chapter 3. As we have seen, Iraq in

---

7. Walt, *The Origins of Alliances.*

FIGURE 5.2 *Alignments, Alliances, and Interstate Bargaining*

The bargaining interaction between State A and State B is determined by the expected outcome of a war between the two states.

However, this interaction changes when State C is expected to join State A in the event of a war. As shown below, when State C's power is added to State A's, the expected war outcome shifts to the right, and State B's costs of war increase. As a result, the set of deals that are preferable to war shifts closer to the ideal point of States A and C, and the range of status quo distributions that State B will challenge shrinks.

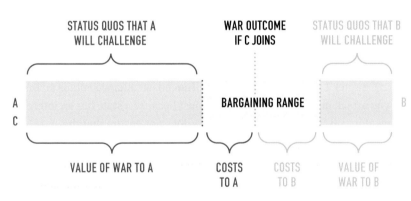

C joins the war as A's ally.

August 1990 did not know whether the United States would defend Kuwait, and its doubts about U.S. threats to that effect helped bring about the Persian Gulf War. Similarly, we saw in the case of the Korean War that the United States was uncertain about whether China would come to the aid of North Korea if U.S. troops crossed the 38th parallel. In the lead-up to World War I, Germany was unsure until the last moment whether Britain would join its allies, France and Russia, in the event of war.

This observation suggests that alliances influence the bargaining interaction between states by influencing the states' beliefs about what third parties will do. While aligned interests are necessary for alliances to form, the main reason that states sign alliances is to signal those interests to others. After all, if it were completely obvious to everyone which states would come to the defense

Allies may engage in joint military exercises in order to improve their ability to fight together and to publicize their commitment to do so. Here, U.S. and South Korean soldiers engage in a May 2013 exercise near the border with North Korea.

of others, then there would be little need to negotiate and sign treaties to this effect.[8]

Because of their role as signals, alliances face the same challenge of credibility discussed in Chapter 3 with respect to threats. Indeed, an alliance entails an implied threat: "If you attack my ally, I will fight you." Just because a state has an interest in the outcome of its ally's bargaining interactions does not ensure that the state will actually fight alongside its ally in the event of war. As a result, an alliance commitment may be questionable for the same reasons that threats are questionable: they are costly to carry out, and there can be incentives to bluff. Alliances are not, after all, binding contracts. There is no external mechanism to compel states to fulfill their treaty obligations. Rather, the promise to come to another's defense in the event of war is precisely that: a promise, which may or may not be fulfilled. In fact, there are many instances in which allies have not lived up to their commitments. Indeed, in June 1941, less than two years after signing the Molotov-Ribbentrop Pact, Germany broke its side of the agreement by invading the Soviet Union and grabbing all of Poland for itself.

This observation suggests that when we talk about alliances, we should be clear to treat them as institutions and not as actors in their own right. It sometimes serves as a useful shorthand to talk about alliances as cohesive actors; for example, we might say that "NATO intervened in Libya." However, we must remember that alliances are institutions formed by states in response to common interests. These

---

8. James Morrow, "Alliances: Why Write Them Down?" *Annual Review of Political Science* 3 (2000): 63–83.

institutions may shape states' interests in a way that helps them to act as a cohesive group, but at all times decision-making power rests with the states, not the alliance itself.[9]

How Alliances Establish Credibility

Whether or not an alliance can successfully further the interests of allied states depends on their willingness to fight on one another's behalf and on their ability to signal this willingness in a credible manner. As a result, alliances must accomplish two key tasks in order to enhance their chances of success. First, they must make it more likely that allies will fight on one another's behalf than they would in the absence of an alliance. This can be accomplished by decreasing the costs of fighting, increasing the benefits of fighting, and/or increasing the costs of not fighting—that is, of abandoning the ally. Second, alliances must do these things in a way that leads adversaries to believe that the allies will indeed fight together. Hence, the goal is both to heighten the allies' interests in aiding one another and to influence the interaction with the rival state by shaping its expectations.

Alliances typically have a number of features designed to further these goals. They increase the benefits and decrease the costs of war by improving the member countries' ability to fight effectively together. Allies may engage in joint military planning and joint military exercises, and they may station troops on one another's soil. By doing so, they make the expected value of fighting together higher than it would be in the absence of an alliance. This coordination is publicly revealed (even if actual war-fighting strategies are not), which serves to put potential adversaries on notice. Some alliances also contain provisions for joint decision making that further enhance their collective war-fighting abilities. NATO appoints a Supreme Allied Commander, Europe, for instance, who is responsible for all troops under the organization's authority.

Alliances can also increase the costs of abandonment—that is, of failing to fight on an ally's behalf. Prior to the nineteenth century, it was common to cement alliances through a marriage between royal families—under the theory that a king would have special motivation to defend an ally if his daughter was married to that ally's monarch. More commonly, the fact that alliance treaties are generally made public—often accompanied by public signing ceremonies and, in some countries, open ratification processes—can bring states' reputations into play.[10] States may fear that the failure to come to an ally's defense, after making such a public commitment, would hurt their credibility in future conflicts. Such hand-tying strategies seek to bolster the credibility of alliances just as they do the credibility of other threats.

---

9. This characteristic distinguishes alliances from empires and more hierarchical relationships between states in which the capabilities of two or more actors are combined but decision-making power rests in a dominant state. On security hierarchies, see David A. Lake, *Entangling Relations: American Foreign Policy in Its Century* (Princeton, NJ: Princeton University Press, 1999).

10. This is generally true of defensive alliances. Offensive alliances, in contrast, may be kept secret if the intended target would otherwise take countermeasures to blunt the effectiveness of the alliance.

Despite the challenges of establishing credibility, states have historically honored their alliance commitments in war about 70 percent of the time.[11] Although it is hard to know with certainty how often states would have fought alongside their allies even without a formal alliance commitment, this is an impressive success rate given the lack of any formal enforcement mechanism for treaties and the often substantial costs of war. Moreover, the states most likely to violate agreements are those that have experienced a significant change either in their power or in their domestic regimes. In the wake of such changes, the alignment of interests between the allies may no longer be as strong as it was when the alliance was first signed.[12] There is also evidence that states with defensive alliances are less likely to be targeted by militarized actions in the first place, suggesting that these agreements generally have the intended effect of deterring challenges.[13] These observations suggest that the institutional mechanisms just described are often effective at heightening states' interests in coming to their allies' aid and at signaling that commitment to potential adversaries.

Why Aren't Alliance Commitments Ironclad?

If states have compatible interests that lead them to form alliances and signal their commitments to one another, why is there often uncertainty about whether or not members will actually fulfill their obligations? Why do allies and other states that are the targets of alliances sometimes have different expectations about whether allies will actually come to one another's aid? To answer these questions, we need to think about the choices facing all sides of a strategic interaction.

While ironclad alliance guarantees can deter challenges to an ally, they also increase the risk that the ally will become more adventurous, making larger and riskier demands on other states. To see this, return to Figure 5.2. Alliances have two effects. As emphasized earlier, an alliance between States A and C deters a challenger, State B, by reducing the probability that it will win a war against the combined might of the two allies. This is why States A and C are interested in forging the alliance in the first place. At the same time, the alliance strengthens State A in its bargaining with State B. As the expected war outcome moves

---

11. Brett Ashley Leeds and Sezi Anac, "Alliance Institutionalization and Alliance Performance," *International Interactions* 31 (2005): 192.

12. Brett Ashley Leeds, "Alliance Reliability in Times of War: Explaining State Decisions to Violate Treaties," *International Organization* 57 (Fall 2003): 801–27.

13. Brett Ashley Leeds, "Do Alliances Deter Aggression? The Influence of Military Alliances on the Initiation of Interstate Disputes," *American Journal of Political Science* 47 (2003): 427–39. Because of the deterrent effect of alliances, the frequency with which states fight on behalf of their allies may understate the true reliability of alliances. We only get to observe whether an alliance is honored if it is challenged by some adversary; absent such a challenge, we do not know if the allies would have fought together had they been challenged. But if third parties are most likely to challenge the alliances that are least credible, then the reliability of those alliances that are challenged is lower than the overall reliability of all alliances. See Alastair Smith, "To Intervene or Not to Intervene: A Biased Decision," *Journal of Conflict Resolution* 40 (1996): 16–40.

to the right, the range of status quo outcomes in which State A has an incentive to challenge State B expands. As a result, State A is likely to demand a better bargain from State B and, following the risk-return trade-off explained in Chapter 3, run a risk of war to obtain its demands. In other words, while the alliance between States A and C weakens State B and deters it from challenging State A, the same alliance strengthens State A and gives it an incentive to demand more of State B.

Why might this situation pose a dilemma? A problem occurs if State C expects to pay greater costs of war than its ally, State A, perhaps because it cares less about the good in dispute. In this case, there are some status quos that State C would prefer to war, but which State A has an incentive to challenge. If State A were to start a crisis under these conditions, then State C would be put in the undesirable position of having to either abandon its ally or risk being dragged into a war that it values less than the status quo. Thus, while State C wants to defend State A from challenges, it must also worry about becoming "entrapped" in a costly war by a reckless ally.[14] In response to this dilemma, states attempt to avoid entrapment by limiting their commitments or leaving those commitments purposely ambiguous. In other words, in an effort to control opportunism by their allies, states rarely forge ironclad agreements that they must fulfill. Rather, states attempt to reserve a measure of discretion for themselves on when, how, and to what extent they will meet their alliance obligations.

An important example of this challenge can be found in the United States' relations with China and Taiwan. Since 1949, the United States has sought to defend Taiwan from mainland China, which regards the island as a renegade province. China has repeatedly warned that if Taiwan officially declares independence, that act would be a cause for war. The dilemma for the United States has been this: how to deter China from attacking without, at the same time, making Taiwan feel that it could declare and win its independence with the help of the United States. On the one hand, China might attack if it believes the United States would abandon Taiwan. On the other hand, an ironclad promise to defend Taiwan might encourage pro-independence politicians there to take the fateful step that would risk a war. In order to navigate this dilemma, the United States has at times pursued a policy of "strategic ambiguity": making its intentions less than fully clear in the hopes that China would be deterred from attacking while Taiwan would act with restraint.

This dilemma shows that there can be a trade-off between the *credibility* of alliances (which requires ironclad promises) and efforts to *control* alliance partners (which can require ambiguity and flexibility). There is seldom any way to avoid this trade-off. The more credible the guarantee to an ally, the greater the incentive for that ally to behave opportunistically. But the greater the discretion the state retains in an effort to limit the risk of entrapment, the less credible is the alliance and the less successful it will be in deterring challengers.

---

14. On entrapment and other forms of opportunism by allies, see Glenn H. Snyder, "The Security Dilemma in Alliance Politics," *World Politics* 36 (1984): 461–95.

Analyzing the European Alliance System, 1879–1990

As we have seen, alliances are institutions that states create in order to facilitate cooperation in support of common interests. They form when states' interests are aligned to an extent that they may be willing to fight on one another's behalf. They work by making it more likely that the states will in fact fight together in the event of war and by signaling this willingness to the adversary. As a result, the success or failure of an alliance depends on (1) the strength of the interests that brought the allies together, (2) the ability of the alliance to alter the members' preferences so that in the event of war, fighting is preferable to abandonment, (3) the effectiveness of the alliance in convincing the adversary of this fact, and (4) the ability of the partners to limit the risk of entrapment.

We can now use these concepts to analyze some of the major events of the last century through the lens of alliance politics. As noted in Chapter 1, the first and second halves of the twentieth century were markedly different in terms of warfare between the world's major powers. In both periods, international politics was shaped by conflicts among the large, industrialized countries in Europe. In both periods, states that felt threatened formed alliances in the hopes of protecting themselves from rivals. Yet the outcomes in these two periods were quite different. The first half of the century witnessed two world wars of unprecedented destructiveness; the second half was remarkable for the absence of war between the two superpowers, in spite of the intense hostility between them. What explains this variation? A complete answer is, of course, quite complicated. Nevertheless, the logic of alliances laid out in the previous sections gives us considerable insight.

Pre–World War I: Two Armed Camps

The story of European alliance formation preceding World War I is driven primarily by the rapid growth of Germany following that country's unification in 1871. Germany's dramatic industrial development and population growth in this period were accompanied by a corresponding increase in the country's international ambitions.

As Germany became more assertive in its foreign policy, it collected both friends and enemies. In 1879, Germany signed an alliance with neighboring Austria-Hungary, uniting the two central powers. In 1882, Italy joined the Austro-German pact to form the Triple Alliance. It would not take long, however, before Germany's newfound power and ambition would lead to the formation of a countercoalition against it. In the late 1880s, relations between Russia and Germany worsened, and Russia went looking for allies. The most likely partner was France, which was still smarting from its defeat at the hands of Germany in their war of 1871. The common fear of Germany led to the formation of the Franco-Russian alliance in 1894. Britain too became fearful of Germany, particularly when the latter began a massive ship-building effort designed to erode Britain's naval superiority. In a set of agreements in 1904 and 1907, Britain cleared up a number of outstanding disputes with France and Russia, paving the way for what became known as the Triple Entente. An entente, which comes from the French word for "understanding," is generally seen as a weak form of alliance, requiring consultation and coordination, not necessarily a strict commitment of military assistance.

Hence, by the first decade of the twentieth century, the major powers of Europe were divided into two armed camps: the Triple Alliance of Germany, Austria-Hungary, and Italy facing off against the Triple Entente of Britain, France, and Russia. Although the apparent symmetry between the two alliances might have created a stable balance, the system was in fact fraught with danger. The alliance network created the possibility that any small conflict could drag all the European powers into war. Of course, since European decision makers understood that a small spark could lead to all-out war, this system did foster some caution and mutual deterrence by raising the expected costs of war to each side. And indeed, several crises in the first decade of the twentieth century were all resolved peacefully, in spite of much saber rattling.

Nonetheless, the system had several features that made it unstable. First, as we saw in Chapter 3, the strategic situation created a number of preventive and preemptive incentives. Germany feared the rise of Russian power, causing some strategists to argue that war with Russia would be better now than later. In addition, Germany's need to plan for a two-front war against France to the west and Russia to the east gave rise to the Schlieffen Plan, with its precise timetables and preemptive logic. Second, the delicate balance made each of the major powers highly dependent on its allies for security; the prospect of losing an ally was seen as particularly dangerous. Hence, the threat to Austria-Hungary from Serbia—a threat that could have caused the empire to break up from within—was also felt keenly in Germany. Thus, Germany gave its ally a blank check in the July crisis, promising to back Austria-Hungary in whatever the latter chose to do. This commitment, however, emboldened Austria-Hungary, leading Austria-Hungary to issue a harsh ultimatum to Serbia.[15] The set of interconnected alliances and Austria-Hungary's unwillingness to back down turned an otherwise local crisis into a war that consumed most of Europe. This process, whereby the actions of a small number of states drag all their allies to war, has been referred to as "chain-ganging," evoking the image of convicts chained together, forced to move in the same direction.[16] Finally, the sheer number of states involved magnified the possibility of miscalculations. Whether or not an ally would actually fight in the event of war was a crucial question in determining how hard a state could push or how much it should give. Uncertainty about who would join a prospective war created considerable scope for errors.

---

15. Some historians argue that Germany issued the blank check precisely to incite Austrian-Hungarian stubbornness and thus provoke war. Among others, see Fritz Fischer, *Germany's Aims in the First World War* (New York: Norton, 1967).

16. Thomas Christensen and Jack Snyder, "Chain Gangs and Passed Bucks: Predicting Alliance Patterns in Multipolarity," *International Organization* 44 (Spring 1990): 137–68.

Probably the most important source of uncertainty in this event was how Great Britain would react in the event of war. Because it had the most powerful navy in the world—larger, in fact, than the next three largest navies combined—whether or not Britain would join a continental war was a crucially important question, and one over which there was a good deal of uncertainty until the very last minute. Although the Triple Entente committed Britain to consult with France and Russia in the event of war, the public and many policy makers in government were not keen to shed British blood over what appeared to be a distant matter. As a result, German decision makers believed for some time that Britain would stand aside while Germany took on France and Russia. Moreover, suggestions by British leaders that Britain would join its allies in war were discounted by German leaders as bluffs. It is unclear whether German leaders would have backed off from war had they been certain that Britain would intervene; it is clear, however, that Germany was encouraged by British wavering to take an aggressive position in the crisis. When Britain belatedly made clear that it would join in the fight, the military actions and diplomatic commitments already made by Germany and Austria were hard to reverse. Once war started, the network of the alliances brought all of Europe into war.[17]

The Interwar Period, 1919–1939 Germany was defeated in World War I, but the underlying problem of its growing power and ambition remained. Still recovering from the devastating war, the European powers "passed the buck" among themselves, hoping others would bear the costs of containing Germany, and failed to form a set of alliances to balance Germany until another war was already imminent.[18]

Until 1939, the alliance system that formed to contain Germany rested on a few thin reeds, which easily snapped under Hitler's pressure. By the Treaty of Locarno (1925), Britain pledged to defend Belgium and France in the event that either was attacked by Germany and to ensure that Germany respected the demilitarization of the Rhineland region, which bordered on those countries. France also signed alliances with several of Germany's neighbors to the east: Poland, Czechoslovakia, Yugoslavia, and Romania. The first of these treaties was tested, and failed, in 1936 when Hitler remilitarized the Rhineland and Britain refused to support France in taking any action to stop it.

The French guarantees to the eastern European countries were also suspect due to the geographic separation between them. The German invasion in World War I, which almost led to the fall of Paris, caused France to adopt a defensive posture in the interwar period, with most of the French forces positioned along a fortified line on the frontier. This meant that France was in a weak position to defend

---

17. In a final example of how the alliance system failed, Italy refused to join its allies, Germany and Austria, when war broke out. After sitting on the sidelines for several months, Italy decided that the Triple Entente powers were more likely to win. Hence, Italy decided to side with the Triple Entente and in May 1915 attacked its former ally, Austria-Hungary, with whom it had a long-standing territorial dispute.
18. Christensen and Snyder, "Chain Gangs and Passed Bucks."

its distant allies from the German threat. The weakness became all too clear in September 1938, when France and Britain acquiesced to German demands for a section of Czechoslovakia called the Sudetenland. Six months later, in March 1939, Germany invaded and conquered the rest of Czechoslovakia, and France did not lift a finger to save its ally. Not until Germany attacked Poland in September 1939 did France and Britain, which had pledged to defend Poland only days earlier, find the resolve to fulfill their commitments.

Hence, rather than being deterred by the states that sought to contain him, Hitler exploited weak alliances that were not backed up by sufficient resolve or capabilities, highlighting the lack of common interests and credible commitments among the allies. Bandwagoning alliances with Italy, the Soviet Union, and eventually Japan only strengthened his hand. The resulting imbalance between a bloc of revisionist powers and a fragmented group of buck-passing allies, combined with a leader ideologically bent on conquest, cast the world into war once more.

In August 1939, Britain formed a defensive alliance with Poland. One month later, Germany invaded Poland, Britain stepped in to defend its ally, and World War II began.

The Cold War: The "Long Peace" in Europe, 1945–1990

Whereas the first half of the twentieth century witnessed two world wars that grew out of European conflicts, the second half of that century was a period of relative peace in Europe. Indeed, the more than five decades that followed the end of World War II are sometimes referred to as the Long Peace, since there were no wars among the major European powers in this period. Of course, the period of relative peace was not due to an absence of conflicts, since most of this time coincided with the Cold War between the United States and the Soviet Union, a rivalry that once again led to the division of Europe into two opposing blocs. Although the Long Peace has a number of causes, some credit must go to the nature of the alliance system that formed in this period.[19]

Within 10 years after the end of World War II, most countries in Europe belonged to either the **North Atlantic Treaty Organization (NATO)** or the **Warsaw Pact** (see "What Shaped Our World?" on p. 204). NATO covered most of the states of Western Europe and bound them in a collective defense treaty with the United States. Its core provision was in Article 5 of the North Atlantic Treaty, which specified that each member would consider an attack against one or more members to be an attack against them all. The Warsaw Pact covered the states of Eastern Europe and the Soviet Union. Germany, which was split after the war into two

North Atlantic Treaty Organization (NATO)

An alliance formed in 1949 among the United States, Canada, and most of the states of Western Europe in response to the threat posed by the Soviet Union. The alliance requires the members to consider an attack on any one of them as an attack on all.

Warsaw Pact

A military alliance formed in 1955 to bring together the Soviet Union and its Cold War allies in Eastern Europe and elsewhere. It dissolved on March 31, 1991, as the Cold War ended.

---

19. John Lewis Gaddis, "The Long Peace: Elements of Stability in the Postwar International System," *International Security* 10 (Spring 1986): 99–142.

countries, was also split between the blocs: with West Germany in NATO and East Germany in the Warsaw Pact. Each bloc formed in response to a perceived threat from the other. NATO was established in 1949 in response to the Soviet military presence in Eastern Europe—a presence that the Soviets used to install puppet governments in those countries. The Warsaw Pact formed in 1955 after West Germany was admitted into NATO, raising the fear in Moscow that its enemy in the two world wars would again be rearmed and active on the European stage.

Although the experience of World War I would seem to suggest that two alliance blocs, roughly evenly divided, can be a cause of war, the Cold War alliance system had a number of features that made it different, and more stable, than what came before. First, the diplomatic landscape in 1914 was much more complicated, with several major powers in competition and highly dependent on their allies for security. During the Cold War, by contrast, the system was dominated by the two superpowers. This meant that there was less scope for miscalculation, as the outcome of any conflict was dependent on the choices of fewer key actors. It also meant that neither superpower would be as threatened by the loss of an ally as the states of Europe were before 1914. Germany at that time considered the possible loss of Austria-Hungary to be extremely threatening, worth risking war over. The United States and Soviet Union, by contrast, had less to fear from the possible defection of allies.[20] And indeed, France's departure from NATO's joint military command in 1966, Yugoslavia's defection from the Soviet orbit in 1948, and Romania's increasingly independent foreign policy starting in the 1960s did not upset the relatively stable equilibrium between the two sides.

A second major feature of the Cold War alliances was their highly institutionalized nature. Both were more than just pieces of paper promising mutual aid in the event of war. Rather, they included a dense set of military, political, and economic relationships. The United States, in particular, needed to demonstrate that it would uphold its commitment to defend its allies an ocean away, as any uncertainty about the U.S. commitment was seen as inviting Soviet aggression against Western Europe. As a result, the NATO alliance provided for close integration of the American and European militaries, a joint command led by an American officer, and the basing of over a quarter of a million U.S. troops on European soil, primarily in West Germany. This forward deployment of U.S. forces served both military and political purposes. It ensured that the United States had capabilities in place to slow a Soviet offensive until much larger reinforcements could come across the sea. It also served to signal the American commitment to the region. In the event of a Soviet attack, U.S. troops would have been quickly involved in the fighting, ensuring that the United States could not remain indifferent.

This political aspect of the American presence in Europe was most clearly evident in the Berlin Brigade, a garrison of about 7,000 troops in West Berlin. Like the rest of Germany, the capital city of Berlin had been divided into western and eastern portions after the war. The city sat in the midst of Communist East Germany,

---

20. Waltz, *Theory of International Politics*, 169–70.

however, so West Berlin was a small island of Western and American influence surrounded by a "red" sea. Given its geographic isolation, the American garrison would have been quickly overrun in the event of a war. Nonetheless, its presence was seen as a crucial signal of the U.S. commitment to defend Western Europe. The theorist Thomas Schelling described its role vividly:

> The garrison in Berlin is as fine a collection of soldiers as has ever been assembled, but excruciatingly small. What can 7,000 American troops do . . . ? Bluntly, they can die. They can die heroically, dramatically, and in a manner that guarantees that the action cannot stop there. They represent the pride, the honor, and the reputation of the United States government and its armed forces; and they can apparently hold the entire Red Army at bay.[21]

Hence, the military presence was a kind of hand-tying strategy (see Chapter 3): an effort to ensure that if the American commitment to NATO were triggered by a Soviet attack, the United States would have little choice but to fulfill that commitment. The strength of this pledge, clearly signaled to the Soviet Union, had a deterrent effect that contributed to the relative stability of Europe during the Cold War. ("What Shaped Our World?" on p. 204 explores NATO's role since the Cold War.)

As this historical overview suggests, alliances were used frequently in twentieth-century Europe by states looking for partners in defense or conquest. Measured in terms of whether allies fought together when war came, most (but not all) of these alliances were successful. Measured in terms of whether they were able to prevent war in the first place, the track record is more uneven. By far the most successful alliances on this score were the Cold War alliance blocs. Anchored by two strong powers, held together by common security interests, and institutionalized through a variety of military, political, and economic ties, NATO and the Warsaw Pact contributed to a period of relative peace in Europe after World War II. By contrast, the alliances in the first half of the twentieth century either abetted aggression—in the case of the Japanese, Italian, and Russian alliances with Hitler's Germany—or failed to contain it, contributing to the outbreak of two catastrophic wars. The inability of alliances to keep the peace would propel the search for a different kind of institution to serve this end: collective security organizations.

Collective Security: When Can the UN Keep the Peace?

As World War I was coming to a close, world leaders began to think about what the postwar world should look like. U.S. president Woodrow Wilson argued that the only way to prevent another such war was to change the nature of world politics.

---

21. Thomas Schelling, *Arms and Influence* (New Haven, CT: Yale University Press, 1966), 47.

NATO after the Cold War

When the Cold War ended in the late 1980s, many analysts thought that NATO's days were numbered. With the Soviet Union unable to maintain its control over Eastern Europe, the Communist regimes in that region fell, the Red Army retreated behind its borders, and the Warsaw Pact dissolved. When the Soviet Union disintegrated in December 1991, it seemed plausible that the NATO alliance would crumble as well.

NATO's obituaries turned out to be premature. The United States did reduce some of its troop presence in Europe, but 67,000 U.S. military personnel remain stationed there today. Rather than withering away, NATO expanded. Twelve additional states, all one-time Soviet allies or former republics within the Soviet Union, have joined (see map on right). The alliance also expanded its mission. From 1993 to 1995, NATO conducted air strikes in support of UN operations in Bosnia (see p. 222). In 1999, NATO went to war against Yugoslavia—not because Yugoslavia had attacked a NATO member but because that country was mistreating some of its own citizens: ethnic Albanians living in a province of Yugoslavia called Kosovo (see "Controversy" on p. 224). The alliance's reach extended even further after the September 11, 2001, terrorist attacks on the United States. The next day, the alliance invoked Article 5 of the North Atlantic Treaty, declaring that the entire alliance had been attacked. NATO subsequently played an important role in efforts to stabilize Afghanistan after the U.S. invasion in 2001. Most recently, in March 2011, NATO initiated a military campaign against Libya in response to that regime's violent crackdown against domestic opponents. How do we explain these developments?

Interests Those who expected NATO to be thrown onto the ash heap of history believed that the common interests and fears that originally brought the alliance into being had vanished and that without a clearly defined purpose it would eventually disappear.[a] Subsequent events suggest that its members still share interests in common. These include a basic concern for security but with an expanded conception of where the main threats lie: particularly, terrorism and the ability of terrorists to take root in chaotic, war-torn regions. Moreover, the Bosnia, Kosovo, and Libya operations showed that the alliance could act on a common commitment to stop massive violations of human rights. NATO members also had an interest in ensuring that former Soviet satellites in Eastern Europe developed stable, democratic, pro-Western regimes; many of those states, for their part, wanted the protection of NATO to guard against a resurgent Russia. Thus, membership in NATO was used as a "carrot" to bolster democratic reformers in those countries.

Institutions NATO's persistence also reminds us that institutions often adapt to changing environments rather than die. Observers draw an analogy to the March of Dimes. This charity was originally formed to combat polio, but when that disease was largely eradicated following the discovery of a vaccine, the organization quickly expanded its agenda to include a host of other childhood illnesses. In taking on new missions and "out of area operations"—that is, operations not confined to territory of the member states—NATO has been transformed from a purely defensive alliance into something more akin to a collective security organization.

Interactions The institution of NATO, along with the dominant or privileged status of the United States within the alliance, helped solve the collective action problem facing Europe and North America in providing the public good of common defense against the Soviet Union during the Cold War. Burden sharing was an essential principle of cooperation within the organization, but the United States—by far the largest member—was nonetheless willing to bear a disproportionate share of the costs of collective defense. If the interests of various European states and the United States diverge, however, bargaining over the costs of collective security will become more intense. The United States has global interests and has diverted many of its military assets to the Middle East and East Asia in its so-called pivot to guard against a rising China (see Chapter 14). It expects Europe to play a more central role in managing

---

a. For an example of this argument, see John J. Mearsheimer, "Back to the Future: Instability in Europe after the Cold War," *International Security* 15 (Summer 1990): 5–56.

conflicts on its borders to the East or across the Mediterranean. Some European allies, in turn, have resisted taking on these responsibilities and the attendant costs. Germany, for example, refused to take part in the NATO operation over Libya. At the same time, the expansion of NATO up to Russia's borders has contributed to renewed conflict. Russian military advances into Georgia (2008) and Ukraine (2014)—both countries that have at times courted NATO membership—created pressure on the alliance to cooperate in containing and sanctioning its former foe. Whether the institution and the common but fraying interests of its members will remain sufficiently robust to overcome the more intense bargaining, both within the alliance and with Russia, remains an open question.

NATO Expansion, 1949–2009

FOUNDING MEMBERS (1949)*

COLD WAR ERA ENLARGEMENT

UNIFICATION OF GERMANY (1990)

ENLARGEMENT 1ST ROUND (1999)

ENLARGEMENT 2ND ROUND (2004)

ENLARGEMENT 3RD ROUND (2009)

FORMER WARSAW PACT COUNTRIES

* NATO members also include the United States and Canada.

League of Nations

A collective security organization founded in 1919 after World War I. The League ended in 1946 and was replaced by the UN.

United Nations (UN)

A collective security organization founded in 1945 after World War II. With over 190 members, the UN includes all recognized states.

collective security organizations

Broad-based institutions that promote peace and security among their members. Examples include the League of Nations and the UN.

genocide

Intentional and systematic killing aimed at eliminating an identifiable group of people, such as an ethnic or religious group.

Wilson was convinced that the prewar pattern, in which major powers jockeyed for advantage against one another in shifting alliances, had to go. Alliances could not prevent wars; they could only cause wars to spread into larger, more destructive events. In their place, there should be a permanent institution that would enable countries to police the international system in the name of peace and security for all. From this vision, in 1919, the **League of Nations** was born; although it limped along until 1946, it effectively died in 1939 with the onset of World War II.

As World War II was coming to a close, world leaders once again turned their thoughts to the question of how to prevent another such war. Like his predecessor, U.S. president Franklin Roosevelt championed the idea of a permanent governing body that would enable the major powers to police the international system. The **United Nations (UN)** was created in 1945 as a successor to the League of Nations. The UN still functions to this day, but its track record in responding to acts of aggression is, at best, mixed. Why is this? Why have efforts to build an effective international organization capable of policing international politics failed to create a lasting peace?

The League of Nations and the UN are both examples of collective security organizations. Like alliances, **collective security organizations** are institutions that facilitate cooperation among their members. These two kinds of institutions, however, form in response to different kinds of interests. Alliances form when two or more states have a common interest in the outcome of bargaining with an adversary or a set of adversaries. They are based on alignments in interests that prompt states to cooperate against a common foe. Collective security organizations, by contrast, form under the presumption that all states have a common interest in preventing war and aggression, regardless of who the perpetrator and victim are. Unlike alliances, their primary purpose is not to alter bargaining outcomes in favor of one state or another but rather to ensure that changes to the status quo, if they occur, happen peacefully. They forbid the use of military force by one member state against another, and they generally provide mechanisms, such as mediators or arbitrators, to help member states resolve their disputes peacefully. An attack by one member against another is considered to be a threat to the whole community. As a result, the entire membership is responsible for coming to the aid of the victims of aggression. This collective response is intended to deter would-be aggressors in the first place and, in the event that deterrence fails, ensure that those who wrong the community by engaging in war will not benefit from the transgression.

Although collective security organizations were born out of the desire to prevent interstate wars, they have also sought to prevent violence within states. Indeed, the UN has been quite active in dealing with civil wars and maintaining peace in their aftermath. In recent years, there also has been pressure to expand its scope to deal with gross violations of human rights, such as cases of **genocide**, the systematic slaughter of an identifiable group of people. In fact, genocidal conflicts have led to the sharpest criticism of the UN in recent years: for inaction in such places as Rwanda, Bosnia and, more recently, Darfur (more on these cases below).

Unlike alliances, whose membership is restricted to a small number of states with common interests, the membership of collective security organizations is

After civil conflict broke out in the Central African Republic in 2013, the African Union (AU), a regional security organization, deployed soldiers to help contain the violence and protect civilians. In September 2014, that mission was replaced by a larger UN peacekeeping operation. Here, Gabonese soldiers from the AU force, in green berets, confer with newly arriving UN troops, in blue.

generally universal, or nearly universal. The UN, for example, includes all internationally recognized states. Universal membership reflects the presumption of a community with universally shared interests in international peace and security. There are also numerous regional security organizations—such as the Organization of American States, the African Union, and the Organization for Cooperation and Security in Europe—that include all or most of the states in each relevant region.

How Does Collective Security Work?

In theory, collective security works as follows. The mechanism is triggered when one state attacks or threatens to attack another. If it is determined that these events constitute an act of aggression—or, in the language of the UN, a "threat to international peace and security"—then all members of the organization are called on to act against the state that has committed the offending action. Depending on the circumstances, the prescribed action can range from economic sanctions to full-scale military intervention. This threat of intervention is primarily intended to deter actors from making aggressive demands against or attacking one another. A state that knows its actions will be opposed by the full weight of the international community should be reluctant to engage in aggression.

While intervention in interstate conflicts reflects the classic view of collective security, in practice the tool kit of collective security organizations has evolved and expanded in at least two important respects. First, largely due to the difficulties of mounting unified responses to international aggression (see "The Dilemmas of Collective Security" section on p. 209), the UN and regional collective security organizations have developed alternative strategies that are intended to foster peaceful

One way that UN forces promote peace is by interposing themselves between hostile factions, making it harder for fighting to resume. Here, UN peacekeepers patrol southern Lebanon to enforce peace between Israel and Lebanon following fighting over territory in southern Lebanon along the Israeli border.

humanitarian interventions

Interventions designed to relieve humanitarian crises stemming from civil conflicts or large-scale human rights abuses, including genocide.

conflict resolution without requiring costly interventions. These include providing mediators to help states identify mutually beneficial bargains and deploying peace-keeping forces—troops from neutral third parties—to help monitor and enforce peace agreements. Second, collective security organizations have in recent years extended their mandate to include stopping or preventing civil conflicts and large-scale human rights abuses. Civil wars and genocides have at times been labeled as "threats to international peace and security," giving rise to **humanitarian interventions**, or collective interventions designed to relieve humanitarian crises. Ironically, while peacekeeping and humanitarian intervention do not fit the original view of collective security, they are, in practice, the bulk of what collective security organizations now do.

The various strategies employed by collective security organizations can influence the bargaining interaction between adversaries in at least three ways, all of them intended to foster peaceful outcomes. First, as with alliances, the prospect of outside involvement makes war less attractive by changing the likely outcome of the interaction between states or, in the case of civil wars, between groups. At the extreme, the combined weight of the entire international community means that the defeat of the challenger is virtually certain. (Consider what Figure 5.2 would look like if State C were replaced with the entire international community.) The status quo is stable if both sides know that they will surely lose if they attempt to change the status quo by force. Under such conditions, neither side can shift the bargain in its favor by threatening war.

Second, outsiders can help resolve the commitment problems identified in Chapter 3 by promising to enforce what would otherwise be an unbelievable commitment by one state not to exploit its power against another. A shift in relative power between two states might be rendered less dangerous if the weakened state can count on others to defend it, thus diminishing any preventive incentive it might have. Likewise, a state may feel secure handing over a piece of strategic territory if it knows that others will come to its aid in the event that its adversary exploits this territory to attack or press further claims. In other words, the state that is made more powerful by the deal can more credibly commit not to exploit its newfound power if it knows that any attempt to do so will be countered by the international community. For example, as noted in Chapter 3, Israel and Syria have a conflict over the strategically valuable Golan Heights, which Israel seized from Syria in 1967. Since control of this territory imparts a military advantage to its owner, Israel has been reluctant to return the land to Syria without guarantees that it (Israel) will remain safe from attack. In 1974, however, the two states agreed to withdraw their forces from the Golan Heights, and the UN inserted over 1,000 peacekeeping troops into observation posts in the hills between the two sides' positions.[22] For four decades, those troops helped ensure that neither side would deploy forces to the area, thereby easing a source of tension in the region. Starting in 2014, the peace-keepers came under attack by militant groups engaged in the Syrian civil war (see Chapter 6), raising doubts on whether the mission could continue.

Third, collective security organizations may play a positive role in promoting peace not through a threat of direct intervention for or against any particular side but by serving as neutral observers and peacekeepers. Peacekeepers diminish first-strike advantages by interposing themselves between two adversarial factions, as in the Golan Heights. Such operations are particularly useful in cases in which previously warring parties have each pledged to disarm and demobilize, but each fears that if it disarms and the other does not, it will be at a dangerous disadvantage. As we will see in Chapter 6, the commitment problem associated with disarmament is a major obstacle to preventing and ending civil wars. The UN often deploys peacekeeping missions into precisely such situations in order to make sure that both sides uphold their promise to disarm and that neither side attempts to exploit the other in the process. For example, following the end of the civil war in Liberia, which claimed almost 150,000 lives from 1989 to 2003, the UN inserted 15,000 peacekeepers to facilitate disarmament and demobilization.

The Dilemmas of Collective Security

Regardless of where and how the organization chooses to intervene, it faces two major challenges: a collective action problem and a joint decision-making problem. The collective action problem arises from the fact that collective security organizations, unlike their members, do not have the power to tax or to raise and field military forces. As a result, the organizations are wholly dependent on their

---

22. For more information on the UN peacekeeping mission in the Golan Heights, see www.un.org/en/peacekeeping/missions/undof/ (accessed 03/02/15).

members to provide troops, funds, and military equipment for any operation. The member states that contribute then face the costs and risks associated with sending troops into combat or forgoing trade due to economic sanctions. Crucially, the international peace and stability that these actions are intended to provide is a public good. Recall from Chapter 2 that a public good can be enjoyed whether or not one actually contributed to its creation. If the community succeeds in preventing or reversing an act of aggression, all members of the community enjoy the benefit—whether or not they took costly action. After all, even if all states have an interest in seeing aggression halted, their first preference will often be to have the aggression halted by someone other than themselves. Hence, collective security organizations necessarily face a free-rider problem: the temptation that member states face to let the burden of providing the public good fall on others. Because of this problem, even if everyone shares an interest in cooperating to stop or prevent a war, their collective effort may fall well short of what is required to do so. Indeed, UN peacekeeping missions are often underfunded and undermanned relative to their mandates; the temptation to free ride, to pass the costs to other states, leads to low levels of cooperation.

The challenges of joint decision making are also severe. Members of the organization need to be able to determine which acts constitute a threat to the community, which states are aggressors, and what actions to take in response. This determination is not always straightforward since collective security organizations permit states to use force in self-defense. Of course, states generally justify their military actions as being in self-defense, so determining which acts are acts of aggression and which are self-defense is necessary for the organization to function. Otherwise, the entire system can collapse as each side accuses the other of being at fault. A finding that a particular act constitutes a threat to international peace and security not only delegitimizes that act as a violation of community interests, but it also grants legitimacy to those who use force to reverse it. As we will see, this grant of legitimacy can be an asset to states that operate under the organization's seal of approval.[23]

Determining whether a given act merits an international response is complicated by the mix of interests that member states have. Although they may share a general interest in halting aggression and promoting the peaceful settlement of disputes, they may also have specific interests that diverge in any particular conflict. Recall that collective security organizations, due to their universal membership, often include states with varying, even opposing, interests. Whereas NATO during the Cold War included only states that perceived a common threat from the Soviet Union, the UN during this period included not only the United States and its NATO allies but also the Soviet Union and its allies, as well as states that were neutral in the superpower rivalry. This mix of interests means that in many situations the members of a collective security organization may not all be neutral outsiders to a particular military action. Some may have reasons to favor one side or the other in

---

23. On the UN's legitimacy role, see Ian Hurd, *After Anarchy: Legitimacy and Power in the United Nations Security Council* (Princeton, NJ: Princeton University Press, 2007); and Alexander Thompson, *Channeling Power: The UN Security Council and American Statecraft in Iraq* (Ithaca, NY: Cornell University Press, 2009).

a dispute, meaning that some will be motivated to see aggression where others will not. Collective security works best when all states are satisfied with the current status quo, a condition that is rarely met.

Institutional Responses to the Challenges of Collective Security

The design of collective security organizations reflects the challenges posed by the dilemmas of collective action and joint decision making. Recall that institutions facilitate cooperation in situations that arise repeatedly. Rather than treating each new crisis in an ad hoc manner, requiring renegotiation of standards and rules each time, institutions embody a lasting set of standards and decision-making rules.

In the two most ambitious collective security organizations attempted in the last century—the League of Nations and the UN—the problems of collective action and joint decision making were addressed by vesting the main decision-making power in the hands of relatively small councils dominated by the strongest states in the system. These councils were given the authority to determine whether a particular action was a threat to international peace and security and to prescribe the organization's response. The League Council began with 4 permanent members—Great Britain, France, Italy, and Japan—and 4 nonpermanent members who were elected every three years.[24] Germany later joined as a fifth permanent member, and the council was expanded to 15. When the UN replaced the League in 1946, its **Security Council (UNSC)** had a similar structure—5 permanent members and 6 (later 10) nonpermanent members—although the identity of the **permanent five (P5)** changed: the United States, Great Britain, France, the Soviet Union (now Russia), and China. In both cases, the privileged few shared a common trait: with the exception of Germany, which was admitted to the League only belatedly, they were the victors of the global wars that gave birth to these organizations.

The voting rules of both councils amplified the influence of these permanent members. In the case of the League Council, all decisions had to be unanimously approved by all 15 members. As a result, any member of the council could block the organization from acting by withholding its support. In other words, every member of the council had **veto power**, and permanent members had permanent veto power. This voting rule was modified in the Security Council. Enacting a substantive resolution in the Security Council requires a "yes" vote from at least 9 of the 15 council members *and* the support of every one of the P5. This change was intended to make decisive action easier—by eliminating the requirement that all members agree—but it also magnified the asymmetrical role of the P5, each of which can block a resolution it does not like.

These arrangements have several virtues. First, vesting decision-making power with a relatively small group of states means that it is not necessary to obtain consensus within the entire membership (which, in the case of the UN, now numbers 193).

Security Council (UNSC)
The main governing body of the UN, which has the authority to identify threats to international peace and security and to prescribe the organization's response, including military and/or economic sanctions.

permanent five (P5)
The five permanent members of the UNSC: the United States, Great Britain, France, the Soviet Union (now Russia), and China.

veto power
The ability to prevent the passage of a measure through a unilateral act, such as a single negative vote.

---

24. Originally, the United States was intended to be the fifth permanent member, but the United States never joined the League because of congressional opposition.

Because of its institutional rules, the UN is unlikely to undertake missions that harm the interests of any of its most powerful members. For example, UN efforts to impose economic sanctions on the government of Sudan, in response to the genocide in the Darfur region, were blocked by China. As a big buyer of Sudanese oil, China has an interest in sparing Sudan from punishment.

This both reduces the costs of coming to an agreement and, in theory at least, makes it possible for the organization to respond to crises quickly. Second, these rules ensure that when the organization acts, it does so with the consent of the strongest powers in the international system. This arrangement can help address the collective action problem by ensuring that any operation that is approved will enjoy cooperation and contributions from those members with the greatest resources and capabilities. Moreover, the veto ensures that at a minimum, the organization's actions will not be forcibly opposed by any of these powerful members.

As with all institutions, however, the effects of these rules are not neutral; rather, they bias policy outcomes in a direction that favors the states that were in a position to dictate the rules at the outset. The organization cannot act on its core mission without unanimity among the most powerful states in the system, any one of which can block action by exercising its veto. Such unanimity can be difficult to achieve. When the major powers disagree among themselves, the permanent member veto introduces a bias toward inaction. The veto also ensures that the organization cannot act in ways that harm the interests of any of the permanent members. As a result, the organization wields its policing powers unevenly: it may respond to the crimes of those who are weak, or who have no friends among the permanent members, while the crimes of the strong, or those with friends in high places, may go unpunished. In the case of Tibet, mentioned at the outset of this chapter, any effective action by the UN against China could have been blocked by its ally, the Soviet Union.[25] More recently, Russia has blocked efforts to sanction the government of Syria, a longtime Russian ally, for indiscriminate killing of civilians during the civil war that has raged in that country since 2011.

In sum, collective security organizations help states cooperate to further their collective interests in international peace by providing rules and standards to address challenges that complicate collective action and joint decision making. Nonetheless, these institutions operate under constraints that limit their ability to act effectively. Collective security organizations are most likely to succeed when two conditions are met. First, the powerful member states that are central to their decision-making processes must all agree on the desirability of collective action. At a minimum, none of these states can be sufficiently opposed that it will block

---

25. Communist China was not, at that time, on the Security Council. Until 1971, China's seat on the council was held by Taiwan.

such action. Second, at least some members must value the collective good highly enough that they are willing to pay the costs in lives and money to ensure that the good is provided. This is most likely when the anticipated costs of intervention are low or when states have some private interest in contributing above and beyond the public interest in stopping aggression. In other words, collective security institutions are useful at promoting cooperation when their key members have strong common interests in protecting the peace; unfortunately, the existence of such common interests is not guaranteed.

The Experience of Collective Security: The United Nations

To see how these predictions have been borne out historically, we consider the experience of the most ambitious collective security organization ever created: the UN. This organization arose from the ashes of World War II with the aspiration, articulated in its founding charter, to "save succeeding generations from the scourge of war"—a goal that had become all the more pressing with the development of nuclear weapons, which had the capacity to kill millions in the blink of an eye. Although the world has not since seen a repetition of global warfare, or the nightmare of nuclear war, the role of the UN in preventing these outcomes is not clear. Indeed, the UN has had uneven success in fulfilling its creators' aspirations. In this section, we briefly review the experience of the UN. As we will see, the challenges facing collective security organizations discussed above play a large role in accounting for this organization's limited success historically.

☆ Goal of UN

What Does the UN Do?
When countries join the UN, they sign on to the organization's charter.[26] Members pledge not to use force in disputes with one another and to seek assistance from the organization in resolving their conflicts peacefully. Chapter VII of the UN Charter authorizes the Security Council to identify acts of aggression and threats to peace and to determine what measures should be taken in response. The charter first provides for economic and diplomatic sanctions to be applied against aggressor states, but it also authorizes the Security Council to "take such action by air, sea, or land forces as may be necessary to maintain or restore international peace and security."

In practice, the Security Council can authorize two different kinds of military operations: peace-enforcement and peacekeeping. A **peace-enforcement operation** is intended to impose a peace upon warring parties by intervening in an ongoing conflict, consistent with the traditional vision of collective security. The Security Council can authorize such an operation under Chapter VII of the charter, after finding that a particular situation is a threat to international peace and security. The invasion of one state by another is a classic example of the kind of act that was intended to trigger intervention under Chapter VII. In recent years, the Security Council has also authorized action under Chapter VII for purely civil conflicts

peace-enforcement operation
A military operation in which force is used to make and/or enforce peace among warring parties that have not agreed to end their fighting.

26. The entire UN Charter can be viewed at www.un.org/en/documents/charter/ (accessed 03/02/15).

when the state in question could not or did not request intervention. Because peace-enforcement operations are generally targeted against one or more sides that are viewed as aggressors, they are not impartial, and the expectation is that troops involved in such operations will engage in combat. Hence, peace-enforcement operations tend to be heavily armed, and one or more P5 members may be centrally involved in providing the necessary resources. The UN efforts in the Korean War and the Persian Gulf War both fall within this category, as does the 2011 NATO-led intervention in Libya, which received UN approval under Chapter VII.

A **peacekeeping operation**, by contrast, typically follows the conclusion of an interstate or civil war. The combatants have agreed to end the fighting, but it is considered valuable to have an impartial force in place to make sure that the war does not resume. In such instances, the UN may assemble a multinational peace-keeping force with the mandate to verify that the terms of the peace agreement are kept: that the cease-fire holds; that any temporary cease-fire lines are respected; that troops are withdrawn or demobilized, if there are provisions to that effect; and so on. In the aftermath of civil conflict, peacekeeping forces have also helped to administer elections and ensure their fairness. Their deployment typically requires that the parties to the conflict agree to invite them in, a requirement known as _host nation agreement_. Hence, except in rare cases, peacekeepers are not imposed on warring parties; rather, they deploy only with those parties' consent. Although peacekeepers may be physically interposed between the adversaries or may patrol in areas where fighting could recur, they are typically lightly armed. Their purpose is not to fight a war but to make sure that a war does not restart. For this reason, their main resource is not military power but rather their perceived impartiality—that is, they are neutral brokers, favoring neither side in the dispute. As a result, peacekeepers are often drawn from distant countries with only weak interests in the conflict, and rarely from the P5. To illustrate, Table 5.1 provides a list of the top 10 contributors to peacekeeping missions in January 2015, none of which is a perma-nent member; the ranking of the permanent members is also shown. Interestingly, peacekeeping operations are not explicitly envisioned by the UN Charter. The diffi-culties of organizing peace-enforcement operations during the Cold War led the UN to innovate this less costly and less controversial strategy for conflict management.[27]

Cold War Paralysis The UN was born with high hopes but soon found its most ambitious aspirations dashed by conflict among the powerful states in the system. The Cold War between the United States and the Soviet Union, which lasted from approximately 1946 to 1989, meant that the Security Council was largely incapable of dealing with issues that cut across this key divide. On many matters that came before the council, one side or the other had an interest in blocking effective action. For example, when the United States put forward proposals in 1947 to help Greece in its civil war against Communist rebels, the Soviet Union exercised its veto. The United States, for its part, wielded its veto quite frequently to stop resolutions that

---

27. When authorizing peacekeeping operations, the UN Security Council typically invokes Chapter VI of the charter, which provides for steps to peacefully resolve disputes that have the potential to threaten international peace and security.

TABLE 5.1 *Top Contributors to UN Peacekeeping Operations, January 2015*

RANK	COUNTRY	NUMBER OF PERSONNEL
1	Bangladesh	9,436
2	Pakistan	8,440
3	India	8,145
4	Ethiopia	7,845
5	Rwanda	5,638
6	Nepal	5,099
7	Senegal	3,024
8	Ghana	2,993
9	Nigeria	2,917
10	Egypt	2,628

Contributions from the P5

RANK	COUNTRY	NUMBER OF PERSONNEL
13	China	2,222
32	France	923
50	United Kingdom	289
66	United States	126
77	Russia	71

Source: UN, Department of Peacekeeping Operations, www.un.org/en/peacekeeping/contributors/2015/jan15_2.pdf (accessed 03/02/15).

it saw as harmful to Israel, such as those censuring Israel for its treatment of Palestinians in the occupied territories. France, Great Britain, and China also exercised their vetoes, though on significantly fewer occasions. All in all, during the period between 1946 and 1989, there were 192 vetoes cast on substantive issues before the council. This compares to 646 resolutions passed in the same period. The UN was most active in cases that did not cut across the Cold War divide, in which case one or both superpowers had little direct interest.

The major exception to this generalization, the UN-sponsored intervention in the Korean War, is the one that proves the rule. Two days after North Korea invaded South Korea, the Security Council passed Resolution 83 authorizing member states to assist South Korea in repelling the attack. While the United States provided the bulk of the forces for this operation, it was joined by 19 other states. Given that North Korea was an ally of the Soviet Union, the latter should have been expected to veto the Security Council resolution. This act would not have prevented American

TABLE 5.2 *The UN during and after the Cold War*

	COLD WAR (1946–1989)	POST–COLD WAR (1990–2014)
Security Council resolutions approved	646	1,549
Vetoed resolutions*	162	29
Peacekeeping missions	18	51

*Vetoed resolutions include vetoes of draft resolutions, and not vetoes of amendments to or subsections of resolutions.

Sources: For information on UNSC resolutions passed, see www.un.org/en/sc/documents/resolutions/ (accessed 03/02/15). For information on vetoes, see http://research.un.org/en/docs/sc/quick/veto (accessed 03/02/15). For information on peacekeeping operations, see www.un.org/en/peacekeeping/ operations/ (accessed 03/02/15).

intervention, but it would have denied the operation UN blessing and perhaps some multilateral support. The veto failed to materialize because the Soviet Union was boycotting meetings of the Security Council at the time owing to a dispute over China's representation on the body. When the UN was created, mainland China was ruled by a pro-American nationalist government. In 1949, however, Communist forces defeated the nationalists in a civil war, and the latter fled to the island of Taiwan. A year later, when the Korean War broke out, China's seat on the Security Council was held by a representative of the nationalist government on Taiwan. The Soviet Union argued that China's seat should be filled by a representative of the Communist government on the mainland, and it refused to attend meetings of the Security Council until that demand was met. Hence, when Resolution 83 came to a vote on June 27, 1950, the Soviet representative was not present to cast a veto. Needless to say, the Soviet Union ended its boycott of the Security Council not long afterward.[28]

The Cold War divide thus crippled the UN for the first five decades of its existence. Although the organization did have a constructive role at times—brokering ceasefires on several occasions and deploying 18 peacekeeping missions—the organization sat on the sidelines of many of the most dangerous conflicts of this period.

The Gulf War and the "New World Order" The end of the Cold War created new possibilities for the UN. In 1989, the central source of the East-West rivalry, Soviet domination of Eastern Europe, receded. And in December 1991, the Soviet Union itself dissolved and was replaced by 15 new independent states, the largest of which, Russia, inherited the Soviet Union's seat in the UN, along with most of its military capabilities. The dramatic realignment of interests and reduction in conflict among

---

28. China's seat on the Security Council remained in the hands of Taiwan until 1971, when warming relations between the United States and the People's Republic of China paved the way for the seat to be transferred to the mainland's control.

the P5 meant that the UN could take on a more active role. And indeed, 1990 marks a major turning point in the activity of the organization. As Table 5.2 shows, the post–Cold War period saw a marked drop in the number of vetoes cast and a corresponding increase in the number of peacekeeping missions and resolutions passed by the Security Council. Map 5.1 on page 218 shows where UN peacekeeping missions were deployed in 2014.

Optimism about the UN's role in the post–Cold War period hit a high point very early on, in the wake of Iraq's invasion of Kuwait in August 1990. As we have seen, U.S. president George H. W. Bush committed almost immediately to ensuring that the conquest of Kuwait would not stand. Bush also made a concerted effort to line up UN support at every step of the way. Between Iraq's invasion of Kuwait and the U.S.-led military operation to reverse it, the Security Council passed 12 resolutions on the crisis. The most important of these, Resolution 678, authorized member states to use "all necessary means" to bring about the unconditional withdrawal of Iraqi forces from Kuwait if Iraq did not comply voluntarily by January 15, 1991. The Security Council's approval of this resolution owed a great deal to the reduction of conflict in the international system with the end of the Cold War. The Soviet Union had long been an ally of Iraq, and in an earlier period it might have been expected to veto a resolution like 678. In the post–Cold War environment, however, when the Soviet Union desired better relations with the West, it was relatively easy to overcome that country's reluctance to approve the use of force against its former ally.

The blessing of the UN meant that the United States had substantial international assistance in the ensuing war. The coalition that fought Iraq included troops from 35 nations. As shown in Figure 5.3, the United States supplied the vast majority of the troops for the operation, but the multinational cast and UN blessing had political, if not much military, significance. The participation of a number

---

FIGURE 5.3 *Allied Troop Contributions to the Persian Gulf War, 1990–91*

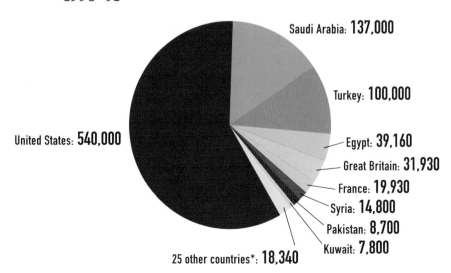

Saudi Arabia: **137,000**

Turkey: **100,000**

United States: **540,000**

Egypt: **39,160**

Great Britain: **31,930**

France: **19,930**

Syria: **14,800**

Pakistan: **8,700**

Kuwait: **7,800**

25 other countries*: **18,340**

Figure source: U.S. General Accounting Office, *Persian Gulf: Allied Burden Sharing Efforts,* GAO/NSIAD-92-71, Appendix II, 16-7, www.gao.gov/products/NSIAD-92-71 (accessed 10/20/08).

*Bangladesh, Morocco, Qatar, United Arab Emirates, Canada, Italy, Australia, Netherlands, Oman, Spain, Bahrain, Germany, Belgium, Senegal, Niger, Argentina, Philippines, Greece, Poland, South Korea, Czechoslovakia, Denmark, Norway, New Zealand, Hungary.

MAP 5.1 *UN Peacekeeping Operations Active in 2014*

UNFICYP
United Nations Peacekeeping Force in Cyprus (Est. 1964)
UNFICYP was established to prevent the reoccurrence of violence between the Greek Cypriot and Turkish Cypriot communities on the island of Cyprus. The mission currently maintains a buffer zone, supervises the ceasefire, and undertakes humanitarian activities.

MINURSO
United Nations Mission for the Referendum in Western Sahara (Est. 1991)
Created to safeguard a transitional period to prepare a referendum through which the people of Western Sahara could choose between independence and integration with Morocco, MINURSO continues to monitor the ceasefire, reduce the threat of mines and unexploded ammunition, and facilitate communication between Saharans in Western Sahara and in Algerian refugee camps.

UNMIK
United Nations Interim Administration Mission in Kosovo (Est. 1999)
UNMIK supports self-governance in Kosovo in the wake of the conflict between Kosovar ethnic Albanians and the Serbian government, which claims the Kosovo Province.

MINUSTAH
United Nations Stabilization Mission in Haiti (Est. 2004)
The latest mission in the UN's prolonged involvement in Haiti, MINUSTAH supports Haiti's transitional government in governing and fostering democracy in Haiti and monitors human rights.

UNMIL
United Nations Mission in Liberia (Est. 2003)
UNMIL supports the transition to democratic rule in Liberia following its civil war. It provides security, assists in reforming the military and police, and supports human rights activities.

MINUSMA
United Nations Multidimensional Integrated Stabilization Mission in Mali (Est. 2013)
MINUSMA assists in providing security and supporting political reconciliation in Mali, where civil unrest led to advances by Al Qaeda–affiliated militants.

UNOCI
United Nations Operation in Côte d'Ivoire (Est. 2004)
UNOCI monitors the cessation of hostilities between government and rebel forces in Côte d'Ivoire, supervising the disbanding of militias, resettlement of displaced persons, and the establishment of democratic governance, and supporting human rights and humanitarian aid.

MINUSCA
United Nations Multidimensional Integrated Stabilization Mission in the Central African Republic (Est. 2014)
MINUSCA protects civilians, facilitates humanitarian assistance, and promotes human rights in response to conflict in the Central African Republic.

Atlantic Ocean

Pacific Ocean

HAITI

UNIFIL
United Nations Interim Force in Lebanon (Est. 1978)
Initially established to monitor the withdrawal of Israeli forces from Lebanon, UNIFIL now oversees the ceasefire, supports the deployment of Lebanese forces into Southern Lebanon, and supports humanitarian services and the return of refugees and displaced persons to Lebanon.

UNDOF
United Nations Disengagement Observer Force (Est. 1974)
UNDOF supervised the withdrawal of Israeli and Syrian forces from the Golan Heights and maintains a ceasefire between them.

UNTSO
United Nations Truce Supervision Organization (Est. 1948)
The UN's first peacekeeping mission, UNTSO supervised the ceasefire between Israel and its Arab neighbors following their 1948 war.

UNAMA
United Nations Assistance Mission in Afghanistan (Est. 2002)
UNAMA is a political mission established by the Security Council in 2002 at the request of the government to assist it and the people of Afghanistan in laying the foundations for sustainable peace and development in the country.

UNMOGIP
United Nations Military Observer Group in India and Pakistan (Est. 1949)
UNMOGIP maintains the ceasefire between India and Pakistan in their dispute over Kashmir.

UNAMID
African Union/United Nations Hybrid Operation in Darfur (Est. 2007)
With ongoing strife in Darfur between the Government of Sudan and rebel militias, UNAMID protects civilians, facilitates the provision of humanitarian aid, and supports implementation of a peace agreement.

UNISFA
United Nations Interim Security Force for Abyei (Est. 2011)
UNISFA exists to oversee demilitarization and monitor peace in the disputed Abyei area of Sudan. The operation will monitor the flashpoint border between north and south, and is authorized to use force in protecting civilians and humanitarian workers in Abyei.

UNMISS
United Nations Mission in the Republic of South Sudan (Est. 2011)
In 2011, South Sudan became the newest country in the world. UNMISS is on the ground to consolidate peace and security and to help establish conditions for development.

MONUSCO
United Nations Organization Stabilization Mission in the Democratic Republic of the Congo (Est. 2010)
MONUSCO took over from an earlier mission (MONUC) to focus on the protection of civilians, humanitarian personnel, and human rights defenders under imminent threat of physical violence and to support the government of the DRC in its stabilization and peace consolidation efforts.

WESTERN SAHARA (MOR.)

SERBIA

CYPRUS

LEBANON

SYRIA

ISRAEL

AFGHANISTAN

PAKISTAN

EGYPT

MALI

CEN. AFR. REP.

SUDAN

S. SUDAN

D. R. CONGO

LIBERIA

IVORY COAST

Indian Ocean

Map source: UN, Map No. 4259 Rev. 21 (E) November 2014.

of Arab and Muslim states was seen as important in blunting Iraq's argument that the United States was waging a war against Islam. The limited mandate of the operation—to liberate Kuwait and not to occupy Iraq—was intended to reassure states in the region that the United States did not have expansionist objectives. International support also reduced the financial costs of the war. Contributions from other countries covered about 90 percent of the $61 billion the United States spent fighting the war—making the Persian Gulf War the least expensive war in America's history on a per capita basis.

The successful operation of the UN machinery in this case led to great optimism about the role this organization could play in the new international environment. Bush, in his State of the Union address just before the war, spoke of the opportunity to create "a new world order, a world where the rule of law, not the law of the jungle, governs the conduct of nations"—a world in which "a credible United Nations can use its peacekeeping role to fulfill the promise and vision of the UN's founders." Indeed, the UN had seemed to meet the first challenge of this new era quite successfully.

The optimism would turn out to be overblown. The Iraqi invasion of Kuwait was in many respects an easy case for effective international action. By invading a weak neighbor, Iraq had committed a flagrant violation of international law. More important, the attack was seen as directly threatening the interests of the United States and its allies. After gobbling up Kuwait, Iraq was in possession of 20 percent of the world's known oil reserves. Furthermore, the attack put Iraq in a position to threaten Saudi Arabia, home to another 25 percent of the world's oil. All told, the Persian Gulf region contained two-thirds of this valuable natural resource. The possibility that so much of the world's oil could come under the control of a hostile power was seen as threatening to vital American interests. As a result, the United States was strongly motivated to take forceful action to reverse the Iraqi invasion. In all likelihood, it would have done so even if it had been unable to secure UN approval.

Hence, the success of the UN in this case owed a great deal to the fact that the United States, the most powerful actor in the international system, perceived a direct threat to its own interests. The international community was, in this instance, what we called in Chapter 2 a privileged group, since a single member was strongly motivated enough to provide the public good. The next several years would provide ample evidence that when such incentives are lacking, the community's collective interests in stopping aggression and/or ending gross violations of human rights are generally not enough to compel effective international intervention.

The "Triumph of the Lack of Will": Bosnia, Rwanda, and Darfur The hard tests of the new world order came only a few years after the victory in the Persian Gulf. The 1990s witnessed a number of bloody and heart-rending crises that transfixed the international community but also exposed the limits of that community's willingness to do much about them.[29]

---

29. We take our heading for this section from the title phrase of an insightful analysis of this period; see James Gow, *Triumph of the Lack of Will: International Diplomacy and the Yugoslav War* (New York: Columbia University Press, 1997).

One visible example of the limited will of the international community played out in the former Yugoslav republic of Bosnia-Herzegovina. The civil conflict in Bosnia was the bloodiest of several violent acts in the breakup of Yugoslavia. Originally composed of five republics—Serbia, Slovenia, Croatia, Bosnia-Herzegovina, and Macedonia—the Yugoslav federation began to dissolve in 1991 as Slovenia, Croatia, and Bosnia sought independence, and Serbia, the largest republic, tried to hold the multiethnic state together by force. The conflict in Bosnia was the most complicated and bloody because this republic was home to three ethnic groups: Serbs (comprising 31 percent of the prewar population), Croats (25 percent), and Bosnian Muslims (44 percent) (see Map 5.2). Many Serbs did not want to live in an independent Bosnia; rather, they wanted to carve out portions of that republic and join with Serbia. The more

Map source: University of Texas at Austin, www.lib.utexas.edu /maps/europe/balkans.jpg (accessed 06/02/15).

MAP 5.2   *Ethnic Divisions in the Former Yugoslavia, 1992*

Groups Comprising 50 Percent or More of the Population of a Given Area

ALBANIANS   CROATS   MACEDONIANS   MUSLIMS   SLOVENES   NO MAJORITY PRESENT

BULGARIANS   HUNGARIANS   MONTENEGRINS   SERBS   TURKS radical Croats had similar thoughts of joining Croatia. When Bosnia declared its independence from Yugoslavia in March 1992, militant Serbs and Croats rebelled, triggering a three-way war.

The ensuring conflict, which lasted three years, was incredibly brutal, with 300,000 killed, mostly civilians, and at least 2 million refugees displaced from their homes. In addition, the combatants engaged in widespread atrocities against civilians: shelling cities, herding men and boys into detention camps where they were malnourished and mistreated, raping women and girls in order to terrorize the population. While crimes were committed by all sides, the greatest offenders were the Serbs, who engaged in a systematic campaign of what became known as "ethnic cleansing": clearing coveted territory of all non-Serbs by either killing them or scaring them into flight.

The international response to these events was feeble and at times counterproductive. Although there was unanimous condemnation of the violence, no one was willing to exert on behalf of Bosnia the kind of effort that had been marshaled to save Kuwait only one year earlier. Without compelling interests, such as securing an important natural resource (such as oil), the UN, at the behest of the United States and European powers, responded in a halfhearted way. A peacekeeping force, comprising mostly European troops, was deployed to the area—despite the fact that there was no peace to keep. Imposed into the war zone under Chapter VII, the UN Protection Force (UNPROFOR) nonetheless had many of the qualities of a traditional peacekeeping force: it was lightly armed, dispersed throughout the country, required to be neutral, and ordered to fire only in self-defense. Its main mission was to distribute food and medicine to civilians and to help keep them out of harm's way. Hence, UNPROFOR sought to treat the symptoms of the war, but it had neither a mandate nor the requisite capabilities to end the war. On several occasions Serb forces took peacekeepers hostage and chained them to artillery pieces in order to deter air strikes against their positions. The UN also declared several Bosnian cities to be "safe havens" where civilians could find safety from the war under its protection. The hollowness of this promise became evident in the worst atrocity of the war. In July 1995, Serb forces overran the safe haven of Srebrenica and proceeded to massacre 8,000 Muslim men and boys. The 600 Dutch peacekeepers charged with defending the city could do little to resist. When Serb forces threatened to kill some Dutch hostages, the Dutch government and the UN commanders on the ground decided to negotiate their troops' surrender.[30]

The massacre at Srebrenica did finally spark tougher international intervention. In August–September 1995, the United States and NATO conducted sustained air strikes against Serb forces. These attacks helped bring about a peace conference in Dayton, Ohio, that led to the Bosnian war's end in December 1995. With a peace to keep, U.S. and NATO forces were deployed as peacekeepers, with the blessing of the UN and alongside international police forces organized by the UN. In a pattern

---

30. Samantha Power, "A Problem from Hell": America and the Age of Genocide (New York: Perennial, 2002), 399–400.

repeated elsewhere (see "The Quiet Successes" section below), the UN mechanism had more success in maintaining a peace already achieved than in ending aggression and gross violations of human rights.

A similar lack of will by the international community was apparent in Rwanda in 1994 and in the ongoing conflict in the Darfur region of Sudan. In Rwanda, conflict between the county's principal ethnic groups, the Hutu and the Tutsi, erupted in genocide in April 1994. In the course of three months, an estimated 800,000 people were killed—many hacked to death by machetes—including 75 percent of the Tutsi population. The international response to this tragedy was very weak. A small UN peacekeeping force already on the ground was overwhelmed. After 10 of its peacekeepers were killed on the first day of the conflict, Belgium withdrew its forces, and other nations followed suit. As the death toll rose, the international community stood by and watched. The killing stopped only after a Tutsi rebel force succeeded in defeating the Hutu forces responsible for much of the slaughter.

In the case of Rwanda, the UN and the international community did little to stop ongoing fighting between Hutus and Tutsis, even when it became clear that civilians were being massacred. Here, Tutsi victims of a Hutu raid on a refugee camp in nearby Burundi are buried in a mass grave.

The case of Darfur is equally tragic. Since 2003, a bloody conflict has raged in western Sudan, where government-supported militias have carried out systematic killings of the people there. In another widely acknowledged genocide, it is estimated that 200,000 to 400,000 people have died, and another 2.8 million have been displaced from their homes. In spite of widespread outrage, the response of the UN has been weak. Member states have been unwilling to support or contribute troops to a robust military operation to end the violence.

This discussion is not meant to imply that the UN mechanism never works. Rather, it suggests that absent compelling national interests, member states are reluctant to pay heavy costs or embrace high risks to further the community's interest in stopping aggression or ending humanitarian crises. In all these cases, the member states cared about the suffering, but they did not care enough to undertake the kind of military operation that would have been needed to end the conflicts that were the cause of the suffering. "Controversy" on page 224 discusses the NATO-led interventions in Kosovo (1999) and Libya (2011) and the challenges that international organizations face when it comes to such interventions.

The Quiet Successes In other cases, however, the costs of intervention are seen as relatively low, and the UN's track record has been more impressive. These cases generally fall under the category of traditional peacekeeping: monitoring and assisting in the implementation of peace agreements. Because the existence of a

Should the International Community Intervene Militarily in Civil Conflicts?

In 2011, Libyans revolted against the dictatorial rule of leader Mu'ammar Qaddafi. A month in, however, Qaddafi's forces were advancing steadily, reclaiming control as they moved east along the coast. The prospect of a bloodbath in Benghazi, Libya's second-largest city with a population of over 650,000, spurred the international community to action. That very day, the UNSC passed a resolution authorizing member states to "take all necessary measures" to protect civilians in Libya. This resolution paved the way for NATO to begin air operations and a naval blockade against Qaddafi's forces. Aided by NATO's bombs and missiles, the rebels beat back the loyalists at Benghazi and then moved on the Libyan capital of Tripoli. Qaddafi was captured and killed two months later.

The Libya operation was the second major humanitarian military intervention undertaken by NATO. Twelve years earlier, in March 1999, Western warplanes had similarly gone into action, this time to end the brutal suppression of civilians in the Serbian province of Kosovo. Nine years of punitive measures by Serbian leader Slobodan Milošević against Kosovo's Albanian majority—including acts of murder, rape, and expulsion—led to international intervention to end a brewing genocide. A three-month

NATO air campaign ultimately resulted in the expulsion of Serb forces from Kosovo, the establishment of an interim administration under the UN, and the return of hundreds of thousands of refugees. Kosovo has since declared its independence, an act recognized by most members of NATO.

While both the Libya and Kosovo operations had successful outcomes, the decision to intervene in these cases was and remains controversial. Should the international community intervene with military force in civil conflicts?

The main argument in favor of military action rests on the urgent moral imperative to protect the interests of unarmed civilians facing death at the hands of their government. When a state has failed in its basic obligation to protect its citizens from massacre, genocide, and other crimes against humanity, it has been argued that other states have a responsibility to intervene, by force if necessary (for more on the emergence of the "responsibility to protect" norm, see Chapter 11). In the case of Libya, the looming attack on Benghazi likely reminded Western decision makers of their countries' failure to act under similar circumstances in June 1995, when Serb forces were allowed to overrun the city of Srebrenica in western Bosnia and massacred 8,000 men and boys. If given the chance to prevent another such atrocity, why not act? A policy of intervention can not only save lives that are at immediate risk, but it may also deter governments from committing atrocities in the first place, by threatening to trigger an international response.

Although this is a compelling argument, opponents of humanitarian intervention have raised a number of concerns over the interests at stake, the appropriateness of the strategy pursued, and the proper institutional processes for deciding when to intervene. One such argument is that because the international community cannot

Benghazi, Libya

possibly protect everyone everywhere in the world, the application of this policy is bound to be inconsistent and driven by interests other than humanitarianism. At the same time that NATO's bombs were falling in Libya, the alliance steered clear of intervention in the Ivory Coast, where violence following a tainted election killed thousands and displaced a million people, and in the Democratic Republic of the Congo, where conflict has, since 1998, claimed more lives than the entire population of Kosovo. Skeptics conclude that humanitarian interests alone do not explain why some conflicts attract intervention and others do not. The fact that Qaddafi was a hostile and unpredictable leader with enormous oil wealth suggests that other interests played a role in the decision to support the rebellion. In Syria, where a bloody civil war has claimed thousands of lives, the United States and regional allies only got involved once a militant group known as the Islamic State started to threaten U.S. interests in neighboring Iraq.

Humanitarian intervention also threatens the interests that states have in exercising sovereign control over internal matters. Milošević claimed that Albanians were engaged in a terrorist campaign that sought to dismember the country; Qaddafi argued that he had the right to put down a violent uprising against his rule. Although the atrocities committed against civilians are unacceptable, states have a legitimate interest in maintaining order domestically and preserving their territorial integrity. While the NATO operations in both Kosovo and Libya served a moral purpose, there is no guarantee that foreign states will not abuse the principle of intervention to pursue less noble interests. For example, Russia has cited the precedent of Kosovo in lending "humanitarian" support—in reality, tanks, guns, artillery, and manpower—to separatists in eastern Ukraine.

Another concern about these operations arises from the strategic disadvantages of military force as a means of promoting humanitarian interests. War is a blunt and costly instrument for achieving policy change. Outside governments worried about casualties to their own forces may not intervene in an effective manner. Both the Kosovo and Libya campaigns were conducted entirely from the air, relying on bombs and cruise missiles. Fighting on the ground was left to the rebels. While this strategy was effective at preventing NATO casualties, it also had drawbacks. In addition to the inevitable civilian casualties caused by errant bombs, the absence of international ground forces limited NATO's ability to influence events. Milošević initially responded to the air campaign by escalating his campaign against the Kosovars; the rebels in Libya were accused of committing atrocities against Qaddafi loyalists, including civilians. Even if an intervention succeeds in easing a crisis, an enduring solution requires a long-term commitment by outside actors that may not be credible. When the foreigners go home, conflict may recur. Tensions between Albanians and Serbs in Kosovo continue to bubble, and Libya has fallen back into chaos as different factions vie to rule that country.

Finally, humanitarian intervention raises the institutional question of who should decide when the international community can get involved. The UN is the natural venue for such a determination. Even so, for the Security Council to authorize intervention in purely domestic conflicts requires an expansive interpretation of what constitutes a "threat to international peace and security." Two members of the Security Council, China and Russia, have been loath to endorse humanitarian intervention, in part because their own human rights records are spotty. Due to the threat of their veto, the Security Council never authorized the Kosovo operation. In the case of Libya, the Security Council (with China and Russia abstaining) approved an operation to protect civilians but did not endorse the goal of ousting Qaddafi. When it became clear that the NATO action would continue as long as Qaddafi was in power, Russia objected that the operation had exceeded its mandate. Supporters of humanitarian intervention argued that NATO, as an alliance of democracies, is well qualified to act in support of human rights. But as a matter of international law the alliance does not have the authority to undertake such an operation on its own. Thus, while it is admirable that the international community has taken steps to protect people in harm's way, it still grapples with the question of how to perform this responsibility well.

peace agreement indicates that the opposing parties are ready to stop fighting and resolve their differences, the risks associated with getting involved are not that high. Keeping peace after a war is generally easier than making peace during a war.

For this reason, UN efforts have been most successful in the area of post-conflict reconstruction.[31] In the case of El Salvador, for example, a UN peacekeeping operation played an important role in that country's recovery from a 12-year civil war that had claimed 75,000 lives. The UN Observer Mission in El Salvador (ONUSAL) comprised about 700 military observers and civilian police from 17 countries, but it had an expansive mandate to help rebuild the country. ONUSAL not only helped to monitor the demobilization of the warring factions after a 1992 peace agreement, but it also assisted in implementing political reforms designed to address the root causes of the conflict, such as reforming the judiciary, forming and training a new civilian police force, and redistributing land to former combatants. ONUSAL also monitored an election in 1994 to ensure that it was free and fair and that all sides would respect the result. The mission's mandate ended in April 1995, leaving in its wake a country that is generally considered free and democratic. Similar stories of success in post-conflict reconstruction can be found in Mozambique, Liberia, Sierra Leone, East Timor, Cambodia, and even Bosnia, where a NATO-led peacekeeping force with a UN blessing went in after the 1995 peace deal and was deemed to have fulfilled its mission and departed in December 2004.[32]

People following the news likely heard much more about the UN's failings in Bosnia, Rwanda, and Darfur than about the quieter victories in places like El Salvador and Bosnia after 1995. Bloodshed naturally draws more attention than do peace and reconciliation, so the failures of the UN get more publicity than do its successes. (See "How Do We Know?" on p. 227 for more evidence on the success of peacekeeping operations.)

From 9/11 to Iraq and After: Consensus Lost During the 1990s, civil conflicts such as the ones in Bosnia and Rwanda were much more prominent on the UN agenda than were cases of international aggression like the Persian Gulf War. As we have seen, the main impediment to effective action in these cases was a lack of will—the absence of compelling national interests that could have justified committing resources and taking risks. The September 11, 2001, terrorist attacks against the United States changed this focus, exposing a threat that many UN member states, including all of the P5, had reason to fear. The unanimous condemnation of the terrorist attacks and international support for the United States' war in Afghanistan suggested that once again the UN mechanism could work effectively in the new international environment.

This optimism would prove short-lived, however. Slightly over a year after the 9/11 attacks, the U.S. effort to mount a war against Iraq divided the Security Council and left the organization alienated from its most powerful member. Although all members were on record demanding that Iraq fully account for its past weapons

---

31. See Michael W. Doyle and Nicholas Sambanis, *Making War and Building Peace: United Nations Peace Operations* (Princeton, NJ: Princeton University Press, 2006).

32. The United Nations force was replaced by a European Union force (EUFOR Althea, named after the Greek goddess of healing).

Does Peacekeeping Keep the Peace?

FIGURE A   *Total Size of UN Peacekeeping Forces, 1946–2015*

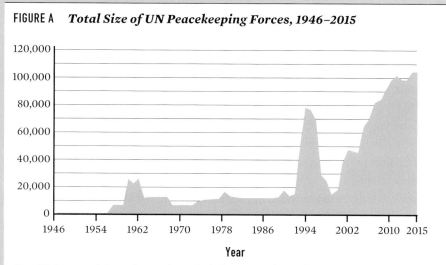

Year

Note: Highest month for each year. Figures include troops, military observers, and police.

Sources: Global Policy Forum, "Size of UN Peacekeeping Forces, 1947–2009," www.globalpolicy.org/component/content/article/102-tables-and-charts/40734-size-of-un-peacekeeping-forces-1947-2009.html (accessed 03/02/15). Updated through January 2015 using data from www.un.org/en/peacekeeping/documents/Yearly.pdf (accessed 03/02/15).

Since its creation in 1946, the UN has undertaken 69 peacekeeping missions in the wake of interstate and civil conflicts. About 3,300 peacekeepers have died in the course of these operations, whose total cost has been about $100 billion. At the time of this writing, over 104,000 uniformed personnel from 128 countries were deployed in 16 ongoing operations around the globe.[a] Given this expenditure of time, blood, and treasure, it is reasonable to ask: Do peacekeeping operations actually work?

A series of studies by Virginia Page Fortna represent a systematic attempt to answer this question.[b] Fortna collected information on cease-fires in interstate and civil

wars since 1946. There is a good deal of variation in how long cease-fires last. Some break down almost immediately, others last for years, and still others form the basis for a permanent peace between the adversaries. To determine whether peacekeepers can affect how long a cease-fire will last, Fortna recorded, for each case, whether or not a peacekeeping force was sent in to monitor and/or enforce the agreement. She also collected information about the severity, duration, and outcome of the war, the issue it was fought over, and features of the combatants—all factors that might affect the durability of a cease-fire.

When these factors are taken into account, the presence of a peacekeeping operation has a substantial effect on the likelihood that a cease-fire will endure. Looking at the 48 cease-fires in interstate wars that ended between 1946 and 1998, Fortna found that the presence of peacekeepers reduced by 85 percent the probability that a cease-fire would break down in any given year.[c] In the case of civil wars, Fortna's analysis focuses on the period from 1989 to 1999, which witnessed an explosion in the number of peacekeepers sent into civil conflicts (Figure A). An analysis of 94 cease-fires in 60 civil wars during this period shows that the presence of peacekeepers reduced the risk of renewed fighting in any given year by around 60 percent.[d] Considering the enormous human and economic costs associated with warfare, peacekeeping operations appear to be well worth their price.

a. Data are from www.un.org/en/peacekeeping/resources/statistics/factsheet.shtml (accessed 03/02/15).

b. See Virginia Page Fortna, *Peace Time: Cease-Fire Agreements and the Durability of Peace* (Princeton, NJ: Princeton University Press, 2004); Virginia Page Fortna, "Interstate Peacekeeping: Causal Mechanisms and Empirical Effects," *World Politics* 56 (July 2004): 481–519; Virginia Page Fortna, *Does Peacekeeping Work? Shaping Belligerents' Choices after Civil War* (Princeton, NJ: Princeton University Press, 2008).

c. Fortna, "Interstate Peacekeeping," 500.

d. Fortna, *Does Peacekeeping Work?* 105.

programs, they parted ways on the desirability of using military force to enforce this demand. For a variety of reasons, a majority of the Security Council members, including France, Russia, and China, refused to back a proposed resolution in January 2003 authorizing the use of force against Iraq. France has a large Muslim population and was worried about the domestic effects of a war on Islamic militancy. France and Russia also had long-standing economic ties to Saddam Hussein's regime and may have been concerned about jeopardizing those relations. Moreover, many members of the council were reluctant to endorse the U.S. doctrine of preventive war (defined in Chapter 3)—which they saw as contrary to the UN Charter's rules on the use of force—or its argument that Iraq posed an imminent threat. Although the U.S.-sponsored resolution never came to an official vote, it looked likely that 11 of the 15 Security Council members, including three of the P5, would have voted against it. Anticipating this defeat, the United States withdrew the draft resolution. Claiming authorization under prior UN resolutions and Article 51 of the UN Charter permitting self-defense, the United States went ahead with the invasion without explicit UN support.

More recently, rising tensions between Russia and the West have been a renewed source of conflict in the Security Council. As noted earlier, Russia has wielded its veto to prevent the UN from imposing economic or military sanctions on Syria, a longtime ally, over the mass killing of civilians and the use of chemical weapons in its bloody civil war. And, in spring of 2014, when Russia tanks and troops moved into Ukraine, the Security Council debated the matter, but there was no chance of that institution acting against one of its permanent members. If the conflict over Ukraine hearkens the onset of a new east-west rivalry, then the UN could once again find itself unable to act on key matters of international security.

As this overview suggests, the UN faces two essential requirements if it is to work as intended. First, none of the veto-wielding members can see a potential operation as threatening to its interests. If this requirement is not met—as it was not through much of the Cold War and in the case of Iraq—then action can be blocked thanks to the voting rule. Second, member states, and particularly the powerful member states, must care enough to devote the necessary resources and take the necessary risks. If those risks are low, as in the case of post-conflict peacekeeping, this requirement may not be hard to satisfy. In the more costly cases of reversing aggression or stopping genocides, a strong interest, such as existed in the Gulf War case, is necessary to ensure that sufficient resources are brought to bear. Thus, effective action can be thwarted in two ways: by self-interest, as in the case of Tibet, or by apathy, as in the case of Rwanda.

A cynical conclusion that one might draw from this observation is that the UN mechanism is most likely to be effective precisely when it is needed least— that is, when the powerful states agree enough and care enough to take action. In a case like the Gulf War, one could argue, the UN served simply to give a stamp of approval to actions that the United States would have taken anyway. Moreover, it is also clear from the experience of the Iraq War that the failure to get UN approval will not always stop a great power from taking actions that it wants to take.

In light of this conclusion, one might question whether the UN matters at all when it comes to war and peace. The answer is that although the UN matters less than one might hope, the organization does indeed make a difference. First, as already noted, it has played a constructive role in organizing peacekeeping missions to help countries reconstruct in the wake of conflict. In these cases, the UN's perceived impartiality bestows a legitimacy on peacekeepers' efforts that is needed for them to play the role of an honest broker. Second, the American experience in its two wars against Iraq, in 1991 and 2003, shows that the UN's blessing can be a valuable resource. In the Gulf War, UN support helped build both domestic and international support for the war effort, which contributed to the United States' ability to prevail at low cost to itself. In the case of the Iraq War, the absence of UN support had important implications for the United States' ability to stabilize the country after toppling Hussein's regime. One study of post-conflict reconstruction showed that in order to have a nation-building effort in Iraq that was the same size per capita as the one that was deployed in Bosnia in 1995, the United States would have needed 480,000 combat troops and 12,600 international police.[33] The absence of UN backing, however, meant that some countries that often contribute peacekeeping or police forces to these kinds of missions, such as Pakistan and India, refused to do so in this case. As a result, the U.S.-led coalition had, in March 2004, 154,000 total combat troops, 85 percent of whom were American. And those troops had to serve double duty as an international police force, because there was no separate deployment of police. Hence, there are costs of going to war without the backing of the UN—even if these costs are not always sufficient to prevent a great power from doing so.

Finally, although cooperation is uneven, the UN facilitates joint decision making. Its rules of procedure in the Security Council and established mechanisms for fielding peacekeeping and peace-enforcement operations keep countries from having to "reinvent the wheel" each time a crisis arises. Vetoes may interfere with decision making; but without clearly established rules, decisions would be harder to reach even in those instances where cooperation has been successful. Indeed, if the UN did not exist, states would need to create some organization very similar to the one we already have.

Conclusion: Are Poor Police Better than None?

At the outset of this chapter, we asked whether and when international institutions can prevent or stop wars between and within states. The track record of both alliances and collective security organizations has been uneven, at best, in this regard.

---

33. James Dobbins et al., *America's Role in Nation-Building: From Germany to Iraq* (Santa Monica, CA: RAND, 2003).

Both are imperfect substitutes for an effective police force of the kind that we take for granted in a well-governed country.

Alliances form in response to common interests—generally, the perception of a common threat. For this reason, allies are often better able to work together in concert than are the more fractious members of, say, the UN. However, the existence of alliances does not ensure that allies will fight together, nor does it ensure that other states will be deterred from making threats. Not all alliances are created equally, as the capabilities and resolve underlying the commitment to defend an ally can vary quite considerably. When these are in doubt, as in the case of the French alliance to Czechoslovakia in the interwar period, the alliance can fail in both deterring threats and defending against them. When states are strongly resolved and take the necessary steps to lock in and demonstrate that commitment, as in the case of NATO, then the alliance institutions can be a source of peace through credible deterrence.

For collective security organizations, like the UN, the primary challenge involves providing a public good in an environment in which there can be competing private interests and the costs of providing the good may be more than anyone is willing to pay. Moreover, the joint decision-making rules set down by the organizations' founding members gave those states important privileges to block actions that they do not like. Hence, these organizations have been most effective only when there has been relatively strong agreement among the powerful states, and they have been crippled when those states are in conflict. They have had their greatest successes when at least one powerful state had a sufficient interest that it was willing to pay costs and take risks to provide the public good for everyone. They have also had more quiet successes when those costs and risks were relatively low, such as in cases of post-conflict reconstruction.

Former UN secretary-general Dag Hammarskjöld reportedly said, "The UN was not created to take humanity to heaven but to save it from hell."[34] This statement reflects a pragmatic understanding of the limits of governance in the international system. States have conflicts of interests that they are willing to fight over, as do people within states. In the absence of an impartial police force, the ability of third parties to enforce peace depends on whether those parties are willing and able to step in. Do outsiders have an interest in intervening? Do the available institutions promote intervention by lowering the costs of getting involved or by increasing the costs of staying out? Does the intervention influence the interaction between combatants in a way that resolves the information and commitment problems that can lead to violence? All these questions have to be answered in the affirmative for outside intervention to have a chance at preventing or reversing acts of violence. In cases like the wars in Korea and the Persian Gulf, these conditions were met, and South Korea and Kuwait owe their continued existence to this fact. Similarly, in places like El Salvador and Liberia, effective outside assistance has helped

---

34. The original source of this well-known quotation is unclear, and slight variations in wording can be found in the secondary literature, possibly because he said something to this effect more than once. For a speech in which Hammarskjöld made this point, see Andrew W. Cordier and Wilder Foote, eds., *Public Papers of the Secretaries-General of the United Nations*, vol. 2, *Dag Hammarskjöld* (New York: Columbia University Press, 1972), 301.

these countries rebuild after decades of civil conflict. But in many other cases these conditions are not met, and the results can be disastrous, as in Bosnia, Rwanda, and Darfur.

And yet, as we survey this uneven record, Hammarskjöld's statement reminds us that even an imperfect police force may be better than none. Although the international system has no central authority analogous to that of a well-governed domestic system, the institutions that have developed in its place have a beneficial—albeit imperfect and uneven—impact on world politics. Alliances and collective security organizations are poor substitutes for an effective and neutral police, but it is likely that the world would be an even more violent place in their absence.

Study Tool Kit

Interests, Interactions, and Institutions in Context

- Alliances form when states have compatible interests that lead them to cooperate militarily. They are institutions created between or among states to facilitate cooperation for the purpose of influencing the outcomes of disputes with outsiders.

- Alliances are successful at deterring or fighting off challenges when allies have a strong interest in coming to one another's aid in the event of war, and when they are able to signal this interest to the opponent in a credible manner.

- Collective security organizations form around a common interest, which all states are presumed to share, in promoting peace. As broad-based institutions, their primary role is to facilitate collective action within the international community so that states can respond effectively to prevent or stop the outbreak of violence whenever and wherever it may occur.

- Collective security organizations are successful when leading states perceive a common and compelling interest in stopping an act of aggression; they fail when leading states have conflicting interests in the outcome of a particular dispute or when they have too little interest in the matter to justify the costs of intervention.

Key Terms

alliances, p. 187

balance of power, p. 190
to Cold war

bandwagoning, p. 191

North Atlantic Treaty Organization (NATO), p. 201

Warsaw Pact, p. 201

League of Nations, p. 206

United Nations (UN), p. 206

collective security organizations, p. 206

genocide, p. 206

humanitarian interventions, p. 208

Security Council (UNSC), p. 211

permanent five (P5), p. 211

veto power, p. 211

peace-enforcement operation, p. 213

peacekeeping operation, p. 214

For Further Reading

Doyle, Michael W., and Nicholas Sambanis. *Making War and Building Peace: United Nations Peace Operations*. **Princeton, NJ: Princeton University Press, 2006.** Examines the track record of UN peacekeeping and peace-enforcement operations in civil wars; finds that while the UN is not well equipped to end wars, it has been helpful in peacekeeping and post-conflict reconstruction.

Lake, David. *Entangling Relations: American Foreign Policy in Its Century.* **Princeton, NJ: Princeton University Press, 1999.** Considers the different ways that states can institutionalize their relationship with other countries, from empire to informal alignments.

Leeds, Brett Ashley. "Alliance Reliability in Times of War: Explaining State Decisions to Violate Treaties." *International Organization* 57 (2003): 801–27. Offers empirical evidence about the conditions under which states do or do not come to the aid of their allies in the event of war.

Power, Samantha. *"A Problem from Hell": America and the Age of Genocide.* **New York: Perennial, 2002.** Graphically details the failings of the United States and the UN in the face of genocide, including the cases of Bosnia and Rwanda.

Snyder, Glenn H. *Alliance Politics*. **Ithaca, NY: Cornell University Press, 1997.** Offers a comprehensive presentation of theory and historical evidence on the origins and maintenance of alliances.

Voeten, Erik. "The Political Origins of the UN Security Council's Ability to Legitimize the Use of Force." *International Organization* 59 (Summer 2005): 527–57. Seeks to explain why people care whether or not the UN authorizes a military operation.

Walt, Stephen M. *The Origins of Alliances.* **Ithaca, NY: Cornell University Press, 1987.** Tests balance of power theory and offers a reformulation that hinges on perceptions of threat, not just power.

Waltz, Kenneth N. *Theory of International Politics.* **New York: McGraw Hill, 1979, esp. chaps. 6 and 8.** Presents a modern formulation of balance of power theory and argues that it explains the relative stability of the pre-1945 and Cold War international systems.

Weiss, Thomas G. *What's Wrong with the United Nations (and How to Fix It).* **Cambridge: Polity Press, 2009.** A very accessible and balanced survey of the strengths and weaknesses of the UN, with suggestions for how the institution could be improved.

6

Violence by Nonstate Actors: Civil War and Terrorism

THE PUZZLE *A great deal of politically motivated violence in the contemporary world is committed by or directed against nonstate actors, particularly rebel groups engaged in civil wars or terrorist networks. Why do some individuals and groups resort to violence against their governments or unarmed civilians?*

Above: Transnational terrorist networks, like Al Qaeda, use violence to try to bring about political change. In March 2004, a group affiliated with the Al Qaeda network detonated bombs on four commuter trains in Madrid, Spain, killing over 191 people and wounding many more.

On September 11, 2001, the United States experienced the worst attack on its homeland since the Japanese bombing of Pearl Harbor. On that day, the threat came not from the naval and air forces of a rival state but from 19 individuals armed with box cutters, who hijacked four airplanes and crashed them into the World Trade Center in New York and the Pentagon in Washington, D.C.; thanks to the heroic efforts of the passengers, a plane likely headed for the White House went down in a western Pennsylvania field. Nearly 3,000 people died in the attacks, which were perpetrated by a terrorist network known as Al Qaeda. In response, the United States launched a "global war on terror," a series of military operations around the world, including most prominently the invasion of Afghanistan, whose government had hosted Al Qaeda. The Bush administration then made the case for war against Iraq based partly on the argument (now largely discredited) that the regime there could transfer chemical, biological, or nuclear weapons to terrorists.

The wars in Afghanistan and Iraq both had two major phases. In the first, the United States and its allies quickly defeated the armed forces of the opposing states. The Taliban regime in Afghanistan collapsed after two months; the Iraqi regime fell after six weeks. In both cases, however, victory in the interstate phase of the conflict was followed by much longer conflicts against a different kind of enemy. Both countries descended into civil war as rebellious factions, including elements of the previous regimes, took up arms against one another and the U.S.-installed governments. The United States' role thus shifted from trying to defeat the military of another state to trying to quell a domestic rebellion. The civil phase of these conflicts lasted much longer and claimed more lives—American, Afghani, and Iraqi—than did the initial invasions. U.S. troops finally left Iraq in 2011, but the lingering conflict there gave birth to a new militant group—the Islamic State (IS)—whose activities drew the U.S. military back to the region only three years later.

Meanwhile, despite being forced to flee Afghanistan, Al Qaeda continued to be a threat. Since 9/11, Al Qaeda-linked militants have carried out terrorist attacks in Europe, South Asia, and the Middle East. U.S. forces finally found and killed the Al Qaeda leader, Osama bin Laden, in May 2011, but this event did not end the threat from this group and its offshoots. In short, the United States has spent much of the twenty-first century engaged in deadly conflict not with other states but with nonstate actors: transnational terrorist networks and rebel groups within Afghanistan and Iraq.

The U.S. experience is representative of broader developments in world politics. Violence by and against nonstate actors has long been a prominent feature of international politics, but its importance has increased in recent years. A great deal of armed conflict in the contemporary world takes place not between states but *within* them (see Figure 6.1). Terrorism has also been a growing international concern, particularly since September 2001, which ushered in a period of increased terrorist violence. How do we explain violence by nonstate actors, particularly civil wars and terrorism?

As a first cut, the tools used to understand interstate war are quite useful in understanding civil war and terrorism. Both phenomena arise when nonstate actors, such as rebel groups or terrorist organizations, have interests that bring them into conflict with states. These disputes can lead to conflict when these actors lack access to political institutions that could address their demands through peaceful means, leading to a bargaining interaction that can bring about violence owing to information problems, commitment problems, and/or issue indivisibility. While some of the specifics may change, we can learn a great deal simply by taking the models from earlier chapters and relabeling State A as "government" and State B as "rebel group" or "terrorist organization."

That said, there is a crucial difference between nonstate actors and states. To understand the problem nonstate actors face, think of a cause that you care about, such as immigration or the quality of the food in your school's dining halls. Imagine that you wanted to form a group that would lobby the government or university administrators to enact policies that further your cause. To do so, you would have to convince people to volunteer their time and raise money to support your activities. It may be hard to find people who are committed to the same cause, and some may sympathize with your goals but not have spare time or money to donate. This challenge can be daunting, and many would-be activists give up. Now imagine that pursuing your cause will require your supporters to take up arms against the police or military, plant bombs in shopping malls, or blow themselves up on a crowded bus. Finding people to contribute is likely to become quite a bit harder. You will also have to figure out how to buy guns, explosives, and other tools of rebellion. Along the way, there is the danger that people you approach will alert the police to your activities. What circumstances would lead you to take these risks? And how could you get others to follow you? This dilemma is the central challenge faced by rebel groups and terrorist organizations.

Thinking Analytically about Civil War and Terrorism

Actors who want to fight together to further their common interests face a collective action problem (see Chapter 2). States, almost by definition, have solved this problem. States generally have some capacity to raise money and to enlist or conscript people to fight their wars. Thus, when we consider the bargaining between states, we typically take it for granted that the participants have some ability to mobilize resources in order to wield power internationally. We cannot make the same assumption when dealing with nonstate actors. For groups seeking to rebel against a government, or for terrorist organizations seeking to enlist people for dangerous, possibly suicidal, missions, the collective action problem is an enduring challenge. Whatever substantive interests they seek to further, all such groups have an organizational interest in finding like-minded individuals and motivating them to participate in the fight. And governments in conflict with such groups have to implement strategies that diminish the pool of potential supporters and/or encourage free riding. These imperatives profoundly affect the likelihood, conduct, and outcome of violence involving nonstate actors. This fundamental dilemma shared by rebel groups and terrorist organizations creates an analytical linkage between these phenomena that justifies our studying them side by side.

This insight suggests two questions: First, what are the factors that bring together groups of individuals who are able and willing to use violence to further their interests, and second, why does the interaction between these groups and their target states sometimes lead to costly, protracted conflicts? We can then ask how the problems faced by nonstate actors shape the strategies they employ and the best strategies for defeating them.

FIGURE 6.1 **Interstate and Civil Wars, 1946–2014**

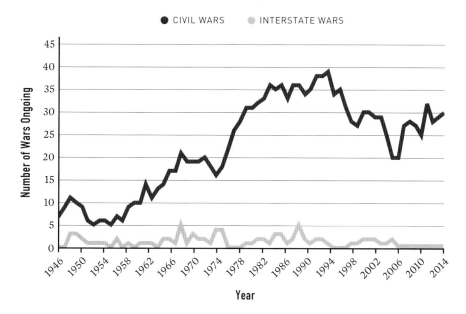

Figure source: UCDP/PRIO Armed Conflict Dataset v4-2015. Nils Petter Gleditsch et al., "Armed Conflict 1946–2001: A New Dataset," *Journal of Peace Research* 39, no. 5 (2002): 615–37, www.pcr.uu.se/research/ucdp/datasets/ucdp_prio_armed_conflict_dataset/ (accessed 07/10/15).

Why Does War Occur within States?

To revisit the definition from Chapter 3, a **civil war** is an armed conflict that occurs between organized actors within a state and that meets some minimum threshold for severity. In most cases, civil wars pit the government of the state against one or more rebel groups, who may also fight among themselves. In some cases, such as Somalia in recent years, there is no functioning central government to speak of, in which case the conflict involves several groups, each trying to assume that role. Scholars conventionally require a conflict to cause at least 1,000 battle-related deaths in order to qualify as a civil war, though lower thresholds are sometimes used. In addition, to be a civil war, casualties need to be incurred by all sides, so that one-sided killings—such as when a government massacres civilians—are not considered in this category.

Figure 6.1 shows the number of ongoing interstate and civil wars in each year from 1946 to 2013. In addition to becoming more numerous, civil wars in this period have tended to be bloodier than interstate wars. From 1945 to 1999, interstate wars were responsible for the deaths of 3 million people, while civil wars killed more than 16 million.[1]

Given that civil wars occur between a government and one or more rebel groups within the same country, why is this topic appropriate to study in a class on international relations, which typically deals with phenomena that cross state borders? There are two main reasons. First, as we will see in this chapter, the theoretical tools

civil war

A war in which the main participants are within the same state, such as the government and a rebel group.

1. James D. Fearon and David Laitin, "Ethnicity, Insurgency, and Civil War," *American Political Science Review* 97 (2003): 75.

that we have developed to explain interstate wars are also very useful in explaining their intrastate counterparts. By examining them side by side, we start to see these two kinds of conflict as instances of a single, broader phenomenon: the use of violence by organized actors to pursue political interests. Seeing them in this way permits useful comparisons that deepen our understanding of both.

Moreover, civil war is an appropriate topic within international relations because while the primary dynamic occurs within a single country, the determinants and effects of a civil war are rarely so contained. External actors often play a significant role in the onset, duration, and outcome of civil conflict. As we will see, foreign states with an interest in the victory of either the government or the rebels often give money, arms, training, and/or sanctuary to their preferred side. This aid can be critical in determining whether a rebel group forms in the first place, how long it can sustain its operations against the government, and which side wins. Indeed, most civil wars experience some outside assistance to the rebels, the government, or both.[2] In addition, civil wars can have spillover effects beyond their borders. They often create refugee flows that can burden neighboring states, and they may involve widespread crimes against humanity that shock the consciences of those far away from the actual fighting. These harms have led to greater international efforts to intervene to stop civil wars, with the United Nations increasingly citing purely domestic conflicts as "threats to international peace and security." Indeed, of the 69 peacekeeping operations undertaken by the United Nations from 1948 to 2014, 39 were deployed to conflicts that were within a single state and another 12 dealt with conflicts involving both international and civil dimensions.[3]

The long-running war in the Democratic Republic of the Congo (DRC) is an extreme but illustrative example of the interdependence between interstate and intrastate violence. The conflict that started in 1996 had its roots in the civil war and genocide that took place in neighboring Rwanda two years earlier (see Chapter 5). The genocide ended when the Tutsi-dominated Rwanda Patriotic Front ousted the Hutu-led government that had perpetrated the killings. Large numbers of Hutu militants then fled across the border into the DRC (then called Zaire) and started carrying out cross-border raids. The Rwandan government responded by arming Tutsis living in eastern Zaire, who then joined with other groups to form a broader resistance movement against the regime. Sensing a chance to rid themselves of a hostile government, Rwanda, Uganda, and Angola openly intervened on the side of the rebels, who unseated Zaire's government in May 1997, at which point the country was renamed the DRC. Conflict restarted the following year when the new government turned on its former allies and asked them to leave. The ensuing war, which officially ended in 2003 but which has continued to smolder to this day, involved 25 different rebel groups supported directly or indirectly by eight different countries. In addition to claiming

---

2. See, for example, Patrick M. Regan, *Civil Wars and Foreign Powers: Outside Intervention in Intrastate Conflict* (Ann Arbor: University of Michigan Press, 2000).

3. Descriptions of UN peacekeeping operations can be found at www.un.org/en/peacekeeping/operations/ (accessed 12/8/14).

millions of lives, the war led to massive atrocities, including horrific levels of rape. The resulting humanitarian crisis spurred the deployment of 20,000 United Nations (UN) peacekeepers in 1999, but these forces have been unable to stop the violence entirely. Given the scale and number of countries involved, this conflict has sometimes been called "Africa's World War,"[4] and it stands as a stark example of how civil conflicts can have their origins in international events and have effects that resonate beyond the borders of a single state.

Why Rebel?

At the root of all civil wars is some conflict of interests between the government and a subset of the population. The literature on civil wars generally classifies these interest conflicts as arising from two different sources: grievances and greed.[5] Grievances can arise when the policies of the government discriminate against members of a particular group, such as by repressing their language or culture, blocking their access to jobs or political office, or denying them government services, such as education, health care, and public infrastructure. These kinds of policies can lead to vast inequalities in wealth and quality of life among groups. Greed refers to a group's desire to control more of the country's economic resources, such as by having a greater share of the profits from natural resource extraction (such as oil or minerals) or privileged access to jobs and government largesse. In either case, conflicts are rooted in individuals' and groups' basic interests in their economic and social well-being, autonomy, and power. When these interests bring them into conflict with their government, dissatisfied groups have three options: they can try to leave the state, they can try to alter its policies, or they can try to take over the state altogether. Thus, intrastate conflicts give rise to demands over the same kinds of issues that we saw in interstate conflicts: territory, policy, and regime. (Map 6.1 on p. 240 shows civil wars from 1990 to 2013, as well as the general underlying issue for each conflict.)

Territorial conflict in this context takes the form of separatism or irredentism. Both arise when a rebel group seeks to carve out a piece of the state's territory. A group is **separatist** if it wants to create its own independent state on the territory. Separatism generally arises when a group that is concentrated in a particular region of the country has grievances with the central government and expects to fare better under its own governance. The newest state in the international system, South Sudan, achieved its independence from Sudan in

The civil war in the Democratic Republic of the Congo that began in 1996 was fueled by the intervention of neighboring states. The war claimed millions of lives, led to atrocities such as widespread rape and torture, and involved the forcible recruitment of thousands of child soldiers.

separatist

An actor that seeks to create an independent state on territory carved from an existing state.

---

4. Gerard Prunier, *Africa's World War: Congo, the Rwandan Genocide, and the Making of a Continental Catastrophe* (New York: Oxford University Press, 2008).

5. Paul Collier and Anke Hoeffler, "Greed and Grievance in Civil War," *Oxford Economic Papers* 56 (2004): 563–95.

MAP 6.1 *Civil Wars, 1990–2014*

This map depicts the countries that experienced a civil war at some point in the period from 1990 to 2014. In each case, the primary aims of the rebel group(s) are indicated. The conflict is categorized as being about territory if rebels were motivated by separatism, irredentism, or a desire for local autonomy. The conflict is categorized as being over government if rebels sought changes in government policy, composition, or regime type. In some cases, rebel groups had both motivations, or the country experienced both kinds of conflict.

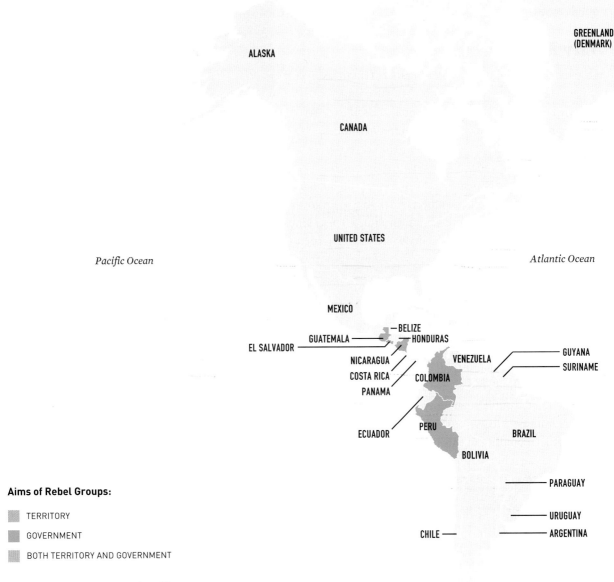

Aims of Rebel Groups:

TERRITORY

GOVERNMENT

BOTH TERRITORY AND GOVERNMENT

Map source: UCDP/PRIO Armed Conflict Dataset v4-2015.
Nils Petter Gileditsch et al., "Armed Conflict 1946–2001: A New Dataset," *Journal of Peace Research* 39, no. 5 (2002): 615–37, www.pcr.uu.se/research/ucdp/datasets/ucdp_prio_armed_conflict_dataset/ (accessed 07/10/15).

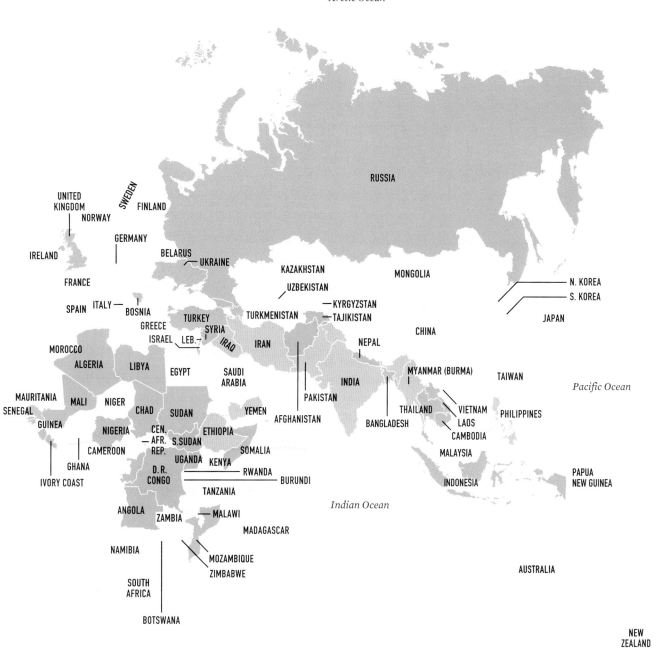

Arctic Ocean

RUSSIA

UNITED
KINGDOM
NORWAY
SWEDEN
FINLAND

IRELAND

GERMANY

BELARUS
UKRAINE

KAZAKHSTAN

MONGOLIA

N. KOREA
S. KOREA

FRANCE

UZBEKISTAN

JAPAN

SPAIN
ITALY
BOSNIA

TURKEY
GREECE
ISRAEL   LEB.
SYRIA
IRAQ

KYRGYZSTAN
TAJIKISTAN

CHINA

TURKMENISTAN

IRAN

NEPAL

TAIWAN

Pacific Ocean

MOROCCO
ALGERIA
LIBYA
EGYPT
SAUDI
ARABIA

MYANMAR (BURMA)

INDIA

PAKISTAN

MAURITANIA
MALI
NIGER
CHAD
SUDAN
YEMEN
AFGHANISTAN

THAILAND

VIETNAM
LAOS
CAMBODIA

PHILIPPINES

SENEGAL
GUINEA

NIGERIA
CEN.
AFR.
REP.
S.SUDAN

ETHIOPIA

BANGLADESH

GHANA
CAMEROON
UGANDA
KENYA
SOMALIA

MALAYSIA

IVORY COAST
D. R.
CONGO
RWANDA
BURUNDI

INDONESIA

PAPUA
NEW GUINEA

TANZANIA

Indian Ocean

ANGOLA
ZAMBIA
MALAWI

MADAGASCAR

NAMIBIA

MOZAMBIQUE
ZIMBABWE

AUSTRALIA

SOUTH
AFRICA

BOTSWANA

NEW
ZEALAND

241

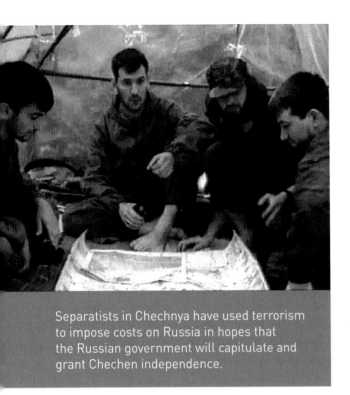

Separatists in Chechnya have used terrorism to impose costs on Russia in hopes that the Russian government will capitulate and grant Chechen independence.

irredentist

An actor that seeks to detach a region from one country and attach it to another, usually because of shared ethnic or religious ties.

2011 after decades of separatist conflict that claimed more than 2 million lives (see "Controversy" on p. 244). Separatist conflicts also gave rise to East Timor, which separated from Indonesia in 2002; Kosovo, which declared its independence from Serbia in 2008; and Eritrea, which won its independence from Ethiopia in 1993. Most separatist conflicts are not as successful. Rebels in Chechnya have been fighting for that region's independence from Russia for over two decades, to no avail. The Liberation Tigers of Tamil Eelam (or Tamil Tigers) fought for a separate state in northern Sri Lanka from 1983 until their defeat in 2009. The United States also experienced a failed separatist movement when the Confederate states seceded in 1861 and were defeated in the ensuing civil war. A rebel group is **irredentist** if members seek to attach their territory to that of a country next door. Irredentism usually arises when people of one state share ethnic or religious ties with the people in the neighboring state and therefore expect that their interests will be better served under its governance.

For example, in the twentieth century Great Britain faced a decades-long conflict with Catholics in Northern Ireland who wanted to join that region with the rest of Ireland, which is majority Catholic. During the conflict in Yugoslavia, ethnic Serbs in Croatia and Bosnia-Herzegovina rebelled in order to attach their lands to Serbia (see Chapter 5).

If leaving is impractical, a group motivated by grievances or greed may threaten civil war in order to change the policies pursued by the central government. Some minority groups in India, for example, have resorted to violence in order to get official recognition of their language, an act that confers a variety of political and social benefits. The civil war in Iraq pitted a variety of groups against each other and the U.S.-led occupation in order to influence policies of the new state. Members of the Sunni Arab minority fought to preserve the privileges that they had enjoyed under Saddam Hussein (himself Sunni), including securing their share of Iraq's oil revenue and protecting their political, civil, and religious rights. Kurds, concentrated in the northern regions, sought to make sure that the new state would be highly decentralized, giving them autonomy in their region, as well as influence over its oil. Even within the Shia majority empowered by the invasion, militant opposition groups emerged contesting a variety of polices, including the pace of a U.S. withdrawal.

Finally, dissatisfied groups might seek to seize control of the central government and establish a new regime (or restore an old one). The civil war in Afghanistan is driven by the desire of those loyal to the former Taliban regime to reclaim power from the U.S.-installed government. During the 1970s and 1980s, white minority governments in Rhodesia (now Zimbabwe) and South Africa faced civil wars against groups pushing for a democratic system that would lead to black majority rule. Political exclusion of a significant group is a common reason that rebels may seek to overturn the existing polity.[6] Clashes over control of the central government are also common in newly independent states, when the retreat of the colonial power creates a space for groups to fight over control of the new state. The conflict between Hutus and Tutsis in Rwanda that resulted in the 1994 genocide had its roots in this kind of struggle. The Tutsi minority had been empowered by the Belgians under their colonial rule, but in 1959, on the eve of Rwanda's independence (which came in 1962), the Hutu majority overthrew the Tutsi leadership and took control of the country. Some Tutsis fled to neighboring countries, and an invasion by Tutsi exiles in 1990 led to a civil war that culminated in a genocide directed against the Tutsi population. The mass killing stopped when the Tutsi forces overran the country and took control.

It should be apparent from this discussion that rebel groups often form on the basis of ethnic and/or religious divisions: Catholic vs. Protestant, Hutu vs. Tutsi, Sunni vs. Shiite, and so on. Indeed, the majority of civil wars have an ethnic or religious component to them. As a result, it might be tempting to assume that civil wars are caused by ethnic or religious differences and that countries that are divided in this way have a higher risk of conflict. In fact, this is not the case, and there are many diverse countries that do not experience internal violence.[7] Ethnic or religious differences alone do not cause the interest conflicts that underlie civil wars. It is when these differences give rise to discriminatory economic and social policies, inequality, political exclusion, and/or intolerance that demands for territory, policy change, or regime change can arise.[8]

When Does Dissatisfaction Lead to Armed Opposition?

Of course, most countries contain dissatisfied people who would like greater control over their territory, more influence over policy, privileged status for their language and culture, a bigger share of the country's wealth, a larger role in government, or a different kind of government altogether. And yet civil wars are relatively rare. Grievances and greed are necessary to fuel emergence of armed opposition groups, but they are clearly not sufficient. Why do some dissatisfied groups organize to further their interests through the threat or use of violence while others, indeed most, do not?

---

6. Lars-Erik Cederman, Andreas Wimmer, and Brian Min, "Why Do Ethnic Groups Rebel? New Data and Analysis," *World Politics* 62 (2010): 87–119.

7. Fearon and Laitin, "Ethnicity, Insurgency, and Civil War."

8. See Donald L. Horowitz, *Ethnic Groups in Conflict*, 2nd ed. (Berkeley, CA: University of California Press, 2000). The danger associated with excluding ethnic groups from power raises an interesting question of why some leaders do it anyway. Although ethnic bias might be to blame, it is also possible that there are short-term political advantages to excluding other ethnic groups from power. For an interesting argument to this effect, see Philip Roessler, "The Enemy Within: Personal Rule, Coups, and Civil War in Africa," *World Politics* 63 (April 2011): 300–46.

Should Every Group Have a State of Its Own?

On July 9, 2011, tens of thousands of people gathered in Freedom Square in Juba, South Sudan, to witness the birth of the international community's newest state. As the joyous crowd looked on, the flag of the Republic of Sudan came down, and the flag of the Republic of South Sudan was raised to the sound of the new national anthem. The country's first president signed its constitution and took the oath of office. Though the mood was jubilant, it was tinged with sadness, since the road to South Sudan's independence had been long and bloody.

Originally colonized and jointly ruled by the British and the Egyptians, the region was joined with northern Sudan prior to the state's independence in 1956. The union of the two Sudans was fraught with tension from the outset. Most northerners are Arabic-speaking Muslims, while most southerners are either Christian or practice indigenous religions. With the bulk of Sudan's population and urban centers, the northern region dominated the country's political and economic life and enjoyed the lion's share of its oil revenues. A rebellion broke out in the south shortly before the Sudan became independent, and over the next 50 years the country experienced civil war for all but 10 of those years, a war that claimed around 2.5 million lives. A deal struck in 2005 provided for a popular vote on South Sudan's future, and in a referendum held in January 2011, 98.8 percent of the region's inhabitants voted for independence.

The creation of a new state is not all that unusual. South Sudan was the twenty-fifth state to join the international system since 1990. Most of these new states were created with the breakups of the Soviet Union and Yugoslavia; two others, the Czech Republic and Slovakia, split up through an amicable process; a few others, Eritrea (1993), East Timor (2002), and Kosovo (2008), won their independence after years of bloody struggle.

Still, there are many other places around the world where people are fighting for a state of their own, to no avail. Somaliland in northern Somalia has been effectively self-governing since the breakdown of central authority in the 1990s, but the international community does not recognize its pleas for independence. The Palestinians in the West Bank and Gaza, South Ossetia and Abkhazia in Georgia, Russian majority areas in Eastern Ukraine, Tibet in China, Aceh in Indonesia, Chechnya in Russia, Catalonia in Spain—all are regions whose people are seeking independence and in some cases exercise de facto statehood that is not internationally recognized.

Should all these regions get states of their own? The main argument in favor of statehood rests on the principle of self-determination: the idea that communities have the right to choose how they are governed and to which authority they are subject. This principle stood in opposition to the practice of imperialism, whereby foreign powers exercised control over conquered lands, and self-determination movements were instrumental in bringing about the end of formal imperialism after World War II. But while there are few colonies remaining in the world, the aftereffects of the imperial era are still ubiquitous in the existence of states whose boundaries were drawn by foreigners without much regard to the interests of the people living there.

On these grounds, there is a strong case for the independence of states like South Sudan. Not only are the people of that region culturally and religiously different from those in the north, the decision to merge the two Sudans into a single state was made not by the inhabitants of the country but by the British. That the people of South Sudan wanted their own state was made clear by decades of costly struggle. By contrast, the north's main interest in a unified state lay in the fact that South Sudan contains about 80 percent of the country's oil reserves. Given these circumstances, the people of South Sudan had a very compelling case for independence. Granting their demand for self-determination earlier would have prevented a great deal of suffering and death. For this reason, some have advocated partition into separate states as a practical solution to ethnic civil wars.[a]

To most Americans, the argument for self-determination likely strikes a chord. The United States was born out of the same desire, as the colonists came to resent being ruled (and taxed) by a faraway government that did not represent them. The U.S. experience also complicates the picture, however. After all, in 1861, the southern region of the United States decided that it no longer wanted to be in a union with the North and declared its independence. The slogan of "states' rights" evoked the idea that people within the Confederate states should have been free to determine their own course, including whether or not to own slaves. Though some Americans look back on that conflict with complex emotions, few regret that the Union was eventually preserved. But if South Sudan deserved its own country, why not the American South?

The main moral argument against independence for the Confederacy was that self-determination for southern whites would have come at a great cost: continued subjugation of black slaves, who had no say in the decision to secede. What if not everyone living in the secessionist region would benefit from a new state? In the case of

South Sudan, opposition to independence was minimal, but in Kosovo, which declared independence from Serbia in 2008, there is a significant minority of ethnic Serbs who did not want separation and who worry about their fate. In such cases, secession may give rise to further conflict, as newly created minorities struggle with the new state. Even if possible, a "clean" partition—that is, one in which no minorities are left on either side—may require large population transfers, which can themselves be quite brutal. The partition of India and Pakistan upon independence from the British was accompanied by the displacement of over 12 million people and intercommunal bloodshed that claimed hundreds of thousands of lives. The two countries have since fought four wars over where the border between them should be. South Sudan's border with Sudan is also contested in places, leading to militarized threats and violence. Thus, partition may lead to new conflicts, both within newly created states and between them.[b]

An even larger complication is that the principle of self-determination is silent with respect to what criteria a group should meet in order to merit its own state. Does everyone need to have the same religion, speak the same language, or have the same skin color? Can any collection of people, no matter how small, proclaim themselves a nation and seek recognition? South Sudan is as much an artificial creation of the colonial era as the state it left. The people come from more than a dozen different ethnic groups, speak many different languages, and follow different religious faiths. Indeed, less than two years after achieving independence, a political struggle between leaders representing the two largest ethnic groups cast the country into a civil war that had, by the end of 2014, killed tens of thousands and displaced almost 2 million people. Given these differences, there could be an argument for breaking South Sudan into ever smaller units. But where does the process end? The international community's hesitation in recognizing new states rests in large part on concerns about a slippery slope that leads to the splintering of the entire system. Thus, those sympathetic to the plight of "trapped" minorities might argue instead for greater democracy and rules protecting minority rights. While partition may be necessary and desirable in some cases, it can be more practical to foster institutions that make it possible for diverse people to live together rather than granting every request to live apart.

a. Chaim Kaufman, "Possible and Impossible Solutions to Ethnic Civil Wars," *International Security* 20 (1996): 136–75.

b. Nicholas Sambanis, "Partition as a Solution to Ethnic War: An Empirical Critique of the Theoretical Literature," *World Politics* 52 (2000): 437–83.

We can illustrate this question more concretely by considering the uprisings that spread across the Middle East and North Africa in winter/spring of 2011. The Arab Spring (so named not only because of the season in which it occurred but also because spring denotes an awakening) involved mass protests in various countries, including Tunisia, Libya, Egypt, Syria, Yemen, and Bahrain. Though local circumstances varied, all were driven to some degree by the same set of factors: a large number of unemployed young men, an increase in food prices, and long-standing dissatisfaction with corrupt and repressive governments. In all cases, the protesters demanded the removal of government officials and/or liberalization of the regimes. And yet, in spite of these similarities, the outcomes varied quite significantly. In Tunisia and Egypt, leaders stepped down in response to mass protests that were largely peaceful. In Bahrain, protests were swiftly put down by the government. The opposition movement in Libya organized into an armed rebel group, which waged open war against the Libyan regime and ultimately succeeded in ousting it. In Syria, a violent crackdown led to the emergence of a full-scale civil war that has claimed hundreds of thousands of lives, caused violence to spread into neighboring states, and at the time of this writing, showed little sign of ending any time soon. What might explain this variation?

In general, three sets of factors help explain the emergence of organized, armed opposition groups: features of the group and its interests, features of the country in which the group resides, and features of the international system that influence the possibilities for external support.

Group-Level Explanations In some cases, the ability of groups to organize is aided by the nature of the interests for which they are fighting. Individuals may be

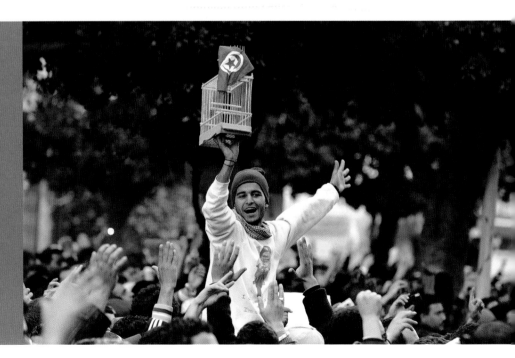

Not all conflicts between dissatisfied groups and the government result in civil war. Mass protests in Tunisia led to the resignation of President Zine al-Abidine Ben Ali in January 2011 and the establishment of a new government without large-scale violence.

motivated by very strong religious or ideological beliefs that lead them to see contributing to the cause as beneficial in its own right. In a study of why individuals participated in El Salvador's civil war, Elisabeth Wood found that many peasants were motivated by a sense of justice and a desire to do something meaningful with their lives.[9] When this is the case, there is no incentive to free ride and the collective action problem does not arise.

Similarly, individuals from the same ethnic or religious group may have higher levels of trust or collective solidarity and feel a stronger social disincentive to free ride when dealing with one another. Indeed, the majority of civil wars involve mobilization along ethnic lines, meaning that the rebels and the government tend to draw support from different ethnic groups.[10] As we already saw, this pattern may reflect interethnic tensions over the division of wealth and political power or the status of a particular religion, language, or culture. But even if ethnicity does not give rise to a grievance, it can be a resource for mobilizing people for or against the government. Because people of the same ethnic group tend to trust one another, it is easier to recruit fighters and raise funds from people of the same ethnicity than from outsiders. Indeed, when people trust their ethnic or religious kin more than they trust others, elites can strategically highlight and manipulate group differences in order to build a base of support. Particularly when accompanied by violence, this strategy can cause a society to polarize along ethnic or religious lines, as individuals seek protection from their "own kind." This process of polarization played out rapidly and with tragic consequences in Iraq's capital city, Baghdad, following the American invasion. Prior to then, Baghdad was home to both Shiites and Sunnis, many living in mixed neighborhoods. In the aftermath of the invasion, radicals on each side started targeting those from the other group. Even if you were, say, a moderate Shiite who preferred to live in peace with your Sunni neighbors, the insecurity of knowing that you and your family might be attacked simply because of your religious identity would lead to you to seek protection from other Shiites. This dynamic caused people to fill the ranks of Sunni or Shiite militias, thereby increasing the power base of the militia leaders who had sparked the violence in the first place. People also fled areas controlled by the other sect, causing mixed neighborhoods to all but vanish from the map.[11]

In addition, some traditional societies may be organized into tribes, which are substate groups with familial or ethnic ties. Tribes generally have their own systems of formal or informal governance, which facilitate collective action. If a tribal leader chooses to join a rebellion, he can bring along other members of the tribe. The civil

---

9. Elisabeth Jean Wood, *Insurgent Collective Action and Civil War in El Salvador* (Cambridge: Cambridge University Press, 2003).

10. Fearon and Laitin, "Ethnicity, Insurgency, and Civil War," report that 51 percent of civil wars in the 1945–99 period were fought along ethnic lines and another 18 percent were mixed or ambiguous. Using different data and criteria, Nicholas Sambanis reports that 77 out of 109 civil wars from 1960 to 1999 were ethnic in nature; see Nicholas Sambanis, "Do Ethnic and Nonethnic Civil Wars Have the Same Causes? A Theoretical and Empirical Inquiry (Part 1)," *Journal of Conflict Resolution* 45 (2001): 259–82.

11. For some detailed maps showing the changes in the ethnic distribution in Baghdad from 2003 to 2009, see http://gulf2000.columbia.edu/maps.shtml (accessed 12/08/14).

war in Libya stemmed in large part from the decision of several key tribes to withdraw their support from the government.

In the absence of strong ethnic ties or ideological motivations, groups that seek to mobilize against the government have to find other ways to encourage participation. One way is to compensate supporters materially. Rebel groups operating in areas of Africa with easy access to diamonds or other precious minerals can sell these goods on international markets, sometimes illegally, and funnel the proceeds to their fighters. The sale of so-called blood diamonds enriched rebels fighting in Sierra Leone (1996–99), while the long-running civil conflict in Colombia was fueled by the cocaine trade. Indeed, some rebel groups are essentially criminal gangs deeply engaged in smuggling, human trafficking, and extortion.[12] Another way rebel groups may amass fighters is through forcible recruitment, or kidnapping. Men, women, and children may be taken from their homes at gunpoint and used as fighters, porters, messengers, spies, or sexual slaves. This practice was shockingly illustrated in April 2014, when nearly 300 Nigerian schoolgirls were kidnapped and forced to marry members of the rebel group Boko Haram. The United Nations estimates that there are more than 300,000 children under the age of 18 participating in civil conflicts around the world.[13]

Country-Level Factors   Certain features of a country can also contribute to the risk that armed opposition will emerge. Three in particular are important to note. The first deals with the country's political institutions or regime type. The incentive to threaten or use violence depends in part of whether the normal political process allows peaceful methods for redressing grievances. After all, fighting is very costly, so it makes sense to seek policy change or influence through existing political channels, if possible. If groups can pursue their goals by running candidates in elections or securing their rights through courts, then they have an alternative to taking up arms. This suggests that democratic countries should have a lower risk of experiencing civil wars, a hypothesis for which there is some evidence.[14] Nevertheless, the relationship between a country's political institutions and civil war is complicated by a second consideration: the ability of a rebel group to form depends in part on the government's repressive capacity—that is, how easily it can prevent, deter, or eliminate armed opposition. In this respect, authoritarian governments can have an advantage owing to extensive police and surveillance activities, a greater willingness to use violence against their own citizens, and the absence of civil liberties. As a result of these competing considerations, there is reason to believe that the risk of civil war is highest in countries that are neither fully democratic nor strongly autocratic, because

---

12. See, for example, John Mueller, "The Banality of 'Ethnic War,'" *International Security* 25 (2000): 42–70.

13. For the UN program on Children and Armed Conflict, see www.un.org/children/conflict/english/index.html (accessed 12/05/14).

14. Håvard Hegre, Tanja Ellingsen, Scott Gates, and Nils Petter Gleditsch, "Toward a Democratic Civil Peace? Democracy, Political Change, and Civil War, 1816–1992," *American Political Science Review* 95 (2001): 33–48.

they lack both effective channels of peaceful participation and an effective apparatus of repression.[15]

A second factor that is known to influence a country's civil war risk is its wealth. That poor countries are much more likely to experience civil wars than rich countries is the strongest and most consistent finding in the scholarly literature. There is some disagreement, however, as to the mechanism underlying this relationship. One natural interpretation is that people in poor countries have greater reason to be unhappy with their lot. Poverty breeds desperation, and a lack of economic opportunities can also lead to a large pool of unemployed young men who can be recruited as fighters. By contrast, people in rich countries may find that their lives are too comfortable to undertake the risks associated with violent strategies.[16] A second interpretation hinges on the government's capacity to prevent and defeat rebellions. Richer states tend to have better and stronger police and military forces as well as better ability to project their authority throughout the country. By contrast, poorer countries often have police and militaries that are not much better trained or equipped than their domestic opponents. With more limited resources, they may also have a hard time exerting their authority outside of one or two main cities. The inability to project forces throughout the country makes it possible for rebel groups to organize in places that are beyond the government's effective reach.[17]

This last insight has led scholars to think about a third set of country-level factors that can affect civil wars: those that make it easier or harder for governments to find and defeat rebels. Civil wars are more likely in populous countries, since rebels can more easily recruit from and hide in large populations. They are also more likely in countries that cover large areas, which are hard to police. Some scholarship has also suggested that civil war risk is higher in countries with rugged terrain, such as jungles and mountains. The difficulty of rooting rebels out of mountainous terrain explains why the English spent considerable effort during the thirteenth and fourteenth centuries to incorporate the rebellious Welsh into their kingdom and why the United States in the twenty-first century has had such a hard time eliminating the Taliban from the mountains that straddle the Afghanistan-Pakistan border. Nevertheless, there is some debate among scholars whether these kinds of examples generalize to a broader pattern.[18]

---

15. There is some controversy on this point. Hegre, Ellingsen, Gates, and Gleditsch, "Toward a Democratic Civil Peace?" and Fearon and Laitin, "Ethnicity, Insurgency, and Civil War" both showed a high risk of civil war in "anocracies"—that is, states that are neither fully democratic nor fully autocratic. This view was called into question by James Raymond Vreeland, "The Effect of Political Regime on Civil War: Unpacking Anocracy," *Journal of Conflict Resolution* 52 (2008): 401–25. It may be that this relationship holds for some kinds of civil wars and not others. For example, Halvard Buhaug argues that "semi-democracies" have the highest risk of civil wars over government or policy, while democracies have a higher risk of territorial conflict; see "Relative Capability and Rebel Objective in Civil War," *Journal of Peace Research* 43 (2006): 691–708. For a recent review of this literature, see Håvard Hegre, "Democracy and Armed Conflict," *Journal of Peace Research* 51 (2014): 159–72.

16. Collier and Hoeffler, "Greed and Grievance in Civil War."

17. Fearon and Laitin, "Ethnicity, Insurgency, and Civil War."

18. Fearon and Laitin, "Ethnicity, Insurgency, and Civil War," show that more mountainous countries experience higher civil war risk. But studies that look at variation within countries have found that mountainous regions are not necessarily more likely to be the site of civil conflict than nonmountainous regions; see, for example, Halvard Buhaug and Jan Ketil Rød, "Local Determinants of African Civil Wars, 1970–2001," *Political Geography* 25 (March 2006): 315–35.

U.S. and Afghan soldiers search for Taliban rebels in the mountains on the Afghanistan–Pakistan border. Rough terrain makes it more difficult for government forces to find and defeat rebels.

International Factors Finally, rebel groups may be able to obtain resources if there are foreign countries that have an interest in their cause. Though civil wars pit rebels against a government within a state, most civil wars witness some meddling by other countries. Foreign states may intervene directly by sending their forces across the border to assist one side or the other; more commonly, sympathetic states may give arms, money, or training to rebel groups. Rebels may also operate from bases in neighboring countries, allowing them to organize and train in sanctuaries that are hard for the government to reach.[19]

There are several reasons why foreign governments might have an interest in supporting or hosting rebels. One possibility is that they share the interests of the rebel group. Just as two states with aligned interests may seek to cooperate militarily to improve the bargaining outcome (see Chapter 5), a state whose interests are aligned with those of a rebel group may look for ways to increase the group's fighting capabilities. Irredentist groups—that is, rebel groups seeking to join their land to that of a neighboring state—are likely to receive such support from the state they hope to join. During the civil war in the former Yugoslavia (see Chapter 5), Serbia gave aid to ethnic Serbs living in Bosnia and Croatia who wanted to carve out a "Greater Serbia" from these lands. Russia has given military support to ethnic Russians in eastern Ukraine who started a separatist war in 2014 with the goal of either joining Russia or creating a new Russian majority state. More broadly, states or individuals may support rebellions that involve ethnic kin in other states.[20] For example, Irish rebels

19. Idean Salehyan, *Rebels without Borders: Transnational Insurgencies in World Politics* (Ithaca, NY: Cornell University Press, 2009).

20. Stephen M. Saideman, *The Ties That Divide: Ethnic Politics, Foreign Policy, and International Conflict* (New York: Columbia University Press, 2001). See also Lars-Erik Cederman, Luc Girardin, and Kristian Skrede Gleditsch, "Ethnonationalist Triads: Assessing the Influence of Kin Groups on Civil Wars," *World Politics* 61 (2009): 403–37.

fighting British rule in Northern Ireland received money from Irish Americans who sympathized with their cause. Rebel groups may also attract foreign support because of their ideology. During the Cold War, movements espousing Communist ideals often received support from the Soviet Union or China. Similarly, Iran has, since its Islamic revolution in 1979, been active in supporting militant Islamist groups such as Hamas, a Palestinian group, and Hezbollah, which operates in Lebanon.

By giving support to groups with aligned interests, a foreign state can force the government to make greater concessions, or it can improve the chances that the rebels will replace the government altogether and implement policies closer to the foreign state's ideal point. This may be a particularly attractive strategy when the foreign state is weak relative to the target. In the case of Somalia, the decision to build up a separatist movement in Ethiopia came after several failed attempts to seize the territory through more conventional means. Thus, supporting rebels was seen as a way around Somalia's military weakness (though this strategy ultimately failed as well).

A second possibility is that outsiders may support rebels not because they care about the rebels' goals per se, but because they have other interest conflicts with the government. In these cases, support for rebels can be a relatively low-cost way for one state to impose costs on another in the hopes of either gaining concessions, to tie down some of the opponent's resources at home, or to hasten the ouster of a hostile government. For example, after Eritrea won its independence from Ethiopia, the Eritrean government gave support to other rebel movements in Ethiopia in order to strengthen its hand in a border dispute that arose after the separation. More generally, states that have long-standing disputes with their neighbors have a high likelihood of supporting and/or hosting rebel groups against their rivals.[21] (See "How Do We Know?" on p. 252 about the spread of civil wars among neighboring states.)

In some cases, the interests of outside parties can cause civil wars to become **proxy wars**, or conflicts in which two opposing states support opposite sides in a civil war in some third state. Such proxy wars were common during the Cold War, when the dangers of a direct confrontation between the superpowers were so great that conflict was often channeled through other actors. Thus, the Soviet Union and China supported Communist rebels in South Vietnam, Laos, and Cambodia, while the United States gave support to the governments of those states. For its part, the United States supported rebels in countries with pro-Soviet governments like Nicaragua, Afghanistan, and Angola. Unfortunately for the inhabitants of these countries, there is a significant cost to being a pawn in other states' conflicts: civil wars in which both the rebels and the government receive external support tend to last longer thanks to additional fuel that outsiders bring to the fire.[22]

All these factors contribute in some measure to explaining why Libya, of all the countries that experienced protests during the 2011 Arab Spring, had the most

proxy wars
Conflicts in which two opposing states "fight" by supporting opposite sides in war, such as the government and rebels in a third state.

---

21. Idean Saehyan, Kristian Skrede Gleditsch, and David E. Cunningham, "Explaining External Support for Insurgent Groups," *International Organization* 65 (October 2011): 709–44.

22. See, for example, Dylan Balch-Lindsay, Andrew J. Enterline, and Kyle A. Joyce, "Third-Party Intervention and the Civil War Process," *Journal of Peace Research* 45 (2008): 345–63.

Why Civil Wars Cluster Together

An important feature of civil wars is that they are not spread evenly around the globe; instead, as Map 6.1 on page 240 shows, they tend to clump together in space. Some regions, like Africa, the Middle East, and South Asia experienced numerous civil wars, while other regions, such as North America and Western Europe, experienced few or none. Even within regions, countries that experienced civil war tend to be neighbors. What explains this clustering?

One hypothesis is that civil wars, like diseases, are contagious. A rebellion in one country might inspire like-minded groups in neighboring states, just as the revolutions of the Arab Spring spread around the Middle East. Armed groups operating in one country might cross into a neighboring state and cause trouble there, just as the flight of militants from Rwanda in 1994 helped bring civil war to neighboring Zaire. After being ousted from power in Afghanistan in 2001, some members of the Taliban fled to Pakistan and helped fuel civil conflict there. A government facing a rebel group financed by a neighboring state might retaliate by supporting a rebellion against its foe. Civil wars can also cause large cross-border flows of refugees, who can impose an economic burden on neighboring states as well as become a pool of recruits (often involuntary) for armed actors.[a]

While the contagion hypothesis is plausible, it is also possible that the clustering of civil wars arises simply because the kinds of states that are most susceptible to civil conflict cluster together. As we saw, poorer countries are much more likely to experience a civil war than richer countries. It is also true that poor countries tend to border other poor countries, and rich countries tend to border other rich countries. Put another way, there are neighborhoods of relatively poor countries in which the risk of civil war is high. Other determinants of civil war, such as regime type, also cluster in space.

So is the clustering of civil wars a product of bad neighbors who spread their disease or of bad neighborhoods in which the risk factors for conflict are high? In a recent study, Halvard Buhaug and Kristian Gleditsch explored this question using data on all countries in the world from 1950 to 2001 and found evidence of contagion effects.[b] Being in a poor region is associated with a higher risk of civil war,

FIGURE A **Conflict Contagion and Civil War Risk**

Sources: Buhaug and Gleditsch, "Contagion or Confusion?" Data available at http://hdl.handle.net/1902.1/11568 (accessed 01/03/12).

Note: The data indicate the percentage of countries per year that experienced the onset of a new civil war as a function of whether or not at least one neighboring state had a civil war ongoing in that year.

but once a country's own level of development is taken into account, the wealth of its neighbors does not have any additional effect: a poor country with relatively poor neighbors is no worse off than an equally poor country with rich neighbors. What matters is whether or not any bordering state is actually experiencing a civil war, in which case there is a real danger of contagion. Buhaug and Gleditsch estimated that a country's chances of falling into civil war double if at least one of its neighbors is experiencing such a conflict (Figure A). They also found that the risk of contagion is particularly pronounced when there are ethnic groups that span the border. These transnational ethnic ties may facilitate the movement of people, arms, ideas, and organizational resources across borders. For example, the Taliban's ability to operate in both Afghanistan and Pakistan is due to its support among the Pashtun people, who live on both sides of the border.

This evidence underscores the fact that civil wars, though primarily a phenomenon that occurs within states, cannot be understood without taking into account the international context. It also suggests that efforts to prevent civil wars need to address not only root problems, such as poverty, repression, and discrimination, but also the mechanisms by which these conflicts can spread.

---

a. Idean Salehyan and Kristian Skrede Gleditsch, "Refugees and the Spread of Civil War," *International Organization* 60 (2006): 335–66.

b. Halvard Buhaug and Kristian Skrede Gleditsch, "Contagion or Confusion? Why Conflicts Cluster in Space," *International Studies Quarterly* 52 (2008): 215–33.

successful armed rebellion. The Libyan rebels benefited from the country's large size combined with the regime's relatively weak grip on its eastern regions, where the rebellion took hold before the government could stamp it out. The strong tribal structure in Libya also facilitated collective action, since tribal leaders who went into opposition brought with them the resources and manpower of their tribes. Rebels also profited, literally, from their ability to seize oil production and exporting facilities. Sales of oil from rebel-controlled ports helped to finance arms purchases. Finally, and most notably, the Libyan rebels benefited from Western intervention on their behalf, which came in the form of air strikes against pro-government forces, arms, and training. Though the NATO intervention was justified primarily as a humanitarian act, the United States had long seen Libyan leader Mu'ammar Qaddafi as a hostile and unpredictable influence in the region. While there had been steps toward rapprochement between Qaddafi and the West following Libya's decision to renounce its nuclear program in 2003, Qaddafi had no powerful protectors in 2011. By contrast, the United States looked the other way when Bahrain, a key strategic ally, cracked down on its protesters, and Russia's support for the Syrian regime constrained the prospects of intervention in support of the rebellion there. Indeed, when the United States and regional allies intervened militarily in Syria in 2014, they did so against the rebel group IS, which was seen as posing a threat to U.S. allies in the region, and not against the Syrian regime.

Civil War as a Bargaining Failure

Thus, the potential for civil violence arises when (1) there are groups of people within the country motivated by greed or grievances that put their interests in conflict with those of the government; (2) those people cannot pursue their grievances through regular political institutions; and (3) those people can, owing to their own resources, foreign support, and/or the state's weakness, overcome the collective action problem to recruit enough fighters and purchase enough weaponry to pose a threat. Once these conditions are met, then the interaction between the rebels and the government can start to look like the bargaining interaction introduced in the interstate context in Chapter 3: two actors with opposed interests bargaining in the shadow of threats to use force.

As with interstate conflicts, civil conflicts can, in theory, be resolved through compromises that would allow the actors to avoid the horrendous costs associated with these wars. A territorial dispute could lead to a negotiated secession or, more likely, a grant of autonomy that would give the rebel group many of the benefits of self-rule in its region. Regime and policy disputes can be diffused through policy concessions or power-sharing arrangements that give rebels greater representation in the government. Thus, once a capable opposition group has emerged, the puzzle of civil war is the same as the puzzle of international war: Why do the actors sometimes fail to reach bargains that would permit them to avoid the costs of war?

The three mechanisms discussed in Chapter 3—information problems, commitment problems, and indivisibilities—are all relevant in answering this question, though, as we will see, commitment problems loom particularly large in this context.[23]

Civil War from Incomplete Information

As in international bargaining, incomplete information can arise if the capabilities and resolve of each side are hard to observe. In the context of civil conflicts, it can be particularly difficult to gauge the size and effectiveness of rebel groups, which often organize covertly and take steps to hide their strength (or weakness) in order to avoid government crackdowns. Moreover, there may be less scope for prewar communication and diplomacy, since representatives of rebel groups do not enjoy the same protection from arrest or execution that international diplomats enjoy. Still, most scholars find informational arguments to be less convincing as explanations for most civil wars because these conflicts tend to last so long. While the median duration of interstate wars since 1945 was three months, the corresponding figure for civil wars was six years.[24] Recalling the argument from Chapter 3 that wars can remove uncertainty about relative strength and resolve (see "How Do We Know?" on p. 252), it seems unlikely that these conflicts would last years, even decades, if the underlying problem were simply a lack of information.

Civil War from Commitment Problems

A more likely explanation for long civil wars is that they are rooted in commitment problems that are particularly difficult to resolve.[25] In this context, several such problems arise. First, as we have seen, anticipated changes to the relative power of two sides can generate incentives for preventive war. When power is changing, the rising actor cannot credibly commit not to exploit its power in the future to revise any deal made today; as a result, the actor that expects to grow weaker may prefer war now to a less desirable deal in the future. In the context of civil conflicts, changes in the relative power of rebels and the government can arise regularly owing to the ups and downs of the state's economy. When the economy falters, the government's tax revenue falls, depriving it of resources that could be used to combat a rebellion; at the same time, popular discontent associated with a poor economy makes it easier for rebels to attract new recruits. As a result, a downturn in the economy creates a window in which rebels are relatively strong and have incentives to press demands. And the government, facing a strong rebellion, has incentives to make concessions.

However, economic downturns are generally temporary, often driven by short-term shocks, such as a change in the price of oil or, in countries that depend heavily on agriculture, too little or too much rainfall in a given year. If everyone expects the economy to recover in the near future, then the rebels' newfound strength is known to be temporary. The rebels may expect that any concessions the government makes

---

23. For a review of how bargaining theory applies to civil wars, see Barbara F. Walter, "Bargaining Failures and Civil War," *Annual Review of Political Science* 12 (June 2009): 243–61.

24. Fearon and Laitin, "Ethnicity, Insurgency, and Civil War," 75.

25. James D. Fearon, "Why Do Some Civil Wars Last So Much Longer than Others?" *Journal of Peace Research* 41(May 2004): 275–301.

under these conditions will be withdrawn once the economy improves. As with a rising state, the government may not be able to commit credibly to abide by the deal once conditions improve. Hence, the anticipated economic recovery creates incentives for rebels to fight now in the hopes of obtaining an irreversible victory while they are relatively strong. This logic suggests that economic downturns should be associated with a higher risk of civil wars, and that is exactly what researchers have found.[26]

A second commitment problem results from the fact that the combatants in a civil war generally have to live together, in the same country, once their conflict is settled. When two states seek to settle a dispute or end a war, their armies can remain or retreat behind their respective borders. As a result, both sides retain the coercive power needed to sustain a deal. In the case of civil conflicts, however, this is usually not an option. A rebel group mobilizes and arms in order to make demands on the government. The government, hoping to avoid war, decides to make concessions but also requires, as part of the deal, that the rebels demobilize and disarm. This is a sensible demand to ensure civil peace and order; unless a new state is created through secession, rebel forces will have to be integrated into the existing state. This demand, however, gives rise to a severe commitment problem: Once the rebels have disarmed, how can they be sure that the government will continue to abide by the deal? The government might simply exploit the rebels' disarmament to crack down and eliminate them as a threat altogether. Hence, any deal that requires disarmament by the rebel group directly affects the future bargaining power of the actors. As we saw in the case of interstate conflict, this dynamic can create an insurmountable obstacle to reaching a negotiated settlement, either before or during conflict.[27]

Partly for this reason, civil wars rarely end with negotiated peace agreements. Indeed, the majority of civil wars end only when one side achieves an outright military victory or when the rebel group simply peters out from a loss of support. Only around 20 to 25 percent of civil wars end with a negotiated settlement, while the rest end with an outright victory of one side or the other.[28] Reaching an agreement either before or during fighting requires some mechanism to ensure that the government will live by the deal once the rebels lay down their arms. In some cases, it might be possible to craft power-sharing agreements that give all sides some control over the military after the conflict so that none can unilaterally exploit the others.[29] A more likely mechanism for these purposes, however, is the presence of some third party, such as peacekeepers from the UN, who can monitor and enforce the terms of the deal. We will revisit this issue below.

---

26. See, for example, Edward Miguel, Shanker Satyanath, and Ernest Sergenti, "Economic Shocks and Civil Conflict: An Instrumental Variables Approach," *Journal of Political Economy* 122 (2004): 725–53.

27. Barbara F. Walter, *Committing to Peace: The Successful Settlement of Civil Wars* (Princeton, NJ: Princeton University Press, 2002).

28. See, for example, Roy Licklider, "The Consequences of Negotiated Settlements in Civil Wars, 1945–1993," *American Political Science Review* 89 (September 1995): 681–90.

29. See, for example, Caroline Hartzell and Matthew Hoddie, "Institutionalizing Peace: Power Sharing and Post–Civil War Conflict Management," *American Journal of Political Science* 47 (April 2003): 318–32.

Just as the government may have a hard time committing to abide by a deal, there can be commitment problems on the rebel side as well. Rebel organizations, unlike states, can often have a hard time controlling all their members. We saw in Chapter 4 that state leaders often have to respond to internal pressures, including from their military, and that these pressures may influence the stances they take in international bargaining. There may also be times when leaders' control over their military organizations is less than total, so that the military may engage in actions over which they have limited knowledge (recall Chapter 4 "What Shaped Our World?" on p. 157). Rebel organizations, which typically lack the capacity and institutional structure of states, face this problem even more acutely. Even if the leaders are willing to accept some deal, they may not be able to guarantee that every member of the group will lay down their arms. Within any group, there may be some members with extreme, even fanatical, views, who are unwilling to accept a compromise and will continue fighting. Unless the rebels can credibly commit to rein in their extreme factions, the government may be unwilling to cut a deal, or bargains may be struck but will not hold. As long as each faction can, on its own, decide to reject a deal and continue the war, fighting will continue until there is a deal that is acceptable to the most extreme faction—or until one side or the other is decisively defeated. For this reason, rebellions that have more factions tend to generate longer wars.[30]

An example of this problem comes from the civil war that has raged since 2003 in the Darfur region of Sudan, a conflict that gained a great deal of international attention because of the genocide carried out by pro-government Arab militias against the non-Arab people of that region (see Chapter 5). Fighting on behalf of the latter are two main rebel groups, the Sudan Liberation Movement (SLM) and the Justice and Equality Movement (JEM), along with a number of smaller groups. Though both groups purport to speak for the same people, they have disagreed over the terms of any peace deal, and there are factions with different preferences within each group as well. The government of Sudan signed an agreement in 2006 with the SLM, but the JEM rejected the deal and continued fighting. The SLM withdrew from the deal in 2010, and since then there have been ongoing, but so far unsuccessful, negotiations between the government and the JEM, as well as a new organization, the Liberation and Justice Movement, which brought together 10 smaller groups. Though the failures of peace in this case are partly the result of the government's unwillingness to compromise, efforts to end the war have been complicated by the multitude of factions within the rebel movement.

Civil War from Indivisibilities   Finally, conflict might be unavoidable if the issue in dispute is valued in such a way that it is difficult to divide. As we saw in Chapter 3, governments and separatist groups might find it hard to compromise over pieces of territory that are imbued with religious or ethnic significance. The more common problem, though, is that the state may have incentives to treat its *entire territory* as indivisible, particularly if there are many possible groups with separatist interests.

---

30. David E. Cunningham, "Veto Players and Civil War Duration," *American Journal of Political Science* 50, no. 4 (2006): 875–92.

Rebellions that involve more factions tend to generate longer wars, as it is more difficult to get all groups to agree to a deal. In Sudan, the government signed a peace deal with the rebel group SLM in 2006, but another group, the JEM, kept fighting, and peace has eluded the region ever since.

Consider the case of Russia, which has fought two bloody civil wars in the break-away region of Chechnya since its predominantly Muslim inhabitants declared independence in 1993. Given the costs of this war, which claimed tens of thousands of lives and sparked terrorist attacks by Islamic militants, Russia might have been better off letting the Chechens take their land and go. If Russia faced a single possible separatist group, the dangers of such a concession might not be too large. But in a large, multiethnic country, concession to one group might encourage others to mobilize for similar reasons. Russia is home to more than 100 different ethnic groups, many of whom seek separation or greater autonomy from the central government in Moscow. If the government appears willing to let one group go, then all other potential claimants have incentives to make their own demand. Although any one set of concessions might not be too painful, the collective costs of making concessions to multiple groups could be quite large. This dynamic means that a state might reasonably see its entire territory as an indivisible good, since the loss of a little can bring about the loss of enormous value. In such cases, a state has an incentive to resist making concessions to any challenger in order to convince all potential challengers that they will similarly face resistance. This suggests that the more potential separatist groups a government faces, the less likely it is to make concessions to any one, a prediction that has been confirmed in recent research.[31]

---

31. Monica Toft, *The Geography of Ethnic Violence* (Princeton, NJ: Princeton University Press, 2005), esp. chap. 5 on Russia and Chechnya; Barbara F. Walter, *Reputation and Civil War: Why Separatist Conflicts Are So Violent* (Cambridge: Cambridge University Press, 2009). Technically, the dynamic described here is, at root, an information problem arising from uncertainty about the government's resolve to fight separatists. Treating the state's territory as indivisible is a strategy that the government employs to build a reputation for toughness, and not something intrinsic to the nature of the good. As we saw in Chapter 3, apparent indivisibilities are often rooted in strategic considerations.

Insurgency and Counterinsurgency: The Strategies of Civil War

If a civil war breaks out, how is it fought? To what extent does the strategy of using violence differ when it is employed by nonstate actors? For most Americans, the term civil war evokes memorable battles between Union and Confederate soldiers, blue uniforms against gray, marching against each other in formation—in other words, a conventional war that happened to be fought by people who previously considered themselves citizens of the same country. The majority of civil wars worldwide bear no resemblance to this image. Most rebel armies do not engage in direct combat with the government forces. Instead, most rebellions take the form of insurgencies.[32] **Insurgency** is a military strategy in which small, often lightly armed units engage in hit-and-run attacks against military, government, and civilian targets. Unlike conventional military strategies, insurgency does not rely on capturing and holding territory. Instead, insurgents usually attack military bases, government buildings, or population centers and then melt back into rural areas, jungles, mountains, civilian populations, or across the border to take sanctuary in neighboring states. In order to blend into their surroundings, insurgents rarely wear distinctive uniforms. Indeed, the Chinese Communist leader Mao Tse-tung argued that insurgents should "swim" among the people just as fish swim in the sea—that is, hidden among the multitude.

The resort to insurgency is a direct response to the collective action problem facing rebel organizations. First and foremost, insurgency is well suited for groups that are small and weak relative to the adversary they face. Insurgency is a form of **asymmetric warfare**, or conflict between actors with highly unequal military capabilities. Generally lacking the ability to raise a large fighting force or acquire sophisticated weaponry, rebels resort to tactics that avoid direct confrontations with usually larger and better-armed government forces. The purpose of insurgency is not to defeat the military but rather to impose costs on the government in order to induce concessions. The hit-and-run strategy means that rebels rarely score decisive victories; at the same time, they are hard to defeat because they are hard to find. This elusiveness helps explain why civil wars often endure for years or decades, even when the rebel forces number only in the hundreds or low thousands.

The strategy of insurgency can also help address the collective action problem by increasing the pool of the individuals who may be willing to side with the rebels. By attacking civilians or police stations, courts, and other official sites, insurgents seek to undermine confidence in the government and encourage people to join them for protection. The Taliban insurgency in Afghanistan, for example, has sought to undermine faith in the U.S.-backed government by making people feel

---

insurgency

A military strategy in which small, often lightly armed units engage in hit-and-run attacks against military, government, and civilian targets.

asymmetric warfare

Armed conflict between actors with highly unequal military capabilities, such as when rebel groups or terrorists fight strong states.

---

32. A recent study classified 147 civil wars in the period 1944–2004 into three types, depending on whether the government, rebels, or both used heavy weapons such as tanks and artillery. Conventional wars, in which both sides used heavy weapons, accounted for 34 percent of the cases. Insurgencies, in which the government used heavy weapons but the rebels did not, accounted for 54 percent. The remaining 12 percent were cases in which both sides lacked heavy weapons. See Stathis N. Kalyvas, "International System and Technologies of Rebellion: How the End of the Cold War Shaped Internal Conflict," *American Political Science Review* 104 (Autumn 2010): 423.

A Sri Lankan military offensive against the LTTE rebel group in May 2009 caused extensive damage to villages in the conflict zone, killing thousands of Tamil civilians.

insecure and then offering to provide protection in exchange for support. Insurgents also, by hiding among the noncombatant population, seek to provoke government forces into attacking civilians, with the hope that these attacks will radicalize people into joining their cause. For example, the Taliban often fire on U.S. and Afghan government forces from populated areas, in the hopes that the retaliation will mistakenly kill civilians. The large number of Afghan civilians killed by U.S. airstrikes has helped fuel opposition to the Western presence and has increased recruitment of new rebels. It is, of course, true that far more Afghan civilians have been killed by the Taliban than by the United States and its allies, but the Taliban have been better able to exploit deaths caused by outsiders.[33] This strategy of provocation is also used by terrorists and will be discussed further below.

The nature of insurgency means that these kinds of rebellions can be hard to defeat through conventional military strategies that characterize interstate combat. Highly mechanized modern forces with tanks, jet planes, and heavy artillery are effective when confronting an opposing force that operates out in the open but not when dealing with a stealthy adversary that hides in the shadows and among civilian populations.[34] One response to this challenge is to engage in indiscriminate attacks against the civilian populations that might be sympathetic to the rebels' cause. Recalling Mao's fish analogy, the purpose of such a policy is to "drain the sea" within which the rebels hide. Not surprisingly, when pro-government forces

---

33. Estimates of civilian deaths in Afghanistan, including efforts to identify those responsible, are reported regularly by the United Nations Assistance Mission in Afghanistan. See http://unama.unmissions.org (accessed 12/08/14).

34. Jason Lyall and Isaiah Wilson III, "Rage against the Machines: Explaining Outcomes in Counterinsurgency Wars," *International Organization* 63 (2009): 67–106.

engage in this kind of strategy, civilian casualties are very high.[35] Whether this strategy can be effective at defeating an insurgency has been the subject of mixed findings in the literature. On the one hand, indiscriminate attacks have been shown in some cases to decisively defeat militants or at least hinder their ability to operate; for example, the Sri Lankan government eliminated the Liberation Tigers of Tamil Eelam (LTTE) in 2009 in the course of an unrestrained offensive that killed as many as 40,000 civilians trapped in the war zone.[36] On the other hand, there is also evidence that attacks on civilians can be counterproductive, spurring people to join the rebellion out of revenge or decreasing the willingness of civilians to cooperate with government forces.[37]

An alternative response to insurgency is one that focuses on winning the support of noncombatant populations in order to undercut the insurgency politically. The basic idea of this strategy is to provide security and support to civilians so that they will not be tempted or coerced into joining the rebellion. To the extent that people see their interests as aligned with the government's, rebels have a harder time recruiting fighters. In addition, greater confidence in the pro-government forces creates incentives for civilians to help identify militants who are hiding among them, thereby neutralizing one of the insurgents' key advantages. Civilians often fear that if they were to "rat out" militants, the government would not be able to protect them from reprisals. Counterinsurgency (COIN) operations are intended to ease this fear by making the government's commitment to defend civilians credible.

Though not new, this idea was at the root of a major rethinking of U.S. military strategy in response to the challenges in Iraq and Afghanistan. Facing persistent insurgencies in both countries, the military articulated a COIN doctrine in 2006 that focuses on using military forces to protect the civilian populations and to create a secure space for economic reconstruction. Rather than emphasizing search-and-destroy missions against insurgent forces, the COIN doctrine instead prioritizes deploying troops within towns and cities, patrolling along with the national army and police forces, to provide security and create confidence in the governments on behalf of which the United States was fighting. The strategy also calls for steps to reduce the danger of accidentally killing civilians, for example, by relying more on ground forces and less on bombs and missiles launched from airplanes, which are responsible for a large share of civilian deaths. In addition, COIN operations involve not just military power but also an injection of economic resources to help jump-start development and undercut rebels' efforts to "buy" new fighters and supporters.

In short, COIN doctrine is an attempt to defeat an insurgency by giving the population an interest in the survival of the government, thereby exacerbating the rebels' collective action problem and eliminating their informational advantages.

---

35. Benjamin Valentino, Paul Huth, and Dylan Balch-Lindsay, "'Draining the Sea': Mass Killing and Guerrilla Warfare," *International Organization* 58 (2004): 375–407.

36. Jason Lyall, "Does Indiscriminate Violence Incite Insurgent Attacks? Evidence from Chechnya," *Journal of Conflict Resolution* 53 (June 2009): 331–62; and Lionel Beehner, "What Sri Lanka Can Teach Us about COIN," *Small Wars Journal* 6 (August 2010): 1–8.

37. See, for example, Luke N. Condra and Jacob N. Shapiro, "Who Takes the Blame? The Strategic Effects of Collateral Damage," *American Journal of Political Science* 56 (January 2012): 167–87.

FIGURE 6.2 *Estimated Civilian Deaths Due to Violence in Iraq, 2003–2015*

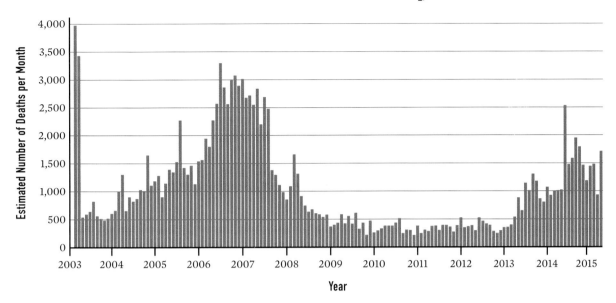

Figure source: The Iraq Body Count project, www. iraqbodycount.org/database/ (accessed 05/18/15).

Note: Data for 2014 and 2015 are preliminary.

This model had success in Iraq in 2007, when the deployment of more U.S. troops and the shift to the new COIN strategy helped bring about a dramatic reduction in insurgent activity and civilian deaths. This "surge" coincided with a split among the rebellious Sunnis, as some local leaders decided to assist the government in combating extremists who were responsible for much of the violence. Though the United States was not primarily responsible for this turn, the surge made credible its commitment not to abandon the government and enabled closer cooperation with local groups. The resulting reduction in violence paved the way for a significant withdrawal of American forces in Iraq as well as their transition out of a combat role.[38] Figure 6.2 shows the trend in Iraqi civilian deaths due to the conflict, including the dramatic reduction after 2007. Taking advantage of this relative calm, U.S. forces left the country at the end of 2011. In the fall of 2009, President Barack Obama decided to try the same model against the Taliban insurgency in Afghanistan, increasing the U.S. troop presence there to 100,000 (together with roughly 40,000 troops from other countries) and implementing the COIN strategy.

Whether these efforts will lead a permanent end to conflict in these countries was, at the time of this writing, in serious doubt. As Figure 6.2 shows, only two years after U.S. forces left Iraq, the civil war there reignited, fed by the emergence of the militant group IS in neighboring Syria. In Afghanistan, the increased troop presence and new strategy had some successes, but there was no marked reduction in violence, nor much prospect that the Taliban could be defeated militarily. Despite limited progress, most U.S. and allied forces withdrew by the end of 2014, and those

---

38. For an analysis of the various factors that brought down violence in Iraq, see Stephen Biddle, Jeffrey A. Friedman, and Jacob N. Shapiro, "Testing the Surge: Why Did Violence Decline in Iraq in 2007?" *International Security* 37 (Summer 2012): 7–40.

that remained transitioned away from combat roles. The frustrations experienced in these countries by the world's most powerful state are a testament to the effectiveness of the strategy of insurgency.

What Can Be Done about Civil War?

Given the enormous human toll of civil wars, it is natural to ask whether there are steps that outsiders can take to reduce the risk of this kind of violence. As mentioned earlier, there is already a great deal of outside interference in civil wars, but much of it takes the form of supporting one side or the other; indeed, this support is often responsible for the onset and long duration of these wars. Can outside actors play a more positive role? As we saw in the previous chapter, there have been attempts, particularly since the 1990s, to extend the reach of collective security organizations like the UN so that they could deal with conflicts that take place within states, not just those that take place between them. The track record in this respect was, at best, uneven. Efforts to end ongoing conflicts in the former Yugoslavia, Rwanda, and elsewhere were ultimately hampered by the fact that few states had strong enough interests to motivate costly action; and in some cases, the international community had conflicting interests. Weak or conflicting interests led to half-hearted, ineffectual measures by international actors. On the other hand, external efforts have played a much more positive role in keeping the peace once the combatants have decided to stop fighting. In particular, cease-fire agreements that are accompanied by some form of peacekeeping operation tend to have a higher likelihood of holding. Moreover, there is evidence that strong international efforts at peace building can not only prevent the resumption of violence but also encourage the emergence of more democratic countries.[39]

International efforts can potentially address several of the factors that can cause peace to break down. First, they can help the combatants resolve commitment problems that arise in the wake of cease-fires. As we saw, agreements that require rebels to disarm create a severe commitment problem owing to the government's incentives to renege on the deal once the rebels have complied. If they can credibly guarantee the safety of disarmed and demobilized rebels, and help them reintegrate into society, peacekeepers may help alleviate this problem. International peace-building efforts may also help with the economic and political reconstruction of the country, which is important to long-term stability. For example, many peacekeeping missions after civil wars help organize and monitor elections, train the civilian police force, and bolster the judicial system. If successful, these efforts can lead to new political institutions through which future disputes can be handled without recourse to coercive bargaining. There have also been some international efforts to reduce the ability of rebel groups to finance themselves through sales of drugs or minerals. For example, the Kimberley Process, initiated in 2003 (and named after the town in South

---

39. Walter, *Committing to Peace*; Virginia Page Fortna, *Does Peacekeeping Work? Shaping Belligerents' Choices after Civil War* (Princeton, NJ: Princeton University Press, 2008); and Michael W. Doyle and Nicholas Sambanis, "International Peacebuilding: A Theoretical and Quantitative Analysis," *American Political Science Review* 94 (2000): 779–801.

Africa where the idea was hatched), is an international process that certifies rough diamonds that did not come from conflict zones. The hope is that if consumers purchase only diamonds that have the certification, the ability of rebels to finance themselves with so-called blood diamonds would be choked off.

Of course, most of these efforts are designed to end civil wars and prevent them from restarting after a peace deal; ideally, we would like to reduce the likelihood that bloody and destructive civil wars will break out in the first place. There are several challenges to this aspiration. As already noted, most countries have dissatisfied groups and individuals that could provide the basis for armed opposition to the government. Although we know some of the factors that increase the risks of civil war, these conflicts are very hard to forecast with much certainty. As a result, it can be hard to correctly anticipate where the next civil war will break out and to target conflict management efforts appropriately. Moreover, there are truly repressive regimes that deserve the opposition of their people. In these cases, reducing the risk of armed rebellion can have the unintended effect of diminishing the government's incentives to liberalize.

In the long run, the best chance for a reduction in civil conflict hinges on economic development and democratization. Relatively wealthy countries have the lowest risk of civil war because their people have less to gain and more to lose by taking up arms and because wealthy governments are better able to buy off dissatisfied groups and/or deter the emergence of armed opposition. Well-functioning democracies provide institutions that enable groups and individuals to pursue their interests through peaceful political processes. Even so, these are long-run developments over which outsiders have only limited influence. Though states and international organizations constantly seek ways to promote development and democratization, these efforts, at best, support internal processes. Moreover, the route to development and democracy can be rocky and dangerous. Though economic growth is good, it can have uneven effects as some groups within a country grow wealthy, while others remain mired in poverty. This kind of inequality can become a grievance that feeds civil conflict. Transitions to democracy can also be risky. During the period of transition, the regime may be too weak to deter violence while at the same time democratic institutions are not strong enough to channel political demands in peaceful ways. There is some evidence to suggest that periods of democratization are associated with an increased risk of civil war.[40]

The promotion of democracy by third parties also has to be done carefully. There is some evidence that foreign aid given for purposes of democracy building can reduce the risk of civil war in countries that are already democratizing.[41] Bringing democracy to countries that are currently autocratic, on the other hand,

---

40. Edward D. Mansfield and Jack Snyder, *Electing to Fight: Why Emerging Democracies Go to War* (Cambridge, MA: MIT Press, 2005). Though the evidence presented in this book is primarily about interstate war, the logic also applies to civil war. For discussion and evidence, see Lars-Erik Cederman, Simon Hug, and Lutz F. Krebs, "Democratization and Civil War: Empirical Evidence," *Journal of Peace Research* 47 (2010): 377–94.

41. Burcu Savun and Daniel C. Tirone, "Foreign Aid, Democratization, and Civil Conflict: How Does Democracy Aid Affect Civil Conflict?" *American Journal of Political Science* 55 (2011): 233–46.

requires some effort to destabilize the existing regime or, as in the case of the U.S. invasion of Iraq, remove it forcibly. As the U.S. experience vividly shows, however, the weakening or destruction of an autocratic regime can itself precipitate civil war.[42] The civil conflict in Iraq that followed the invasion is estimated to have claimed tens of thousands if not hundreds of thousands of lives. And, as we have seen, while U.S. forces helped bring about a reduction in violence after 2007, Iraq's civil war reignited only a few years after those troops left, dimming the prospects that Iraq will emerge prosperous and democratic.

Terrorism: Why Kill Civilians?

terrorism

The use or threatened use of violence against noncombatant targets by individuals or nonstate groups for political ends.

Though a variety of definitions abound, **terrorism** is conventionally described as the premeditated threat or use of violence against noncombatant targets by individuals or subnational groups to obtain a political or social objective through intimidation of a larger audience.[43] Unlike conventional warfare, terrorism is an attempt to win concessions not by defeating the armed forces of another actor but by attacking civilians or civilian police forces or military units not engaged in combat. These attacks sow fear among some target population in the hope that this target will concede to the terrorist's political or social demands. The existence of such demands is crucial, as otherwise terrorism is no different from simple criminality.

Terrorism is transnational, and thus the subject of international relations, when it crosses an international border by involving a perpetrator and victim from different countries or when it aims to alter the behavior of a foreign government. Figure 6.3 shows the number of international terrorist attacks per year, along with their estimated fatalities. Though terrorism rose to high levels in the 1970s and '80s, it was generally on the decline until September 2001, which ushered in a new spike of activity.

Most terrorism, however, is purely domestic and does not cross national borders. Indeed, there is an overlap between terrorism and civil wars, since many rebel groups engage in systematic violence against civilians. The Irish Republican Army (IRA), the main Protestant group fighting British rule in Northern Ireland in the twentieth century, and the Tamil Tigers, the secessionist group that fought in Sri Lanka for decades until its defeat in 2009, were armed actors in civil wars that used terrorism extensively. One study estimated that about 30 percent of rebel groups involved in civil wars used indiscriminate violence against civilians as part

---

42. For a general finding to this effect, see Goran Peic and Dan Reiter, "Foreign-Imposed Regime Change, State Power, and Civil War Onset, 1920–2004," *British Journal of Political Science* 41 (2010): 453–75.

43. This definition, used by scholars, is similar to that in the *United States Code*, title 22, chap. 38, sec. 2656f(d). Any definition of terrorism is itself a political statement. *Terrorist* is a term of opprobrium intended to delegitimize the action and, in turn, the cause for which violence is used. Thus, who is and is not a terrorist is often contested. State-sponsored terrorism involves government funding or support of terrorists. State terrorism, which we do not consider here, involves the targeting of noncombatants by the government with the intent of influencing an audience.

FIGURE 6.3 *International Terrorist Attacks and Fatalities, 1968–2008**

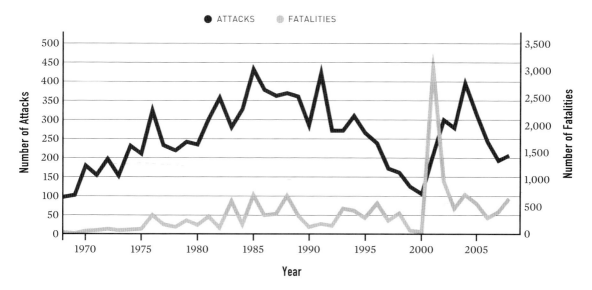

Figure source: RAND Database of Worldwide Terrorism Incidents, www.rand.org/nsrd/projects/terrorism-incidents.html (accessed 12/18/14).

*The RAND Database of Worldwide Terrorism Incidents, the most comprehensive source for identifying attacks with an internationl component, was discontinued in 2009.

of their effort to coerce the target government.[44] Moreover, as we will see, strategies of insurgency and terrorism have similar logics. Nonetheless, many groups that engage in terrorism are much smaller and less centrally organized than are rebel groups capable of waging a civil war.

How can we understand people who hijack airliners and fly them into skyscrapers or blow themselves up on crowded trains and buses? A common explanation for terrorism is that terrorists are hate-filled, irrational extremists who win glory by taking the lives of others. This is too simplistic. Rather, terrorism, like war, is a product of a strategic interaction between the terrorists and the governments they hope to influence. As such, violence can be understood as a bargaining failure prompted by incomplete information, commitment problems, and indivisibilities. At the same time, terrorists, like the rebel groups considered in the previous section, face a challenge in finding resources and recruits willing to undertake dangerous, possibly even suicidal, missions and in organizing collective action without being detected or ratted out. These organizational imperatives affect the nature of terrorist groups and the strategies they select.

Are Terrorists Rational?

In popular discussions, it is often implied that terrorists are irrational, crazed "fanatics." If so, this characterization would significantly challenge our ability to

---

44. Virtually all rebel groups attack civilians to some degree, primarily to dissuade them from collaborating with the government or to coerce them into aiding the rebellion. Virginia Page Fortna, "Which Rebels Use Terrorism? Data from Civil War" (unpublished manuscript, Columbia University, New York, October 2010).

analyze their behavior within the analytic framework developed in this textbook. There are at least three reasons for this perception that must be examined before turning to an explanation of terrorism.

First, groups that resort to terrorism often possess interests that are not widely shared, especially by the target audience. Describing terrorists as irrational may simply mean that terrorists rank alternative outcomes in ways that are "unreasonable," at least from the broader population's perspective. However, as we saw in Chapter 2, rationality refers to purposive behavior or the strategies by which individuals or groups pursue their interests; the term *rational* is not a statement about the substance of an individual's or group's preferences. We may not agree with the preferences of terrorists and their supporters, but the fact that we disagree does not necessarily imply that the strategy they choose in pursuit of their interests is irrational. Indeed, there is substantial evidence that given their interests, terrorist networks choose targets, respond to risk, and adjust to counterterrorist efforts in quite purposeful or rational ways. One common explanation for the expanding number of suicide attacks in recent years, for instance, is that as sites have become harder to destroy by more conventional methods, terrorists have upgraded from "dumb bombs" controlled by a timer, to "smart bombs" in the form of well-trained suicide bombers who can adapt to countermeasures and react to events on the scene.[45] Reflecting a highly rational calculus, terrorists appear to select targets according to how well they are defended, the chances of a successful attack, and the targets' political impact.

Second, a person's choice to become a terrorist—especially to become a suicide bomber—may entail costs larger than the gains to that individual and thus appears not to be an effective strategy for obtaining one's goals. It is true that we do not currently possess good explanations for why any particular individual chooses to become a terrorist or a suicide bomber. After all, the sacrifice of one's own life seems a high price to pay for any cause. However, we also lack complete explanations for why an individual man or woman may voluntarily choose to join a national military and go into battle to risk death for his or her country. For any individual, such choices may be irrational in that the personal costs (the risk of death) exceed the personal gains. Acknowledging this point, however, does not imply that a terrorist organization lacks purpose and careful strategizing in how it deploys its forces, including suicide bombers.

Third, terrorist attacks sometimes appear to be random. In some cases, of course, it is clear why terrorists chose a certain target, as the selection of the World Trade Center and Pentagon as targets on 9/11 demonstrates. These sites were chosen because they represent the core of America's international power—business and the military. More generally, the most frequent targets of terrorists are businesses and diplomatic missions, which also serve as emblems of the target state's power. But certainly some terrorist attacks are random, as when a suicide bomber selects one crowded pizzeria rather than another. Random selection of targets and

---

45. Eli Berman and David Laitin, "Hard Targets: Theory and Evidence on Suicide Attacks," NBER Working Paper W11740, National Bureau of Economic Research, Cambridge, MA, November 2005.

times, however, is often part of a terrorist's strategy. After all, one objective of terrorism is to strike fear into the target population. If terrorist attacks are systematic and predictable, the population will adjust accordingly and avoid likely targets when an attack is anticipated. By selecting random times and places, terrorists can make people feel unsafe everywhere and greatly magnify the threat they pose and the fear they instill. In other words, randomness can be quite rational.

Why Terrorism?

A key point in understanding terrorism is that terrorist organizations are weak in two key senses: they are weak relative to their targets (usually, states), and they are weak relative to the extensive demands they make. This weakness arises from the nature of the interests that motivate them.

People and groups that use terrorism may be motivated by any number of interests. They may seek to overthrow a government, expel a foreign power from their homeland, or create a new utopian society based on some economic or religious ideology. Al Qaeda has sought to eradicate Western influence from the Middle East in order to bring about Islamist governments in the region. Palestinian terrorist groups like Hamas have sought the destruction of the state of Israel. The Shining Path is a Marxist terrorist group that has operated in Peru since the 1980s and sought to destabilize the government and bring about a Communist revolution.

Whatever interests they seek to promote, terrorists are typically **extremists** in the sense that their interests are not widely shared by others, or, at least, their willingness to pay costs to achieve those interests is not widely shared. In any population there is a range of individual interests over issues such as the most appropriate political system, the distribution of resources, proper religious beliefs, and so on. For most issues the range of interests is distributed in a bell-shaped curve, with most people being "moderate" and clustered in the middle of the distribution (Figure 6.4). When we call someone extreme, we typically mean that his or

extremists

Actor whose interests are not widely shared by others; individuals or groups that are politically weak relative to the demands they make.

FIGURE 6.4 *Extremist Interests*

Terrorists sometimes carry out seemingly random attacks on public places as a purposeful strategy to strike fear into the target population, as in the 2013 attacks on a social club in Quetta, Pakistan, which killed more than 80 people.

her interests are significantly different from those of the majority. In the curve illustrated in Figure 6.4, extremists exist in the "tails" of the distribution to either the left or the right of the moderate majority. In fact, what it means to be an extremist is relative: someone who is an extremist in one society might not be in another. For example, moderates in Britain may have very different interests from moderates in Pakistan. But extremism implies that relatively few other individuals share their political preferences. And even if others share the terrorists' ultimate objectives—for example, many peaceful individuals in the Middle East resent Western influence there and would like to see it end—they may not care so intensely that they are willing to kill or die for that goal.

Almost by definition, therefore, extremists are small groups of individuals who face a much larger majority that does not share their views and that will likely resist having those beliefs imposed on it. The result is that extremists tend to be weak politically relative to the demands they make. This condition means that the problem of recruitment is particularly acute, since the pool of motivated individuals is relatively small, and extremists have difficulty in convincing others to share their interests and join their cause. Moreover, their fringe status means that they will seldom be able to further their interests by participating in the normal political process, making use of existing institutions, even in a democracy. Instead, their hope lies in using violence to coerce concessions or somehow alter the status quo in their favor.

The resort to violence is further complicated by the fact that terrorists are weak not only relative to their demands but also relative to their targets. Like insurgency, terrorism is a form of asymmetric warfare. States are nearly always stronger politically and militarily than the terrorist networks they face. Whereas states have populations and economies they can tax for resources and standing militaries they can deploy, terrorist organizations are often starved for resources, quite small in numbers, and poorly armed, especially in their formative stages when they are most vulnerable to government countermeasures. Like rebel groups, they often must resort to such criminal activities as drug running or bank robbery to acquire their initial funding, although some grow out of legitimate religious and service activities, such as Hamas, or depend on the personal wealth of their founders, such as Osama bin Laden in the case of Al Qaeda (see "What Shaped Our World?" on p. 277). This weakness is central to understanding why terrorism involves attacks on civilians, government embassies, and other official buildings. The object of terrorism is to bypass the other side's military, as direct confrontation would result in certain defeat, and inflict pain and suffering on the target population so as to induce political change.

The weakness of terrorists also influences the way they choose to organize. Terrorists adopt organizational forms that make it difficult for traditional military forces to defeat them. First, they typically form networks of small self-contained cells that are loosely connected to one another and, in some cases, to a central directorate.[46] Unlike states, which have internal hierarchies, terrorists are organized in networks of individuals and groups that cooperate to achieve common aims. Terrorists do not routinely share information within the network; each cell is largely responsible for its own activities and acquires resources and information from other cells or the central directorate only as necessary. This loose network insulates the individual cells and allows the organization to survive when penetrated or attacked. If the potential target state successfully infiltrates or destroys a cell, there is minimal impact on the rest of the network. In addition, transnational terrorist groups may try to spread their message through publications and social media in order to inspire followers into committing "lone wolf" attacks, that is, attacks by individuals who are not actually members of the group but who share its goals. The April 2013 attack on the Boston Marathon, which killed three people and injured over 250, was committed by two brothers who were allegedly radicalized by extremist propaganda and learned bomb-making skills from an online Al Qaeda publication. Such lone wolf attacks are rarely as lethal as those planned by an organization, but they are very hard to prevent because the perpetrators have no observable connection to a terrorist group.

Second, just as rebels take refuge in jungles, mountains, and cities, terrorists hide within sympathetic populations. In cases where the group is not too extreme and thus has affiliated individuals who share their interests, or in which the local population has been radicalized and now shares the extremists' beliefs, terrorists can live within a larger population that protects and supports them. Palestinian extremists, for example, can blend into the wider Palestinian community, which supports many of their goals, if not always their methods. In other cases, terrorist groups can buy support from a corrupt, failed, or sympathetic state to gain refuge, as Al Qaeda did when, having been expelled from Saudi Arabia, it set up bases in Sudan and, after the Taliban seized power, subsequently returned to Afghanistan. Hidden within larger populations, terrorists are difficult to identify. Attempts to eliminate them, in turn, are likely to cause collateral damage to the larger population and thus raise the costs of any retaliatory or preemptive attack by the target state. Indeed, networks of loosely connected cells hidden in sympathetic populations make terrorist groups hard to eradicate.

Terrorism as a Bargaining Failure

Like states, terrorist organizations use violence or threats of violence to raise costs to the other side in hopes of eliciting concessions. In this way, terrorism and threats of terrorism are a form of bargaining. But if the target state knows the costs that terrorists can inflict on it, and the terrorists know that they are unlikely to defeat the state but can extract some concessions by threatening violence, why can the two

---

46. Note that this is not necessarily the case with rebel groups that use terrorism, which may be more centrally organized.

The bombing at the Boston Marathon in 2013 showed the danger of lone wolf attacks by people who are inspired by, but not members of, a terrorist group.

sides not reach a compromise that reflects their relative bargaining positions? If such a bargain were possible, then the terrorists would be spared the costs of carrying out the attack and the target would not incur the damage and subsequent widespread fear. Given that the costs of violence theoretically make a mutually beneficial deal available, can we understand terrorism, like international and civil war, as a bargaining failure?

One natural reaction against this view is that terrorists' goals may be so extreme that compromise is simply not possible. If terrorists want everyone in the target population to convert to a different religion, or they seek the elimination of the target state, then it may be difficult to imagine some compromise settlement that would be acceptable to both sides. In the extreme case where the adversary seeks your death or the obliteration of your identity, then the costs of concessions and the costs of conflict may be indistinguishable, and there is little choice but to fight. But while we do not rule out the possibility of this extreme case—for example, Hamas and other Palestinian terrorist groups have called for the destruction of Israel—what separates terrorists from mass murderers is that they kill in order to advance a political objective, not as an end in its own right. Therefore, a mutually beneficial bargain generally exists in theory, even if there are significant barriers to identifying and achieving such a bargain in practice. As in the case of international and civil war, we can group these barriers as relating to information problems, commitment problems, and indivisibility.

Terrorism from Incomplete Information Like states in conflict, terrorists have private information and incentives to misrepresent that information to targets. Precisely because terrorist networks are small, weak, and often shadowy organizations that hide within sympathetic populations or in fragile states, targets usually possess incomplete information about their size, capabilities, and resolve. Often, the first time anyone learns of a new terrorist group is after it claims credit for an attack. Even when targets have intelligence sources within the terrorist group, they may acquire relatively little information: the cell that is infiltrated or monitored may know little about other cells. Terrorist networks, in turn, have incentives to misrepresent their capabilities and resolve. By exaggerating claims of strength and commitment, these organizations seek to negotiate better deals from their targets. The targets, knowing that the networks have incentives to exaggerate, discount their claims. As we now know, there were numerous hints about the impending attacks before 9/11, and bin Laden made no secret of the fact that he saw himself at war with the United States.[47] These warning signals were ignored in part because the separate agencies of the U.S. government were not able to put together the disparate pieces of the puzzle they had before them and because officials saw other threats as more important. But the warning signs were also downplayed because they could be interpreted as the normal blustering of terrorists whose aspirations seemed to far exceed their reach.

As we saw in Chapter 3, overcoming information problems requires finding ways for actors to communicate their capabilities and resolve in a credible manner. But the nature of terrorist organizations makes credible communication particularly difficult. Since their ability to carry out attacks against militarily more powerful targets typically hinges on the element of surprise, terrorists cannot reveal their true capabilities or strategies in advance without undermining their effectiveness. If Al Qaeda had announced before 9/11 that unless the U.S. government conceded to its demands it would fly hijacked airliners into the World Trade Center and the Pentagon, the United States would have quickly responded by grounding all airplanes (which it did immediately after the attacks) and surrounding New York and Washington, D.C., with constant air patrols. By tipping its hand in advance, Al Qaeda would have lost the ability to implement those very attacks on the United States. The use of attacks to signal capabilities and resolve distinguishes terrorist organizations from states engaged in coercive diplomacy. States often communicate using strategies short of force, such as public statements and mobilizations. The goal is to demonstrate a willingness to use force in the hopes of winning concessions without actually having to use force. The nature of terrorist organizations, however, means that they cannot engage the same kind of public displays without exposing themselves to the authorities and risking a crackdown. Instead, they tend to mobilize their efforts in secret, and the attack becomes the public signal.[48] Thus, unlike in interstate relations, there may be no bargaining between terrorists and states before the violence starts.

---

47. See *The 9/11 Commission Report: Final Report of the National Commission on Terrorist Attacks upon the United States* (New York: Norton, 2004), 254–77.

48. Harvey E. Lapan and Todd Sandler, "Terrorism and Signaling," *European Journal of Political Economy* 9 (1993): 383–97.

Terrorism from Commitment Problems   Problems of credible commitment also loom large in this context.[49] As part of any agreement reached before or after an attack, the target will insist that the organization promise not to employ violence in the future. After all, the whole point of making concessions is to reduce the threat and fear of future attacks. If the commitment to refrain from further attacks is not credible, however, this can prevent the conclusion of agreements that both sides prefer. Achieving credibility can be particularly hard in this context since the target must judge not only the trustworthiness of the terrorist leadership but also its ability to exert control over potential defectors within its ranks. Given their organization as decentralized networks of loosely connected individuals and cells, centralized control is often difficult to achieve. Even if the group's leadership is willing to make a deal, it may not be able to rein in all the "loose cannons" that might want to continue the fight.

Terrorists can most credibly demonstrate their commitment to peace by publicly renouncing terror, disarming, and giving the target or some neutral third party full access to the network so as to alleviate any lingering information problems. This approach has been key to the still-fragile peace between Catholics and Protestants in Northern Ireland, where the IRA has disavowed terrorism, disarmed, and joined the political process. As in the case of civil wars, however, the need for disarmament creates another commitment problem: If the terrorists disarm, how can they be certain that the target will honor its side of the agreement? After all, it was the fear of continuing attacks that gave terrorists power over the target in the first place. Once that ability is given up, the target no longer has any incentive to compromise with the terrorists. Credibly agreeing not to fight may be more difficult than credibly making threats in the first place. Indeed, the difficulties of committing to peace have been a source of continued fighting in many terrorist conflicts—including that between the Basque separatist group Euskadi Ta Azkatasuna (ETA) and Spain, where both sides now appear to want peace but still have difficulty in credibly committing to a plan for disarmament and regional autonomy.

States may also see fighting terrorists, rather than compromising with them, as a solution to a different commitment problem. A common argument for not negotiating with terrorists is that even if it makes sense to compromise with any one group, doing so will simply encourage others to emerge with new demands. After all, if any individual or group that threatens to detonate a bomb can wrest concessions from the target government, then a government faces a potentially endless list of demands from an ever-increasing set of adversaries. This is similar to the problem, mentioned earlier, of governments that face many potential separatist groups: though making concessions to any one might make sense, buying off every group is too costly. When faced with a large number of potential adversaries, the government would like to commit itself not to negotiate with any of them. Resisting any

---

49. Ethan Bueno de Mesquita, "Conciliation, Counterterrorism, and Patterns of Terrorist Violence," *International Organization* 59, no. 1 (2005): 145–76; and Navin Bapat, "State Bargaining with Transnational Terrorist Groups," *International Studies Quarterly* 50, no. 1 (2006): 213–29.

ETA erakundeak zigilatutako materialaren inbentarioa
Inventaire du matériel scellé par l'organisation ETA
Inventario del material precintado por la organización ETA

ZM-01/2014

Euskadi Ta Askatasunak, Nazioarteko Egiaztatze Batzordea lekuko, honoko materialaren zigilatzea burutu du.

Euskadi Ta Askatasuna, en présence de la Commission Internationale de Vérification, a réalisé le scellé du matériel qui suit.
Euskadi Ta Askatasuna, en presencia de la Comisión Internacional de Verificación, ha realizado el precintado del material detallado a continuación.

Armak eta munizioa (armes et munition/armas y munición):

G3 fusil luzea (fusil G3 long/fusil G3 largo) 1

Smith&Wesson 22 long rifle pistola (Pistolet Smith&Wesson 22 long rifle/pistola Smith&Wesson 22 long rifle) 1

Smith&Wesson Lady Smith errebolberra (Revolver Smith&Wesson Lady Smith) 1

Arminius HW1G errebolberra (Revolver Arminius HW1G) 1

Balak 38 SP (cartouches 38 SP/balas 38 SP) 300

Karga hutseko Hepat granada (Grenade de charge vide Hepat/granada de carga hueca Hepat) 2

Leherkariak (explosifs, explosivos):

Pentrita (pentrite/pentrita) ....4,50 Kg

Kazkabarra (mélange explosif chloraté: soufre et chlorate de sodium/Cloratita: azufre y clorato de sodio) ....8,00 Kg

Sodio kloratu xehatua (chlorate de sodium en poudre/clorato de sodio molido) ....4,00 Kg

Nitromanitola (nitromannite/nitromanita) ....10 g

Pentritaz osatutako 15 g-ko lokarri detonatzaile industriala (Cordon détonateur industriel de 15 g/cordón detonante industrial de 15 g) ....120 m

Pentritaz osatutako 12 g-ko lokarri detonatzaile industriala (Cordon détonateur industriel de 12 g/cordón detonante industrial de 12 g) ....70 m

Gailuak (dispositifs/dispositivos):

AKT-Atzera Kontaketa Tenporizadorea (temporisateur compte-à-rebours/temporizador cuenta-atrás) 2

ET-Eguneko Tenporizadorea (temporisateur de 24h/temporizador de 24h) 3

Dardar Lapa-Mugimendu sentsore elektronikodun tenporizadorea (temporisateur avec senseur de mouvement electronique/temporizador con sensor electronico de movimiento) 1

Merkurio Lapa-Merkurio bidezko mugimendu sentsoredun tenporizadorea (temporisateur avec senseur de mouvement en mercure/ temporizador con sensor de movimiento de mercurio) 3

Euskal Herrian, 2014ko urtarrilean
En Euskal Herria, Janvier 2014
En Euskal Herria, Enero de 2014

Nazioarteko Egiaztatze Batzordea
Commission Internationale de Vérification
Comisión Internacional de Verificación

Euskadi Ta Askatasuna
E.T.A.

On February 21, 2014, international monitors reported that the Basque separatist group ETA had taken the first steps toward disarmament as part of a ceasefire pledge. Pictured here is the inventory list of firearms, explosives, and detonators turned over by the group.

single group's demands, even at the risk of experiencing new attacks, is a way to signal this commitment and thereby deter the emergence of new challengers.

Terrorism from Indivisibilities
Finally, bargaining may fail if the goods in dispute are such that they cannot readily be divided or subject to compromise. The view that it is not possible to negotiate with terrorists is often driven by the perception that these organizations have goals that are nonnegotiable. The connection between religion and terrorism furthers this perception, since goods that are connected to religious identities may be particularly hard to split. Hamas and other Palestinian terrorist groups do not want a Jewish state on the land between the Jordan Valley and the Mediterranean Sea; if given the choice, they would institute an Islamic regime in what is now Israel. Most Israelis want their state to be a Jewish state, though one that permits other religions to be practiced openly. In principle, there are middle positions between a Jewish state and an Islamic state on this land. One could imagine a state with no officially sanctioned religion in which all faiths can

FIGURE 6.5 *The Number of Attacks and Fatalities by Group Goal, 1968–2005*

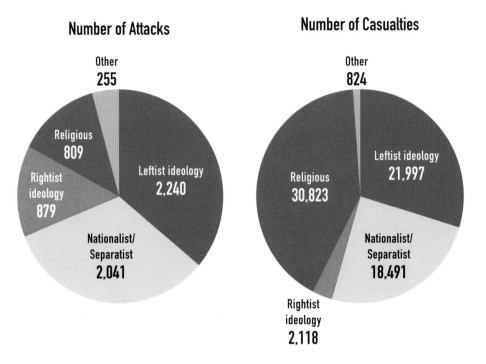

Number of Attacks

Other
255

Religious
809

Rightist
ideology
879

Leftist ideology
2,240

Nationalist/
Separatist
2,041

Number of Casualties

Other
824

Religious
30,823

Leftist ideology
21,997

Nationalist/
Separatist
18,491

Rightist
ideology
2,118

Figure source: James A. Piazza, "Is Islamist Terrorism More Dangerous? An Empirical Study of Group Ideology, Organization, and Goal Structure," *Terrorism and Political Violence* 21 (2009): 63. Leftist ideology includes groups whose goals were characterized as anarchist, antiglobalization, Communist, Socialist, and environmental. Rightist ideology includes groups whose goals were characterized as racist, right-wing conservative, and reactionary.

be freely practiced (as the United States) or a state in which both religions are officially sanctioned. But while such compromises exist both in principle and in practice, there are those on both sides who see the state's religious identity as an all-or-nothing issue.

The connection between religion and terrorism is real but also should not be overstated. It is not the case that most terrorism is religiously motivated. Figure 6.5 breaks down international terrorist groups by the type of goal they were pursuing and shows the number of attacks and casualties (killed and wounded) caused by each type of group in the period 1968–2005. According to these figures, only 13 percent of terrorist attacks in this period were committed by religious terrorists. However, attacks by religious groups were particularly lethal, accounting for 42 percent of all casualties. Religion also plays a pronounced role in suicide terrorism, as the belief that a reward is waiting in the afterlife seems important in motivating this kind of behavior. Though not all groups that use suicide terrorism draw on explicitly religious ideologies, most do, and the vast majority of suicide attacks involve perpetrators and targets from different religions.[50] If the individuals engaged in terrorism believe that they are pursuing ideals that cannot be compromised, then there may be little scope for bargaining.

---

50. Eli Berman and David D. Laitin, "Religion, Terrorism, and Public Goods: Testing the Club Model," *Journal of Public Economics* 92 (2008): 1942–67. See also Robert A. Pape, "The Strategic Logic of Suicide Terrorism," *American Political Science Review* 97 (August 2003): 351–55.

As we noted in Chapter 3, however, while indivisibility is not a trivial issue, we should be cautious about accepting this explanation too readily. Actors often have incentives to make others believe that their demands are all or nothing. The belief that you are unable to compromise can be an asset in bargaining, so actors may try to present issues as indivisible, or they may try to commit themselves to treat an issue as indivisible. One of the goals of suicide terrorism is to convey precisely this message: our followers would rather die than give up their ideals. Thus, indivisibility can be the product of a bargaining and signaling strategy rather than a quality inherent in the dispute.

How Can Terrorists Hope to Win?
Strategies of Violence

We have already seen that terrorist organizations are generally small and weak relative to their adversaries. Given that they cannot defeat the target in any conventional sense, how can they hope to succeed? What purpose does killing people serve? When bargaining fails and a group turns to terrorism, there are four principal strategies by which it may use violence to further its interests: coercion, provocation, spoiling, outbidding.[51] These strategies are not mutually exclusive, and any particular attack can involve elements of more than one. The key to understanding them is to recognize that terrorists act in front of at least two audiences: (1) the government and population of the target state and (2) the "home" population—that is, the people on whose behalf they claim to act. The different strategies of terrorism seek to impress these audiences in order to advance the organization's twin interests in wresting concession from the target and winning supporters among the home population. In particular, coercion and spoiling are intended to influence the beliefs of the target, while provocation and outbidding are intended to influence the beliefs of the home population.

Coercion Terrorists can attack or threaten to attack in order to coerce a target into making concessions. **Coercion** induces policy change by imposing costs—usually civilian deaths and casualties—on the target. More specifically, it is the *threat* of imposed costs that matters. The target may change its policy or offer concessions to avoid the costs. But if a threat is carried out and the costs are realized—people are killed, buildings are destroyed—the target has no incentive to alter its behavior. At that point, only the threat of *future* attacks will lead it to change its policy. By threatening to inflict harm on the target, terrorists aim to intimidate potential victims, using the fear of future attacks to motivate individuals to press their own government to change its policy or to change the governing party.

Since it is the fear of future attacks that may induce policy change, it follows that actual attacks occur primarily to make the threat of future violence credible. This is necessary, in turn, because the target is uncertain about the terrorists' capabilities or resolve. The terrorist group might threaten costs of a certain magnitude

coercion

A strategy of imposing or threatening to impose costs on other actors in order to induce a change in their behavior.

---

51. Andrew Kydd and Barbara Walter, "The Strategies of Terrorism," *International Security* 31 (Summer 2006): 49–80. We combine their strategies of attrition and intimidation into a single strategy of coercion.

unless appropriate concessions are made, but the target knows that the group has incentives to bluff and exaggerate its capabilities or willingness to bear the costs of carrying out the attack. To demonstrate its capabilities or resolve, the terrorist group must then attack the target to show that it is willing and able carry out similar attacks in the future.

In this way, attacks are a form of costly signaling intended to make credible the terrorists' threats of future violence unless their demands are met. This type of signaling can entail small demonstration attacks such as bomb scares, which are not designed to kill people or destroy property but rather to call attention to the network and signal that it has the ability to kill and destroy in the future if its demands are not met. In a form of pure signaling, the Basque separatist group ETA often gave warnings of its attacks so that people would not be killed. More spectacularly, Al Qaeda's attacks on 9/11 were an attempt to coerce the United States into withdrawing its troops from the Arabian Peninsula and ending its support for the Saudi regime. The simultaneous hijacking of four airliners and the destruction of the twin towers and severe damage to the Pentagon were intended to demonstrate an ability to carry out great violence at the core of America's centers of power.

Provocation Terrorists may attack in order to provoke the target government into a disproportionate response that alienates moderates in the terrorists' home society or in other sympathetic audiences. Particularly dramatic and heinous attacks often leave the target government with little political choice but to respond with a vigorous counterstrike. After 9/11, there was significant domestic support—even pressure—for the administration of President George W. Bush to strike back forcefully against Al Qaeda. The Israeli government has long maintained a policy of at least "an eye for an eye," responding aggressively to all terrorist attacks on its soil or citizens. When terrorists are hiding within their home population, any counterstrike is likely to inflict collateral damage, that is, deaths and injuries to innocent bystanders. If the target government is already feared by the terrorists' home population, such a vigorous counterstrike can further radicalize that population and increase its support for the terrorists. Other audiences outside the terrorists' home society may also be alienated and possibly threatened by what are regarded as overly aggressive responses by the target. Thus, this strategy helps address the organization's collective action problem by creating a larger pool of extremists or sympathetic moderates.

Key to any strategy of **provocation** is the uncertainty of the terrorists' home population about the target's interests.[52] For example, many people in the Middle East fear that the United States is an imperialist state aligned with Israel to impose its will on their countries, with little regard for Muslim lives. This is precisely the message that Al Qaeda uses to mobilize people to its cause (see "What Shaped Our World?" on p.277). The group hopes that a disproportionate

provocation

A strategy of terrorist attacks intended to provoke the target government into making a disproportionate response that alienates moderates in the terrorists' home society or in other sympathetic audiences.

52. On provocation strategies, see Ethan Bueno de Mesquita and Eric S. Dickson, "The Propaganda of the Deed: Terrorism, Counterterrorism, and Mobilization," *American Journal of Political Science* 51 (2007): 364–81.

The Rise of Al Qaeda

Most Americans who woke up to the sight of burning towers on September 11, 2001, had never heard of Al Qaeda, the group that was responsible for the attacks of that day. But by 2001, the terrorist organization had been in existence for over a decade.

Interests Al Qaeda (translated as "the base") was forged during the 1980s in the resistance to the Soviet Union's occupation of Afghanistan. The struggle against the Soviets was waged by Afghan opposition groups who were fighting for control of their country. The resistance attracted a large number of outsiders who saw the struggles in religious terms—as an opportunity to evict non-Muslim invaders and establish Islamic rule. Among them was Osama bin Laden (right), who became the prime financier for an organization that recruited fighters from around the Muslim world.

When the Soviet Union withdrew in 1989, bin Laden formed Al Qaeda as a way to maintain the existing organization and networks. While his ultimate goal was to install Islamist governments throughout the Muslim world, he concluded that this was impossible as long as the United States and the West were actively involved in the region. Thus, he shifted his focus from the "near enemy," local governments viewed as anti-Islamist, to the "far enemy," the United States. Al Qaeda's grievances against the West in general, and the United States in particular, focused on their support for Israel; their backing of dictatorial governments in the Middle East, especially those of Saudi Arabia and Egypt; and their military bases in Saudi Arabia.

Interactions To further its interests, Al Qaeda employed a strategy of coercion against the United States and its allies, waging attacks that grew bolder and more damaging over time. In 1996, after a series of smaller attacks for which the group neither claimed credit nor made any public demands, bin Laden allied himself with the Taliban in Afghanistan, an Islamist movement that was close to controlling the entire country after years of civil war. He subsequently issued two fatwas (or religious rulings) declaring jihad against "Jews and Crusaders." These declarations were followed by three major terrorist attacks: against the U.S. embassies in Kenya and Tanzania (1998); against the USS *Cole*, a navy ship docked for resupply in Yemen (2000); and the attacks of September 11, 2001.

In response to this growing threat, the United States pursued a strategy that targeted bin Laden and his organization. Following the East African embassy bombings, President Bill Clinton retaliated by launching cruise missiles at Al Qaeda training camps in Afghanistan and placing a $25 million bounty on bin Laden. After the 9/11 attacks, the United States invaded Afghanistan both to hunt down the Al Qaeda leadership and to deny it a safe haven in that country. Though scattered, the group retained its capacity to kill, and Al Qaeda–linked militants carried out mass-casualty bombings in Istanbul (2003), Madrid (2004), and London (2005). Bin Laden and many other leaders, after initially fleeing to Pakistan, have since been captured or killed.

Institutions The persistence of Al Qaeda owes a great deal to a decentralized institutional structure that makes it hard to defeat. While formed around a central core originally led by bin Laden, regional groups and individual operatives scattered around the world possess a measure of autonomy. In addition, the group's ideology attracts a diffuse set of sympathizers who supply resources, convey information, or carry out lone wolf attacks. Al Qaeda has been successful also in creating offshoots in other regions. After the U.S. invasion of Iraq, a Jordanian militant formed Al Qaeda in Iraq, which became the most prolific terrorist group in that country and eventually gave rise to the IS. Al Qaeda offshoots are also active in Yemen, Saudi Arabia, Syria, and Northern Africa. Thus, even after his death, the brand bin Laden created continues to attract extremists bent on violence.

U.S. response that kills innocent civilians will essentially confirm this narrative. After 9/11, the invasion of Afghanistan and the overthrow of the Taliban regime by the United States received generally broad support because the war could be understood as a response to the attacks; however, the subsequent invasion of Iraq, which had no role in the 9/11 attacks, was widely seen internationally as unjustified. In the words of a U.S. national intelligence estimate released in 2006, Iraq became a "'cause célèbre' for jihadists, breeding a deep resentment of U.S. involvement in the Muslim world and cultivating supporters for the global jihadist movement."[53] The war also led to increased anti-American sentiment around the world, complicating U.S. relationship with other countries. Disproportionate responses may lead the terrorists' home population to believe that it has more to fear from the target than from the extremists. Through multiple applications of this strategy, terrorist organizations hope to expand their base of support within their home populations and increase their political power over time.

Spoiling Terrorists may also attack to spoil, or sabotage, a prospective peace between the target and the moderate leadership from their home society.[54] Target states are often uncertain whether an opponent, even if led by moderates, wants to settle the conflict and can control its extremists. Targets want to negotiate with trustworthy and capable moderates who want to and can make peace, but they do not want to negotiate with untrustworthy or incapable moderates who cannot or will not prevent further terrorist attacks. Unable to judge the sincerity or capability of the opponent's leadership, target governments watch for terrorist attacks to occur and break off negotiations when they do. By attacking, the terrorists can thus scuttle an agreement they oppose and hold out for terms they hope will be more favorable.

The purpose of the violence in **spoiling** is not to apply pressure on the target per se but to play on doubts in the target state about whether the opponent can be trusted to implement a peace agreement and abide by it in the future. In this case, the target is uncertain about the home population's interests and capabilities and whether it will be able to honor and enforce an agreement. When terrorists attack the target, the latter learns that the terrorists' home government either does not want to or cannot control its extremists, and thus it is more likely to reject agreements as not credible. Paradoxically, the effect of terrorist attacks on the target's willingness to make peace is greatest when the target initially believes the opponent's moderates are strong and able to restrain the terrorists. If the terrorists then attack, the target is more likely to conclude that the moderates are not sincere about making peace,

spoiling
A strategy of terrorist attacks intended to sabotage a prospective peace between the target and moderate leadership from the terrorists' home society.

---

53. Office of the Director of National Intelligence, "Trends in Global Terrorism: Implications for the United States," National Intelligence Estimate," April 2006, www.dni.gov/files/documents/Special%20Report_Global%20Terrorism%20NIE%20Key%20Judgments.pdf (accessed 03/09/15).

54. Andrew Kydd and Barbara F. Walter, "Sabotaging the Peace: The Politics of Extremist Violence," *International Organization* 56 (2002): 263–96.

as they apparently could—but chose not to—control the terrorists. Attacks motivated by this logic are most likely to occur during or shortly after peace negotiations.

Outbidding Finally, terrorist organizations may use violence in order to outbid potential rivals for support among their home population. In poker, a player may raise the bet to convince others that she is holding a stronger hand. Likewise, when two or more terrorist networks or factions compete for support within their home populations, they may attack a target in an effort to outbid the other and demonstrate their capability for leadership and commitment to the cause for which they are fighting. **Outbidding** arises when the home population is uncertain about which of several organizations is best able to represent and further its interests. In these cases, an organization may mount dramatic attacks not simply to coerce the target but also to impress the audience at home.

Rivalries among different factions of the Palestinian movement have led to this kind of dynamic. Since the early 1990s, a number of groups have competed for the support of the Palestinian people, most prominently Fatah and Hamas. Though originally a terrorist group, Fatah renounced violence and is no longer considered a terrorist organization; it has argued instead for a process of negotiation leading to the creation of a Palestinian state. Hamas continued to engage in terrorist attacks, as did Islamic Jihad and other militant factions, some of which spun off from Fatah. For these groups, attacks against Israel are intended to demonstrate their credentials for leadership among Palestinians who are uncertain about which group best serves their interests. These rivalries have led to cycles of escalation wherein attacks by one group require attacks by others so as not to be outdone; in some cases, multiple groups would claim credit for the same attack.[55] Similarly, when Peru returned to democratic rule in 1980, the Shining Path group turned to violence to distinguish itself from rival groups that chose instead to participate in the electoral process.

The actors we call *target, terrorist*, and *home population* are convenient abstractions but obvious simplifications. Within any particular instance, these actors may need to be disaggregated further to reveal internal divisions. Likewise, the four strategies of terror are not exclusive. Terrorist networks can attack simultaneously to coerce a target into making concessions, provoke the target into a disproportionate response that radicalizes their home population, undermine prospective peace agreements, and build support for their factions over others within their home populations. In any long-term struggle (such as that between Israel and the Palestinians or between the Tamil Tigers and the government of Sri Lanka), all four strategies are likely to be employed at some point. We isolate the strategies here merely to highlight their different logics. Understanding the multiple strategies of terrorism is also important in designing effective counterterrorist responses.

outbidding

A strategy of terrorist attacks designed to demonstrate superior capability and commitment relative to other groups devoted to the same cause.

---

55. Mia M. Bloom, "Palestinian Suicide Bombing: Public Support, Market Share, and Outbidding," *Political Science Quarterly* 199 (2004): 61–88.

Can Terrorism Be Prevented?

Like the war on drugs, the war on poverty, or the war on crime, the "global war on terror" is likely to be a struggle without any clear end. As long as actors have different interests, and as long as individuals retain the ingenuity and ruthlessness that enabled 19 terrorists to use simple box cutters to transform airplanes into maneuverable kerosene-filled bombs, terrorism will remain a possibility. Extremism, combined with problems of information and credible commitment, will continue to lead terrorist organizations to launch attacks simply to demonstrate that they can. As with civil wars, economic development and political liberalization might in the long run diffuse some of the grievances that fuel or enable terrorist violence, but there is actually little evidence that poverty, on its own, breeds extremism or drives people to join terrorist organizations.[56] Since ideological, religious, and nationalist extremists can arise in a variety of political and economic contexts, promoting development, while no doubt desirable, is also unlikely to be a magic bullet. Nonetheless, states can adopt certain counterterrorist strategies to make future attacks less likely and, perhaps, less destructive when they do occur. The same strategies also allow states to make smaller concessions to terrorists even when bargaining works and violence is avoided.

Can Terrorists Be Deterred? As discussed in Chapter 3, deterrence is a strategy to preserve the status quo by threatening challengers with unacceptable costs. Terrorism can in principle be deterred by potential targets threatening massive retaliation against terrorist organizations should attacks occur. Although deterrence worked to avoid nuclear war between the superpowers during the Cold War, and although it may operate on a daily basis between states that might otherwise challenge one another if they thought the other would not fight back, many analysts are skeptical that in practice deterrence can work against terrorist networks.

Unlike states, terrorists do not possess a clearly identifiable location against which targets may respond. If a terrorist organization believes it can escape retaliation by hiding in unknown locations, it is less likely to be deterred from attacking. This consideration is real. However, investigative work can often find the trail leading back to a terrorist organization. In the event that terrorists turn to weapons of mass destruction, such as nuclear, chemical, biological, or radiological weapons, the materials may be traceable, and large nuclear processing facilities are hard to hide. Given today's advanced technological devices, it is quite likely that targets could, with time, identify who manufactured the weapons and where they originated. Thus, it is not the absence of a location against which to retaliate that undermines deterrence as much as two, more subtle, problems.

---

56. See, for example, Alan B. Krueger and Jitka Malečková, "Education, Poverty and Terrorism: Is There a Causal Connection?" *Journal of Economic Perspectives* 17 (Fall 2003): 119–44; and James A. Piazza, "Do Democracy and Free Markets Protect Us from Terrorism?" *International Politics* 45 (2008): 72–91.

First, when terrorists use a strategy of provocation, retaliation by the target may simply play into their hands. Retaliating against a terrorist stronghold will likely kill a significant number of members of the home society, confirming for previously undecided moderates that the target really is a threat to their own security. Unless the retaliating target succeeds in eradicating the terrorist network, a cycle of attacks and counterattacks may over time serve only to increase political support for the terrorists. Second, and closely related, the threat of retaliation by the potential target may not be credible. Since terrorists hide in larger populations and massive retaliation would likely kill many individuals who are unrelated to the terrorist network, a target state may be unwilling to attack. If a terrorist sets off a nuclear explosion in New York, would the United States be willing to annihilate hundreds of thousands of likely innocent people to destroy a terrorist cell operating in, say, Somalia? In a country allied with the United States in the global war on terror, such as Pakistan? Or perhaps even in another advanced democratic country, like Germany (where much of the planning for the 9/11 attacks took place)? Nuclear deterrence in the Cold War, and especially extended deterrence in which the United States promised to launch a retaliatory attack against the civilian population should the Soviet Union invade West Berlin or Paris, always rested on the possibility that the threat would be carried out. Although the United States might not have started another world war in response to a limited Soviet incursion in Europe, the risk that it might do so was sufficient to deter Russia. The risk that the United States or any other target would retaliate massively against terrorist attacks is not as likely or as clear. Knowing this, terrorists are less likely to be deterred than states. For these reasons, deterrence may not be as robust against terrorism as it has been against interstate violence.

Preemption   If the threat of retaliation after an attack cannot deter terrorists, an alternative strategy is for states to take the initiative and attempt to disrupt or destroy terrorists and their networks before they attack. This strategy of preemption was the most distinctive response of the Bush administration to the attacks of 9/11. In his *National Security Strategy for the United States of America* outlined in September 2002, President Bush placed emphasis, for the first time, on preempting attacks from terrorists and states that may possess weapons of mass destruction. The invasion of Afghanistan was not just in retaliation for the attacks but was also intended to prevent future attacks. The goals of the war included capturing or killing the organization's leadership and foot soldiers and dismantling the infrastructure that had been used to plot and train

Countries can attempt to stop terrorists before they strike—a strategy known as preemption. The United States has used remotely piloted drones to kill suspected terrorists in Pakistan, among other countries. This practice has bred resentment because of collateral damage from missile strikes.

for attacks. Although Afghanistan was the main theater of "Operation Enduring Freedom," this operation spanned the globe, leading to the killing and detention of suspected terrorists. The United States has also made extensive use of drones—remote-controlled aircraft armed with missiles—to kill suspected terrorists in a variety of countries, including Pakistan, Yemen, and Somalia. And, of course, the war in Iraq was justified by President Bush, in part, as a preemptive war on terror.

Preemption can also take nonmilitary forms. Surveillance can be used to identify terrorist networks and future attacks, such as by monitoring phone calls, e-mail, and other communications and by tracking international financial transactions. Intelligence agencies may also detain and interrogate terrorism suspects in order to unravel plots or to identify other members of an organization. A report released by the U.S. Senate in 2014 detailed an extensive program of detention that was enacted after 9/11, as well as the use of interrogation techniques that are commonly understood to constitute torture.[57] In resorting to such methods, the United States is not alone. The use of torture, as well as other violations of civil rights, such as imprisonment without due process and extrajudicial killings, is not uncommon among states that are targeted by terrorism.[58]

Preemption is costly in many ways. The wars in Afghanistan and Iraq came at very high prices. By the end of 2014, the United States had spent $3.3 trillion on those wars, which claimed the lives of over 6,000 Americans, over 1,500 from allied countries, and hundreds of thousands in both Afghanistan and Iraq. Even less forceful measures entail costs. Surveillance is expensive relative to the number of attacks prevented. Like all police patrols, surveillance must be continuous—not just when attacks are under way—and comprehensive; otherwise, intelligence efforts are likely to be deployed elsewhere when actual attacks are being planned. Monitoring possible terrorist activities is akin to looking for the proverbial needle in the haystack, but in this case a potential terrorist attack is a well-hidden needle that we are not even sure exists. Moreover, surveillance is likely to infringe on the civil liberties of innocent civilians.

Preemption can also impose political costs by playing into the provocation strategy used by terrorists. Preemptive actions may be perceived by foreign populations as disproportionate responses that are threatening to those very populations. As we saw above, the invasion of Iraq, which was never linked to the 9/11 attacks except rhetorically by the Bush administration, became a recruiting tool for extremist groups. Even smaller operations, like U.S. drone attacks in Pakistan, have the potential to kill civilians and breed resentment that can feed terrorist recruitment. There is also evidence that the systematic use of torture, extrajudicial

---

57. Senate Select Committee on Intelligence, *The Senate Intelligence Committee Report on Torture* (New York, NY: Melville House, 2014).

58. James A. Piazza and James Igoe Walsh, "Transnational Terror and Human Rights," International Studies Quarterly 53 (2009): 125–48. The authors find that terrorist attacks are associated with increased use of "disappearances" and extrajudicial killings but not necessarily torture. They note, however, the challenge of detecting and confirming torture complicates any analysis of this relationship.

Defensive measures against terrorists in Israel include a fortified wall between Israeli and Palestinian-controlled territory, with numerous checkpoints manned by armed guards. These measures appear to have reduced the number of terrorist attacks in Israel, but they are expensive and inconvenient for everyone, not just the terrorists.

killings, and imprisonment without due process can increase, rather than decrease, the number of attacks a country experiences.[59] Thus, in considering preemptive action, targets must balance the probability that they will make themselves safer in the short term against the risk that they will undermine their support within the terrorists' home population or internationally over the longer term.

Defensive Measures As an alternative to offensive or retaliatory military operations, states can and do employ defensive measures to guard against attacks.[60] This has been a significant response in the United States since the attacks on 9/11. Airports now possess even more elaborate security procedures than those implemented after the rash of airplane hijackings in the early 1970s. American embassies abroad have been fortified. National monuments are protected by barrier defenses and, sometimes, armed guards. Border security forces and inspection regimes have been expanded. Numerous sites remain vulnerable, including the nation's shipping ports, but across the country homeland security efforts have been significantly increased. Similarly, after a campaign of suicide bombings, Israel constructed a wall separating it

---

59. James A. Piazza and James Igoe Walsh, "Physical Integrity Rights and Terrorism," *PS: Political Science and Politics* 43 (July 2010): 411–14.

60. On the limits of defensive measures, see Robert Powell, "Defending against Terrorist Attacks with Limited Resources," *American Political Science Review* 101, no. 3 (2007): 527–41. On collective action problems in defensive responses, see Todd Sandler, "Collective versus Unilateral Responses to Terrorism," *Public Choice* 124, nos. 1–2 (2005): 75–93.

from Palestinian-controlled areas of the West Bank, with dramatic results in reducing the number of attacks. Defensive measures work to reduce terrorism by raising the costs to groups of carrying out attacks. As it becomes more expensive to strike a target, whether in terms of resources deployed or time and effort consumed to evade security procedures, terrorism becomes less likely overall. Defensive measures can also have the advantage that they do not inflict collateral damage on the terrorists' home population, though the Israel security barrier in the West Bank has caused a great deal of hardship and resentment among Palestinians.

Defensive measures are not cheap. The U.S. Department of Homeland Security's budget for 2015, for instance, was $38.2 billion. Indirectly, such measures may impose even greater costs on society. Passengers must now arrive at airports earlier to clear security before boarding their planes, making air travel less efficient and more unpleasant than before. Trucks are subject to longer delays at the nation's borders. Measured by hours of productivity lost, these indirect costs may well dwarf the direct costs. That said, when measured relative to the costs of the Iraq and Afghanistan wars, these costs may seem like a bargain.

Still, defensive measures will never be totally effective. Terrorists select among sites based on the difficulty of penetrating defenses and the likely success of carrying out their attacks. When the United States stepped up its internal security measures after 9/11, Al Qaeda shifted its attacks to embassies abroad and American troops in Iraq. It is widely believed that Al Qaeda attacked three trains in Spain on March 11, 2004, because they were softer targets than airports. Given the many possible sites, it is prohibitively expensive to protect them all equally. But protecting some may only divert attacks onto the next less well-defended target.

Criminalization States can criminalize terrorism and pursue specific individuals and groups for the attacks they have planned or carried out. Along with airport security measures, this was the primary response to the airplane hijackings that occurred in the late 1960s and early 1970s. By 1973, a series of international conventions on skyjackings were put into place through which states agreed not to harbor hijackers and to turn them over to appropriate authorities. Individual terrorists and groups were pursued and brought to justice in criminal proceedings. Combined with the use of metal detectors at airports, this strategy led to a sharp decline in the number of airplane hijackings.

Criminalization is mostly reactive, seeking to arrest terrorists for attacks after they have been committed. By bringing individuals and groups to justice, states hope not only to disrupt terrorist groups but to deter others from carrying out attacks as well. For transnational terrorism, this strategy hinges on effective international cooperation. Nearly all countries would agree that airplane hijackings are odious and against their interests. Even the United States and Cuba, which cooperate in few other areas, have been able to work together effectively in capturing and prosecuting hijackers; the two nations signed a bilateral pact in 1973 in which they agreed to return immediately any planes, passengers, crew members, and hijackers to the country of origin. The growth of transnational networks may require the development of new international institutions to combat terrorism in the future.

Yet countries do not always share such clearly compatible interests. States that sympathize with the goals pursued by terrorists and grant them safe haven, like the Taliban regime in Afghanistan, or states that are too weak internally to prevent terrorist groups from operating from within their territory, like Somalia, can effectively undermine the ability of other countries to capture indicted terrorists. Even Pakistan, a country that is nominally allied with the United States in the war on terror, has chafed at U.S. efforts to track down Al Qaeda leaders there. The killing of bin Laden on Pakistani soil in 2011 added to tensions in the relationship.

The same forces of globalization that allow terrorists to attack anywhere around the world also permit terrorists to hide anywhere. To limit terrorism, states need to share intelligence and coordinate their counterattacks. To date, progress on this front has been slow, a problem deepened by international disagreements over the Iraq War and America's treatment of terrorist suspects. To expand efforts to track and prosecute terrorists will require greater compromise on policy differences with other states and increasingly effective institutions to secure compliance with antiterrorist efforts.

Negotiation and Compromise Finally, states can attempt to negotiate and compromise their differences with terrorist groups.[61] As explained above, bargaining failures are likely to be inevitable, and thus negotiations will not eliminate the problem of terrorism. Most states today maintain a policy of not negotiating with terrorists for fear of recognizing the legitimacy of their demands and tactics— and for fear of being charged with appeasement by domestic critics. Countries are also reluctant to negotiate with terrorists so as not to spur other groups making greater demands. Thus, few explicit negotiations occur between states and terrorists.

Nonetheless, states have at times made concessions sought by terrorist groups. In the wake of terrorist campaigns, American and French military forces withdrew from Lebanon in 1983, and Israel withdrew from occupied portions of southern Lebanon in 2000 and from the Palestinian-controlled Gaza Strip in 2005. Most prominently, in the so-called Good Friday agreement, signed in 1998, Britain made concessions favored by the IRA, granting Northern Ireland a great deal more autonomy and ensuring an influential role for "unionists" (that is, those seeking union with Ireland) in the region's governance. Terrorists may

---

61. On bargaining, see Harvey F. Lapan and Todd Sandler, "To Bargain or Not to Bargain: That Is the Question," *American Economic Review* 78, no. 2 (1988): 16–21.

never get everything they say they want (actors rarely do in any bargain), and there have been many cases in which no concessions were made. But terrorism persists and may even be growing as a tactic because it works at least some of the time.[62]

Conclusion: A Challenge to States?

Violence pursued by rebel groups and terrorist organizations represents a challenge to states in several respects. For the states that are targeted by these actors, insurgency and terrorism represent a threat to their people and to their ability to govern. Civil wars in particular exact a very high toll on the countries that suffer them, in terms of lives lost, resources spent and destroyed, and even death and disease that linger long after the fighting stops.[63] Terrorism kills many fewer people but, by design, can lead whole nations to live in fear. Though in some cases we might share or sympathize with the interests that lead these groups to violence, the enormous costs involved are always tragic.

Rebellion and terrorism also pose a challenge to states in a more fundamental sense. Many models of international relations start with the assumption that states are the main actors in world politics. This assumption is sometimes made only to simplify the analysis, as we did in Chapter 3 when we used states as actors, a simplification that allowed us to focus on bargaining dynamics. In other theoretical approaches, however, particularly those derived from the realist school, the state-centric view represents a substantive claim about which actors really matter and, by implication, which do not. The pride of place given to states usually rests on two assertions: (1) interactions in international politics are dominated by the threat and use of force, and (2) states, and particularly large states, are the main actors capable of mobilizing and wielding military power. In this view, then, the world stage is dominated by the clash of great powers.

The importance of rebellion and terrorism call this view into question. As we have seen, nonstate actors, while lacking the size and organizational advantages of states, have developed strategies of violence that can be quite effective. Insurgency and terrorism, the main weapons of asymmetric warfare, seek to neutralize states' power in several ways: by evading the target state's conventional military power; by exploiting vulnerabilities, such as civilians and other "soft" targets; and, at times, by using the state's power against it, by provoking counterattacks that may swell the ranks of the group's supporters. We have also seen that states often wield nonstate actors against one another. When direct confrontation with

---

62. On the success of terrorist campaigns, see Pape, "The Strategic Logic of Suicide Terrorism," 351–55. For an alternative view, see Max Abrahms, "Why Terrorism Does Not Work," *International Security* 31, no. 2 (Fall 2006): 42–78.

63. On this last point, see Hazem Adam Ghobarah, Paul Huth, and Bruce Russett, "Civil Wars Kill and Maim People—Long after the Shooting Stops," *American Political Science Review* 97 (2003): 189–202.

another state is likely to be too costly (as during the Cold War) or ineffective (as when a weak state confronts a stronger one), sponsoring a rebel group or terrorist organization may be an effective alternative. Thus, even the bargaining interaction between states can be fundamentally influenced by the presence of nonstate actors willing to use violence.

In short, rebel groups and terrorist organizations violate the view that states monopolize the means of coercion in international politics. What strong states have is an institutional structure capable of overcoming the collective action problem inherent in wielding coercive power. This is no small matter, as many dissatisfied groups and extremist individuals will never mobilize the people, arms, and money necessary to make an impact. But those that have found a way to do so have managed to kill large numbers of people, consume vast resources, overthrow governments, and at times, dominate the foreign policy agenda of even the most powerful states.

Study Tool Kit

Interests, Interactions, and Institutions in Context

- Civil conflict can arise when individuals have interests that conflict with those of the central government, leading to demands over territory, policy, or government composition. But conflicting interests are not sufficient for organized opposition to emerge. Whether a rebel group can overcome the collective action problem depends on its own resources, the capacity of the government, and the willingness of foreign states to lend support.

- As in interstate relations, bargaining between a government and a rebel group can lead to war as a result of information problems, commitment problems, and issue indivisibilities. In the context of civil war, there are particularly severe commitment problems that often make disputes hard to resolve without the outright victory of one side or the other.

- International terrorist organizations are composed of relatively small numbers of individuals with extreme preferences. Their weakness relative to their targets and relative to their goals drives their strategy of attacking civilians and their organization into loose networks that are hard to root out.

- Rebel groups and terrorists employ strategies of violence that are intended both to coerce their targets and to address their collective action problem by attracting supporters. For this reason, efforts to defeat these groups often require strategies that take account of their effects on noncombatants.

Key Terms

civil war, p. 237

separatist, p. 239

irredentist, p. 242

proxy wars, p. 251

insurgency, p. 258

asymmetric warfare, p. 258

terrorism, p. 264

extremists, p. 267

coercion, p. 275

provocation, p. 276

spoiling, p. 278

outbidding, p. 279

For Further Reading

Blattman, Christopher, and Edward Miguel. "Civil War." *Journal of Economic Literature* 48 (2010): 3–57. A rigorous review of theoretical and empirical scholarship on civil war, with suggestions for future research.

Bloom, Mia. *Dying to Kill: The Allure of Suicide Terror*. New York: Columbia University Press, 2005. A study of the origins of and motives behind suicide terrorism.

Enders, Walter, and Todd Sandler. *The Political Economy of Terrorism*. New York: Cambridge University Press, 2006. Provides an excellent introduction to current research on terrorism.

Kilcullen, David. *The Accidental Guerrilla: Fighting Small Wars in the Midst of a Big One*. New York: Oxford University Press, 2009. An examination of counterterrorism and counterinsurgency doctrine as applied to the "war on terror."

Kydd, Andrew, and Barbara Walter. "The Strategies of Terrorism." *International Security* 31, no. 1 (Summer 2006): 49–80. Develops the four strategies of terrorism explained in this text.

Regan, Patrick M. *Sixteen Million One: Understanding Civil War*. Boulder, CO: Paradigm Publishers, 2009. An accessible blending of academic research on civil wars with a vivid account of the lives and motives of those who fight in them.

Sageman, Marc. *Understanding Terrorist Networks*. Philadelphia: University of Pennsylvania Press, 2004. Explores the network structure of terrorist organizations.

Salehyan, Idean. *Rebels without Borders: Transnational Insurgencies in World Politics*. Ithaca, NY: Cornell University Press, 2009. Examines how civil wars often spill over into neighboring countries owing to weak states, international rivalries, and refugee flows.

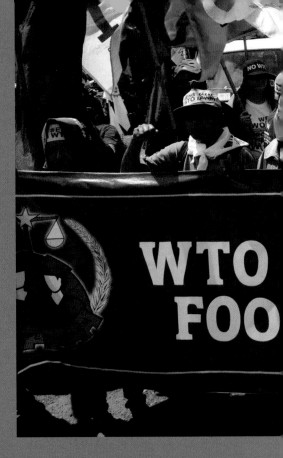

7

International Trade

THE PUZZLE *Virtually all economic analysis concludes that trade is economically beneficial. Why, then, does every country restrict trade in some way? Why have policies toward trade varied so much from country to country and over time?*

Above: Economies as a whole benefit from freer trade, but trade policies often create winners and losers. Critics of the WTO claim that its policies enrich some countries and groups at the expense of others. These marchers believe the WTO benefits companies that export goods but harms local farmers.

The American steel industry employs about 150,000 people. Yet this relatively small industry has received massive assistance from the U.S. government, primarily in the form of protection from foreign competition. This trade protection raises the cost of steel in the United States and thus raises the cost American consumers pay for goods made with steel. By one estimate, since 1970 protection and other aid to the American steel industry have cost American consumers and taxpayers between $145 billion and $230 billion dollars—a staggering amount for an industry with just 150,000 employees.[1]

The steel industry is hardly alone in being protected from imports, to the benefit of producers and the detriment of consumers. Footwear, dairy products, motorcycles, clothing, cotton, automobiles, and sugar are among the many other goods whose import has been restricted by the U.S. government. One group of scholars estimated that if all barriers to international trade were removed, the U.S. economy would gain between $500 billion and $1.5 trillion dollars a year, equivalent to between $5,000 and $15,000 a year for every American household.[2] And the United States is hardly alone in erecting obstacles to international commerce: to varying degrees, every country has such trade barriers.

People have traded across borders for as long as borders have existed. In the modern world, international trade has been one of the two most important economic relationships among countries (the other is international investment, which we will examine in Chapter 8). Dramatic reductions in trade barriers and dramatic increases in international trade itself are a major component of the globalization of the contemporary world economy. Yet governments have always attempted to control trade across their borders. In fact, trade policy—the restriction

1. William H. Barringer and Kenneth J. Pierce, *Paying the Price for Big Steel* (Washington, DC: American Institute for International Steel, 2000); and William H. Barringer, Kenneth J. Pierce, and Matthew P. McCullough, *Still Paying the Price* (Washington, DC: American Institute for International Steel, 2007).

2. Scott Bradford, Paul Grieco, and Gary Hufbauer, "The Payoff to America from Global Integration," in *The United States and the World Economy: Foreign Economic Policy for the Next Decade*, ed. C. Fred Bergstein, 65–109 (Washington, DC: Institute for International Economics, 2005). Figures have been updated from their original 2003 dollar terms. It should be noted that these numbers have been questioned by other scholars, who think they are either too high or too low.

of imports and the promotion of exports—has long been one of the most important economic policies, foreign or domestic, that governments undertake. Today's very high levels of international trade, and the continued attempts of governments to control trade, serve as the basis for this chapter's discussion.

We first ask why international trade takes the form it does. Most poor countries export almost exclusively farm products and raw materials, and they import manufactured goods. Most rich countries, in contrast, import much of their food and raw materials and export mainly manufactured goods. Those poor countries that do export industrial products typically sell such simple goods as clothing, footwear, and furniture; rich countries' manufactured exports primarily include sophisticated goods, such as commercial aircraft and elaborate machinery. How can we explain these patterns of international trade?

Our exploration of this question raises the further question of why international trade is so commonly restricted. Although many of us take for granted that protecting national products is good, why should a government purposely raise the prices that domestic consumers pay?

Another question results from the fact that barriers to international trade vary a great deal. Some countries restrict trade very little while others come close to prohibiting it. In addition, trade barriers have changed dramatically over time: both globally and in individual countries, trade has gone from generally unhindered to tightly regulated over relatively short periods. Today, international trade is quite free (that is, unrestricted). Finally, government trade policies themselves often differ among industries, with some goods being strongly protected and others not at all.

Thinking Analytically about International Trade

Because trade policy stands at the intersection of international and domestic politics, it involves powerful interests, important interactions, and influential institutions at both the domestic and international levels. Foreign trade has powerful effects on domestic producers, consumers, and others. Those who sell or buy from abroad have a great deal at stake in international trade; so too do those who face competition from foreigners, which can threaten their jobs or businesses. The conflicts of interest between those in a country who want access to world markets and those who want protection from foreign competition help determine a nation's trade policy.

Domestically, trade interests interact in a battle over national policy, with supporters and opponents of freer trade squaring off according to their own economic interests. Interactions among contending domestic interests are mediated through the national political institutions of trade policy making: parties, legislatures, executives, and bureaucracies.

While important domestic interests, interactions, and institutions determine a country's goals in world trade, this is only half the story. In addition, a given nation's trade policies affect other nations' trade, such that all national policies are made in interaction with those of other governments. Sometimes governments cooperate closely to maintain and expand their trade relations; at other times, bargaining among governments over trade policy is conflictual and even hostile. Indeed, international trade interactions have often spilled into broader interstate relations—sometimes in a positive way, sometimes negatively.

A network of global and regional institutions has evolved to facilitate bargaining over trade policies. These institutions include treaties among countries as well as regional and global trade agreements. The most prominent trade institutions have been the two international organizations that have governed world trade for 60 years: first, the General Agreement on Trade and Tariffs (GATT); and, since 1995, the World Trade Organization (WTO). At the regional level, trade-based institutions include the European Union (EU), which addresses many other issues as well as those relating to trade, the North American Free Trade Agreement (NAFTA), and the Southern Common Market (Mercosur). All these factors help determine how open a country will be to trade and which domestic industries it will likely protect. When we consider global networks, these factors affect how open or closed international trade as a whole will be.

What's So Good about Trade?

Actors engage in foreign trade for the same reason that they trade with each other within countries: to realize the benefits of specialization. Only a household that produces everything it wants to consume, at a lower cost than available elsewhere, would have no reason to trade. But such a household is unlikely to exist. For example, a farm family could make its own tractor but is better off expending its energy in farming and using the proceeds to buy or rent a tractor. Modern societies are based on specialization—some people farm or manufacture; others transport or build—and on trade among people with different specialties. The division of labor permits diverse segments of society to focus on different economic activities in ways that benefit society as a whole. After all, if all households or all villages had to be self-sufficient, they would produce only a fraction of what they could if they specialized.

Specialization—that is, the division of labor—was central to the argument made by Adam Smith in his 1776 founding text of classical economics, *The Wealth of Nations*. Smith and his fellow economic liberals argued, against the then dominant mercantilists, that self-sufficiency was foolish because a greater division of labor made societies wealthier. In a famous example, Smith pointed out that an individual pin maker working alone could make at best 20 pins a day. However, in the workshops of Smith's time, pin making was divided into about 18 steps, with each worker specializing in 1 or 2 steps. In this way, a pin factory with 10 workers produced 48,000 pins a day—making each individual some 240 times as productive as he would be if working alone.[3] Specialization increased productivity, and productivity fueled economic growth.[4]

The classical economists emphasized that specialization required access to large markets—after all, a village could hardly use 48,000 pins a day. They argued that restricting market size slowed economic growth. A village cut off from the rest of the world and forced into self-sufficiency would have to produce everything it needs, but if that village were part of a larger national or global market, it could specialize in what it does best. Producers need ample markets in order to specialize; the division of labor depends on the size of the market.

The division of labor allows gains from international trade. In farming, temperate countries, such as the United States and Argentina, specialize in temperate crops, such as wheat, while tropical countries, such as Brazil and the Philippines, specialize in tropical crops, such as sugarcane. The nations around the Persian Gulf, with their rich oil deposits, base their economies on oil while countries with plentiful iron ore gain economic advantages by mining it. Similarly, countries with

---

3. Adam Smith, *An Inquiry into the Nature and Causes of the Wealth of Nations* (New York: Modern Library, 1937), 4–5. Originally published 1776.

4. Productivity in this context refers to the amount produced by one unit of labor with the other factors of production—especially land and capital—at its disposal. In farming, for example, the same amount of labor is more productive on good soil than on poor, more productive with machinery and fertilizer and irrigation than without.

The Scottish thinker Adam Smith's ideas about division of labor help explain the benefits of trade.

comparative advantage

The ability of a country or firm to produce a particular good or service more efficiently than other goods or services such that its resources are most efficiently employed in this activity. The comparison is to the efficiency of other economic activities the actor might undertake, not to the efficiency of other countries or firms.

absolute advantage

The ability of a country or firm to produce more of a particular good or service than other countries or firms using the same amount of effort and resources.

many unskilled laborers, such as Bangladesh and Egypt, produce goods that require lots of unskilled labor, including clothing, footwear, and furniture. Countries with many skilled technicians, such as the European nations, produce goods that require sophisticated technical skills, such as complex machinery and aircraft. Such specialization among countries leads to economic gains based on trade.

Comparative advantage is the core concept of the economics of trade. (See the "Special Topic" appendix to this chapter on p. 334.) It applies the principle of specialization to countries: like people, they should do what they do best. Thus, comparative advantage implies that a nation gains most by specializing in producing and exporting what it produces most efficiently. By doing so, it can earn as much as possible in order to pay for imports of the best products of other countries. The principle of comparative advantage leads to the conclusion that each country will be best off if it produces what it is best at producing and exchanges its products with other countries in return for imports of things it is not so good at producing.

The word *comparative* in the term *comparative advantage* refers to a comparison among the things a country can do—not between one country and another. Just as personal specialization implies that each individual should do what he does best—not what he does better than all others—the specialization involved in comparative advantage implies that countries should produce what they produce most cost-effectively. In other words, it is not necessary for a country to have an **absolute advantage** (that is, the ability to do something better than others) in producing something for it to be profitable to produce and export it; all that is necessary is a comparative advantage.

The principle of comparative advantage has clear implications for free trade. Since a country gains from following its comparative advantage and engaging in exchange with other nations for goods in which it does not have a comparative advantage, and since barriers to trade impede its ability to do so, trade protection is harmful to the economy as a whole. Government policies that keep out imports force the country to produce goods that are not to its comparative advantage to produce. Indeed, trade protection raises the price of imports and reduces the efficiency of domestic production. Were national governments to follow the principle of comparative advantage, they would unilaterally remove trade barriers and implement free trade. In this state of affairs, trade policy would be fundamentally cooperative in that all countries would gain from the elimination of obstacles to international trade.

Many people find the economic argument for free trade counterintuitive. Policy makers often argue, like the mercantilists did 300 years ago, that exports are good because they create jobs, that imports are bad because they take away jobs, and that governments should stimulate the national economy by restricting imports and encouraging exports. Economic logic insists the opposite: that imports are the gains from trade while exports are its costs. A country imports goods that it cannot make very well itself, which allows the nation to focus its productive energies on making (and exporting) the goods that it produces best.

Free trade induces a country to follow its comparative advantage, and economic logic implies that it is the ideal policy. This is true even if free trade is pursued unilaterally. Protection only serves to raise costs to consumers. If other countries impose trade barriers that raise prices to their own consumers, that is no reason for us to harm our own consumers in response. Countries should undertake open trade policies regardless of what other countries do.

There is a clear parallel between the comparative advantage argument and the choices available to a household. A farm family, for example, "exports" (sells its crops) in order to "import" (buy the goods and services it wants). Because the farm family wants to maximize the imports it buys, it needs to earn more; the best way to do so is to produce more of what it produces best. The principle of comparative advantage illustrates how farmers, workers, and firms gain by specializing and trading, just as countries do.

Why Do Countries Trade What They Do?

The principle of comparative advantage suggests that countries will produce and export what they do best. But how can we know what a country does best, other than by observing what it exports? And if the only way to predict a country's exports is to observe them, the theory is not of much value—especially given that trade flows are affected by many noneconomic factors, such as trade barriers. In the 1920s, Swedish economists Eli Heckscher and Bertil Ohlin addressed this puzzle and extended the classical view.

The Heckscher-Ohlin approach tries to explain national comparative advantage and therefore national trading patterns. The two economists recognized that comparative advantage is not simply a result of effort: for example, the productivity of farmers depends primarily on characteristics of their land, not on how hard they work. In countries where land is in short supply and expensive, farming is costly; where it is plentiful and cheap, farming is low in cost.

Heckscher-Ohlin trade theory describes the basic economic characteristics of a country in terms of the material and human resources it possesses. Typically, these economic features are summarized according to basic factors of production, resources essential for economic activity. Such factors of production include:

- Land, an essential input into agricultural production

- Labor, usually meaning unskilled labor

- Capital for investment, which refers both to the machinery and equipment with which goods are produced and to the financial assets necessary to employ this machinery and equipment

- Human capital, which refers to skilled labor, so called because the labor has been enhanced by investment in training and education

Countries differ greatly in how they are endowed with these factors of production. Some are rich in land, others have abundant unskilled labor, others have abundant skilled labor (human capital), and still others are wealthy in investment capital.

Heckscher–Ohlin trade theory

The theory that a country will export goods that make intensive use of the factors of production in which it is well endowed. Thus, a labor-rich country will export goods that make intensive use of labor.

Heckscher-Ohlin trade theory relies on these "factor endowments" to explain what determines national comparative advantage and, in turn, what countries produce and export. A country with a large population and poor farmland is likely to have a comparative disadvantage in farming; a country with few people but vast supplies of farmland is likely to have a comparative advantage in agriculture. Different products too require different mixes of resources: typically, farm goods require a lot of land, simple manufactured goods require a lot of unskilled labor, and complex machinery requires a lot of investment capital. Heckscher-Ohlin trade theory argues that a country will export goods that make intensive use of the resources the country has in abundance, and it will import goods that make intensive use of the country's scarce resources. Countries with lots of land, where land is cheap, specialize in producing farm goods: for example, the United States in the nineteenth century was relatively sparsely populated but was rich in very fertile land and exported massive quantities of cotton, tobacco, and wheat. In contrast, countries with very little farmable land import many farm goods—such as Great Britain in the nineteenth century, which relied heavily on imports for its food. Countries rich in investment capital focus on making products whose production requires a great deal of capital: for example, most North American and western European nations' industries today specialize in sophisticated manufactured goods, such as complex machinery, construction equipment, and commercial aircraft. Regions with abundant labor produce labor-intensive goods: China and other rapidly developing labor-rich nations concentrate on making products that require a great deal of labor, such as clothing, toys, furniture, and other relatively simple manufactures.

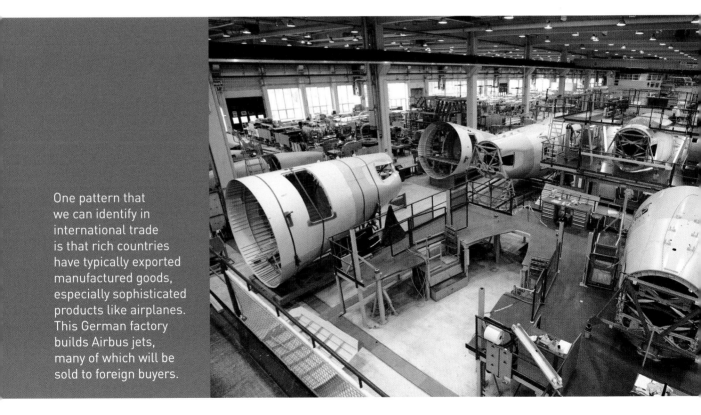

One pattern that we can identify in international trade is that rich countries have typically exported manufactured goods, especially sophisticated products like airplanes. This German factory builds Airbus jets, many of which will be sold to foreign buyers.

This pattern of specialization leads to analogous trade patterns. Poor countries with little capital import the capital-intensive products they need. Today, for example, poor agricultural nations tend to import their farm machinery from capital-rich industrialized nations, just as the United States did in the early nineteenth century. China and India export their labor-intensive manufactures to North America and Western Europe and import capital-intensive industrial goods—including the complex machinery needed to operate their domestic factories.[5] Within North America, the capital-rich United States exports capital-intensive machinery (and capital) to Mexico while labor-rich Mexico sends labor-intensive manufactured products (and labor) to the United States.

Each of the *factors* of production can be associated with different socioeconomic *actors*. A country abundant in land will also, typically, have many farmers. Unskilled or skilled laborers have unskilled and skilled labor to sell on the labor market, respectively. Investors hold much of the investment capital of a country. When we say that a country that is abundant in land will export products that make great use of land, we are saying that farmers and farmworkers will be heavily engaged in producing goods for export. The relative abundance or scarcity of factors of production has a powerful impact on the economic activities of actors within a society.

The Heckscher-Ohlin theory helps explain the broad outlines of international trade. The industrial countries are rich in capital and skilled labor (human capital), and they export manufactured goods that make intensive use of these resources. Most developing countries are rich in land, raw materials, or unskilled labor (or some combination of the three), and they export agricultural products, minerals, or labor-intensive manufactures. The theory also helps explain changes over time in a country's trade relations. A poor country with abundant land and labor but little capital will export farm goods and simple labor-intensive manufactures. As the country develops, it accumulates capital and its workers become more skilled such that its endowments change and, with them, its export patterns. This explains, for example, why the United States in the nineteenth century exported almost exclusively raw materials and farm goods, yet today it exports almost exclusively goods and services that require large amounts of capital and skilled labor to produce. In addition to explaining aspects of world trade patterns, Heckscher-Ohlin trade theory has important implications for the domestic politics of trade policy, as we discuss below.[6]

---

5. This argument applies to movements of capital and people as well as to trade. Countries rich in capital should export capital, and countries rich in labor should export labor. (Land, of course, cannot be traded across borders without changing the borders!)

6. Other economic links among countries also encourage trade. Countries that share a currency, such as those in the European Union that use the euro, trafde with one another much more than those that do not. Countries that invest heavily in one another's economies also tend to trade heavily with one another. There are other potential economic sources of patterns of international trade. A great deal of modern international trade is related to the activities of multinational corporations, such as sales from overseas affiliates of American corporations to their headquarters. This sort of "intrafirm" trade may not be due primarily to the forces that Heckscher-Ohlin trade theory suggests but rather to production and distribution networks within firms. In addition, a great deal of international trade is in goods whose attraction to consumers has to do as much with brand name, reputation, or other related considerations as it does with price. North America, for example, both imports automobiles from Europe and exports automobiles to it. This sort of "intraindustry" trade is not the result of fundamentally different factor endowments (and prices) between Europe and North America—both regions are rich in capital and skilled labor and poor in unskilled labor—but rather of European consumer interest in American car brands and American consumer interest in European car brands.

According to the Heckscher-Ohlin trade theory, developing countries that are rich in unskilled labor should export labor-intensive manufactured goods. Indonesia's primary exports are textiles and clothing.

Noneconomic factors also affect both what and with whom countries trade. Countries that are geographically close together trade more since transport costs are lower. Diplomatic and military relations between nations also influence their trade patterns. Countries whose governments are hostile to one another are likely to trade little whereas those on friendly terms are likely to trade more. There are two reasons for this. First, trade between hostile nations is riskier than trade between friendly nations: businesses avoid engaging in trade that may very well be disrupted by the outbreak of hostilities. Second, governments often pursue close economic ties with their allies in order to cement the alliance and help friendly nations. After all, if trade is good for a national economy, a government might shy away from encouraging trade with an unfriendly nation in order to keep from strengthening a potential enemy. During the Cold War, as we mentioned in Chapter 5 when discussing NATO, the United States and its allies purposely limited their economic ties with the Soviet Union, just as they encouraged ties among themselves.

Some analysts believe that trade encourages friendly relations as much as friendly relations encourage trade. For example, Cordell Hull, American secretary of state before and during World War II, wrote: "It is a fact that war did not break out between the United States and any country with which we had been able to negotiate a trade agreement. It is also a fact that, with very few exceptions, the countries with which we signed trade agreements joined together in resisting the Axis. The political line-up followed the economic line-up."[7] After World War II, the two superpowers used their trade relations to reinforce their alliances: the United States and the Soviet Union each encouraged its allies to build a common

---

7. Quoted in Richard Gardner, *Sterling-Dollar Diplomacy in Current Perspective: The Origins and Prospects of Our International Economic Order*, expanded ed. (New York: Columbia University Press, 1980), 9.

trading order that excluded members of the other alliance. After the Cold War ended, many policy makers in Europe wanted to encourage trade with the former Communist countries of Eastern and Central Europe as a way to encourage cooperative diplomatic relations with them. Regardless of the pattern of cause and effect, international diplomatic realities and international trade are closely related.

But the most important noneconomic source of international trade patterns is national trade policies, undertaken to address the interests of domestic constituencies. Discussions of international trade often overlook the fact that while it takes place among countries, it really involves individuals and firms with well-defined interests. We say that "Mexico" exports a million tons of steel to "the United States," but in fact companies in Mexico sell the steel to companies in the United States. Companies in one country profit from the sale, and companies in the other profit from the purchase. For trade is the stuff of domestic politics, as governments attempt to respond to the interests of corporations and consumers, farmers and workers, all of whom have something at stake in their countries' policies toward foreign trade. We now consider how domestic political and economic factors affect trade policy and trade itself. In this context, we examine the interests, institutions, and interactions that lead to national trade policies.

Trade Restrictions Are the Rule, Not the Exception

Despite the powerful economic arguments for free trade, every country currently has at least some restrictions on trade with the rest of the world. Some countries have very high barriers to trade; others have much lower ones. Yet government policies to control and contain trade are the norm, today as in the past. **Protectionism**, the use of specific measures to shield domestic producers from imports, has long been one of the most common government policies worldwide.

Virtually all governments restrict at least some imports. For hundreds of years, governments have imposed a wide variety of **trade barriers**, impediments to the importation of foreign goods. Historically, the most common barrier is a **tariff**, a tax on imports levied at the border and paid by the importer. A tariff raises the price of the import directly, so a consumer of the imported good has to pay more for it. Another common form of trade barrier is a **quantitative restriction, or quota**, which limits the quantity of a foreign good that can be sold domestically. Because the reduced quantity typically causes an increase in its domestic price, a quantitative restriction has an effect like that of a tariff: it makes the imported good more expensive to domestic consumers. There are many other **nontariff barriers to trade**, such as regulations targeted at foreign goods or requirements that governments purchase from national producers. In all instances, the effect of these policies is to shelter domestic producers from foreign competition. Before we analyze the effects of these policies, it is important to emphasize how common they have been and continue to be.

protectionism
The imposition of barriers to restrict imports.

trade barriers
Government limitations on the international exchange of goods. Examples include tariffs, quantitative restrictions (quotas), import licenses, requirements that governments only buy domestically produced goods, and health and safety standards that discriminate against foreign goods.

tariff
A tax imposed on imports; this raises the domestic price of the imported good and may be applied for the purpose of protecting domestic producers from foreign competition.

quantitative restriction (quota)
Limit placed on the amount of a particular good that is allowed to be imported.

nontariff barriers to trade
Obstacles to imports other than tariffs (trade taxes). Examples include restrictions on the number of products that can be imported (quantitative restrictions, or quotas); regulations that favor domestic over imported products; and other measures that discriminate against foreign goods or services.

TABLE 7.1 *Merchandise Exports as a Percentage of GDP, 1820–1998**

	1820	1870	1913	1929	1950	1973	1998
France	1.3%	4.9%	7.8%	8.6%	7.6%	15.2%	28.7%
Germany	NA	9.5	16.1	12.8	6.2	23.8	38.9
Netherlands	NA	17.4	17.3	17.2	12.2	40.7	61.2
Great Britain	3.1	12.2	17.5	13.3	11.3	14.0	25.0
Spain	NA	3.8	8.1	5.0	3.0	5.0	23.5
United States	2.0	2.5	3.7	3.6	3.0	4.9	10.1
Mexico	NA	3.9	9.1	12.5	3.0	1.9	10.7
Brazil	NA	12.2	9.8	6.9	3.9	2.5	5.4
China	NA	0.7	1.7	1.8	2.6	1.5	4.9
India	NA	2.6	4.6	3.7	2.9	2.0	2.4
Japan	NA	0.2	2.4	3.5	2.2	7.7	13.4
World	1.0	4.6	7.9	9.0	5.5	10.5	17.2

*Exports and GDP at 1990 prices. While more recent data may better reflect changes in the past two decades, such as the dramatic increase in exports from China, these more recent data are not directly comparable to the data collected before 1960 and thus don't give an accurate sense of the longer-term trend.

Sources: Angus Maddison, *Monitoring the World Economy* (Paris: Organisation for Economic Co-operation and Development, 1995), Table 13; Angus Maddison, *The World Economy: A Millennial Perspective* (Paris: Organisation for Economic Co-operation and Development, 2001), Table F-5.

The degree to which the world's major nations have been open to trade has varied greatly over time and among countries (Table 7.1). As we saw in Chapter 1, for more than 300 years after 1492, the major European nations followed the trade policies of mercantilism, a system by which great powers used their military might to control trade with and extract wealth from their colonial possessions. The colonial powers' mercantilist regulations kept foreign goods out of their markets and reserved their colonies' markets for themselves.

However, around the middle of the nineteenth century, Great Britain and other leading industrial countries moved in the direction of trade liberalization: they pursued policies that involved fewer restrictions on trade. Great Britain adopted free trade, permitting foreigners to sell anything to Britain without tax or restriction. More generally, from the 1860s until 1914 international trade among the principal industrialized nations was quite free. There were tariffs and other barriers, to be sure, and some countries were very protectionist—especially such industrializing nations as the United States. Nonetheless, most of the world's major economies were open, and world trade grew at a very rapid rate.

With the outbreak of World War I in 1914, however, international trade relations entered 30 years of crisis and closure. Efforts to rebuild the trading system after the war were not very successful, especially once the Great Depression hit in 1929. The major powers divided up the world into more or less hostile trading blocs: the British, French, Italian, Japanese and other empires, along with the less formal German and American spheres of influence.

After 1945, the Western world under American leadership moved gradually to reduce trade barriers among the developed nations. The Communist countries and most developing countries protected themselves from world markets, but the industrialized world significantly liberalized its trade. Although the reduction of trade barriers has remained controversial, by the 1980s the rich countries had become very open to world trade, as part of the broader march toward economic globalization. Eventually, most developing and formerly Communist countries joined the liberalizing and globalizing trend. Since the early 1990s, international trade has once more—as before 1914— been quite open. Thus, in terms of global trade relations over time, we see a pattern in which mercantilist closure gave way to freer trade, then to interwar closure, then to liberalization after 1945 and further liberalization leading to globalization after 1980.

Many nations have, at some point, gone from very closed to very open to trade, or in the opposite direction. Great Britain jettisoned mercantilism in the 1840s. The United States was one of the most protectionist nations in the world through most of the nineteenth and early twentieth centuries, started moving toward freer trade in the 1930s, and by the 1950s and 1960s was leading the charge for trade liberalization. As Figure 7.1 shows, trade became an increasingly large part of the U.S. economy after the 1960s. Developing nations such as Brazil and India were among the world's most

Figure source: World Bank, World Development Indicators, http://data.worldbank.org/ indicator/NE.TRD.GNFS.ZS/ countries/US?display=default (accessed 02/02/14).

FIGURE 7.1 *Importance of Trade to the U.S. Economy, 1960–2013*

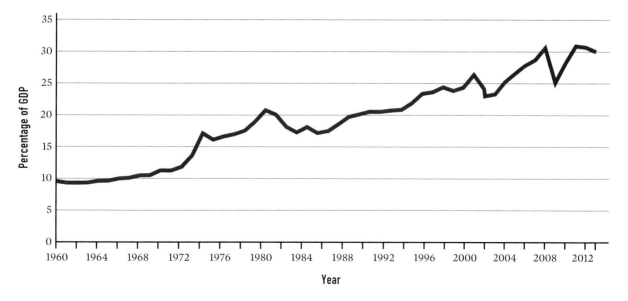

closed economies until the 1980s, after which they reduced their barriers dramatically. Trade among European countries was quite free from the 1860s until 1914; in the 1920s and 1930s, the region's nations erected highly strict barriers to trade among themselves; today, trade among the 28 EU members is completely unrestricted.

Even within a single country, there can be significant differences among policies toward trade in different goods—some protected and some not. Almost all developed nations protect agricultural producers much more heavily than manufacturers. Developing nations, meanwhile, tend to protect manufactured products more than farm products. The United States, as well as many other industrial nations, generally protects the steel industry more than most other industries. And despite the industrial countries' rhetoric in favor of freer trade, they have imposed restrictions on many goods that might be imported from developing nations. Why are some producers—farmers, or certain kinds of farmers; industries, or certain kinds of industries—more favored by trade policy than others? Why do different countries' trade policies vary so much? Why has the world's general openness to trade changed so dramatically over time? And, perhaps most central, why have governments almost always, and almost everywhere, ignored economic analysis and advice and imposed restrictions on foreign trade?

Why Do Governments Restrict Trade? The Domestic Political Economy of Protection

For over 200 years, economic analysis has been unambiguous about the benefits of trade for national income, output, and efficiency. This is reflected in the opinions of professional economists, more than 90 percent of whom believe that barriers to trade reduce national well-being (according to one survey of American economists).[8] Yet economists' confidence in the benefits of trade is not shared by most people. Public opinion is much less favorable to trade: 60 percent of respondents in another survey of American views were favorable to trade protection, as opposed to less than 5 percent of economists.[9] Indeed, many people seem wary of openness to international trade, despite the overwhelming support of economists. Such wariness is evident in the fact that almost all countries, almost all the time, have substantial barriers to trade that protect their own producers.

Trade barriers usually reflect domestic concerns, despite the fact that they implicate foreign relations. William McKinley, a leading protectionist member of the U.S. Congress before he became president, once said of a tariff he was

---

8. Cletus C. Coughlin, "The Controversy over Free Trade: The Gap between Economists and the General Public," *Federal Reserve Bank of St. Louis Review* 84, no. 1 (January–February 2002): 1.

9. Coughlin, "The Controversy over Free Trade," 1.

shepherding through the House of Representatives, "This is a domestic bill; it is not a foreign bill."[10] This statement remains a common view of protection for domestic interests.

Trade policy typically reaches the public consciousness, and the media, when some national producers complain that there is too much or too little trade in the goods they produce. Often, producers are concerned because imported goods cut into their profits or cost them their jobs. Other producers may complain that foreign barriers to their goods keep them out of markets abroad and similarly cut into profits and cost jobs at home. To understand the domestic politics of trade, we need to know the interests in question, the institutions through which these interests are expressed, and how competing interests interact with one another.

There are both benefits and costs to trade barriers. Virtually all tools of trade protection—tariffs, quotas, and other restrictions—make imports more expensive, which allows domestic producers to sell more of their products, to raise their prices, or both. When tariffs are imposed on foreign steel imported into the United States, American steelmakers can expand sales at higher prices. This may allow them to increase profits, raise wages, and hire more workers. Quotas, which restrict the quantity of foreign goods sold in the national market, ultimately have a similar impact in that the reduction in imports reduces supply, thus raising prices. So trade barriers assist national producers. What could be wrong with that?

The most direct cost of protection is to consumers of the protected good. Tariffs and quotas raise the domestic price of imported goods and may lead to price increases for similar domestically produced goods: for example, a barrier to steel imports makes imported steel more expensive and allows domestic steelmakers to raise prices too. Producers gain and consumers lose from protection; the *redistributive effect* is such that income is redistributed from domestic consumers to the protected domestic industry. But there is another cost as well: in this case, to efficiency or the welfare of the society as a whole—the ability of society to use its resources most effectively. For a trade barrier introduces economic inefficiencies. It leads domestic producers to make more goods that they are not particularly good at making (otherwise, they would not need protection). It also leads consumers to consume less of those goods that protection has made artificially expensive. Trade protection leads to an allocation of domestic resources—labor, capital, land, skills—that is not to the country's comparative advantage. Protection of European wheat leads European farmers to

The former Soviet Union imposed strict controls on trade, which meant that many goods had to be produced domestically (such as these shoes stitched in a factory in Armenia), even if the country was not well equipped to do so.

10. Cited in David Lake, *Power, Protection, and Free Trade: International Sources of U.S. Commercial Strategy, 1887–1939* (Ithaca, NY: Cornell University Press, 1988), 111.

use their land for wheat farming when it might make more sense, from the stand-point of the region's overall economy, to use that land for dairy or vegetable farming or to build houses. (For more on the economic effects of trade restrictions, see the "Special Topic" appendix on p. 334.)

Winners and Losers in International Trade

The domestic politics of trade is infused with battles between winners and losers from protection and with debates over the importance of any inefficiencies it may promote. The potential winners and losers constitute the principal actors in national debates over trade policy.

Domestic industries protected by trade barriers receive clear and concentrated benefits. Protection creates returns above the normal rate of profit by artificially restricting competition and supply. However, at least three groups of actors stand to lose from trade protection. First are consumers of the imported good. This group includes consuming industries, which—unlike average consumers—may be powerful and well organized. When the U.S. government imposed tariffs on imported steel in 2002, the American users of this steel—especially in the automobile industry—mobilized strongly against it (as did foreign governments), and the policy was eventually reversed. A second group that tends to oppose protection is exporters. They worry that their country's protective barriers might provoke retaliation in foreign markets. American farmers, for example, have opposed American barriers to Chinese goods—largely to avoid Chinese retaliation against the many billions of dollars of American farm goods that China imports. Third, citizens in general may be willing and able to punish politicians for the costs that protection imposes on them, especially if the connection is clear and the issue is prominent. In the 1980s, many people in Soviet-bloc (Communist) countries blamed the stagnation of their economies on their governments' pervasive trade controls, and this may have created popular sympathy for the subsequent opening of these nations to international trade. Also, there is evidence that consumers in developing countries favor freer trade because they understand that it will lead to reduced prices for themselves.[11]

Because of the diverse array of industries that compete with imports, use imports, and sell exports, as well as the range of producers and consumers, trade is politically controversial. Which actors do we expect to have an interest in support-ing and opposing trade protection within national political systems?

Economic Interests and Trade Policy

The economic characteristics of a country, and of particular groups within it, help explain who might be in favor of and against trade. There are two leading theories of trade-policy interests; each predicts different sets of actors who will support or oppose trade protection. The first theory described in this section emphasizes the interests of broad factors of production—land, labor, capital. Remember that

---

11. See, for example, Andy Baker, "Who Wants to Globalize? Consumer Tastes and Labor Markets in a Theory of Trade Policy Beliefs," *American Journal of Political Science* 49, no. 4 (October 2005): 924–38.

the Heckscher-Ohlin approach expects that a country's exports will make intensive use of resources the country has a lot of. A labor-rich country will export labor-intensive goods; a capital-rich country will export capital-intensive goods. This pattern, in turn, affects which groups trade will help or hurt. If the country exports labor-intensive goods, for example, the demand for labor goes up and so do wages. This first theory argues that trade primarily affects broad factors of production: labor, capital, land, skilled labor. On the other hand, the second theory described in this section, the Ricardo-Viner approach, emphasizes specific sectors of the economy, such as the steel industry or cotton farmers. Both help us think analytically about support for and opposition to trade.

The Stolper–Samuelson Approach

The **Stolper-Samuelson theorem** is one explanation of who will support and who will oppose protection. It predicts that trade protection benefits the scarce factor of production. This is simply the counterpart of the argument that more trade helps the abundant factor: as discussed above, in a labor-rich country, labor benefits most from trade. Logically, this implies that reducing trade in a labor-rich country will harm labor. Consider Bangladesh, a poor country with lots of unskilled labor and very little capital. Bangladesh exports mainly clothing and leather goods, which make intensive use of its abundant unskilled labor; it imports such capital-intensive products as machinery, equipment, and chemicals. Trade barriers artificially make imported capital-intensive goods more expensive or harder to buy, which means that at least some of them will have to be produced in Bangladesh. Some Bangladeshi capital will have to be diverted from labor-intensive production in order to produce these capital-intensive goods (from garment factories to chemical plants, for example), which raises the domestic demand for capital and reduces the local demand for labor. This, in turn, raises the return on Bangladeshi capital (profits) and reduces Bangladeshi wages. Protection in a capital-scarce country helps owners of capital and hurts workers; we expect investors to support protection and workers to oppose it.

We can apply the Stolper-Samuelson theorem to a labor-scarce country, such as the United States. The opposite of Bangladesh, the United States has abundant capital but scarce unskilled labor. The United States imports labor-intensive goods, such as clothing and furniture, and exports capital-intensive goods, such as airplanes. Protection restricts the American supply of labor-intensive products and raises their price. This, in turn, increases American production of these labor-intensive products, raises the American demand for unskilled labor, and raises the wages of American unskilled workers. By the same token, protection in land-scarce countries (such as those of western Europe as well as Japan) helps farmers and hurts workers and owners of capital.

So which actors would we expect to support and oppose trade barriers? We expect owners of the scarce factors of production in a country to be protectionist and owners of the abundant factors to favor free trade. In rich societies, which typically have abundant capital and skilled labor but are scarce in unskilled labor, capitalists and skilled workers should be free traders while unskilled workers should be protectionists. In countries with abundant land, farmers should support trade; in countries

Stolper–Samuelson theorem
The theorem that protection benefits the scarce factor of production. This view flows from the Heckscher-Ohlin approach: if a country imports goods that make intensive use of its scarce factor, then limiting imports will help that factor. So in a labor-scarce country, labor benefits from protection and loses from trade liberalization.

where land is scarce, farmers should support protection. In poor societies, which typically have abundant unskilled labor and scarce capital, workers should support trade while capitalists should be protectionists. An important feature of the model is that actors' attitudes toward trade are not fixed but vary with the country's resources of land, labor, capital, and human capital (skills). Thus, the model expects farmers to be protectionists in land-poor Japan but free traders in land-rich Argentina.

There is a great deal of evidence to support this model. Labor movements in the United States and other rich countries do seem to be relatively protectionist while people with a lot of capital appear more favorable to free trade. Japan and Europe have relatively little land, and their farmers are strongly protectionist; Australia and Canada are rich in land, and their farmers usually favor free trade. Notice that the Stolper-Samuelson predictions are about very broad groups or actors—owners of production factors (roughly the same as social classes) such as laborers, investors, and farmers.

But observers of economic policy making in the United States and elsewhere note that many demands for protection come from specific *industries*—the steel industry, sugar growers, shoe manufacturers. Often, everyone in an industrial sector-skilled and unskilled workers, managers, and owners of firms—works together to ask for trade barriers or support for their exports. For example, we tend to think of the American steel industry as relatively protectionist because we group together everyone associated with the industry. This flies in the face of the Stolper-Samuelson focus on labor as a class or investors (capital) as a class. Indeed, one study of lobbying behavior by corporate and labor groups over a trade bill in the early 1970s found that labor and investors (capital) were almost always on the same side of the trade-policy issue. Twenty-one industries appeared before the relevant congressional committee. Labor unions and corporate management both were in favor of protection in 14 industries while they were both in favor of free trade in 5 industries. In only 2 industries were unions and management on opposite sides of the trade-policy debate.[12] Many detailed studies of trade policy, and of attitudes toward trade, confirm the idea that the industry in which people work has a powerful impact on their trade-policy opinions.[13]

The Ricardo-Viner or Specific-Factors Approach

Ricardo–Viner (specific-factors) model

A model of trade relations that emphasizes the sector in which factors of production are employed rather than the nature of the factor itself. This differentiates it from the Heckscher–Ohlin approach, for which the nature of the factor—labor, land, capital—is the principal consideration.

A second way of predicting trade-policy preferences focuses on why whole industries often act together. The **Ricardo-Viner or specific-factors model** has one key feature that differentiates it from Stolper-Samuelson: some factors of production are tied to their industry-that is, they are *industry-specific*. This makes the relevant actors not classes but industrial sectors. The approach is based on the principle that the factors of production are not very mobile, that it is difficult for labor or capital to move from use to use. For example, capital in the steel industry largely takes the form of steel factories and

12. Stephen Magee, "Three Simple Tests of the Stolper-Samuelson Theorem," in *Issues in International Economics,* ed. Peter Oppenheimer, 138–53 (London: Oriel Press, 1980).

13. See, especially, Anna Maria Mayda and Dani Rodrik, "Why Are Some People (and Countries) More Protectionist Than Others?" *European Economic Review* 49 (2005): 1393–1430.

machinery; it cannot simply be turned into capital in the food-processing industry. Since they are "stuck" in the steel industry, steel manufacturers care not about the profits of capital in *general* and in the country as a whole but rather about the profits available only in steel. The same may be true of workers or farmers, whose job skills or land can be inherently "specific to" (some might say "trapped in") a particular industry or crop. This gives the owners, workers, or farmers a strong incentive to safeguard their current use—for example, by obtaining government protection from foreign competition.

In this model, the interests of individuals flow from the sectors of the economy in which they are employed. Given the limited mobility of labor and capital, actors associate their interests with the sector in which they are employed. A worker or manager in an industry that faces stiff import competition will be protectionist; a worker or manager in an exporting industry will want free trade. Unlike in the Stolper-Samuelson approach, people's interests are tightly bound up with the interests of others in their sector of the economy, and the pertinent actors in domestic trade-policy debates are economic sectors, not factors.

There is evidence that both kinds of actors matter in the politics of trade protection. Broad classes—farmers, workers—sometimes mobilize for or against protection. But at the same time, much lobbying for protection is industry-based, consistent with the view that the benefits of protection accrue to industries, not to broad classes or factors. The accuracy of each view may vary among industries and countries, and over time. One study has found, for example, that in the late

The U.S. steel industry, whose capital equipment is specific to the production of steel, has urged the U.S. government for protection from what it views as unfair "dumping"—that is, selling steel in the United States below the true cost of production. Cheap steel benefits consumers, but hurts the steel industry.

nineteenth century American labor was quite interchangeable, which contributed to the working class having a clear, distinctive interest in trade policy; in contrast, today's American working class is much more differentiated, so industry-based sectoral interests predominate.[14]

It can also be the case that groups support trade policies because they believe those policies help make possible other policies they favor. The economist John Maynard Keynes wrote that protectionism "rests on the principle of making things relatively scarce. To those who are concerned with making these things, this is no doubt advantageous. But it causes an amount of distress more than equivalent elsewhere. The community as a whole cannot hope to gain by making artificially scarce what the country wants."[15] This is a powerful argument; but later, in the midst of the Great Depression of the 1930s, Keynes came to believe that there could be equally powerful political arguments against free trade. In 1933, in fact, Keynes spoke in favor of "the policy of an increased national self-sufficiency . . . not as an ideal in itself, but as directed to the creation of an environment in which other ideals can be safely and conveniently pursued." Keynes had come to believe that trade barriers might usefully give national governments breathing space as they attempted to combat mass unemployment and economic collapse. Keynes felt that protectionism might permit governments to implement policy measures to alleviate the social and economic distress of the Great Depression.[16]

Understanding the economic interests that are in contention over trade is only a start to understanding national trade politics and policies. At best, this can tell us which actors want more or less protection and what the interests of different groups in trade policy might be. But what determines who wins and who loses in the battles among supporters and opponents of trade liberalization?

Domestic Institutions and Trade Policy

Since there are always supporters and opponents of protection in any country, how are trade-policy decisions made? Why are some countries more open to trade than others? Why do governments protect some industries and not others? There are many steps between raw economic interests and the actual results in economic policy. Most of them have to do with the institutions of national politics, including the organization and representation of interests, and the ways in which policy decisions are made.

National political institutions can be of stunning variety and complexity, but a general rule of thumb can help orient our understanding of their implications for trade policy. Let's start with the observation that trade protection tends to help relatively narrow and concentrated groups—the steel industry, skilled workers—but tends to harm the economy and consumers as a whole. It follows that those political

---

14. Michael Hiscox, "Commerce, Coalitions, and Factor Mobility: Evidence from Congressional Votes on Trade Legislation," *American Political Science Review* 96, no. 3 (September 2002): 593-608.

15. Cited in Robert Skidelsky, *John Maynard Keynes*, vol. 1, *Hopes Betrayed 1883–1920* (New York: Penguin, 1983), 227.

16. John Maynard Keynes, "National Self-Sufficiency," *Yale Review* 22, no. 4 (June 1933): 755–69.

institutional forms that are particularly responsive to the interests of more concentrated groups—a particular class, a particular industry—will be more favorable to protection while those that respond especially to broad national pressures will be less favorable. So an important question about domestic institutions has to do with whether they favor particularistic interests, in which case they would incline toward protectionism, or whether they favor broad economic and consumer interests, in which case they would incline toward less protectionist policies.

The Organization of Interests Trade protection affects large groups, both positively and negatively. This raises the possibility of free riding, a concept we introduced in Chapter 2. If a trade barrier is imposed, it helps all the beneficiaries of trade protection—whether a factor of production or an industry—regardless of whether they worked to get protection or not. This means that some members of the winning group—some companies, some individuals—have reasons to sit back and wait for others to fight for them. But if all the actors in a class or industry attempt to free ride, nothing will get done. In other words, both supporters and opponents of trade protection face problems of collective action.

As we've discussed in previous chapters, the logic of collective action implies that smaller groups will be better able to organize than larger groups. We saw in Chapter 4 how smaller, highly motivated groups were better able to influence foreign policy in matters of war and peace. The same principle applies in matters of trade policy. There are typically relatively few producers and a great many consumers, which leads to the expectation that producers will win over consumers in many circumstances. This helps explain, for example, how a relatively small number of steel workers are able to obtain a policy that benefits them at the expense of the vast mass of American consumers of goods that are made with steel.

Economic interests organize themselves very differently in different societies. In some western European countries, for example, most workers are members of a centralized labor federation that devises policies for virtually the entire labor movement. Even where workers in different industries might disagree, the existence of a class-wide labor federation helps create a common working-class political position and overcome collective action problems. In the United States, by contrast, labor unions tend to be organized by industry; even if there were common trade-policy interests among American workers, it might be difficult for them to express those interests in a common way.

The implication is that an organization reflecting the concerns of broad groups—such as all workers—is more likely to ignore the demands of specific groups or industries. In contrast, interests that are organized into narrower groups are more likely to pursue the particular goals of such special interests.

The Representation of Interests through Political Institutions Just as narrowly based social groups are more likely to favor protection than broader ones, so political institutions that are more closely tied to narrow interests are more likely to favor trade protection than institutions that reflect broader interests. This is an example of the sort of bias that political institutions can create or intensify. Generally, to the extent that democracies reflect broad interests while dictatorships are restrictive, we would expect democracies to be less protectionist than dictatorships. Indeed, scholars have found that democratic developing countries are much more likely to liberalize their trade than dictatorships are.[17]

Apart from such broad institutional features as democracy, societies differ in the ways their partisan, electoral, and legislative institutions represent the interests of their citizens, and these differences are likely to affect the way trade policy is made. For example, many European countries have strong class-based parties: the working class votes for the socialist parties, and other parties associate themselves more or less explicitly with farmers or business. Although the American labor movement has close ties to the Democrats and working-class voters tend to vote Democratic, these connections are weak by European standards. This affects the expression of interests and their bias toward special or general interests, and thus toward protection or freer trade.

National electoral systems vary greatly, and they may cause differences among national party structures. Most industrial countries are parliamentary and have a legislature elected on a proportional basis in which voters choose the party they prefer rather than the individual local candidate. American voters elect the president on a national basis but elect individual local candidates (for the House of Representatives and the Senate) whose ties to the national party may be weak. And there are systems in between, such as the Westminster system (in Great Britain) and hybrid presidential-parliamentary systems (in much of Latin America).

How might these institutions affect trade policy? Politicians with local political constituencies tend to be more responsive to local interest groups while nationally elected politicians have less reason to cater to particular local concerns. Consider two otherwise identical countries: one with strong national parties and a powerful national executive and the other with weak national parties and a weak national executive. Politicians in the former are more likely to focus on national effects of policy and favor free trade while politicians in the latter are more likely to emphasize local concerns and thus favor trade protection to local special interests.

The same holds within a country, where one branch of government may be more sensitive to local pressures than another. The American president, elected nationally, has a strong incentive to consider the impact of trade policies on the country as a whole. Members of Congress, however, have little reason to think about anything other than the effects of the policy on their district. For example, most members of Congress or senators from Michigan feel bound to support protection for the automobile industry, but the president needs to consider the electoral implications of higher car prices nationally.

Partisan features of government can also affect trade policy, especially if parties are associated with well-defined social groups with preferences for particular trade policies. For example, in the Stolper-Samuelson framework, labor has well-defined interests in trade: if labor is scarce, laborers will be protectionist; if

---

17. Helen V. Milner and Keiko Kubota, "Why the Move to Free Trade? Democracy and Trade Policy in the Developing Countries," *International Organization* 59, no. 1 (Winter 2005): 107–43.

Farmers in France grew angry when the European Union reduced the benefits they would receive as compensation for sales lost to import. They protested by depositing manure in front of a government building.

labor is abundant, laborers will support free trade. In most of the world, labor typically supports left-wing parties. Given this observation, governments of the Left in labor-rich countries (mainly poor nations) should be more open to trade than governments of the Left in labor-scarce countries (mainly rich nations). Similarly, because business typically is associated with right-wing parties, governments of the Right in capital-rich countries (usually rich nations) should be more open while in capital-poor countries (usually poor nations) they should be more protectionist. Thus, leftist governments should support free trade in poor countries and protection in rich countries; rightist governments should support free trade in rich countries and protection in poor countries. One study of a large number of countries indeed found strong support for this joint impact of partisan politics and Stolper-Samuelson interests. For example, Bangladesh and Senegal are similarly labor rich and capital poor, but in the 1980s Bangladesh's right-wing (presumably anti-labor) government had tariffs twice as high as Senegal's left-wing (presumably pro-labor) government.[18]

Costs, Benefits, and Compensation in National Trade Policies

Even if trade liberalization makes a country's economy as a whole better off, it can seriously harm groups within the country. Concentrated groups of potential losers with a lot at stake could conceivably block policy changes that would improve conditions for the nation overall. This means that the country would be better off if it "bought off" the actors whose interests would be harmed, to give them a reason to

---

18. Pushan Dutt and Devashish Mitra, "Endogenous Trade Policy through Majority Voting: An Empirical Investigation," *Journal of International Economics* 58 (2002): 107–33.

cooperate with trade policies that benefit the society as a whole. Such an approach would represent a movement toward the Pareto frontier in the model presented in Chapter 2. Movement toward the Pareto frontier, called a Pareto improvement, makes everyone better off (or at least unharmed) and nobody worse off. While trade liberalization might hurt some people in the first instance, the overall gains to the national economy are large enough that the losers can be fully compensated for their losses and the benefits will still be left over for the rest of society. Indeed, it is not uncommon for a government to arrange compensation for people who lose from trade liberalization, in order to diminish opposition to a removal of trade barriers that the government wants to pursue. The United States, for example, provides Trade Adjustment Assistance to workers harmed by the country's foreign trade; the assistance ranges from tax credits, to money for retraining, to outright grants.

More generally, the very structure of the post-1945 political economy of most Western societies has to some extent been based on the logic of compensation. As the industrialized world substantially reduced trade barriers after World War II, its governments implemented sweeping social policies that provided a safety net to workers, farmers, and others who might be negatively affected by the reopening of world trade. This strategy reflects a kind of compromise between supporters of economic integration, on the one hand, and defenders of the welfare state, on the other.[19] The Bretton Woods System (introduced in Chapter 1) permitted, even encouraged, this compromise, and it was quite successful at achieving its goal of an integrated world economy and extensive social welfare policies in the industrialized nations.

The issue of compensation has attracted recent attention because many observers believe that trade has led to reduced wages for unskilled workers in the industrial countries. Trade puts unskilled American workers in direct competition with unskilled workers in poor countries with much lower wages, which may depress the wages of the former. This is a clear implication of the Heckscher-Ohlin approach: trade will tend to make wages, profits, and other earnings more similar across countries. In this process, the prices of factors of production (the wages of labor, the profits of capital, the returns to land) tend to become more equal across countries. Trade leads countries to export goods that use factors of production in which they are well endowed: labor-rich countries export labor-intensive goods. This increases the demand for labor and raises wages. At the same time, labor-poor countries import labor-intensive goods rather than producing them at home, and this reduces the demand for labor—thus lowering wages. The implication is that wages in poor countries will rise toward the levels of those in rich countries while wages in rich countries will fall toward the levels of poor countries.

For example, the wages of unskilled workers in the United States have in fact been stagnant or declining since the early 1970s, and trade with developing countries may have contributed to this process. The issue is controversial; some analysts

---

19. John Ruggie called this compromise "embedded liberalism." See John Gerard Ruggie, "International Regimes, Transactions, and Change: Embedded Liberalism in the Postwar Economic Order," *International Organization* 36, no. 2 (1982): 379–415.

think that the decline in unskilled wages in the United States is largely due to technological changes that have made computer-based skills more valuable in the workplace. Nonetheless, there is little doubt that globalization has created winners and losers in rich countries and that working people are more likely to be on the losing side. This observation has led some analysts to suggest that rich countries may face social and political conflict over economic openness unless they develop more extensive social safety nets to reduce the negative impact of the world economy on some groups in society. (We will return to this issue in Chapter 13.)

Clearly, the interests, interactions, and institutions that characterize different national political economies have a powerful impact on national trade policies. Nonetheless, a focus on the *domestic* sources of trade policies misses an important part of the story, because each country's trade relations are part of a broader international environment. While trends in French or Indian trade depend on French and Indian domestic politics, they also depend on the global economic and political situation. It would be difficult to understand the French turn toward protectionism in the 1930s without the context of the Great Depression, that country's reduction in protection after 1950 without situating it within the Cold War, or its current trade policies without knowing France's place in the single market of the European Union. Similarly, it would be difficult to explain India's protectionism upon independence in 1947, or its turn toward freer trade in the 1990s, without knowing that in both instances it was following policies shared by most other developing countries. The *international* environment—especially the global strategic and institutional setting—has a powerful impact on national trade policies and patterns.

How Do Countries Get What They Want? The International Political Economy of Trade

What a national government wants from trade is only a starting point, for every country's commercial relations depend on the international environment. Certainly, a country can pursue a unilateral trade policy; it can open its borders or close them, regardless of what other countries do. But what a country achieves depends on the actions of others. How can governments get what their constituents want out of the world economy? How do factors abroad, including the policies of other countries, affect the ability of a national government to deliver goods to its people? What is the international political economy of trade?

International economic conditions, for example, have a powerful impact on both the policies a country might like to pursue and their likely effects. The collapse of the world economy in the 1930s drove many countries inward—foreign markets were small and shrinking, and the benefits of openness shrank with them. In contrast, the rapid expansion of world trade since 1945 has given many countries strong incentives to link their economies to dynamic world markets. In addition to global market conditions, the policies of other governments can have an enormous impact: for example, the opening of China and India to world trade has profoundly affected other developed and developing nations. How, then, can we understand the national politics of trade within the broader international context? How does the strategic and institutional environment affect whether countries get what they want from world trade?

Strategic Interaction in International Trade Relations

When governments make national trade policies, they take into account what other governments are likely to do in response. A government that raises tariffs dramatically, for example, might find other countries retaliating with even higher barriers to its exports—so that the benefits to domestic producers sheltered from imports might be canceled out by costs to exporters frozen out of foreign markets. In 1930, for example, the U.S. Congress attempted to provide relief to farmers by raising the tariff on eggs from 8¢ to 10¢ a dozen. This reduced the already small number of Canadian eggs bought in the United States by 40 percent, from 160,000 to fewer than 100,000. The British imperial trade area (which included Canada) countered by increasing the tariff on eggs to the same 10¢ a dozen, from the previously low 3¢. This move drove America's very considerable egg exports to Canada down by 98 percent, from 11 million to fewer than 200,000. The British-Canadian response meant that American protectionism had backfired.[20]

By the same token, attempts to create regional trading areas such as the European Union or NAFTA, or to affect the international commercial order such as the United States did after World War II, rely on the joint behavior of different nation-states. One government cannot achieve many of its trade-policy goals without considering the actions of other governments. (See "What Shaped Our World?" on p. 315 for a discussion on the evolution of the European Union.)

Two or more governments involved in trade-policy negotiations are engaged in strategic interaction and must take into account the behavior of other governments in trying to do their best. For example, suppose that American farmers decide they would be better off if they had access to Europe's market for farm goods and are willing to reduce American agricultural trade barriers in return. American trade negotiators offer the Europeans a joint reduction of farm trade protection, and the Europeans agree. But the Americans are wary: the Europeans might find hidden ways to maintain their barriers, such as by imposing regulations that apply only to American crops. In fact, some American farmers argue that European bans on the import of genetically modified food, or of meat from animals whose feed contains hormones, are in fact trade barriers in disguise. In other words, the Europeans might find ways to "cheat" on the agreement and gain greater access to the American market without providing anything substantial in return. The Europeans,

---

20. Cordell Hull, *The Memoirs of Cordell Hull* (New York: Macmillan, 1948), 355–56.

The Creation of a Single European Market

In 1945, Europe emerged from the most devastating war in history, the culmination of multiple rivalries that tore the continent apart. Today, the 28 countries (and counting) of the European Union constitute a single market for goods, services, capital, and even people. How did the single European market emerge from such a troubled past?

Interests European integration was based on the common interests among the states of Western Europe and the United States in the wake of World War II. The war had devastated European economies, and all countries were looking for a way to rebuild. At the same time, the Soviet Union had taken advantage of its control of Eastern Europe to install Communist regimes. The threats of unrest from within and attack from without created shared interests among the Western European states in security and economic growth. Although these immediate threats dissipated with time, cooperation continued to rest on common interests, particularly the joint gains that could be achieved through the free flow of goods, money, and people.

Interactions Although common interests are necessary for cooperation, they by no means ensure that it will happen. In the aftermath of war, fear and distrust among states of Western Europe, particularly toward West Germany, complicated the interaction. In this regard, the United States played a major role, not only providing security through the presence of U.S. troops, but also by injecting money though the famous Marshall Plan. The Europeans had to cooperate among themselves to distribute U.S. aid, and this spirit

of cooperation continued into the next decade. Given the emerging Cold War competition with the Soviet Union, an early priority of these cooperative efforts was the production of coal and steel, which were vital to both the economic development and military might of the west. Cooperation in this sphere gave rise to the European Coal and Steel Community, established in 1951 among six countries—France, West Germany, Italy, Belgium, the Netherlands, and Luxembourg—which forged a common market for these two industries and placed them under the control of a supranational governing body.

Institutions From these relatively modest beginnings, institutional growth took off. The original six countries moved toward greater integration with the Treaty of Rome in 1957, which created the European Economic Community (EEC), or European Common Market. The EEC was a regional trade agreement of a particular type: a customs union. This meant that the members agreed to allow free trade among themselves for all goods and to impose a common external tariff on imported goods.

Trade among the original six countries more than doubled during the period from 1960 to 1972. However, the customs union was not a single market in the same way that national states, such as the United States, constitute a single market. Trade in services remained outside its scope, as did many informal barriers to trade in goods, such as product standards and regulatory differences. The next institutional steps—the 1986 Single European Act and the 1991 Maastricht Treaty—were designed to create a single European market for goods and services, along with capital and people.

Today, the European Union is close to reaching the ideal of a truly open market, free of barriers to trade and investment. Citizens of an EU country can move freely to any other member country to live, work, study, or retire. There are no formal trade barriers among members, and nontariff barriers (such as licensing requirements and environmental safeguards) have been substantially harmonized throughout the European Union. Cross-national investment occurs without impediment. And 19 of the 28 members of the European Union share a common currency, the euro, with a common central bank, the European Central Bank (see Chapter 8).

for their part, have similar concerns: the United States, they fear, will promise them open markets but find devious ways to keep European goods out. Given this threat, both the United States and the European Union decide not to take the chance, farm trade is not liberalized, and both sides are left worse off than they would have been with an agreement. This scenario is an example of how international trade bargaining problems can resemble a Prisoner's Dilemma (see Chapter 2 "Special Topic" appendix on p. 82): both sides would be better off cooperating to reduce trade barriers, but concern that the other side will cheat leads both sides to act noncooperatively, to their common detriment.

This sort of cooperation problem is common in trade relations among countries. To be sure, the logic of comparative advantage discussed above implies that countries would maximize their overall economic welfare by unilaterally liberalizing trade. However, governments respond to pressures other than that of the economy as a whole. For this reason, a government's first choice of trade policy is almost never to remove its trade barriers unilaterally; typically, it wants to get concessions from other countries in return for its own.

However, as the example of the Prisoner's Dilemma shows (see Chapter 2), it can be difficult for political actors to arrive at a mutually beneficial accord when there is no way to guarantee that all parties to the agreement will cooperate. Just as in the security relations among countries discussed in Chapters 3 through 5, in the international trade realm governments that want to collaborate may be hampered by the fear that they will be taken advantage of in an interaction that can have very high stakes. No government can take lightly the possibility that its farmers, companies, or workers might lose money or jobs because the government mismanaged an international trade negotiation. Countries face inherent difficulties in making credible commitments to abide by the terms of trade agreements; as in military matters, this can lead to a breakdown of trust and, eventually, an inability to cooperate.

Strategic problems can also arise when countries try to work out a common approach to a problem, such as what legal rules to use to govern trade. One of the most common difficulties arises when one country accuses another of unfairly subsidizing its exports with grants, loans, and other programs to raise profits artificially. Disputes in world trade often involve accusations that one country's exporters are *dumping* their goods—that is, selling them below the true cost of production in order to drive out competitors. Dumping is widely accepted to be an unfair trading practice, but it is extremely hard to define, let alone measure. Similarly, government subsidies to exporters encounter widespread disapproval. But such subsidies can take many indirect forms (such as regulation of shipping costs, complicated accounting or tax rules, or manipulation of the exchange rate), and there is often no easy way to determine whether in fact an actual subsidy is being used. In these cases, even where countries would like to work out their conflicts amicably, there may be serious disagreements about the standards to be used to govern fair trading relations.

For example, one of the longest-standing disputes in world trade has been between the United States and Canada, two countries with generally very friendly relations. Starting in the early 1980s, the U.S. government argued that the Canadian federal and provincial governments, which own most of the country's timber-bearing land, were charging lumber producers artificially low prices. This would constitute an unfair subsidy to the country's exports of softwood lumber; the Canadians reject the charge. Both countries wanted to maintain their cooperative trade relations, but this cooperation was threatened by conflicting interpretations of trade rules. In these cases of coordination problems, the parties typically want to find a common position or standard but have trouble deciding which one is best.

Overcoming Problems of Strategic Interaction The international politics of trade is full of examples of problems of cooperation and coordination; it is also full of attempts to make it easier for governments to overcome these problems. In Chapter 2, we saw that several factors can facilitate cooperation and coordination: small numbers, information, repeated interaction, and linkage politics. These all affect international trade relations.

Small numbers make it easier for governments to monitor each others' behavior; there is likely to be less free riding among small groups of countries than in the world at large. An extreme version of this observation is the theory of *hegemonic stability*, which argues that the existence of a single very powerful nation facilitates the solution of problems of collective action and free riding; the hegemonic power is large and strong enough to be both willing and able to solve these problems for the world as a whole. In economic affairs, this approach argues that when there has been such a hegemonic power over the past two centuries (Great Britain after 1860 and the United States after 1945), trade liberalization was facilitated by the leadership of an overwhelmingly influential world economic power. Less

Mercosur began as a regional trade agreement among Argentina, Brazil, Paraguay, and Uruguay in 1991. However, it has not achieved the same level of success in the freer movement of goods, capital, or people as the European Union.

extreme versions of the approach suggest, more modestly, that smaller numbers of countries—privileged groups (see Chapter 2)—will find it easier to monitor and enforce trade agreements than very large groups of nations or the world as a whole. Because of the greater ease of monitoring and enforcement, small numbers of countries are more likely to succeed at liberalizing trade.[21] This might help explain why so many trade agreements take the form of regional accords among a few neighboring nations, such as the European Union, NAFTA, and Mercosur.

Small numbers might also help explain why the United States and Canada have been able to negotiate successfully even in the bitter dispute over softwood lumber, which involved billions of dollars and one of Canada's more important industries. In 1986 and again in 1996, despite long-standing conflict over whether Canada was in fact subsidizing its lumber industry, the two countries reached compromise agreements. In the first instance, the United States agreed to reduce its tariff on Canadian imports; in the second instance, Canada agreed to limit its exports to the United States.

Information can also be an important consideration in trade negotiations. Many failures of cooperation are due to fears of hidden actions—such as the fear that one government might use its superior knowledge of its own domestic conditions to take advantage of other governments. In the case of dumping and subsidies, decisions are often made by national bureaucratic agencies about which foreigners may know little. For example, in 2001 the United States and Canada were unable to negotiate a renewal of the 1996 Softwood Lumber Agreement. Immediately after the agreement expired, the U.S. International Trade Commission and the Department of Commerce found that Canadian lumber was being subsidized, so the United States unilaterally imposed a 27 percent tariff on Canadian imports, triggering a new round of acrimonious conflict. If the Canadians had known about this finding, perhaps they might have reached an agreement with the Americans, but the Canadians did not have access to advance information about the American government decision. This example suggests that transparency may lead to trade cooperation. It also suggests that establishing some manner by which partners can provide information to one another may facilitate cooperative relations.

Repeated interaction (iteration) between governments on a continuing basis provides a reason to avoid cheating, or even the appearance of cheating. The possibility that the collapse of a current deal might sour future deals can impose a powerful discipline on government behavior and can encourage greater efforts to cooperate. This is especially the case in a trading relationship, which is likely to go on indefinitely. By the same token, governments with a long history of dealing with one another are likely to have more information about each other—and, in good circumstances, more reason to trust one another.

Linking concessions granted in one arena to concessions received in another may also facilitate cooperation on trade. A government that would otherwise

---

21. For a reasoned summary, see David A. Lake, "Leadership, Hegemony, and the International Economy: Naked Emperor or Tattered Monarch with Potential?" *International Studies Quarterly* 37, no. 4 (December 1993): 459–89.

be uninterested in negotiating lower barriers in, say, steel might be willing to exchange concessions in steel if its partner gives it concessions in some other industry. Governments can, in other words, trade among trade policies—"giving" in an area they care less about, in return for "getting" in an area they care more about. These exchanges can benefit governments and their citizens. Countries might link agreements in trade (steel for apparel, for example), or they might link agreements in trade with agreements on something else, such as foreign aid or military cooperation.

All these considerations help explain why countries are more likely to have friendly, collaborative trade relations in some circumstances than in others. This is true of pairs or groups of countries: bilateral or regional trade agreements (RTAs) are more likely with smaller numbers, where information about the partners is readily available, when the partners have a long history of interaction, and where trade relations are linked to other economic or noneconomic relations. It may also be true for the world as a whole: when these conditions are met, at least for the leading countries in the international trading system, trade cooperation is more likely. But when there is great uncertainty about the true intentions of some of the major powers (such as Germany and Japan in the 1920s and 1930s), coupled with a real concern for the short term and the absence of a dense network of other relationships among the major powers, international trade cooperation is difficult or impossible.

Because it can be inherently difficult for governments to ensure cooperative trade relations among themselves, they have created international institutions that help overcome the variety of collective action and other strategic problems that have beset international trade relations. International institutions may indeed be the most powerful factor in affecting whether trade relations among countries are collaborative or conflictual. They run the gamut from global organizations, such as the WTO, to regional agreements, such as NAFTA, to bilateral treaties between countries. Most such institutional arrangements have the goal of facilitating trade cooperation among their member states.

International Institutions in International Trade

International organizations represent the principal systematic attempts to bring order to contemporary international trade policy. As we saw in Chapter 2, institutions can play an important part in providing a setting within which cooperation is facilitated. They can help mitigate all the problems that stand in the way of interstate cooperation on trade. Institutions can set standards of behavior that governments are expected to follow. They can gather information to assist member states in monitoring and enforcing compliance with their agreements. By providing an expectation of repeated interaction, they can restrain defection. International institutions can reduce the costs to governments of making joint decisions—a real problem in the very complex trade realm—and can help governments resolve disputes. For all these reasons, over the years countries have developed institutional

reciprocity

In international trade relations, a mutual agreement to lower tariffs and other barriers to trade. Reciprocity involves an implicit or explicit arrangement for one government to exchange trade-policy concessions with another.

most-favored nation (MFN) status

A status established by most modern trade agreements guaranteeing that the signatories will extend to each other any favorable trading terms offered in agreements with third parties.

World Trade Organization (WTO)

An institution created in 1995 to succeed the GATT and to govern international trade relations. The WTO encourages and polices the multilateral reduction of barriers to trade, and it oversees the resolution of trade disputes.

General Agreement on Tariffs and Trade (GATT)

An international institution created in 1947 in which member countries committed to reduce barriers to trade and to provide similar trading conditions to all other members. In 1995, the GATT was replaced by the WTO.

arrangements to facilitate their trade negotiations. One is the concept of **reciprocity**, by which a concession granted by one government is met by another, a sort of linkage politics that helps bind agreements. A more general provision of this nature has developed over the course of more than a hundred years to serve a similar purpose: **most-favored nation (MFN) status**. Countries that grant one another MFN status agree to extend to each other the same concessions that they provide to all other nations with that status—for example, a tariff reduction given to one country is automatically given to all countries with MFN status. This system, called normal trade relations in the United States, serves to link negotiations between two countries to all their multilateral trade relations.

The World Trade Organization The most important international institution in commercial relations has a global reach: the **World Trade Organization (WTO)**, which succeeded the **General Agreement on Tariffs and Trade (GATT)**. The GATT was created in 1947 as one of the original Bretton Woods institutions, and it oversaw a dramatic liberalization of trade relations, in particular among developed countries, for more than 40 years.[22] By the early 1990s, GATT members had come to believe that the GATT's somewhat loose structure was insufficient in an environment in which almost all countries—developed, developing, and formerly centrally planned—were joining the international trading system. The WTO, which opened its doors in 1995, is more structured, more formal, and more encompassing than the GATT, although its goal is very similar: to encourage the expansion of an open international trading system.

Both the GATT and WTO have been enormously successful in their stated purpose of reducing barriers to trade among member nations, with world trade growing faster than world output for virtually all the postwar period. The principal achievement of both organizations has been to organize a series of "rounds" during which member states negotiate multilateral reductions in trade barriers. The negotiations take place under a loose rule of reciprocity that balances the dollar value of concessions, which are then automatically extended to all other member states under the MFN rule. There are also rules about when and how countries can use safeguards to temporarily protect domestic industries.

Although all members of the WTO have a formally equal vote, in practice negotiations are dominated by the largest trading states—in particular, the United States, the European Union (which negotiates as a single actor in the WTO), and Japan. The power of the largest members comes in part from their ability to set the agenda for negotiations. Their power also flows from the fact that they have more attractive outside options—they can more easily contemplate "going it alone" without the WTO. For all these reasons, developing countries have found it difficult to get their concerns onto the international trade agenda.

---

22. To be entirely accurate, the original Bretton Woods institution for trade was to be an International Trade Organization, but it foundered and was never created; the GATT was an interim replacement that lasted far longer than its initiators had expected.

Conflicts between developed and developing nations have pervaded the most recent series of WTO negotiations, the Doha Round that began with a meeting in Doha, Qatar, in 2001. Developing nations have accused the rich world of ignoring their concerns. Their principal demand has been for the liberalization of agricultural trade, as many developing countries would benefit from greater access to rich-country markets for food. This, however, has been blocked by politically powerful farmers in the developed countries. For their part, developed countries would like greater liberalization of trade in services—most developed countries are major exporters of such services as finance and telecommunications—and stricter rules to protect intellectual property. The Doha Round has been stalled for many years, and there are widespread fears that it may never be completed.

Although the Doha Round has been a disappointment, and unequal power among countries have been a source of conflict, most WTO member states understand that the WTO, like the GATT before it, facilitates international cooperation: it helps set standards of behavior, verify compliance, ease joint decision making, and resolve disputes. The WTO makes available a great deal of information about trade and trade policies, including monitoring national compliance with international agreements. The WTO monitors a country's compliance in two primary ways. First, members must report actions taken to restrict trade, as well as on any RTAs they may enter into (such as NAFTA). Second, countries that believe that foreign exporters or importers are not complying with the rules can file a complaint with the WTO. Complaints are referred to the Dispute Settlement Body, composed of all member states, which then appoints a panel of experts in consultation with all parties to the dispute. The panel investigates the alleged rule violation and issues a report that becomes a ruling within 60 days. Each side can appeal (but not block) the ruling to the WTO's standing seven-member Appellate Body. If not overturned, the ruling becomes binding. A country held to be in violation of WTO rules must bring its policy into conformity with the rules; if it does not, it is subject to sanctions authorized by the organization itself.

As the world's largest trader, the United States is the most frequent defendant at the WTO. It is surprising to some observers that the United States usually abides by WTO rules and rulings, even when the complainant is a small country like Costa Rica that the United States could easily ignore. The reason is probably that the United States believes that it is more likely to be a complainant than a target and would like rulings in its favor to be obeyed, which is less likely to occur if the United States itself does not respect WTO rulings. This point applies more broadly: states usually obey the rules of the WTO because they value the WTO's promotion of an open trading system. They fear that defiance of WTO rules and decisions would threaten the whole system of trade rules and the gains from trade.

Regional Trade Agreements   In addition to the WTO—and perhaps in reaction to some of the concerns about its organization and progress—many similar institutions have arisen at the regional level. In fact, the number and range of **regional trade agreements (RTAs)** has grown very rapidly in the past 20 years, and by 2011 the WTO counted 489 RTAs in force (Map 7.1). The three most prominent are the

regional trade agreements (RTAs)
Agreements among three or more countries in a region to reduce barriers to trade among themselves.

MAP 7.1 *Selected RTAs*

NO DATA

NAFTA
North American Free Trade Agreement
Members: 3
Established: January 1, 1994
NAFTA is a trilateral trade bloc that also imposes some environmental restrictions on its participants.

ECOWAS
Economic Community of West African States
Members: 15
Established: May 28, 1975
ECOWAS strives for "collective self-sufficiency" for its member states.

CARICOM
The Caribbean Community
Members: 15 full, 5 associate, 8 observers
Established: August 1, 1973
CARICOM promotes economic cooperation and mutually beneficial foreign policy among its members.

SICA
Central American Integration System
Members: 8
Established: December 13, 1991
CACM is the trade element of a broad intergovernmental coalition of Central American states.

Andean Community
Members: 4 full, 5 associate, 1 observer
Established: May 26, 1969
The Andean Community fosters economic development among its members and works cooperatively with Mercosur.

Mercosur
Southern Common Market
Members: 5 full (plus Bolivia, currently becoming a full member), 4 associate
Established: March 26, 1991
Mercosur pursues economic development and integration among its member states, including favorable trade and foreign policy.

CEMAC
Economic and Monetary Community of Central Africa
Members: 6
Established: 1994
CEMAC, a bloc of Central African states using the common currency of the CFA Franc, seeks to promote trade and establish a genuine common market among its members.

Map note: Bolivia is part of both Mercosur and the Andean Community and Belize is part of BOTH SICA and CARICOM.

ALASKA (U.S.)
CANADA
GREENLAND (DENMARK)
ICELAND
UNITED STATES
Pacific Ocean
Atlantic Ocean
CUBA
HAITI
JAMAICA
DOMINICAN REPUBLIC
MEXICO
BELIZE
DOMINICA
GUATEMALA
ST. LUCIA
EL SALVADOR
HONDURAS
NICARAGUA
GUYANA
VENEZUELA
COSTA RICA
SURINAME
COLOMBIA
PANAMA
ECUADOR
PERU
BRAZIL
BOLIVIA
PARAGUAY
URUGUAY
CHILE
ARGENTINA

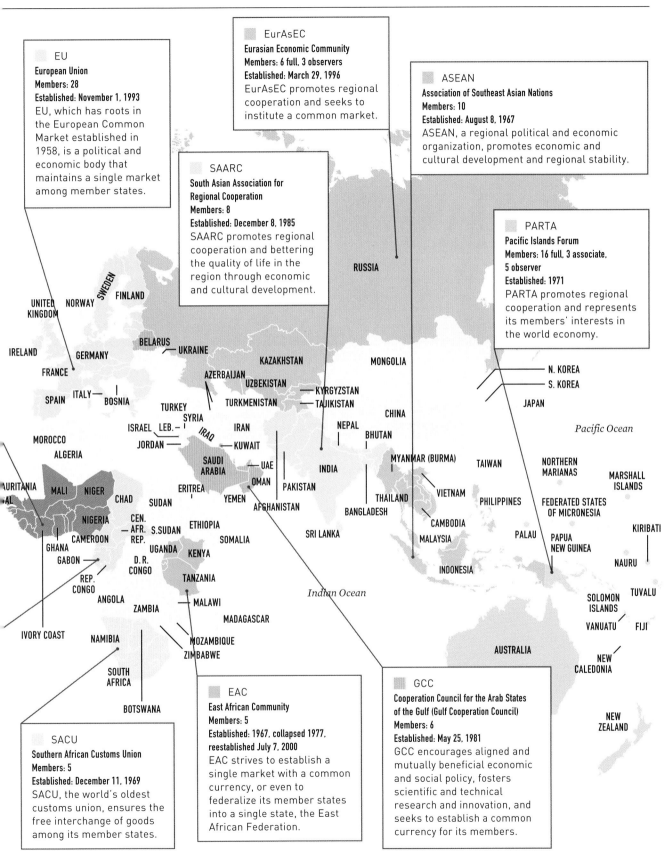

EU
European Union
Members: 28
Established: November 1, 1993
EU, which has roots in the European Common Market established in 1958, is a political and economic body that maintains a single market among member states.

EurAsEC
Eurasian Economic Community
Members: 6 full, 3 observers
Established: March 29, 1996
EurAsEC promotes regional cooperation and seeks to institute a common market.

ASEAN
Association of Southeast Asian Nations
Members: 10
Established: August 8, 1967
ASEAN, a regional political and economic organization, promotes economic and cultural development and regional stability.

SAARC
South Asian Association for Regional Cooperation
Members: 8
Established: December 8, 1985
SAARC promotes regional cooperation and bettering the quality of life in the region through economic and cultural development.

PARTA
Pacific Islands Forum
Members: 16 full, 3 associate, 5 observer
Established: 1971
PARTA promotes regional cooperation and represents its members' interests in the world economy.

SACU
Southern African Customs Union
Members: 5
Established: December 11, 1969
SACU, the world's oldest customs union, ensures the free interchange of goods among its member states.

EAC
East African Community
Members: 5
Established: 1967, collapsed 1977, reestablished July 7, 2000
EAC strives to establish a single market with a common currency, or even to federalize its member states into a single state, the East African Federation.

GCC
Cooperation Council for the Arab States of the Gulf (Gulf Cooperation Council)
Members: 6
Established: May 25, 1981
GCC encourages aligned and mutually beneficial economic and social policy, fosters scientific and technical research and innovation, and seeks to establish a common currency for its members.

Country labels on map: SWEDEN, FINLAND, NORWAY, UNITED KINGDOM, IRELAND, GERMANY, FRANCE, SPAIN, ITALY, BOSNIA, BELARUS, UKRAINE, RUSSIA, KAZAKHSTAN, MONGOLIA, AZERBAIJAN, UZBEKISTAN, KYRGYZSTAN, TURKMENISTAN, TAJIKISTAN, TURKEY, SYRIA, ISRAEL, LEB., IRAQ, IRAN, CHINA, NEPAL, BHUTAN, JORDAN, KUWAIT, SAUDI ARABIA, UAE, INDIA, OMAN, PAKISTAN, N. KOREA, S. KOREA, JAPAN, TAIWAN, NORTHERN MARIANAS, MARSHALL ISLANDS, MOROCCO, ALGERIA, MAURITANIA, MALI, NIGER, CHAD, SUDAN, ERITREA, YEMEN, AFGHANISTAN, MYANMAR (BURMA), VIETNAM, PHILIPPINES, FEDERATED STATES OF MICRONESIA, KIRIBATI, NIGERIA, CEN. AFR. REP., S.SUDAN, ETHIOPIA, THAILAND, BANGLADESH, SRI LANKA, CAMBODIA, MALAYSIA, PALAU, PAPUA NEW GUINEA, NAURU, GHANA, CAMEROON, GABON, REP. CONGO, D.R. CONGO, UGANDA, KENYA, SOMALIA, IVORY COAST, ANGOLA, TANZANIA, ZAMBIA, MALAWI, MADAGASCAR, INDONESIA, SOLOMON ISLANDS, TUVALU, VANUATU, FIJI, NAMIBIA, MOZAMBIQUE, ZIMBABWE, AUSTRALIA, NEW CALEDONIA, SOUTH AFRICA, BOTSWANA, NEW ZEALAND

Pacific Ocean

Indian Ocean

Although the WTO has lowered barriers to international trade, it has often provoked opposition from actors whose interests may be harmed by trade liberalization. The 2009 demonstrations against the WTO in Geneva turned violent as angry protesters torched cars.

European Union, which started in 1958 as a customs union of six countries and now encompasses 28 nations in a single market; NAFTA, made up of the United States, Canada, and Mexico; and Mercosur, originally comprising Argentina, Brazil, Paraguay, and Uruguay. There are many other such RTAs, of varying size and involving varying degrees of commitment to openness among their members. Many are bilateral, involving only two countries; others involve dozens of countries.[23]

Some observers applaud these regional agreements, arguing that they, like the WTO, constitute institutional structures that help mediate or avoid divisive trade-policy conflicts among countries. Others see them more negatively, believing that they may serve to limit trade with nonmembers. In the words of economist Robert Lawrence, the question is whether the RTAs will be "building blocs" or "stumbling blocks" on the road to an integrated world economy.[24] While questions remain, most observers today regard such regional institutions as complementary to the WTO.

To state that the WTO (or the European Union or NAFTA) facilitates cooperation among governments on trade policy is not to pass judgment on whether its actions are good or bad, ethically, economically, or otherwise. Governments may cooperate for purposes that leave some consumers, workers, or businesses worse off. Antiglobalization critics complain that the WTO is too pro-business, that it privileges international corporations over other interests. They charge that WTO

23. For more information on RTAs, see the WTO's RTA website at www.wto.org/english/tratop_e/region_e/ region_e.htm (accessed 01/02/12).

24. Robert Z. Lawrence, "Emerging Regional Arrangements: Building Blocs or Stumbling Blocks?" in *Finance and the International Economy*, vol. 5, *The AMEX Bank Review Prize Essays*, ed. Richard O'Brien, 25–35 (New York: Oxford University Press, 1991).

rules and procedures are biased, especially in their disregard for environmental, health and safety, labor, and social policies. Indeed, WTO rules do tend to focus on trade itself and exclude consideration of other concerns that many analysts regard as important. Whether this is justifiable depends largely on value judgments about the relative importance of trade, and economic relations more generally, as compared to concerns about human and social rights (see "Controversy" on p. 326). Nonetheless, in many instances cooperation among governments is preferable to conflict among them, and the international institutions of trade contribute to this cooperation.

Explaining Trends and Patterns in International Trade

We can now return to some of the questions about international trade relations with which we began, bringing together what we have learned from the preceding sections to try to explain them. Let's recall the major ways in which trade policies vary.

Why, within a Country, Are Some Industries Protected and Some Not?

Governments often favor some industries over others, some regions over others, some groups over others—and this is certainly true of trade policy. Perhaps the most striking such difference is that virtually all developed countries protect agriculture, whereas they have relatively open trade in manufactured products. Why are America's farmers (in particular, its sugar producers) strongly protected while so many other producers are not?

We can look at the actors involved and their interests to determine which groups or industries are most likely to benefit from protection. Land is scarce in most developed countries, certainly relative to capital and skilled labor; this explains why their farmers are protectionist. We can then explore how well the actors are able to overcome their collective action problems; the more cohesive and powerful interests are likely to get more government support. Farmers are well organized, whereas consumers of food are rarely organized at all. Perhaps the country's political institutions are biased for or against some regions, classes, or industries. Many nations' electoral institutions favor farm regions over cities, as does the U.S. Senate, which allots a sparsely populated farm state the same number of senators (two) as a densely populated, mostly urban state. Farmers and their parties are often pivotal in parliamentary systems, as they occupy the crucial center of the political spectrum. All these considerations help explain why some sectors receive more trade protection than others and, in particular, why farmers in rich countries are so commonly favored. In the case of American sugar producers, they have very high stakes in protection—the country's sugar farms might shut down without

Does the WTO Hurt the Global Poor?

In the late 1980s, Lee Kyung-Hae led a rewarding life as a thriving farmer in South Korea. He had succeeded in transforming a difficult area of land in the mountains south of Seoul into a prosperous cattle farm and a model of modern agriculture for the farmers in his poverty-stricken region. However, this success story ended abruptly when, under pressure from the WTO, South Korea opened its markets to imports of cheaper cows from Australia. Beef prices collapsed, and Lee, now unable to make the repayments on his loans, was forced to sell his farm. This experience, and the similar experience of many other farmers and fishermen in his country, caused Lee to become a prominent antiglobalization activist. After a series of hunger strikes over a period of years, on September 10, 2003, at a demonstration outside the WTO meeting in Cancún, Lee climbed a police barricade and stabbed himself in the heart, surrounded by 150 of his countrymen and the television cameras of the world.[a] Some observers consider Lee a hero for calling the WTO to account for its treatment of the global poor. His signature phrase, "The WTO kills farmers," continues to be displayed on placards by protesters worldwide. Others consider Lee's death a pointless tragedy. Well meaning as his action was, it displayed a fundamental misunderstanding of the impact of trade liberalization on the world's disadvantaged. Who is right?

When thinking about the effects of the WTO on the global poor, it helps to distinguish two questions. The first is whether trade liberalization has indeed hurt the world's poor. There is no doubt that certain people—such as Lee and the poor South Korean farmers he represented—have suffered great hardship as a result of some WTO-related policies. But assessing the overall effects of the WTO regime on the poor is difficult. This is because, partly, trade liberalization has varying impacts on a range of interests (income, food security, health, education, and life expectancy)—some impacts are negative, others positive; and partly, because the interests of different actors, both within and across countries, are affected differently by trade liberalization. The Stolper-Samuelson theorem projects that trade liberalization will benefit a country's abundant factor of production and harm the country's scarce factor. This implies, for example, that in South Korea, where land is scarce but labor is abundant, trade liberalization will harm farmers but help workers. More generally, trade liberalization will harm the producers of previously protected goods and help their consumers. Again, this means that in South Korea, liberalization would hurt farmers—because farm products were protected—but help the consumers of farm products. As sympathetic as we might be to Lee Kyung-Hae's plight, these perspectives on the economic impact of trade liberalization remind us that Lee's livelihood was sustainable only as a result of his government's agricultural protectionism—a policy that hurts not only South Korean consumers (including the poor) by raising the prices of agricultural goods but also poor farmers in other countries, such as China, who are denied a market for their produce. It is difficult to know how we should weigh the negative effects of trade liberalization on those harmed by it—such as Lee and his fellow South Korean farmers—against the positive impact it might have on those benefited by liberalization—such as South Korean consumers and farmers elsewhere.

Whatever we decide on this first question, it leaves the following one unaddressed. Has the bargain represented by the WTO been fair to the global poor? Our interest here is not the nature of the benefits and burdens produced but the way in which those benefits and burdens have been distributed. Some aspects of the WTO system may seem unfair in this sense. While rich countries have pressured poor or middle-income countries such as South Korea to open their markets to the developed world, they themselves have maintained extensive protectionism in precisely the markets that matter most to the developing world. And global inequality has, by some measures, increased over the past several decades, suggesting to some analysts that the gains of free trade have been unevenly distributed. These facts appear to violate, respectively, reciprocity and nondiscrimination, two core norms of fairness.

This argument is related to the broader charge that the major international economic institutions are biased

---

a. Jonathan Watts, "Field of Tears," *Guardian*, September 16, 2003, www.theguardian.com/world/2003/sep/16/northkorea.wto (accessed 02/05/15).

against poor countries. The WTO (and the GATT before it) was set up by the industrialized nations, and many observers believe that they have largely reflected the concerns and priorities of these rich countries. For example, the WTO has made very little progress on the opening of world markets in agricultural products—a matter of grave concern to many developing countries, but one that is strongly opposed by most developed countries. If the WTO were unbiased, it could have exerted as much pressure on developed countries to liberalize trade in farm products as it exerted on poor countries to open trade in manufactured goods—a policy that benefits primarily the industrialized nations.

However, proving that the WTO is biased against the developing world runs up against difficulties similar to those discussed above. While agricultural subsidies in richer countries have burdened the poor in food-producing countries, such subsidies may have helped people in less developed countries that import food, such as those of North Africa and the Middle East. And it is difficult to decisively attribute changes in the relative economic fortunes of different countries to the WTO system in the absence of knowing what the world would have looked like without it. Some scholars argue that any increase in inequality in recent decades is the result of technological change, the collapse of Communism, or the AIDS crisis and civil war in Africa rather than WTO policies.

Some scholars wonder, finally, whether it matters if the WTO is unfair, provided that the aggregate gains from free trade are large enough. One way in which it may matter is if the perception that the WTO is unfair undermines the public support necessary to sustain it—as indicated by the demonstration during which Lee Kyung-Hae met his death.

Source: OECD, Producer and Consumer Support Estimates Database, www.oecd.org/unitedstates/producerandconsumersupport estimatesdatabase.htm (accessed 02/5/15).

FIGURE 7.2 *Agricultural Subsidies in Selected Countries, 2013*

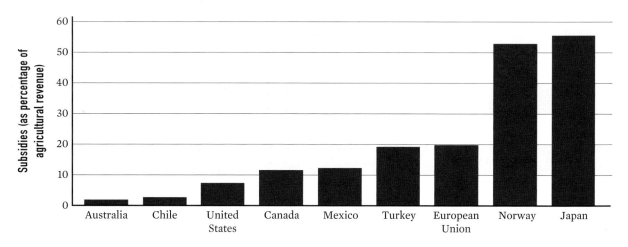

Figure source: OECD, Producer and Consumer Support Estimates, www.oecd.org/ unitedstates/producerand consumersupportestimates database.htm#tables (accessed 1/30/14).

it—and their numbers are small enough to be extremely well organized and well represented in Congress. Figure 7.2 shows selected examples reflecting the protection of farmers in various countries.

Why Have National Trade Policies Varied over Time?

There have been many striking instances of countries shifting from openness to closure or from protectionism to trade liberalization. The United States in the 1920s was one of the most protectionist industrial nations on earth; starting after 1945, however, it led the Western world toward substantial trade liberalization. How can we explain such shifts?

Interests may change: for example, a nation's ability to compete in world markets might improve, giving rise to more actors favorable to trade and reducing the concerns of those actors opposed to trade. Institutions may change too: perhaps democratization gives more pro-trade groups, such as consumers, access to political influence and reduces a bias toward protectionist producers. Some such national changes may be driven by changes at the international level that affect the nation in question, such as a dramatic change in the price of its principal export product. The winners and losers from trade policy may change in such a way that affects national policy, as when one factor becomes more abundant or one industrial sector develops powerful export interests. And national political institutions can affect policy by strengthening the hands of groups that want to push policy in a certain direction.

For example, several explanations have been offered for the American shift from very high levels of trade protection to support for liberalization. The destruction of foreign economies by World War II reduced support for protection: the United States faced very little serious industrial competition, which made it relatively easy for the country to opt for trade liberalization. As the Cold War began, the geopolitical concerns associated with a desire to bind together a pro-American Western alliance reinforced support for an open Western trading system. At the same time, the rise of powerful American manufacturing industries interested in exporting and in investing overseas increased the range of actors in support of economic integration. This too was encouraged by institutional changes in the making of American trade policy in the 1930s, which gave the generally more trade-friendly president greater influence than the usually relatively protectionist Congress. All these factors and more may have affected American policy. Scholars continue to present arguments and evidence for and against these hypotheses. They may not, in fact, be mutually exclusive. National policy changes may be better explained in some cases by the global context, in others by the domestic interests engaged, and in still others by domestic institutions.

Why Do Some Countries Have Higher Trade Barriers than Others?

Even within a common international trading system, national policies can differ. In the late 1930s, as the United States and some Western European nations began moving away from trade protection and toward liberalization, most other industrial countries—especially Germany, Italy, and Japan—erected extremely high barriers to trade. In the 1980s, China became a global exporting powerhouse while many other developing nations remained very closed to trade.

Again, actors and their interests matter: these differences among nations may be driven by different factor endowments or sectoral features. In line with the Stolper-Samuelson approach, for example, the interests of landowners in two countries might be diametrically opposed: in favor of trade in a land-rich country, opposed to it in a land-poor country. If identical pro-farmer parties were in power in the two nations, one would reduce trade barriers while the other would raise them. A country whose economy is dominated by well-organized exporters will tend to be less protectionist than one that has very few exporters.

The source of the difference, however, might be in national institutions, such as a party system or legislative structures biased in favor of the protectionist class (scarce factor) or protectionist sectors and regions. A democracy might give labor or consumers more influence than a dictatorship would. (See "How Do We Know?" on p. 330 for the connection between democracy and free trade in developing countries.) Anything that affects the domestic interests, institutions, or interactions of a country may well affect its trade policies.

Why Has the World Trading Order Been More or Less Open at Different Times?

Global trends are usually best explained by international factors, and trade is no exception. Three causes of the ebb and flow of open trade relations are most prominent: international economic conditions, the role of one or a few very large

Why the Move to Free Trade in Developing Countries?

Since the 1970s, developing countries around the world have reduced their barriers to trade and embraced the global economy. One by one, countries as diverse as the Philippines, Bangladesh, Mexico, and Ghana dismantled their tariffs on imported manufactured goods and agricultural products and shifted to an export-oriented development strategy. This change puzzled many observers who believed that entrenched special interests would prevent governments in these countries from opening their economies to foreign competition.

Helen Milner and Keiko Kubota tackled this important puzzle by demonstrating the connection between trade liberalization and democratization.[a] In authoritarian countries in which the majority of citizens cannot vote, many people who would benefit from free trade—such as unskilled workers in a labor-abundant country—are not able to directly influence the government's trade policies. Elites, however, such as owners of scarce capital and land, might have special channels in which to press the government for continued trade protection. Figure A provides evidence of this protectionist equilibrium through the 1980s, with developing countries sustaining high average tariff levels. Milner and Kubota argue that the process of democratization—defined as a movement toward majority rule with universal voting in competitive elections—disturbed this historical equilibrium. After a country transforms from autocratic rule to democracy, elected leaders must adjust their policies to respond to the preferences of the expanded electorate. Previously disenfranchised groups, including women, unskilled workers, and individuals who do not own land, are suddenly able to assert their preferences and influence trade policy. As the authors note, "Democratic political competition meant that leaders were likely to liberalize trade to appeal to these new groups to ensure their political survival."[b]

Testing this argument was no easy task. First, Milner and Kubota needed to find data on trade policy for a large number of developing countries. Trade-policy data for each country and each year over a long period is difficult to find because there are so many different ways to restrict trade, including tariffs, quotas, regulations, and other tools. The authors settled on two different measures: the average statutory tariff rate (used in Figure A), and a simpler binary indicator which takes the value of 1 (liberalized trade) if a variety of trade restrictions fall below certain thresholds, and 0 otherwise. Second, the authors had to find a reliable measure of democracy. Here, they used a well-regarded index of democratization from the Polity Project, which measures whether or not countries have regular competitive elections, universal suffrage, and a number of other indicators. Using these measures and a series of statistical models, the authors found that as countries transition to democratic rule, they are more likely to reduce their trade barriers.

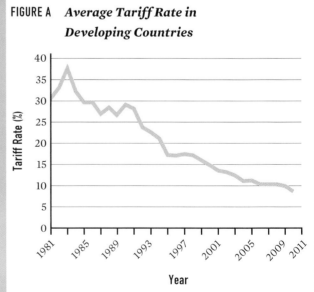

FIGURE A *Average Tariff Rate in Developing Countries*

Source: World Bank, Data on Trade and Import Barriers, http://go.worldbank.org/LGOXFTV550 (accessed 02/01/14).

---

a. Helen Milner and Keiko Kubota, "Why the Move to Free Trade? Democracy and Trade Policy in Developing Countries," *International Organization* 59, no. 1 (Winter 2005): 107–43.

b. Milner and Kubota, "Why the Move to Free Trade?" p. 113.

countries, and the creation of international institutions. Forbidding world economic conditions in the 1930s were a major source of the protectionist turn of many countries' trade policies, just as global economic growth in the 1990s encouraged trade liberalization among developing and formerly Communist countries. The ability of one or a few large countries to organize a leadership role in international trade relations—Britain and France in the late nineteenth century, the United States and its principal allies after World War II—also appears to have been important in affecting global trade. Further, the presence of such institutions as the WTO can help countries overcome some of the problems of cooperation that bedevil international trade relations, encouraging and facilitating collaborative trade ties among governments.

Conclusion: Trade and Politics

International trade is the centerpiece of international economic relations, and government policies toward trade have long been among the most hotly contested. They are controversial *within a country*, as supporters and opponents of freer trade clash. Trade policies can also be controversial *among countries*, as governments contend over their respective policies. This contention often breeds further discord; as the American statesman Cordell Hull said of the 1930s, "The political line-up followed the economic line-up."[25]

National policies toward foreign trade have been important to the development of the world economy and to international politics more generally. How open a nation is to trade affects its pattern of economic and social development as well as its relations with other nations. In turn, a country's trade policies are determined by the nature of its prevailing economic interests and political institutions and by its interactions with other nations.

---

25. Quoted in Gardner, *Sterling-Dollar Diplomacy*, 9.

Study Tool Kit

Interests, Interactions, and Institutions in Context

- Economists are virtually unanimous in concluding that international trade brings important benefits and that reducing trade barriers—trade liberalization—is good for a nation's economy.

- While trade may be beneficial for a country as a whole, it can harm the interests of groups and individuals in the society. Trade can create both winners and losers.

- The nature of a country's economy determines which groups have an interest in expanding or restricting trade with the rest of the world. National political institutions shape the outcomes when these interests come into conflict.

- The politics of international trade also involves strategic interaction among national governments. Governments can face difficult problems of bargaining and cooperation, which sometimes lead to trade conflicts among nations.

- The institutions of the international trading system can facilitate cooperation among governments as they confront the demands of both their own constituents and their foreign counterparts.

Key Terms

comparative advantage, p. 294

absolute advantage, p. 294

Heckscher-Ohlin trade theory, p. 295

protectionism, p. 299

trade barriers, p. 299

tariff, p. 299

quantitative restriction (quota), p. 299

nontariff barriers to trade, p. 299

Stolper-Samuelson theorem, p. 305

Ricardo-Viner (specific-factors) model, p. 306

reciprocity, p. 320

most-favored nation (MFN) status, p. 320

World Trade Organization (WTO), p. 320

General Agreement on Tariffs and Trade (GATT), p. 320

regional trade agreements (RTAs), p. 321

For Further Reading

Busch, Marc I. *Trade Warriors: States, Firms, and Strategic-Trade Policy in High-Technology Competition.* **New York: Cambridge University Press, 1999.** Analyzes why governments intervene in trade to support industries and firms regarded as strategically important to their economies.

Chase, Kerry. *Trading Blocs: States, Firms, and Regions in the World Economy.* **Ann Arbor: University of Michigan Press, 2005.** Describes and analyzes why countries decide to form RTAs such as NAFTA and the European Union.

Davis, Christina. *Food Fights over Free Trade: How International Institutions Promote Agricultural Trade Liberalization.* **Princeton: Princeton University Press, 2005.** Analyzes the interests and institutions that have structured the complex politics of trade in farm products.

Destler, I. M. *American Trade Politics.* **4th ed. Washington, DC: Peterson Institute for International Economics, 2005.** Surveys and analyzes the political economy of trade policy in the United States.

Hiscox, Michael. *International Trade and Political Conflict: Commerce, Coalitions, and Mobility.* **Princeton, NJ: Princeton University Press, 2002.** Evaluates the relative importance of factoral (class) and sectoral (industry) demands for protection and of variation among these considerations over time.

Hoekman, Bernard, and Michel M. Kostecki, *The Political Economy of the World Trading System.* **3rd ed. New York: Oxford University Press, 2009.** Comprehensive overview of the structure and functioning of the WTO and international institutions in the international trade arena.

Irwin, Douglas. *Against the Tide: An Intellectual History of Free Trade.* **Princeton, NJ: Princeton University Press, 1997.** Presents the theory, economics, and politics of debates over trade in the modern era.

Irwin, Douglas. *Free Trade under Fire.* **3rd ed. Princeton, NJ: Princeton University Press, 2009.** Makes a strong argument for trade liberalization, addressing many common sources of opposition.

Mansfield, Edward D., and Helen V. Milner. *Votes, Vetoes, and the Political Economy of International Trade Agreements.* **Princeton, NJ: Princeton University Press, 2012.** Analyzes the domestic political forces that lead countries to undertake RTAs.

Rogowski, Ronald. *Commerce and Coalitions: How Trade Affects Domestic Political Alignments.* **Princeton, NJ: Princeton University Press, 1989.** Develops an analysis, based on the Stolper-Samuelson theorem, of how trade affects politics within nations.

Comparative Advantage and the Political Economy of Trade

Economists generally agree that international trade is good for the aggregate welfare of societies. Where does this consensus come from? In this section, we introduce the concept of comparative advantage, which for centuries has been the backbone of economic thinking on international trade. We also illustrate the redistributive and welfare effects of opening the domestic economy to international trade and the countervailing effects of imposing a tariff.

Comparative Advantage

At the heart of economic analyses of international trade is *comparative advantage*. In short, the idea of comparative advantage implies that all countries benefit from trade if each country specializes in the production of certain goods. Which goods should countries produce? Economist David Ricardo[a] provided the straightforward answer in the early 1800s: countries should focus their production only on goods that they can produce most efficiently relative to other goods. If a country is good at mining copper or growing coffee beans or producing steel, then it should focus its productive capacities on producing these goods and rely on international trade to obtain all the other goods that it needs.

What if a country is not very good at producing anything? To answer this question, it is important to distinguish between *absolute advantage* and comparative advantage. A country has an absolute advantage if it can produce a good more efficiently than any other country. Comparative advantage, on the other hand, is determined within a country: of all the possible goods in the world, a country can produce some goods more efficiently than others. This means that *all* countries have a comparative advantage in something. A country might not be the most efficient in the world at producing coffee, but it still has a comparative advantage in coffee if it can produce coffee more efficiently than steel, airplanes, or any other good.

Consider the following example used by Ricardo himself to explain the concept of comparative advantage. Assume that there are two countries in the world, Portugal and England, and that these two countries can produce only cloth and wine. Further assume that the only input in the production process is labor, such that one unit of each good (a bolt of cloth or a barrel of wine) has a cost in man-hours. For example, in England it takes 15 man-hours to produce a bolt of cloth and 30 man-hours to produce

---

a. The idea of comparative advantage—not the term itself—was introduced by David Ricardo in Chapter 7 of his *On the Principles of Political Economy and Taxation*, www.econlib.org/library/Ricardo/ricPCover .html (accessed 01/10/12).

TABLE A.1

COUNTRY	CLOTH	WINE
	Cost in Man-Hours per Bolt	Cost in Man-Hours per Barrel
England	15	30
Portugal	10	15

a barrel of wine. In Portugal, it takes 10 man-hours to produce a bolt of cloth and 15 man-hours to produce a barrel of wine. Note that it takes fewer man-hours to produce both cloth and wine in Portugal than in England; indeed, in this example, Portugal has an absolute advantage in the production of both goods, cloth and wine (Table A.1).

To understand the impact of each country's choice of which goods to produce, it is helpful to examine the *opportunity cost of production*. This is the value that a country forgoes in order to make one product rather than another. The resources (in this example, labor) that each nation uses to make cloth are unavailable to make wine, so that it must forgo a certain amount of wine in order to make cloth. How many bolts of cloth must a country give up to produce a barrel of wine and vice versa?

England must give up two bolts of cloth to produce an additional barrel of wine (30 ÷ 15); alternatively, it can give up a half barrel of wine to produce a bolt of cloth (15 ÷ 30). In contrast, Portugal must give up one and a half bolts of cloth to produce an additional barrel of wine; alternatively, it can give up two-thirds of a barrel of wine to produce an additional bolt of cloth. Table A.2 presents these results.

Note that the opportunity cost of producing cloth is lower in England than in Portugal, whereas the opportunity cost of producing wine is lower in Portugal than in England. From these figures, we can conclude that England has a comparative advantage in the production of cloth, and Portugal has a comparative advantage in the production of wine.

What happens if these two countries engage in international trade? If England focuses all its man-hours on producing cloth, and Portugal does the same for wine,

TABLE A.2

COUNTRY	OPPORTUNITY COST OF PRODUCING . . .	
	One Bolt of Cloth	One Barrel of Wine
England	$1/_2$ barrel of wine	2 bolts of cloth
Portugal	$2/_3$ barrel of wine	$1^1/_2$ bolts of cloth

then the total world production of cloth and wine will be considerably higher than if the two countries did not specialize or engage in trade. Ricardo's simple model tells us that international trade based on comparative advantage increases aggregate welfare, measured by the total amount of goods produced in this two-country world. The increase in aggregate welfare occurs even though England does not have an absolute advantage in the production of either good.

Distributional and Welfare Effects of Trade

Economists largely agree that international trade is welfare improving for societies, whereas tariffs and other forms of trade protection are inefficient and costly for societies. A few simple graphs can illustrate the logic behind these claims. Consider first a country in a state of autarky, in which there is no international trade. The domestic price of any good is therefore determined by the intersection of the two lines of domestic supply and domestic demand. All else being equal, producers will supply more of a good as its price increases, and consumers will demand more of a good as its price falls. Therefore, the supply line is upward sloping and the demand line is downward sloping. The intersection indicates the good's domestic price (*P*) and quantity demanded (*Q*), as shown in Figure A.1.

The effects of the production of the good in autarky are measured by the concepts of *consumer surplus* and *producer surplus*. Consider first the fate of consumers. Based on the downward-sloping demand line, some people in the country would be happy to pay more than *P* for the good. The shaded region represents the aggregate welfare benefit for consumers; it is called a surplus because it represents the gains to consumers who would be willing to pay more than *P* for the good. Similarly, there are some producers in the country who would happily supply the good at a

FIGURE A.1 *Autarky*

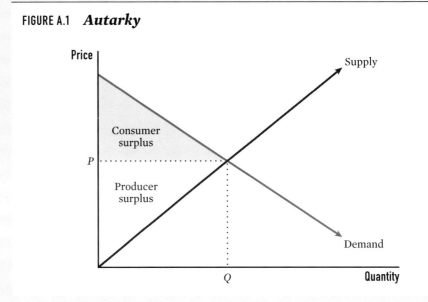

lower price than P. The region beneath P and bounded by the two lines represents the producer surplus. This region captures the gains to producers who benefit from a higher price than they would otherwise tolerate for selling the good.

Now consider how the price and quantity of the good change as the country begins to trade freely with other countries. Note that the world price of the good will be lower than the domestic price in autarky. The world price is determined by the intersection of global, not domestic, supply and demand. For simplicity, we assume that the country in this example is small relative to the world economy. In other words, it is a "price taker": its own domestic supply and demand of the good will not appreciably affect global supply or demand. Figure A.2 indicates that the new domestic price declines to the (lower) world price (P_w) after the country moves from autarky to international trade openness. At this lower price, domestic consumer demand increases to Q_d because more people can enjoy the good at the new lower price. Domestic supply of the good decreases to Q_s because fewer producers are willing to produce the good at the lower price. The larger consumer demand is satisfied by imports from the rest of the world (equal to the distance between Q_s and Q_d). Note that under free trade, the consumer surplus increases considerably because consumers are better off with the lower price. The regions labeled A and B represent the additions to consumer surplus that result from free trade. The producer surplus declines as a result of the lower world price. However, note that the combination of consumer and producer surplus—an overall measure of aggregate welfare—is larger under free trade than in autarky. There are two important implications: opening to trade redistributes income from producers to consumers, and opening to trade makes society as a whole better off.

As a final exercise, consider the implications to redistribution and to aggregate welfare of a tariff on the good. The tariff—which is a tax by the government on the imported good—increases the domestic price of the good to P_t, as shown in

---

FIGURE A.2 *Free Trade*

FIGURE A.3 *Tariff*

Figure A.3. The quantity demanded by consumers falls to Q_d^t because of the higher price, whereas the quantity supplied by domestic suppliers increases to Q_s^t. As expected, the consumer surplus declines, because many consumers who wish to purchase the good cannot afford the higher price. The producer surplus increases by the amount represented by Region A, as more producers benefit from a higher price than what they would normally receive. What of the remaining regions? The amount represented by Region C accrues to the government as a result of the tariff revenue. But the two dark triangular regions on either side of Region C do not benefit anyone! Known as the *deadweight loss* of the tariff, they represent the efficiency losses to society of trade protection.

Where does the deadweight loss come from? The best way to understand this loss is to reflect on the concept of comparative advantage. The tariff causes an artificially higher price, which leads domestic producers to shift their production away from whatever they were previously producing and toward the higher-priced good. Suppose the country in question is England, which has a comparative advantage in the production of cloth. If England imposes a tariff on imported wine, then more English producers will shift their production away from cloth and toward wine to take advantage of the higher price, even though they are relatively inefficient in producing wine. In other words, a tariff interferes with the efficient allocation of production and works against the concept of comparative advantage. By the same token, the artificially high price of the protected good leads consumers to reallocate their consumption away from it and toward a good they would not otherwise purchase, which is another loss to society. The losses to efficiency are represented by the dark triangles in Figure A.3. When we combine these efficiency losses with the decline in domestic consumption caused by the higher price, we can see why economists are generally in agreement that tariffs cause society as a whole to be worse off compared to free trade.

This simple set of graphs captures the essence of the political economy of trade policy. First, international trade improves aggregate welfare. However, certain producers who previously produced exclusively for the domestic market can be harmed when the country moves toward free trade. Trade tariffs lead to a decline in aggregate welfare and cause deadweight losses to society. They also result in an increase in the producer surplus and a reduction in the consumer surplus. If producer groups can successfully lobby the government for protection, they can reap great benefits. These benefits come at the expense of consumers, in the form of a reduced consumer surplus (owing to higher prices), and at the expense of the country as a whole, in the form of an efficiency loss.

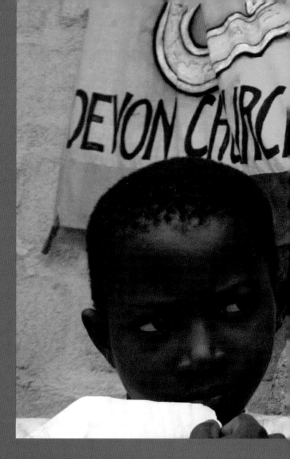

8

International Financial Relations

THE PUZZLE *Every year, approximately $5 trillion is invested abroad. Why is so much money invested in foreign countries? And why do relations between foreign investors and the countries in which they invest often become hostile and politically controversial?*

Above: International financing from international organizations and private investors has provided many countries with loans for infrastructure and other development projects. Today, there is a debate about whether asking poor countries to repay their debt is helpful or hurtful.

The Global Financial Crisis that began in late 2007 hit Europe almost immediately with a major debt crisis. A number of governments in the eurozone had built up large debts and appeared unable to service them. The crisis came to be known as the European Sovereign Debt Crisis (sovereign debt is debt owed by governments to private financial institutions and investors) and was the most serious sovereign debt crisis since the 1930s, endangering the international financial system and its economy.

The four principal eurozone debtors were Greece, Ireland, Portugal, and Spain. In Spain and Ireland, households had borrowed heavily to finance a major housing and construction boom, as happened in the United States. When housing prices collapsed, the two national governments started running large deficits by borrowing from abroad to avoid massive national banking crises and stimulate their economies. Portugal and Greece, on the other hand, were running budget deficits due to the very creation of the eurozone, which were principally paid for by foreign borrowing.

The difficulties of the eurozone debtors were not just a problem for them, since major northern European financial institutions and investors were the ones that had made most of these loans. If the debtors defaulted—were

unable to service their debts—trillions of dollars in loans on the books of northern European banks, investors, and pension funds would go bad, just as the housing loans had gone bad in the United States. The weight of so many bad loans and investments endangered the very integrity of the financial systems of even the richest northern European countries, especially Germany and France. The sovereign debt crisis threatened both the sovereign debtors and their creditors—and, in fact, the entire European economy.

Faced with this looming catastrophe, leaders of the eurozone member states put together a trillion-euro package to shore up the finances of the major debtors and the region's financial system. In return, they insisted that the debtor countries impose severe austerity measures, including raising taxes, cutting government spending, laying off government workers, reducing pensions, increasing the retirement age, and selling off public enterprises. Mass protests rocked the debtor nations, and there were even talks of leaving the euro.

Eight years after the crisis began, eurozone economic output was still substantially below what it was at the outset of the crisis, and unemployment was at nearly 12 percent; in Greece and Spain, unemployment stood at a staggering 25 percent. The result was a widespread dissatisfaction with both national governments and, more generally, the European Union (EU). All over Europe, it seemed, 50 years of consensus in favor of European integration and a moderate centrist vision of society had collapsed.

The eurozone crisis is a recent example of how international finance can become a highly political issue. Today, capital flows around the world in unimaginably large quantities. Nearly half of all the world's investment goes across borders—every year about $5 *trillion* in foreign loans or investments. Total international investments in 2011 were about $140 trillion, and *every day* many trillions of dollars in foreign currencies are traded. Even the United States has financed large trade and budget deficits with money from abroad, borrowing about $5 trillion between 2005 and 2012—increasing its debt to foreigners in those years by nearly $40,000 for every American household.[1]

International finance has long been the leading edge of global economic integration. Massive investment flows drove the integrated world economy of the nineteenth and early twentieth centuries; then they dried up during the years between World Wars I and II, when the world's nations turned inward. Since 1960, international finance has revived and is once again the most globalized component of the world economy, dwarfing international trade and migration.

Some analysts regard the emergence of a worldwide market for capital as one of globalization's main attractions. Companies, investors, and borrowers around the world now can tap into an enormous pool of capital. Home buyers in Arkansas can have their mortgages underwritten by investors in Germany; start-ups in India can be financed by Canadian pension funds; shopkeepers in South Africa can borrow money that comes from small savers in Japan.

Yet international finance is also extremely controversial, and critics of global economic integration have long targeted international bankers. Many policy makers in the developing world see international finance as a source of economic and political problems and as a potential threat to their nations' sovereignty.

The global economic crisis that erupted in 2007 has focused attention on how financial developments in one country can affect others. Problems that started in the market for housing finance in the United States ended up causing the most serious international financial panic since the 1930s. Meanwhile, loans gone similarly bad in Europe threatened to tear the European Union apart. Even the world's largest and richest economies seemed highly susceptible to the volatility of international financial markets.

Thinking Analytically about International Finance

Governments, firms, and individuals sometimes pursue international finance avidly and sometimes attack it mercilessly. This discrepancy raises questions about why international investment is so controversial. As we will see, within borrowing nations, there are many actors who value access to foreign funds. However, there are others who resent the constraints and burdens that foreign investments sometimes impose on debtors. Similar conflicting interests exist within lending nations.

At the international level, lenders and borrowers have a shared interest in sustaining capital flows, but they may disagree about how the benefits from loans are divided. For example, most Europeans favor allowing capital to flow among EU member countries, but they may disagree profoundly about who should be asked to make the sacrifices necessary to resolve the region's debt crisis. Similarly, international investors and the recipients of investment may enter into conflict. These interactions frequently involve bargaining over the investments, as each side tries to get the best deal.

International institutions, such as the IMF, structure interactions in the international financial realm. However, like international finance generally, the role of the IMF is very controversial: some analysts think it contributes to the cooperative resolution of financial problems while others think that it takes unfair advantage of struggling debtor nations. In this chapter, we take a closer look at these questions.

1. Except where otherwise noted, all data in this section are from M. Ayhan Kose et al., "Financial Globalization: A Reappraisal," *IMF Staff Papers* 56, no. 1 (2009); and the Updated and Extended External Wealth of Nations Dataset, 1970–2011, from Philip Lane and Gian Maria Milesi-Ferretti, "The External Wealth of Nations Mark II: Revised and Extended Estimates of Foreign Assets and Liabilities, 1970–2004," *Journal of International Economics* 73, no. 2 (2007), supplemented and updated from the IMF's International Financial Statistics and the U.S. Department of Treasury.

How and Why Do People Invest Overseas?

There are many ways in which those with capital can invest in foreign lands. The principal varieties of foreign investments can be grouped into two broad categories: portfolio investments and direct investment. A **portfolio investment** gives the investor a claim on some income but no role in managing the investment. Loans are portfolio investments. So are shares of a company's stock (equities), for each share of stock represents a minuscule portion of ownership in the corporation.[2] If, for example, an investor buys the bonds of an Indian corporation or the Indian government, or if a bank lends money to an Indian corporation or the Indian government, the Indian debtor commits itself to make interest and principal payments but has no obligation to involve the creditor in figuring out how or when to use the borrowed money. Even if the Indian corporation or Indian government has a bad year, it is obligated to pay off its creditors at the preestablished interest rate.[3] Portfolio investors take little or no part in running their investment; their interest is simply in the rate of return.

A substantial portion of the portfolio investment that goes to developing countries is **sovereign lending**, that is, loans from private financial institutions to sovereign governments. Loans by European or American financial institutions to the governments of Indonesia or Brazil—or to government-owned or -controlled companies or agencies in those countries—are sovereign loans. So too are purchases by foreigners of the bonds of the French or American governments, for example. In some instances, loans made to private firms in foreign countries are considered to be sovereign loans, if the government of the debtor has an explicit or implicit commitment to ensure the creditworthiness of its nation's borrowers. For example, loans to an Indonesian or Brazilian private bank or corporation may implicate the Indonesian or Brazilian government, because these governments can facilitate or impede repayment of those loans.

Foreign direct investment (FDI) is made by a company that owns facilities in another country, facilities over which the company maintains control. For example, when Toyota opens a truck factory in Thailand or when Disney opens a theme park in France, these are instances of FDI. FDI differs from foreign portfolio investment most importantly because the investor maintains managerial control—and also bears the full long-term risk of the investment. If a Toyota truck

portfolio investment

Investment in a foreign country via the purchase of stocks (equities), bonds, or other financial instruments. Portfolio investors do not exercise managerial control of the foreign operation.

sovereign lending

Loans from private financial institutions in one country to sovereign governments in other countries.

foreign direct investment (FDI)

Investment in a foreign country via the acquisition of a local facility or the establishment of a new facility. Direct investors maintain managerial control of the foreign operation.

---

2. Equities (stocks) can be ambiguous; if an investor owns enough of the company's shares, he or she might, in fact, take control of the company, which would make the investment direct. But almost all international equity investment is of the portfolio variety, meaning that it does not involve actual managerial control of the firm.

3. This distinction is blurred in instances in which foreigners buy large quantities of corporate equities— so at some point they could, in fact, exercise control over the corporation. Traditional portfolio investors, as discussed here, are not interested in control; they buy equities solely as financial instruments.

factory in Thailand is not profitable, Toyota loses money. Direct investors have full authority to run their investments, but they take most of the associated risks as well.

Why Invest Abroad? Why Borrow Abroad?

Banks, corporations, and individuals make investments overseas with a clear goal: to make money. Those with capital want to move their money from where profits are lower to where profits are higher. Thus, many international investors want to take money from capital-rich developed countries to capital-poor developing ones. Banks, corporations, and individuals in rich countries invest more than $800 billion every year in developing- and emerging-market nations, about two-thirds of it in direct investment from multinational corporations (MNCs), the other third in loans and investments in equities (stocks).[4] (Figure 8.1 illustrates the rapid growth of foreign investment in emerging markets over recent decades.) The Heckscher-Ohlin theory presented in Chapter 7 explains why. A country's average profit rate depends on how plentiful capital is. Where land or labor is scarce, it is expensive; where it is plentiful, it is cheap. The same is true of capital, recognizing that the interest rate is the "price" of capital— more expensive capital means a higher rate of return. In a poor country, capital is scarce and therefore expensive: borrowers pay higher interest rates for something in short supply. In a rich country, capital is abundant, so interest rates and

Figure source: World Bank, World Development Indicators, http://data.worldbank.org/indicator (accessed 10/10/14).

Note: Measures are "net inflows" in current U.S. dollars for low- and middle-income countries as defined by the World Bank. See http://data.worldbank.org/income-level/LMY for countries included.

FIGURE 8.1   *Foreign Investment in Emerging Markets, 1970–2012*

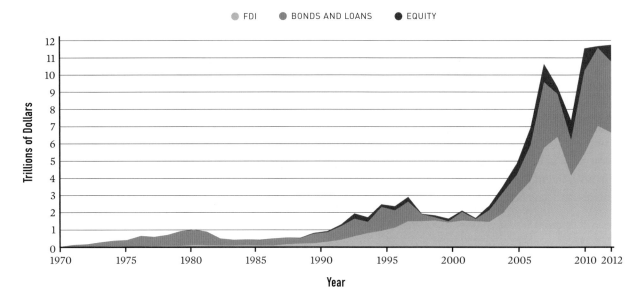

4. This is an annual average for 2007 to 2012 based on the data in Figure 8.1.

profit rates are much lower. For example, in 2014 the prevailing rate of interest on short-term loans in most developed countries was below 2 percent while in Latin America it was typically 10 percent and often higher.

The greater scarcity of capital, as well as higher interest rates, in developing than in developed countries encourages capital to flow from richer to poorer countries. For example, Mexico is poor in capital while the United States is rich in capital. Thus, profits and interest rates are higher in Mexico, which helps explain why American investors have over time accumulated investments worth over $300 billion there.

If the only consideration in international investment were differential rates of return, as in our simple Heckscher-Ohlin discussion, then all foreign investment would flow from capital-rich countries to capital-poor countries. But it decidedly does not. In fact, most international investment is among rich countries, and only a relatively small but growing fraction of international investment in the past couple of decades has gone to the developing world. This is due to the lower risk of cross-border investment in rich countries. International banks, corporations, and other investors care not just about the promised interest or profit rate on foreign investments but also about the likelihood that they will actually get the money. (See Figure 8.2 for the share of total FDI to developing countries since 1970.)

The United States presents a low-risk environment for foreign investors because it is stable and rich. Many American brands and landmarks are owned by corporations based overseas, such as Budweiser beer, owned by Belgian–Brazilian Inbev, and New York City's Waldorf Astoria hotel, sold to a Chinese insurance company in 2014.

Although all investment is risky, international investment involves a very specific risk: that a foreign government over which the investor has no influence may do things that reduce the value of the investment. This is especially true about loans to a foreign government, which involve a government's promise to pay debt service (interest and principal). Unlike in domestic lending, this promise cannot be enforced by the threat of foreclosure or bankruptcy. For international corporate investment, the concern is that the local government will undertake policies that devalue the investment—up to and including taking over the investment itself.

Investment among rich countries is much less risky than investment in poor countries. After all, the industrialized nations are more economically and politically stable, and they have a longer and more reliable history of treating foreign investors well. For investors to be willing to take a chance on the greater risk in the developing world, they need either higher interest rates and profits or some reason to think that they can effectively manage the investment risks. This need can lead to negotiations between lenders or investors, on the one hand, and developing countries, on the other hand, to try to ensure a more reliable investment environment. This effort, in turn, draws international investment into international politics.

FIGURE 8.2 ***FDI to Developing Countries, 1970–2012***

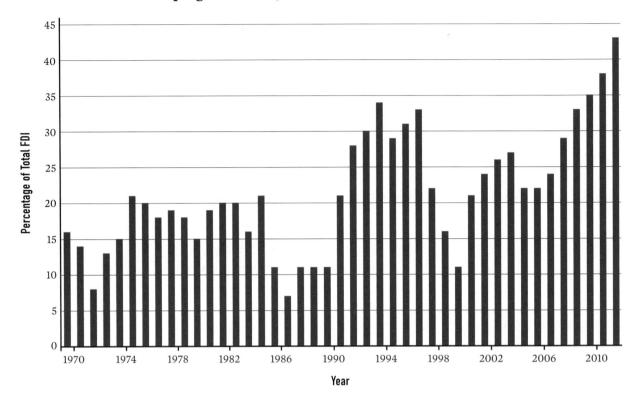

Figure source: World Bank, World Development Indicators, http://data.worldbank.org/ indicator (accessed 10/10/14).

Note: Includes low- and middle-income countries as defined by the World Bank. See http://data.worldbank. org/income-level/LMY for countries included.

What's the Problem with Foreign Investment?

International investment is controversial because not only can it provide great benefits to both investors and the countries they invest in, but it can also impose real costs on both sides of the relationship. This is yet another example, discussed in Chapter 2, of how many issues in international politics contain elements of both cooperation and bargaining. Both sets of actors stand to gain by an amicable resolution of their differences, so they have an interest in cooperating; but each side wants to get as much as possible out of the relationship, which leads their interaction down the path to bargaining.

In international investment, there are many common interests among borrowers and lenders, among investors and the countries they invest in. Both sides of the interaction gain from successful international investments and loans. The receiving country gets capital it would not otherwise have. Companies that borrow from abroad can expand their businesses. Governments that borrow from abroad can finance projects that spur development, such as roads and power plants. An inflow of foreign funds can increase the availability of credit to small business owners and homeowners. Meanwhile, the foreign investor who has sent the money overseas gets higher profits than are available at home. Borrowing and lending nations alike gain from the ability of capital to flow across borders.

But there may also be major conflicts of interest between the two sides of the relationship. Each party wants to get as much as possible from the other and to give as little as possible. Lenders want their debts repaid in full, and corporations want to bring home high profits from their foreign investments. Debtor nations, however, would rather pay less of what they owe, and host countries would rather that foreign corporations have less to take away. This situation creates both a commonality of interests in maintaining a flow of capital and a conflict of interests in distributing the benefits of the flow.

Within countries, domestic politics may also contribute to conflict between capital-sending and capital-receiving nations. In most countries, there is little disagreement when money is flowing in. Foreign capital allows the country to consume more than it produces and allows the government to spend more than it takes in through taxes; the foreign capital increases domestic consumption, investment, and economic activity, and this outcome tends to be popular. However, eventually lenders must be repaid and profits taken out, an outcome that is less universally popular. Making debt service payments can require raising taxes, reducing government services, restraining wages and consumption, importing less while exporting more, and generally imposing austerity on the national economy. Debt crises throughout history—including recent ones in both developing and developed countries—have been associated with slow growth, unemployment, cuts in social spending, and general economic hardship. And there is no guarantee that the people and groups who are asked to bear the greatest burden of austerity will be those who benefit most from the capital inflow. Even if foreign borrowing and foreign investment are unambiguously good for a nation, the benefits and costs do not accrue equally to all people in the country. This fact has made international finance a contentious issue within developing—and many developed—countries.

Overseas loans and investments can be controversial within lending and investing nations too. While those making the foreign investments stand to gain, there are also workers and firms that resent money going abroad that could be lent or invested at home. And when debt crises erupt, it is common for creditor-country governments to expend time, energy, and money to try to resolve the crisis. This is partly because a crisis abroad can have grave repercussions at home: in the midst of the debt crisis of the 1980s, for instance, many Americans were shocked to learn that American banks had lent more money to Latin American governments than the value of the capital base of the entire American banking system. This meant that the Latin American debt crisis could conceivably have bankrupted many of America's largest banks and caused a more general financial and economic crisis in the United States itself. Similarly, northern Europeans were startled to find out after 2008 that their banks, and often pension funds, had invested trillions of dollars in American, Spanish, and Irish mortgages and in the government bonds of Greece and Portugal—and that as these investments went bad, their financial systems were under serious threat. But even if it is in the general interest of creditor nations as a whole to "bail out" their troubled banks and their borrowers, it may not be in the interests

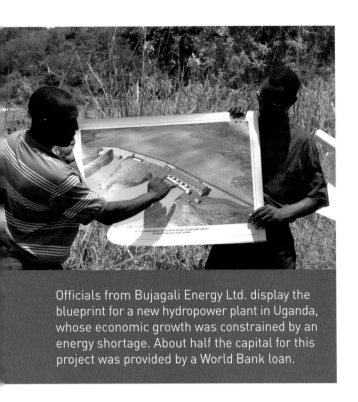

Officials from Bujagali Energy Ltd. display the blueprint for a new hydropower plant in Uganda, whose economic growth was constrained by an energy shortage. About half the capital for this project was provided by a World Bank loan.

of everyone in these nations. So international investment gives rise to plenty of potential sources of conflict, and these conflicts of interest give rise to complex interactions among the sources and targets of global capital movements.

Concessional Finance

There is another, smaller and somewhat less controversial, part of international finance: money lent to developing countries by government agencies and intergovernmental organizations. Rich countries give to poor countries or lend to them at below-market interest rates, something on the order of $130 billion a year. Such concessional finance differs from that discussed above because it is typically lent at interest rates well below those available in the marketplace—World Bank loans to the poorest nations, in fact, bear no interest. Many of the countries that borrow these concessional funds would not be able to borrow from private creditors, who are wary of particularly poor and unstable nations. Most countries in sub-Saharan Africa and South Asia have little access to private loans; to the extent that they can borrow, it is from North American, European, and Japanese governments or from such institutions as the World Bank and the Asian Development Bank.

Concessional loans from foreign governments are more a form of aid than of finance. They reflect, as does aid generally, both economic and political motivations of the donors and lenders. The international development banks and related agencies—the World Bank, Inter-American Development Bank, Asian Development Bank, and so on—are somewhat less directly political, as they are controlled by a number of rich countries. Their lending programs emphasize basic development projects, such as economic infrastructure (power plants, dams, highways) and social infrastructure (schools, housing).

As we saw in Chapter 1, the two major international economic institutions established at Bretton Woods after World War II were the World Bank and the IMF. The **World Bank** (officially, the International Bank for Reconstruction and Development) was charged with making loans to promote economic development. The IMF was originally focused primarily on exchange rates and monetary relations, but as we will see later in this chapter, its focus has shifted to international finance in recent decades. Like the IMF, the World Bank is headquartered in Washington, D.C.—in fact, the two international financial institutions are across the street from each other. The World Bank gets most of its money by borrowing on major financial markets—typically at very low rates, as its bonds are guaranteed by the governments of the markets in which it borrows. Funds raised in this way

World Bank

An important international institution that provides loans at below-market interest rates to developing countries, typically to enable them to carry out development projects.

are lent out to developing countries to help them build major infrastructural and other development projects. Because the World Bank can borrow at much lower interest rates than developing countries, it can relend to them at very attractive rates. The World Bank also receives some money from developed member states that is lent out at extremely low or no interest to the poorest nations. The World Bank is primarily oriented toward financing long-term investments in such things as roads, dams, and power plants, all of which are considered essential for broader economic growth and development.

There has been less political controversy about concessional finance, as loans from individual governments are negotiated directly and, like loans from the World Bank and its related institutions, are relatively cheap. Nonetheless, countries with severe economic problems often complain about the cost of these loans, and for extremely poor nations concessional debt can be a heavy burden—despite the loans' lower interest rates. This situation has led to calls for debt forgiveness, a measure that would alleviate some problems in very poor nations but that would come at the expense of rich nations' taxpayers. These issues, ethically important as they may be, do not have much impact on private international finance. The amounts at stake are relatively small, and private investors are typically not involved. In any case, much government-to-government concessional debt has been canceled, and the World Bank and IMF are in the process of writing off the debt of the most heavily indebted poor countries.[5] Moreover, the major economic and political issues related to international investment have to do with other, nonconcessional, finance.

Why Is International Finance Controversial?

We start our analysis with what has historically been the most important—and most politically conflictual—component of international investment: private lending to foreign governments. Shakespeare may have been right about the pitfalls of borrowing and lending when he wrote:

> Neither a borrower nor a lender be;
> For loan oft loses both itself and friend,
> And borrowing dulls the edge of husbandry.
> —Polonius, in Shakespeare's *Hamlet*

Indeed, the parties might end up enemies, and the borrowers could have little incentive to use the money wisely. However, there is nothing economically suspect

---

5. For further information on the reduction of debts owed by the heavily indebted poor countries (HIPC), see International Monetary Fund, "Debt Relief under the Heavily Indebted Poor Countries (HIPC) Initiative," September 20, 2014, www.imf.org/external/np/exr/facts/hipc.htm (accessed 02/01/15).

about borrowing or lending in principle. In the case of a private corporation, it makes sense to borrow if the borrowed funds are used in ways that increase the firm's earnings by more than the money costs. If General Motors borrows at an interest rate of 10 percent but uses the money to make investments that only pay out 5 percent, it will suffer a loss; but if the investments pay out 15 percent, both the borrower and the lender can benefit. The logic is similar for a government.

Who Wants to Borrow? Who Wants to Lend?

Borrowing is usually quite popular within borrowing countries—at least while the money is flowing in. As more capital comes into the nation, it is cheaper and easier for people in the recipient country to borrow. Companies, consumers, and the government can benefit from this easier credit.

From the standpoint of the economy as a whole, it generally makes sense for a country to borrow if the borrowed funds are used productively, in ways that increase the country's output by more than it will take to repay the debt. Loans might be used to raise national output directly, such as to make productive use of a government-owned natural resource (oil or copper, for example). The money could also be used to increase national output indirectly, such as by building new roads that allow the opening or improvement of agricultural lands or by building a hydro-electric power plant that makes national industry more efficient. As national output rises, the government gets more tax revenue and can service its debts more easily. If borrowed funds are used to increase the productivity of the national economy, they can pay for themselves.

Because developing countries are by definition short of capital, most of their governments are eager to borrow abroad. The prospect of using borrowed money to speed growth and increase national output gives developing economies today a powerful interest in attracting loans from international investors, and it makes borrowing relatively uncontroversial within debtor countries—as long as times are good.

But sovereign debts can quickly become a burden to debtor nations, which makes them much less popular. Governments attempting to service their debts often impose unpopular measures. They cut spending and raise taxes in order to earn the money they need to pay off loans. They raise interest rates to restrain wages, profits, and consumption, which in turn reduces imports and increases exports, so that the country can earn more foreign currency to pay its creditors. These austerity measures typically weaken the domestic economy in order to allow the government to continue paying debt service to foreign creditors. Such measures can cause a **recession** and or even **depression**, incurring the wrath of labor, business, and other groups. For example, in the wake of a 1997 debt crisis, the Thai government pushed interest rates to 25 percent, cut government spending by 20 percent, and raised taxes. The economy collapsed, shrinking by 12 percent in two years as unemployment more than doubled.[6] In Thailand, as in many such cases,

recession

A sharp slowdown in the rate of economic growth and economic activity.

depression

A severe downturn in the business cycle, typically associated with a major decline in economic activity, production, and investment; a severe contraction of credit; and sustained high unemployment.

---

6. Joseph Kahn, "I.M.F. Concedes Its Conditions for Thailand Were Too Austere," *New York Times*, February 11, 1998.

people regarded debt-driven austerity as doubly unfair: they were being asked to sacrifice to repay borrowed money that did not help them, and their sacrifice was going to enrich huge international financial institutions.

One potential source of debt difficulties is international conditions, which can change in ways that make it harder for governments to pay their debts. Between 1980 and 1982, for example, American interest rates rose by 10 percent as the Federal Reserve attempted to reduce American inflation. Most of the debts owed by developing countries to international banks were at floating interest rates, adjusted every six months in line with American interest rates; as American rates went up, so did the cost of outstanding loans. This was, in fact, one of the causes of the debt crisis of the 1980s. Similarly, an international recession that reduces demand for debtors' exports can make it hard to service loans: when the Great Depression of the 1930s drove down prices and demand for debtors' products, it caused almost every debtor nation to **default**. When circumstances, especially conditions beyond their control, make it harder for debtor governments to keep up their payments, some people in debtor nations prefer that their government simply default in order to force a reduction in the debt burden. There are, then, contending interests within debtor countries over whether to service foreign debt. Those who expect to benefit from maintaining access to international loans will disagree with those who have more to lose from the economic sacrifices required to maintain good relations with foreign creditors.

Within lending countries, when foreign debts are performing well there is usually little conflict over them. Some local companies and individuals may resent the fact that money that could be lent to them is being sent abroad, but this is counterbalanced by the profits being brought home. Overall, creditor countries and their governments tend to support their lenders.

Domestic conflict within creditor nations over foreign debts arises most commonly when the loans run into trouble. In these conditions, creditors and their governments often step in with billions of dollars of new loans and aid to alleviate a debtor country's financial crisis. They do so in the belief that if such a crisis were allowed to broaden and deepen, it could spread to other nations and eventually hurt the creditor nation itself. But many people in North America, Europe, and Japan resent their governments' spending of billions of dollars to "bail out" debtors and creditors whose plight may be the self-inflicted result of greed, venality, and bad judgment.

For example, in 1994, in the aftermath of another Mexican crisis, the U.S. government provided many billions of dollars to the beleaguered Mexican government to try to keep the crisis from spreading and affecting American domestic finances as well. In reaction, conservative Republican political activist Patrick Buchanan charged: "What's going down is not just a bailout of Mexico, but a bailout of Wall Street. [President] Clinton and Congress are rushing to recoup for Wall Street bankers and brokers their enormous losses from the plunderings of [Mexican] ex-President Carlos Salinas and friends."[7] From the Left, the liberal

default

To fail to make payments on a debt.

---

7. From http://buchanan.org/blog/congress-saves-wall-streets-bacon-172 (accessed 01/03/08).

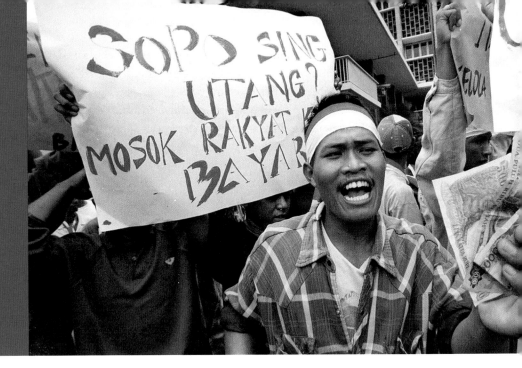

When the Indonesian government sought the IMF's help during the 1997–98 Asian financial crisis, it was forced to cut spending on popular programs, and poor Indonesians suffered. These protesters in Jakarta hold a sign asking, "The country's debt—why should the people pay?"

magazine the *Progressive* observed: "It's amazing how our government can find money for . . . bailing out some banks or shoring up some brutal regimes, but not for solving the pressing social needs of our own country, like health care, housing, and jobs at a living wage."[8]

Many people in creditor nations regard the trillions of dollars spent in financial rescue packages over the past 30 years as money doled out to undeserving banks and investors who benefited from their ability to put pressure on policy makers. In the aftermath of the Mexican and East Asian financial rescues, the U.S. Congress enacted a number of measures that limited the authority of the executive branch to use taxpayer money for such bailouts. Supporters of the bills presented them as a clear case of Wall Street versus Main Street: bailing out banks while many small farms and businesses were allowed to go under.[9] Many American and European taxpayers were similarly angry with the financial rescues mounted by the governments of the United States and the European Union in the context of the global financial crisis that began in 2008.

Attitudes toward the IMF and other international financial institutions are often related to broader attitudes toward global economic integration. Both supporters and opponents of globalization tend to think of the IMF and its allies as important pillars of the contemporary international economy. Those wary of globalization distrust global finance and the IMF; those who favor globalization support them.

---

8. "Bailout for Whom?" *Progressive* 62, no. 2 (February 1998): 9–10.

9. J. Lawrence Broz, "Congressional Politics of International Financial Rescues," *American Journal of Political Science* 49, no. 3 (July 2005): 496–512.

Whatever domestic disagreements there may be, in general the interests of debtor and creditor countries are clear. Both sides of the relationship stand to benefit from continued lending: borrowers get access to foreign money, and lenders get profits. But each side would prefer to gain more from the relationship. Thus, there are incentives to cooperate to keep the lending going and incentives to bargain for the best possible deal. This sets the stage for complex interactions between debtors and creditors.

Debtor-Creditor Interactions

In the modern era, there have been many cycles of lending and debt crises. All through the nineteenth and early twentieth centuries, rapidly growing countries borrowed heavily from the major European financial centers—primarily London but also Paris, Amsterdam, and Berlin. Foreign borrowing was, in fact, important to the economic development of the principal developing regions of the day: the United States, Canada, Australia, Argentina, Brazil, and others. In most instances, debts appear to have contributed to economic development, but that did not diminish the attendant crises and political disputes. The United States, the world's largest borrower throughout the nineteenth century, was not immune: many of its state governments defaulted in the 1840s, and the state of Mississippi, whose banks borrowed heavily from London financiers in the 1830s and defaulted in 1841, has ever since continued to refuse to make payments on its London debt.

Concern about getting embroiled in debt disputes helps explain why today's private international financial flows to the developing world are restricted to the more advanced and successful developing countries. Countries facing severe developmental difficulties, or about which there is little reliable information, are simply unattractive to private creditors. For example, the government of Brazil is able to attract substantial loans from foreign investors (it had over $116 billion in outstanding debt to private creditors in 2012), whereas the governments of Burkina Faso, Nepal, and Yemen must rely overwhelmingly on concessional lending from the World Bank and other aid agencies.[10] Even in the case of well-known debtor countries, however, debtor-creditor interactions are inherently complicated by the strategic interactions that are inherent in the relationship.

When debtors and creditors enter into conflict, each side in the interaction has clear interests at stake. For debtor nations in crisis, making prompt and full debt service payments can mean restraining consumption, increasing taxes, reducing government spending, and cutting wages—in a word, **austerity**. So debtor governments want to reduce the amounts they have to pay so as to reduce the demands on their citizens. On the other hand, creditors' profits depend on the debt service payments they receive. So creditors want to be paid in full for the loans they have extended. The two sets of interests are, of course, in conflict.

austerity
The application of policies to reduce consumption, typically by cutting government spending, raising taxes, and restricting wages.

---

10. World Bank, World Development Indicators, http://data.worldbank.org/data-catalog/world-development-indicators (accessed 02/19/15).

This graffiti in Lisbon, Portugal, depicts German chancellor Angela Merkel manipulating the strings of Portuguese leaders. Many Portuguese blamed Merkel for the austerity measures the government enacted in order to receive an emergency loan from eurozone partners during the crisis.

As we have seen, when two actors have conflicting interests, they engage in a bargaining interaction to determine whether some mutually acceptable deal is possible. Each side has tools in its arsenal that can be used to extract favorable terms. The principal bargaining weapon available to the debtor government is the threat of default, or suspension of payment on the debt.[11] In August 1998, the Russian government responded to national economic difficulties with a default that affected as much as $80 billion in foreign debt; in December 2001, the Argentine government defaulted on $93 billion in foreign debt, and controversy over its repayment continues to this day.[12] Any sensible creditor would prefer to get some money rather than to get no money at all and therefore has an incentive to reduce the burden of debt. But creditors also have financial weapons available: they can cut off debtor governments from future lending, and they may be able to retaliate in related areas, such as freezing debtor governments' bank accounts or taking other government-owned properties. Creditors can also try to get their home governments to use broader foreign policy considerations to induce compliance, such as threatening a cutoff of aid or even military action. In short, each side can threaten to impose costs on the other in order to extract a better deal at the bargaining table. The ability of each side to get concessions from the other depends on how powerful and how credible these threats are.

11. Legally, a default is invoked by the creditor when the debtor misses payments, but the term is used more generally to describe a suspension of debt service.

12. The amounts involved are unclear, especially for Russia. See International Monetary Fund, *World Economic Outlook* (Washington, DC: International Monetary Fund, 1998), chap. 2. On Argentina's most recent default controversy, see "Everything You Need to Know about Argentina's Weird Default," *Washington Post*, August 3, 2014, www.washingtonpost.com/blogs/wonkblog/wp/2014/08/03/everything-you-need-to-know-about-argentinas-weird-default/ (accessed 02/01/15).

The bargaining between creditors and debtors over existing debt is analogous to the bargaining between countries we described in Chapter 3, which can sometimes lead to war. Because of the costs associated with default and retaliation, there is usually a bargaining solution to their interaction that makes both sides better off than financial warfare. Both sides would prefer to restructure the debt so that payments can continue to be made; this is what negotiators, arbitrators, and bankruptcy courts do in the case of domestic debt problems. However, as in the case of security relations, international debtor-creditor interactions are characterized by incomplete information. The debtor may claim not to be able to make payments, but the creditor does not know if the claim is true. Thus, creditors cannot know if the threat to default will, in fact, be carried out in the face of potentially dire consequences for the debtor, which may simply be bluffing in order to get a better deal. The creditor, for its part, may threaten to retaliate, but the debtor does not know if the threat will be carried out. In these circumstances, cooperative relations between debtors and creditors can collapse into bitter conflict. Many debt conflicts drag on for years or even decades and can have a powerful impact on other dimensions of interstate interaction. Debt-related conflicts have even been blamed for invasions, wars, and colonialism. In some instances, the issue is resolved amicably with a negotiated settlement; in other instances, the parties remain far apart.

Of course, cooperation between debtors and creditors is not necessarily a good thing for everyone involved. This is especially the case when debtor or creditor governments pursue policies that impose major costs on domestic groups. Whether an amicable resolution of debtor-creditor interactions is a good thing or a bad thing, it is important to try to understand the conflict and how it develops. One prominent aspect of international debt interactions is that it has come to involve important international institutions that can play an important part in debtor-creditor relations.

Institutions of International Finance

During the twentieth century, there were frequent attempts to regulate debtor-creditor relations by creating institutions to mediate their interactions and perhaps facilitate mutually acceptable outcomes. These institutions have, to a certain extent, helped alleviate the problems that can make lending difficult or impossible and that cause conflict when debtors run into trouble. In the interwar period, the League of Nations' Economic and Financial Committee attempted to work with debtors and creditors to manage the financial difficulties of troubled nations in central and eastern Europe, with mixed results. The **Bank for International Settlements** was established in 1930 explicitly to help oversee relations between one of the world's most problematic debtor nations, Germany, and its international creditors. This too met with mixed results. Nonetheless, by the 1940s there was a common view that some form of international financial institution might be beneficial to the resolution of sovereign debt problems.

Bank for International Settlements

One of the oldest international financial organizations, created in 1930, its members include the world's principal central banks, and under its auspices they attempt to cooperate in the financial realm.

International Monetary Fund (IMF)

A major international economic institution that was established in 1944 to manage international monetary relations and that has gradually reoriented itself to focus on the international financial system, especially debt and currency crises.

The International Monetary Fund Today, many aspects of international financial affairs are overseen by one of the world's most powerful international organizations, the **International Monetary Fund (IMF)**. The establishment of the IMF was agreed on at Bretton Woods (see Chapter 1) in order to manage the international monetary system. After the Bretton Woods monetary regime collapsed in the early 1970s (as we will see in Chapter 9), the IMF gradually took on a more directly financial role. Today, its principal concern is financial crises in developing nations, although it has also played a role during crisis periods in developed countries.

The IMF is a membership organization that includes both borrowing and lending countries. All member states have a vote on its activities, but these votes are proportional to the member's financial contribution to the IMF resources, its "quota." These financial contributions are in turn a function of the size of the country's economy and its importance to world trade and payments. As a result, the United States provides nearly 18 percent of the IMF's total resources; the member states of the European Union provide another 32 percent. Because IMF decisions require an 85 percent supermajority, this gives both the United States and the European Union (acting as a group) a veto over fund actions. This has led to complaints that the IMF is largely a tool of its richer and most powerful members—to which those members sometimes respond that this is appropriate inasmuch as they are the ones footing most of the bills.

The IMF, indeed, needs substantial funds to carry out its activities. The total of quotas from its members is currently nearly $400 billion, and the fund can call upon pledges from its members of another $1 trillion. This gives the IMF, in theory, access to nearly $1.5 trillion dollars, although it has never come close to using all these resources. Nonetheless, one of the things that leads many to regard the IMF as the most important, and most powerful, international economic institution is that it can mobilize an extraordinary amount of money in a relatively short time. And because debt crises often erupt suddenly, and often involve vast amounts of money, the IMF is uniquely suited to intervene in such crises. Typically, a country facing debt difficulties turns to the IMF to negotiate a program of economic policies intended to address the sources of the difficulties. In return for implementing a program that meets the IMF's standards, the debtor government receives relatively inexpensive loans from the IMF. Probably more important, the debtor country is "certified" as being in compliance with IMF norms, which makes it more attractive to creditors. This certification is meant to encourage private lenders to renegotiate with the debtor government and perhaps to extend it new loans to help it overcome temporary difficulties. For example, during the debt crisis of the 1980s, the IMF signed dozens of agreements with troubled debtors, typically requiring policies of economic austerity and adjustment in return for assistance with working out their debt problems. The IMF's agreement with Indonesia in the midst of the 1997–98 Asian financial crisis obliged the Indonesian government to cut subsidies to—and therefore raise the prices of—sugar, wheat flour, corn, and soybeans, as well as fuel and electricity. All these factors imposed hardships on Indonesia's poor and working people. The IMF also required the government to shut down 16 banks controlled by relatives or cronies of the country's dictatorial president, Suharto. This move may have been less objectionable to ordinary people, but it was, of course, unpopular with the Indonesian government.[13]

While the IMF largely dealt with developing debtor nations from the 1970s until the 2000s, the financial crisis that began in 2008 drove many industrialized countries to the fund. By 2014, the fund's largest programs were with Greece, Ireland, and Portugal, countries that fell into debt crises after 2008. The IMF's operations in these instances were similar to those in other debt crises, although in the European cases it worked in concert with the authorities of the European Union itself.

The IMF, like other international institutions, can facilitate cooperative interactions among actors in a variety of ways. It provides a set of financial and macroeconomic standards, and a wealth of other information, that can be used to assess the behavior of debtor nations. By increasing the likelihood that debtor-creditor relations will be iterated (repeated), the fund can make cooperation more attractive. The IMF can also help verify a debtor government's compliance with commitments to pursue economic policies that creditors want to see. And the IMF can act on behalf of the collectivity of creditor nations, which might otherwise have difficulties working out common decisions about how to deal with financial crises.

In one sense, though, the IMF is unusual. While many international institutions act primarily to facilitate bargaining among nation-states, the IMF negotiates agreements directly with an individual country's government. And, perhaps even more unusual, the IMF's involvement is typically closely tied to relations between the debtor government and private international creditors. While the IMF does not represent foreign creditors, there is normally an understanding that an agreement with the IMF will facilitate agreement with private lenders, and sometimes the IMF, member governments, and private creditors make this connection explicit. In this sense, the IMF plays a major part, directly or indirectly, in negotiations between sovereign governments and private financiers. This unusual relationship has also led to charges that the IMF is biased in favor of creditors and against debtors (see "Controversy" on p. 358).

Supporters of the IMF believe that it plays an important role in managing the international financial system, allowing for an orderly resolution of debtor-creditor problems. They focus on the informational difficulties endemic in sovereign debt, as well as the need for reliable monitoring of compliance with agreements. Supporters emphasize how the IMF can help debtors and creditors arrive at cooperative arrangements. They believe that the IMF's power comes from its central

---

13. Stephan Haggard, *The Political Economy of the Asian Financial Crisis* (Washington, DC: Institute for International Economics, 2000).

Is the IMF Unfair?

In February 1989, facing a protracted fiscal crisis, Venezuela's president, Carlos Andrés Pérez, negotiated a loan with the IMF. In a reversal of preelection promises he had made only weeks earlier, Pérez implemented a package of market-based reforms under the IMF's recommendation, including import liberalization and tariff elimination measures, privatization of state companies, restrictions on state spending, relaxation of price controls, and deregulation of exchange and interest rates. On February 27, the people of Caracas took to the streets in violent protests that came to be known as the Caracazo ("Caracas smash"). Considered by some observers to mark the birth of the antiglobalization movement, the Caracazo also played a key role in the demise of Pérez's government and the rise of Hugo Chávez to the Venezuelan presidency. In April 2007, Chávez, by then one of the world's most vocal critics of the IMF, announced that he would pull Venezuela out of the IMF.

The IMF provides a source of economic assistance to nations that would otherwise risk protracted fiscal crises and be cut off from the foreign capital that is vital to their development. Why, then, does such a useful institution cause such controversy? The answer stems in part from the IMF's nature as a bargaining forum. Although the IMF facilitates mutually beneficial international cooperation, critics claim that it distributes the benefits and burdens of that cooperation unevenly across member nations. Whereas IMF policies often appear to directly promote the interests of (certain influential investors within) creditor countries, benefits to debtor countries are not always as immediately apparent.

Two of the chief criticisms leveled by Chávez at the IMF reflect these distributive concerns. The first charge is that the IMF violates national sovereignty (or, in Chávez's interpretation, that it is an "agent of U.S. imperialism"). This charge derives from the "conditionalities" routinely attached to IMF loans. For decades, the IMF has required that countries requesting balance-of-payments assistance commit to what are known as structural adjustment programs, designed to solve debtor nations' fiscal crises. Such programs have included not only economic reforms of the kind Venezuela enacted but also specific political reforms. Pérez, for instance, was asked to institute direct elections of state governors in place of presidential appointments. Although acceptance of such conditions is supposedly voluntary, the high price of refusal—ineligibility for IMF assistance—creates an impression of coercion. Moreover, when developed countries sign on to the IMF, they do not suffer a similar risk of diminished sovereignty. As they are more often lenders rather than borrowers, developed countries impose rather than submit to the IMF's conditionalities.

Chávez's second main criticism derives not from the use of conditionalities per se but from the particular nature of the conditions the IMF routinely imposes. Those conditions are said to exhibit scant concern for the most needy debtor nations. Indeed, the immediate result of IMF economic austerity measures is often hardship for such nations' poorest citizens, who face higher taxes, wage cuts, unemployment, and reduced social services—all at a time of rising prices. Again, the world's affluent countries, as lenders rather than borrowers in these situations, do not face comparable hardship through IMF membership. Although Chavez died in 2013, critics of the IMF continue to charge that it unfairly favors the affluent creditor countries of the developed world. (The cartoon on the right depicts the IMF as pirates set to plunder the Jamaican economy when called upon to provide assistance in 2012.)

Defenders of the IMF respond to both of these criticisms by stressing the mutual gains from cooperation. The IMF's policy recommendations are essential for restoring fiscal balance and access to foreign credit, they say, and the benefits of achieving these goals over the long term outweigh the temporary diminishment of a nation's sovereignty and the short-term suffering of its poorest citizens. Once these longer-term effects are taken into account, defenders argue, it becomes clear that debtor nations derive substantial benefit from membership in the IMF, so that talk of an unfair bargain is inappropriate.

Supporters further argue that the IMF is essential to the international financial system and is at least as beneficial to debtor nations as it is to creditors. If the IMF were not there to help guarantee creditors of good debtor behavior, creditors would not lend. This is why member states *voluntarily* go to the IMF: they want its "seal of approval" in order to gain access to global financial markets. Typically, the reason the government has gotten into trouble in the first place is that it is pursuing unsustainable policies, and the IMF can help it get back on track and regain access to international finance. The medicine the IMF dispenses may not be pleasant, but it is essential to help sick economies recover. Without the IMF, there would be little or no international lending, and the poor nations would be far worse off.

Critics counter that the IMF's main goal is keeping creditors happy. If social progress, economic growth, and equity are sacrificed, the IMF appears unconcerned. There is little moral justification for subjecting the people of a country to terrible austerity measures solely to pay billions to wealthy foreign banks and investors. Even if in principle the IMF could be beneficial, in practice its current orientation is far too heavily skewed toward regressive policies. Many IMF programs fail even on their own terms, providing little economic relief in return for mass suffering. The allegedly "voluntary" nature of IMF programs is a fiction: a developing country that does not "voluntarily" subject itself to IMF dictates will be severely punished. As a result, critics argue that the IMF is a tool of the creditor nations and their investors, and its policies benefit only the rich and powerful.

The plausibility of these arguments depends on how well the IMF in fact delivers on its promise. It must be shown that standard IMF measures actually do rectify debtor nations' trade deficits, that this in turn contributes to economic growth, and that the growth in question benefits the poor. The evidence is currently mixed: while IMF programs may improve a nation's balance of payments, their record on economic growth and poverty reduction is unclear.

role in resolving financial problems in ways that are beneficial to both debtors and creditors.

However, opponents see the IMF as a tool of international financiers. They regard the IMF as a biased agency whose actions reinforce the subordinate position of debtor nations and do little to assist them in achieving economic growth and development. Similar conflicts arise over the involvement of the home governments of creditors, primarily from North America, Europe, and Japan. Debtor nations often resent political pressure from these powerful governments, which they regard as unduly concerned with insisting that "their" bankers get repaid. Creditors can be politically influential at home, and defaults can threaten to bankrupt major financial institutions in industrial nations, which would, in turn, destabilize their own financial markets. This situation leads creditor governments and the IMF, in the eyes of many opponents, to serve as debt collectors for international banks.

Recent Borrowing and Debt Crises

Lending to developing nations has been an important part of the international economy since the mid-1960s. At the same time, there have been many debt crises since international financial markets reopened to developing countries. The first such crisis started in 1982, with the Mexican default. Like most financial crises, this one had a self-reinforcing nature. As in a bank panic, as lenders worried that developing-country governments might not repay them, they stopped lending. This left developing-country governments without a financial cushion, and in desperation they stopped making payments to their creditors—thereby scaring international bankers even further. The more the developing countries ran out of money, the less bankers lent; the less bankers lent, the more the developing countries ran out of money. In the space of weeks, some of the most rapidly growing economies in the world were suddenly cut off from the bank lending they had relied on for 15 years.

One after another, the major debtor governments struggled to generate the foreign currency and government revenue needed to pay their creditors, until eventually their economies collapsed. By 1983, as many as 34 developing and socialist countries were formally renegotiating their debts, and a dozen more were in serious trouble. Latin America was spending nearly half of its export earnings to pay interest and principal on its foreign debt, leaving little to buy the imports it needed. Most debtor economies remained depressed for years, and the crises were not fully resolved until 1990. Austerity programs and economic reforms in debtor nations coupled with concessions from lenders to reduce the debt burden gradually allowed the problems to be worked out. (See "What Shaped Our World?" on p. 361 for details about this debt crisis.)

Eventually, lending resumed, but debt crises continued to occur. In 1994, Mexican finances once again collapsed. In 1997 to 1998, combined debt and currency crises hit a series of East Asian countries from Indonesia and Thailand to the Philippines and Korea. This was a particularly startling shock, as these nations had

The Latin American Debt Crisis

In the 1960s, the governments of Latin America discovered a valuable resource: foreign loans. International investors had not lent money to developing countries since 1929, having been burned during the Great Depression when most countries stopped paying their debts. But by 1965 memories had faded, and international banks resumed lending to governments in the developing world.

Interests Latin American governments needed the money to build factories and roads, power plants and steel mills, schools and houses. For 15 years, governments in Latin America, as well as a few other developing regions, borrowed frantically to try to catch up with the industrialized world. Loans poured in, public and private projects lined up for money, and economies expanded. The region's total debt grew in 10 years, from 1973 to 1982, from $40 billion to $330 billion. The borrowing boom came to a crashing halt late in the summer of 1982. In August, the Mexican government announced that it could not pay the interest and principal on its $100 billion debt to foreign banks. International banks panicked. If Mexico, a major oil producer, couldn't or wouldn't pay its debts, perhaps other nations couldn't or wouldn't either. Investors stopped lending within weeks, and heavily indebted developing nations around the world were thrown into crisis. Within four months, about 40 countries had fallen behind on their debt payments.

Institutions The debt crisis that began in 1982 led to an economic collapse that was, for many countries, the most catastrophic in modern history. The crisis had dire effects on domestic political institutions. Latin America spiraled downward into recession and depression, unemployment, and hyperinflation (price increases of more than 50 percent a month). In 1983, as demonstrations and strikes roiled the country, Mexico's principal opposition party won control of some of the country's major cities for the first time.

At the international level, the governments of creditor and debtor nations, as well as the world's principal international financial institution, the IMF, all were important. The IMF orchestrated a multibillion-dollar bailout package even as it played an intermediary role between the creditor banks and the debtor nations. Debtor countries typically found themselves forced to enter an IMF program if they wanted to work out a better deal with their bank creditors.

Interactions The interplay among creditor governments, creditor banks, debtor governments, and the IMF made the politics of the debt crisis particularly complex. Lengthy and often bitter negotiations ensued over who would make the major sacrifices needed to address the accumulated debt burden. Most of the costs were borne by debtor nations. After decades of rapid growth, income per person in Latin America declined over the 1980s by 10 percent, real wages fell by at least 30 percent, and investment fell even further; inflation in many nations rose above 1,000 percent.[a] The 1980s became known in the region as the lost decade. Eventually, in 1989, creditor governments and banks offered some debt relief and the region began growing again.

Domestically, throughout the developing world, protests erupted over the debt crisis and the unemployment, inflation, and government cutbacks it had brought. The economic and political crisis eventually drove most of Latin America's military dictatorships from power. But this advance was overshadowed by the fact that the debtor nations had fallen even further behind economically as they struggled to shoulder their debt. What had originally seemed a golden opportunity—readily available foreign loans—now seemed a terrible burden.

The Banco de México, Mexico's central bank.

---

a. Eliana Cardoso and Ann Helwege, *Latin America's Economy: Diversity, Trends, and Conflicts* (Cambridge, MA: MIT Press, 1995).

long been regarded as models of developmental success. Their apparently endless potential had drawn in considerable amounts of foreign money: Thailand's foreign debt tripled from $30 billion to $90 billion in three years to 1996, while Indonesia's doubled from $25 billion to $50 billion. During the early 1990s, about $50 billion a year flowed into East Asia from global financial markets, with tens of billions more in direct investment from MNCs.

Once the crisis hit in the summer of 1997, however, money ran out of the East Asian debtor countries as fast as it had run in. The $50 billion annual inflow of the early 1990s turned into an outflow of over $230 billion between 1997 and 1999. After years of extraordinary growth—10 percent a year was common—the economies of Indonesia, Thailand, and Malaysia contracted by 15, 12, and 8 percent, respectively, in a matter of months. It would be years before they would recover their pre-crisis levels.

The East Asian crisis was followed by crises in Russia and Brazil in 1998 to 1999, Argentina in 2000 to 2001, and others since then. In all these cases, intervention by the IMF alone was not sufficient—the debt problems were so large that creditor governments also stepped in, to the tune of over $50 billion for Mexico, almost $120 billion for the three principal Asian crisis nations (Indonesia, Korea, and Thailand), and another $70 billion for Russia and Brazil. Critics charged that taxpayers were being forced to bail out foolish investors and dissolute governments, but financial leaders insisted on the need for a quick response to avoid financial contagion.

The international politics of developing-country debt is a striking example of how actors with different interests interact strategically in a highly institutionalized context. The parties have not only clear conflicting interests but also clear interests in common. Even though creditors want to be repaid and debtors want to pay as little as possible, both sides have an interest in continuing their relationship: the creditors to earn profits, the debtors to maintain access to foreign finance. This mix of cooperative and conflictual motives leads to complicated strategic interactions. And the role of the IMF highlights the role of international institutions—seen by some as effective at helping resolve conflicts, by others as tools of the powerful.

These debt crises in developing and transitional economies were dwarfed by a financial collapse that hit the advanced industrial economies in 2008. Some of the aspects of this crisis were familiar from previous debt crises—although it had been decades since an industrialized country had been so affected—while other features were very novel. Together, they plunged the world into the most serious economic downturn since the Great Depression of the 1930s.

A New Crisis Hits the United States— and the World

The 2008 financial crisis originated in the United States, the world's largest economy and most developed financial system. The country had embarked on a major foreign borrowing spree. In 2001, substantial tax cuts drove the American federal government into a large deficit. Much of the deficit was financed by borrowing from abroad. Government borrowing spurred the economy, reinforced by a monetary policy of very low interest rates; in turn, these low interest rates encouraged American households to borrow heavily. Much of the borrowing went for housing, as many Americans refinanced their homes or bought new homes. Foreigners eager to buy American investments they regarded as safe and profitable provided large portions of the lending directly or indirectly.

From 2001 to 2007, the United States experienced a traditional borrowing boom. Every year, the country borrowed between a half-trillion and a trillion dollars from the rest of the world. A significant portion of the debt went to finance the government budget deficit; much of the rest went into the flourishing housing market. As financial markets grew at a dizzying pace, banks developed ever more complex ways of investing, borrowing, and lending. Some observers warned that not enough of the new debt was going into productive investments that would increase the efficiency of the U.S. economy, such as new factories or new technologies. Other observers were concerned that American regulators were inadequately supervising the freewheeling, increasingly complex financial system. However, the U.S. government resisted stricter financial oversight, especially given its general commitment to deregulation. Meanwhile, most Americans were happy to

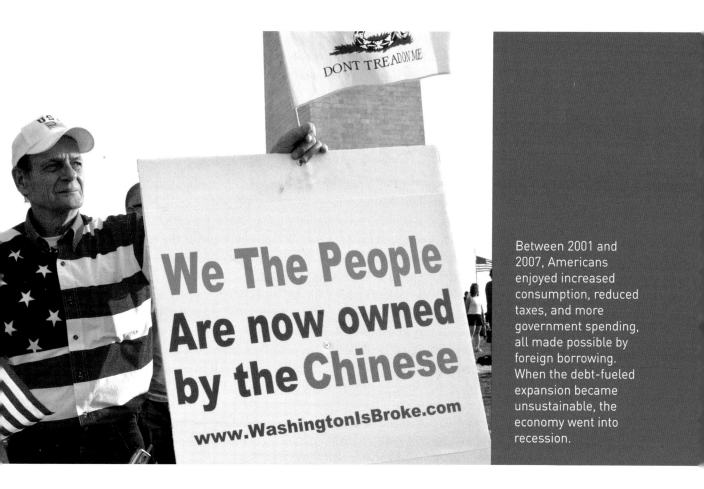

Between 2001 and 2007, Americans enjoyed increased consumption, reduced taxes, and more government spending, all made possible by foreign borrowing. When the debt-fueled expansion became unsustainable, the economy went into recession.

enjoy a dramatic expansion in consumption, reduced taxes, increased government spending, and a striking increase in housing prices—all made possible by foreign borrowing.

America's debt-fed expansion eventually became an unsustainable bubble, especially in the housing market. In some parts of the country, housing prices doubled in the space of four or five years. Much of the lending was predicated on the unrealistic expectation that housing prices would continue to rise at this pace. For example, financial institutions extended mortgages to borrowers who would otherwise not have qualified, because they expected that the homes being bought would rise in value. Both borrowers and lenders were thus gambling that housing prices would continue to go up.

Eventually, housing prices stopped soaring and began to fall. Overextended mortgage holders could not pay their debts; overextended lenders faced massive losses. During 2007 and 2008 financial difficulties spread, as hundreds of billions of dollars worth of mortgages and related financial assets went bad. Fear spread from bank to bank, culminating in September 2008, when Lehman Brothers, one of the world's leading investment banks, collapsed. This was the largest bankruptcy in American history, and it caused near panic in financial markets.

Within a few months, the crisis was transmitted around the world, and virtually every economy was in decline. Some countries faced circumstances much like those of the United States: the United Kingdom, Spain, Portugal, and Greece. Also hard hit were some developing and transition economies that had been borrowers over the course of the decade. When the U.S. spiraled downward into crisis, so did the other debtor nations. But the damage was even more widespread, because the collapse of the debtor economies affected the creditors who had extended trillions of dollars in loans to them. As the crisis spread from debtor to debtor, and from debtor to creditor, it became the first truly global financial crisis since the 1930s, resulting in the deepest global economic downturn since that decade.

Individual governments attempted to stem the decline. The U.S. government stepped in with trillions of dollars to bail out affected financial institutions and try to get financial markets working again, taking over some of the country's largest financial corporations in order to avoid their collapse. And the U.S. government enacted a massive deficit-funded spending package to attempt to stimulate an economy in its steepest recession since the 1930s.

Within the United States, political battles broke out over the response to the financial crisis. The principal question confronting the nation was who would pay for the country's financial follies. Many Americans were furious that the government was spending taxpayer dollars to bail out imprudent banks and corporations. Others argued that attempts to stimulate the economy were simply throwing taxpayer money at the problem without any guarantee it would work. As in other debt crises, many felt that the interests of working-class and middle-class Americans were being sacrificed to address problems created by wealthy financiers. As the recovery stalled, political battles heated up, and the country became increasingly polarized over how best to confront the aftermath of the debt crisis and how best to distribute the burden of economic adjustment among Americans.

A similar dynamic played out in Europe, with the added complication that the problem divided the eurozone, the group of EU member countries that had created a common currency in 1999. As with the world at large, eurozone countries were divided into those that borrowed heavily during the decade before 2008, and those that lent heavily. The big borrowers were largely in southern Europe—Greece, Spain, Portugal, and Italy—but also included Ireland. They borrowed for different purposes: Greece to fund an overgrown public sector and huge budget deficits; the rest, like the United States, largely to fuel a consumption and housing boom. The big lenders were the northern Europeans, especially Germany.

Internationally, too, the crisis caused tension among contending interests. Governments everywhere scrambled to protect their economies, even at the expense of other countries. For example, the U.S. Congress insisted that government spending to stimulate the failing economy be used preferentially to buy American goods; trading partners insisted that this was protectionist and violated the rules of the WTO. Developing countries complained that the heavy borrowing by industrialized-country governments to deal with the crisis was making it impossible for poor nations to get the funds they needed to confront their dire problems. The European Union was torn by conflicts among member states with widely different views as to the appropriate response to the crisis. Neither existing levels of international cooperation nor existing international institutions seemed adequate to address a global financial crisis of this magnitude.

As the crisis exacerbated disputes among major governments, many observers wondered whether the world would descend into the kind of trade, currency, and debt conflicts that characterized the interwar years. More generally, people everywhere wondered whether the deep recession that began in 2008 might spiral downward into a global depression similar to that of the early 1930s. As it turned out, the worst experiences of the 1930s were not repeated. Nonetheless, the crisis had a profound impact on both domestic and international politics around the world, and demonstrated the potential for political controversy inherent in international financial affairs.

Foreign Direct Investment: What Role Do Multinational Corporations Play?

FDI is another important form of international capital movement. It differs from foreign lending because it is carried out explicitly by corporations that maintain control over the facilities they establish overseas; the corporations involved have come to be known as **multinational corporations (MNCs)**. FDI occurs when Volkswagen sets up an auto factory in Brazil, or Telefónica de España buys the Czech telephone company, or ExxonMobil drills for oil in Angola. In all these instances, what is involved is far more than a simple transfer of capital. Volkswagen could export cars to Brazil but chooses to build them there instead; individual foreign investors could buy shares in the Czech telephone company, but instead a global telecommunications corporation adds the Czech system to its network; the Angolan government could borrow money to drill for oil but instead gives a concession to an American company.

Why Do Corporations Go Multinational?

It is not easy for a corporation to set up facilities in a foreign country. Volkswagen could simply build cars in Europe and export them to Brazil rather than building them in Brazil, and one might imagine that a local company could run the Czech telephone system better than a Spanish company could. There must be a reason for firms to invest abroad rather than exporting, and for a foreign firm to have some advantage over a domestic one, despite the inherent difficulties of doing business abroad. What makes it attractive for the corporation to establish or purchase subsidiaries across borders, and what gives the host country an interest in permitting this foreign investment?

Corporations may want to establish overseas affiliates to gain access to the local market or to take advantage of local resources—in both instances presumably because doing so through trade is less attractive or impossible. Some FDI is driven by resource location: American and European oil companies, with ample experience in exploring for oil, may be more effective at getting Angola's oil out of the ground than local entrepreneurs could be. The case of Volkswagen in Brazil illustrates that there are often advantages to producing in the local market: cheaper transport costs, or the ability to avoid trade barriers, or better access to market information. In the decades right after World War II, most FDI was by American manufacturers and was motivated by trade protection in Europe and developing countries. Ford, GE, and other big U.S. corporations faced tariffs and other restrictions imposed on their exports to Europe and the developing world. To get around these barriers, they established local affiliates.

More recently, as trade barriers have come down, other motivations have surfaced. MNCs today often place different components of their production network in different countries: the labor-intensive work is done in countries with cheap labor, such as Vietnam, while the work that requires more skilled labor and technicians is done in countries with ample skilled labor, such as Ireland. Other types of FDI, such as that by Telefónica de España, are in service sectors in which companies may have substantial experience or a famous brand name—banking or entertainment, for example. What ties all FDI together is that the corporations involved believe that overseas direct investment is profitable.[14]

---

14. For more on the economics of FDI, see Richard Caves, *Multinational Enterprises and Economic Analysis*, 3rd ed. (Cambridge: Cambridge University Press, 2007).

Within the home countries of MNCs (that is, the countries in which they are headquartered), there is generally support for their foreign activities. After all, American corporations are constituents of American politicians, and it is part of the job of the government to support their constituents, corporate or otherwise. So the U.S. government, like all governments, typically acts to promote and protect the interests of American corporations abroad.

However, FDI can be controversial in the countries from which it originates. Groups and people in North America and western Europe often fault MNCs for not investing at home. Labor unions in North America and western Europe often criticize MNCs, especially for "outsourcing" jobs to countries with lower wages. The American labor federation, the AFL-CIO, has complained: "In the global economy, multinational corporations move capital and jobs half-way around the world with the click of a mouse. These companies—many of them American—seek out the lowest possible labor costs and weakest worker protections. Even if the jobs are not moved, corporate executives use the threat of moving to coerce concessions from their U.S. workers."[15] Labor unions and others have demanded stricter controls on "sweatshop labor" in the developing countries, reflecting both working-class solidarity and a more prosaic desire to reduce competitive pressure.

Some human rights activists and environmentalists also eye MNCs with apprehension. Just as corporations can seek lower wages, they can look for pollution-friendly regimes, dictatorships that allow violations of human rights, and other ethically lax governments. In the words of a European campaign to "clean up" the world garment industry, "incentives for foreign investors include not only low wages, but also the suspension of certain workplace and environmental regulations. If a government does attempt to strictly enforce these regulations, you can bet that many investors will quickly pack their bags for another country that is even less strict and is more accommodating."[16] And there is a cultural component to some complaints about MNCs, arguing that MNCs reduce diversity and encourage the homogenization of world culture. Nonetheless, in general, home-country governments see their interests as closely tied to those of their corporations.

Nike is one of Vietnam's largest private employers. Abundant cheap labor in countries like Vietnam makes it profitable for companies like Nike to invest in factories there.

Why Do Countries Let Foreign Multinationals In?

Most countries that host FDI have an interest in allowing MNCs to operate within their borders—otherwise, of course, they would keep the corporations

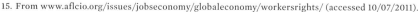

15. From www.aflcio.org/issues/jobseconomy/globaleconomy/workersrights/ (accessed 10/07/2011).
16. From www.cleanclothes.org/intro.htm#7 (accessed 08/21/04).

out. Certainly, in the nineteenth century it was common for such rapidly growing nations as the United States, Canada, Argentina, Russia, and Australia to rely on foreign companies to build up such important industries as railroads.

Today, governments generally welcome foreign corporations. This is because MNCs bring in managerial, technological, and marketing skills that might not otherwise be available, as well as investment capital. Some less developed countries (LDCs) lack the trained personnel and capital necessary to access and develop their own natural resources; without foreigners, they might not be able to profit from their resources. However, if they allow foreign companies to pump oil or to mine copper, the government can then tax some of the profits. Other poor nations with weak or small private sectors may welcome foreign corporations to provide jobs for their citizens and to gain access to world markets for their products.

Most nations are eager to attract the technological or other expertise that MNCs can mobilize. This may especially be the case in high-technology industries, where such multinationals as IBM or Siemens can be the sole source of crucial modern technologies. When Intel opened production facilities in Costa Rica in 1997, it transformed that country's economy. The firm soon accounted for one-third of total exports, with Intel's sales alone surpassing the country's traditional banana and coffee exports. Overall, Intel invested about a billion dollars in a country of 3.5 million people, and it employed about 5,000 people directly or indirectly; it had a network of almost 500 local supplier companies; and its presence spurred the creation of a high-technology cluster with over 50 other companies. There were years when Intel's activities alone accounted for more than half of the growth of the Costa Rican economy.[17]

Yet host countries—the countries in which MNCs invest—do not always have such positive views of FDI. There is always scope for disagreement over the division of the benefits. Conflict can arise over how much in taxes an oil company should pay to the local government or over the wages an automobile factory should pay to local workers. Local competitors may complain about foreign firms' presence in the domestic market. Some people may be concerned that foreign managers will be insensitive to national social, cultural, and political norms. Interactions between MNCs and national governments have been particularly fraught in the case of developing countries, many of which have gross domestic products (GDPs) smaller than the sales of the MNCs they host.

Even where there is agreement when the investment is made, views may change over time. One common pattern is that when countries are very poor, they are eager to attract FDI to bring natural resources and other national products to market. Over time, however, as the local economy becomes more sophisticated, local investors become better able to undertake the activities dominated by the MNCs. As the LDC develops, its government may want its own citizens to get more of the

---

17. World Bank, Multilateral Investment Guarantee Agency, *The Impact of Intel in Costa Rica* (Washington, DC: World Bank, 2006).

benefits of the investment. National businesses may come to resent the foreign competition, and local managers and technicians may feel they no longer need the MNC. Even the case of Intel in Costa Rica is hardly clear-cut. Just as Intel's expansion spurred the country's economy, its difficulties have held it back: in 2000, when the firm's growth slowed, Intel's problems depressed Costa Rican growth to half of what it would have been otherwise. And in order to attract Intel, the Costa Rican government had exempted it from all taxes for eight years and from half of its taxes for another four, and had freed it from many regulations that apply to other domestic and foreign firms. And in 2014, Intel announced that it would close its main production facility in Costa Rica and move its operations to Malaysia, Vietnam, and China.[18] Costa Rica certainly gained from having Intel invest there; but the presence of this huge firm—whose total worldwide sales are larger than the GDP of Costa Rica— also imposed real constraints on the small Central American nation, and its sudden departure will lead to job losses and economic contraction. In this context, there is plenty of scope for conflict between MNCs and host governments.

Host-Country Interactions with MNCs

Like debtors and creditors, foreign corporations and host-country governments have some common interests and some conflicting interests. This mix defines the scope of interactions between national governments and MNCs. As with foreign debt, each side has reasons to work to ensure that the investment can take place. But, again as with foreign debt, each side has strong incentives to bargain for a greater share of the benefits from FDI. This bargaining can involve negotiations over tax rates, or the company's training of local citizens for more skilled jobs, or the MNC giving some of its business to local suppliers. The host country's weapons include its ability to regulate and tax companies within its borders, up to and including nationalizing them—essentially, forcing them to sell out to local investors or to the government itself. The MNC's weapons include withholding its capital, its technology, or its expertise and ultimately pulling out of the local economy.

Interactions between host countries and MNCs have gone through many phases. Among the most conflictual have been relations over FDIs in the raw materials sector. Before World War I, most FDI was in mining, agriculture, or utilities. These investments, which may have been popular at the outset, eventually became controversial. The case of the United Fruit Company in Central America (see Chapter 4) is a good example: many people in developing nations came to see plantation and raw-materials investments as exploitative. Indeed, after the 1920s, more and more LDCs tended to buy out, take over, or limit foreign investment in these sectors, favoring their own investors instead. One study of forcible takings of MNCs in developing countries between 1960 and 1976, for example, found that while FDI in extractive industries (agriculture and raw materials) and utilities

---

18. See "Intel Outside," *Economist*, April 19, 2014, www.economist.com/news/americas/21600985-chipmaker-shuts-factory-slicing-away-one-fifth-countrys-exports-intel-outside (accessed 02/01/15).

was just one-fifth of the total, these sectors accounted for more than half of the takings.[19]

Political considerations about the role of FDI have added to purely economic concerns. Especially over the course of the 1960s, LDC governments began to believe that large foreign corporations could have a powerful and unwelcome impact on local politics. The activities of the U.S.-based International Telephone and Telegraph Company (ITT) in Chile demonstrated the threat. ITT first tried to keep Socialist Party candidate Salvador Allende from being elected president in 1970 for fear that his government would nationalize its investments. When this attempt was unsuccessful, ITT participated in a series of plots to try to overthrow President Allende. The story ended with a coup that destroyed one of Latin America's sturdiest democracies and brought the murderous dictatorship of Augusto Pinochet to power. The notion that American companies could be complicit in such matters, long derided by Westerners as feverish imaginings, was soon proven to be accurate by a congressional investigation, and this finding fueled sentiment against MNCs.

For both economic and political reasons, many countries began restricting MNCs in the 1960s. This was even true of some developed nations: Canada monitored and controlled new investments while both France and Japan limited foreign companies. But the most sweeping efforts were in the developing world, where foreign corporations were excluded from many industries, and foreign ownership was strictly limited, often to a minority share. Many developing countries nationalized foreign corporations, transferring ownership to local private companies or to the government. Others allowed FDI only if the foreign company did not compete with local firms, shared ownership with local investors, or agreed to reinvest most of its profits in the host country. The turning away from MNCs in the 1960s and 1970s went hand in hand with the turn toward foreign borrowing: by borrowing, developing countries could get foreign capital without allowing foreign ownership of the projects.

But the debt crisis of the 1980s, along with the increased acceptance of global economic integration in the 1990s, eroded resistance to multinationals. Developing countries were desperate for foreign capital, especially after loans dried up. And it appeared that attracting foreign corporations was important to ensuring a nation's integration into global markets. Previous restrictions on FDI were loosened or removed, and many LDCs actively sought to encourage foreign corporations to locate production facilities within their borders. The amounts involved were enormous: while MNCs invested about $2 billion a year in the developing world in the early 1970s, they have averaged over $350 billion a year since 2000. Even accounting for inflation, this is more than a 30-fold increase. As most developing countries have opened their economies to world markets, FDI has become less politically sensitive and more broadly desired.

---

19. Stephen J. Kobrin, "Foreign Enterprise and Forced Divestment in LDCs," *International Organization* 34, no. 1 (Winter 1980): 65–88.

20. Paul Sigmund, *Multinationals in Latin America* (Madison: University of Wisconsin Press, 1980).

This does not mean that MNCs are not controversial. Indeed, many people in the developing world continue to regard foreign corporations as economically, politically, or culturally undesirable. Restrictions persist on their activities in developing nations. In industrialized countries too there are continuing concerns about the exporting of jobs, and in some quarters about the possibility that foreign investors might compromise national sovereignty. Nevertheless, in the past 25 years the prevailing attitude toward FDI has been quite positive.

Why Aren't There International Institutions Related to FDI?

There are no effective international institutions associated with FDI. This is in striking contrast to international lending, where there are both regional and global multilateral institutions: the IMF, the World Bank, the Inter-American Development Bank, and so on. One possible reason is that there are fewer (if any) widely accepted truly global concerns associated with FDI than with international finance. In the latter area, it has been generally agreed for over a century that there is a risk of financial crises in one country affecting other countries. This risk creates incentives for countries to find ways, including institutionalized ways, to cooperate to avoid such financial contagion, and international institutions facilitate cooperation in pursuit of these types of common goals. Such incentives are not as strong in the case of FDI.

Nor is there a particularly strong demand for cooperation among countries in bargaining with MNCs. Individual countries that wish to limit or regulate MNCs can do so on their own, and it is not clear that IMF-style international institutions would help with this effort. The role of international institutions in providing information or establishing standards seems less relevant in the case of FDI, where each investment has different characteristics and where host governments are often well equipped to supervise foreign companies.

There have been occasional suggestions that some international agreement or organization might help to create a common set of standards for FDI. Codes of conduct have been proposed, and there has been an increase in private voluntary compliance with such codes of conduct, but this falls far short of an organized intergovernmental institution. Initiatives to institutionalize and regularize relations between MNCs and host nations have made little progress. There are thousands of **bilateral investment treaties** signed between two countries, providing protection for each other's investors, but nothing even remotely similar to an IMF has emerged.

Despite the absence of any multilateral institution, since the 1980s interactions between foreign corporations and national states have been less conflictual than they were before then. Certainly, FDI today leads to much less debate than conflict between debtors and creditors. FDI is widely accepted as an important component of an integrated world economy and as a generally positive factor in economic development.

bilateral investment treaty

An agreement between two countries about the conditions for private investment across borders. Most of these treaties include provisions to protect an investment from government discrimination or expropriation without compensation, as well as establishing mechanisms to resolve disputes.

International Migration: What Happens When People— Rather than Capital— Move across Borders?

Like capital, labor is a factor of production that moves across borders. In fact, international movements of labor and capital can be thought of as responding to similar economic factors and having similar economic effects. Capital can leave one country in order to hire workers in another—this is what happens when a corporation sets up production abroad. Alternatively, labor can leave one country in order to work for capital in another—this is what happens when workers migrate to a new country to be employed by a corporation there. Whether GM moves a factory to Mexico to hire Mexican workers, or Mexican workers move to Detroit to work for GM, the effect is similar. It therefore makes sense to think about the politics of immigration as part of the broader integration of the world economy and as simply another example of the movement of factors of production from country to country.

In fact, international migration has long been a feature of a globalized world economy. In the nineteenth and early twentieth centuries, international labor migration occurred at much higher levels than today. Over the decades before World War I, some 100 million people left their homelands in Europe and Asia for other parts of the world. The cities of such rapidly growing countries as Canada, Australia, Argentina, and the United States were full of foreign-born workers. For the most part, before 1914 Europeans could move and work wherever they pleased, without complicated legal proceedings or documents (Asian immigration was much more heavily restricted). While international labor movements in recent years have been very large, they are proportionately much smaller than those of the nineteenth and early twentieth centuries. However, labor migration has been significant—and also politically controversial.

Today, about one American resident in seven was born in a foreign country, approximately half of them in Latin America. The immigrant share of the population of other developed countries is generally similar to that of the United States (14 percent). It is a bit lower in some countries (9 percent in Italy, 11 percent in France) and substantially higher in some others (20 percent or more in Canada, New Zealand, and Switzerland).[21] Table 8.1 shows the countries with the largest number of immigrants. In almost every developed country, immigration is a politically contentious issue, with some residents favoring more open borders to

---

21. United Nations Population Division, Trends in International Migrant Stock: The 2013 Revision, http://esa.un.org/unmigration/TIMSO2013/migrantstocks2013.htm (accessed 10/10/2014).

TABLE 8.1 *Countries with the Largest Number of International Migrants, 2013*

	TOTAL MIGRANTS	AS % TOTAL POPULATION
United States	45,785,090	14.3
Russia	11,048,064	7.7
Germany	9,845,244	11.9
Saudi Arabia	9,060,433	31.4
United Arab Emirates	7,826,981	83.7
United Kingdom	7,824,131	12.4
France	7,439,086	11.6
Canada	7,284,069	20.7
Australia	6,468,640	27.7
Spain	6,466,605	13.8

Source: United Nations Population Division, "Trends in International Migrant Stock: The 2013 Revision," http://www.un.org/en/development/desa/population/migration/data/estimates2/index.shtml (accessed 10/10/2014).

immigrants and others wishing to limit immigration.[22] What explains these controversies over immigration?

There are many ways in which the movement of labor from one country to another is similar to the movement of capital, and it can be similarly analyzed. Labor, like capital, responds to differential rates of return: higher wages in rich countries attract workers from poor countries. This is true of both unskilled labor and skilled labor, which is typically called human capital because its "owners" have invested in advanced skills. Unskilled workers from El Salvador or Morocco migrate to the United States or Germany in search of higher-paying jobs, just as unskilled workers from Italy and Sweden migrated to the United States and Australia a hundred years ago. Skilled workers from India or Argentina too move to Europe or North America in search of higher incomes.

In this sense, immigration can be explained in terms of the Heckscher-Ohlin theory discussed in Chapter 7. Countries with abundant unskilled labor will export unskilled labor; countries scarce in unskilled labor will import it. Differences across countries in labor endowments (and, consequently, wages) mean that there are

22. A useful resource on this highly controversial topic is the Migration Policy Institute, www.migrationpolicy.org (accessed 01/25/11).

economic incentives for a labor-rich country such as Mexico or China to export both labor-intensive goods and labor.

The economic impact of labor migration can also be understood in terms of the Heckscher-Ohlin theory. An inflow of unskilled labor from abroad will tend to reduce the wages of local unskilled workers while an inflow of skilled labor will tend to reduce the wages of local skilled workers. Thus, for example, unskilled workers in developed countries are likely to be harmed by the immigration of unskilled workers from countries with lower wages. Concerns about this labor-market competition are one source of unease about immigration in developed countries (see "How Do We Know?" on p. 375). This is not a new phenomenon. In the century before 1914, immigration probably also exerted downward pressure on wages in migrant-receiving countries: two scholars have estimated that in such countries as the United States, Australia, and Argentina, unskilled wages were between one-eighth and one-third lower with immigration than they would have been without it.[23] While this outcome may have been bad for unskilled workers, it was probably good for the countries' economies as a whole, supplying them with much-needed labor.

Immigration benefits people in receiving countries in several ways. Employers gain from the lower wages they can pay. This is especially true for those who hire a lot of unskilled labor; in parts of the United States, sectors such as agriculture, restaurants, and construction have come to rely on cheaper immigrant labor. The economy as a whole profits from having a larger labor force and from the lower cost of production that lower wages can provide. As usual, the benefits for some are counterbalanced by costs to others: if immigration lowers the wages that employers have to pay, it also lowers the wages paid to native workers who compete with immigrants.

The domestic distributional effects of immigration, coupled with national political institutions, help explain changes in policies over time. In the nineteenth century, there was substantial anti-immigrant sentiment among workers in such countries as the United States, Canada, and Australia. But a century and more ago, employers were far more politically powerful than labor—after all, unions were barely organized. So while there were some restrictions on immigration, especially from Asia, most countries remained open. As the political influence of labor grew, restrictions on immigration expanded and until the 1960s were very stringent. During the 1960s, labor shortages began to develop in industrialized nations, and pressure to permit more immigration grew. The result was a loosening of restrictions; this may also have been due to the rising influence of skilled workers in rich countries, who are less concerned about competition from unskilled immigrants. Today, there are many countervailing economic interests at play: workers who would compete with immigrants and workers who would not, employers who depend on immigrant labor and those who do not.

---

23. Kevin O'Rourke and Jeffrey Williamson, *Globalization and History: The Evolution of a Nineteenth-Century Atlantic Economy* (Cambridge, MA: MIT Press, 1999), Tables 8.1 and 8.3.

Explaining Public Opinion on Immigration

Immigration is one of the most politically controversial issues in developed countries. Politicians frequently invoke immigration in their campaigns, and surveys suggest that immigration policy is an important issue for an overwhelming majority of voters. How do voters decide whether they favor or oppose immigration?

To answer this question, some scholars begin with the same frameworks used to analyze international trade. The Heckscher-Ohlin model, introduced in Chapter 7, demonstrates that the relative abundance or scarcity of factors of production (land, labor, and capital) are critical for understanding trade patterns. For example, countries that have abundant labor are likely to export labor-intensive products. The related Stolper-Samuelson theorem assumes that trade protection benefits the scarce factor of production. The same logic can be used to explain patterns of immigration and its distributional consequences. Labor-abundant countries, such as India, the Philippines, and Mexico, are likely to experience the largest out-migration of residents, and the relatively labor-scarce rich economies, such as Britain, the United States, and Saudi Arabia, are likely to experience the largest inflows of people (see Table 8.1). By the same logic, restricting immigration benefits labor in the receiving country when it is scarce.

Political scientist Kenneth Scheve and economist Matthew Slaughter have used the logic of the Heckscher-Ohlin model to explain American voters' responses to surveys about immigration policy.[a] They measured immigration preferences by responses to a question that appeared in three successive American National Election Studies nationwide surveys in 1992, 1994, and 1996: "Do you think the number of immigrants from foreign countries who are permitted to come to the United States to live should be increased a little, increased a lot, decreased a little, decreased a lot, or left the same as it is now?" The authors assumed that respondents believed that U.S. immigrant inflows increase the relative supply of low-skilled workers, which is a reasonable assumption given that nearly one-third of U.S. immigrants lack a high school

diploma or equivalent.[b] The survey also asked respondents about their wages and years of education, which serve as useful proxies for respondents' skill levels. Scheve and Slaughter analyzed the survey data using a statistical model and found that public opinion toward immigration reflects the basic logic of the Heckscher-Ohlin framework: respondents with lower skills prefer a more restrictive immigration policy whereas high-skilled respondents prefer a more open policy. In their interpretation, domestic labor competition is key: unskilled workers—who constitute a relatively scarce factor in the United States—fear that low-skilled immigrants will cause a drop in their wages.

Scheve and Slaughter's findings caused considerable controversy among political scientists, some of whom were skeptical that voters could correctly calculate the income effects that are predicted by the Heckscher-Ohlin model. Other scholars were skeptical that wages and education actually measure skill level rather than noneconomic attributes like open-mindedness and experience with foreign cultures.[c] Public opinion toward immigration remains a very active research area, with political scientists devising new experiments to determine which economic or noneconomic factors drive individual preferences toward this highly politicized issue.

a. Kenneth F. Scheve and Matthew J. Slaughter, "Labor Market Competition and Individual Preferences over Immigration Policy," *The Review of Economics and Statistics* 83, no. 1 (February 2001): 133–45.

b. See Pia Orrenius and Madeline Zavodny, "Immigrants in the U.S. Labor Market," Working Paper 1306, Federal Reserve Bank of Dallas, Dallas, TX, September 2013, www.dallasfed.org/assets/documents/research/papers/2013/wp1306.pdf (accessed 02/19/15).

c. See Jens Hainmueller and Michael J. Hiscox, "Attitudes toward Highly Skilled and Low-Skilled Immigration: Evidence from a Survey Experiment," *American Political Science Review* 104, no. 1 (February 2010): 61–84.

The political economy of immigration involves other economic and noneconomic considerations. One economic consideration is the potential cost of social programs that immigrants may use disproportionately, inasmuch as they tend to be poorer than natives. However, immigrants typically pay taxes, so that the overall (net) effect may be hard to distinguish.[24] In some contemporary American debates, opponents of immigration express particular concern about the fiscal effects of large-scale immigration.

Supporters and opponents of immigration often raise noneconomic issues as well. Unlike capital, labor is a factor of production that inherently involves people. Capital can move across borders without having much, or any, noneconomic impact on sending or receiving nations. But immigration changes the nature of both the countries from which immigrants come and the countries to which they go. Some people feel that immigrants pose a cultural threat to host societies and that immigrant communities will change the social and political nature of the local society. Others welcome the diversity; for many citizens, new immigrants may well be family members or former neighbors. Some people regard immigrants as a threat to national security and national identity. Others see immigration as a way of spreading Western values and of rewarding allies in poor countries.

Certainly, immigration is one of the more prominent and visible features of contemporary globalization. It raises many of the same economic issues as do factor movements involving capital. But it also provokes responses on a very human level—about culture, rights, and identity. It promises to continue to be a controversial topic.

Conclusion: The Politics of International Investment

International finance is the most globalized portion of the international economy. People and governments worldwide try mightily to attract foreign corporations and to qualify for loans from foreign lenders. There are substantial advantages to having access to the world's enormous pool of capital. This gives governments powerful reasons to try to collaborate with foreign investors to smooth the path of capital as it moves from country to country.

However, international finance is not an unmitigated blessing. Foreign loans can be a boon to a developing nation, but they can become an oppressive burden that forces the population to make huge sacrifices in order for their government to keep up interest payments. Foreign investment by MNCs can bring a country

---

24. Like many other aspects of immigration, the fiscal costs and benefits of immigrants are hotly debated, even among scholars. For two contending views, both from conservative think tanks, see Robert E. Rector, Christine Kim, and Shanea Watkins, "The Fiscal Cost of Low-Skill Households to the U.S. Taxpayer," *Heritage Foundation Special Report* 12 (April 4, 2007); and Daniel Griswold, "The Fiscal Impact of Immigration Reform: The Real Story," *Free Trade Bulletin* 30 (May 21, 2007).

valuable technology and expertise, but it can also impose severe constraints on the room for maneuver of the host nation. Governments have many interests in common with international financiers, but they also have many conflicting interests.

International finance is inherently political because powerful private actors, governments, and international institutions all come together to bargain over the terms of international financial relations. Such negotiations—over foreign loans, debt bailouts, IMF packages, the role of MNCs, and other financial issues—can be contentious. The policies associated with them are also often very controversial within nations, which adds to the problems' politicization.

Certainly, international financial flows can be a powerful force for development and economic progress. Many countries, past and present, have used foreign capital to finance rapid economic growth and development. And many individuals, groups, and companies have benefited from their access to international finance. However, when things go wrong in the international financial system, they can go spectacularly wrong in ways that can profoundly impact international politics—and the lives of billions of people.

Study Tool Kit

Interests, Interactions, and Institutions in Context

- Within borrowing nations, there are many actors who value access to foreign funds. However, there are others who resent the constraints and burdens that foreign investments sometimes impose on debtors. Similar conflicting interests exist within lending nations.

- At the international level, both lenders and borrowers, like investors and recipients of investment, have a common interest in sustaining capital flows, which benefit both sides. Nonetheless, they may enter into conflict—especially over how the benefits from the loans or investments will be divided.

- Lenders and borrowers, and investors and recipients, bargain over the investments that tie them together. There is frequent disagreement over debt payments to foreign creditors and profit payments to foreign corporations.

- An array of important and influential international institutions structure interactions in the international financial realm. The most prominent is the IMF, which has often played a major role in managing the problems of heavily indebted countries. Like international finance generally, the role of the IMF is very controversial: some analysts think it contributes to the cooperative resolution of financial problems while others think that it takes unfair advantage of struggling debtor nations.

Key Terms

portfolio investment, p. 343

sovereign lending, p. 343

foreign direct investment (FDI), p. 343

World Bank, p. 348

recession, p. 350

depression, p. 350

default, p. 351

austerity, p. 353

Bank for International Settlements, p. 355

International Monetary Fund (IMF), p. 356

multinational corporation (MNC), p. 366

bilateral investment treaty, p. 371

For Further Reading

Chinn, Menzie D., and Jeffry A. Frieden. *Lost Decades: The Making of America's Debt Crisis and the Long Recovery.* New York: Norton, 2011. Analyzes the politics and economics of the biggest financial crisis since the Great Depression.

Copelovitch, Mark. *The International Monetary Fund in the Global Economy: Banks, Bonds and Bailouts.* Cambridge: Cambridge University Press, 2010. Analyzes the politics and economics of the role of the IMF in resolving international debt conflicts.

Mosley, Layna. *Labor Rights and Multinational production.* Cambridge: Cambridge University Press, 2011. Assess the impact of FDI on the rights and oppotunies available to workers in developing countries.

Obstfeld, Maurice, and Alan Taylor. *Global Capital Markets: Integration, Crisis, and Growth.* Cambridge: Cambridge University Press, 2004. Provides a detailed description and analysis of the history and contemporary nature of international financial markets.

Pandya, Sonal. *Trading Spaces: Foreign Direct Investment Regulation, 1970–2000.* Cambridge: Cambridge University Press, 2014. Analyzes the politics and economics of national responses to foreign corporations.

Singer, David. *Regulating Capital: Setting Standards for the International Financial System.* Ithaca, NY: Cornell University Press, 2007. Analyzes the economics and politics of international financial regulation in a world of global financial markets.

Tomz, Michael. *Reputation and International Cooperation: Sovereign Debt across Three Centuries.* Princeton, NJ: Princeton University Press, 2007. Explores the politics and economics of private lending to governments historically and in the present.

Vreeland, James. *The International Monetary Fund: Politics of Conditional Lending.* New York: Routledge, 2007. Presents an analytical survey of one of the world's most controversial international organizations.

Walter, Stefanie. *Financial Crises and the Politics of Macroeconomic Adjustments.* Cambridge: Cambridge University Press, 2013. Explains the causes and consequences of financial crises, and government responses to them, with both historical and contemporary applications.

International Monetary Relations

THE PUZZLE *In the absence of global government, how are international currencies supplied and international monetary relations regulated?*

Above: International monetary relations are often controversial. Today, the European Central Bank in Frankfurt, Germany, implements monetary policies for the entire eurozone, which comprises 19 member countries that gave up their national currencies for the euro.

On December 18, 2001, rioters swept through the cities of Argentina. They were furious about three straight years of economic stagnation and government economic policies that seemed to make matters worse. Most recently, the government had frozen bank deposits so that Argentines could take only small amounts of cash out of their bank accounts—and nothing out of the very popular accounts that many people had in U.S. dollars. In response to the rioting, President Fernando de la Rúa declared a state of siege, but the following day the disorder spread as hundreds of thousands of middle-class Argentines joined the protests in the streets. That evening, the economy minister stepped down. A day later, violent clashes with the police led to more than two dozen deaths around the country, and huge crowds surrounded the presidential palace in Buenos Aires. At the end of the day, de la Rúa resigned and was evacuated by helicopter from the presidential palace to avoid the hostile crowds.

The president of the Senate, a member of the opposition Peronist Party that controlled both houses of Congress, assumed the interim presidency. Two days later, the Peronists installed provincial governor Adolfo Rodríguez Saá as president until national elections could

be held. Rodríguez Saá declared the largest default in history—on $93 billion in sovereign debt. But he too faced protests and resigned a week after taking office. This time the president of the Chamber of Deputies, also a Peronist, stepped in as interim president. After further turmoil, the legislature appointed to the presidency Eduardo Duhalde, the Peronist candidate who had lost the 1999 presidential election to the now disgraced de la Rúa. Meanwhile, the country had entered full-fledged economic collapse. Argentine gross domestic product (GDP), which had declined by 8 percent over the three previous years of recession, dropped by 11 percent in 2002, and unemployment soared above 20 percent.

The ultimate reason for these extraordinary events—nationwide riots, five presidents in less than two weeks, the biggest default in history, economic disintegration—was the Argentine government's policies toward its currency. Ten years earlier, the government had made the Argentine peso equal to one U.S. dollar and fixed it at this exchange rate. The currency policy led to rapid growth and many other economic achievements in Argentina. But by 2001 the commitment was dragging the economy downward. It was widely blamed for general economic stagnation and for the specific banking policies that provoked popular outrage. Argentina's fortunes rose dramatically, and fell even more dramatically, with its currency policies.

Many people who find currencies confusing or boring may be surprised that exchange rates could be responsible for such striking developments. But the Argentine events are not alone in illustrating the importance of currencies and currency policies to economics and politics—and to people's everyday lives. A couple of weeks after Argentine society exploded into violence over the exchange rate, and halfway around the world, came another, unrelated but equally remarkable, currency development. Twelve European countries abandoned their national monies, some of which had existed for centuries. In place of the Deutschmark, franc, lira, and other currencies, they adopted the euro, a common European currency. The creation of the euro dominated European politics and economics for most of the 1990s, and the early 2000s were spent consolidating, managing, and expanding the new currency. Then, in 2008, the global financial crisis hit the eurozone. The international economic slowdown brought a European borrowing boom to an end and plunged the continent into recession. The euro's problems festered until 2011, when accumulated sovereign debts plunged the eurozone, and the European Union (EU), into a crisis that constituted the gravest threat in its history. European currency politics—the euro's rise, creation, evolution, and crisis—have been central to the continent's political economy for 30 years. Argentina and Europe are not alone: in many countries, currency policy is one of the most hotly contested economic and political issues.

National governments have pursued very different policies toward their national currencies. Today, most governments choose among three monetary paths. One option is to give up the national currency in favor of another money—as has occurred in a number of Caribbean and Latin American countries, which have adopted the U.S. dollar, and in most European countries, which have adopted the euro. Other governments have tied the national currency's value to that of another country, such as the dollar or the euro (as we will discuss in more detail below). Finally, many governments continue to maintain a separate national currency whose value is allowed to change in response to markets and other forces. How and why do governments choose any one of these three monetary paths? The international monetary order has also varied enormously over the years. As we saw in Chapter 1, from the 1870s until 1914 most of the world's major economies were on a classical gold standard that tied their currencies together. After World War II, a revised version of this approach, the Bretton Woods monetary system, reigned until 1973. Since then, international and regional currency arrangements have been in flux.

Thinking Analytically about International Monetary Relations

This chapter makes several points about the interests, interactions, and institutions associated with international monetary policy. First, within each country, there are many actors who have an interest in the country's monetary affairs, which leads to conflict over the appropriate currency policy to pursue. We will see, briefly, how national currency policies are set and which groups have a stake in those policies.

In addition to individual national choices, there are important global monetary issues. Indeed, international monetary affairs—the interrelationships among national monies—are central to the international economy and thus to world politics. Stable relations among national currencies allow actors in one country to make payments to actors in other countries, making it easier for goods, people, and capital to move across borders—all important forms of international interaction. Just as it is hard to imagine national economies without national money, it is hard to see how the modern world economy could function without some arrangement for cooperation in the use of money among countries.

Yet, while national governments supply national monies, there is no international government to organize international monetary affairs. Virtually everyone has an interest in the existence of a functioning international monetary system, but different arrangements benefit some actors more than others. This leads to disagreements about how such a system should be organized. How is such a quintessentially governmental function as the provision of currencies carried out at the global level in the absence of global government?

What Are Exchange Rates, and Why Do They Matter?

A national monetary system allows for the convenient exchange of goods, services, and capital. It is a classic public good (see Chapter 2): it benefits everyone, but because people cannot be excluded from its benefits and charged for them, there is little incentive for private firms to provide it. This is why national governments typically determine the currency, print bills, mint coins, and control the money supply. It is also why governments try to instill trust in the national currency. Almost everyone in a country can agree on the desirability of a recognizable, trustworthy national money and stable prices. But in addition to a currency's domestic use, it exists in relation to other national currencies. For example, the U.S. dollar can be used not only to buy goods and services in the United States but also to buy euros, Canadian dollars, and Mexican pesos, among other currencies. The price of a national currency relative to other national currencies is its **exchange rate**, and like other prices, the exchange rate can go up or down. When the dollar goes up in value against some other currency—such that, for example, a dollar can buy more pesos—it is said to strengthen or **appreciate**. When the dollar's value goes down against that of some other currency—such that, for example, a dollar can buy fewer pesos—it is said to weaken or **depreciate**, or to be **devalued**.

When a country's currency appreciates, it is more expensive for foreigners to buy the country's goods and services; when the currency depreciates, it is cheaper to do so. The most direct experience that many people have with currency movements is as tourists or, if they live near a national border, with prices around the border. American travelers to Europe find, for example, that when the dollar is strong, local prices in Europe seem relatively low. The hotels they stay in, the restaurants they go to, and the souvenirs they purchase are relatively inexpensive. However, when the dollar weakens, local prices get much higher. For example, in May 2014 an American staying in an Italian hotel charging 100 euros a night would have been paying about $140 a night, because the euro was worth 1.40 dollars; a year later, with the euro worth 1.09 dollars, the same hotel room at the same euro price would have cost the American $109 a night. The dollar had appreciated by about 20 percent against the euro, so goods and services in euro countries, such as Italy, cost 20 percent less. (See Figure 9.1 for an indication of how the value of the dollar has fluctuated against the euro.)

The same is true of goods bought and sold across borders. If a currency goes up or down, the prices that foreigners pay for goods priced in that currency rise or fall as well. So a pair of Italian shoes that cost 100 euros in Italy in May 2014 could have been exported to the United States and sold for around $140 dollars (plus shipping costs), while a year later, after the euro had depreciated by about 20 percent, the same 100-euro Italian shoes would have sold for $114 dollars. When the U.S. dollar is weak against other currencies, foreign goods are expensive to Americans;

exchange rate
The price at which one currency is exchanged for another.

appreciate
In terms of a currency, to increase in value in terms of other currencies.

depreciate
In terms of a currency, to decrease in value in terms of other currencies.

devalue
To reduce the value of one currency in terms of other currencies.

FIGURE 9.1   *The Value of the U.S. Dollar, 1975–2014*

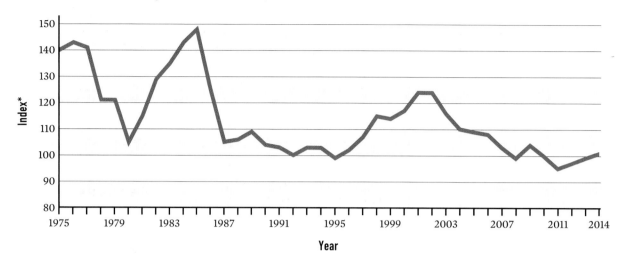

Figure source: World Bank, World Development Indicators, http://data.worldbank.org/indicator (accessed 06/01/15).

*Real effective exchange rate index. The real effective exchange rate index is a measure of the value of the dollar against a weighted average of the currencies of the United States' major trading partners. The base year, 2010, is given the value of 100. Higher values indicate a stronger (more appreciated) dollar relative to the world's major currencies, and lower values indicate a weaker (depreciated) dollar.

however, when the U.S. dollar is strong against other currencies, foreign goods are inexpensive to Americans.

Although the attractiveness of a given country to foreign tourists is not particularly important to most nations, the attractiveness of that country's goods, services, and investment opportunities is crucial. Thus, the exchange rate is a very important part of a country's international economic relations.

How Are Currency Values Determined?

Like other prices, an exchange rate goes up or down in response to changes in supply and demand. There are many factors that can affect supply and demand for a national money. Perhaps the most relevant is relative interest rates. As we saw in Chapter 8, foreigners considering investing in a country weigh relative interest rates; if interest rates are higher in the United States, investments in the United States are more attractive (everything else being equal).[1] But in order to invest in the United States, investors need dollars. Higher interest rates make it more profitable for people to put (or keep) their money in the country, so higher interest rates increase the demand for the currency and lead to its appreciation. Of course, the relationship works in the opposite direction as well: if people want fewer dollars, its exchange rate will go down. Lower interest rates can lead to a depreciation of the currency, just as higher interest rates can lead to an appreciation. More generally, if foreigners want to invest in a country, they have to buy its currency; so if there is a lot of investment into an economy, demand for its currency will rise and the exchange rate will tend to appreciate. When foreigners invest heavily in the United States, all else equal, the dollar strengthens.

---

1. For convenience, we ignore trade-related sources of currency movements. It should be clear that anything that makes a country's goods and services more attractive to foreigners will increase demand for the country's currency and lead to an appreciation (and vice versa).

The relationship between interest rates and the value of the national currency is particularly important because governments routinely raise and lower interest rates as part of their **monetary policy**. Indeed, monetary policy is a powerful tool of national governments; in most developed countries, it is implemented by the **central bank** (for example, the Federal Reserve in the United States). National monetary policy refers to government attempts to affect macroeconomic conditions—unemployment, inflation, overall economic growth—by manipulating monetary conditions. Central banks most commonly affect monetary conditions by raising or lowering interest rates. If the central bank wants to stimulate the economy, it lowers interest rates. Lower interest rates make it easier for people and companies to borrow and allow the economy to expand. If the central bank wants to restrain the economy, typically because prices are rising and there is concern about inflation, it raises interest rates; this makes it harder to borrow and restrains demand.

Because interest rates also affect the exchange rate—higher interest rates make the currency more attractive and tend to raise its value—national monetary policy can also have a powerful impact on the value of the national currency. And this too can be a tool of national economic policy. For example, if a government wants to stimulate demand for its country's products in world markets, it can lower interest rates so that the currency depreciates. The weaker currency makes local goods cheaper to foreigners and spurs exports; it also makes foreign goods more expensive to local residents and reduces imports. In this way, a monetary policy that weakens the currency can help the nation's producers. Of course, a weaker currency means citizens can buy less with their money, so the government has to choose which effects it finds most appealing.

Allowing the Exchange Rate to Change

There are other choices facing a national government with respect to its currency. Among these, the most important is whether and how to let the exchange rate change relative to others. The simplest choice is whether to "fix" the exchange rate or let it "float." A **fixed exchange rate** is one whose government promises to keep the national money at some established value in terms of another currency or of a precious metal such as gold. During the period of the classical **gold standard**, from the 1870s to 1914, a country's government "went on gold" by promising to exchange its currency for gold at an established rate (in the United States, it was one troy ounce of gold for $20.67). This move made the country's currency equivalent to gold and interchangeable at a fixed rate with the money of any other gold-standard country. Much of the world, as a result, essentially shared one currency. Gold-backed money invested by Germans in Japan, or by Belgians in Canada, would be paid back in equivalent amounts of gold-backed money. Contracted prices would not fluctuate, for exchange rates did not change. A government that commits itself to a fixed exchange rate also commits itself to the policies necessary to maintain the set rate. For example, if the currency was posed to depreciate against other currencies, meaning the

monetary policy
An important tool of national governments to influence broad macroeconomic conditions such as unemployment, inflation, and economic growth. Typically, governments alter their monetary policies by changing national interest rates or exchange rates.

central bank
The institution that regulates monetary conditions in an economy, typically by affecting interest rates and the quantity of money in circulation.

fixed exchange rate
An exchange rate policy under which a government commits itself to keep its currency at or around a specific value in terms of another currency or a commodity, such as gold.

gold standard
The monetary system that prevailed between about 1870 and 1914, in which countries tied their currencies to gold at a legally fixed price.

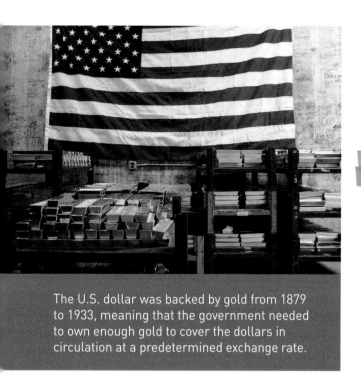

The U.S. dollar was backed by gold from 1879 to 1933, meaning that the government needed to own enough gold to cover the dollars in circulation at a predetermined exchange rate.

exchange rate would fall, the government might raise interest rates to have money keep coming into the country—in other words, so foreigners would buy the country's currency. This increase in demand for the currency would make the exchange rate go back up to the set level.

At the other extreme is a **floating exchange** rate, under which a currency's value is allowed to change more or less freely, driven by markets or other factors. This is the regime currently in place for most major currencies, including the U.S. dollar, the Japanese yen, and the euro. If a government chooses this exchange rate regime, the price of the currency moves around in line with changes in supply and demand. Map 9.1 on p. 388 indicates which countries worldwide follow fixed versus floating exchange rate regimes.

There are intermediate steps between a fully fixed currency and a freely floating one. A government can allow its currency to vary but only within limits, or it can fix the exchange rate for short periods, changing the currency's value as desired. This approach avoids some of the costs of each system but also forgoes some of the benefits. At the global level, the **Bretton Woods monetary system**, which followed the classical gold standard and prevailed from 1945 to 1973, was something of a compromise. It was based on a fixed rate and a gold standard for the United States and on a "fixed but adjustable rate" for other currencies that were on a dollar standard. This system of fixed but adjustable rates (an **adjustable peg**) required that governments keep currency values fixed for relatively long periods but permitted them to alter ("adjust") them if and when governments found it desirable to do so. In practice, the Bretton Woods monetary system meant that the U.S. dollar's value could not change (it was fixed at $35 per ounce of gold). Other governments also fixed their currency against the dollar, but the national government of a country other than the United States could devalue or readjust its currency's value if it felt a change was necessary. Typically, such changes were infrequent, occurring once every five to seven years. The Bretton Woods monetary system was seen as a middle ground between gold-standard rigidity and complete unpredictability. As under the gold standard, exchange rates were stable enough to encourage international trade and investment. As under a more flexible system, the exchange rates could be varied as necessary, albeit rarely.

As these examples indicate, a national government's decisions about the exchange rate often depend on international monetary conditions. While national policies are important, from the standpoint of international economics and politics more generally it is the *global* nature of international monetary relations that is most relevant. We will return to these international issues below. First, however, we evaluate the potential for *domestic* conflicts of interest over exchange rate policy.

floating exchange rate

An exchange rate policy under which a government permits its currency to be traded on the open market without direct government control or intervention.

Bretton Woods monetary system

The monetary order negotiated among the World War II allies in 1944, which lasted until the 1970s and which was based on a U.S. dollar tied to gold. Other currencies were fixed to the dollar but were permitted to adjust their exchange rates.

adjustable peg

A monetary system of fixed but adjustable rates. Governments are expected to keep their currencies fixed for extensive periods but are permitted to adjust the exchange rate from time to time as economic conditions change.

Who Cares about Exchange Rates, and Why?

A national government's decision about its exchange rate leads the country to take other policies to support its decision. Both the initial currency policy and the other economic measures needed to sustain it affect different domestic groups differently. This can lead to disagreement over the appropriate currency policy to pursue.

Governments

A government deciding what to do with its currency must consider important trade-offs and domestic interests that are often in conflict. One dimension of conflict involves whether the currency should be fixed, floating, or in between. Each choice helps some domestic actors and hurts others.

Fixed exchange rates, such as the gold standard or a peg to the dollar, provide currency stability and predictability, which greatly facilitate international trade, investment, finance, migration, and travel. Under the gold standard, businessmen, investors, and immigrants did not have to worry about changes in exchange rates or about major impediments to moving money around the world. The stimulus to trade was substantial; being on gold in this period is estimated to have raised trade between two countries by between 30 and 70 percent.[2] Generally speaking, a fixed currency provides stability that facilitates international economic exchange; it also provides a monetary anchor that keeps prices stable. It is thus very much in the interest of those engaged in cross-border trade, investment, finance, and travel, as well as those who want to keep inflation low.

However, there are costs to fixing the exchange rate, so some people and governments are strongly opposed to it. By definition, a government on a fixed exchange rate is committed to maintaining its currency's value, even if economic conditions could be improved with a change. A fixed rate reduces or eliminates a government's ability to have its own independent monetary policy, which can be costly. For example, if an economy is in recession, a common economic policy response is to lower interest rates and thereby promote borrowing to expand consumption and investment. This move stimulates the economy, as mentioned above, and may help alleviate the recession. But if a country is on a fixed exchange rate, its interest rates are dictated by the need to keep the currency's value constant. For example, the government will raise interest rates if the exchange rate threatens to depreciate, in order to encourage investors to buy the currency. This is the case even in difficult economic times, when there can be strong pressures

---

2. See, for example, A. Estevadeordal, B. Frantz, and A. M. Taylor, "The Rise and Fall of World Trade, 1870–1939," *Quarterly Journal of Economics* 118 (May 2003): 359–407; and J. Ernesto Lopez-Cordova and Christopher M. Meissner, "Exchange-Rate Regimes and International Trade: Evidence from the Classical Gold Standard Era," *American Economic Review* 93, no. 1 (2003): 344–53.

MAP 9.1 *Exchange Rate Regimes, 2013*

Today, several of the world's major economies, including the United States and Japan, allow the value of their currency to float independently. However, exchange rate regimes around the world span a wide spectrum, from those that have given up their national currency, such as countries in the eurozone, to those that peg the value of their currency to the dollar, the euro, or other currencies. Countries with a "crawling peg" or "managed floating currency" can be considered to have a floating exchange rate, though with some limits on changes in the value of the currency.

FIXED RATE REGIMES

No national currency

- USES DOLLAR
- USES EURO
- USES CFA FRANC

Fixed peg arrangements

- PEGGED TO DOLLAR
- PEGGED TO EURO
- PEGGED TO "OTHER"

FLOATING RATE REGIMES

- CRAWLING PEG
- MANAGED FLOATING CURRENCY
- INDEPENDENTLY FLOATING CURRENCY

GREENLAND (DENMARK)

ICELAND

ALASKA

CANADA

Pacific Ocean

Atlantic Ocean

UNITED STATES

BAHAMAS
HAITI
DOMINICAN REP.
PUERTO RICO
DOMINICA

MEXICO
CUBA
BELIZE
GUATEMALA
HONDURAS
EL SALVADOR
NICARAGUA
COSTA RICA
PANAMA

VENEZUELA
GUYANA
SURINAME
COLOMBIA

ECUADOR
PERU
BRAZIL
BOLIVIA

PARAGUAY
URUGUAY
ARGENTINA
CHILE

Map source: International Monetary Fund, "De Facto Classification of Exchange Rate Regimes and Monetary Policy Frameworks," April 31, 2008, www.imf.org/external/np/mfd/er/2008/eng/0408.htm (accessed 10/27/14).

388

Arctic Ocean

RUSSIA

UNITED
KINGDOM
NORWAY
SWEDEN
FINLAND

GERMANY
NETH.
IRELAND
FRANCE
BELARUS
UKRAINE
SLOVAK
GEORGIA
KAZAKHSTAN
MONGOLIA
N. KOREA
S. KOREA
JAPAN

ITALY
SERBIA
PORTUGAL SPAIN GREECE
TURKEY
UZBEKISTAN
KYRGYZSTAN
TURKMENISTAN TAJIKISTAN
CHINA
HONG KONG

ISRAEL LEB. SYRIA
IRAQ IRAN
MOROCCO
JORDAN
KUWAIT
NEPAL BHUTAN
MYANMAR
(BURMA)
TAIWAN

ALGERIA LIBYA EGYPT
SAUDI
ARABIA
UAE
OMAN
PAKISTAN
INDIA
VIETNAM

MAURITANIA MALI NIGER CHAD
ERITREA
YEMEN
AFGHANISTAN
THAILAND
PHILIPPINES

NEGAL
SUDAN
BANGLADESH
LAOS
CAMBODIA
PALAU

GUINEA NIGERIA
CEN.
AFR.
REP. S. SUDAN ETHIOPIA
SOMALIA
SRI LANKA
MALAYSIA
MICRONESIA

GHANA
CAMEROON
UGANDA
KENYA

IVORY COAST
D.R.
CONGO
INDONESIA
PAPUA NEW GUINEA

TANZANIA
Indian Ocean

ANGOLA
MALAWI

ZAMBIA
MADAGASCAR

NAMIBIA
MOZAMBIQUE
ZIMBABWE
AUSTRALIA

SOUTH
AFRICA

BOTSWANA

NEW
ZEALAND

Pacific Ocean

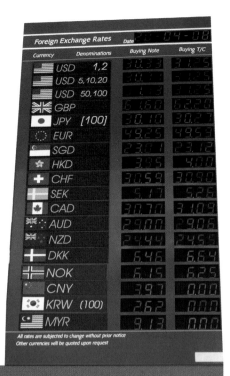

Foreign Exchange Rates	Date		
Currency	Denominations	Buying Note	Buying T/C
USD	1,2		
USD	5,10,20		
USD	50,100		
GBP			
JPY	[100]		
EUR			
SGD			
HKD			
CHF			
SEK			
CAD			
AUD			
NZD			
DKK			
NOK			
CNY			
KRW	(100)		
MYR			

All rates are subjected to change without prior notice
Other currencies will be quoted upon request

Travelers to foreign countries find that their money goes further when their country's currency is strong relative to the local currency. The same is true when goods are traded across borders; buyers find that foreign goods are less expensive when their own currency is relatively stronger.

for the government to allow the currency to depreciate so as to make the country's goods more attractive to foreign consumers. The government's commitment to a fixed exchange rate makes this impossible. More generally, producers of goods that compete on import or export markets might want the government to be able to change the currency's value so that it becomes easier for them to sell their products. But this is impossible with a fixed exchange rate.

Both of these fixed-currency constraints were at work in the run-up to the 2001 Argentine crisis, and in the eurozone crisis that began in 2008. In 2001, the Argentine peso had been tightly fixed to the U.S. dollar for 10 years, but the Argentine economy was in great distress. There were powerful pressures for the government to address broader economic conditions—in particular, to lower interest rates and to depreciate the currency so that Argentine goods would become more competitive on international markets. To carry out this strategy, the Argentine government needed to loosen the peso's link to the dollar. But at the same time, many Argentines did not want to see the peso's value change; among them were millions of homeowners whose mortgages were in dollars and who would have had to pay substantially more in pesos if the currency were devalued. With powerful interests on both sides, the Argentine government was paralyzed.

Members of the eurozone faced a similar instance of the constraints of a fixed exchange rate after 2008. As the global financial crisis deepened, and the European debt crisis worsened, some countries that used the euro, such as Greece, Spain, and Portugal, faced severe economic difficulties. If those countries had their own national monies, they could have loosened monetary policy and depreciated their currencies. This would have made their goods cheaper for other countries, increasing the amount of goods they exported, and thus bringing more money back into the country. By selling more, their economies would grow faster, and perhaps, they could have exported their way out of recession. But these nations were part of a multicountry currency union, whose monetary and exchange rate policies were set in Frankfurt by the European Central Bank (ECB) on behalf of the entire eurozone. This meant that the governments of these nations simply did not have the tools of monetary and exchange rate policy in their arsenals as they attempted to confront the crisis.

As these examples demonstrate, the great advantage of a floating exchange rate is that it gives a government more freedom to pursue its own monetary policies, as it is not hampered by the need to keep the exchange rate fixed. But this advantage is countered by the fact that floating exchange rates can move around a great deal, which can impose costs on those engaged in international trade and investment, and which more generally can impede international economic exchange. Volatility (that is, frequent significant shifts) in currency values almost certainly makes international trade and investment, travel, and finance more difficult.[3]

Consumers and Businesses

Different actors have different interests, and often conflicting views, about how the national currency should be managed, depending on their position in the economy. Those whose economic activities are entirely domestic are likely to favor a floating exchange rate, because they are indifferent to currency fluctuations but want the government to be able to affect the national economy as necessary. Those with international economic concerns have an interest in a fixed currency, because too much volatility in exchange rates can be harmful to their activities.

Just as people, firms, and groups may have conflicting interests over whether a currency should be fixed or floating, actors' interests may also differ over a currency's desirable value (that is, whether it should be stronger or weaker). Government policy can have a powerful impact on whether a currency's value rises or falls in the short and medium run, which in turn can affect important domestic interests.

A strong exchange rate allows consumers and others to buy more of the world's products, thereby increasing national purchasing power. But there is a trade-off: a strong exchange rate makes domestic goods more expensive to foreigners, which harms national producers who compete with foreigners on local or world markets. This is why manufacturers and farmers typically complain about a strong currency: it leads to a surge of cheaper imports, and it dampens exports. For example, the U.S. dollar appreciated by more than 50 percent between 1981 and 1985. This was associated with a big increase in Americans' purchasing power and ability to buy goods from the rest of the world—all of which contributed to a sense of prosperity among American consumers. However, the strong dollar led to a flood of cheaper imports into the United States and made American exports more expensive to foreigners. This caused serious problems in American manufacturing industries and led to the loss of 1.5 million manufacturing jobs. The strong dollar was particularly damaging to firms that either sold many of their products abroad or competed with imports; it led the president of one such firm, Caterpillar Tractors, to call the strong dollar "the single most important trade issue facing the U.S." Under this pressure, in 1985 the Senate passed a unanimous resolution calling on the administration to depreciate the dollar.[4] Eventually, the dollar did decline, and complaints subsided.

---

3. The specific constraints on exchange-rate policy are known as the Mundell–Fleming conditions, after the two economists who pioneered the approach. They imply, simply put, that in a financially integrated country the government must choose between a stable exchange rate and an independent monetary policy; it cannot have both. See, for example, Jeffry Frieden, "Invested Interests: The Politics of National Economic Policies in a World of Global Finance," *International Organization* 45, no. 4 (Autumn 1991): 407–31.

4. Jeffry Frieden, "Economic Integration and the Politics of Monetary Policy in the United States," in *Internationalization and Domestic Politics*, ed. Robert Keohane and Helen Milner, 127–30 (Cambridge: Cambridge University Press, 1996).

A weak currency gives a big boost to national producers. This is why countries that are trying to encourage exports—such as many developing countries—typically keep their currencies weak. It is also why manufacturers and farmers, who compete with foreign producers both at home and abroad, have an interest in a relatively weak exchange rate. But there is a trade-off here, too: a weak currency reduces national purchasing power, making consumers worse off. As the dollar declines, Americans can buy less of the world's products—and tourists cannot afford foreign vacations so easily. As a currency declines and prices of foreign goods rise, this can also contribute to overall price rises and inflation.

Both strong and weak currencies have advantages and disadvantages, and there is no particular reason that one or the other is better for a country. A strong currency helps consumers (and tourists) but hurts producers who compete with foreigners; a weak currency helps producers but hurts consumers. These conflicts of interest make currency policy controversial within countries and can make governments sensitive to the domestic political and economic effects of their currency arrangements. Such conflicts are evident when the possibility arises that a government might devalue its currency. Because the devaluation makes foreign goods more expensive and domestic goods relatively cheaper, it is in the interests of national producers. But the devaluation also reduces consumers' ability to buy goods and services. In this context, it is perhaps not surprising that governments in democratic systems typically avoid currency devaluations or depreciations in the run-up to elections, for fear that the negative impact on consumers will cost them votes.[5]

A government's interest in exchange rate policy depends on the structure of its economy, its interest groups, and its political system. In a country with many firms and individuals engaged in economic activities across borders, the government is likely to face powerful pressure to stabilize or fix the currency's value. This is why the smaller economies of Europe that were extremely open to trade with other European countries (the Netherlands, Belgium, Luxembourg, Austria, Ireland) were among the strongest supporters of the creation of the euro. However, some larger European economies that traded and invested less across European borders (like France and Italy) were less enthusiastic. This is also why, in the Western Hemisphere, small countries that are tightly tied in to U.S. trade, investment, and tourism (such as Caribbean island nations, El Salvador, and Panama) have been the most likely to adopt the U.S. dollar or to fix their currencies to it. Larger, more self-sufficient economies (like Mexico and Brazil) have typically allowed their currencies to vary.

One currency policy has been the source of much controversy in recent decades, and that is the tendency of some governments to keep their currency very weak over long periods of time in order to stimulate their exports. The most prominent example is that of China, which since 1979 has organized its development

---

5. S. Brock Blomberg, Jeffry Frieden, and Ernesto Stein, "Sustaining Fixed Rates: The Political Economy of Currency Pegs in Latin America," *Journal of Applied Economics* 8, no. 2 (November 2005): 203–25.

strategy around the promotion of manufactured goods for export. A major part of this strategy has involved keeping the Chinese currency, the renminbi, artificially weak. The export promotion policy has been very successful, and China has become one of the world's greatest exporters. But if the government let the dollars its exporters earned come back into the Chinese economy, they would be used to buy renminbi for local purchases, and the renminbi would appreciate against the dollar. However, this would make Chinese exports less attractive on world markets. So the Chinese government uses a series of measures to keep its currency depreciated. It controls capital flows and the domestic market for foreign currency; and the government also holds very large reserves of dollars overseas (keeping them from coming back to China to be spent).

The Chinese government's currency policies have been very successful at promoting the nation's exports. But they have created problems both at home and abroad. Within China, the weak-currency policy is effectively taxing consumers to benefit export producers. An artificially weak renminbi means that Chinese residents have artificially low purchasing power. There have been complaints from Chinese consumers and the country's growing middle class that the average Chinese has not gotten the full benefit of the country's rapid economic growth and that disproportionate benefits have gone to the export producers. Another set of problems is international: China's trading partners, in particular the United States, have complained with increasing vehemence that the artificial weakness of the renminbi is an unfair trading practice. This dispute has threatened to break

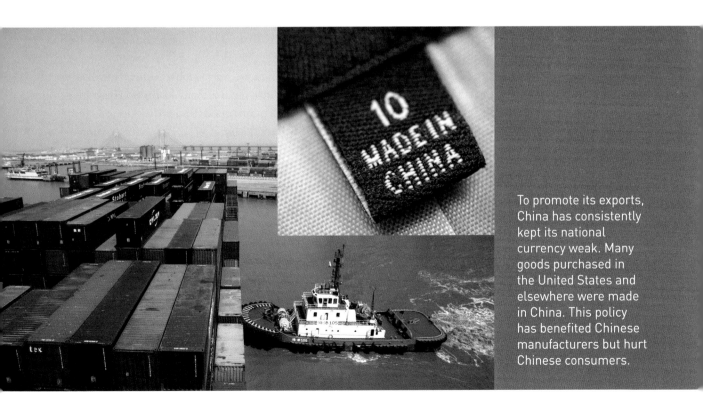

To promote its exports, China has consistently kept its national currency weak. Many goods purchased in the United States and elsewhere were made in China. This policy has benefited Chinese manufacturers but hurt Chinese consumers.

into open trade conflict between the United States and China on many occasions since 2000.

National currency policy implicates contending interests and complex institutions within countries. As disputes over China's currency indicate, the matter is doubly complicated because one government's exchange rate policy inevitably affects other countries' policies. This observation takes us to the international level, where national governments with interests in conflict, and in common, interact over the structure of the international monetary system.

Can There Be World Money without World Government?

A monetary system is crucial to any modern economy; this is also true of the international economy, which requires some institutional arrangement to permit trade, investment, and other payments across borders. A *national* monetary order provides predictability in the value of a trusted money and thus in the prices of goods; this is widely seen as one of the core functions of the institutions of national government. An *international* monetary order does the same for prices across borders—which means that it has to provide predictability in currency values. If traders, investors, tourists, and others had no idea what exchange rates would be tomorrow or next week, they would be very reluctant to engage in exchange across borders. For the international economy to work well, there must be some predictability to currency values so that people can reasonably expect that the dollar or peso they are earning today will be worth something tomorrow.

However, there is no global institution to provide a global monetary order. In the absence of world government and a world money, many institutional arrangements have emerged to provide this global public good. Under the classical gold standard of the nineteenth and early twentieth centuries, gold was the common denominator for international transactions. Under the Bretton Woods monetary system, which prevailed from 1945 to 1973, the dollar was the centerpiece of the monetary order. Some form of functioning global monetary system is in the interest of almost everyone.

But there can be disagreements over the nature of the international monetary system and every country's place in it; the different actors in the international political economy may have conflicting interests about the kinds of international monetary institutions they would like to see in place. As we will see later in this chapter, the classical gold standard was popular with some people but unpopular with others. Similarly, Americans were quite satisfied with a Bretton Woods monetary system that put the dollar at its center, but Europeans were less enthusiastic. Just as there are conflicting interests within countries over national policy, there are trade-offs and conflicts of interests among countries over international monetary arrangements.

When and Why Do Governments Agree on the Monetary Order?

Although there are many conflicts of interest in international monetary affairs, in the broad sense international agreement on a common monetary regime or system can be in everyone's interest, because it facilitates international exchange. After all, almost everyone wants to have a stable and predictable monetary arrangement that allows firms and people to compare prices and transact business from one nation to another. Governments and people tend to share a desire for a general commitment to a common regime. In this sense, a common international monetary order is a Pareto improvement over a world in which there is no agreement on global monetary relations.

However, governments and people often differ on the standard they would prefer. During the days of the classical gold standard, for example, there were many people and governments—including some powerful political movements—that preferred a silver standard to a gold standard. Supporters of silver typically believed that if money were the more plentiful silver, prices would be higher than with scarce gold and this would help raise the prices of goods they produced. During the decades of the Bretton Woods monetary system, there were frequent complaints by non-Americans over the role of the United States in the international monetary order. International monetary relations are infused with this tension between sources of conflict and reasons for cooperation.

International Monetary Cooperation and Conflict

It can be difficult for governments to agree on global monetary relations. At the international political level, the difficulties stem from inherent characteristics of international monetary affairs. Agreement on a monetary regime has many features of a public good: everyone benefits if there is a smoothly functioning way to carry out international economic transactions. However, as with most public goods, the provision of this monetary order is not automatic or easy. A functioning monetary order can require conscious efforts by national governments to alter their policies, or to contribute funds to stabilize currencies, or otherwise to help sustain the system. However, it can be difficult to organize collaboration among governments to provide such a public good because there are powerful incentives to free ride on the efforts of others. Governments of smaller countries might reason that their contributions are too trivial to matter and thus not participate; if enough governments follow this path, cooperation will break down. For example, a global fixed-rate system such as the gold standard can facilitate international trade and investment, but the government of a small country might decide that it can benefit from the global system without fixing its own currency and tying its hands. If enough countries take this route, the system will collapse.

A successful international monetary regime depends on interactions among the governments of the world's major economies. Their behavior sets the standards for the regime as a whole, and they need to address problems as they arise. However, governments also face major temptations to "cheat" on their international monetary commitments. In a fixed-rate regime, for example, one government might decide to devalue in order to make its producers' goods more competitive on world markets. Other countries might respond by also devaluing to allow their producers to match. The result is akin to the undesirable outcome of a Prisoner's Dilemma game (see the Special Topic appendix to Chapter 2). If every nation engages in competitive devaluations, the result is that all currencies end up being devalued, and nobody gains any advantage. Meanwhile, the currency turmoil can throw international monetary relations into disorder and uncertainty, thereby interfering with normal economic activities.

Interactions among national governments, facing incentives both to cooperate and to enter into conflict, have determined the character of international monetary relations, including the emergence of global and regional monetary institutions. In the following section, we take a closer look at the evolution of international monetary arrangements over the past couple of centuries.

International Monetary Regimes

international monetary regime

A formal or informal arrangement among governments to govern relations among their currencies; the agreement is shared by most countries in the world economy.

National government decisions to float or to fix their currencies interact to create an **international monetary regime**—that is, an arrangement, which may be formal and institutionalized or informal, that is widely accepted to govern relations among currencies and that is shared by most countries in the world economy. There may also be regional monetary regimes that prevail in particular geographical regions, such as Europe with the euro.

The existence of a generally accepted international monetary regime has clear benefits for the international community in general, as it facilitates international economic exchange. It may come, however, at the cost of national sacrifices, which we will discuss below. First, we define the characteristics of international monetary regimes.

International monetary regimes have two principal features. The first makes clear whether currency values are expected to be fixed or floating or a mix of both. As discussed above, the classical gold standard and the Bretton Woods monetary system were international fixed-rate regimes (although the Bretton Woods monetary system allowed for occasional adjustments). The contemporary regime is based on floating rates; there is no general agreement that national currency values should be fixed.

The second feature of an international monetary regime is agreement about whether there will be a mutually accepted benchmark against which values are measured, some common base or standard to which currencies can be compared. Three such standards have been used over time: a commodity standard, a commodity-backed paper standard, and a national paper currency standard.

A *commodity standard* uses a good with value of its own as the basic monetary unit. Typically, this involves a precious metal such as gold or silver. Under the classical gold standard that prevailed from the 1870s until 1914, for example, all major national currencies had a fixed value in terms of gold, and they could be exchanged freely on the basis of their gold equivalent. This was a fixed-rate regime based on gold as the commodity standard.

A *commodity-backed paper standard* is similar to the Bretton Woods monetary system that prevailed from 1945 to 1973. Under such a regime, national governments issue paper currency with a fixed value in terms of gold (or some other commodity). This is one step removed from a pure gold standard, as it requires that governments be able to commit credibly to stand ready to redeem the currency for gold. Nonetheless, under such a standard, national currency values are comparable because they are all expressed in terms of a common commodity: gold. Under the Bretton Woods monetary system, the U.S. dollar was fixed to gold, while all other currencies were fixed to the dollar.

Under a *national paper currency standard*, national currencies are only backed by the commitments of their issuing governments to support them. In this context, people want to know that the government will act to ensure that the national currency continues be valuable. This may not mean committing to a fixed rate; it does mean committing to the currency not losing so much value as to become undesirable. Foreigners who hold dollars or euros, or who accept promises to pay in dollars or euros, do so with the expectation that even if exchange rates do change, dollars and euros will continue to be valuable national monies. Typically, only a few major currencies are used for international exchange—usually, the currencies of the world's most important trading and financial powers. This is the system that has prevailed since 1973. Today, most international exchange is measured and conducted in the dollar and the euro.

A Short History of International Monetary Systems

The modern international economy has experienced all three of these kinds of international monetary regimes.

The Gold Standard Under the classical gold standard, most of the world's major economies had gold or gold-backed currencies tied together at exchange rates that did not change for decades. The portion of the world that was on gold—which eventually came to include every major economy except China and Persia—effectively had a common money: gold.

The stability of the classical gold standard relied on close ties among the three leading financial powers of the day—Britain, France, and Germany—along with support from smaller European nations. For example, when the 1890 collapse of Barings, a major British bank, threatened to destabilize the London markets, the central banks of France and Russia lent large sums to the Bank of England. The mere knowledge that enough money was available to address the problem helped calm investors. In 1898, the British and French helped stabilize German financial markets; a few years later, the Austrians helped calm the Berlin market. And at least seven more times between 1900 and 1914, the French stepped in to assist the British in order to stabilize the gold standard.[6]

The gold standard provided currency stability and predictability, which greatly facilitated international trade, investment, finance, migration, and travel. Most of the world's governments and many countries' citizens agreed that this common monetary standard was generally beneficial. Such confluence of interests among the major financial centers allowed them to interact cooperatively to sustain the gold standard for many decades.

However, the costs to being on gold were such that some people and governments were less enthusiastic. As we saw in our discussion of a fixed-rate system, a government on the gold standard gave up its ability to run its own independent monetary policy, which implied a serious loss of economic policy influence. In the United States, the gold standard was very controversial; in fact, the 1896 presidential campaign was largely fought around it. William McKinley and the Republicans ran in favor of maintaining the American commitment to gold, but many Americans were hostile to the gold standard. The anti-gold forces, led by the Populists, wanted the government to take the dollar off gold and put it on silver at a different rate. This move would have accomplished two things: it would have devalued the dollar, making American exports more competitive, and it would have raised American prices. Farmers in particular liked the idea of a devaluation, as many of them produced for export markets. They, and others, also liked the idea of raising prices, as many of them were heavily indebted, and a rise in prices could have reduced their debt burden (the debts would have remained the same, while prices for farm products would have risen). As a result, the Democratic Party and the Populists united around William Jennings Bryan, who famously said to gold supporters, "You shall not crucify mankind upon a cross of gold!" Bryan lost in 1896 and again in 1900 and 1908, although the anti-gold movement he represented remained strong. (See "What Shaped Our World?" on p. 399 for more on this episode.) Nonetheless, there was enough domestic political support for the international cooperation necessary to sustain the gold standard that it was solid and extensive for almost 50 years, from the 1870s until 1914.

In the 1920s and 1930s, attempts to restore the classical gold standard were largely unsuccessful. Most countries did go on gold again after World War I ended, but the sort of international monetary cooperation that had allowed the classical gold standard to succeed had become difficult to organize. Countries such as France and Germany were on very poor terms diplomatically, which created an atmosphere of distrust that impeded efforts to negotiate monetary collaboration. As interests diverged, interactions among the major financial players became more hostile.

---

6. For a classic account of the gold standard era and its interwar collapse, see Barry Eichengreen, *Golden Fetters: The Gold Standard and the Great Depression, 1919–1939* (New York: Oxford University Press, 1992).

The Wizard of Oz and the Gold Standard

The gold standard was a central institution of the late nineteenth and early twentieth centuries. This international monetary system, and political battles over it, were so prominent that one of the most famous children's stories of all time may well be a parable about the politics of exchange rates in the gold-standard era.

The book *The Wonderful Wizard of Oz* was first published in 1900; it was turned into the film in 1939. The story chronicles the adventures of Dorothy, a girl from Kansas whose house is swept up in a tornado and transported to a magical place populated by munchkins, witches, and other strange creatures. The Good Witch of the North counsels Dorothy to follow the yellow brick road to the Emerald City and seek the help of the Wizard of Oz to return home to Kansas. The Good Witch also gives her a pair of magic slippers. Dorothy skips along the yellow brick road and meets a brainless scarecrow, a tin man without a heart, and a cowardly lion. Together, this motley team battles the Wicked Witch of the West to gain access to the venerable Wizard. At the end of the story, they realize that the Wizard is a fraud, but fortunately the Good Witch reappears and informs Dorothy that she can return home simply by clicking together her magic slippers.

What does *The Wizard of Oz* have to do with exchange rate politics? A little background on the gold standard will help to elucidate the symbolism in the story.

Institutions Starting in the 1870s, the U.S. government officially agreed to exchange dollars for gold at a fixed

rate of one ounce of gold for $20.67. This institution was intended to facilitate international trade and financial flows. However, one problem with this policy was that the domestic money supply was fixed based on the availability of gold. If businesses produced more goods and services but the stock of gold remained steady, then prices would fall. This was indeed the case throughout much of the 1880s and 1890s. Because the United States was on the gold standard, it was not able to lower interest rates or allow the currency to depreciate, both of which would have boosted prices and stimulated the economy.

Interests Falling prices harmed nearly everyone, but they were especially harmful to farmers who sold their grain on world markets and borrowed money from banks to finance their operations. With the price of grain declining, farmers had difficulty earning enough to repay their debts. Industrial workers also faced tough times as unemployment increased. The dire economic conditions of the 1890s helped to fuel the Populist movement, led by Democratic presidential candidate William Jennings Bryan. He wanted to replace the gold standard with an alternative system that would help increase the money supply—in particular, a system that included silver, a much more plentiful commodity. Bryan ultimately lost the 1896 election to William McKinley, a Republican who supported the gold standard.

Interactions With this background in mind, it is easy to see the symbolism in *The Wizard of Oz*, which was written just a few years after the 1896 election. Dorothy, representing the naive American public, believes that her problems will be solved if she simply follows a winding road paved with gold bricks. She meets a scarecrow (a farmer), a tin man (an industrial worker), and a lion whose roar masks his cowardice (Bryan). When Dorothy finally meets the Wizard (McKinley), she realizes that he is a fraud. In response, she simply clicks her slippers together to transport herself back home. In the original book, the slippers were silver.

The symbolism in *The Wizard of Oz* (note that *oz* is an abbreviation for *ounce*) reflects the political and cultural importance of different monetary systems.

This failure to cooperate in the 1920s was exacerbated by the Great Depression, which began in 1929. Faced with massive crises, governments were unwilling to forgo an economic policy that might allow them to alleviate the suffering of their citizens. After 1929, virtually all the governments that had gone on gold in the 1920s went back off it as they tried to resuscitate their failing national economies. The result was a floating-rate system based on paper national currencies. This led to a great deal of currency volatility and instability, including many competitive devaluations, and probably contributed to the overall collapse of the international economy in the 1930s. In any case, monetary disorder was overwhelmed by the economic and military conflicts of the 1930s and 1940s.

The Bretton Woods Monetary System As World War II drew to a close, the United States and Great Britain led the victorious Allies in designing an international monetary order—called the Bretton Woods monetary system because the agreements were negotiated at the Bretton Woods resort in New Hampshire— that represented a fundamental reform of the gold standard.[7] The Bretton Woods monetary system was organized around the U.S. dollar, and the dollar was tied to gold at the fixed rate of $35 per ounce. While other currencies were tied to the dollar, and thus indirectly to gold, they were permitted to be adjusted as necessary. This was seen as a middle ground between gold-standard rigidity and interwar insecurity. Like under the gold standard, exchange rates were stable enough to encourage international trade and investment. Unlike under the gold standard, governments other than the United States could change their currencies' values as needed, although frequent changes were frowned upon. The Bretton Woods monetary compromise kept currency values stable and currency markets open, contributing to the growth of international trade and investment while allowing national governments to pursue national policies in line with national conditions.

Like the gold standard, the Bretton Woods monetary system relied on collaboration among its leading members. It was sustained in large part because the Western allies after World War II saw it as an important component of their economic and military alliance structure, just as the West's willingness to undertake international trade liberalization was related to its geopolitical alliance. There was thus a confluence of both economic and noneconomic interests among Western nations that facilitated cooperation. This cooperation was reminiscent of that which prevailed during the classical gold standard: under Bretton Woods, as under the gold standard, for example, it was common for the world's major national central banks to lend money to each other in times of crisis.

Under the Bretton Woods monetary system, the International Monetary Fund (IMF) was established as the principal institution to monitor interstate interaction on exchange rates. During this period, the IMF was charged with overseeing

---

7. The term *Bretton Woods System* is sometimes used to describe the post–World War II international economic order more generally; we use the term *Bretton Woods monetary system* more narrowly to describe the currency order.

Representatives of 44 countries met at the Bretton Woods conference in 1944 and negotiated a new monetary system organized around the U.S. dollar. After the turbulence of the interwar years and World War II, the Bretton Woods monetary system succeeded in bringing stability to currency values.

currency relations and with providing support to countries in need of short-term assistance in keeping their exchange rates stable. The IMF made information available to members and provided standards of behavior that countries were expected to follow with respect to their currencies. The backing of the major Western financial powers, along with the institutional support of the IMF, were central to the stability of the Bretton Woods monetary system.

Eventually, however, international monetary cooperation failed because of fundamental disagreements among countries. By the early 1970s, the U.S. government was unwilling to make the sacrifices necessary to keep the dollar fixed to gold. President Richard Nixon felt that the Bretton Woods commitments constrained American economic policy more than was acceptable. The U.S. government felt itself too constrained by the rigid link between the dollar and gold, eventually breaking that link in order to give itself more monetary independence.

Today's International Monetary System   Since 1973, international monetary relations have been based on floating exchange rates among a small number of major currencies, typically those of the principal industrial and financial nations (especially the United States, Japan, Germany, and Great Britain). While today's international monetary system does not depend on explicit commitments to fixed exchange rates, its orderly functioning still requires the major national governments to work together, especially in times of crisis. And although the IMF was originally designed to monitor and assist the functioning of a modified fixed-rate international monetary order, it has remained important even after the shift to floating rates. When the major governments believe that exchange rates are fluctuating too wildly, they can coordinate their monetary policies to try to reduce these wide swings; the IMF sometimes serves as the venue for discussions of this sort of coordination. At times, currency problems in developing countries have led the major financial powers to intervene to attempt to stabilize exchange rates and keep a crisis from spreading; again, the IMF frequently participates in such attempts at crisis management and sometimes leads them.

Different alignments of national interests, and different patterns of strategic interaction among states, help account for different international monetary outcomes. It is striking that both the gold standard and the Bretton Woods monetary system each relied in major ways on the leadership of one country—Great Britain and the United States, respectively. Nonetheless, the participation of other major financial and monetary powers was needed to keep the systems going, so a sense of common interests was also crucial. As the collapse of both systems indicates, such participation can be difficult to sustain. It can be impeded by fundamental disagreements over how to share the costs of stabilizing the system or by a lack of trust among governments that the commitments of others will be honored.

Today's world of floating exchange rates presents a related set of problems. While the major powers do interact, generally cooperatively, to try to avoid major monetary disturbances, exchange rates still fluctuate quite widely. Since 1980, for example, the U.S. dollar has risen and fallen by very large amounts against other major currencies. While few people in the United States seem overly worried about this volatility, in smaller countries that trade more with the rest of the world, these currency fluctuations can be widely unpopular.

The current system is not monolithic, as was the gold standard, or organized, as was Bretton Woods, but it does have some clear defining features. Countries can allow their currencies to float freely, and large countries typically do; but smaller countries appear less enthusiastic about this currency volatility, and they often link their currency to that of a larger nation or bloc. The absence of an established global monetary system has in fact led some countries to try to develop regional monetary systems that can at least stabilize exchange rates among groups of countries.

Regional Monetary Arrangements: The Euro

In the absence of a global agreement on stabilizing currencies, some countries have tried to work out regional arrangements. Where countries can resolve problems of cooperation, a more orderly system can be maintained regionally even as it disintegrates globally. This was the strategy pursued by most of the members of the European Union after the collapse of the Bretton Woods monetary system. Most EU countries trade and invest a great deal with one another, an arrangement that leads them to want to limit exchange rate fluctuations. Starting in 1973, they committed themselves to stabilize exchange rates among EU member countries and eventually to work toward a common currency.

But the road to the euro was not an easy one, for both domestic and interstate political reasons. Within countries, some interests were often less than enthusiastic about a common monetary policy. In practice, fixing EU exchange rates meant pegging them to the German currency (the Deutschmark), for Germany was the largest economy in the European Union and had a long-standing commitment to keeping its currency, as well as its prices, stable. In countries with higher inflation than Germany, pegging the currency to the Deutschmark meant that governments would have to bring inflation down. This typically involved raising interest rates and implementing austerity measures, such as restraining wages and cutting government spending. In France and Italy, labor unions and public employees, especially, felt that their interests would be sacrificed to the currency peg. It was not until 1985 that supporters of a fixed rate won out in these two countries. In Great Britain and Sweden, there were even fewer supporters of a fixed rate, and for most of the period these two nations kept their distance from the growing currency union.

At the regional level, interactions among the governments of the European Union were complex and often conflictual. Because other EU currencies were fixed to the Deutschmark, Germany's monetary policy had to be followed by other countries. This arrangement was satisfactory as long as they all agreed on the course of German policy. However, in 1991, in the aftermath of the reunification of the eastern and western parts of Germany, the German central bank was very concerned about inflation. To restrain prices, it raised interest rates very high. This measure, taken for entirely domestic reasons, forced the rest of the currency bloc to make a difficult choice. They could raise interest rates and drive their economies into recession; or they could keep interest rates low, in which case money would flow out of their countries, toward Germany's higher interest rates, and force them to leave the peg. The eventual result was a currency crisis—and the decision by many EU members to break the Deutschmark link.

Movement toward currency union continued, nonetheless, because there was a domestic consensus in most EU countries on the desirability of stabilizing currencies—even at the cost of giving up a national policy and even, in many cases, a powerful national symbol, the currency. The next move was to plan for a common currency, the euro, to be managed by a common ECB. This measure appealed to countries other than Germany, because it meant that European monetary policy would be made by a European, rather than a German, central bank and would presumably take European conditions as a whole into account. Germany went along for several reasons. First, the ECB was to be based in Frankfurt, Germany, and its constitution was drafted so as to ensure that it would be very similar to the German central bank. This helped allay German fears that the new institution would stray too far from the low-inflation principles Germans preferred. Second, Germany itself wanted a reduction in currency volatility in Europe, and it was clear that other EU members would not accept a continuation of the Deutschmark-based system. Third, the creation of the euro and the ECB was connected to a broad array of cooperative ventures among EU member governments on a wide range of issues. Just as economic cooperation between the United States and western Europe was facilitated

MAP 9.2 *Members of the EMU, 2015*

ORIGINAL MEMBER COUNTRIES

COUNTRIES THAT JOINED BETWEEN 2001 AND 2015

COUNTRIES IN THE PROCESS OF JOINING

NOT MEMBERS

by their military alliance, monetary union among western European countries was facilitated by the fact that they had come to cooperate in so many other dimensions, from trade policy and antitrust to foreign policy.

The combination of gradually emerging domestic consensus within most EU member countries and increasingly cooperative interaction among EU governments led to the adoption of the euro and its successful introduction as Europe's circulating money in 2002. As of 2015, most EU members share the euro, which is used by more than 300 million people in 19 countries. (See Map 9.2 for members of the European Monetary Union in 2015.) Britain and Sweden remain outside the monetary union; Denmark has not adopted the euro but has fixed its own currency against the euro very tightly. Another seven or so more recent and prospective members of the European Union are considering joining the eurozone. But the eurozone has also been wracked by a crisis that threatened its very unity (see below).

The creation of this regional currency union reflected the interests of many countries to stabilize their exchange rates in a time of turbulence. There are several other such regional currency arrangements. For example, 14 Central and West African countries share a common currency, which is pegged to the euro; and eight Caribbean island nations and territories share a common East Caribbean dollar, pegged to the U.S. dollar.

Many other countries deal with concern over currency volatility by pursuing unilateral measures, such as adopting another currency (for example, Panama, Ecuador, and El Salvador use the U.S. dollar as their currency) or linking their currency to that of another country. All these strategies are aimed at achieving the desired balance between currency stability and policy independence—either on one's own or in collaboration with other national governments. While they may succeed in reducing threats to individual countries or groups of countries, they do not address problems at the global monetary level, which some analysts regard as a matter for concern. Nor do they address the continuing problem of spreading currency crises, to which we turn in the next section of this chapter.

What Happens When Currencies Collapse?

Even those who pay little attention to international monetary affairs notice the occasional spectacular currency crises, such as those that affected Europe in 1992 to 1993 and again in 2011, East Asia in 1997 to 1998, or Argentina in 2001. Indeed, currency crises have been a frequent feature of the modern international political economy. They are one of the more dramatic effects of national currency policy. Currency crises have been closely related to the financial and debt crises discussed in Chapter 8 and have been associated with all-encompassing economic and political upheavals.

Currency crises usually result when government exchange rate commitments are not fully credible. In this sense, they are analytically comparable to crises in military affairs that result when the threats and promises of governments are not fully credible (see Chapter 3). In the case of currency affairs, when private economic actors do not believe the promises of a government with respect to its exchange rate, they can react in ways that cause a major crisis.

Effects on Government

Up to now, we have assumed that when a government fixes its exchange rate, it stays fixed until the government decides, on its own, to alter the arrangement. But we also know that it can be economically and politically difficult for a government to sustain a fixed currency, because a government with a fixed exchange rate may not be able to undertake monetary policies desirable to address national economic conditions. This was the problem in Argentina in 2001, when the tight dollar-peso link made it virtually impossible for the Argentine government to reverse a three-year recession. It was also the problem in a number of countries in the eurozone in the aftermath of the crisis that began in 2008, for the fact that they had given up their national currencies made it very difficult for them to act to ease the impact of the Great Recession. In these circumstances, expectations that the government will not be able to sustain its commitment to a fixed rate or to membership in a currency union can create concern among economic actors about the future course of the currency. And this concern can feed on itself until it becomes a panic.

A typical currency crisis follows a fairly predictable trajectory. In order to reap the benefits of a fixed currency, the government commits itself to a particular fixed exchange rate—a peg to gold, the dollar, or the euro at a specific rate. This move presumably has all the advantages we have identified, but it also imposes costs. Over time, for some reason, the government faces economic and political difficulties in maintaining a fixed exchange rate. Perhaps the local economy is doing poorly, or exporters are clamoring for a devaluation that will make their goods more attractive abroad, or the country's main exports are losing markets to competitors.

As the government faces increasing pressures to devalue the currency, people begin to lose faith in the government's commitment to keep the exchange rate stable. This unease gives investors strong reasons to sell the nation's currency. After all, nobody wants to hold on to an asset, in this case a currency, that is going to lose value. So investors at home and abroad start converting the local currency into more reliable foreign currency. The government usually continues to assure the public that the exchange rate will be maintained, in an effort to keep people from selling the currency. But as doubts about the government's credibility grow, more and more people may go to the banks to exchange their local currency for more reliable dollars or euros.

The government itself is torn. On the one hand, there are powerful domestic interests in favor of keeping the currency's exchange rate where it is. Companies and others that have borrowed in a foreign currency, for example, are anxious to make sure the national currency is not devalued. For those with foreign currency debts, a devaluation would increase the cost of their debt by requiring more of the national currency to buy the foreign currency they must use to repay the debt. Also, a devaluation would reduce national purchasing power—an unpopular move with consumers, who would have to pay more for many goods as a result. On the other hand, there are good reasons to allow the currency's value to drop: it might alleviate the economic distress and help national farmers and manufacturers compete with foreigners. ("How Do We Know?" on p. 408 looks at the decision to devalue the currency in several European countries.) At the same time, sustaining the fixed rate can be very difficult. The government would have to take some action to convince people to hold on to the national currency rather than buying dollars or some other foreign currency. Most commonly, a government trying to convince investors and others to hold on to the national money has to raise interest rates in order to make the local currency more attractive—and raising interest rates is likely to exacerbate the country's economic difficulties.

When the Argentine government devalued the peso in 2001, many homeowners whose mortgage was denominated in dollars saw the value of their debt triple compared to their salary (paid in pesos) in a span of just two months. This fueled public anger.

Eventually, the government runs out of time, money, or patience, and the currency is devalued. When the currency drops in value, this may have a positive effect by helping national producers compete with foreigners. But it also usually has some very powerful negative effects. Anyone in the country with substantial foreign currency debts, including the government, faces serious trouble. As the local currency drops, the burden of foreign currency debt rises. In early 2002, the Argentine peso dropped from 1 to the dollar to 3 to the dollar in two months, so a 1-million-dollar debt went from being a 1-million-peso debt to a 3-million-peso debt. In these circumstances, large numbers of debtors go bankrupt, which in turn leads many banks to fail as their customers cannot pay their debts. A recession almost always ensues, which can even turn into a deep financial and debt crisis. Indeed, most currency crises eventually turn into broader banking crises. This scenario has been repeated dozens, perhaps hundreds, of times, from the nineteenth century through the present in developed and developing countries.

International Repercussions

The international aspect of currency crises can be particularly troubling. Currency crises can be transmitted from one country to another as uncertainties about one country feed uncertainties about others. Investors looking at countries that are economically or politically similar may believe that the collapse of one country's currency portends the collapse of others like it. Throughout the nineteenth century, currency crises (often originating in the United States, then a heavily indebted developing country) had repercussions all over the industrialized world. When, in 1931, Austria was hit by a currency and banking crisis, the resulting fears soon affected neighboring Hungary, leading to

Devaluation or Depression in the European Union

When the global financial crisis hit in 2007, governments in central and eastern Europe had to figure out how they would respond. These nations had recently entered the EU, and many of them were on track to adopt the euro. Most had currencies that were tightly tied to the euro.

As the world economy spiraled downward, each faced a serious exchange rate policy choice. On the one hand, in order to move forward toward adoption of the euro, the government could hold fast to its peg to the euro. However, this would restrict it from adopting an independent policy, such as devaluing its currency. And this was a major restriction: one of the typical recommendations for small open economies in crisis is to devalue in order to make national goods more attractive on world markets and stimulate exports. However, if the government chose to devalue, it would forego the opportunity to join the eurozone.

Political scientist Stefanie Walter analyzed the political economy of this choice.[a] She focused on the interests at play in different central and eastern European societies and, in particular, on their citizens' debts in foreign currency. In the Baltic states of Estonia, Latvia, and Lithuania, for example, between 60 and 90 percent of total loans were in foreign currency. A devaluation would have dramatically increased the cost of this debt. If a Latvian homeowner took out a 100,000 euro mortgage in 2005, this would have been equal to about 70,000 Latvian lats (at the then current exchange rate of one lat being equal to 1.42 euro). But if the lat had been devalued by 30 percent (so that the exchange rate was one lat equal to about one euro), the mortgage would have increased in local value to about 100,000 lats.

In some other countries, citizens had not borrowed very much in foreign currency. In Poland, foreign-currency debts were barely 30 percent of the total, and in the Czech Republic there were few foreign-currency debts. People in these countries were less vulnerable to devaluation.

Walter argues that the countries whose economic interests were most vulnerable to devaluation chose to keep their currency peg (Table A). Lithuania, Estonia, and Latvia, in fact, underwent massive recessions—unemployment approached 20 percent and GDP dropped by over 15 percent in just one year. Nonetheless, they held on to their euro dreams, and all three countries are now in the eurozone.

Poland and the Czech Republic, whose economic interests were less vulnerable to devaluation, opted to devalue their currencies. Their exports boomed, and as a result, they experienced little or no increase in unemployment. The Czech Republic had only a shallow recession, and Poland had none. On the other hand, neither country will be able to join the eurozone.

TABLE A *Foreign-Currency Debt and Currency Depreciation*

	LOANS IN FOREIGN CURRENCY[a]	MAXIMUM DEPRECIATION OF NATIONAL CURRENCY[b]	REAL GDP GROWTH RATE, 2009[b]	CHANGE IN UNEMPLOYMENT RATE, 2007–2010[b]
Estonia	85.3%	0%	−14.3%	12.2%
Latvia	88.4%	1.2%	−17.7%	13.3%
Lithuania	64.0%	0%	−14.8%	13.5%
Poland	32.6%	43%	1.6%	0%
Czech Republic	13.6%	21%	−4.7%	2%

a. Martin Myant and Jan Drahokupil, "International Integration, Varieties of Capitalism, and Resilience to Crisis in Transition Economies," *Europe-Asia Studies* 64, no. 1 (2012): 1–33.
b. Stefanie Walter, *Financial Crises and the Politics of Macroeconomic Adjustments* (Cambridge: Cambridge University Press, 2013), Table 7.1.

a. Stefanie Walter, *Financial Crises and the Politics of Macroeconomic Adjustments* (Cambridge: Cambridge University Press, 2013), 181–217.

a follow-on crisis there. Then the crisis hit Germany, then the rest of Central Europe, then Great Britain; eventually, most of Europe was brought down by a "contagious" currency crisis that almost certainly deepened the Great Depression.

In the past 30 years, there have been many rounds of currency crises. The first was associated with the less developed countries' sovereign debt defaults of the early and middle 1980s. In this case, the currency crises followed, rather than led, the larger financial crisis. As country after country found itself unable to sustain its currency's value in the face of massive debt problems, currencies collapsed as well. Since the early 1990s, it has become more common for currency crises to be the source of broader financial and economic difficulties.

Case Study: Europe, 1992

One of the first major modern currency crises affected European countries that were moving toward currency union. In this process, most EU countries had pegged their currencies to that of Germany, the Deutschmark. In 1991, the German central bank raised interest rates quickly and steeply to keep prices from rising after the eastern and western parts of the country had been unified. This presented the other European countries whose currencies were tied to the Deutschmark with a difficult choice. On the one hand, they could keep interest rates low, which would cause investors to pull their money out of other countries in favor of the higher German interest rates. As investors pulled out and sold the non-German currencies, these countries would eventually have to devalue their currencies against the Deutschmark and break the peg. On the other hand, the other countries could raise interest rates along with Germany, which would shove them into a recession made in Germany. In sum, German policy confronted European governments with a stark choice between continued membership in the Deutschmark bloc, on the one hand, and avoiding a recession, on the other. The rest of Europe was already mired in slow growth and double-digit unemployment, and there was little enthusiasm for more austerity measures that would slow inflation but also reduce wages and public spending.

In the summer of 1992, investors and currency traders began anticipating that Great Britain and Italy would not maintain their currencies' pegs to the Deutschmark. Investors sold off their holdings of these currencies, which intensified speculation that the pound and the lira would be devalued. The British and Italian governments pushed interest rates up to try to convince investors to hold on to their pounds and liras, but in the end, the cost seemed extreme and both devalued their currencies. Foreign exchange traders started selling off other currencies in the months that followed. Governments tried to hold on to the link to the Deutschmark (at one point, the Swedish central bank pushed interest rates to 500 percent), but the cost was too high. Eventually, six other European nations followed Britain and Italy in devaluing their currencies. The damage to monetary unification was repaired quickly and effectively enough to move forward with plans for the euro. But it was clear that even the world's richest nations were not immune from currency crises that could force governments to devalue and change policies. The perception began to grow that there might be a common interest in trying to limit the negative effects of currency crises, as they could be transmitted from nation to nation.

Case Study: Mexico Within a year, this point was brought home to Mexico. With the North American Free Trade Agreement in effect, the Mexican government wanted to hold the peso steady against the U.S. dollar. And in the run-up to a hotly contested presidential election campaign, the government wanted to keep the peso strong and Mexican incomes high. But in January 1994, a rebellion broke out in southern Mexico, and in March, one of the ruling party's leading presidential candidates was assassinated. This worried investors, who came to believe that the government's position was shaky. As the election year of 1994 wore on, the government struggled to maintain its commitment to the peso, both to uphold its reputation and, through the strong peso, to increase the purchasing power of Mexican consumers.

But currency traders did not believe that the government could hold to its promises. Investors became more and more skittish, and the narrowness of the victory won by the ruling Partido Revolucionario Institucional (PRI), or Institutional Revolutionary Party, in the August 1994 presidential election was not reassuring. The PRI's secretary general was assassinated in September, which further scared investors who worried that the new government would be too unstable to commit credibly to the currency peg. As the new government took office in December, currency traders sensed they could take a "one-way bet" against the peso: if it was devalued, they won; if it wasn't, they didn't lose. As the speculators sold off the currency, the government tried desperately to keep the currency stable, but a few days before Christmas 1994, it floated the peso—which promptly sank. Yet another government had been forced to devalue its currency.

Following the common pattern of currency crises leading to financial crises, Mexico was next hit by a crippling banking crisis as a result of the currency collapse. When the peso was strong, many banks and companies borrowed heavily in dollars. The devaluation of the peso triggered mass bankruptcies as the real cost of dollar debts soared. The peso dropped in the space of a month from about 30 cents to about 15 cents, so the real burden on a Mexican company of a $1 million foreign debt doubled from about 3.3 million to 6.6 million pesos. Many indebted firms collapsed, followed by their domestic bankers, and within weeks the country was in the throes of a financial panic. The country's output dropped by 6 percent, and inflation soared above 50 percent. The fallout of the Mexican crisis affected all of Latin America, which was plunged into recession.

Case Study: East Asia The next round of currency and financial crises was even more dramatic. In 1997, the East Asian economies were booming, as about $50 billion a year flowed into East Asia from global financial markets, with tens of billions more in direct investment from multinational corporations. The region seemed well on the way to rapid economic development. But there were a few warning signs of slowing growth and a bubble in housing and financial markets. By 1996 and early 1997, exports were lagging, inflation was rising, and banks were taking on more and more debt. Soon investors began to anticipate devaluations and started selling off East Asian currencies.

In a now-familiar spiral, the movement away from the region's currencies became a flood, then a stampede, then a panic. The sell-off spread from Thailand and the Philippines to Indonesia and Malaysia, then to Taiwan and Korea. The size and efficiency of international financial markets seemed to facilitate the attacks by making it remarkably easy for investors to speculate against government attempts to defend their currencies. Joseph Stiglitz, then chief economist at the World Bank, gave an example of the process:

> Assume a speculator goes to a Thai bank, borrows 24 billion baht, which, at the original exchange rate, can be converted into $1 billion. A week later the exchange rate falls; instead of there being 24 baht to the dollar, there are now 40 baht to the dollar. He takes $600 million, converting it back to baht, getting 24 billion baht to repay the loan. The remaining $400 million is his profit—a tidy return for one week's work, and the investment of little of his own money. . . . As perceptions that a devaluation is imminent grow, the chance to make money becomes irresistible and speculators from around the world pile in to take advantage of the situation.[8]

As more and more investors did as Stiglitz described, expectations of devaluations grew. As no investor wanted to hold on to currencies that would lose value, billions of dollars flooded out of the East Asian economies and eventually governments were in fact forced to devalue. Within weeks of the initial attack, the currencies of Korea, the Philippines, and Malaysia dropped by 40 percent, that of Thailand by 50 percent, and that of Indonesia by 80 percent. The political fallout was also intense: the government of Thailand fell, and after more than 30 years in power, the Suharto dictatorship in Indonesia collapsed.

Case Study: Europe, 2011–2015   The most recent currency crisis was different: it involved the threat that a multicountry currency union might break up. The member states of the eurozone have very different economies and have grown at different rates, but as long as the zone as a whole was growing, this did not cause many problems. When the global financial crisis began in 2008, however, it put major strains on the very structure of the euro.

A group of eurozone member states—especially Greece, Ireland, Portugal, and Spain—had borrowed very heavily after the euro was created. Their economies had boomed, but at the same time these debt-financed booms raised prices

---

8. Joseph Stiglitz, *Globalization and Its Discontents* (New York: Norton, 2002), 94–95.

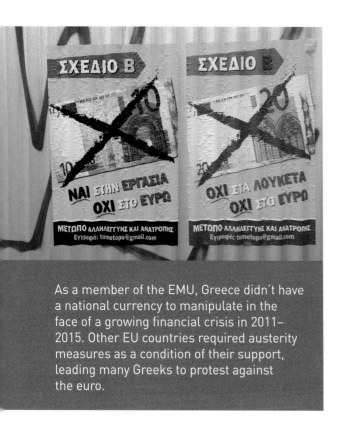

As a member of the EMU, Greece didn't have a national currency to manipulate in the face of a growing financial crisis in 2011–2015. Other EU countries required austerity measures as a condition of their support, leading many Greeks to protest against the euro.

and wages and made it harder for them to compete. Faced with the worldwide recession, the major debtor countries had trouble servicing their debts. Soon they were in full financial crisis and had to be bailed out by their EU partners to the tune of over a trillion euros (see Chapter 8).

As the debt crisis dragged on, it appeared that it might threaten some countries' membership in the eurozone. The hardest-hit member state, Greece, certainly might have benefited from the ability to devalue its currency—except that it no longer had a currency to devalue. And it was not clear that the other members of the eurozone were enthusiastic about Greece staying in. Indeed, in 2015, Greece appeared to come very close to being forced out of the eurozone, due to its continuing difficulties in servicing debts to banks and governments in other eurozone member countries. Nonetheless, the threat of the breakup of the euro helped push the eurozone's leaders toward a resolution of the crisis, involving a combination of painful austerity measures in the debtor nations, bailouts from the rest of the eurozone, and a small amount of debt restructuring. Thus far, the euro's unity has been preserved, but at a very high cost.

The dramatic economic and political effects of the crises in Europe, Mexico, Argentina, and East Asia, and of others in Turkey, Russia, Brazil, and elsewhere, caught the world's attention. So too did the fact that currency and banking crises could spread quickly from country to country, as they did in East Asia in 1997 to 1998. This realization led many of the world's economic leaders to see these currency crises as threats to the international monetary order and the world economy more generally. One nation's currency collapse could be transmitted to others, to an entire region, or to the whole world. Currency and financial instability had, after all, lengthened and deepened the Great Depression of the 1930s. The currency crises of the 1990s and the 2000s led many to believe that in a globalized financial system, such attacks had the potential to destabilize the entire world economy. "Controversy" on p. 414 explores the debate over what, if anything, should be done to prevent them.

Containing Currency Crises

Concern that currency crises can have broad international effects makes attempts to counter them something of an international public good. Thus, major governments have a common interest in containing such crises—although, as with all public goods, there is often conflict over how to distribute the cost of providing such containment. This challenge has given rise to complex interactions in which governments, private investors, and international institutions both cooperate and contend over attempts to limit the damage caused by currency crises.

Indeed, over the past 20 years, governments of the major financial centers and the leading international financial institutions have often cooperated to try to slow the spread of currency crises. The IMF, other international institutions, and creditor governments have often mobilized tens of billions of dollars to try to support governments facing a currency crisis. The reasons for major governments to cooperate in the face of currency crises are closely related to the reasons for cooperation to address sovereign debt crises, as discussed in Chapter 8. Cooperation among national governments can help avoid, or mitigate the international impact of, currency crises; indeed, developed-country governments and the IMF have spent hundreds of billions of dollars since 1980 in attempts to control these crises.

However, such cooperation has not always been easy to organize and sustain. As with all public goods, there are incentives for each government to free-ride and hope that other governments will pay the price of stabilizing the monetary order. Even more, many people believe that it is not a good idea to spend billions to support a failed or failing currency: such an effort may prop up undeserving governments and banks. This highlights the fact that currency crises can be controversial in domestic politics: governments are often blamed for allowing the crisis to take place, for not dealing with it effectively, or for inappropriately setting the currency in the first place.

Supporters have regarded these currency crisis interventions as striking examples of international cooperation to sustain the global monetary order, and with it the global economy more generally, with a quick response to avoid the proliferation of contagious crises. But critics have charged that taxpayers were being forced to bail out foolish investors and overextended governments, encouraging a continuation of irresponsible government and private behavior. The clash has largely pitted contending interests against one another (see Chapter 8 for similar debates over financial bailouts), and it is sure to continue. The mix of common interests and contentious issues ensures that currency crises, and controversies over them, will continue to plague many currencies and globalized financial markets.

Conclusion: Currencies, Conflict, and Cooperation

Argentines and Greeks are not alone in learning from experience that currency policy can make a significant difference to economic and political life. Over the past 20 years, billions of people in dozens of countries have experienced both the

Should Currency Traders Be Permitted to "Attack" Weak Currencies?

In summer and early fall of 1997, Malaysia faced the gravest economic crisis in its history. Trouble had started when the currency of Thailand came under speculative pressures in early summer. On July 2, after months of desperate measures to maintain the value of the baht, Thai authorities devalued the currency. Within a few days, the Philippines, Malaysia, Singapore, and Indonesia faced attacks on their currencies; eventually Vietnam, Hong Kong, Taiwan, and South Korea joined the list of victims. By September 1997, all of East and Southeast Asia was engulfed in a financial crisis that threatened to reverse decades of economic progress. In a scorching speech at the annual meeting of the World Bank and the IMF, the prime minister of Malaysia, Mahathir bin Mohamad, blamed international currency traders. "Society must be protected from unscrupulous profiteers," he raged.[a] International financier George Soros, whom Mahathir had previously singled out as a key culprit, lashed back the following day. Soros called the suggestion of a trading ban "so inappropriate that it does not deserve serious consideration," and he labeled Mahathir "a menace to his own country."[b]

Most people—including Mahathir in calmer moments—agree that international currency markets are, on balance, highly beneficial. By supplying liquidity, currency trade greases the wheels of international trade and investment, and the market signals sent by speculators provide a helpful check on unsustainable inflationary policies within domestic economies. The controversy is chiefly over the way in which the benefits and burdens of this generally useful institution are distributed across distinct interests, both within and across countries. Those who join Mahathir in condemning the current system, such as Nobel prize–winning economist Joseph Stiglitz, make three main complaints. The first is that currency speculation can result in economic disaster in developing countries, especially for the poor. Devaluation allegedly spurred by speculation increases the prices of foreign goods, bankrupts debtors, and can cause a society-wide recession. In their quest to profit from betting against a currency, speculators cause grave hardships to residents or the target country. The second complaint is that in their current form, international currency markets allow speculators to ride roughshod over the policy autonomy of developing nations. Not only do speculators have the power to decimate national budgets and disrupt economic planning, but they also appear to use that power to favor particular economic measures. Critics charge that it is only when economies violate the IMF's core tenets of liberalization, deregulation, balanced budgets, and privatization that currency speculators, sensing imminent trouble, step in. Whether the speculation is justified or not on economic grounds, governments must respond.

A third, related, complaint is that speculators often attack a currency for reasons that have nothing to do with the fundamental economic circumstances or the target country. There may be no good macroeconomic reason why a particular currency should depreciate. But if speculators "gang up" on the national government, they can mobilize so much money that the government cannot resist, and speculation can force the exchange rate down despite the absence of any real economic basis for the depreciation. In these cases, currency markets are causing changes in currency values only as part of their "gambling" strategies rather than as a reflection of underlying economic conditions.

Defenders of the current currency market system reject all these criticisms. To begin with, they claim that currency speculation is hardly the chief cause of currency crises. In most cases, they argue, speculation simply hastens or exacerbates a crisis that would have happened anyway owing to underlying domestic problems. Soros claimed, for instance, that Malaysia's crisis stemmed from an excessive expansion of credit and that Mahathir was using Soros "as a scapegoat to cover up his own failure" to deal with that issue.[c] There are few demonstrable

---

a. "Premier of Malaysia Spars with Currency Dealer," *New York Times,* September 22, 1997.

b. "Premier of Malaysia Spars with Currency Dealer."

c. "Premier of Malaysia Spars with Currency Dealer."

instances in which speculation in and of itself caused currency movements; it is much more common for analyses to find that speculation only sped a process that was inevitable due to national policy failures.

Second, defenders argue, the suggestion that international financiers intentionally mold the domestic policy of foreign nations and willfully impoverish the poor is overblown. Traders in international currency are no different from traders in other goods: their motivation is simply to realize profits through market exchange. Defenders characteristically finish by reemphasizing the idea that international currency markets are not solely of benefit to international financiers but also promote the interests of most everyone, including, ultimately, the poor.

Third, advocates of free markets for currencies insist that currency trading provides a valuable discipline on exploitative or unsustainable government policies. In the absence of a market test, governments could evade their macroeconomic responsibilities for longer—and typically, the longer bad policies persist, the bigger is the crisis at the end of the downward spiral. As with most markets, currency markets reflect economic realities, and

governments can only ignore economic realities in the short run.

How should we evaluate this debate? Soros's defenders may be right that individual traders, pursuing their own interests within an established system, are not necessarily doing anything wrong. And there is often value in the signals that currency markets can provide. However, Mahathir is arguably equally right to question the aggregate consequences of those individual actions—the product of their interactions. If the rapid flow of large amounts of money in and out of a country does not alone cause a crisis, it may nonetheless aggravate one, especially in the case of emerging economies such as Malaysia's. So while currency markets can provide valuable signals, they can also exaggerate the impact of economic trends in ways that exacerbate underlying problems rather than help address them. This is yet another instance in which individually rational actions that may have some economic justification can lead to collectively undesirable effects. The contradiction suggests to some observers that the institutions of international currency markets need to be reformed.

positive and negative effects of national currency policies. The exchange rate is controversial within countries because its impact differs among groups, firms, regions, and individuals with contending interests. There are many who benefit if the currency is fixed, and others who are harmed. For every firm that gains as a currency depreciates, there is another that loses. This clash of interests, mediated through national political institutions, determines national attitudes toward the exchange rate.

International monetary relations too have a profound impact on international economic and political affairs. There is a reason that the classical gold standard and the Bretton Woods monetary system gave their names to entire economic eras: the ordering principles of these currency regimes were central to their respective international economies. Without functioning international monetary arrangements, global economic activity would be immensely difficult.

Governments have powerful reasons to collaborate in devising international monetary arrangements, but they also have significant interests that conflict. Inasmuch as an international monetary regime is a public good, governments have strong incentives to free ride and let others provide it; they also have strong reasons to try to make sure it is provided, and they have reasons to want the regime to be organized in ways favorable to themselves. Such a mix of incentives for cooperation and incentives to bargain hard characterizes the politics of international monetary relations today, as it has for centuries. This can be seen through the currency policy issues that are likely to preoccupy national governments, and the world community, over the coming years.

The first contentious issue has to do with the overall structure and functioning of the international monetary system, and also cooperation among the world's major financial and monetary powers. Many scholars believe that more organized collaboration among major governments is desirable to avoid future problems and crises. Certainly, there is a desire among many governments to collaborate in devising a new monetary order. Yet there are also powerful interests in conflict, as governments disagree about the desirable characteristics of such an order.

In the absence of global agreement on international monetary relations, many countries in specific geographical regions continue to devise regional currency arrangements. The eurozone is scheduled to expand to incorporate new members of the European Union in eastern, central, and southern Europe, and many countries in Africa and the Middle East have already linked their currencies to the euro or have plans to do so. There have been similar proposals for informal or formal currency unions in Latin America, North America, and parts of Asia. As many governments find these regional proposals an appealing way to reduce currency instability, some observers have suggested that we may be heading toward a world of currency blocs: an expanded eurozone eventually encompassing all of Europe, much of the Middle East and Africa, and parts of Asia; a dollar zone in the Western Hemisphere; and an East Asian currency area.

The future of such arrangements depends both on the interests governments have in developing them and on their interactions to pursue their monetary goals. Whether national governments come together on the global level to forge a new international monetary regime, or devise regional arrangements such as the euro, international monetary relations will profoundly shape the world economy.

Study Tool Kit

Interests, Interactions, and Institutions in Context

- There are many contending interests over monetary affairs within countries, which leads to domestic conflict over the appropriate currency policy to pursue.

- Although every country can set currency policy as it wants, the fact that exchange rates value currencies relative to one another means that outcomes are the product of interactions among countries' policies. As a result, countries may have reasons to cooperate with one another to create arrangements that are mutually beneficial.

- Virtually everyone has an interest in the existence of a functioning international monetary system. But different arrangements benefit some actors more than others, which leads to disagreement about how such a system should be organized and about how the burdens and benefits should be distributed among countries.

- International monetary institutions, such as the gold standard, the Bretton Woods monetary system, or Europe's EMU, can create rules that facilitate cooperation in international monetary policy.

Key Terms

exchange rate, p. 383

appreciate, p. 383

depreciate, p. 383

devalue, p. 383

monetary policy, p. 385

central bank, p. 385

fixed exchange rate, p. 385

gold standard, p. 385

floating exchange rate, p. 386

Bretton Woods monetary system, p. 386

adjustable peg, p. 386

international monetary regime, p. 396

For Further Reading

Eichengreen, Barry. *Exorbitant Privilege: The Rise and Fall of the Dollar and the Future of the International Monetary System.* **New York: Oxford University Press, 2011.** Surveys the rise of the U.S. dollar as an international currency and evaluates how the dollar's role—and international monetary relations—are likely to evolve in the future.

Eichengreen, Barry. *Globalizing Capital: A History of the International Monetary System.* **2nd ed. Princeton, NJ: Princeton University Press, 2008.** Presents a general historical survey of the economics and politics of the international monetary order.

Eichengreen, Barry. *Golden Fetters: The Gold Standard and the Great Depression, 1919–1939.* **New York: Oxford University Press, 1992.** Serves as a classic analysis of how the gold standard collapsed in the interwar period.

Frieden, Jeffry. *Currency Politics: The Political Economy of Exchange Rate Policy.* **Princeton: Princeton University Press, 2015.** Explains the politics and economics of government exchange rate policy choices, with applications to the gold standard, European monetary integration, and Latin American currency policies and currency crises.

James, Harold. *International Monetary Cooperation since Bretton Woods.* **Oxford: IMF and Oxford University Press, 1996.** Surveys the evolution of the international monetary system from the end of World War II through the rise of the system of floating exchange rates up to the mid-1990s.

Kenen, Peter, and Ellen Meade. *Regional Monetary Integration.* **Cambridge: Cambridge University Press, 2008.** Summarizes and analyzes international experience with the creation of regional monetary unions.

Klein, Michael, and Jay Shambaugh. *Exchange Rate Regimes in the Modern Era.* **Cambridge: MIT Press, 2010.** Analyzes the different exchange rate policy choices available to governments and explores how and why they have chosen their currency regimes.

10

Development: Causes of the Wealth and Poverty of Nations

THE PUZZLE *Why are some countries rich and others poor? How do international politics and economics affect development?*

Above: Despite the overall growth of the world economy in recent decades, billions of people still live in poverty. For example, citizens of Zambia are significantly worse off today than they were when Zambia achieved independence in 1964. The average Zambian lives on the equivalent of about $1,200 per year.

In 1964, the African nation of Zambia and the East Asian country of South Korea were at roughly equivalent levels of development. Indeed, when Zambia achieved its independence in 1964, its prospects appeared far more promising than those of South Korea. Zambia was rich in copper, and its newly elected president, Kenneth Kaunda, was popular at home and respected abroad for his intelligence and seriousness of purpose. South Korea, in contrast, had no resources to speak of, was ruled by a despised and ridiculed military dictatorship, and depended heavily on American aid, which was being cut back.

Five decades later, the two countries could not be more different. The economy of Zambia has failed miserably. By the mid-1990s, the average Zambian had barely half the income he did at independence. Kaunda had been voted out of office in disgrace, political unrest was rife, and food riots were widespread. The government's failures were compounded by the AIDS epidemic that was sweeping through Africa. In 2014, Zambia has one of the lowest standards of living in the world. Life expectancy is just 58 years, more than one-third of the adult population is illiterate, child labor rates are high with over 40% of children ages 5 to 14 in the work force, and

three-quarters of the population lives on less than $1.25 a day.[1] Today, Zambia is a developmental disaster.

Meanwhile, South Korea has become a modern industrial nation. In 1996, the Organisation for Economic Co-operation and Development recognized Korea's progress and made the country a member of this club of rich countries. South Korea had "graduated" from the developing to the developed world. As of 2014, it has a standard of living comparable to that of France. Life expectancy is 82 years, adult literacy is practically universal, and per capita income is around $30,000 a year. Although the two nations had similar starting points 50 years ago, today South Korea is an industrialized, developed nation, while Zambia is desperately poor.

This comparison illustrates two realities of contemporary economic development. First, billions of people live in conditions of poverty. For example, average incomes in Africa today are comparable to what they were in western Europe 200 years ago; African life expectancy and literacy rates are similar to those of western Europe 100 years ago.

---

1. Data from the UN Human Development Reports 2014, http:// hdr.undp.org/en/ (accessed 11/21/14).

In sub-Saharan Africa, nearly one-third of all children under age five are malnourished, fewer than one-third of children of secondary school age attend school, and barely half the population has access to clean water.

Second, developmental experiences have varied widely. In 1960, countries such as South Korea and Taiwan were dismally poor—poorer than most of Africa. Today, these two nations are advanced industrial countries with per capita incomes comparable to those in western Europe. And the world's two most populous countries, China and India—home to over one-third of the world's people—have been growing very rapidly for over 30 years. China's living standards are today over five times higher than they were in 1980; India's are three times higher. The differences among developing nations are enormous: for example, the gap between Latin America and sub-Saharan Africa is substantially bigger than the gap between Latin America and the industrialized nations.

In fact, the proportion of the world's population living in abject poverty has declined since the 1980s. Most international organizations use an international absolute poverty line equivalent to about $1.50 a day per person in today's dollars, taking into account differences in the cost of living across countries. By this measure, while 52 percent of the developing world's population lived in absolute poverty in 1981, by 2011 the proportion was 17 percent.[2] This improvement is largely the result of successful development in China and India.

Nonetheless, the stark fact remains that some 6 billion of the total world population of about 7 billion live in poor countries. While not everyone in poor countries is poor, these nations have an average income per person of just one-quarter that of the rich countries. Most of the world's people are poor.

The continued poverty of much of the world's population leads us to ask why so many countries are poor. Why have some countries developed successfully while others have stagnated? Why have the experiences of less developed countries differed so widely? Within these questions lie related issues about the relationship between developing countries and international politics: How has the international political economy affected the development of poor nations? Has it been a hindrance or a help to them?

Thinking Analytically about Development

This chapter makes several points about the politics and economics of development. First, we note that although everyone in poor countries prefers more development to less, individuals and groups within countries may have conflicting interests with respect to how development is achieved. Powerful domestic groups that pursue policies to enrich themselves might prevent the adoption of other measures that would improve economic conditions for everyone else. Domestic social and political institutions can have a major impact on how conflicts of interest among different domestic groups affect a country's development. Some institutional arrangements empower special interest groups, while others overcome those who would stand in the way of development. In addition, a country's institutions can either facilitate or impede cooperation to promote policies that are conducive to economic growth.

At the international level, rich and poor nations generally have a common interest in accelerating the economic growth of the developing world. As poor nations grow, their demand for the products of rich nations grows, and they are better able to supply rich nations with goods and services they need. However, there have been many instances of rich countries supporting policies and institutions that disfavor less developed countries. For example, agricultural policies in Europe, North America, and Japan help farmers in rich countries at the expense of farmers in poor countries. Given these conditions, successful economic growth requires that a country overcome both the domestic obstacles posed by interests and institutions that are detrimental to development and the international obstacles created by conflicts of interest with wealthy nations.

---

2. The best source on the issue, from which most of these data are taken, is Branko Milanovic, *Worlds Apart: Global and International Inequality 1950–2000* (Princeton, NJ: Princeton University Press, 2005). The numbers cited here are from the World Bank, www.worldbank.org/en/topic/poverty/overview (accessed 01/02/15).

If Everyone Wants Development, Why Is It So Hard to Achieve?

Less developed countries (LDCs) want to develop, and few people would deny them the opportunity to do so.[3] However, steps to improve a nation's developmental prospects sometimes threaten the interests of certain actors at home or abroad. Recognizing this fact, we can identify three prominent approaches that explain why such a universally accepted goal appears to be so difficult to attain. These approaches consider geography, domestic factors such as a nation's political economy, and domestic institutions.

Geographic Location

One view is that the geographic realities of some countries impede their growth. The fact that the world's tropical regions are generally poor, while its temperate regions are generally rich, suggests that geography and climate affect development, directly or indirectly. There is little doubt that such factors play some part in explaining patterns of development. Landlocked countries, regions with diseases that are difficult to control or cure, and areas that are very far from major markets for their goods are all at a developmental disadvantage—and this disadvantage was probably greater in an earlier era, when medical knowledge was limited and transportation and communications costs were much higher. By virtue of weather and disease, tropical environments in particular may be less conducive to urbanization and industrialization than temperate zones. Some scholars ascribe a substantial portion of the developmental problems of such tropical regions as sub-Saharan Africa, for example, to geography itself.[4]

But geographic factors cannot be the whole story, as there is a great deal of variation among countries within the same regions. Indeed, if we compare LDCs with very similar geographic characteristics, we find that some have done extremely well, while others have done very poorly (see "What Shaped Our World?" on p. 424). While the climate and geography of a nation shape its development, they do so by way of their impact on the people, social structures, politics, and policies of the nation.

Two other approaches dominate attempts to explain patterns of development. One focuses on domestic factors, another on domestic institutions. International factors are relevant as well, and we return to them below. However, the fact that

---

3. Observers use a variety of terms for these countries. During the Cold War, it was common to refer to them as *third world* countries, to distinguish them from the capitalist *first world* and the Communist *second world*. Today it is more common to use the label *less developed country* or, more optimistically, *developing country*. Another convention is to refer to these countries collectively as *the South* because they tend to be located geographically to the south of the richer countries. We will use some of these terms interchangeably.

4. For prominent statements on geography and development, see Jared Diamond, *Guns, Germs, and Steel* (New York: Norton, 1997); David Bloom and Jeffrey Sachs, "Geography, Demography, and Economic Growth in Africa," *Brookings Papers on Economic Activity* 2 (1998): 207–95; and Jeffrey Sachs, Andrew Mellinger, and John Gallup, "The Geography of Poverty and Wealth," *Scientific American*, March 2001, 70–75.

Paths to Development

Why have some countries prospered, with their economies growing over time, while others have stagnated or even declined? One way to understand the interests, interactions, and institutions that lead some countries to prosper while others struggle is to compare countries that began their modern developmental experience under similar conditions, especially when they now diverge substantially.

Interests Consider the cases of Zambia and Botswana. These two southern African countries gained their independence from Great Britain in 1964 and 1966, respectively. Both countries are landlocked and have substantial mineral wealth. At independence, Zambia was much richer than Botswana, perhaps twice as rich.[a] The interests that dominated Zambian politics were largely urban: the business community and the urban middle and working classes, along with workers in the country's major copper mines. In contrast, the new Botswanan government presided over an economy with few initial natural resources: the main economic activity was cattle ranching, with most cattle in the hands of indigenous political leaders (the tribal chiefs). This difference meant that the Zambian government had incentives to channel its resources from the countryside and the copper belt to the cities, while Botswanan government had incentives to develop the country's cattle-ranching economy.

Institutions Following independence, the new Zambian government created institutions that centralized power. The country's rulers institutionalized a single-party state, destroying most of the country's democratic institutions. The government also created institutions to take over the country's copper mines from private owners. This monopoly of power allowed the government to use its copper earnings to award benefits to its core supporters. It also permitted the government to discriminate against farmers to provide cheap food to urban interests that were its power base, and raise high barriers to imports to encourage local industries. Thus, Zambian

The Botswanan parliament in Gaborone.

political institutions served the interests of the business community and the urban middle and working classes, while leaving other domestic groups, notably farmers, in poverty.

The new Botswanan government pursued a different path. Rather than centralizing power in the hands of one political party, it maintained and strengthened democratic political institutions. It invested in public goods to promote farming, especially cattle ranching; spent heavily on education and infrastructure; provided a stable environment for private investment; and encouraged foreign investment in the country's natural resources. Eventually, rich diamond deposits were discovered, which helped speed up economic growth.

Interactions The structure of Zambia's dominant interests, and the institutions that allowed them to control political power, led the government to pursue policies that primarily served to reinforce the position of the minority of urban-dwellers to the detriment of the society as a whole. In contrast, the principal interests in Botswana led the government to encourage agrarian development and maintain inclusive democratic institutions. Today, Botswana is a thriving, democratic nation with a 2013 per capita GDP of $7,770; while Zambia is an economically, politically, and socially troubled country, whose 2013 per capita GDP is $1,810—less than one-quarter that of its neighbor.

There are many reasons why one country develops while another does not. Whether it is divergent domestic interests, different national political institutions, or varied interactions among them, they all have powerful impact on government policies and domestic politics.

---

a. Real GDP per capita here and elsewhere in this section comes from Alan Heston, Robert Summers, and Bettina Aten, Penn World Table Version 7.0, Center for International Comparisons of Production, Income, and Prices, University of Pennsylvania, Philadelphia, May 2011, http://pwt.econ.upenn.edu/php site/pwt_index.php (accessed 3/21/15); and World Development Indicators, http://data.worldbank.org/country (accessed 01/02/15).

there is so much variation among countries that are similarly situated and that face similar international conditions implies that domestic factors and institutions are crucially important.

Domestic Factors

Within developing nations, there are interests, interactions, and institutions that can speed or impede economic growth. While every country is different and every experience is unique, certain common features of national political economies can help explain why some nations have been more successful than others. At the outset, it is crucial to recognize that a government's policies have a powerful impact on economic growth because they can either encourage or retard it. In fact, almost all explanations of development and underdevelopment consider the results of the actions (or inactions) of governments.

A very important policy that governments can undertake to boost development is to provide public goods that contribute to economic growth and prosperity. One such public good is the economic **infrastructure**. This includes a physical infrastructure of roads, railroads, airports, utilities, ports, and the like, which are necessary to allow trade and exchange. It also includes such economic institutions as financial and monetary systems, which permit people to carry out payments and investments easily. A social infrastructure too—public health and sanitation, education, urban planning—can encourage growth and development by allowing citizens to focus their efforts on economic activity in a productive way. In contrast, if the government does not build and maintain roads and schools, impedes normal banking operations, allows prices to spiral out of control, and fails to control disease and social problems, it is hard to imagine how the economy can develop.

Another crucial function for government is to ensure the security of property. After all, economic growth requires everyone from farmers to factory owners to invest in improving their ability to produce, and such improvements are unlikely to be made if property rights are not safe. Secure property rights—which people in developed countries take for granted—mean that a property owner can be confident that his or her material goods will not be seized arbitrarily. A commitment to protect private property is not necessarily something that benefits only the rich: in most poor societies, the principal property owners are farmers. For them to take advantage of new economic opportunities, they have to set aside time, energy, and money to improve the soil. Farmers have to put their livelihood on the line in order to plant coffee trees, clear woodland, or irrigate. How can they undertake such risky investments if they cannot be sure that the benefits can come back to them? If marauders can steal their animals and torch their fields? If local government officials can extort any wealth they saw being earned? If the national government taxes away all their earnings?

Long-term economic growth requires a stable and reliable environment within which people can make economic plans for the future. A government that invests in education and public health, creates an efficient economic infrastructure, and ensures a stable monetary and financial system can do a great deal to facilitate economic growth. In all these instances, people need a credible commitment that the

infrastructure
Basic structures necessary for social activity, such as transportation and telecommunications networks, and power and water supply.

Some countries, including Malaysia and Indonesia, have recently chosen to pursue a policy of infrastructure development to facilitate trade and exchange, attract foreign investment, grow their economies, and ultimately join the ranks of wealthy nations.

government will abide by its promises to provide such public goods. Governments that cannot or will not credibly promise to provide such public goods inhibit their citizens' ability to take advantage of economic opportunities.

Why might a government not be willing or able to commit to creating a favorable environment for economic growth? After all, even the most selfish rulers presumably stand to benefit from a prosperous economy. And all societies have workers, farmers, and businesspeople with an interest in active and effective government policies to expand the range of economic opportunities.

Some countries' governments might simply lack the technical expertise to manage modern economic growth, in which case foreign assistance, in the form of both money and skills, may be needed. More often, unfortunately, the answer is not so easy.

In many societies, certain actors have interests that go against broad-based economic development. This is not to say that such actors consciously desire to limit growth but that a pursuit of their own interests can ultimately harm the economy. (This is, of course, not a phenomenon specific to LDCs; every country has actors with an interest in manipulating the economy to benefit themselves, even at the cost of slowing economic growth.) In developing countries, such actors are often engaged in traditional economic sectors whose livelihood would be threatened by the growth of a more modern economy. For example, wealthy landowners may prefer that the property rights of poor farmers not be protected so that the rich can encroach on the land being farmed by the poor. Owners of labor-intensive plantations or mines may have little reason to support urbanization, industrialization, or education, because these developments would draw workers away and raise labor costs. Powerful corporations that receive generous subsidies and protection want to maintain them, even if they are a burden on taxpayers and consumers. Bureaucrats who can extort bribes in return for favors have nothing to gain from a more open and efficient administration.

The dismal experience of sub-Saharan Africa since independence provides an example of how actors whose interests are at odds with the general social interest can impede economic growth. As Map 10.1 shows, many of the world's poorest countries are found in sub-Saharan Africa. Development policy in the region has largely served to benefit small groups and to harm the rest of society. For decades, governments systematically drained resources from the countryside in order to channel them into the cities, by direct taxation of farmers, by keeping farm prices artificially low, or by other means. These policies were often justified as a way of speeding urbanization and industrialization, and they may indeed have had that effect. But in societies that were 80 or 90 percent rural, this process amounted to impoverishing the masses to benefit a narrow urban elite. However, the urban elite was a politically important base of support for African governments. It included urban businessmen, government employees, and the military, on which many governments relied to stay in power. As a result, many African governments pursued economic policies that depleted the farm sector—which represented most of the population and most of the meaningful economic opportunities—in the interest of catering to inefficient urban enterprises and bureaucracies.[5]

Self-serving groups whose goals conflict with those of the rest of society can significantly impede development, but interests alone are insufficient to explain countries' different paths of development. After all, every country has powerful special interests, including groups who may be inimical to broader development, but every country also has masses of farmers, workers, businesspeople, and others who stand to benefit from policies that promote economic growth. What ultimately determines the character of government policies toward development is not just the interests in play but also the nature of their interactions: how politicians, social groups, and the public bargain, fight, cooperate, and negotiate their way toward an outcome.

In some societies, there may be conditions that make it easy for actors to come together in pursuit of shared goals, but in others there may be endemic divisions that make this collaboration very difficult. Hostility and conflict among ethnic or regional groups can impede both political stability and effective national government policies if rivalries between groups overcome a concern for the common good. Because many LDCs have boundaries that were determined by colonial powers without regard to preexisting ethnic, religious, and racial features of the population, they can be very diverse, and competition among groups can complicate the making of economic policy in these countries.[6]

Generally speaking, as we saw in Chapter 2, the larger the group, the more difficult collective action is. This means that, as we saw with respect to trade policies in Chapter 7, broad social interests are less likely to be organized than narrower special interests. Thus, special interest groups have an advantage in influencing policy. Nonetheless, sometimes the existence of a powerful common national goal (such as national unification or resistance to an external threat) can lead groups to set aside

5. Robert Bates, *Markets and States in Tropical Africa* (Berkeley: University of California Press, 1981), is the classic examination of this process.

6. For a survey, see Alberto Alesina and Eliana LaFerrara, "Ethnic Diversity and Economic Performance," *Journal of Economic Literature* 63 (September 2005): 762–800. This is not a problem only for poor countries, but it can be particularly troubling there.

MAP 10.1 *Income around the World*

As this map shows, per capita income varies greatly around the world. People in many African and South Asian countries live on less than $1,000 per year on average, a small fraction of the per capita income in North American and European countries. However, per capita income tells only part of the story, as it is an average. Some countries with relatively high per capita income, such as Brazil or South Africa, nonetheless have serious problems with poverty owing to the highly unequal distribution of wealth within the country.

Per capita income, 2014

- LOW, $1,045 OR LESS
- LOWER MIDDLE, $1,046 – $4,125
- UPPER MIDDLE, $4,126 – $12,745
- HIGH, $12,746 OR MORE

Map source: World Bank, World Development Indicators, http://data.worldbank.org/indicator (accessed 11/21/14).

Arctic Ocean

RUSSIA

UNITED
KINGDOM
NORWAY
IRELAND
GERMANY
FRANCE
PORTUGAL
SPAIN
ITALY
GREECE
MOROCCO
TUNISIA
ALGERIA
LIBYA
MAURITANIA
EGAL
GUINEA
MALI
NIGER
CHAD
SUDAN
NIGERIA
CEN.
AFR.
REP.
CAMEROON
GHANA
IVORY COAST
D.R.
CONGO
UGANDA
S. SUDAN
ETHIOPIA
KENYA
SOMALIA
ANGOLA
ZAMBIA
MALAWI
TANZANIA
MADAGASCAR
NAMIBIA
MOZAMBIQUE
ZIMBABWE
SOUTH
AFRICA
BOTSWANA

SWEDEN
FINLAND
BELARUS
UKRAINE
GEORGIA
KAZAKHSTAN
UZBEKISTAN
TURKMENISTAN
KYRGYZSTAN
TAJIKISTAN
MONGOLIA
TURKEY
SYRIA
ISRAEL
LEB.
JORDAN
IRAQ
IRAN
EGYPT
SAUDI
ARABIA
UAE
OMAN
ERITREA
YEMEN
PAKISTAN
AFGHANISTAN
NEPAL
BHUTAN
INDIA
CHINA
MYANMAR
(BURMA)
MACAU
N. KOREA
S. KOREA
JAPAN
HONG KONG
TAIWAN
THAILAND
VIETNAM
LAOS
CAMBODIA
BANGLADESH
SRI LANKA
MALAYSIA
PHILIPPINES
INDONESIA
PAPUA NEW GUINEA
Pacific Ocean
Indian Ocean
AUSTRALIA
NEW
ZEALAND

429

their differences and focus together on developmental requirements. It has been suggested that South Korea and Taiwan were strongly motivated to grow rapidly in part because of their competition with North Korea and China, respectively. The economist Mancur Olson was optimistic that development could be spurred, and self-interested special interests denied, when societies were dominated by encompassing coalitions—that is, alliances that include enough of society to be concerned for broad social welfare.[7]

Whether important social actors interact in a cooperative manner to spur development also depends on domestic political institutions. These institutions affect the influence of those pressing for the public interest and for the goals of specific groups. More representative political institutions, for example, are likely to give more weight to broad public concerns about overall economic growth. Countries with more democratic political institutions appear to provide more public goods than do authoritarian political systems—more basic education, more public health, more equitable and efficient distributions of land.[8] In fact, part of the problem in postcolonial Africa has been the very undemocratic nature of most of the region's political systems, which allowed a narrow urban elite to use the government to exploit the masses of farmers and other rural dwellers.

Domestic Institutions

How and why have certain societies developed institutions that are conducive to economic growth, while others have not? Of course, the interests that characterize a society, the interactions among them, and the institutions that develop within them are all interrelated. Nonetheless, some scholars emphasize how the human and material resources that societies possess give rise to interests and institutions that may be more or less favorable to development. This view incorporates the geographic features of different regions of the world into a broader interpretation of developmental paths. For example, societies that rely on the exploitation of rich natural resources with the use of plantation agriculture or mining are often dominated by powerful elites whose interests work against development. Elites in these societies can create political institutions that are strongly biased against popular participation and that serve to retard broad-based participation in economic growth (see "How Do We Know?" on p. 432).

This perspective helps explain the surprising fact that many regions that are extremely rich in natural resources are developmental disasters. The relationship between resource wealth and underdevelopment is strong enough to have prompted theories of a "resource curse" in which initial wealth gives rise to

---

7. Mancur Olson, *The Rise and Decline of Nations: Economic Growth, Stagflation, and Social Rigidities* (New Haven, CT: Yale University Press, 1982).

8. See, for example, David Lake and Matthew Baum, "The Political Economy of Growth: Democracy and Human Capital," *American Journal of Political Science* 47, no. 2 (April 2003): 333–47; Nancy D. Lapp, *Landing Votes: Representation and Land Reform in Latin America* (New York: Palgrave/Macmillan, 2004); David Stasavage, "Democracy and Education Spending in Africa," *American Journal of Political Science* 49, no. 2 (2005): 343–58; and David S. Brown and Wendy A. Hunter, "Democracy and Human Capital Formation: Education Spending in Latin America, 1980 to 1997," *Comparative Political Studies* 37, no. 7 (2004): 842–64.

Many countries that are rich in natural resources remain poor. Nigeria is one of the world's largest oil exporters, but the average Nigerian has hardly benefited from this natural wealth. Poor Nigerians frequently risk death to pilfer oil from pipelines.

subsequent poverty. One such idea is that the government of a country with a natural resource that can be easily and lucratively exploited may have few reasons to encourage productive activities other than those associated with the resource. In addition, the effortless inflow of money to the government may provide a fertile ground for corrupt practices. In contrast, the government of a country with few natural resources, if it wants economic growth, has little choice but to undertake measures that will make the economy more productive. Recalling the comparison of Zambia and South Korea noted at the outset of this chapter, it may be that Zambia's copper wealth gave its rulers little incentive to increase the country's ability to produce anything other than raw materials by improving education, public health, and the economic infrastructure; by contrast, South Korea's lack of any major exportable raw materials forced its government to focus on improving the productive capacities of its people.[9] The broader point is that geographic and other inherent features of a country are important for subsequent development inasmuch as they have a substantial impact on the kinds of interests and institutions that arise on their basis.

In sum, to understand why countries have developed in a certain way, we need to understand people's interests and their ability or inability to interact in ways that foster cooperation, as well as the political institutions that determine how people's interests are translated into policy. Domestic factors, and especially national

---

9. See, for example, Michael Shafer, *Winners and Losers: How Sectors Shape the Developmental Prospects of States* (Ithaca, NY: Cornell University Press, 1994); Halvor Mehlum, Karl Moene, and Ragnar Torvik, "Institutions and the Resource Curse," *Economic Journal* 116 (2006): 1–20; and Macartan Humphreys, Jeffrey D. Sachs, and Joseph E. Stiglitz, eds., *Escaping the Resource Curse* (New York: Columbia University Press, 2007). But for a different view see Yu-Ming Liou and Paul Musgrave, "Refining the Oil Curse," *Comparative Political Studies* 47, no. 11 (September 2014): 1584–1610.

Explaining Developmental Differences: North and South America

What explains the major developmental differences among countries with relatively similar economic starting points? One instructive comparison is between North and South America. The two regions were colonized by Europeans at roughly the same time and got their independence within a few decades of each other; since then, however, they have diverged in important ways.

Two economic historians, Stanley Engerman and Kenneth Sokoloff, have argued that the kinds of economic activities the regions undertook early in their history had a lasting impact on their subsequent social, political, and economic evolution. The early patterns of economic organization created powerful interests that could craft institutions with an enduring effect on subsequent political, social, and economic development. Engerman and Sokoloff have brought many different kinds of evidence to bear in comparing North and South American developmental paths.[a]

Many Latin American colonies and countries were drawn into the world economy on the basis of plantation agriculture (such as sugar, cotton, or coffee, as in the plantation pictured above) or labor-intensive mining (silver, gold). These economic activities created highly unequal societies made up of wealthy landowners or miners, on the one hand, and poorly paid workers or slaves, on the other. Naturally, the wealthy landowners and miners were the dominant interests in these societies. These powerful interests played a major part in creating undemocratic political institutions, which reflected

and reinforced the great inequalities in society and helped the wealthy hold on to power.

The bias in colonial and postcolonial political institutions can be seen through their rules on who was eligible to vote. All 13 original colonies that made up the United States restricted voting to those with property, sometimes substantial property. But over the decades after independence, these property restrictions were gradually relaxed and eventually eliminated. By 1850, white male adult Americans could vote whether or not they owned property or were literate, while every Latin American country restricted voting to those who both owned property and were literate. As a result, at a time when 13 percent of the American population voted in elections, the proportion in Latin America was at most 1 or 2 percent. To be sure, the United States would not qualify as a democracy by our current standards: African Americans and women could not vote. Nonetheless, the difference in the extent to which politicians faced a broad electorate is striking. The image on the right depicts a lively scene from the 1852 U.S. elections.

These differences in the right to vote persisted for decades, even centuries. Around 1900, 18 percent of Americans voted—although this advance was marred by the fact that the southern states had imposed literacy requirements in order to restrict the rights of African Americans to vote. In most Latin American countries, the proportion voting was still below 5 percent. Even in 1940,

a. A summary of their work is in Stanley Engerman and Kenneth Sokoloff, "History Lessons: Institutions, Factor Endowments, and Paths of Development in the New World," *Journal of Economic Perspectives* 14, no. 3 (2000): 217–32. Other components can be found in Stanley Engerman and Kenneth Sokoloff, "Factor Endowments, Institutions, and Differential Paths of Growth among New World Economies: A View from Economic Historians of the United States," in *How Latin America Fell Behind,* ed. Stephen Haber, 260–304 (Stanford, CA: Stanford University Press, 1997); Stanley Engerman and Kenneth Sokoloff, "The Evolution of Suffrage Institutions in the New World," *Journal of Economic History* 65, no. 4 (December 2005): 891–921; and Kenneth Sokoloff and Eric Zolt, "Inequality and the Evolution of Institutions of Taxation: Evidence from the Economic History of the Americas," in *The Decline of Latin American Economies: Growth, Institutions, and Crises,* ed. Sebastian Edwards, Gerardo Esquivel, and Graciela Márquez, 83–136 (Chicago: University of Chicago Press, 2007).

the share of Americans voting was still two to four times as great as the share of Latin Americans.

The institutions that restricted the access of Latin Americans to the political system had a powerful effect on what governments had incentives to do. Where only the wealthy could influence politics, policies reflected the interests of the wealthy. This is seen, in the case of Latin America, in the lack of government policies to improve education, public health, or the economic opportunities of the poor. Such biased institutions, and such a lack of developmentally oriented policies, retarded economic growth.

In most of North America, however, early economic activities created fewer inequalities. Small-scale wheat farming in the United States and Canada, for example, produced a class of independent family farmers and a society that was quite equal. This equality was reflected in democratic political institutions as well as in substantial government investments in infrastructure, education, and other economically important activities. Here, the developmentally oriented institutions and policies encouraged economic growth. As early as 1850, literacy for white adults in the United States was above 90 percent, a level that many Latin American countries have reached only recently—if at all. Of course, because literacy was actively discouraged (even prohibited)

among slaves, literacy among African American adults in the United States was under 20 percent.

In fact, the experience of the American South underscores the argument that economic activities affect interests, which in turn affect institutions, which in turn affect development paths. In the southern United States, unlike in the North and Midwest, there were substantial slave plantation regions growing cotton and tobacco. In this way, the South was more like Latin America than like the North. Engerman and Sokoloff show that in the former plantation areas in the eighteenth and nineteenth centuries, inequalities were much greater than elsewhere in the United States; the right to vote was much more restricted, and, of course, these restrictions persisted for a century after slavery was abolished; and there was much less spending on education and other public works. The highly unequal nature of southern American society, Engerman and Sokoloff argue, created an enduring legacy that was reflected in the South's institutions and that held back its economic growth for many decades.

The experiences of Latin America, and of the American South, demonstrate how domestic economic, political, and social interests and institutions created early in a region's economic history can have a long-lasting impact on its subsequent development.

government policies, are crucial to understanding national developmental success or failure.

Nonetheless, there are many ways in which the international environment shapes the constraints and opportunities faced by developing countries—and not always in a positive way. Many people in the LDCs argue that international conditions have not been helpful to their prospects and indeed that the current poverty of much of the world is due to the structure of the international system.

Are Rich Countries Responsible for the Problems of the Developing World?

There is evidence that interests, interactions, and institutions at the international level are responsible for at least some of the current problems of poor nations. While developed and developing countries have many interests in common, there are also many real and potential conflicts of interests among them.

Rich and poor nations have many shared interests. Economic growth in the developing world can create enormous opportunities for wealthy countries. As we saw in Chapters 7, 8, and 9, rich-country corporations can profit from investing in and selling to developing nations, while poor countries can benefit from the capital, technology, and expertise that such corporations bring. LDC exports provide cheap goods for industrial-country consumers while they make money for the exporters. Banks from the industrialized world are eager to make loans to developing countries, in part because poor countries that are short of capital are willing to pay higher interest rates than can be earned elsewhere. The growth of poor countries' economies expands investment opportunities and markets for rich-country businesses. All these factors suggest why the relationship among rich and poor nations could be cooperative and the scope for mutually beneficial exchange very large.

By the same token, all countries have a common interest in the successful management of international economic affairs. Developed and developing countries alike benefit from well-functioning international trading, financial, and monetary systems. Few, if any, nations stand to gain from a breakdown of the international economy or from the transmission of financial crises from one country to another. International collaboration to smooth the operation of the world economy and to deal with problems that may arise is generally in the interest of all countries. Indeed, most international economic organizations—including the International Monetary Fund (IMF), the World Bank, and the World Trade Organization (WTO)—have both rich and poor nations as their members.

However, the interests of developed and developing countries may also clash. As we have seen in other areas of international politics, agreement over the desirability of cooperation coexists with disagreement over how to distribute the benefits of cooperation. A multinational mining company and an LDC government have a common interest in getting minerals out of the ground and to market, but they are likely to disagree about the division of the profits. Similarly, LDC companies and governments may appreciate being able to borrow from international banks, but there is likely to be political controversy about making the sacrifices necessary to pay back their debts—especially in hard times. The fact that rich countries' corporations can profit from low wages in the LDCs can give them little interest in encouraging development that will raise wages. Such a mix of interests in common and in conflict is central to the international political economy of development. It can be seen in many historical and contemporary examples.

Did Colonialism Hamper Development?

One aspect of the international order that is often blamed for underdevelopment is the legacy of colonialism. As we discussed in Chapter 1, from the sixteenth through the twentieth centuries colonial rule was often justified as being in the interests of both the colonial powers and the colonized. Indeed, there are many instances of colonialism that encouraged broad-based economic growth in poor countries, for sometimes the interests of rulers and ruled were similar. Some colonial regimes supplied roads, railroads, ports, and other infrastructure both to facilitate their rule and to gain access to the colonies' resources; this infrastructure facilitated the economic and political development of the colonial society overall. After all, some of today's most developed nations—the United States, Canada, Australia, New Zealand—were longtime colonies.

Nonetheless, the interests of the colonizers and the colonized were frequently in conflict, so the enduring impact of colonialism was frequently negative. Most imperial powers wanted to use their colonies for the mother country's benefit even if this was not beneficial to the colonial society. They often reserved economic advantages to their own citizens and restricted the access of colonial subjects to

This 1933 French illustration shows an idealized vision of colonialism, one in which the European settlers fostered development through education and industry. In reality, however, the interests of colonial rulers were often at odds with local development.

economic opportunity. And when the colonial rulers' interests were inconsistent with local development, it was the rulers' interests that prevailed. This situation led to interactions that subordinated colonial societies and economies to the needs of the empire.

Colonialism, indeed, institutionalized a relationship in which the interests of the colonies were secondary to those of the mother country. For example, colonial policy commonly directed colonial trade toward the mother country, restricted manufacturing in the colonies, and otherwise gave trading privileges to the colonial power. (This was true of British policy toward the 13 colonies in North America; see Chapter 1.) Such preferential policies were intended in part to benefit residents of the great power, in part to deny benefits to real or potential enemies in other empires. This approach can hardly have been beneficial for development, and it may have been highly detrimental.

There are many instances of colonial rule that was negligent at best, predatory at worst. One famous example is that of Leopold II, king of the Belgians, in the Congo (the former Belgian Congo, now known as the Democratic Republic of the Congo). When the European powers colonized Africa in the late nineteenth century, they permitted Leopold to turn the Congo into his own personal possession. For decades, Leopold exploited the indigenous people mercilessly, forcing them to gather ivory, rubber, and other raw materials and to turn them over to his own colonial government.[10]

In one study, three scholars analyzed how the form colonialism took had a systematic impact on subsequent development. Daron Acemoglu, Simon Johnson, and James Robinson suggest that the countries and regions of the colonial world can be divided into two types. The first includes countries where European settlers could live easily, without fear of high mortality owing to tropical diseases or other threats. In these regions, settlers from the colonial powers, the scholars write, "went and settled in the colonies and set up institutions that enforced the rule of law and encouraged investment."[11] European settlers, in other words, went where they could survive, and they established social, political, and economic institutions that were conducive to economic growth. These institutions persisted, and in such countries as Canada and Australia the result was successful development.

In other regions, where European settlers were much more likely to die of disease or other factors, the colonial powers engaged in predatory policies. There, the scholars say, the Europeans "set up extractive states with the intention of transferring resources rapidly to the metropole. These institutions were detrimental to investment and economic progress."[12] In other words, where large-scale European immigration and settlement were not feasible, the colonial powers simply exploited the region for their own benefit, establishing institutions that were not conducive to

---

10. A classic analysis of the Congo's experience is Adam Hochschild, *King Leopold's Ghost* (Boston: Houghton Mifflin, 1998).

11. Daron Acemoglu, Simon Johnson, and James Robinson, "The Colonial Origins of Comparative Development," *American Economic Review* 91, no. 5 (December 2001): 1395.

12. Acemoglu, Johnson, and Robinson, "The Colonial Origins of Comparative Development," 1395.

In regions with climates hospitable to European immigrants, such as the American West, settlers moved in and established political institutions that set the stage for successful economic development.

economic growth. These institutions too persisted and served to impede successful development.

To evaluate their argument, Acemoglu, Johnson, and Robinson looked at the death rates of early European settlers in colonial regions between the 1600s and the 1800s. There is little reason to think that these death rates would in themselves have a direct impact on modern economic growth, but in fact the settlers' mortality rates were strongly correlated with underdevelopment today. This is powerful evidence for the kind of effects the three scholars anticipated. It seems clear that different types of colonial experiences, and the different institutions put in place by colonial powers, have had enduring effects on development. Where the common interests of colonial powers and people in the colonies predominated, the impact of colonialism was favorable (or at least neutral). However, where the colonial powers' interests went against those of the local population—such as in extracting labor and resources from the colony by force—and the colonialists imposed their will, the impact of colonialism was detrimental.

While the lasting effects of colonialism explain some of the disparity between rich and poor nations, they cannot explain all of it. After all, most Latin American nations have been independent for nearly 200 years—longer than many developed countries have been in existence—and even most former colonies in Africa, Asia, and the Caribbean have been independent for at least 50 years. Some poor countries—such as China, Thailand, Iran, Liberia, and Ethiopia—have never been colonies[13] and yet have suffered from severe developmental problems. However, other international factors are often invoked as barriers to development as well.

---

13. However, parts of China were occupied by foreign powers, and Ethiopia was invaded and occupied by Italy for several years.

Is the International Economy Biased against LDCs?

Some analysts believe that general features of the international economy impede the development of poor nations. One prominent argument was made in the 1950s by Raúl Prebisch, an Argentine economist and for many years the head of the UN Economic Commission for Latin America (ECLA).[14] Prebisch accepted that in principle trade was good for both rich and poor countries. However, he noted that LDCs produced mostly raw materials and agricultural products while rich countries produced mostly manufactured goods. He contended that this very fact meant that trade worked against the interests of the LDCs and in favor of the interests of the developed countries.

The problem, Prebisch said, was that the prices of the LDCs' products tended to decline over time relative to the prices of the industrialized countries' products. This occurred because LDCs sold mainly **primary products**—that is, agricultural goods and raw materials. And because markets for the LDCs' primary products were very competitive (there were millions of cocoa or coffee farmers), prices moved up and down very easily. However, markets for manufactured goods (automobiles, machinery) were controlled by a few large **oligopolistic** firms—that is, firms that could control their markets. Such firms could ensure that prices rose whenever possible and did not fall even in adverse market conditions.[15] The result was that the **terms of trade**—the relative movement of export and import prices—of countries that specialized in primary products deteriorated: they got less for what they sold, and they paid more for what they bought. Countries that specialized in producing raw materials and farm products for world markets, Prebisch and his supporters argued, were at a fundamental disadvantage.

Prebisch and his followers in ECLA concluded that the very structure of the world economy was biased against the developing world. In this view, the industrialized countries had an interest in maintaining a structure of international trade that was detrimental to the LDCs. Although many scholars were skeptical of the argument, it was very popular in the developing world. Indeed, it justified policies that many LDCs were pursuing—of protecting the home market and artificially spurring industrialization.

Are International Institutions Biased against LDCs?

Even among those who accept that the world economy can benefit the LDCs, many scholars believe that international political factors are responsible for exacerbating the problems of development. They emphasize the relative powerlessness of developing nations in their interactions with richer countries. In this view, the principal obstacle facing LDCs is not global markets but the character of the international order

---

primary products

Raw materials and agricultural products, typically unprocessed or only slightly processed. The primary sectors are distinguished from secondary sectors (industry) and tertiary sectors (services).

oligopoly

A situation in which a market or industry is dominated by a few firms.

terms of trade

The relationship between a country's export prices and its import prices.

---

14. For a survey and analysis, see Joseph L. Love, "Raúl Prebisch and the Origins of the Doctrine of Unequal Exchange," *Latin American Research Review* 15 (1980): 45–72.

15. Prebisch also observed that because manufacturing was usually unionized, wages were also less flexible, which contributed to the rigidity of industrial prices.

and of international institutions whose rules are written by rich nations in order to serve their own interests.

While all countries can benefit from international economic exchange, the greater power of rich countries to influence patterns of international trade and finance can certainly work against the interests of the LDCs. Indeed, rich countries often pursue their own interests in ways that harm prospects for development in poor countries. The problem is not that the industrialized nations purposefully or maliciously attempt to impoverish poor countries. Rather, it is that rich countries' policies to safeguard their own interests (or at least the interests powerful enough to matter to their governments) create problems for poor countries. Farm trade policy is a good example. As we saw in Chapter 8, almost all industrialized countries extensively subsidize and protect their farmers. This policy has the effect of restricting the opportunities of LDC farmers, many of whom would otherwise be able to undersell farmers in North America, western Europe, and Japan. There is no intellectual or economic justification for these protectionist policies; they are simply the result of the interests of American, European, and Japanese farmers, which are in conflict with the interests of developing-country farmers.

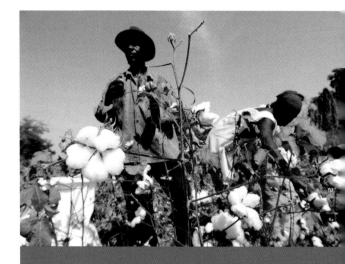

Farmers in the developing world have a comparative advantage in providing agricultural products (like cotton) to world markets, but Western governments subsidize their farms so heavily that developing nations' farmers are hampered in their ability to compete.

American cotton policy illustrates the point. The U.S. government spends several billion dollars a year to subsidize American cotton farmers. This is lucrative for the recipients of the subsidies and politically attractive for American politicians. The subsidy program pays farmers extra to produce cotton, which increases American output of cotton beyond what it would otherwise be; it therefore raises the world supply of cotton and lowers its price. This in turn drives down the price received by cotton farmers in developing countries, who may be lower-cost producers than the American farmers but who do not have the luxury of expensive farm support programs. The upshot is that the U.S. government has since 1995 paid about $2 billion a year in subsidies to American cotton farmers—almost all of which has gone to about 25,000 farmers. Cotton farmers in Texas alone have received nearly $11 billion in subsidies since 1995.[16] Meanwhile, several million cotton farmers in Africa, Asia, and Latin America have their incomes cut by the resultant reduction in the world price of cotton.

The power disparity between rich and poor countries clearly works against the LDCs. The governments of the developing world have been almost entirely unsuccessful at getting their farmers greater access to the markets of the industrialized nations. Meanwhile, the governments of the rich countries have been quite successful in getting the LDCs to open their markets to manufacturers, multinational

16. Full data are available at http://farm.ewg.org/progdetail.php?fips=00000&progcode=cotton (accessed 01/05/15).

FIGURE 10.1 *Voting Power in the International Monetary Fund, 2014**

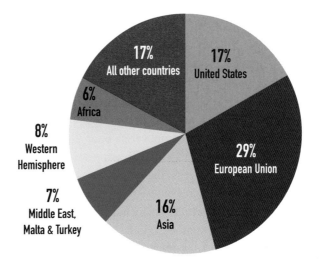

Figure source: IMF, www.imf.org/external/np/sec/pr/2011/pdfs/quota_tbl.pdf (accessed 12/11/14).

*Projected vote shares after implementation of 2008 and 2010 reforms.

corporations, and international banks from the developed world. The weakness of the LDCs relative to the developed nations means that they often lose out in international interactions of this sort, to the ultimate detriment of their economic prospects.[17]

The same pattern prevails within the major international economic institutions. While the LDCs participate in international economic institutions—most are members of the IMF, the World Bank, and the WTO—these institutions are dominated by the rich countries and biased against the interests of the poor nations.

We saw in Chapter 9 that many critics in the developing world regard the IMF as a tool of the rich nations. Indeed, in the IMF, voting is weighted by the financial and economic size of the member states, such that rich countries effectively control the institution (Figure 10.1). In fact, the United States has enough votes to veto any proposal, as do the member states of the European Union. This means that the rich countries can bend IMF policies and procedures in their favor—for example, to deal lightly with their allies or harshly with their enemies—even when such action is not generally consistent with the IMF's own rules.

International trade agreements similarly reflect the interests of the rich and powerful. Initiatives of the developing countries are frequently ignored, even when they clearly would go in the direction of the WTO's purported goal, trade liberalization. Many developing-country exports face protectionist barriers in the industrialized nations, provided at the behest of affected industries that do not want to face such stiff competition. Perhaps most important is the attempt by the developing nations (and a few industrial countries that export farm products) to push for the WTO to encourage greater openness to farm products, especially on the part of the highly protectionist rich countries. Agricultural trade liberalization would open up

17. Joseph Stiglitz discusses many such examples in *Making Globalization Work* (New York: Norton, 2006); see pages 85–86 for the cotton example mentioned above.

important new opportunities to farmers in developing countries, many of whom are low-cost agricultural producers. But because the principal losers would be farmers in developed countries, the rich nations have adamantly resisted including trade in farm products on the agenda for liberalization.

The interests of developed- and developing-country governments clash in many arenas. The power disparities between rich and poor countries typically mean that interactions among them are decided in favor of the rich. Moreover, the international institutions that govern the international economy were largely created by rich and powerful countries, so their policies and decision rules reflect their own concerns. In all these ways, the alignment of interests, interactions, and institutions in the international order can limit the prospects for successful development of poor nations.

Development Policies and Development Politics

Over the past century, poor countries have experienced many changes in the domestic and international spheres that have affected their development. Conditions both at home and abroad have had an impact on the interests, institutions, and interactions that structure the development process. Before 1914, most developing regions—whether they were independent, as in Latin America, or colonial, as in most of the rest of the world—focused their efforts on primary products (agricultural goods and raw materials). Dominated as they were by those with interests in selling their goods abroad, they welcomed access to global markets and foreign capital as they strove to develop their mineral wealth and their farmland. The importance of export-oriented interests was reinforced by their control over political institutions, a situation that occurred in both autocratic independent countries and colonial systems. Despite the lack of democracy, many poor nations did quite well in the late nineteenth and early twentieth centuries, selling copper, coffee, cotton, and other primary goods to Europe and North America. In the process, they usually accepted general economic openness: relatively free trade, the gold standard, and inflows of foreign capital.

But after 1914, as the world economy experienced serious trouble, most developing regions turned inward. World War I, the troubled interwar years and the Great Depression of the 1930s, World War II, postwar reconstruction, and the start of the Cold War all kept the developed world preoccupied—and relatively uninterested in the developing regions. International investors were otherwise engaged at home; the foreign markets into which the LDCs had previously sold their products were stagnant or heavily protected, or both. The developing regions, both independent and colonial, were forced to fend for themselves as their ties to the developed world began to dwindle.

Import-Substituting Industrialization

In the context of these international trends, beginning in the 1930s a different set of interests came to the fore in many developing countries. With the collapse of foreign markets, export interests could no longer claim primacy, and initiative often shifted to economic groups interested in domestically oriented growth. Many developing countries therefore adopted policies that encouraged industrial development so that domestic producers could supply goods that had previously been imported. Latin America led the way in practice as in theory, adopting measures to stimulate industry.

The initial turn inward may have been forced by international events, the dislocations of the two world wars, and the Great Depression, but eventually it became a more conscious strategy. As domestic industrial interests grew in size and strength, they were able to push for a complex of policies known as **import-substituting industrialization (ISI)**. These policies had the goal of substituting local products for imports. It was in this context that Raúl Prebisch and his followers argued that such enforced self-sufficiency was actually desirable and should be deepened.

There were powerful domestic interests in favor of ISI. Most generally, developing-country governments wanted their economies to move away from primary (raw materials and agricultural) production and toward industry. This interest grew out of such theoretical conceptions as those of Prebisch, that accelerated industrialization would aid broader development; out of the belief that modern societies required a manufacturing base; out of a national security desire for indigenous industrial capacity; and out of other broad goals. At the same time, there were more specific interests in favor of the new policies. The previously predominant emphasis on primary production for export was associated with the political dominance of producers of these goods—copper miners, oilmen, plantation owners, ranchers. As foreign markets collapsed, these internationally oriented groups lost influence. They were supplanted by such pro-industrial groups as the urban business and middle classes and the industrial working class, who strongly supported ISI. The institutional evolution of developing societies, particularly the emergence of more representative political systems—democracies, in some cases—reduced the influence of the old exporting elites and increased the power of the urban groups.

Both broad and narrower interests in ISI were also at play in the former colonies in Africa and Asia as they won their independence. Colonialism had been associated with selling primary products to the colonial power, but decolonization was associated with efforts to replace raw materials and agricultural production with urban manufacturing. And just as colonial societies were often dominated by colonial or local miners, oilmen, or farmers, postcolonial societies came to be dominated by such urban interest groups as businessmen, the middle classes, labor, and government employees. For these reasons, after 1945, almost all the long-independent developing nations of Latin America and the newly independent ones of Africa, Asia, and the Caribbean reduced their economic ties with the rest of the world, protected and subsidized local manufacturing, and attempted to stimulate domestic industrial development. In important ways, these policies reflected the view that engagement with the world economy could be an impediment to national economic development.

import-substituting industrialization (ISI)

A set of policies, pursued by most developing countries from the 1930s through the 1980s, to reduce imports and encourage domestic manufacturing, often through trade barriers, subsidies to manufacturing, and state ownership of basic industries.

For decades, most LDCs followed the broad outlines of import substitution, including:

- Trade barriers to protect domestic manufacturers from foreign competition and encourage national industrial development

- Government incentives to industry, including tax credits, cheap loans, and other subsidies to draw investors into the modern industrial sector

- Government provision of basic industrial services by public enterprises—electric power, telecommunications, transport, finance—to supplement or replace private provision that was seen as too expensive or too limited

All over the third world, government policies encouraged the development of large state sectors behind high protectionist barriers. The result was rapid industrialization in many areas. Between 1950 and 1970, for example, Brazil and Mexico developed large automobile industries where none had previously existed, and by the 1970s the two countries were producing a million cars a year. By the 1970s, indeed, most of the larger developing countries pursuing ISI—India, Brazil, Mexico, Argentina—were largely self-sufficient in manufactured products.

However, ISI had weaknesses. The industries it encouraged were not efficient and had difficulty selling their goods abroad. After all, they had grown up in protected markets and were not originally expected to be competitive in international markets. Over time, as countries continued to need to earn money to pay for essential imports, the difficulties the new manufacturers encountered in exporting were worrisome.

As problems accumulated, the inward-looking self-sufficiency of ISI began to lose support. In part, the Prebisch-ECLA view declined for intellectual reasons: evidence accumulated that the argument might not be correct or that economic ties with developed countries might not have as negative an impact as had been suggested. There were also pragmatic and political reasons why the LDCs turned toward global integration. Many producers with previous interests in ISI came to believe that selling only to a small and poor home market restricted their potential. The insularity of protected markets left many manufacturers technically backward, making products of low quality—a fact that became increasingly worrisome with the rise of modern electronics and computing. The bias against producing for export meant that developing countries sold little in world markets. This meant they could not buy much abroad, which left them vulnerable to crises when, for example, oil prices skyrocketed in the 1970s. And the ISI bias against agriculture impoverished many farmers, leading to mass internal migrations that flooded the cities with the formerly rural poor. By the early 1980s, ISI was in trouble.

Export-Oriented Industrialization

There was also an alternative available, for a handful of countries in East Asia had tried something different. Beginning in the mid-1960s, South Korea, Taiwan, Singapore, and the British colony of Hong Kong had turned toward **export-oriented industrialization (EOI)**. These governments had encouraged their manufacturers to produce for foreign, especially American, consumers. They used many

export-oriented industrialization (EOI)

A set of policies, originally pursued in the late 1960s by several East Asian countries, to spur manufacturing for export, often through subsidies and incentives for export production.

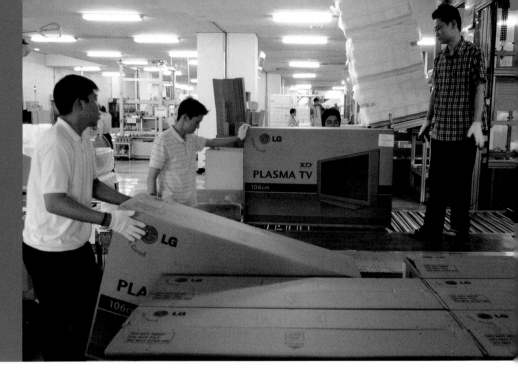

A strategy of export-oriented industrialization led some developing countries to produce high-quality goods to be sold overseas. By the 1980s, this strategy had proved highly successful for countries like South Korea. Here, workers in a South Korean factory produce plasma TVs.

techniques to push exports: low-cost loans and tax breaks to exporters, and a very weak currency to make their products artificially cheap. While the rest of the third world turned industry inward in the 1960s and 1970s, the export-oriented countries pushed it outward. This meant relying on often volatile international markets, but it had the advantage of forcing national manufacturers to produce goods that met rigorous technological, quality, and price standards.

By the late 1970s, the four East Asian economies were flooding world markets with toys, clothing, furniture, and other simple manufactures. South Korean exports skyrocketed from $385 million in 1970 to $15 billion in 1979, 90 percent of them manufactured goods. On this basis, South Korea's government pursued heavy industrial development by sponsoring modern steel mills, chemical factories, and a new auto industry. By the early 1980s, the country had the world's largest private shipyard and largest machinery factory.[18]

The Turn toward Globalization

While the EOI model was pursued by a relatively small number of countries prior to the 1980s, only a decade later it became the dominant strategy throughout the developing world. The devastating debt crisis that hit the developing world in the early 1980s (see Chapter 9) dealt a fatal blow to ISI. For one thing, the ISI economies were particularly severely affected because they had so much trouble increasing exports and generating the money they needed to service their debts. But the East Asian EOI economies weathered the crisis with less trouble. Their businesses were used to selling abroad and could increase exports rapidly to service their debts.

18. Jeff Frieden, "Third World Indebted Industrialization: International Finance and State Capitalism in Mexico, Brazil, Algeria, and South Korea," *International Organization* 35, no. 3 (Summer 1981): 426.

After a couple of difficult years, the so-called Asian Tigers resumed rapid growth. Meanwhile, the deep crisis in the ISI economies eventually drove them to turn toward export promotion themselves. By the late 1980s, almost all developing countries had abandoned ISI and opted to integrate their economies into global markets. The positive experience of EOI, and the negative experiences of ISI, seemed to point the way toward a new, globalized economic future for the developing world.

The debt crisis also left the LDCs vulnerable to pressure from the industrialized countries—and from such international institutions as the IMF and World Bank—to change their economic policies. In return for having their debts restructured, LDCs came under pressure to implement reforms favored by governments and institutions from the rich world. For both domestic and international reasons, then, over the course of the 1990s many LDCs adapted to the new interest in globalization. The economist John Williamson dubbed the complex of policies associated with this transformation the **Washington Consensus**, which came to connote the general acceptance of market-oriented policies.[19] Among the policies that were, in varying degrees, adopted by the LDCs were the following:

- *Trade liberalization*, the removal of barriers to imports and exports in an attempt to make national producers more competitive on world markets

- *Privatization*, the selling off of many government enterprises to private investors who would presumably run them more efficiently

- *Fiscal and monetary policies* to avoid large deficits and high inflation

- *Openness* to foreign investment and to international capital flows more generally

These policies were also generally embraced by the governments of countries in eastern and central Europe and the former Soviet Union, as they made their way from Communist central planning toward market societies in the 1990s.

The shift away from economic nationalism toward economic openness had both international and domestic sources. As the rest of the world economy grew rapidly, and as globalization advanced elsewhere, it was hard for poor nations to continue to deny themselves access to the opportunities the world economy might make available. Powerful domestic actors in the developing world increasingly saw their interests as being served by tapping into global markets, global capital, and global technologies. And economic integration seems to have worked relatively well. Countries such as China and India have grown very rapidly since they turned toward world markets, and they have been followed by dozens of other LDCs. Meanwhile, demands from the developed countries and the international institutions they dominated pushed even many reluctant LDCs in the direction of globalization. This move highlights the fact that many actors in the developing world resent the perceived bias of international economic institutions and that many LDC governments have attempted to counter the power imbalance with the power of numbers.

Washington Consensus

An array of policy recommendations generally advocated by developed-country economists and policy makers starting in the 1980s, including trade liberalization, privatization, openness to foreign investment, and restrictive monetary and fiscal policies.

---

19. John Williamson, "What Washington Means by Policy Reform," in *Latin American Readjustment: How Much Has Happened*, ed. John Williamson (Washington, DC: Institute for International Economics, 1989).

Attempts to Remedy the Bias of International Institutions

Developing countries confronted their problems at the international level as well as through national policies. Beginning in the 1950s, many countries in Asia, Africa, and the Caribbean that gained their independence after World War II grouped themselves into an international organization focused on economic and political issues that are of concern to developing nations, the Non-Aligned Movement, and pledged to avoid alliances with either the American-led West or the Soviet-led East. The Non-Aligned Movement eventually gave rise to developing-country coalitions at the UN and in international institutions more generally. The UN variant was formed in 1964 with 77 members and has since been known as the **Group of 77** (although it currently has over 130 member countries). These developing-country-based institutions attempt to use the collective power of numbers in the world political arena to reform the economic order in favor of the developing world.

The most systematic efforts along these lines came in the 1970s, when developing countries fought in the UN and elsewhere for what they called the New International Economic Order. Its purpose was to renegotiate the bargain that had constituted the international economic order so that it would be more in line with the economic needs of poor nations. The proposals included curtailing the rights of foreign investors in developing countries, revising trade agreements to favor the products of the developing world, and enhancing the influence of LDC governments in international economic organizations. These efforts resulted in some UN resolutions and other initiatives, but little of a concrete nature was accomplished.

The LDCs were more successful at using their control over natural resources to strengthen their bargaining position with the rich nations. The most striking example came from the members of OPEC, a group of developing-country oil producers whose creation in 1960 had gone almost unnoticed. But in 1973, in the midst of a war between Israel and its Arab neighbors, OPEC's Arab members doubled the price of oil to more than $5 a barrel, then two months later doubled it again to nearly $12 a barrel. They did so by purposely restricting their supply of oil to world markets, a move that drove up world oil prices. As the price increases persisted, it was clear that a small group of developing countries had dramatically changed the terms on which they sold their goods. Tens of billions of dollars flowed into the coffers of developing-country governments, and for the first time a group of developing nations appeared to have the upper hand in economic dealings with the West. In the wake of this electrifying development, other third-world commodity producers—of copper, coffee, iron ore, bauxite, and bananas—tried to emulate OPEC in creating international **commodity cartels**, organizations of producers who cooperate to restrict the supply and raise the price of their products.

Some of the other commodity cartels had an impact, but the oil sector was unique in the scale of its achievements. Oil producers were particularly successful for several reasons. There were few readily available substitutes for oil, so price increases did not reduce consumption very much. Also, just a few OPEC members

Group of 77

A coalition of developing countries in the UN, formed in 1964 with 77 members; it has grown to over 130 members but maintains the original name.

commodity cartels

Associations of producers of commodities (raw materials and agricultural products) that restrict world supply and thereby cause the price of the goods to rise.

controlled a very large share of the world's oil: Saudi Arabia, Kuwait, Qatar, and the United Arab Emirates together had nearly half the world's oil reserves. They did not need to sell oil quickly and could hold it off the market to keep prices high. An additional source of power was the solidarity of OPEC's Muslim members in and around the Middle East, who shared cultural and political ties.

OPEC was able to obtain enormous amounts of money for its members. Some of this income was shared with other developing countries, although many poor countries that did not have oil themselves were harmed by the oil shocks. In addition, oil states were able to leverage their resources into increased influence at the IMF and World Bank. For a while, it appeared that commodity cartels would have a more general effect on third-world power, strengthening demands for a new economic order. But, by the early 1980s, LDC attempts to achieve far-reaching international reforms had largely failed. Some natural resource producers had gotten richer, but the underlying institutions of the international political economy had not fundamentally changed.

The very rapid growth of some large developing countries—in particular China, India, and Brazil—has led to their gradual inclusion in some of the international discussions that had previously been the sole domain of the rich countries. In fact, in the aftermath of the global financial crisis that began in 2008, the Group of 20 Finance Ministers and Central Bank Governors played a major role in attempting to address the crisis. The Group of 20 includes representatives of nine developing nations—Argentina, Brazil, China, India, Indonesia, Mexico, Russia, Saudi Arabia, and Turkey. Many observers believe that this expansion of the "leadership group" in international economic affairs reflects an opening up of at least some global discussions to the concerns of developing countries. Nonetheless, the countries represented tend to be the largest and richest nations in the developing world, and on balance it is still the case that LDCs find themselves subject to international economic trends and constrained by international institutions, over which they have little or no control.

Is Foreign Aid an Answer?

Many people believe that problems of development could be substantially alleviated by increased foreign aid from the rich nations of the world (see "Controversy" on p. 448). And there are certainly examples of places and projects where foreign aid has made a difference to the quality of life of people in poor nations. However, foreign aid is unlikely to play a major role in overcoming problems of underdevelopment for at least two reasons.

First, the amounts of aid given are quite small and are unlikely to grow. In recent years, total foreign assistance has been about $100 billion a year. This may seem like a lot, but it averages out to less than $20 per person in the LDCs, and it is dwarfed by the amounts of private investments and loans that come into the developing world from abroad. Although the rich countries have often expressed support for increasing aid, few countries have followed through in practice. In 1970, the rich nations set a target of 0.7 percent of their GDP as aid, but the actual number today is about one-third of that target. There is very little popular support for foreign aid in most developed nations, and there seems to be little prospect that it will change.

What Responsibilities Do Rich Countries Have to the Global Poor?

In 1998, a severe famine hit southern Sudan. The region's farmers, who barely subsist at the best of times, found themselves facing a chronic shortage of food and water following a two-year drought. Widespread malnutrition, starvation, and disease resulted. As many as 70,000 people died, and more than that number were displaced into surrounding regions in a desperate search for food. Thanks to an international aid effort and improved weather conditions, the immediate crisis subsided. But famine warnings continued at regular intervals throughout the succeeding decade. Today, other regions in Sudan again risk suffering a famine that could be at least as serious as that of 1998. This case is but one example of the many ways in which extreme poverty continues to cripple the lives of much of the world's population. Perhaps eventually we will see a world in which all countries enjoy a level of economic development sufficient to secure their citizens' basic needs, but that goal is currently distant. In the meantime, millions of people continue to suffer. What responsibility do citizens of the developed world have to assist them?

In 1972, in one of the best-known papers in ethics, the philosopher Peter Singer proposed a simple and startling answer to this question.[a] The argument depends on an analogy between two cases. In the first case, imagine you are walking past a shallow pond and see a child drowning. Should you jump into the pond and rescue the child? Clearly, Singer says, you should. Although your clothes will get wet, that fact is morally insignificant in comparison to the child's drowning. In the second case, imagine that people are starving overseas. Should you donate the money needed to help save them? Again, Singer claims, clearly you should, and for the same reason. Although you may have to sacrifice some luxuries, those things are morally insignificant in comparison to saving the starving people. And the same argument applies, Singer claims, to every starving person in the world. In practice, this means that you ought to give away all resources beyond those necessary to support yourself and your dependents, until global poverty is eradicated.

This conclusion calls for radical redistribution of wealth. Some opponents of Singer's perspective assert that his argument underestimates the role of conflicting interests, cooperation failures, and weak institutions in undermining the effectiveness of aid interventions. For example, consider that aid donations must pass through several hands before they reach their intended beneficiaries. And the interests of some of the intermediaries involved may not be well aligned with those of the poor. Governments that receive aid may use it to avoid providing relevant services; worse, they might simply appropriate the aid and use it for their own purposes, including repressing the poor. Nongovernmental organizations that receive aid have themselves been accused of setting priorities that are not in line with the real needs of the poor.

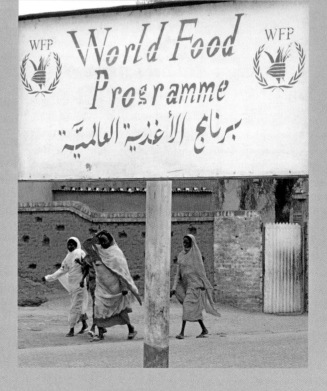

a. Peter Singer, "Famine, Affluence and Morality," Philosophy and Public Affairs 1, no. 1 (1972): 229–43.

Those who are skeptical about the potential of foreign aid to be of much assistance also point to the fact that the problems the aid is meant to solve are often due to long-standing political or economic failures of national governments, problems that the aid does little to alleviate and may actually prolong. As this chapter indicates, economic growth may be the surest way to overcome poverty in a developing country, and the obstacles to economic growth are typically highly political. In addition, ethnic or other political conflicts are often at the root of such development failures as famines.

In the recipient countries, aid typically is subject to the oversight—and sometimes the direct control—of the local government, and the local government may be biased toward existing local elites. In this case, all that the aid would do is strengthen the domestic interests and institutions that are responsible for the problem in the first place. In this case, the aid would actually *contribute* to the problems it is meant to help alleviate. Foreign aid of this sort has been characterized as poor people in rich countries giving money to rich people in poor countries.

Famines in the Sudan, for instance, have not primarily been caused by lack of rain. Throughout recent decades, as a tactic in an ongoing civil war, the Sudanese government and associated militias intentionally impoverished the country's poorest civilians, sometimes by seizing and diverting aid supplies for military purposes. Eventually the southern part of the Sudan seceded and created an independent state of South Sudan. However, the current threats of famine involve two states that border the new country, and which are once more the object of conflict between the Sudanese government and secessionist rebels.

Those that do have the interests of the starving at heart—international aid organizations—often struggle to effectively cooperate with the communities they aim to serve. Their struggle is partly a function of geographic and cultural distance and partly a function of weak domestic institutions in LDCs. These common problems suggest that the private aid recommended by Singer may in many cases be ineffective or even counterproductive. The effectiveness of foreign aid has been hotly debated for decades.

A second response to Singer's argument sidesteps these empirical disputes and questions Singer's moral premise more directly. It is commonly held that there are limits to the extent to which we are morally required to sacrifice our own interests for the sake of others, however desperate their situation may be. A moral requirement to save a drowning child, should we come across one, is unlikely to run up against these limits, since most of us will rarely if ever find ourselves in such a situation. A moral requirement to save every person suffering from severe deprivation, on the other hand, may well run up against these limits, given the sheer magnitude of global poverty. At the limit, attempts to meet such a moral requirement could require that all individuals in rich countries impoverish themselves. The extreme demand that this moral requirement makes may be enough to undermine it. Nonetheless, scenes like those we see today in Sudan and around the developing world make the question of how to respond to poverty and suffering hard to ignore.

Second, and perhaps more important, there is good reason to believe that even increased levels of aid would not go very far toward solving the basic problems of developing countries. LDC governments that act in the narrow interests of themselves or their supporters are likely to use the aid they receive for similarly narrow purposes. There is substantial evidence that much foreign aid is misused by recipient governments. By the same token, there is evidence that much foreign aid is given by developed-country governments for geopolitical and military reasons and not to alleviate poverty.

To be sure, humanitarian assistance can make a difference in the lives of people in the developing world. However, sustained economic development provides the best hope for achieving the broader goal of lifting poor countries out of poverty. Governments that are willing and able to pursue policies aimed at stimulating growth may use aid effectively as a supplement to good policies. But aid alone, especially in the small amounts currently available, cannot go far toward satisfying the massive needs of impoverished people in developing countries.[20]

Globalization and Its Discontents

Over the past 25 years, developing countries have gradually committed themselves to more engagement with the global economy. In this context, their interests may be more in line with those of the developed nations. The LDCs have also tended to participate more fully in international economic institutions. This reflects a widespread acceptance of the desirability of economic integration and a broader belief that there is scope for some of the common interests of developed and developing nations to create opportunities that will speed economic growth and development in Africa, Asia, and Latin America.

But the turn toward globalization in the developing world has not been without difficulties and critics. One source of stress has been the series of financial and currency crises that have affected a score of developing countries (see Chapters 8 and 9). While such developing countries as Mexico, Thailand, and Argentina benefited from massive inflows of capital, they also suffered debilitating crises when these flows stopped. As developed countries had themselves discovered, integration into world markets has costs as well as benefits, creates losers as well as winners. The depth of the currency and financial crises led many observers to question whether the benefits of openness to international investment truly outweighed its costs.

The threat of crisis was heightened by the concern that the new economic openness was not delivering the kind and rate of economic growth many analysts had anticipated. Economic reform was, in the minds of many, justified by pointing to how rapidly such countries as South Korea had rushed to modernity and at how relatively equitable their societies had become in the process. This justification was immensely attractive to people in developing countries whose economies had been stagnant and in which the gap between rich and poor had been growing. But many developing

---

20. For two divergent views on aid, see William Easterly, *The White Man's Burden: Why the West's Efforts to Aid the Rest Have Done So Much Ill and So Little Good* (New York: Penguin, 2007); and Jeffrey Sachs, *The End of Poverty: Economic Possibilities for Our Time* (New York: Penguin, 2006).

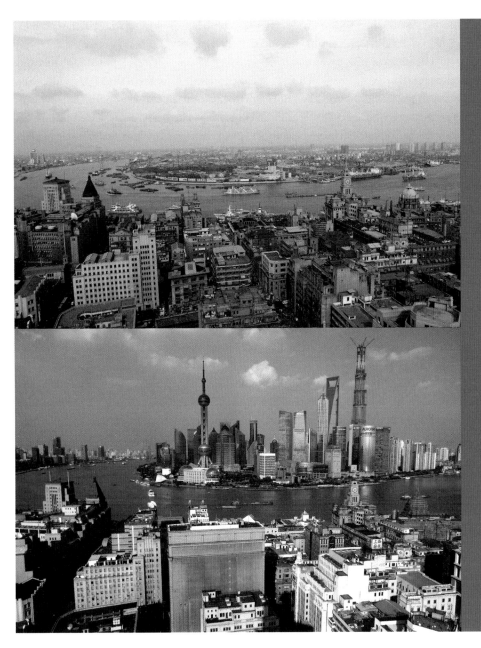

Between 1987 (top) and 2013 (bottom), China increased its GDP per capita from just $250 to $6,810. These images show the effects of economic development on Shanghai's Pudong district. However, extreme inequality has accompanied the rapid development.

countries grew only slowly or not at all, an outcome that disappointed those who had hoped to see tangible results of the economic reforms. Even more disturbing was that income appeared to be getting more unequally distributed in many of the reformed developing countries. Then there were true developmental disasters, countries that seemed to be sinking ever further into destitution and, in some cases, social chaos.

While there have been success stories, the overall picture is still troubling. Many of the developing world's people still live in poverty. While the impoverished are a smaller share of LDC population than 25 years ago, because of population growth there has still been an increase of about 100 million people in the ranks of the poor. Meanwhile, many developing countries—including some of the fastest growers—have become more unequal as they have grown.

The sense of disappointment with the past 25 years of development policies and outcomes has led to a backlash against the economic reforms of the 1980s and 1990s. Some of this backlash has taken the form of electoral successes by politicians who have been very critical of current policies—such as Hugo Chávez in Venezuela, Evo Morales in Bolivia, and more broadly the government of the Islamic Republic of Iran. Even governments that remain fully committed to integration in the world economy have searched for ways to reduce the social costs of this integration and to address the political discontent that has become common in much of the developing world.

Conclusion: Toward Global Development

At the human level, the most pressing issue today is how to improve the living standards of the billions of people in the developing world who live in or near poverty. This is why so many nongovernmental organizations (which we discuss more in Chapter 11) focus on development issues. Generally, finding an effective path toward the goal of broad-based economic development requires a clear understanding of how and why countries have failed or succeeded in developing. While scholars and others continue to debate the matter heatedly, the discussion above points to several components of a reasonable diagnosis of the sources of underdevelopment and suggestions about what might be done to overcome them.

Addressing International Factors

While developed and developing countries have many interests in common, there are also important areas in which their interests conflict. And interactions between developed and developing countries almost always favor developed countries. Industrialized nations are richer and more powerful than the LDCs and can usually get their way in bilateral and multilateral negotiations. Although scores of developing nations have been involved in international trade bargaining rounds, the outcomes of these interactions have been far more reflective of developed-country concerns than of developing-country preferences. International institutions tend to reflect inherent power relations among nations, which means that they favor developed over developing nations. The principal international economic organizations—the IMF, the World Bank, the WTO—all have an implicit or explicit bias toward the interests of the rich nations. Sometimes the bias is formal, as when votes are weighted by economic size in the IMF; sometimes it is informal, based only on the greater wealth and power of the industrialized world. Either way, the policy bias of these international institutions can bend outcomes in ways that are not favorable to the developmental prospects of poor nations.

The developed countries are unlikely to cede influence over the outcome of international bargaining, or over international institutions, for purely humanitarian reasons. Yet there are common interests between rich and poor nations, and there may be scope for agreement on reforming international institutions to make them more responsive to the LDCs. Indeed, the IMF and World Bank have undertaken reform efforts to address some LDC criticisms of their activities. But there are many observers who believe that reform of international institutions has to go farther in order to have a substantial impact on development prospects.[21]

To the extent that these international factors impede LDC progress, addressing them might speed it. Because both the developed and the developing world can benefit from faster growth and more stability in the LDCs, there is scope for LDC and developed-country interests to emphasize shared goals over individual ones. However, a diagnosis of failures of development that rests too strongly on international constraints faces the reality that the same international conditions seem to allow for strikingly different national economic outcomes—for example, Botswana and Zambia. While the external environment may not be as favorable as LDCs might like, it has permitted the emergence of some very striking success stories in addition to spectacular failures. This observation leads us back to the conclusion that domestic forces are probably the principal factors affecting economic growth and development.

Addressing Domestic Factors

As we have seen, interests within a poor country can stand in the way of its overall economic progress. Powerful groups may hamper the government's ability to improve education, social services, or the economic infrastructure. But even the most malevolent interests can only impede economic progress if they are successful in dominating society and politics. Where the impact of self-interested groups is countered by broad public pressure, the result is less likely to impede economic development. Where groups can cooperate to support the provision of public goods, rather than fighting over private benefits, all of society will be better off in the long run. Likewise, the political institutions of developing nations have a powerful impact on whether their citizens are able to overcome obstacles to development. A well-functioning electoral democracy, for example, can reduce the impact of venal private interest groups and can serve as a brake on the activities of corrupt public employees.

The conclusion that domestic features of LDCs are key to understanding their problems is guardedly optimistic. It is optimistic because it suggests that the future of the developing nations is in their own hands rather than being hostage to geographic destiny or the nature of the international system. Indeed, a growing number of countries have succeeded in narrowing the development gap. But this optimism must be guarded. For where economic development has been held back for decades, even generations, by domestic interests, interactions, or institutions, it is likely to be difficult to change these conditions. Nonetheless, this would appear the most promising path forward in the continuing effort to reduce the enormous disparity between the world's rich minority and its poor majority.

---

21. Stiglitz, *Making Globalization Work*, is a prominent statement of the position that lays much of the blame on the structure of the international order and that presents proposals for global reform.

Study Tool Kit

Interests, Interactions, and Institutions in Context

- Although everyone in poor countries prefers more development to less, individuals and groups within countries may have conflicting interests with respect to development policy. The pursuit of private interests by powerful groups can impede the adoption of measures that would spur economic growth.

- Domestic social and political institutions can have a major impact on how these conflicts of interest affect development. They can either empower or overcome special interest groups that stand in the way of development. They can either facilitate or impede the ability of actors to cooperate to promote government policies conducive to economic growth.

- At the international level, rich and poor nations generally have a common interest in accelerating the economic growth of the developing world. However, there have been many instances of rich countries supporting policies and institutions that disfavor less developed countries.

- Successful economic growth requires that a country overcome both the domestic obstacles posed by interests and institutions that are detrimental to development and the international impediments created by conflicts of interest with wealthy nations, which can draw on superior reserves of economic and political power.

Key Terms

less developed countries (LDCs), p. 423

infrastructure, p. 425

primary products, p. 438

oligopoly, p. 438

terms of trade, p. 438

import-substituting industrialization (ISI), p. 442

export-oriented industrialization (EOI), p. 443

Washington Consensus, p. 445

Group of 77, p. 446

commodity cartels, p. 446

For Further Reading

Banerjee, Abhijit V., and Esther Duflo. *Poor Economics: A Radical Rethinking of the Way to Fight Global Poverty*. **New York: Public Affairs, 2011.** Presents both illuminating analyses of poverty in developing countries as well as concrete proposals for policies to alleviate poverty, based in large part on the authors' many years of work in the field.

Bates, Robert. *Markets and States in Tropical Africa*. **Berkeley: University of California Press, 1981.** Offers a classic analysis of how political factors can lead developing-country governments to pursue policies that impede economic growth.

Diamond, Jared. *Guns, Germs, and Steel*. **New York: Norton, 1997.** Makes a striking argument about the fundamental impact of geography on the development of nations and continents.

Milanovic, Branko. *The Haves and the Have-Nots: A Brief and Idiosyncratic History of Global Inequality*. **New York: Basic, 2011.** Offers an impressive and historically informed summary of the level of and trends in international inequality.

Rodrik, Dani. *One Economics, Many Recipes: Globalization, Institutions, and Economic Growth*. **Princeton, NJ: Princeton University Press, 2007.** Presents a prominent economist's ideas about how globalization can be made more compatible with the needs of developing countries.

Stiglitz, Joseph. *Making Globalization Work*. **New York: Norton, 2006.** Provides a critical look by the Nobel laureate and former World Bank chief economist at how the contemporary international economic order impedes economic growth and development and what might be done about it.

11

International Law and Norms

THE PUZZLE *In a world of sovereign states, how can the international community constrain their actions? When and why do states do what is "right"?*

Above: The international community's failure to stop the genocide that took place in Rwanda in 1994, which killed 800,000 and exiled millions, inspired a reexamination of the norms related to intervention.

Shocked by the suffering of wounded soldiers after the Battle of Solferino, fought in 1859 as part of the Italian wars of unification, Swiss social activist Henry Dunant began a campaign to reform and limit the conduct of states during wartime. The result of Dunant's efforts, and the efforts of many others mobilized to the cause, was the first Geneva Convention on the treatment of wounded soldiers, adopted in 1864. This agreement was followed by a second convention on the treatment of members of armed forces at sea in 1906 and a third convention on the treatment of prisoners of war in 1929. These three agreements were revised in 1949 and joined by a fourth convention on the protection of civilians in wartime.

This set of treaties outlining the laws of war is typically referred to as the Geneva Conventions, and they form one of the most clearly articulated and respected bodies of international law in today's world. War between states might seem an unlikely interaction to be governed by such an international institution. At the same time that states are sending their soldiers into battle to kill their enemies and possibly die for their country, they generally follow international laws regulating how that killing is done and how prisoners and civilians are to be treated.

The Geneva Conventions are monitored and supervised by the International Committee of the Red Cross, part of the International Red Cross and Red Crescent movement. The conventions have now been ratified by all 193 members of the United Nations (UN), firmly establishing their provisions as near universally acknowledged and respected international law.

The conventions, however, have not ended all atrocities, especially within countries. In 1994, Hutu extremists in Rwanda began a mass murder of ethnic Tutsis. Although a minority, Tutsis had been favored under colonial rule and remained politically dominant within Rwanda. A civil war that began in 1990, which pitted Hutus against Tutsis, ended with the signing of the Arusha Accords in 1993, signed by then President Juvénal Habyarimana. Seeking to overturn the agreement, Hutu extremists allegedly killed the president and then carried out systematic killings of Tutsis and Hutus they believed had collaborated with the regime. Roughly 800,000 people are believed to have been killed within 100 days, although estimates range from 500,000 to 1,000,000. A small UN force in Rwanda to implement the Arusha Accords was overwhelmed and proved ineffective in controlling the violence. The killings ended only when the Rwandan Patriotic Front, a militia of mostly Tutsi rebels who had originally started the civil war, reentered the conflict and seized control of the country.

The international community watched and condemned this unmistakable act of genocide but did little to stop it. In 1999, then UN secretary general Kofi Annan challenged the international community to define its obligations to protect endangered peoples when their governments either cannot or will not protect vulnerable populations themselves. Grasping the lead, Canada sponsored the International Commission on Intervention and State Sovereignty in September 2000. In December 2001, the commission issued its report with the provocative title *The Responsibility to Protect*.[1] The report argued that the international community not only must prosecute crimes against humanity but also has a responsibility to protect at-risk populations through military means if necessary. This new obligation was quickly dubbed R2P, after the title of the report. In April 2006, the UN Security Council affirmed R2P, recognizing it as a new norm of international behavior.

The Geneva Conventions are international treaties in which states consent to treat armed personnel and civilians in humane ways. The conventions have had an important impact, but the agreements do not diminish the sovereignty of states, as the principle of sovereignty includes the right to freely enter into agreements that constrain one's actions. R2P, on the other hand, stands in stark contrast to this principle. The UN, with the consent of its member states, has championed a new international norm that explicitly limits national sovereignty in cases of widespread human rights abuses and state-sponsored violence. This is important because it legitimates the intervention of states in the internal affairs of other states whether or not the targets give their consent. Nonetheless, the Geneva Conventions and R2P are both part of a growing collection of laws and norms, respectively, broadly referred to as *global governance*.

The puzzle, though, is why would sovereign states agree to be bound by international rules? This is especially curious in the case of norms like R2P, to which individual states have not necessarily agreed to bind themselves but to which they may be held to account.

As we saw in Chapter 2, sovereignty implies that states are the ultimate authorities over their own territories. Yet states today are increasingly governed by laws and norms promoted by the international community in general, and nongovernmental organizations (NGOs) in particular. Why and how do states collectively constrain their own behavior? How are other, private actors, who are supposedly subject to states under the concept of sovereignty, able to alter state behavior?

Thinking Analytically about International Law and Norms

International law and norms are institutions that seek to shape how states understand their interests and that constrain the many ways in which states interact. States create and abide by international law because of the cooperation it facilitates. Indeed, where we observe strong international laws, the benefits of cooperation to states are generally large enough that international laws are often self-enforcing, or in the interests of states to follow willingly. International law clarifies the obligations of states, defines violations that are subject to retaliation, and sometimes provides for independent tribunals to resolve disputes. Through these mechanisms, international law helps states to understand, meet, and manage their obligations to one another.

International norms affect world politics by changing how individuals and, in turn, states conceive of their interests and appropriate actions in their interactions with other states. Norms are standards of behavior that reflect a community's beliefs about what is appropriate behavior for an actor in a specified condition. Norms affect interactions because they are understood by states to be rules of conduct that are right and morally correct.

As we will see, transnational advocacy networks (TANs) have an important effect on world politics by promoting normative values, which are then reflected in international law or norms. In addition to changing conceptions of interest, TANs facilitate cooperation between states by providing information about international agreements and monitoring compliance.

---

1. The full report is available at http://responsibilitytoprotect.org/ ICISS%20Report.pdf (accessed 02/01/14).

What Is International Law?

International law is established by states through either custom or convention as a way to facilitate international cooperation. The Geneva Conventions are one example, but others abound. For instance, the World Trade Organization (WTO) sets rules on the exchange of goods and services and increasingly on investment and property rights; the UN Convention on the Law of the Sea (UNCLOS) governs the use of the oceans and seabed resources; and the Convention on the Prohibition of the Use, Stockpiling, Production, and Transfer of Anti-Personnel Mines and on Their Destruction, more simply known as the Ottawa Convention, outlaws the use and production of land mines and mandates the clearing of existing mine fields. International human rights law, which we will examine in more detail in Chapter 12, intrudes deeply into national political practices. Precisely because the specific rules of international law matter, states often bargain intensely over the rules and their interpretation. Law does not mean the end of conflict between states but is itself the product of political interaction and struggle. Nonetheless, international law is valued and typically followed for the cooperation that it helps bring about.

International law is "a body of rules which binds states and other agents in world politics in their relations with one another and is considered to have the status of law."[2] This definition might appear circular at first, with law being constituted by rules having the status of law, but two aspects of the definition help us understand international law more precisely. First, international law is a *body of rules* linked together in a common logical structure. Law is not simply an ad hoc list of rules issued or even enforced by some authority. Rather, to stand as law, rules must be woven together by one or more unifying principles. In contemporary international law, the primary unifying concept is sovereignty, especially the notion that all states have equal rights to make international law and can be bound by law only by their own consent. Even though sovereignty is often violated in practice, it still forms the foundation on which rules governing state and nonstate behavior become international law.

Second, to have the *status of law*, a body of rules must include both primary and secondary rules.[3] Primary rules are the negative and positive rules regulating behavior. They may take the form of "Don't do *x*," where *x* is some more or less clearly specified action. The Ottawa Convention, for instance, explicitly prohibits the use of land mines. Or primary rules may require that actors "must do *y*," where *y* is also some specified action. The Ottawa Convention also stipulates that states destroy their stockpiles of land mines within four years of the treaty's coming into force.

To have the status of law, primary rules must be made in accordance with secondary rules. One can think of secondary rules as the constitution that structures

international law

A body of rules that binds states and other agents in world politics and is considered to have the status of law.

---

2. Hedley Bull, *The Anarchical Society: A Study of Order in World Politics* (New York: Columbia University Press, 1977), 127.

3. This conception of the status of law follows from H. L. A. Hart, *The Concept of Law* (Oxford: Clarendon Press, 1961).

the making of primary rules, or the rules about how rules are made. To be governed by the "rule of law" is thus to set and enforce primary rules in ways that are consistent with secondary rules. It is the existence of primary rules enacted in compliance with existing secondary rules that gives a rule the status of law. Once again, sovereignty is the central unifying principle. In the case of international law, sovereignty implies a rule about how other rules are made: under sovereignty, only states can bind themselves to international law.

It is this body of rules, duly enacted under secondary rules, that separates international law from norms (taken up later in this chapter) and other international institutions. Norms are often singular rules, disconnected from any larger body of rules, and can contradict secondary rules, especially sovereignty. Thus, R2P is an emerging norm and not law, even though it was affirmed by the UN Security Council, because it explicitly violates the principle of sovereignty by calling for intervention into the internal affairs of states under some circumstances and has not been accepted as binding by those states most likely to be subject to those interventions.

How Is International Law Made?

States establish and abide by international law, like any other institution, because it facilitates cooperation. States may also bargain over international law, with some preferring one rule over another. For instance, the UNCLOS, enacted in 1982, took 9 years of hard negotiations, largely over rules on the exploitation of mineral resources on the ocean floor. It did not come into force until 12 years later, after being ratified by the required 60 countries. Even though 165 countries have now joined the treaty, and it is widely acknowledged as international law governing the use of the seas, the United States was so opposed to some of the provisions that it has refused to sign the final document. Most of the time, however, it is the benefits of cooperation made possible by rules and adherence to those rules that lead states to create and abide by international laws.

In international relations, there are two principal mechanisms for making international law.[4] The first is custom, or accepted practice, that is carried out by states based on a subjective belief that an action is a legal obligation. **Customary international law** usually develops slowly, over time, as states recognize some practices as appropriate and correct. The law of diplomatic immunity, whereby ambassadors and other embassy staff are exempt from a host nation's law, is a classic example. This practice became law by custom because it was in the interests of both home and host countries. Diplomatic immunity permits embassy personnel to carry out their jobs of reporting on the host country, negotiating with host country representatives, and generally promoting the interests of their home country without fearing possibly politically motivated prosecutions for

customary international law
International law that usually develops slowly, over time, as states recognize practices as appropriate and correct.

---

4. The sources of international law are formally defined by Article 38 of the Statute of the International Court of Justice. In addition to conventions and custom, discussed here, the statute also allows for law to follow from "general principles of law recognized by civilized nations" and, as a subsidiary means, "the teachings of the most highly qualified publicists of the various nations." The statute is available at www.icj-cij.org/documents/index.php?p1=4&p2=2&p3=0 (accessed 08/13/11).

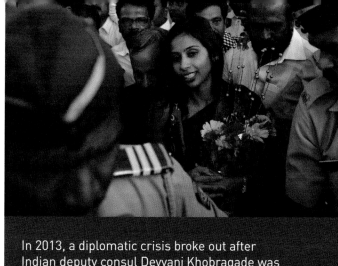

In 2013, a diplomatic crisis broke out after Indian deputy consul Devyani Khobragade was arrested for visa fraud in the United States. To avoid further dispute, the United States granted Khobragade diplomatic immunity and asked her to leave the country.

"trumped up" crimes. It also prevents potential misunderstandings between countries over the activities of their diplomats from escalating into larger disputes. Countries have learned that rather than imprisoning and punishing diplomats, it is best just to send them home if they violate national laws. Despite occasional abuses, such as diplomats racking up a large number of parking tickets for traffic violations, the practice of diplomatic immunity was sufficiently beneficial to home and host countries that, over time, it came to be recognized as international law. Although in effect for centuries, this law was codified in the Vienna Convention on Diplomatic Relations enacted in 1961. Freedom of the seas is another important rule that was accepted as customary international law long before it was codified in the UNCLOS. Finally, the concept of crimes against humanity also developed largely as customary law and was finally codified in the Rome Statute of the International Criminal Court (ICC), which went into effect in 2002 (see "What Shaped Our World?" on p. 462).

Secondary rules for the establishment of customary international law remain vague, however. How many countries must recognize a practice as legitimate and for how long before it is accepted as law is not specified by any other rule. Increasingly, as the examples of diplomatic immunity, freedom of the seas, and crimes against humanity suggest, customary international law is for this reason being codified in formal international agreements.

The second mechanism for creating international law, as just suggested, is international treaties, which are negotiated and then ratified by states. International treaties typically originate in a convention that brings together a large number of states, but not necessarily all countries, to negotiate a new agreement. Some agreements are easily reached, such as the first Geneva Convention, though the original negotiations involved just 12 states. As in the UNCLOS negotiations, however, hard bargaining may ensue precisely because substantial gains are at stake and states seek a deal more favorable to their interests. As explained in the next section, agreements differ in their obligations, precision, and delegation, sometimes in order to address differences in interests that would otherwise prevent agreement. Once finalized by international negotiations, the agreement must then be ratified by each member state in accordance with its domestic constitutional provisions. By ratifying treaties like the Geneva Conventions, states voluntarily take on the constraints of international law. This is not interpreted as a violation of the principle of sovereignty. With international conventions, the secondary rules of international law are quite clear. Countries that sign an international convention are bound to respect the terms of the agreement.

Crimes against Humanity

The concept of crimes against humanity is one of the most significant developments in international law in the last century.

Institutions The Rome Statute of the ICC, adopted in 1998 and entered into force in 2002, defines crimes against humanity as any of the following acts when committed as part of a planned and systematic attack directed against any civilian population: (1) murder; (2) extermination; (3) enslavement; (4) deportation or forced population transfer; (5) imprisonment or other severe deprivation of liberty in violation of fundamental rules of international law; (6) torture; (7) rape and other forms of sexual violence; (8) persecution against any identifiable group based on political affiliation, race, nationality, culture, religion, or gender; (9) enforced disappearance of persons; and (10) apartheid. In contrast, war crimes are single, isolated instances of abuse carried out during armed conflict. Crimes against humanity are intentional systematic violent acts against civilians.

Interests The interests of states in prosecuting crimes against humanity have evolved and grown over time. The first known use of the phrase *crimes against humanity* was in the 1860 Republican Party platform, on which President Abraham Lincoln was elected; it described the reopening of the African slave trade as "a crime against humanity and a burning shame to our country and age." In May 1915, the Allied powers in World War I denounced the Armenian genocide carried out by the Ottoman government as a "crime against humanity." The term, however, was first developed systematically in the London Charter of the International Military Tribunal, under which the Nuremberg trials of Nazi leaders were conducted after World War II. A traditional understanding of war crimes did not allow for the prosecution of government officials for crimes carried out against their own citizens. The Holocaust, in which 6 million Jews were systematically exterminated by the Nazi regime, was not then illegal under international law. Faced with an interest in punishing officials of the Nazi regime for the Holocaust and other atrocities, the drafters of the London Charter gave first real form to the doctrine of crimes against humanity. The doctrine was carried over into the International Military Tribunal for the Far East and the so-called Tokyo trials, which prosecuted Japanese government officials for atrocities carried out during the war as well, especially the Nanking Massacre in which hundreds of thousands of Chinese civilians and disarmed soldiers were murdered and tens of thousands of women raped by the Japanese Imperial Army. As is clear from this history, the concept of crimes against humanity originated in the desires of the victors of World War II to punish the losing states for atrocities conducted in the course of the conflict and to prevent similar behaviors from recurring in the future.

Interactions Through the charters and military tribunals created after World War II, crimes against humanity became international law largely through custom, being formally codified only with the Rome Statute creating the ICC. Government officials are now held responsible for widespread abuses of their own citizens, potentially subject to punishments for violations of basic rights and possibly even to armed intervention to halt abuses. This relatively recent innovation in international law is important because, like human rights law more generally (see Chapter 12), it explicitly defines international law as resting on a common humanity that is superior to that of any state. This law clearly constrains and limits the rights and, more important, actions of states within the international community. R2P is an extension of the doctrine of crimes against humanity. It not only allows for the prosecution of such crimes after they have happened, as at Nuremberg and Tokyo, but calls for active responses by the international community to stop the abuses.

As of May 2015, there are nine official investigations and 22 cases under way at the ICC, all including indictments of individuals for crimes against humanity. These investigations include high-level government officials, including President Omar Hassan al-Bashir of Sudan and Uhuru Kenyatta of Kenya. The first conviction by the ICC was handed down in early 2012 against Thomas Lubanga Dyilo for war crimes in the Democratic Republic of the Congo, though three years later the case is still under appeal. The indictment of heads of state for crimes against humanity confirms the status of international law in this area and puts leaders on notice that they will be held responsible for abuses of their citizens by the international community.

Is All International Law the Same?

Even when states have a shared interest in establishing international law to facilitate cooperation, they must still agree on what form the law will take. International law varies across several dimensions. First, international law varies in **obligation**, or the degree to which agents are legally bound by a rule. High-obligation rules "must be performed in good faith regardless of inconsistent provisions of domestic law" and changing state interests, subject to certain exceptions such as self-defense or necessity.[5] High-obligation laws, like the Geneva Conventions or crimes against humanity, are unconditional and, if breached, require reparations to an injured party. Low-obligation laws are merely aspirational, urging states to live up to some standard of behavior. As we will explain in Chapter 12, much early human rights law took this form. Even high-obligation laws are often contingent or contain escape clauses. The 1994 Framework Convention on Climate Change (FCCC), which we will discuss in Chapter 13, requires parties to the agreement to reduce greenhouse gas emissions but only after considering "their specific national and regional development priorities." Likewise, the Limited Test Ban Treaty enacted in 1963, which outlaws certain forms of nuclear weapons testing, permits states to withdraw from the agreement if they decide "extraordinary events" jeopardize their "supreme interests."

Second, law differs in its **precision**, or how specific are the obligations states incur. More precise laws narrow the scope for reasonable interpretation. Importantly, "for a set of rules, precision implies not just that each rule in the set is unambiguous, but that rules are related to one another in a noncontradictory way, creating a framework within which case-by-case interpretation can be coherently carried out."[6] Much of international law is quite precise, with international treaties running to hundreds and sometimes thousands of pages of definitions, terms, and rules. The UNCLOS treaty, for example, contains 17 parts, 320 articles, and nine annexes, plus an additional agreement (with nine more annexes) elaborating on Part XI of the treaty. States often seek to retain control over international law, and to limit future interpretations, by being as precise as possible in the treaty itself. Other agreements, however, are remarkably imprecise. Commercial treaties, for instance, typically require states to create "favorable conditions" for investment and avoid "unreasonable regulations." Such imprecise terms are usually not the product of poor legal draftsmenship but rather reflect continuing disagreement between states over the exact nature of the obligations being specified. Vague terms ensure that law will not bring bargaining to a close and that states will continue to negotiate albeit now within a legalized framework.

obligation
The degree to which states are legally bound by an international rule. High-obligation rules must be performed in good faith and, if breached, require reparations to the injured party.

precision
The degree to which international legal obligations are fully specified. More precise rules narrow the scope for reasonable interpretation.

---

5. We owe these dimensions, and the examples used here, to Kenneth W. Abbott, Robert O. Keohane, Andrew Moravcsik, Anne-Marie Slaughter et al., "The Concept of Legalization," in *Legalization and World Politics*, ed. Judith L. Goldstein, Miles Kahler, Robert O. Keohane, and Anne-Marie Slaughter, 25 (Cambridge, MA: MIT Press, 2001).

6. Abbott et al., "The Concept of Legalization," 29.

Under some international laws, states agree to delegate extensive rule-making powers to specialized agencies, such as the ICAO. The ICAO establishes rules and standards that help states cooperate on the common goal of safe and orderly air transport.

Finally, law also varies in its degree of **delegation** to third parties, wherein courts, arbitrators, mediators, or others are given the authority to implement, interpret, and apply the rules specified; to resolve disputes over the rules; and to make additional rules. In domestic law, courts often have tremendous delegated powers to interpret the law and, in so doing, to fill in legal gaps left in the original statutes. When delegation is high and statutes are imprecise, courts through their interpretations may actually make new law, a result sometimes decried by critics as judicial activism. In international relations, states are generally reluctant to delegate significant legal authority to third parties. The power to interpret law and possibly make new law has the potential to bind states in ways they did not anticipate and would not have approved if considered in advance. In dispute settlement, delegation ranges from international courts with relatively broad jurisdiction, binding decision-making powers, and the ability to set legal precedents, as in the ICC in the enforcement of crimes against humanity, to limited dispute settlement bodies with more narrow mandates and national vetoes of decisions, as under the old General Agreement on Tariffs and Trade. With even less delegated authority are various arbitrators and mediators who can recommend more or less binding solutions to disagreements. In rule making and implementation, administrative bodies can have sweeping powers, usually found only in specialized agencies like the International Civil Aviation Organization (ICAO). In most cases, administrative bodies have more conditional powers subject to override by states, as in the International Monetary Fund (IMF) and World Bank.

By considering these three dimensions—obligation, precision, and delegation—we can distinguish between hard and soft law.[7] Hard law is obligatory; precisely defined; and delegates substantial authority to third parties, particularly international courts. Soft law is aspirational, ambiguous, and does not delegate significant powers to third parties. Countries often adopt soft law because it is easier to achieve, is more flexible and therefore better suited to dealing with uncertain futures, infringes less on state sovereignty, and facilitates compromise. Soft law is not a failure of law making but reflects intentional choices by states to write law appropriate to the issue area or to the extent of cooperation they are currently prepared to accept. Although there is no guarantee that soft law will lead to hard law, agreements in new issue areas often begin as soft law that sets goals for states and creates frameworks for continuing negotiations and may eventually become hard

delegation

The degree to which third parties, such as courts, arbitrators, or mediators, are given authority to implement, interpret, and apply international legal rules, to resolve disputes over the rules, or to make additional rules.

---

7. Kenneth W. Abbott and Duncan Snidal, "Hard and Soft Law in International Governance," in Goldstein, Kahler, Keohane, and Slaughter, *Legalization and World Politics*, 37–172.

law as states gain experience, bargain out specific issues, and write more detailed treaties. A clear example is the FCCC, dismissed by critics as toothless when first signed, but which later led to the effective Montreal Protocol, in force since 1999, and to the Kyoto Protocol (see Chapter 13). At the extreme, soft law blends into international norms, like R2P, which we will consider further below.

Does International Law Matter?

Can international law "domesticate" international politics? That is, can international law become more like domestic law found within states? Can the use of force in international relations be tamed by international law? Perhaps no questions have vexed scholars of international relations and diplomats more.

Supporters of international law view it as an effective—perhaps essential—tool in facilitating cooperation and managing conflicts. International lawyer Louis Henkin has observed that "almost all nations observe almost all principles of international law and almost all of their obligations almost all of the time."[8] Sometimes high levels of compliance result from more or less explicit enforcement mechanisms in international law (see "How Do We Know?" on p. 466). Yet, states may comply with international law even without enforcement provisions. International lawyers Abram Chayes and Antonia Chayes argue that states typically do comply with international law, and when they fail to do so, it is either because the law itself is imprecise or because they lack the capacity to fulfill their obligations.[9] In their view, states want to observe, say, the Geneva Conventions on the rules of war, but they may not have effective control over their own soldiers, who may abuse prisoners, as in the infamous Abu Ghraib scandal that shocked the world in 2004 when pictures of American soldiers abusing Iraqi prisoners surfaced on the Internet. Proponents point to the high rates of compliance as evidence of international law's potential. In this view, law can be a significant constraint on the interactions of states.

More skeptical observers see international law as unrealistic and utopian or at least a reflection of state interest rather than as a severe constraint on state action. Two main problems exist. First, law is seldom precise enough to deal with every possible interaction between actors. Indeed, in domestic politics, lawyers earn their livings and courts are clogged with cases where the parties disagree on what the law says or requires in their specific circumstances. We should hardly expect international law to be more precise and less open to creative interpretation than domestic law. In one telling instance, when NATO was considering intervening in Kosovo, British foreign secretary Robin Cook told U.S. secretary of state Madeleine Albright that he had "problems with our lawyers" over using force without the approval of the UN Security Council. Albright responded that he should "get new lawyers."[10]

---

8. Louis Henkin, *How Nations Behave: Law and Foreign Policy* (New York: Columbia University Press, 1981), 47. Italics omitted.

9. Abram Chayes and Antonia H. Chayes, "On Compliance," *International Organization* 47, no. 2 (1993): 175–205.

10. Michael J. Glennon, *Limits of Law, Prerogatives of Power: Interventionism after Kosovo* (London: Palgrave Macmillan, 2003), 178.

Enforcing International Law

The majority of international agreements do not contain explicit enforcement provisions. Indeed, the political scientist Barbara Koremenos[a] has found that only one-third of international treaties make any reference to possible punishments for noncompliance. As shown in Figure A, agreements on economic issues and human rights are most likely to contain enforcement provisions. As one example, the International Coffee Agreement seeks to raise prices for coffee beans by establishing export quotas for members. If a state exports more than its quota, the treaty specifies that the excess is to be deducted from its next year's quota, a second infraction doubles the amount deducted from the next quota, and a third instance ejects the state from the organization.

Security and environmental agreements are much less likely to include formal rules on enforcement. International environmental treaties are often aspirational, soft law agreements that may eventually mature into hard law. The absence of enforcement provisions in such agreements is perhaps not surprising. But security agreements without enforcement provisions are especially puzzling. States appear most concerned about defection and cheating on these types of agreements, but few actual treaties make any reference to enforcement. The Treaty on the Non-Proliferation of Nuclear Weapons (NPT), signed in 1968 to prevent the spread of nuclear weapons is typical in this regard. Dealing with one of the most central concerns of the great powers, the agreement is silent on how it should be enforced.

Koremenos's findings are based on a random sample of 234 agreements registered with the UN since 1946 and all agreements previously filed with the League of Nations. She has coded the treaties for many institutional features, including punishment provisions.

Based on this sample of agreements, Koremenos also found that enforcement provisions are more likely when states have large incentives to defect, face larger difficulties in committing credibly to the agreement, and are more uncertain about the behavior of their treaty partners. The less confident states are that others will comply, the more

FIGURE A *Treaties Containing Punishment Provisions*

likely they are to write punishment provisions into their agreements. The selection effect discussed in the text, however, still makes it difficult to know whether enforcement provisions really "matter" for behavior. When enforcement is very difficult, states may not be able to design appropriate mechanisms to punish one another and, therefore, may not reach an agreement. In this case, no treaty will be filed with the UN and therefore will not appear in the database. This implies that the agreements we observe may be solving relatively "easy" problems of international cooperation.

However, just because agreements do not contain explicit enforcement provisions does not mean there are not informal mechanisms by which states can punish noncompliance. Koremenos also finds that states are more likely to rely on informal mechanisms when differences in the size and power of states are large. In the case of the NPT, for instance, the U.S. National Security Council actually recommended against attempting to include any formal enforcement provisions in the treaty. Rather than specify in advance how the treaty would be enforced, the United States wanted to retain the full range of diplomatic tools at its disposal to make the punishment "fit the crime." Thus, the absence of explicit enforcement provisions does not imply that states lack means to punish each other for failing to comply with their agreements.

a. Barbara Koremenos, *The Continent of International Law: Explaining Agreement Design* (New York: Cambridge University Press, 2016).

If international law is malleable and can be interpreted to justify whatever states might want to do, it is a weak constraint at best on their actions.

Second, as we have seen, international law is the product of states' interests and interactions. States decide the rules by which they will constrain themselves, including the degree to which these rules are obligatory, precise, and delegated. That states therefore comply with rules they have written is, at one level, hardly surprising. This is sometimes described as the "selection problem" in international relations.[11] For skeptics, therefore, international law does not constrain states, despite seemingly high levels of compliance with the law. Rather, countries only sign agreements and make laws that serve their interests and obligate them to undertake actions they would want to do anyway. With states crafting the laws that constrain them and then interpreting their meaning for their own purposes, it is very difficult for scholars to demonstrate conclusively that international law has an effect on state behavior over and above state interest.

The truth likely lies somewhere between these extremes. The questions here are how, when, and why does international law alter state behavior. International cooperation requires that states often subordinate their short-term interests for long-term benefits. Can international law constrain states to act in ways that are not in their short-term interests?

The enforcement of international law, even when specified in the agreement, is dependent on the principle of national self-help. It is a truth of world politics that there is no central authority higher than the state that can enforce law between all states. As we discussed in Chapter 5, there are no police in international relations. At most, international law sets the terms and conditions under which victims can legally and legitimately retaliate against countries that violate rules of behavior. Even in world trade, an area of international relations with strong and well-developed international laws, the WTO only permits victims of illegal trade barriers to retaliate by imposing punitive duties on goods purchased from the violator. The WTO cannot punish violators itself, nor can it mandate that other states punish violators. Each victimized country must, on its own, decide whether to seek and carry out retribution for clearly illegal acts. This dependence on self-help necessarily limits the effectiveness of international law.

At the same time, international law is generally followed because of the very real and important benefits of cooperation it enables. Like all institutions, international law facilitates cooperation by setting more or less obligatory standards of behavior, helping to verify compliance by articulating more or less precise rules, lowering the costs of decision making by creating rules that do not need to be renegotiated for each interaction, and managing disputes. In analyzing the problem of restraints on violence during war, as one example, the political scientist James Morrow argues that cooperation is dependent on reciprocity.[12] A state is more likely

---

11. George W. Downs, David M. Rocke, and Peter N. Barsoom, "Is the Good News about Compliance Good News about Cooperation?" *International Organization* 50, no. 3 (1996): 379–406.

12. James D. Morrow, *Order within Anarchy: The Laws of War as an International Institution* (New York: Cambridge University Press, 2014).

to treat enemy prisoners of war (POWs) well if it expects its opponent to treat its captive soldiers well, and violations by one state are likely to provoke retaliation by another. The Geneva Conventions, especially when ratified by both parties, make clear that the states understand, accept, and are likely to follow international laws regulating the treatment of POWs. This makes it easier for states to presume that others will treat POWs humanely, and for them to do the same for theirs, and defines relatively clearly what constitutes a violation that would then be punished through retaliation. By setting rules that help clarify expectations on both sides, the Geneva Conventions reinforce the equilibrium of treating POWs well as long as the other state treats POWs well that might otherwise prove more fragile or tend to erode under the stress of war.

In facilitating cooperation, obligation and precision may actually be the most important dimensions of international law, for as just explained they set expectations for the behavior of others and reduce the range within which states can argue that the law does not apply to their interactions in a particular instance. Simple words matter here because they define which behaviors are consistent with cooperation and which are not. It is the anticipated benefits of cooperation that lead states to create international law in the first place, and it is the actual benefits of cooperation that lead them to comply with the rules once they are in place. Widespread transgressions of law undermine the gains from cooperation that states seek, and states fear that the set of rules will unravel and destroy cooperation. This fear of cooperation breaking down prevents states from violating law in pursuit of their short-term interests. The greater the benefits of cooperation, and the more evenly these benefits are shared, the more constraining international law will be on the policies of all states. The more states have to lose, the more international law will shape their interactions and alter outcomes.

International law is also more effective when it is delegated to courts. When states disagree on what the law says, or how it should be applied in specific situations, it helps prevent conflicts from escalating to refer the dispute to an independent body for decision. Domestic courts, however, are also important to the enforcement of international law. In many countries, including the United States, international treaties are superior to domestic laws, meaning that once enacted they override domestic laws that contradict their provisions and cannot be changed by subsequent legislation. The treaty thereby becomes part of "domestic" law and is enforced in the same way as all other laws in the ratifying country. Domestic courts are also increasingly appealing to international law in interpreting strictly domestic statutes. In *Roper v. Simmons* (2005), which overturned laws on the death penalty for juvenile offenders in the United States, the U.S. Supreme Court cited as support the UN Convention on the Rights of the Child, previously signed by the president but never ratified by the Senate. Writing for the majority, Justice Anthony Kennedy argued it was "proper that we acknowledge the overwhelming weight of international opinion against the juvenile death penalty. . . . The opinion of the world community, while not controlling our outcome, does provide respected and significant confirmation of our own conclusions."[13] By being directly and indirectly incorporated into domestic law, the enforcement powers of states within their own jurisdictions are being harnessed to international law.

In addition, some international law also creates *compliance constituencies* within states that then have interests in ensuring that their governments follow the rules.[14] Even when some domestic groups might benefit from breaking international laws, other constituencies have a strong interest in upholding the law. WTO law, for instance, opens foreign markets to trade and helps ensure nondiscriminatory treatment for goods from different countries. Although import-competing industries that favor protection might advocate policies that violate WTO rules, export industries that are dependent on foreign markets have an interest in ensuring that their governments uphold their obligations. Similarly, militaries are often staunch advocates of upholding the Geneva Conventions, especially the treatment of prisoners. TANs that propagate norms that are subsequently embedded in international law, as discussed in the next section, are also likely to be continuing advocates for compliance.

Thus, the benefits of cooperation, both to states as a whole and to particular groups within states, can make international law self-enforcing. Although still reliant on and limited by the principle of self-help, states have an interest in following international law so as to help ensure that other states also follow the rules. In this way, international law can significantly influence and constrain the interactions of states even without any external enforcement mechanism. Nonetheless, international law is unlikely to end the bargaining failures that lead states into war or resolve other sources of conflict. Like other institutions, international law facilitates cooperation, but it does not ensure that cooperation will always prevail. It is a useful tool in altering the interactions of states in more constructive directions and in bringing about desirable outcomes in world politics, but it is not a panacea. The difficulty of demonstrating the independent effect of international law, however, ensures that the debate about how effective law is will continue. As we shall see, the selection problem is central in the debate about the effectiveness of international human rights law in Chapter 12.

What Are International Norms?

International norms are also a type of international institution that constrains states. **Norms** are standards of behavior for actors with a given identity defined in terms of rights and obligations. They rest on a community's beliefs about what is appropriate for an actor under some specified condition. Norms may be codified

norms
Standards of behavior for actors with a given identity; norms define what actions are "right" or appropriate under particular circumstances.

---

13. Quoted in Robert Delahunty and John Yoo, "Against Foreign Law," *Harvard Journal of Law and Public Policy* 29, no. 1 (2005): 291–330. The trend toward citing foreign law is strongly opposed by conservatives who see it overturning democratic processes within the United States.

14. Miles Kahler, "Conclusion: The Causes and Consequences of Legalization," in Goldstein, Kahler, Keohane, and Slaughter, *Legalization and World Politics,* 283–84.

into international law, but norms as institutions can exist and be respected by members of a community even when they are not written down in formal agreements. In our everyday life, many of our interactions are regulated by norms that have nothing to do with law. You are not required by law to hold an elevator for others, for instance. But to intentionally—or even unintentionally—allow the doors to close on someone rushing to the elevator is regarded as rude, and you may even apologize for letting the door close even though the now excluded passenger cannot hear you. Similarly, and with greater political importance, norms of fairness—which are not required in any way by law but reflect deep-seated social understandings—shape political appeals and policies in many countries, although exactly what is "fair" is not always clear and has varied considerably over time. In this same way, many now recognize a nuclear "taboo" in international relations—a normative prohibition against the use of nuclear weapons—even though the norm is nowhere found in international law.

Like law, international norms shape the behavior of states in important ways. Norms affect the interactions of states because they are understood by people within those states to be rules of conduct that are right and morally correct. In other words, norms define what it is we *should* do and thereby shape our understanding of our interests. In our everyday lives, of course, individuals and countries do many things they should not. Norms are often violated. They are standards of behavior, not prohibitions or straitjackets. But even if we choose to violate norms, we must then excuse our behavior, justify it, or risk being ostracized by the community.

We can group most norms into three broad categories. The first category, which we refer to as constitutive norms, defines who is a legitimate or appropriate actor under what circumstances. What it means to be a state, for instance, is largely defined by norms.[15] At the level of everyday diplomacy, all states have flags, national anthems, and—even in the poorest states—ministries of science and technology. No law requires this, but there is remarkable similarity in the form and practices of states in the world today. To show that they are indeed modern states, many countries also buy advanced military equipment for which they have little use and even less ability to maintain—most notably fighter jets, which appear to have enormous symbolic value. More broadly, norms shape what it means to be sovereign at any point in history. This includes evolving ideas about when states can legitimately intervene in one another's "sovereign" areas of control, as reflected today in the new norm of R2P.

The second category, procedural norms, defines how decisions involving multiple actors should get made. As such, procedural norms are analogous to secondary rules in international law. In domestic politics, procedural norms are often well structured. In legislatures, for instance, ramming through a major bill late at night without due warning to the opposition, though permitted by the rules, is usually regarded as unfair and illegitimate and taints the resulting legislation.

---

15. Statehood and sovereignty are defined as law through the UN Charter and other international agreements. What "rights" sovereignty entails, however, has varied dramatically over time depending on how states choose to interpret the law.

In international relations, procedural norms are generally less robust. Sovereignty implies that all states are formally equal, and thus each state is entitled to an equal voice in world affairs—at least in principle. This is an important support for multilateralism, the practice of "diffuse reciprocity" in international relations in which states are expected to offer one another roughly equal benefits over time.[16] Yet more powerful states are often acknowledged to have special rights and greater responsibilities in recognition that their support is necessary for multilateralism to be effective. The United States and other major donors are often consulted, for instance, by the IMF staff before loan agreements are formally presented to the executive directors for approval.[17] This gives more powerful states a larger voice in diplomatic circles than the formal equality of sovereignty otherwise allows.

Finally, the third category, regulative norms, governs the behavior of actors in their interactions with other actors. R2P is one example, as is the norm of election monitoring. The nuclear taboo is also a regulative norm.[18] Although the United States did drop two atomic bombs on Japan in 1945, ending World War II, no country since has used nuclear weapons, despite the fact that at least nine countries are now believed to possess workable bombs. Although they are held in reserve as the ultimate defense—a lingering threat to all enemies—political leaders are reluctant to contemplate the use of nuclear weapons even when they are technically feasible and possibly efficient. To destroy hardened underground bunkers—whether of the type that hid Saddam Hussein during the Iraq War or those that protect the Iranian or North Korean nuclear programs—the United States has devoted considerable resources to developing large conventional "bunker busting" bombs, even when existing tactical nuclear weapons could likely accomplish the same task more effectively. That countries do not use nuclear weapons for fear of retaliation is undoubtedly part of the explanation for this norm. But such weapons are not used—and not contemplated for use—even when the target does not have nuclear weapons or the capacity to retaliate against the user directly. Deterrence alone cannot explain the taboo. Leaders appear reluctant to cross the nuclear threshold for fear of being branded as immoral, either personally or on behalf of their country.

Norms are often difficult to identify. When not written down, they exist only by collective assent. In turn, when norms are deeply internalized, actors typically do not even consciously contemplate violating them, meaning that behavior consistent with the norm appears entirely voluntary or as the exercise of free will. To take an extreme example, nearly all societies have strongly internalized norms against cannibalism, yet this norm almost never appears to affect our conscious choices. We do not wake up in the morning and consider eating our neighbor for breakfast. That we

---

16. John G. Ruggie, ed., *Multilateralism Matters: The Theory and Praxis of an Institutional Form* (New York: Columbia University Press, 1993), 11.

17. Randall W. Stone, *Controlling Institutions: International Organizations and the Global Economy* (New York: Cambridge University Press, 2011).

18. Nina Tannenwald, "The Nuclear Taboo: The United States and the Normative Basis of Nuclear Non-Use," *International Organization* 53, no. 3 (2003): 433–68.

The taboo against the use of nuclear weapons is an example of a regulative norm. Since the U.S. bombing of Hiroshima (above) and Nagasaki in 1945, no country has resorted to a nuclear attack, at least in part because of the international norm against the use of such weapons.

do not want to violate the norm is not evidence that the norm is unimportant but rather that it is so deeply internalized that we are not even aware it constrains our behavior. In a far less extreme form, the nuclear taboo works in similar ways. That nuclear first strikes are not on the list of options that leaders in diplomatic disputes consider does not mean that the norm is not having an effect but instead suggests that the norm is sufficiently internalized that we are not aware of how fundamentally it shapes our interests and interactions.

Norms are often most easily observed when they are violated. Their presence is revealed both by the censure of others and, usually, by the justifications or excuses given by the offending party. To continue with the extreme example just noted, the depth of the norm against cannibalism can be best seen when breached even under extraordinary circumstances. In 1972, an airplane carrying a college rugby team from Uruguay to a match in Chile crashed in the Andes Mountains. Isolated and without significant supplies, the survivors eventually resorted to eating the flesh of their deceased teammates. The survivors later were broadly and stridently condemned in the press, indicating widespread agreement with the norm, even though many commentators and the Catholic Church later observed that under the circumstances the survivors had had little choice. Similarly, since 1945, there has been a growing international norm against changing international borders through the use of force, described as the "territorial integrity" norm.[19] When Saddam Hussein invaded and seized Kuwait in August 1990, the international community quickly condemned his actions. Although Saddam challenged the prior border as an anachronism of British colonial rule—trying to reframe the issue as one of decolonization—and proclaimed Kuwait to be the long-lost nineteenth province of Iraq, his justifications for the land grab were broadly rejected by the rest of the international community—and the United States and a coalition of other states fought a war to return Kuwait to sovereignty. Similar objections were raised when Russia annexed the Crimea from Ukraine in 2014, claiming it as part of its historic territory. Although no state or coalition rose to reverse Russia's action in this case, it was nonetheless in the reactions of norm-abiding others and the types of justifications or excuses offered by Russia that we see most clearly the territorial integrity norm at work.

---

19. Mark W. Zacher, "The Territorial Integrity Norm: International Boundaries and the Use of Force," *International Organization* 55, no. 2 (2001): 215–50.

No actor needs to justify its behavior to others unless it is at risk of transgressing a norm held by the community of which it is part.

Unlike law, norms need not be consistent with one another or secondary rules. Indeed, the norm of national self-determination conflicts with sovereignty: if the state is the ultimate authority within a territory, how can a nation within that territory freely decide to secede? We have already discussed how R2P conflicts with sovereignty, and the same holds for many of the human rights norms examined in the next chapter. The tension between norms creates opportunities for actors to interpret rules selectively for their own advantage. When faced with two morally just but conflicting rules, which one do you follow? Germans faced exactly this kind of choice in deciding whether to back NATO's intervention in Kosovo. On the one hand, many Germans were committed to a foreign policy that eschewed war and the use of force and, simultaneously, pledged to never again stand idly by as a genocide unfolded. Despite contradictions such as these, however, norms—as with law—can serve as important constraints on states in their interactions.

How Are International Norms Created?

For a principle or idea to become institutionalized as a norm, the standard of behavior it specifies must be accepted as morally right and appropriate by a sufficiently large proportion of any given population, although that proportion is not always clear. Norms change. Where once it was acceptable to own slaves, we now find the practice morally repugnant—although many people around the world are still held in various forms of bondage, not least in the sex trade. Something is not considered immoral until a sufficiently large number of us decide that it is wrong or objectionable. Child labor is one such principle that remains contested and thus has failed to attain the status of a norm (see "Controversy" on p. 478). Once we agree, in turn, practices that once might have been common become odious or at least inappropriate and even sometimes unimaginable. Over time, norms can develop a "taken for granted" quality, an unquestioned and perhaps unquestionable status. But all norms were originally just principles or ideas without widely accepted moral implications.

Some principles become norms simply by the force of their own inherent moral standing. The nuclear taboo may be one such example of a principle that so obviously improves human welfare that almost everyone accepts it. Other norms are propagated by powerful states or through international organizations. The Washington Consensus on economic liberalism (see Chapter 10, p. 445), which held broad sway in the 1990s and early 2000s, was heavily promoted by the United States through its policies and the IMF and World Bank. Still other norms may be championed by virtuous leaders seeking to distinguish themselves from the perhaps less virtuous. This has been a factor in spreading the norm of inviting monitors to oversee elections in new democracies.

Norms typically begin with individuals or groups who seek to advance a principled standard of behavior for states and other actors. Transnational advocacy networks (TANs) are central to spreading norms throughout the international system. Comprising individuals and NGOs deeply committed to ethical beliefs, TANs aim to persuade other individuals and groups to share their commitment. We call these individuals and groups **norms entrepreneurs.**

norms entrepreneurs

Individuals and groups who seek to advance principled standards of behavior for states and other actors.

The International Campaign to Ban Land Mines (ICBL), for instance, is a clear example of how a group of committed activists were able to call attention to an issue and convince many other people around the globe that existing practices were morally wrong. The ICBL is a network of hundreds of NGOs in some 100 countries, working to outlaw and remove land mines, which still kill and maim well over 3,500 people worldwide each year. It was the primary force behind the negotiation and adoption of the Ottawa Convention. The convention was negotiated and signed in 1997 and entered into force in March 1999. As of February 2015, 162 states have joined the convention and only 35 countries remain outside the treaty entirely, including China, Egypt, India, Israel, Pakistan, Russia, and the United States.[20] In 1997, the ICBL and its coordinator, Jody Williams, were awarded the Nobel Peace Prize for their work. In making the award, the Norwegian Nobel Committee applauded the campaign for moving the ban from "a vision to a feasible reality" and acclaimed the organization as a model for international disarmament and peace.

Once norms are adopted, supporters of those norms then hold their governments accountable to acceptable standards of international behavior. Political leaders who hold deep normative commitments may decide to rule out certain policy options, deeming them immoral in the face of these international standards. Even if tempted to violate norms, leaders may fear punishment by their constituents for violating widely accepted standards of behavior. Political leaders may also be held to account by citizens of other states, who press their governments to enforce compliance to norms they hold dear, as in the anti-apartheid movement, which we will discuss in Chapter 12. In this way, even authoritarian governments that are not accountable to their own people can be pressed to uphold international norms.

transnational advocacy network (TAN)

A set of individuals and nongovernmental organizations acting in pursuit of a normative objective.

TANs: Changing Minds, Altering Interests **Transnational advocacy networks (TANs)** are, as the name implies, sets of activists allied in the pursuit of a common normative objective, including (in the contemporary era) human rights; the environment; economic and social justice; democracy; women's rights; and abortion rights or, conversely, the right to life (Figure 11.1). The actors that make up TANs may include (1) international and domestic NGOs involved in research and advocacy; (2) local social movements; (3) foundations and other philanthropic organizations; (4) the media; and (5) churches, trade unions, and consumer and other civil organizations. The number of TANs has grown dramatically over the past

---

20. See www.icbl.org/en-gb/the-treaty/treaty-status.aspx (accessed 02/05/15).

21. Margaret E. Keck and Kathryn Sikkink, *Activists beyond Borders: Advocacy Networks in International Politics* (Ithaca, NY: Cornell University Press, 1998), 9. We exclude international organizations and governments from this list, although individuals in these organizations may interact with transnational networks. On public transnational networks, see Anne-Marie Slaughter, *A New World Order* (Princeton, NJ: Princeton University Press, 2004).

FIGURE 11.1 *Issue Focus of Transnational Advocacy Networks, 2000**

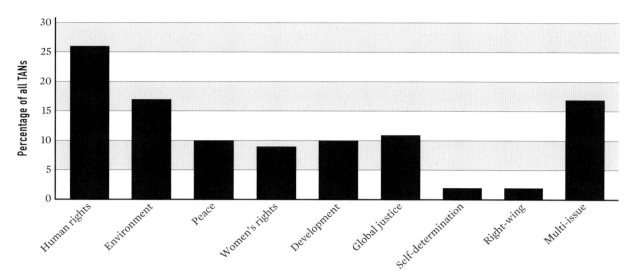

50 years: in 1953, there were about 100 identifiable TANs; today, they number well into the thousands—so many, in fact, that a proper count is nearly impossible.[22] Nearly all the major issues that engage citizens within countries now have an international counterpart. For example, the Planned Parenthood Federation of American, often on the front lines of the movement to make or keep abortion legal, has 10 foreign affiliates and cooperates with hundreds of other organizations and countless individuals worldwide in the women's rights and legalized abortion movement. Heartbeat International, a network of pro-life pregnancy centers, has affiliates in more than 47 countries and works with many churches and other organizations to promote the right to life. Gaining momentum in the United States, the struggle over abortion has become an international political issue with transnational networks on both sides of the question coordinating action, sharing information and tactics, and mobilizing new members. TANs coordinate the activities of participants around the globe and initiate, lead, and actively direct collective action on issues of concern.

TANs promote norms to alter interests and change interactions at the individual and state levels. TANs alter the way actors first define their interests by bringing new knowledge to public attention. For example, as evidence of global warming has become increasingly clear, it has been brought to the attention of people around the globe by environmental TANs such as Greenpeace and former vice president Al Gore's Alliance for Climate Protection. By increasing public

Figure source: Jackie Smith, "Exploring Connections between Global Integration and Political Mobilization," *Journal of World System Research* 10, no. 1 (2004): 266, Table 2.

*The most recent data available are from 2000 but are still useful in providing a sense of the issue areas contemporary TANs focus on.

---

22. For the last available figures, see Kathryn Sikkink and Jackie Smith, "Infrastructures for Change: Transnational Organizations, 1953–1993," in *Restructuring World Politics: Transnational Social Movements, Networks, and Norms*, ed. Sanjeev Khagram, James V. Riker, and Kathryn Sikkink, 30, Table 2.1 (Minneapolis: University of Minnesota Press, 2002); and Jackie Smith, "Exploring Connections between Global Integration and Political Mobilization," *Journal of World System Research* 10, no. 1 (2004): 266, Table 2.

awareness, TANs have persuaded at least some individuals to place a higher priority on reducing global warming. New public pressure, in turn, has helped to elevate the issue on the political agenda, even if action on policy remains halting and tentative (see Chapter 13). Responding to new public pressure, some politicians are beginning to place greater emphasis on protecting the environment.[23] Yet scientific or technical knowledge seldom translates directly into policy change. Expert consensus can call attention to new problems and point to possible solutions, but groups negatively affected by the proposed policy changes will also mobilize politically to influence government decisions. For example, the scientific community agreed for decades on the hazards of smoking before the tobacco industry lobby in the United States was finally defeated and policy altered. In many countries, government policy still favors smokers even in the face of nearly universal scientific agreement on the harmful effects of smoking. Similarly, despite widespread scientific concern about carbon dioxide emissions into the atmosphere, policies to limit global climate change are often blocked by countries and industries that use carbon intensively. Knowledge is power—but it alone may not be enough to create a norm or set policy.

Perhaps more important, TANs also change how actors conceive of their interests by promoting new moral values. In essence, TANs urge actors to have preferences over some actions—owning slaves, using land mines—rather than just the possible outcomes they confront, such as greater wealth or victory on the battlefield. Of course, norms existed and spread throughout the world system prior to the recent growth in TANs. After all, not all norms are connected with TANs and their activities. But one important function of TANs is to encourage and support socially appropriate behavior and help spread norms across national borders. Martha Finnemore and Kathryn Sikkink, two leading scholars of norms in international relations, posit a three-stage **norms life cycle** that can help us understand how TANs shape norms and interests and, thus, political outcomes.[24]

norms life cycle
A three-stage model of how norms diffuse within a population and achieve a "taken for granted" status.

In the first stage, norms entrepreneurs actively work to convince a critical mass of other individuals in other states to embrace their beliefs. As we saw above, the norm that medical personnel on the battlefield and wounded soldiers be treated as neutral noncombatants, now embodied in the Geneva Conventions, was rooted in the crusade by Henry Dumont, a Swiss banker, who helped found the International Committee of the Red Cross. Similarly, the National Rifle Association (NRA) is working globally to promote the principle that owning a gun is a natural right. Although its charter prohibits the organization from funding groups in other countries, it is building a network of like-minded organizations around the world. Whether the NRA will succeed in establishing gun ownership as a right outside the United States is not clear, but its efforts helped defeat a national gun control law in

---

23. Communities of technical experts who create and promote new knowledge are often called epistemic communities but are in practice similar to TANs. See Peter M. Haas, ed., *Knowledge, Power, and International Policy Coordination* (Columbia: University of South Carolina Press, 1997).

24. Martha Finnemore and Kathryn Sikkink, "International Norm Dynamics and Political Change," *International Organization* 52, no. 4 (1998): 887–917.

Brazil in October 2005.[25] It is during this first stage that most TANs develop as vehicles for the dissemination of new norms.

Norms entrepreneurs frame "issues to make them comprehensible to target audiences . . . [and] attract attention and encourage action."[26] Perhaps most important, they find creative ways to connect the behavior they wish to encourage to other, preexisting norms; because these norms are already widely accepted, audiences are likely to see the value in the desired behaviors or ends. Activists "win" by framing principles they want to promote so that they connect to principles that are already accepted in a community.

One effective frame is to redefine undesirable behaviors as perpetrating violence against innocent persons, which is nearly universally abhorred. The women's rights movement, for instance, failed to make progress for many years in the 1980s and 1990s because it was caught among three competing frames: one of discrimination, emphasizing the principle of gender equality articulated in the 1979 Convention on the Elimination of All Forms of Discrimination against Women; one of economic development and the need to improve the quality of life for women; and one of general human rights, claiming that civil and political rights for everyone could not be secured without protecting the rights of women as well, adopted at the 1993 World Conference on Human Rights. Seeking to build an integrated transnational movement, activists finally framed the issue as one of violence against women and made this approach the centerpiece of the UN Conference on Women in Beijing in 1995, successfully bridging the competing orientations and rallying the women's rights network behind a unified message of opposition to all forms of violence against women.[27] In the case of female genital cutting, opponents framed the practice simply by changing the name from female circumcision (thereby breaking its association with the traditional practice of male circumcision, which does not produce the same long-term health problems) to female genital mutilation, which carries stronger connotations of violence against women. Traditionalists, in turn, attempted to frame the issue as one of local culture against Western values imposed by colonial governors and Christian missionaries.[28]

TANs and other groups try to frame issues in a way that will win sympathy for their position. In the case of female circumcision, opponents have framed it as female genital *mutilation* to emphasize the violence of the practice.

25. David Morton, "Gunning for the World," *Foreign Policy* (January–February 2006), 58–67.

26. Keck and Sikkink, *Activists beyond Borders*, 2–3.

27. Keck and Sikkink, *Activists beyond Borders*, chap. 5.

28. See, for example: Makau Mutua, *Human Rights: A Political and Cultural Critique* (Philadelphia: University of Pennsylvania Press, 2002).

Toys Made for Children, by Children

Tariq was 12 years old, stitching soccer balls for the equivalent of 60¢ a piece in Pakistan. It took him all day to make one ball, for an average of about 6¢ per hour. Featured in *Life* magazine in 1996, Tariq became the face of child labor in the developing world and sparked a major global civil society action to stop the commercial exploitation of children. Today, over 167 million children ages 5 to 17, about 1 in 6 worldwide, are still engaged in some form of child labor. Over 35 percent of all child laborers in that age range live in sub-Saharan Africa.[a] Children work in a host of occupations, including rug weaving, the production of surgical instruments, mining and construction, and—like Tariq—in the making of toys for other children.

Some forms of child labor are universally abhorred, such as child sex workers, numbering about 960,000 worldwide, down from 1.8 million in 2002.[b] Likewise, some practices like bonded labor—where children are sold into a form of slavery, often by their own families— are broadly condemned. And there is no doubt that children are exploited. Working conditions are often worse for children than adults, with breaks, fresh air, and even sanitation facilities in short supply. Although employers will sometimes claim that children are better than adults at some tasks, they are almost always paid less than their mature counterparts, suggesting strongly that they are not employed because they are more productive but rather because they are cheaper than adults.

Since Tariq appeared in *Life*, TANs devoted to ending the practice of child labor have grown significantly, and at least in developed countries there appears to be an emerging norm against child labor. Consumers in rich countries are increasingly avoiding goods that are known to be produced by child labor. There has been an equal expansion in NGOs that monitor child labor—although since they are unable to inspect factories and especially home work sites

frequently, it is not clear just what their product certifications entail.[c] We are witnessing in real time the growth of a norm. For many in developed countries, the concept of child labor is now abhorrent, nearly unthinkable, and is assumed to be exploitative. Nonetheless, this principle has probably not yet hit the tipping point where enough individuals accept the principle that it acquires a broad moral status. Why?

The issue of child labor is more complicated than it first appears. Clearly, the economic exploitation of children is wrong. But the evil of child labor must be balanced against the alternatives to work for children in the poorest countries. And these alternatives are often quite dismal. Most children and their families are not choosing between work and play or even education, but between work and starvation. Given that choice, children in poor countries are often sent to the factory—to make toys for children in rich countries, among other items.

Although low, the wages earned by children are often essential to supplement the meager incomes of their parents. In families living on mere dollars a day, a child's earnings might be the difference between subsistence and starvation. In turn, for most villages where children work, schools are typically few and far away. Moreover, families dependent on child labor can rarely afford even the small fees required for schooling where it exists. In the end, banning child labor may only force child workers further into the informal economy, outside government oversight and regulation, where they are even more easily exploited, or into the sex trade. Indeed, after the Child Labor Deterrence Act was introduced in the U.S. Senate in 1992, the mere threat of prohibitions on child-produced garments led business owners in Bangladesh to summarily dismiss many children from their jobs. According to a unique follow-up study that tracked those children, some were forced to take jobs "in more hazardous situations, in unsafe workshops where

a. International Labour Office, *Marking Progress against Child Labour: Global Estimates and Trends*, 2000–2012 (Geneva, Switzerland: International Labour Office, 2013), 3–5. The number of child laborers is down from 182 million in 2003.

b. International Labour Office, *Marking Progress against Child Labour*, 22.

c. Irfan Nooruddin and Sarah Wilson Sokhey, "Credible Certification of Child Labor Free Production," in *The Credibility of Transnational NGOs: When Virtue Is Not Enough*, ed. Peter Gourevitch, David A. Lake, and Janice Gross Stein, 62–85 (New York: Cambridge University Press, 2012).

they were paid less, or in prostitution."[d] Although even employers rarely give a principled defense of child labor, the core problem is the lack of other opportunities for child laborers.

Under these circumstances, banning child workers can be seen as another form of Western cultural imperialism—a projection of values that are now dominant in the richest countries onto individuals and families struggling to sustain themselves in some of the world's poorest areas. After all, minimum age requirements for employment in the United States were not enacted until 1938. In 1910, 2 million children, 18 percent of the total, were employed outside the agricultural sector in the United States—and this number would be much larger if we included farm labor. The first national attempt to set a minimum age for workers in the United States, the Keating-Owen Act of 1916, was later declared by the Supreme Court to be an unconstitutional infringement of a child's right to contract his or her own labor. Although the states had moved individually to regulate child labor, only during the Great Depression—when unemployment rates rose to extraordinary levels—could Progressives in the United States finally enact national minimum age standards for workers. This standard, combined with free primary schooling, led the proportion of children working to drop rapidly to under 1 percent. Even today, the Fair Labor Standards Act sets 14 as the minimum age for most nonagricultural work in the United States and permits youth of any age to deliver newspapers; perform in radio, television, and other media; engage in minor chores at a private home; or work in businesses or farms owned by their parents. Child labor was common in the now-developed countries before they became rich. Why should consumers or voters in these countries now seek to deny employment to children in the poorest countries?

Clearly, it is not enough to simply ban child labor. Advocates must couple ending child labor with expanded educational opportunities and financial support for poor families to replace lost income. It is not just a matter of ending a practice that is increasingly seen as immoral but of building new opportunities for children in areas where they do not now exist. This will be expensive, at least in the short term. The International Labor Organization demonstrates clearly that the long-term benefits of shifting children from

work to education are enormous. More education not only frees children from labor but increases their earning capacity over the course of their lifetimes. But paying to educate cohorts of children, monitoring compliance with anti–child labor laws, and subsidizing families to replace the income lost incurs substantial net costs for approximately the first 20 years of any program.[e] Only after generations of children have completed their educations and entered the adult workforce do the economic gains begin to outweigh the costs. Politicians everywhere are notoriously short-sighted. To bear costs for 20 years before the gains arrive is a challenge, and one even farsighted leaders may not easily manage. To ask the poorest countries to incur such costs over two decades is, perhaps, to expect too much.

A norm against child labor is taking hold in developed countries. More and more consumers are avoiding goods produced with child labor, whether these be athletic gear, rugs, or clothing. Governments are considering legislation to ban goods produced by children. This hardly seems objectionable. These moral consumers and politicians, however, may not actually be helping children unless they also support expanded education and income transfers to those they leave with fewer—rather than more—opportunities in the world's poorest countries.

d. UNICEF, *The State of the World's Children* (New York: Oxford University Press, 1997), 23, www.unicef.org/sowc97/report/ (accessed 09/08/14).

e. International Labour Office, *Investing in Every Child: An Economic Study of the Costs and Benefits of Eliminating Child Labour* (Geneva, Switzerland: International Labour Office, 2003), 6.

By connecting the practice to the larger anticolonial struggle, they ensured some continuing support among local communities and, thus, continuing controversy.[29] Similarly, the NRA attempts to frame the issue of gun ownership by linking it to the concept of human rights, while advocates of gun control emphasize firearm safety and the threat to children.

During the second stage, once a new frame has taken hold, a *norms cascade* occurs as the number of adherents passes a tipping point beyond which the idea gains sufficient support that it becomes a nearly universal standard of behavior to which others can be held accountable. The tipping point is often hard to identify in advance; it is determined not only by the number of actors that adopt the new belief but also by those actors' leadership or visibility within the international community. Conformity to the new norm can then be established through coercion (such as economic sanctions in the case of human rights norms) or through socialization (a process akin to peer pressure in which, say, states adopt new behaviors because that is what "good" states do). The norm of national election monitoring appears to have recently crossed this threshold. Although the norm was essentially unknown before 1978, virtually all democratizing states now invite other governments or transnational NGOs to monitor their first elections (see Chapter 2 "How Do We Know?" on p. 71). It is not clear, given the prominent countries that have not yet committed to eliminate their use, whether the ban on land mines has reached this stage.

In the third stage, norms are internalized or become so widely accepted that they acquire the taken-for-granted quality that makes conforming almost automatic. Indeed, even contemplating the violation of the deeply internalized norms against, say, cannibalism or eating certain foods can make some people feel ill. Norms against slavery or violence against political prisoners, once the subjects of TAN activity, are now at least partially internalized within many countries, although violations still occur. Few norms governing interactions between states have reached this final stage, although the nuclear taboo may be close.

Once internalized, norms affect the way in which actors conceive of their interests. Prior to this stage, norms are enforced by the sanctions or moral disapproval of others. These forms of punishment raise the costs of engaging in behaviors that violate the norm, thereby affecting the choices actors make in particular interactions. But once a norm is internalized, certain actions are simply not considered because they are normatively prohibited (taboo) and others are favored as appropriate or correct. At this deepest level, internalized norms lead actors to reconceive their interests by reordering how they evaluate alternative political outcomes and the appropriate means of achieving them.

Do Norms Matter?

Norms constrain states and other actors in two principal ways, first by redefining interests and, second, by changing their interactions. In both cases, isolating the

---

29. Keck and Sikkink, *Activists beyond Borders*, 67–71.

effects of norms on policy is difficult. To the extent that norms define how individuals and states perceive their interests, the selection problem identified above in the case of international law becomes even more acute. If norms shape interests, and states act on those intests, distinguishing the independent effect of norms on action is nearly impossible. Nonetheless, there is reason to believe that the effects of norms on state action may be considerable.

Norms define interests by shaping what actors believe is right and appropriate behavior under specific circumstances. Countries as a whole may respect norms out of concern for their reputations as honorable or norm-abiding states. Such a reputation may have intrinsic value. It may also be valued because it facilitates cooperation with other countries. As individuals, leaders may seek for their own egotistic reasons to be seen as moral and "upstanding." Other leaders may do the right thing simply because it is right. Even if leaders are cross-pressured by circumstances or self-interested groups to act in ways that contravene norms, however, they can be held to account by their own citizens, and especially by voters.

TANs play an important role in enforcing norms by calling attention to violations of widely held beliefs—a practice known as naming and shaming. States and their leaders typically value their reputations as "good" countries or individuals that respect and comply with standards of appropriate behavior. By calling attention to violations of norms, TANs mobilize domestic citizens as well as the "court of world opinion" to castigate and shame states into altering abhorrent behavior. They also challenge and potentially damage the reputations of offending states. If countries violate norms frequently and are called to account repeatedly by TANs, they risk becoming international pariahs that other states will be reluctant to trust. Although naming and shaming might seem like a weak tool to leverage good compliance from otherwise strong states, over the long run it can severely weaken a state's reputation and put potentially profitable cooperation at risk.

Norms also change the interactions of states and their outcomes by invoking the coercive power of other states. In the **boomerang model** proposed by Margaret Keck and Kathryn Sikkink, NGOs in one state are able to activate transnational linkages to bring pressure from other states to bear on their own governments (Figure 11.2).[30] This process is most likely to be effective when NGOs are blocked from influencing their own governments, as is common in many nondemocratic regimes. Unable to appeal to their own governments, NGOs activate their transnational network and bring their plight to the attention of NGOs and individuals in other countries, who, in turn, press their governments or, perhaps, international organizations into action. These other governments then demand that the first state alter its behavior or remove the block on its own NGOs. In this way, foreign states are mobilized to try to influence the offending state. Reflecting the importance of domestic political institutions, the boomerang model is most likely to be activated by NGOs originating in nondemocratic regimes and directed at

boomerang model
A process through which NGOs in one state are able to activate transnational linkages to bring pressure from other states on their own governments.

---

30. Keck and Sikkink, *Activists beyond Borders*, 12–13.

FIGURE 11.2   *The Boomerang Model*

This stylized depiction of the boomerang model shows how NGOs that are blocked from influence within their own state (State A) can appeal to other transnational NGOs, which can press their states (State B) or an international organization to press State A to change its policy.

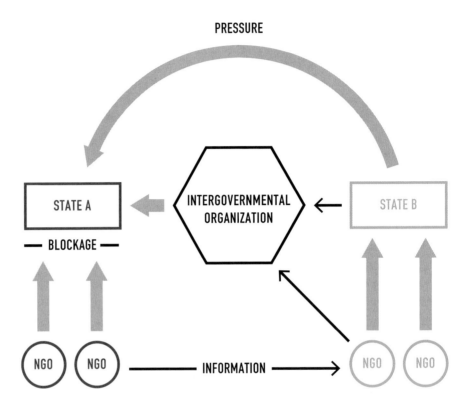

Figure source: Margaret E. Keck and Kathryn Sikkink, *Activists beyond Borders: Advocacy Networks in International Politics* (Ithaca, NY: Cornell University Press, 1998), 13.

NGOs in more democratic states, where governments are more sensitive to social demands pressed by their voters. New forms of social media have likely accentuated the strength and speed of the boomerang effect as news and, importantly, often graphic video of state repression can be transmitted broadly across the globe instantaneously.

The anti-apartheid movement in South Africa is a good example of the boomerang model in action (see Chapter 12). Excluded from power and influence in the white-dominated government, black South Africans, their NGOs, and their allies in the society appealed to foreign TANs in their struggle. These advocacy networks mobilized opinion and voters in other countries—mostly in Western democracies—whose governments placed sanctions on South Africa and eventually helped topple the apartheid regime. As this example suggests, the essence of the boomerang process involves domestic NGOs bringing greater pressure to bear on their government than they would be able to exert on their own. The process does not require any actor to alter its perceived interests; instead, the activation of transnational ties changes the nature of the political interactions in which the domestic actors are engaged and makes socially inappropriate behavior most costly.

Beyond Norms: TANs and International Cooperation

In addition to promoting norms, TANs can also affect behavior and outcomes by providing information to states both as endorsers before a final agreement is reached and as monitors afterward. In both cases, the information provided by TANs facilitates interstate cooperation that would otherwise fail. In this way, TANs provide important support for international cooperation that goes beyond their role as norms entrepreneurs.

TANs as Endorsers International agreements can be quite complex. We assume that the negotiators themselves know and agree on the terms of any given treaty or executive agreement they sign, although many agreements contain imprecise language to paper over differences between parties or do not consider all possible contingencies under which the agreement might hold. But members of the legislature that must ratify the agreement or implement its terms typically do not have a detailed understanding of its provisions. Furthermore, the voters who must reelect the executive who negotiated the deal, or the legislators who concurred, almost certainly do not know much about the agreement undertaken in their name.

Legislators and voters can learn whether to support or oppose an agreement from TANs that track the negotiations, study the final text, and endorse or reject its provisions. Legislators or voters need not know a great deal about the substance of the policy issue or the agreement, but they can make informed choices by taking cues from groups that (1) share their preferences or have some external incentive (such as penalties for lying) to truthfully reveal what they know and (2) possess real knowledge about the agreement.[31] Thus, in considering whether to support a proposed environmental treaty, a legislator need not study the text closely but can observe whether representatives of a trustworthy TAN have endorsed the agreement and decide how to vote accordingly. Legislators who support tighter environmental regulations will vote for treaties endorsed by, say, the Sierra Club, Greenpeace, and similar organizations; those who prefer less stringent regulations will vote against treaties endorsed by those same groups.

The endorsements by TANs provide an informational shortcut that allows legislators or voters to make decisions (nearly) identical to those they would make if they were completely informed. TANs are often particularly effective endorsers precisely because they are perceived as principled actors with strongly held normative beliefs. When they speak for or against an issue on which they are perceived to possess expertise, their voices are typically quite loud and are heard clearly by legislators and voters.

---

31. This discussion draws on Arthur Lupia and Mathew D. McCubbins, *The Democratic Dilemma: Can Citizens Learn What They Need to Know?* (New York: Cambridge University Press, 1998).

By helping voters or legislators to make appropriate decisions on the basis of limited information, TANs enhance the prospects for cooperation between states. Whenever a domestic legislature must ratify an international agreement, the effect is to make cooperation between two countries either the same or less likely than it is when only the executive is directly involved.[32] If the legislature is uncertain about the content and meaning of the agreement negotiated between the executive and the foreign state, it may mistakenly reject agreements that all three parties would prefer. Similar to the problem of bargaining in war (see Chapter 3), uncertainty makes bargaining inefficient and more likely to fail. TANs can reduce such uncertainty and improve the likelihood of cooperation by providing information to all the parties. In this way, TANs facilitate cooperation between states that would otherwise not occur.

TANs as Monitors   TANs can also monitor whether and how states comply with international law and other agreements as well as international norms. By revealing information about compliance, TANs allow states to have greater confidence that present and future agreements will be honored.

Having enacted a law, reached an agreement, or recognized a norm, states acquire information about compliance in one of three ways. First, they can rely on the self-reports of others. Many international agreements depend on this mechanism, requiring states to report on their efforts to reduce atmospheric emissions, for instance. This mechanism is, in fact, relatively weak, as states that have incentives to cheat on agreements are also likely to have incentives to lie about their cheating. Self-reports are only useful when they can be verified by one of the other mechanisms.

Second, states can monitor one another's behavior directly. For example, the arms control agreements negotiated between the United States and the Soviet Union during the Cold War depended on direct monitoring. Yet direct monitoring is often quite expensive, as each state must expend resources in collecting information about often hard-to-observe behaviors by others. Direct monitoring is sometimes likened to police patrols actively circulating on their "beats" looking for violations of the law.[33] Such direct monitoring can be inefficient, as monitors must be in the field even when violations are not occurring. It can also be imperfect, as monitors may be occupied or distracted elsewhere when violations do occur. Nonetheless, this practice is a common means of monitoring compliance in international relations.

Third, states can monitor indirectly by listening to the testimony of trustworthy third parties. Here TANs can be useful in identifying and calling attention to

---

32. See Helen Milner, *Interests, Institutions, and Information: Domestic Politics and International Relations* (Princeton, NJ: Princeton University Press, 1997). The existence of an effective legislature never makes cooperation more likely.

33. See Mathew D. McCubbins and Thomas Schwartz, "Congressional Oversight Overlooked: Police Patrols versus Fire Alarms," *American Journal of Political Science* 28, no. 1 (February 1984): 165–79.

TANs may monitor compliance with international laws and call attention to violations. Greenpeace frequently monitors compliance with laws against whaling, pollution, and deforestation.

violations of international agreements. Having championed the ban on land mines into international law, the ICBL now monitors state compliance very closely. Indirect monitoring is common in the human rights issue area, where organizations like Amnesty International and Human Rights Watch track practices globally and issue calls to their members and states when violations are observed. Similar practices are emerging in the issue area of the environment. Nearly 10,000 NGOs were officially permitted to participate in the 1992 Earth Summit, the largest-ever gathering of national leaders to discuss protecting the environment. Not only did these organizations conduct a parallel summit and make policy proposals to the interstate meeting, but through their participation they were accredited and legitimated as the watchdogs of the agreements made at the conference. With their new acceptance and prominence, this transnational environmental network has played an important role in calling international attention to poor environmental policies and practices worldwide. Indirect monitoring is similar to fire alarms: when problems arise, concerned parties pull the alarm and alert others who respond, but only when necessary.[34] When trustworthy monitors are available, indirect monitoring is far less expensive to states and more efficient than the alternatives. By facilitating monitoring and reducing its costs, TANs help promote cooperation that states would otherwise be reluctant to pursue.

---

34. McCubbins and Schwartz, "Congressional Oversight Overlooked." On the credibility of transnational NGOs, see Peter Gourevitch, David A. Lake, and Janice Gross Stein, eds., *The Credibility of Transnational NGOs: When Virtue Is Not Enough* (New York: Cambridge University Press, 2012).

Conclusion: Can States Be Constrained?

Can state behavior be changed by international law and norms? This remains a lively debate in which scholars do not have settled answers. On one side, traditionalists argue that international law only binds states to the extent they want to be bound; in turn, transnational networks exist only because states that might otherwise regulate, control, and limit their interactions permit them to flourish. From this perspective, international law is at best a soft constraint, and TANs and the norms they promote reflect the interests and international prominence of liberal, democratic states that have active domestic civil societies and project these onto the global system. Were these states to weaken or choose otherwise, both international law and international norms might be undercut by less supportive governments.[35]

On the other side, globalists argue that international law and transnational networks are emerging as effective forms of global governance. In this view, political authority previously exercised by states is migrating to new supranational authorities, which can regulate states through international law, and to TANs, which are gradually assuming some responsibilities formerly fulfilled by states.[36] Here, law is respected because of the large gains from cooperation it facilitates, and TANs are promoting new norms of global civil society and pressing states to change their behavior. For the globalists, international law and norms are increasingly constraining states in their actions both at home and with one another.

As with all such debates, there are no easy answers. The growth of international law and norms does appear to be changing patterns of state interaction in some areas, including human rights and the environment, discussed in the following chapters. International law constrains some actions of some states at least some of the time, punishing or at least sullying the reputation of states that violate legitimate rules. TANs make cooperation between countries more likely by serving as endorsers and monitors of international agreements. They perform essential roles in supporting and observing compliance with both the international human rights and environmental regimes. Although the traditionalists may be correct in their view that states in principle still have the authority to set

---

35. Among other traditionalists, see Robert Gilpin, *Global Political Economy* (Princeton, NJ: Princeton University Press, 2001), chap. 15; and Stephan D. Krasner, "Power Politics, Institutions, and Transnational Relations," in *Bringing Transnational Relations Back In: Non-State Actors, Domestic Structures and International Institutions*, ed. Thomas Risse-Kappen, 257–79 (New York: Cambridge University Press, 1995).

36. See David Held, Anthony G. McGrew, David Goldblatt, and Jonathan Perraton, *Global Transformations: Politics, Economics, and Culture* (Stanford, CA: Stanford University Press, 1999), especially chap. 1; Walter Mattli, "Public and Private Governance in Setting International Standards," in *Governance in a Global Economy: Political Authority in Transition,* ed. Miles Kahler and David A. Lake, 199–225 (Princeton, NJ: Princeton University Press, 2012); and Virginia Haufler, "Globalization and Industry Self-Regulation," in Kahler and Lake, *Governance in a Global Economy*, 226–52.

international law and control transnational groups, it is not clear that they retain the ability or political will to do so. Precisely because international law and norms are often useful to states, it will become increasingly difficult for states to ignore their restraints.

Globalists, however, may exaggerate the extent to which international law and TANs can substitute for government at the global level. International law is still hampered by the need for self-enforcement. TANs that are active in promoting social causes are voluntary associations that cannot legally bind their members, even less so others. Lacking the political authority attributed to states, they must rely on voluntary compliance from their targets, which is often uneven. Despite the hopes of some, international law and norms appear not to have displaced the central role of states on the world stage. States make international law. Even though TANs are influencing interests, the norms advocated by TANs are still very much norms about appropriate *state* behavior. It is the human rights, environmental, economic, and political practices of *states* that TANs typically seek to change. Similarly, although TANs activate transnational linkages, they do so to mobilize foreign groups to urge their *states* to press the offending state to change its policy. Finally, although TANs facilitate cooperation, it is cooperation between and among *states* that is altered, and the information the TANs provide is about states to other states. Even as law and TANs have proliferated and grown in prominence, world politics remains very much an arena of states.

Study Tool Kit

Interests, Interactions, and Institutions in Context

- International law and norms are institutions that seek to shape how states understand their interests and to constrain the ways in which they interact.

- States create and abide by international law because of the cooperation it enables. Although states are typically dependent upon "self-help" for enforcement, the benefits of cooperation to states are often large enough that international laws are self-enforcing, or in the interests of states to follow apparently willingly.

- International norms affect world politics by changing how individuals and, in turn, states conceive of their interests and appropriate actions in their interactions with other states.

- TANs have an important effect on world politics by promoting normative values. TANs also alter interactions between states and facilitate cooperation by providing information about international agreements and monitoring compliance.

Key Terms

international law, p. 459

customary international law, p. 460

obligation, p. 463

precision, p. 463

delegation, p. 464

norms, p. 469

norms entrepreneurs, p. 474

transnational advocacy network (TAN), p. 474

norms life cycle, p. 476

boomerang model, p. 481

For Further Reading

Adler-Nissen, Rebecca. "Stigma Management in International Relations: Transgressive Identities, Norms, and Order in International Society." *International Organization* 68, no. 1 (2014): 143–76. Demonstrates that international order is formed in part by stigmatizing nonconforming and norm-violating states.

Goldstein, Judith L., Miles Kaher, Robert O. Keohane, and Anne-Marie Slaughter, eds. *Legalization and World Politics*. Cambridge, MA: MIT Press, 2001. Some of the best contemporary research on international law by political scientists.

Guzman, Andrew T. *How International Law Works: A Rational Choice Theory*. New York: Oxford University Press, 2008. Explains how international law can succeed even in the absence of third-party enforcement through reciprocity, reputation, and retaliation.

Henkin, Louis. *How Nations Behave: Law and Foreign Policy*. 2nd ed. New York: Columbia University Press, 1979. A classic study on international law and politics.

Keck, Margaret E., and Kathryn Sikkink. *Activists beyond Borders: Advocacy Networks in International Politics*. Ithaca, NY: Cornell University Press, 1998. Serves as a classic study of the growth and role of TANs.

Morrow, James D. *Order within Anarchy: The Laws of War as an International Institution*. New York: Cambridge University Press, 2014. Examines how law conditions expectations and state behavior in the context of the Geneva Conventions.

Raustiala, Kal. "States, NGOs, and International Environmental Institutions." *International Studies Quarterly* 41, no. 4 (December 1997): 719–40. Explains the role of NGOs in monitoring compliance with international agreements.

Reus-Smit, Christian. *The Moral Purpose of the State: Cultural, Social Identity, and Institutional Rationality in International Relations*. Princeton, NJ: Princeton University Press, 1999. A survey of international norms that shape the basic constitutional structure of world politics.

Towns, Ann E. *Women and States: Norms and Hierarchies in International Society*. New York: Cambridge University Press, 2010. Examines the changing norms that govern the relationship between women and the state.

12

Human Rights

THE PUZZLE *Why do states undertake costly actions to protect the human rights of people outside their borders? In light of the widespread support for the principle of human rights, why has the movement to protect those rights not been even more successful?*

Above: Under apartheid, the South African government systematically denied the human rights of non-White citizens. Here, participants at the 1986 Nelson Mandela Freedom Festival in London call for South Africa to free the anti-apartheid leader. Mandela was released from prison in 1990.

For over 40 years, the White-dominated government of South Africa pursued a strict policy of racial segregation and inequality called apartheid. Distinguishing among Whites, Indians, Coloureds, and Africans or Blacks, this policy assigned everyone to a "homeland" within the territory of the state, regulated movement into the cities and employment, and created a system of racial discrimination designed to perpetuate the political and economic dominance of the White minority. Human rights abuses under apartheid were widespread. In addition to denying the political, economic, social, and cultural rights of more than three-quarters of the country's population, the White government engaged in arbitrary arrests and detentions without trial, as well as torture and executions without judicial review. The full extent of the abuses perpetrated by the regime was revealed only by the postapartheid Truth and Reconciliation Commission.[1]

Transnational advocacy networks (TANs; see Chapter 11) worked closely with South African opposition groups to bring international pressure against the apartheid regime. In November 1962, the United Nations (UN) General Assembly adopted Resolution 1761 condemning apartheid and calling for all countries to terminate economic and military relations with South Africa. The country was excluded from the Organization of African Unity at the institution's founding in 1963 and was expelled from Olympic Games membership in 1968. The UN Security Council adopted a mandatory embargo on weapons sales to the White regime in 1977. As domestic unrest flared in 1984 following constitutional reforms that gave political rights to Indians and Coloureds but not to Africans, the government began a brutal crackdown. To signal their displeasure with the widespread human rights abuses, by 1986 all of South Africa's major trading partners—including the United States—had adopted economic sanctions. Often under pressure from student protests that forced universities to flex the power of their endowments, some foreign firms ended their investments in South Africa.[2]

Increasing internal dissent, both nonviolent and violent, combined with international censure to finally end

1. David Black, "The Long and Winding Road: International Norms and Domestic Political Change in South Africa," in *The Power of Human Rights: International Norms and Domestic Change,* ed. Thomas Risse, Stephen C. Ropp, and Kathryn Sikkink, 80 (New York: Cambridge University Press, 1999).

2. Audie Klotz, *Norms in International Relations: The Struggle against Apartheid* (Ithaca, NY: Cornell University Press, 1995).

apartheid in 1990 and start the peaceful transition to Black majority rule in 1994. Primary credit for the repeal of apartheid goes to the brave South African men, women, and children of all backgrounds who stood up against the racist regime. Nonetheless, the anti-apartheid struggle stands out for two larger effects on the global human rights movement. First, the national struggle played out on a global stage. Blocked at home from influencing the White regime, the Black majority appealed to allies abroad for support. By documenting and publicizing abuses and by mobilizing activists worldwide, TANs helped bring about the end of the long-standing practice of systematic racial discrimination. The struggle against apartheid set a visible precedent for TAN activity and success in the broad area of human rights. Second, the anti-apartheid struggle demonstrated that states are, at times, willing to bear costs to express their disapproval of other governments and to support the victims of widespread human rights abuses. Not all states cooperated in the movement to repeal apartheid, and some were pushed into doing so only by vigorous pressure from activists. Nonetheless, opposing apartheid was an important turning point for states in using their influence to isolate and punish regimes that systematically abuse their own people.

Despite the success in ending apartheid, the effort to promote human rights in other countries is highly uneven. Concerns remain about human rights practices in many places, including China, Myanmar, Russia, and even in the United States with regard to the death penalty and the treatment of detainees in the global war on terror. Although nearly everyone supports human rights in principle, and many rights are codified in international law, disagreement continues on what constitutes a human right and when they should be protected. Human rights violations in one country rarely affect the material welfare of other countries, the principal exception being when political conflict within a country generates significant refugee flows into other countries. Moreover, noninterference by others in a state's internal affairs is a defining and often highly treasured principle of national sovereignty—a principle that the apartheid regime appealed to repeatedly in an effort to insulate itself from foreign scrutiny. By condemning the human rights abuses of others, states not only violate this norm of noninterference but risk opening themselves to foreign interference. Why do states undertake costly actions, such as sanctioning South Africa, with no immediate benefit to themselves or their own citizens?

As the example of South Africa makes clear, human rights practices around the globe are undoubtedly better than they would be without broad support for human rights, international laws governing how states treat their citizens, TANs "naming and shaming" abusers, and states occasionally punishing those violators with sanctions. Yet few countries respect all human rights, and a significant number of countries violate many of these rights. Why isn't international human rights law more effective?

Thinking Analytically about Human Rights

In addressing this puzzle, our discussion considers the interests, interactions, and institutions involved in international human rights. First, we will see that international human rights law is an institution created by and largely reflecting the political norms and values of Western, liberal democracies. The norms embodied in these laws are not shared equally by all countries and have not yet been internalized by many societies and governments. Thus, even when formally codified, they remain controversial.

The interests and interactions involved in enforcing human rights help explain both why some actors work hard to promote human rights abroad and why states that violate human rights do so despite international norms. Individuals have an interest in international human rights, and this is why they sometimes encourage their leaders to take action to punish states that violate rights. But, as we will see, these interests are rarely strong enough to compel states to pay the high costs to protect vulnerable individuals and groups outside their own borders. Thus, states that violate human rights anticipate that in their interactions with other states they probably will not face serious consequences for their behavior and, therefore, can abuse individuals and groups without significant penalties. Unfortunately, these states are most likely correct. International human rights law does indeed promote improved practices. Its full promise, however, has not yet been realized.

What Are International Human Rights?

Human rights are rights that all individuals possess by virtue of being human, regardless of their status as citizens of particular states or members of a group or organization. These rights are, by definition, universal and apply to all humans equally.

The concept of human rights has a long philosophical tradition, dating from the Enlightenment in the eighteenth century. English philosopher John Locke (1632–1704) first developed the modern notion of natural rights, the idea that people are by nature free and equal and, therefore, possess certain basic rights that are not contingent on the laws, customs, or beliefs of any particular society or government. This idea then informed the American and French Revolutions, embodied in the famous second sentence of the Declaration of Independence, which states "that all men are created equal, that they are endowed by their Creator with certain unalienable rights, that among these are life, liberty and the pursuit of happiness."

The first concrete international steps toward regulating how governments treat their citizens were undertaken in the UN Charter, adopted in 1945. This movement was spurred by the atrocities of World War II, especially the Holocaust, in which over six million Jews and other minorities were systematically "dehumanized" and killed. Article 55 of the charter states that "based on respect for the principle of equal rights and self-determination of peoples, the United Nations shall promote . . . universal respect for, and observance of, human rights and fundamental freedoms for all without distinction as to race, sex, language, or religion."

Soon after the United Nations was founded, work began on an effort to clarify which rights Article 55 embodied and which rights states would be expected to protect. The **Universal Declaration of Human Rights (UDHR)**,[3] adopted by the UN General Assembly in 1948, is the product of those deliberations. Defined as a "common standard of achievement for all peoples" and broadly accepted as the foundation of modern human rights law, its 30 articles identify a diverse set of rights (see "What Shaped Our World?" on p. 494). Although governed only by soft law (see Chapter 11), the UDHR is today considered to be the authoritative standard of human rights.

René Cassin, one of the main authors of the UDHR, described the document as having four pillars supporting "dignity, liberty, equality, and brotherhood." Each of the pillars represents a different historical principle and philosophy of human rights. The first two articles of the UDHR stand for a timeless human dignity shared by all individuals regardless of race, religion, nationality, or sex. Articles 3 to 19 of the declaration define a first generation of civil liberties and other rights founded in a Western philosophical and legal tradition begun during the Enlightenment, such as freedom of speech and association. Articles 20 to 26 focus on political, social, and

human rights
The rights possessed by all individuals by virtue of being human, regardless of their status as citizens of particular states or members of a group or organization.

Universal Declaration of Human Rights (UDHR)
Adopted by the UN General Assembly in 1948, this declaration defines a "common standard of achievement for all peoples" and forms the foundation of modern human rights law.

---

3. See www.hrweb.org/legal/udhr.html.

The Universal Declaration of Human Rights

The UDHR was adopted by the General Assembly of the United Nations on December 10, 1948. It seeks to set a standard for human rights practices around the globe.

Interests The origins of the UDHR lie in the Great Depression of the 1930s, the New Deal of U.S. president Franklin Delano Roosevelt, and World War II. By pushing millions into poverty, the Depression reinforced the people's interest in their government's commitment to a basic level of economic security. The violence of World War II, the Holocaust specifically, exposed people's vulnerability to a government committed to enslavement or extermination. Furthermore, the experiences in World War II suggested that a government that carried out atrocities against its own citizens was likely to turn its aggression against its neighbors. These events combined to create new interests in promoting human rights around the world. In laying out his vision of a postwar peace, Roosevelt identified his famous four freedoms in a speech delivered on January 6, 1941, even before the United States entered the war: (1) "freedom of speech and expression"; (2) "freedom of every person to worship God in his own way," or freedom of religion; (3) "freedom from want" or poverty; and (4) "freedom from fear," especially aggression and war. This was a new and expanded vision of a postwar order founded on respect for human rights as a bulwark against economic crisis and Fascism.

Interactions Negotiations for the UDHR were extraordinarily rapid for an international compact of this sort. The UN at the time was composed mostly of countries allied during World War II and states from Latin America, all of which (except for the Soviet Union and its clients, South Africa, and Saudi Arabia) were comfortable with the philosophy of fundamental individual rights that informed the agreement.[a] Prior to the outbreak of the Cold War in the late 1940s, many citizens in the United States supported the notion of broad economic and social rights. Indeed, President Roosevelt himself had proposed an economic bill of rights within the United States in 1944. Building on this broad base of agreement, Eleanor Roosevelt, then chairwoman of the UN Human Rights Commission, used her stature and leadership skills to facilitate quick agreement on a broad statement of rights. This was a relatively rare moment in history when the interests of states were aligned in favor of establishing new rights and responsibilities. In a short time, and with the astute leadership of key individuals, a consensus to promote human rights was reached.

Institutions The UDHR is a soft-law institution, lacking in obligation or precision, that enumerates a variety of rights available to all "without distinction of any kind, such as race, colour, sex, language, religion, political or other opinion, national or social origin, property, birth or other status." The rights include:

- Life, liberty, and the security of person (Art. 3)
- Recognition everywhere as a person before the law (Art. 6)
- Equal protection under the law (Art. 7)
- Fair and public trials (Art. 10)
- The presumption of innocence until proven guilty (Art. 11)
- Freedom of movement and residence (Art. 13)
- Asylum from persecution (Art. 14)
- Marriage, freely entered into, and procreation and family (Art. 16)
- Property (Art. 17)
- Employment, equal pay for equal work, and just remuneration necessary for an existence worthy of human dignity (Art. 23)
- An adequate standard of living (Art. 25)
- Education, including compulsory free education in the elementary and fundamental stages (Art. 26)

The UDHR also recognizes as inherent rights the freedoms of:

- Thought, conscience, and religion (Art. 18)
- Opinion and expression (Art. 19)
- Peaceful assembly and association (Art. 20).

In turn, the UDHR prohibits:

- Slavery or servitude (Art. 4)
- Arbitrary arrest, detention, or exile (Art. 9)
- Ex post application of law (Art. 11)
- Arbitrary interference with privacy, home, or correspondence (Art. 12)

---

a. These states abstained from voting on the UDHR; all the successor governments except Saudi Arabia have since publicly disavowed their abstentions.

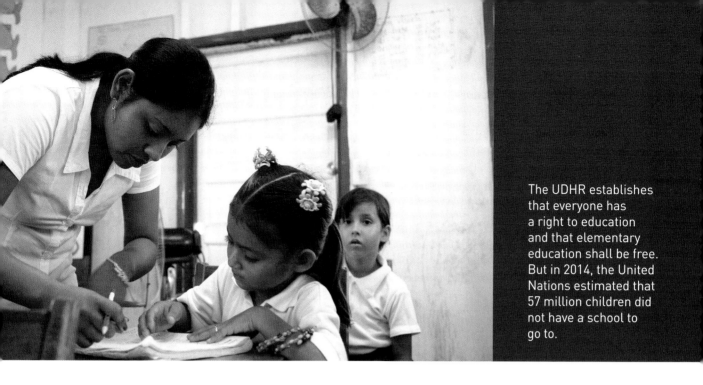

The UDHR establishes that everyone has a right to education and that elementary education shall be free. But in 2014, the United Nations estimated that 57 million children did not have a school to go to.

economic equality, a second generation of rights that emerged during the Industrial Revolution and that is often associated with socialist thought. This second generation includes the rights to employment, form trade unions, and education. Articles 27 and 28 address rights of communal and national solidarity, first developed in the late nineteenth century and championed by the states emerging from colonialism.[4] This last generation of rights, however, is far less developed in the UDHR than the first two.

In tandem with the UDHR, the UN negotiated the Convention on the Prevention and Punishment of the Crime of Genocide, the first human rights treaty with clearly defined obligations and precise rules. The term *genocide* was coined by Raphael Lemkin, a Polish lawyer of Jewish descent who immigrated to the United States in 1941, to capture the essence of what happened during the Holocaust. It combines the Greek word *genos*, for "race" or "people," with the Latin word *cidere*, "to kill." The Genocide Convention, as it is widely known, follows Lemkin closely in defining genocide as "acts committed with the intent to destroy, in whole or part, a national, ethnical, racial or religious group." Pushed to the forefront of the human rights agenda because of the Holocaust, the Genocide Convention became the first piece of hard international human rights law. With 146 state parties to the agreement and 41 additional signatories, this is one of the more widely recognized and supported treaties ever written. The United States signed the treaty in 1948 but did not ratify it until 40 years later. Senator William Proxmire (D-WI), a major supporter, was well known for his daily speeches in favor of ratification (a total of 3,211), given on the floor every day the Senate was in session between 1967 and the Senate vote on the treaty in 1986.

4. Micheline R. Ishay, *The History of Human Rights: From Ancient Times to the Globalization Era* (Berkeley: University of California Press, 2004), 3–4.

International Covenant on Civil and Political Rights (ICCPR)

The agreement completed in 1966 and in force from 1976 that details the basic civil and political rights of individuals and nations.

International Covenant on Economic, Social, and Cultural Rights (ICESCR)

The agreement completed in 1966 and in force from 1976 that specifies the basic economic, social, and cultural rights of individuals and nations.

After negotiating the UDHR and the Genocide Convention, the UN then began the much more difficult task of translating the UDHR into legally binding and internationally enforceable treaties. Unfolding over 18 years, the negotiations eventually produced two separate agreements: the **International Covenant on Civil and Political Rights (ICCPR)** and the **International Covenant on Economic, Social, and Cultural Rights (ICESCR)**.[5] Although there was nearly universal agreement on the UDHR, the attempt to write hard international law protecting human rights got caught, like so many other attempts at cooperation, between the superpowers during the Cold War. The solution was to write two separate treaties: one focusing on the civil and political rights of liberty then favored by Western states and one focusing on the economic, social, and cultural rights of equality and brotherhood supported by the then Communist states and others in the developing world. As formal treaties completed in 1966 and in force from 1976, the twin covenants are considered legally binding for all states that have signed them.

The ICCPR details the basic rights of individuals and nations, defining in sometimes more precise terms the political and civil rights first claimed in the UDHR. The ICCPR affirms the rights to life, liberty, and the freedom of movement; the presumption of innocence; equal standing before the law; legal recourse when rights have been violated; and privacy. In addition, all individuals are guaranteed freedom of thought, conscience, and religion; freedom of opinion and expression; and freedom of assembly and association. The covenant forbids torture and inhumane or degrading punishment, slavery and involuntary servitude, and arbitrary arrest and detention. It also prohibits propaganda advocating war or hatred based on race, religion, national origin, or language. The treaty provides for the right of all people to choose freely whom they will marry and to found a family, and it requires that the duties and obligations of marriage and family be shared equally between partners. It guarantees the rights of children and prohibits discrimination based on race, sex, color, national origin, or language. It restricts the death penalty to the most serious of crimes, guarantees condemned people the right to appeal for commutation to a lesser penalty, and forbids the death penalty entirely for people under 18 years of age.

As of June 2015, 168 of the UN's 193 member countries were parties to the ICCPR. The United States ratified the treaty in 1992, but only after declaring that its provisions were "not self-executing"—meaning that although the agreement is binding as a matter of international law, its provisions would not automatically become domestic law without further legislation by the U.S. Congress. Human rights practices under the covenant are monitored by the UN Human Rights Committee, a group of 18 experts who meet three times a year to consider periodic reports submitted by member states on their compliance with the treaty and interstate complaints of violations.

The parallel ICESCR reiterates and affirms the basic economic, social, and cultural rights of individuals and nations, including the right to earn wages sufficient to support a minimum standard of living; equal pay for equal work; equal opportunity for advancement; the right to form trade unions and strike; paid or otherwise compensated maternity leave; free primary education and accessible schools at all levels; and

---

5. For more information on the covenants and their texts, see www.ohchr.org/EN/ProfessionalInterest/Pages/InternationalLaw.aspx (accessed 09/18/14).

copyright, patent, and trademark protection for intellectual property. The treaty forbids the exploitation of children and requires all countries to cooperate to end world hunger. Each nation that has ratified this covenant is required to submit annual reports on its progress in providing for these rights to the secretary-general of the UN. The ICESCR currently has 164 members. The United States signed the covenant in 1977 under President Jimmy Carter but has never ratified it because of continuing opposition to provisions that would go substantially beyond existing domestic laws.

Together, the UDHR and the twin covenants are often referred to as the **International Bill of Rights**. Over time, additional rights have been added through supplementary conventions as summarized in Table 12.1. The agreements listed there highlight the range of rights that are now more or less protected under international law, including in certain cases the right of individual petition through which victims of human rights abuses can seek redress directly from international courts. In short, as demonstrated by Table 12.1, the international community now possesses an extensive body of international human rights law, albeit one that remains controversial and possesses varying degrees of national support for different provisions.

Why Are Human Rights Controversial?

Because of differing legal traditions, domestic political regimes and institutions, and philosophies, states often have different interests in human rights. Even though human rights are by definition universal, states do not necessarily have the same interests in promoting the same rights to the same extent. States have interests in supporting rights that they already respect domestically and in fighting against new rights that they see as costly to protect. They also have an interest in preserving

International Bill of Rights

Refers collectively to the UDHR, the ICCPR, and the ICESCR. Together, these three agreements form the core of the international human rights regime.

There are 81 parties to an optional protocol to the ICCPR aimed at abolishing the death penalty. The protesters here delivered a petition to the U.S. embassy in Hong Kong, calling for the United States to stop executions.

TABLE 12.1 *UN Human Rights Agreements*

TREATY	DATE SIGNED/IN FORCE	BRIEF DESCRIPTION
Universal Declaration of Human Rights (UDHR)	1948	Outlines basic human rights.
Convention on the Prevention and Punishment of the Crime of Genocide	1948/1951	Bans acts committed with the intent to destroy, in whole or part, a national, ethnic, racial, or religious group.
International Convention on the Elimination of All Forms of Racial Discrimination (ICERD)	1965/1969	Bans all racial discrimination, with particular attention to policies and practices of apartheid.
International Covenant on Economic, Social, and Cultural Rights (ICESCR)	1966/1976	Details the basic economic, social, and cultural rights of individuals and nations.
International Covenant on Civil and Political Rights (ICCPR)	1966/1976	Details the basic civil and political rights of individuals and nations. Optional protocol (1966/1976) permits petitions from individuals. Second optional protocol (1989/1991) commits state parties to abolish the death penalty.
Convention on the Elimination of All Forms of Discrimination against Women (CEDAW)	1979/1981	Bans discrimination against women, focusing on education, employment, health, marriage, and the family. Optional protocol (1999/2000) permits petitions from individuals.
Convention against Torture and Other Cruel, Inhuman or Degrading Treatment or Punishment (CAT)	1984/1987	Bans torture under all circumstances. Optional protocol (2002/2006) establishes regular visits to monitor state practice.
Convention on the Rights of the Child (CRC)	1989/1990	Details the special rights of children. Optional protocol (2000/2002) bans children in the armed forces from participating in hostilities. Second optional protocol (2000/2002) prohibits the sale of children, child prostitution, and child pornography.
International Convention on the Protection of the Rights of All Migrant Workers and Members of Their Families (ICRMW)	1990/2003	Details the special rights of workers outside their country of origin.
Convention on the Rights of Persons with Disabilities	2007/2008	Mandates equal status and treatment for individuals with disabilities. Optional protocol (2007/2008) permits petitions from individuals.
International Convention for the Protection of All Persons from Enforced Disappearance	2007/2010	Prohibits arrest, detention, or abduction of individuals without acknowledgment by the state.

Note: For texts and updated membership information, consult www.ohchr.org/EN/ProfessionalInterest/Pages/InternationalLaw.aspx (accessed 09/18/14).

their own sovereignty. States may also have a strategic interest in promoting rights that their adversaries will deny or find costly to implement.

Many of the rights defined in the UDHR—especially many of the economic and social rights—are directly drawn from President Franklin D. Roosevelt's New Deal, adopted during the Great Depression of the 1930s. Through the 1950s, many people in the United States and other Western countries remained supporters of economic and social rights. As the New Deal lost popularity, however, support for enshrining many of its progressive policies into international law diminished. Human rights also became caught up in the Cold War competition of ideas. In public forums, Western states tended to emphasize first-generation civil and political rights already enshrined in their own systems while the countries of the Soviet bloc and many countries in the developing world trumpeted their superior progress on second-generation economic, social, and cultural rights. This Cold War division and historical legacy continues to undermine support for the ICESCR in the United States today. Many conservatives in the United States, for instance, question whether economic, social, and cultural rights are actually rights at all since they pertain to particular classes or groups of people (for example, workers) rather than to all human beings.[6]

Critics of the rights specified in the UDHR point to their origin in a Western, liberal philosophical tradition that emphasizes first-generation individual rights over second- and third-generation collective rights. This is correct—to a point. The modern idea of human rights is rooted in a moral vision that sees all humans as equal and autonomous individuals. Political scientist Jack Donnelly observes that "it is a relatively simple matter to derive the full list of rights in the Universal Declaration from the political principle of equal concern and respect."[7] Although the rights founded in this tradition may now be accepted because of their status as international standards and law, the philosophical tradition itself is not universally shared. An alternative philosophy, for example, is the notion of "Asian values," which elevates the rights of families and communities and the goal of social and political stability over the rights of individuals. Supported by such leaders as Mahathir bin Mohamad, prime minister of Malaysia from 1981 to 2003, this philosophy resonates strongly with some populations. Although the Asian financial crisis of 1997 called into question the "Asian tigers" model of political and economic development, this differing philosophical tradition continues to pose a direct challenge to the human rights norms now enshrined in international law.

The debate over which rights individuals have continues, underscoring the point that rights are an institution that evolves over time. International human rights are not fixed but are a product of struggle, debate, and social interests. Although nearly everyone may agree that some human rights exist in principle, debate continues on exactly which rights humans possess.

This continuing debate also demonstrates that human rights have not been internalized as norms in all societies and governments. Although more deeply held

---

6. Jack Donnelly, *Universal Human Rights in Theory and Practice*, 2nd ed. (Ithaca, NY: Cornell University Press, 2003), 28.

7. Donnelly, *Universal Human Rights in Theory and Practice*, 45.

Some human rights activists have argued that the U.S. government violates the rights of detainees held at Guantánamo Bay, Cuba. They are concerned about harsh interrogation methods and the lack of due process of law.

in Western, democratic countries, few human rights have obtained the taken-for-granted quality in which violations are considered taboo or inappropriate except in the most dire circumstances. Freedom from torture is likely one of the most widely and deeply held human rights, but the recent debate in the United States on the treatment of terrorist suspects suggests that even for some Americans, torture or practices that border on torture remain acceptable instruments of government policy. The power of the anti-torture principle was evident in the President George W. Bush administration's attempt to deny it was engaging in torture by redefining some practices, such as waterboarding, as not inconsistent with international law—an interpretation not supported by most other states. But actual practice suggests that the norm is, in fact, ambiguous and fails to significantly constrain government behavior. That human rights norms have not yet been internalized or, at best, are only weakly internalized implies that individuals and states still act on human rights and enforce laws only when it is in their self-interest to do so.

Are Some Rights More Important than Others?

Although the UDHR specifies a wide range of rights, it appears that (to paraphrase George Orwell's *Animal Farm*) although all rights are equal, some are more equal than others. Although few if any human rights are internalized as norms, some rights in the UDHR and ICCPR do have a special status in international law and, along with the Genocide Convention, appear to have broader support than others.

In the ICCPR, Article 4 permits the suspension of some rights in cases of social or public emergency, but it simultaneously identifies a small number of other rights that cannot be suspended for any reason. These **nonderogable rights** include freedom from torture or cruel and degrading punishment, recognition as a person before the law, and freedom of thought, conscience, and religion.[8] In contrast, none of the rights identified in the ICESCR are nonderogable, and all can be limited by states acting under the law. Despite their special status, however, nonderogable rights are not automatically enforced more than other rights, as the continuing practice of torture in countries around the world makes clear.

In turn, many of these nonderogable rights have gained special support within human rights TANs. Amnesty International, generally considered the world's leading human rights organization, identifies its core mission as protecting individuals from torture; cruel or inhuman or degrading punishment; and arbitrary arrest, detention, and exile, as well as defending the freedoms of thought, conscience,

nonderogable rights
Rights that cannot be suspended for any reason, including at times of public emergency.

---

8. Specifically, Article 4 prohibits the suspension of Articles 6 (inherent right to life, referring to the death penalty), 7 (torture), 8 (paragraphs 1 and 2, on slavery and servitude), 11 (imprisonment from contractual obligation), 15 (ex post criminal offenses), 16 (recognition before the law), and 18 (freedom of thought, conscience, and religion).

religion, opinion, and expression.[9] Individuals imprisoned solely for the peaceful expression of their beliefs are what Amnesty International calls **prisoners of conscience (POCs)**. One prominent contemporary POC is Noble Peace Prize winner Liu Xiaobo, who was jailed in 2009 simply for coauthoring a proposal for political and legal reform in China. The focus of Amnesty International, overlapping to a considerable extent with the nonderogable rights of the ICCPR, is shared by many human rights organizations. In focusing on these more limited rights and publicizing violations of only these rights, Amnesty has done much to influence notions of what human rights are today. To the extent that certain rights have become or moved toward becoming international norms, as explained in Chapter 11, Amnesty International and the other major human rights organizations that make up the TAN have had much to do with shaping this process.[10] Building support for human rights and changing conceptions of interests for both individuals and states on human rights practices has been a major achievement of TANs.

Finally, by examining when states are willing to incur costs in order to punish human rights violations in other states, we can infer something about which rights are most important to them. Economic sanctions are a common tool that states use to punish violators of human rights (see "Controversy" on p. 502). Since sanctions inflict costs on states that impose them, these states must weigh their interest in defending certain rights against their other priorities. Indeed, many violations of human rights go entirely unpunished, sometimes even unnoticed. Actual sanctions by states against violators are relatively rare. But when states have taken steps to impose sanctions against human rights abusers, these steps have almost always been for unfair political detentions and torture and the suspension of peaceful political opposition.[11] For instance, the United States imposed sanctions on South Korea and Chile in 1973 for the detention and treatment of political prisoners, and on Paraguay, Guatemala, Argentina, Nicaragua, El Salvador, and Brazil in 1977 for the same issues. Even in the case of South Africa, sanctions were not imposed against the country for its policy of apartheid in general but only after the insurrection began and the South African government brutally repressed political opponents. States clearly act to enforce some rights more frequently than others. Through practice, the rights that states appear ready to defend are narrower than the full range of rights articulated in the UDHR and may, in fact, be limited to the nonderogable rights identified in the ICCPR.

Overall, as an institution, international human rights remain a work in progress. Although codified in at least soft law, rights are themselves objects of political struggle, defining what is and is not acceptable government behavior toward its own citizens. Countries differ in their views on which rights they are bound to protect. They also differ on which rights they should seek to enforce when abused by others. Thus, we must examine not just human rights law but also the interests and interactions of states to account for the politics of international human rights.

prisoners of conscience (POCs)

A label coined and used by the human rights organization Amnesty International to refer to individuals imprisoned solely because of the peaceful expression of their beliefs.

---

9. Articles 5, 9, 18, and 19 of the UDHR.

10. See David A. Lake and Wendy Wong, "The Politics of Networks: Interests, Power, and Human Rights Norms," in *Networked Politics: Agency, Power, and Governance,* ed. Miles Kahler (Ithaca, NY: Cornell University Press, 2009).

11. Lake and Wong, "The Politics of Networks," 148.

CONTROVERSY

Should Economic Sanctions Be Imposed on Governments That Violate Human Rights?

Four days after Saddam Hussein's 1990 invasion of Kuwait, the UN Security Council passed a resolution imposing economic sanctions on Iraq, including a trade embargo on all exports to the country other than basic food and medical supplies.[a] Although in the ensuing Gulf War Iraqi troops were expelled from Kuwait within seven months, the sanctions continued for the next 12 years. One justification for maintaining the policy was that restrictions on international trade and finance would sap Hussein's power and thereby end the human rights abuses that the autocrat had inflicted on the Iraqi people. Yet the World Health Organization reported in March 1996 that sanctions-related deprivations in Iraq had caused infant mortality to rise by a factor of six, equivalent to the deaths of hundreds of thousands of children under age five.[b] At the same time Iraqi industry, employment, and education collapsed, crime and violence escalated, and vital public infrastructure failed to be rebuilt after the war. Denis Halliday, the UN humanitarian coordinator for Iraq, condemned the sanctions. Resigning in 1998 after a 34-year career with the UN, he described the sanctions against Iraq as "satisfying the definition of genocide."[c] Although sanctions had little to no effect in eventually removing Hussein from power, they did have a severe impact on Iraq's economy and society.

The sanctions program in Iraq poses a difficult moral question found in all cases where economic leverage is used to try to promote better human rights practices: If sanctions can reduce human rights abuses by governments but only at the cost of increased suffering by average citizens, are they justified? Is it legitimate to victimize the victims if this helps bring about long-term political change? To address this question, we must understand how sanctions work and when they are effective. But even a better understanding of what sanctions can and cannot accomplish does not fully alleviate the moral issue.

Sanctions are sometimes intended to satisfy domestic audiences in the countries imposing the sanctions. Many people do not want to be complicit in human rights violations by doing business with governments that abuse their citizens. In these cases, sanctions are an expressive act designed to distance a country from policies in the target country that are offensive and odious, regardless of their effect on politics and policy within that target country. But sanctions are also used with political intent to impose economic hardship on the target country sufficient to cause it to alter its policies. As such, sanctions are a form of coercion (see Chapter 2). Sanctions impose costs on, first, consumers by restricting access to foreign goods and, second, exporters who cannot sell their output on foreign markets. Both effects reduce the gains from trade and economic welfare and reduce the standard of living of the country as a whole. By creating economic hardship in the target country, sanctions are expected to mobilize consumers and exporters to press their governments for change, and in the case of Hussein in Iraq and other human rights abusers, to end repugnant human rights practices. But with authoritarian regimes that already ignore the wishes of their citizens and have demonstrated their willingness to abuse human rights, sanctions are likely to have small political effect. Either the public will still be deterred from political mobilization by the repressive abilities of the government, or protests—even if they occur—will likely evoke only a harsh crackdown on dissent. Authoritarian leaders who control the press, moreover, can often "spin" the sanctions as a foreign assault on the nation's sovereignty and thereby place the blame for economic hardship on other countries rather than themselves. The effect of broad-based sanctions, regardless of whether they are merely expressive or coercive, is often to impose pain on the victims of political abuses without forcing the government to change its ways.

So-called smart sanctions, which the United States and others tried to implement in the later stages of the

a. UN Security Council Resolution 661 Iraq/Kuwait, August 6, 1990.
b. World Health Organization, "The Health Conditions of the Population in Iraq since the Gulf Crisis," WHO/EHA/96.1, March 1996.
c. John Pilger, *Paying the Price: Killing the Children of Iraq*, documentary broadcast on ITV, Carlton Television, March 6, 2000.

program against Iraq, are intended to limit hardship to high government officials and specific elite groups allied with authoritarian regimes. Smart sanctions attempt to target pro-government elites by freezing their foreign assets and banks accounts, limiting their ability to travel, and cutting off trade in luxury goods and items used by the military and police to repress society. The aim is to impose pain only on the regime's supporters so that they will want to change policy to alleviate their own suffering. Even with such carefully designed smart sanctions, however, it appears difficult to impose sufficient pain on the elite that they will turn against the regime, since they are its primary beneficiaries. It is also hard to limit the effects of sanctions to the elite alone. Even smart sanctions, however carefully designed they may be, will nearly always impose some costs on the public in target states.

Yet, despite their costs, citizens in target countries may welcome sanctions if they contribute to beneficial political change. Economic sanctions were imposed on South Africa for 32 years in the effort to end apartheid. As explained in the introduction to this chapter, beginning with a ban on only a few items and relying on only loosely enforced restrictions, the sanctions were steadily broadened and tightened over time, especially in the mid-1980s. The sanctions were fully supported—indeed, demanded—by anti-apartheid groups in South Africa. Although anti-apartheid leaders did not underestimate the impact of sanctions on Black South Africans, they argued that the hardships were necessary to help bring down the racist regime. As with all opposition tactics, some short-term sacrifice was required to bring long-term political gains.

In the case of South Africa, the effects of sanctions on the economy were, for most of their history, relatively small. The anti-apartheid movement was also sufficiently mobilized that it could evaluate the effects of sanctions and decide autonomously to call for their implementation. The Iraq case was different. The sanctions were more painful, given the prior damage of the 1991 Persian Gulf War. The sanctions were also imposed not at the request of opposition groups within Iraq—who at the time were still heavily repressed by the regime—but by the United States and its allies.

The issue is not just whether sanctions work to bring about improved human rights practices, although the more effective they are the stronger the case for their use. (The record on success is quite mixed.[d]) Rather, the more perplexing moral question is how much pain is political change worth to members of the target society? And who has the right to determine the answer to this question? In the midst of the sanctions against Iraq, then U.S. ambassador to the United States Madeleine Albright was asked in a *60 Minutes* interview about the possibility that up to a half-million children had died as a result of the trade and financial restrictions. Albright responded that "we think the price is worth it." Although she later said she was pressed on a "loaded" question and regretted her answer, she did not disavow it.[e] Was she right?

---

d. The classic study on the effectiveness of sanctions is Gary Hufbauer, Jeffrey Schott, and Kimberly Elliott, *Economic Sanctions Reconsidered: History and Current Policy*, vol. 1 (Washington, DC: Peterson Institute, 1990).

e. Madeleine Albright, *Madam Secretary: A Memoir* (Norwalk, CT: Easton Press, 2003), 274–75.

Why Do Individuals and States Care about the Human Rights of Others?

Proponents of improving human rights, including TANs such as Amnesty International, Human Rights Watch, and hundreds of other nongovernmental organizations (NGOs), clearly suggest that individuals and states possess and act on an interest in the human rights of others around the globe. But the puzzle still remains. Why would individuals and states care about the way other states treat their citizens? Why is it in their interests to promote and potentially enforce laws governing the human rights practices of other states? In turn, as sovereign entities, why would states want to constrain the way they deal with their own people and open themselves to the scrutiny of others? In answering these questions, we begin by addressing why states violate human rights in the first place.

Why Do States Violate Human Rights?

States violate human rights for many reasons. Some violations arise from a lack of state capacity. Many poor countries, for instance, may sincerely want but simply cannot afford to provide free primary schooling to everyone, as required under the ICESCR. Other governments may not be able to control their militaries or police sufficiently to stem human rights abuses. Recognizing varying capacities to implement standards, many human rights are soft law, understood to be aspirations or goals toward which states should strive rather than strict rules to which they can and should be held accountable.

In other cases, however, states violate human rights in defense of their national security. Violent or potentially violent opposition to the state is illegal everywhere, and thus it counts as criminal, not political, behavior. Amnesty International specifically excludes as POCs any individuals who use or advocate violence. Nelson Mandela, a leader of the anti-apartheid movement in South Africa, was originally designated a POC in 1962 after his arrest for organizing strikes to protest apartheid. Nonetheless, Mandela's status was revoked by Amnesty after he was convicted of trying to overthrow the government violently in 1964. Yet the dividing line between criminal and political activities is often ambiguous, and some states prosecute individuals as criminals for political actions that would be considered legal elsewhere. Even when actions are clearly criminal, however, prosecution and punishment may be abusive when individuals are not given due process under the law.

When under attack or perceived attack, states are sometimes tempted to violate the rights of groups or individuals they fear may be allied with a foreign power. Thus, the United States violated the civil and political rights of many of its own citizens in the infamous Red Scare of 1917 to 1920, following the Bolshevik revolution in Russia. During the first Red Scare, between 4,000 and 10,000 individuals were arrested, denied due process, and sometimes beaten during questioning. The United States also violated the rights of approximately 110,000 Japanese Americans who were interned in concentration camps following the attack on Pearl Harbor and the start of World War II. And, in the second Red Scare of 1947 to 1957, the U.S. government blacklisted, jailed, and deported Americans suspected of following a Communist or other left-wing ideology. Today, following the terrorist attacks of September 11, 2001, the United States has been criticized for violating the human rights of citizens or residents accused of planning additional attacks or associating with terrorist organizations abroad.[12] Targeted drone attacks authorized by President Obama against U.S. citizens abroad accused of planning terrorism have been especially controversial. Other countries have responded similarly to attacks on their own people or soil. Indeed, the existence of an interstate or civil war is strongly associated with increased human rights violations.[13] In justifying these violations, governments often claim that national security trumps the human rights of individuals.

Governments also violate the human rights of their citizens to preserve their own rule. This differs from the national security rationale just described. In these cases, the country is not under attack, but political opponents are abused in an effort to suppress internal dissent. To weaken and deter opponents, governments in essence declare war on their own citizens. One of the most egregious cases of such abuse occurred in Argentina following a military coup in March 1976. The three-man junta, led by General Jorge Rafael Videla, immediately began a seven-year campaign known as the Dirty War against suspected political dissidents and opponents of the military regime. Although some were publicly detained, many more individuals were "disappeared." While denying any official knowledge or involvement, the military eventually kidnapped, tortured, and killed nearly 10,000 perceived political opponents.[14] Many of the disappeared, we now know, were taken on death flights on which they were pushed from airplanes high above the Atlantic Ocean. As many as 500 newborns were taken from their imprisoned mothers and given to childless military families because, as General Ramón Camps (head of the Buenos Aires Provincial Police) later attempted to explain, "Subversive parents will raise subversive children."[15] This was government-sponsored cruelty on a dramatic scale intended to crush and intimidate political opponents and keep the military regime in power. Like the case of apartheid in South Africa, the Dirty War in Argentina was critical

---

12. The United States is also accused of violating international humanitarian law, specified in the Geneva Conventions, when it treats foreign detainees as "enemy combatants" supposedly outside international law. On the Geneva Conventions and laws of war, see James D. Morrow, "The Institutional Features of the Prisoners of War Treaties," *International Organization* 55, no. 4 (2001): 971–91.

13. Steven C. Poe and C. Neal Tate, "Repression of Human Rights to Personal Integrity in the 1980s: A Global Analysis," *American Political Science Review* 88, no. 4 (1994): 853–72; Matthew Krain, "State-Sponsored Mass Murder: The Onset and Severity of Genocides and Politicides," *Journal of Conflict Resolution* 41, no. 3 (1997): 331–60.

14. The Argentine National Commission on the Disappeared provides an "official" figure of about 9,000 "disappeared" between 1976 and 1983. Internal documents from the Argentine security services suggest a figure of 22,000. Human rights organizations estimate that the total number of casualties of this Dirty War may be as high as 30,000.

15. Translated from Nancy Berger-Levraut, *Disparus: Rapport à la Commission Indépendente sur les questions humanitaires internationales* (London: Zed Books, 1986), 29. For more on Camps, see "Ramon Camps, 67, Argentine General In the 'Dirty War,'" *New York Times*, August 23, 1994, www.nytimes.com /1994/08/23/obituaries/ramon-camps-67-argentine-general-in-the-dirty-war.html (accessed 09/18/14); and Francisco Goldman, "Children of the Dirty War," *New Yorker*, March 19, 2012, www.newyorker.com /magazine/2012/03/19/children-of-the-dirty-war (accessed 09/18/14). There have been 77 documented cases of kidnapped newborns.

Argentina's Dirty War, which began in 1976, provoked a strong response from a vast transnational human rights network. Here, the Mothers of the Plaza de Mayo in Argentina gather to protest abuses by the junta and to demand information on their "disappeared" children.

in mobilizing the human rights TAN, and that network, in turn, was instrumental in bringing about political change in Argentina.

Fear of "others" within a society who may undermine the state, as well as fragile governments seeking to preserve their rule, often come together in genocides, the most extreme form of human rights abuse, in which entire identity groups are singled out for systematic persecution and murder. Genocide is one of the extreme crimes against humanity. The Armenian Genocide in Turkey during World War I and the Holocaust perpetrated by Germany during World War II led to the concept of genocide and modern human rights law. More recently, genocides have occurred in Rwanda (see Chapters 5 and 11); the former Yugoslavia, where perpetrators of the Srebrenica massacre were prosecuted for the crime; and in Sudan, where President Omar Hassan al-Bashir has been indicted by the International Criminal Court (ICC) on three counts of genocide.

More generally, autocracies and unstable democracies are significantly more likely to violate the human rights of their citizens than established democracies, where political competition is respected and channeled through regular elections in which incumbent governments accept defeat and leave office.[16] Overt acts of torture (and possibly other human rights abuses as well) are most likely to occur in multiparty dictatorships. In single-party or personalist dictatorships, political opponents are sufficiently repressed that fewer acts of torture are necessary. These states

---

16. Christian Davenport, "Multi-Dimensional Threat Perception and State Repression: An Inquiry into Why States Apply Negative Sanctions," *American Journal of Political Science* 39, no. 3 (1995): 683–713; and Steven C. Poe, C. Neal Tate, and Linda Camp Keith, "Repression of the Human Right to Personal Integrity Revisited: A Global Cross-National Study Covering the Years 1976–1993," *International Studies Quarterly* 43 (1999): 291–313. Todd Landman, *Protecting Human Rights: A Comparative Study* (Washington, DC: Georgetown University Press, 2005), finds that more recently democratic states are more likely to engage in human rights abuses.

might use torture if necessary, and broad civil liberties are typically denied, but opponents are deterred from challenging the government; thus, the regime does not often need to use violence against individuals to maintain its rule. In multiparty dictatorships, however, the political opposition usually remains visible and viable, and the government is tempted to use torture to suppress opponents to stay in power.[17] In all cases, the weaker or less legitimate the government, the more likely it is to abuse human rights.

There is no single explanation for why countries violate human rights. In turn, there is no single explanation for why individuals, groups, and states seek to protect human rights at home and abroad. Repressing human rights is a political strategy that states and governments employ to protect themselves from real and perceived threats. It should be no surprise, then, that protecting human rights is also a political strategy that a variety of political actors use for a variety of aims.

Why Do States Sign Human Rights Agreements?

Some states have an interest in imposing human rights law on themselves as a means of demonstrating their commitment to democracy and political liberalization. While some governments have an interest in repressing human rights to retain political power, liberal or liberalizing governments often have an interest in promoting human rights as a means of committing themselves and their successors to political reforms.

Political scientist Andrew Moravcsik argues that democratizing states that sincerely seek to shed their autocratic and possibly abusive pasts sign human rights agreements in an attempt to lock in their new institutions and improved practices.[18] By committing to international agreements that may carry some cost if they are violated—even if that cost is only a loss of international reputation—new democratic leaders and coalitions attempt to make political backsliding more costly and, thus, less likely. By obliging themselves to follow international human rights law, newly democratizing states aim to commit themselves credibly to political reform. This observation implies that the countries most eager to ratify human rights treaties should be newly democratic or democratizing states, a proposition for which Moravcsik and others find some support. In this conception, international human rights law is a tool that states use strategically to alter their own domestic political incentives.

This notion of using international human rights treaties to lock in domestic political reforms also explains the weaker tendency and sometimes outright reluctance of established democracies to ratify human rights agreements. To the extent that human rights are already secured at home through constitutional protections and the rule of law, stable democracies have less need to bind themselves through

17. James Raymond Vreeland, "Political Institutions and Human Rights: Why Dictatorships Enter into the United Nations Convention against Torture," *International Organization* 62, no. 1 (2008): 65–101.

18. Andrew Moravcsik, "The Origins of Human Rights Regimes: Democratic Delegation in Postwar Europe," *International Organization* 54, no. 2 (Spring 2000): 217–52.

international agreements.[19] Thus, with its own Bill of Rights and stable democratic institutions, the United States, for instance, relies on its own, internal processes for protecting human rights and is reluctant to cede any authority to international treaties like the ICCPR or international bodies like the UN Human Rights Commission or the ICC (see below) to oversee its practices. Increasingly, however, democracies are recognizing the contradiction inherent in advocating human rights for others while failing to ratify international human rights treaties themselves. Established democracies are now signing agreements they had previously rejected and shrinking the difference in treaty ratification between new and established democracies. The United States remains a visible exception to this trend, however, in its continuing reluctance to accept international human rights accords.

Finally, some states may sign international human rights treaties because they are induced to do so by contingent rewards provided by others, a form of linkage (see Chapter 2). Established democracies often provide inducements for new democracies to join such regimes. Inducements may include financial assistance or the promise of future membership in international organizations, such as NATO, that provide benefits on other dimensions. The European Union, for instance, has required countries applying for membership to sign and comply with a host of human rights treaties before being accepted. Turkey's human rights practices—especially its repression of the Kurds—have been one of the major stumbling blocks in its attempt to join the European Union. By imposing human rights standards as a condition for assistance or membership in international organizations, other states hope to facilitate the lock-in of democracy in transitional governments—and to use the threat of expulsion to persuade states to live up to their promises.

As the example of the established democracies suggests, states also ratify international human rights treaties not to bind themselves but to constrain the human rights practices of others. They accept international oversight of their own affairs in order to secure their ability to scrutinize others. There are both altruistic and self-interested reasons why individuals and states seek to influence human rights in other countries.

Moral and Philosophical Motivations

Many individuals identify with a common humanity and feel personally affected by the welfare and treatment of others, including those in countries other than their own. As social animals, humans possess a degree of empathy that is weaker in some, stronger in others, but present in all.[20] This is evident most dramatically in the international responses to natural disasters when individuals across the globe donate to relief efforts. The tsunami of December 2004, which wreaked havoc across Southeast Asia, for instance, generated billions of dollars in donations from governments and private individuals worldwide. When others suffer, we may hurt as well; this response can be a

---

19. These states will, however, also have lower costs for signing agreements that already accord with domestic practice. See Jay Goodliffe and Darren G. Hawkins, "Explaining Commitment: States and the Convention against Torture," *Journal of Politics* 68, no. 2 (2006): 358–71.

20. For more on social preferences in humans, see Samuel Bowles and Herbert Gintis, *A Cooperative Species: Human Reciprocity and Its Evolution* (Princeton, NJ: Princeton University Press, 2011).

profound motivator of political action. Empathy produces support not only for victims of natural disasters but also for victims of human rights abuses. Indeed, human rights for all, and especially for the disadvantaged, is a cause that many individuals feel deeply about and are driven to try to protect by strong feelings of empathy. Gross violations of human rights, like genocide, strongly affect and motivate individuals and states to respond.

Closer to home, our own human rights depend on state respect for the individual. It is our status as humans that creates and sustains our rights. It follows in the views of some philosophers and human rights advocates that we cannot secure these rights domestically unless we also seek to promote respect for rights abroad. If it is acceptable for some governments to abuse the rights of some people, what principled defense can we give if our own government wants to abuse our rights? In this view, human rights are only secure if they are universal not merely in principle but also in practice.

Finally, as much if not more so than on other issues, we have been socialized to identify with universal human rights. Human rights NGOs and the larger human rights advocacy network have played a critical role in educating the public about human rights and human rights practices, calling attention to human rights abuses, and eventually bringing pressure to bear on states. As discussed in Chapter 11, the human rights TAN has successfully framed the issue of international human rights in terms that resonate with the political freedoms and civil rights that already exist in established democracies. Given the wide acceptance of these principles within states, it is easier to persuade people to actively defend these rights abroad. The international human rights TAN has vigorously promoted concern with human rights among broad publics and has emphasized to many groups and individuals the

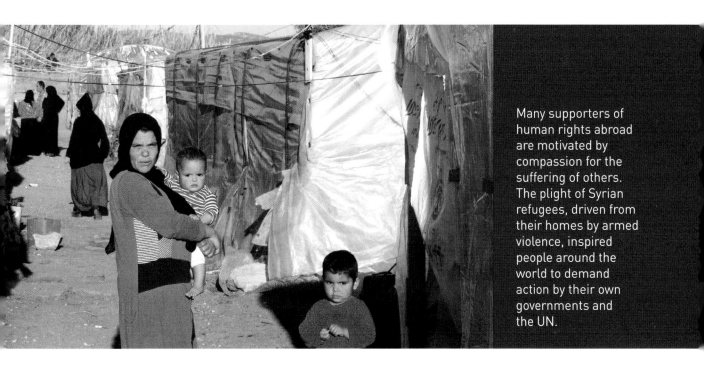

Many supporters of human rights abroad are motivated by compassion for the suffering of others. The plight of Syrian refugees, driven from their homes by armed violence, inspired people around the world to demand action by their own governments and the UN.

extent to which human rights practices abroad affect our daily lives. It is in framing issues and socializing individuals to see their interests in different ways that TANs may have their greatest impact on the international politics of human rights.

Self-Interest Motivations Even if we do not have altruistic interests in protecting the human rights of others, we do have self-interests in promoting peace and prosperity, which, in a globalizing world, cannot flourish at home without flourishing abroad too. Modern human rights originated in the depths of the Great Depression and World War II. Reflecting on the causes of these twin disasters, President Roosevelt and others drew the conclusion that protecting human rights against Fascism and other forms of totalitarianism was essential to the maintenance of international peace. By connecting human rights to the epic struggles against totalitarianism that defined much of the twentieth century, Roosevelt laid out the case that promoting human rights abroad was in the self-interest of both Americans and the citizens of other countries. This observation may be no less true today. As the *democratic peace* discussed in Chapter 4 shows clearly, there is an increasing recognition that democracy and the protection of political freedom can promote peace, economic interdependence, and growth that are of direct benefit to all countries.

More immediately, to the extent that suppressing human rights creates domestic political unrest and possible insurrection, such civil conflicts may spill into neighboring states either directly or indirectly. As a result, all states have an interest in preventing abuses in neighboring countries. The United States was forced to become involved in Haiti's internal political unrest in 1994 to stem the flow of people escaping by boat to southern Florida over treacherous waters. European countries sent troops into Bosnia to prevent political instability and ethnic violence in the former Yugoslavia from spilling over into the rest of the Balkans and possibly beyond. In an interdependent world, political instability and repression in one country can have direct consequences for others.

Images of police beating mostly peaceful protesters in Egypt in 2011 were transmitted around the globe almost instantly via the Internet and drew international attention to the harsh practices of the Mubarak government.

In addition to general self-interest motivations, particular interests within countries have promoted human rights law abroad for their own instrumental purposes. This is most evident in the labor movements within the United States and Europe, which now demand that human rights (and environmental) clauses be inserted into nearly all regional trade agreements (RTAs).[21] The North American Free Trade Agreement (NAFTA), for instance, includes extensive labor provisions that guarantee freedom of association and the right to organize, the right to bargain collectively and strike, freedom from discrimination, access to labor tribunals, and effective employment standards and minimum wage laws; it even establishes a tri-national ministerial commission to monitor the labor provisions of the agreement.[22] Labor unions promote such clauses to level the political and economic playing fields on which their own workers compete. To protect their ability to organize and strike for higher wages at home, unions want to ensure that workers in labor-abundant and low-wage countries have similar rights and, indeed, possess the broader political rights necessary to protect their ability to form effective trade unions. In this way, the economic self-interest of workers in developed states can dovetail with the interests of citizens in developing countries in more effective protections for human rights.

Labor demands for human rights clauses, however, may also disguise a form of trade protectionism. By inserting human rights clauses into RTAs, the unions may be making free-trade pacts less appealing to foreign trading partners and, therefore, less likely to be approved. For example, the Mexican government strongly opposed the human rights clauses of NAFTA. Moreover, human rights provisions open up the opportunity for subsequent claims that the trading partner is violating the terms of the agreement and that the trade concessions made by the home country should be withdrawn. For labor in the developed countries, human rights provisions in RTAs may be "poison pills" that are used to prevent further movements toward free trade.

Together, these various motivations for protecting human rights abroad suggest that interests are multiple and often quite complex. Each reason, however, prompts individuals or groups to press their governments to promote international human rights law. One person may be particularly motivated by a general concern for human well-being, another by a concern with protecting democracy at home, and a third by a hidden desire for trade protection, but all combine to bring pressure to bear on their governments to make international human rights a priority.

Such pressure on governments may be increasing. As human rights TANs grow and succeed, as they have done in a more globalized world, they influence the views of more and more individuals. In turn, the same technology that facilitates

---

21. Emilie M. Hafner-Burton, "Trading Human Rights: How Preferential Trade Agreements Influence Government Repression," *International Organization* 59, no. 3 (2005): 593–629.

22. Collectively, the labor provisions of NAFTA are referred to as the North American Agreement on Labor Cooperation. On the purview and powers of the Commission for Labor Cooperation, see www.naalc.org (accessed 09/18/14).

the growth of TANs also brings the horror of human rights abuses to immediate public attention. In 2003, photos from Abu Ghraib prison that showed American soldiers abusing detainees in Iraq flashed around the globe in moments. The genocide in the Darfur region of Sudan was brought into our homes via television and the Internet. In the summer of 2014, protests of democratic activists in Hong Kong were watched in real time around the globe. It is now much harder to ignore human rights abuses or to deny that we knew about the violations while they were occurring. This realization heightens awareness and may prompt individuals to demand that their governments be more aggressive in promoting international human rights.

Rarely would we expect governments to promote human rights abroad to the exclusion of all other interests they might be seeking in their relations with other states. Nonetheless, founded in the tragedy of World War II, supported by a growing transnational human rights movement, and accelerated by new technologies that bring abuses to the public's immediate attention, individuals and groups now increasingly recognize international human rights as part of their nations' interests and demand that their governments act accordingly.

Do States Observe International Human Rights Law?

Given a now extensive body of international law, broad agreement on human rights norms, and growing interests in promoting rights, do states actually protect human rights abroad? Is interest reflected in practice? In the case of human rights practices, we can view the proverbial glass as half empty or half full. Although international human rights institutions are being developed, large-scale abuses continue to occur. Maps 12.1 to 12.3 graphically illustrate the extent of the problem. While it can be difficult to measure such rights and some of the information in the maps may seem surprising, the data reflected in the maps are the best available and, on the whole, indicate that human rights violations still occur across the globe. (See "How Do We Know?" on p. 516 about the difficulty of measuring human rights practices.) At the same time, however, it appears that human rights practices have improved substantially since 1980. Even if, in the view of optimists, the glass of human rights practices is half full, it is still possible to ask why has there not been even greater improvement given the development of a body of robust international human rights law, an extensive transnational advocacy network, and growing norms of appropriate state behavior?

The most frequent and deadliest form of violence in the world today is by governments against their own citizens (including governments fighting civil wars). In violation of the ICCPR, governments continue to inflict violence against political dissidents. Defying the ICESCR, governments also violate the human rights of their citizens by misguided economic or social policies that lead to widespread suffering

MAP 12.1 *Imprisonment for Nonviolent Politics: Beliefs and Actions, 2011**

■ MANY PEOPLE IMPRISONED FOR RELIGIOUS, POLITICAL, OR OTHER BELIEFS

▨ SOME PEOPLE IMPRISONED FOR RELIGIOUS, POLITICAL, OR OTHER BELIEFS

☐ NO PEOPLE IMPRISONED FOR THE ABOVE REASONS

NO DATA AVAILABLE

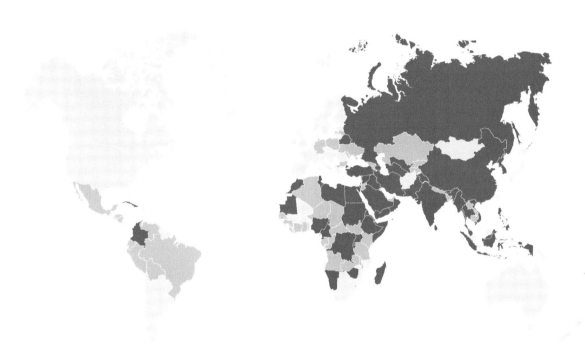

and deaths. For example, the Great Leap Forward in China (1958–62) created a nationwide famine and left as many as 38 million people dead. R. J. Rummel, who coined the word *democide* to describe such government-sponsored killing, graphically writes:

> In total, during the first eighty-eight years of [the twentieth] century, almost 170,000,000 men, women, and children have been shot, beaten, tortured, knifed, burned, starved, frozen, crushed, or worked to death; or buried alive, drowned, hung, bombed, or killed in any other of the myriad ways governments have inflicted death on unarmed, helpless citizens or foreigners. . . . This is as though our species has been devastated by a modern Black Plague.[23]

According to political philosopher Thomas Hobbes (1588–1679), states were created to lift humans out of the state of nature in which life was "solitary, poor,

Map source: David L. Cingranelli and David L. Richards, *The Cingranelli-Richards Human Rights Dataset,* http://humanrightsdata.com (accessed 9/18/14).

Note: The data presented in this map measure the incarceration in 2011 of people by government officials because of their speech; their nonviolent opposition to the government; their religious beliefs and practices; or their membership in a group, including an ethnic or racial group.

*The data for maps 12.1, 12.2, and 12.3 is no longer being compiled by David Cingranelli and David Richards, and as of 2015 no new data have replaced theirs.

23. From www.hawaii.edu/powerkills/POWER.ART.HTM (accessed 09/20/14).

MAP 12.2 *Torture, 2011*

TORTURE PRACTICED FREQUENTLY

TORTURE PRACTICED OCCASIONALLY

TORTURE NOT PRACTICED IN GIVEN YEAR

NO DATA AVAILABLE

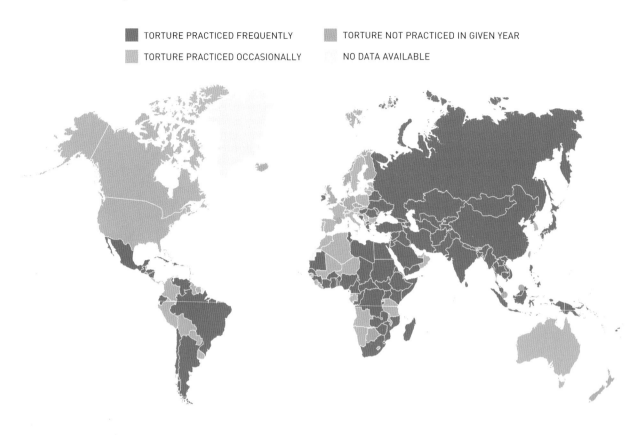

Map source: David L. Cingranelli and David L. Richards, *The Cingranelli-Richards Human Rights Dataset,* http://human-rightsdata.com (accessed 9/18/14). http://ciri.bingham-ton.edu/-(accessed 1/12/12).

Note: The data presented in this map measure in 2011 the purposeful inflicting of extreme pain, whether mental or physical, by government officials or by private individuals at the instigation of government officials. Torture includes the use by police and prison guards of physical and other force that is cruel, inhuman, or degrading. This also includes deaths in custody due to negligence by government officials.

nasty, brutish, and short." This statement may be true; we do not know how dangerous life would be without states to provide a measure of social order and protection against other individuals—although failed states like Somalia suggest that life in the state of nature may be close to that envisioned by Hobbes. But today, governments around the world may themselves be the biggest threats to our human rights and, indeed, to our very lives.

Unfortunately, there are few systematic compilations of the human rights practices of states over an extended period. Rummel's data do show that the twentieth century appears to have been more violent and deadly than past centuries, but this may have more to do with the "improved" technology of state killing than with any change in state intent or practice. The modern Black Plague he describes, moreover, does not include human rights abuses that do not result in death, for which we have no data on long-term trends.

Thus, we do not know whether states today treat their citizens better than, worse than, or about the same as in the past. The best evidence indicates, however, that human rights practices on average have improved fairly significantly in recent decades, especially in South America, which enjoyed a wave of democratization in

MAP 12.3 *Women's Political Rights, 2011*

- ■ GUARANTEED IN LAW BUT SEVERELY PROHIBITED IN PRACTICE
- ▨ GUARANTEED IN LAW BUT MODERATELY PROHIBITED IN PRACTICE
- ▢ GUARANTEED IN BOTH LAW AND PRACTICE
- NO DATA AVAILABLE

the 1980s, supported in part by popular outrage at the human rights abuses of the prior military regimes, and Central and Eastern Europe, which democratized in the 1990s after the fall of Communism.

Does International Human Rights Law Make a Difference?

Given the pattern discussed above, does international human rights law make a difference? Even if abuses continue to occur, do countries that sign human rights treaties protect the rights of their citizens better than those that have not signed the agreements? Do these human rights institutions constrain state behavior in significant ways?

The accumulating evidence on the impact of international human rights agreements on state practice is mixed. This is, as discussed in Chapter 11, a difficult problem for researchers due to the fact that the countries most likely to sign human rights agreements are also those most likely to respect human rights. If we simply examined the relationship between signing agreements and protecting human

Map source: David L. Cingranelli and David L. Richards, *The Cingranelli-Richards Human Rights Dataset,* http://humanrightsdata.com (accessed 9/18/14).

Note: The data presented in this map measure in 2011 women's political rights to vote, run for political office, hold elected and appointed government positions, join political parties, and petition government officials. Many countries in which rights are guaranteed in law but moderately prohibited in practice have only limited proportions of women (less than 30 percent) in elected or appointed government office.

Measuring Human Rights Practices

Observing trends in human rights practices is quite tricky. Violations of human rights are typically not advertised by governments, and some, like torture, are usually carried out in secret with few witnesses or traces of physical evidence. Even when observers suspect that governments are violating human rights on a fairly widespread and persistent basis, lawyers often lack the kinds of evidence necessary to prosecute offenders in traditional courts of law.[a] Amnesty International and the U.S. Department of State track violations as best they can, drawing on many forms of evidence, including local sources, and issue annual reports on human rights practices for every country. Political scientists, in turn, have developed scales of human rights violations based on these reports, which then give us an approximate measure of the pattern over time and across countries.[b] In Figure A, the gray line represents rights practices around the globe based on the reports of Amnesty International and the U.S. Department of State. The "whiskers" around the estimates indicate the degree of uncertainty about that estimate. This gray line is essentially flat, indicating that there has been virtually no improvement since 1950 despite the considerable efforts of the international community. Estimates such as this one have fueled controversy about the effectiveness of international human rights law.

Recently, however, Christopher Fariss has developed a new measure of human rights protection that uses the available information on actual, observed violations of human rights, and compares this to the traditional measure based on the Amnesty and State Department reports. He finds that the standards for assessing and including information about violations used by Amnesty and the State Department have changed in subtle ways over time, perhaps because of better information and monitoring. It now takes fewer cases of documented torture by governments, for instance, to be rated as a "frequent violator" than in the past. It may also be the case that as practices actually improve, the international community, as reflected in these annual reports, has become less tolerant of violators. When rescaled to reflect these changing standards, depicted in the blue line in the figure, we see that human rights practices have improved considerably, especially since about 1980. Overall, this is good news for international human rights. Even though it reminds us that human rights practices are difficult to measure accurately and consistently, this research suggests that those practices really have improved over the last generation.

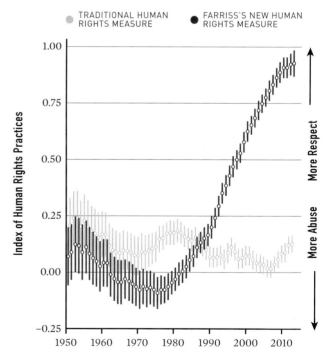

FIGURE A **Estimates of Human Rights Practices around the World, 1950–2013**

a. Yonatan Lupu, "Best Evidence: The Role of Information in Domestic Judicial Enforcement of International Human Rights Agreements," *International Organization* 67, no. 3 (2013): 469–503.

b. See David L. Cingranelli and David L. Richards, The Cingranelli-Richards Human Rights Dataset, http://humanrightsdata.com (accessed 09/18/14).

Source: Christopher J. Fariss, "Respect for Human Rights Has Improved over Time: Modeling the Changing Standard of Accountability," *American Political Science Review* 108, no. 2 (2014): 297–318.

rights we would conclude, perhaps incorrectly, that the agreements were having a huge effect on practice when, in fact, these two factors simply occur together as a reflection of some underlying trait, such as democracy and a concern for political and civil rights, that leads states both to sign agreements and protect those rights. As a result of these difficulties, as well as the measurement problems discussed in the previous section, different analysts have found different results.

Some researchers find that international human rights agreements make no difference on practice or even have a negative effect once other factors (like income per capita and economic growth) that affect state practice are taken into account. This implies that signing agreements is associated with worse human rights practices,[24] suggesting that international human rights law just might not matter very much. After all, international law, like most international agreements, is dependent on self-help. In the absence of any third-party enforcers, international law places the burden of enforcement on the victims of the crime, who in the case of human rights law are the politically powerless individuals and groups who were abused in the first place. The burden of enforcement, therefore, rests on others who can speak and act on behalf of these victims. Yet not all states have a strong interest in penalizing violators of human rights; thus, international human rights law is, at best, sporadically enforced. Knowing this, states can choose to violate human rights with a degree of impunity.

As described by international law professor Oona Hathaway, countries may sign international human rights agreements for their "expressive value" rather than as a commitment to better behavior.[25] By signing human rights agreements, she suggests, states may hope to give the appearance of conforming to civilized norms of behavior while continuing to engage in actual practices that violate human rights behind the scenes or out of the public eye. Our most developed explanation for the negative effect of international agreements on practice comes from political scientist James Vreeland. Focusing on the Convention against Torture and Other Cruel, Inhuman or Degrading Treatment or Punishment (CAT), Vreeland shows that the negative relationship is rooted primarily in multiparty dictatorships that both sign the CAT and use torture at higher than average rates. Multiparty dictatorships, he argues, are pressed by domestic political opponents, who have some influence, to ratify international conventions in hopes of changing the government's behavior over the long run. But since domestic opponents remain viable and their rule is unstable, dictators are also most likely to abuse human rights, including the use of torture against insurgents.[26] In the case of the despotic rule of Paul Biya in Cameroon, for instance, levels of torture were rated as "isolated" and infrequent, but once multiple parties were permitted in 1992 the practice became "common."[27] Putting

---

24. Linda Camp Keith, "The United Nations International Covenant on Civil and Political Rights: Does It Make a Difference in Human Rights Behavior?" *Journal of Peace Research* 36, no. 1 (1999): 95–118; Oona Hathaway, "Do Human Rights Treaties Make a Difference?" *Yale Law Journal* 111, no. 8 (June 2002): 1935–2042; and Daniel W. Hill Jr., "Estimating the Effects of Human Rights Treaties on State Behavior," *Journal of Politics* 72, no. 4 (2010): 1161–74.

25. Hathaway, "Do Human Rights Treaties Make a Difference?"

26. Vreeland, "Political Institutions and Human Rights."

27. See Vreeland, "Political Institutions and Human Rights," 76, for this and other examples.

these two trends together appears to explain why multiparty dictatorships sign human rights agreements and are also more likely to abuse those rights.

By contrast, other researchers find that signing international human rights agreements actually improves practice.[28] They reach this conclusion either by modeling the selection process directly or adjusting for the changing standards of human rights over time (see "How Do We Know?" on p. 516). Others find that the effects of international agreements are contingent or exist only when combined with certain other factors. Agreements "work" in essence only when combined with specific domestic political institutions, strong domestic courts and the rule of law, large NGO contingents, the expected tenure of political leaders, and legal standards of proof for particular rights violations.[29] Taken together, this more recent research appears to be gaining the upper hand, indicating that international human rights law is having a positive effect but in subtle ways and only under certain limited conditions.

As reflected in these inconsistent results, however, it is very difficult to isolate the effect of international human rights agreements on state behavior. Joining human rights conventions might indeed be leading to better protections of human rights than otherwise; but at the same time, the effect on practice is overwhelmed by a number of countries signing agreements to hide their practices and insulate themselves from international pressure. Isolating the impact of international institutions from the underlying interests of states to join agreements is difficult. Although additional research is still necessary, there may be some grounds for optimism by advocates of international human rights law.

Even if the effect of international human rights institutions is limited in the short term, they may exert a more beneficial effect on human rights norms and practices in the long run.[30] Rather than just binding states, international human rights law also empowers social actors to conceive of their interests in new ways, provides a shared vocabulary of judgment, and emboldens societies to advocate for their own rights, sometimes leading to massive political change. For instance, the Helsinki Final Act of 1975, which established the applicability of human rights in all of

---

28. In *Protecting Human Rights*, 157, Landman uses a broader set of agreements and longer time period than other studies, as well as a nonrecursive model, and reports a positive effect of human rights agreements on practice. In a later survey of this debate, however, he concludes judiciously that no conclusive evidence exists; see Todd Landman, *Studying Human Rights* (New York: Routledge, 2006), 103. Using his dynamic standard measure (see "How Do We Know?" on p. 516), Christopher J. Fariss, in "The Changing Standard of Accountability and the Positive Relationship between Human Rights Treaty Ratification and Compliance," *British Journal of Political Science* (forthcoming), finds consistent support for a positive relationship. See also Yonatan Lupu, "The Informative Power of Treaty Commitment: Using the Spatial Model to Address Selection Effects," *American Journal of Political Science* 57, no. 4 (2013): 912–25.

29. Eric Neumayer, "Do International Human Rights Treaties Improve Respect for Human Rights?" *Journal of Conflict Resolution* 49, no. 6 (2005): 925–53; Beth Simmons, *Mobilizing for Human Rights: International Law in Domestic Politics* (New York: Cambridge University Press, 2009); Amanda N. Murdie and David R. Davis, "Shaming and Blaming: Using Events Data to Assess the Impact of Human Rights INGOs," *International Studies Quarterly* 56, no. 1 (2012): 1–16; Courtenay R. Conrad and Emily Hencken Ritter, "Treaties, Tenure and Torture: The Conflicting Domestic Effects of International Law," *Journal of Politics* 75, no. 2 (2013): 397–409; Yonatan Lupu, "Best Evidence: The Role of Information in Domestic Judicial Enforcement of International Human Rights Agreements," *International Organization* 67, no. 3 (2013): 469–503.

30. The statistical evidence on long-term effects is, at best, ambiguous as well. See Emilie Hafner-Burton and Kiyoteru Tsutsui, "Justice Lost! The Failure of International Human Rights Law to Matter Where Needed Most," *Journal of Peace Research* 44, no.4 (2007): 407-25.

Human rights TANs, including groups like Amnesty International, promote public awareness of human rights issues and monitor states' compliance with international laws. In these ways, they pressure other states to take action against governments that violate human rights.

Europe, served as the opening wedge that allowed human rights activists to mobilize within the Communist bloc countries of Eastern Europe. Three years earlier, the 35-country Conference on Security and Cooperation in Europe had convened to resolve political and territorial issues left over from World War II and to expand economic contacts between East and West. Much against the wishes of the Communist regimes, the countries of Western Europe insisted on the inclusion of human rights on the agenda. Trading concessions on other issues, the Western states were eventually able to gain the assent of their Eastern counterparts to the principle of "respect for human rights and other fundamental freedoms, including freedom of thought, conscience, religion or belief."[31] Although the Communist countries first attempted to suppress publication and discussion of this principle, word spread and domestic groups began to agitate for their rights and make contact with their transnational counterparts in the West. In the bright lights of public awareness, the societal groups activated by the Helsinki Accords were eventually able to mount effective challenges to the autocratic regimes that had long suppressed all dissent. Although many factors contributed to the fall of the Communist regimes in Eastern Europe in 1989, the political freedom first created by the Helsinki agreement is broadly seen as a contributing cause of that political earthquake.[32]

In addition, international human rights law permits TANs to bring pressure to bear on governments to enforce human rights standards. Human rights TANs, of course, have no legal standing to issue mandatory sanctions or other punishments,

31. Conference on Security and Cooperation in Europe, Final Act, Helsinki, August 1, 1975, Section 1, (a) VII, www.osce.org/mc/39501?download=true (accessed 09/20/14).

32. Daniel C. Thomas, "The Helsinki Accords and Political Change in Eastern Europe," in Risse, Ropp, and Sikkink, *The Power of Human Rights*, 205–33.

but they do exert an important effect by naming and shaming violators of human rights.[33] Equally if not more important, by promoting public awareness and monitoring state human rights practices, TANs create political pressure that may eventually force states to act. TANs are not superseding the role of the state, but they do shape the political context in which states interact with their citizens and one another. Thus, even if international human rights law may not cause governments to change their behavior in the short run, it may lead to significant political change over time by legitimating and encouraging the mobilization of domestic political forces.

What Can Lead to Better Protection of International Human Rights?

Few human rights violators are actually punished. States do sanction one another for human rights abuses, as discussed, but such penalties remain rare. Although states may be named and shamed by transnational human rights organizations, and some may modify their behavior to avoid public condemnation, most escape any significant costs for violating the rights of their citizens.

The key problem in human rights is that the gains from cooperation that make international law self-enforcing, as explained in Chapter 11, are small or nonexistent, meaning that states have few incentives to bear high costs for enforcing the law. States that violate human rights, of course, have no interest in enforcing the law against themselves. This much is obvious. But although other states have interests in supporting human rights in principle, as discussed below, few gain directly from better human rights practices abroad. They have some interest in enforcing human rights standards but only if the costs are not too high. This combination of mostly empathetic interests in human rights practice abroad and few incentives to actually punish violators produces for most states an inconsistent human rights policy. Even the United States, a strong promoter of human rights, has often chosen not to act against abuses by states it supports—including the use of poison gas against his country's Kurdish minority in the late 1980s by Saddam Hussein, who was then being backed by the United States in his war against Iran, and widespread abuses by the military junta in Chile following an American-backed coup in 1973. At the same time, the United States did press human rights concerns against the White-majority regime in South Africa, contributing to the peaceful revolution that eventually led to Black-majority rule, and spoke out in support of the pro-democracy protesters in Egypt and Libya during the Arab Spring in 2011.

This inconsistent enforcement may explain why international human rights law is often ineffective. Facing opposition to their rule at home, states may be

---

33. The effectiveness of naming and shaming is open to debate. See Emilie M. Hafner-Burton, "Sticks and Stones: Naming and Shaming the Human Rights Enforcement Problem," *International Organization* 62, no. 4 (2008): 689–716.

willing to take the small risk of international punishment to secure their tenure in office. That is, for some governments the temptation to ignore human rights law to secure their hold on power may be stronger than the fear of international penalties. With regime survival as a strong core interest and minor punishments carried out only a small percentage of the time by the international community, few leaders may feel tightly constrained by international human rights institutions or the laws that they themselves have accepted as binding.

It is costly for states to enforce international human rights laws. Naming and shaming may anger a violator whose cooperation is needed on some other diplomatic issue. Pressing the human rights provisions of the Helsinki agreement, for instance, meant that European states gave up bargaining leverage on other issues they also cared about. Economic sanctions impose costs on the target state, but they also impose costs on exporters within the home state who lose a potential market for their goods. Businesses strongly resisted divesting from South Africa when it meant forgoing access to raw materials, cheap labor, and Africa's wealthiest consumers. If sanctions hurt the target state, they will also hurt the home state as well (see "Controversy" on p. 502). Promoting human rights always carries a price. But states do sometimes act to punish human rights violations. When do they do so?

When Do States Take Action on Human Rights?

States are most likely to pay the costs of enforcing human rights law under three conditions. First, states act when faced with domestic pressure to "do something" to stop human rights abuses. As noted, few governments have intrinsic interests in promoting international human rights, and most do so only in response to domestic political pressure. Governments normally weigh demands to stop abuses, however, against costs to business interests or other diplomatic initiatives. Domestic pressure often produces merely toothless condemnations of the abuse or loose and ineffective economic sanctions. Nonetheless, the more outrageous the abuse, the greater will be the domestic pressure on governments to act. In this way, the boomerang effect (described in Chapter 11) employed by TANs plays an important role in protecting human rights. Victims or other advocates in one country who are blocked from influencing their own states can bring their plight to the attention of concerned others in foreign countries who can then press their own governments into action against the offending regime. Domestic pressure also explains why democratic states are typically the most important promoters of international human rights. Not only are such rights more consistent with their own practice, but they are more susceptible to the demands of their citizens to undertake costly efforts to advance human rights abroad.

In turn, domestic demands for action are more likely the better informed are citizens about abuses in other countries. It is here, as monitors of practices around the globe, that human rights TANs play perhaps their most important role. Almost by their very nature, human rights abuses are hidden. They are typically perpetrated against individuals and groups that, though perhaps a potential threat to the regime, are nonetheless excluded from political power. Governments that violate human rights, in turn, are also likely to control access to the international media and other routes by which the abused might publicize their plight. It is through the links between domestic activists, who are often the victims of abuses, and transnational activists, who largely operate out of established democracies, that human rights violations are most often brought to light. Amnesty's annual reports are an important vehicle for documenting state practice. Even though the U.S. Department of State also issues its own annual reports, many of the abuses in that document are first uncovered and brought to public attention by TANs. Without TANs, many more governments would be able to abuse their citizens, being confident that their odious practices would escape international scrutiny. This is one issue area where the networks of individuals and groups promoting new international norms, and pressing their governments to make greater efforts in pursuit of those goals, have had a significant effect on state practice.

Second, states are more likely to act against human rights violators when doing so serves larger geopolitical interests. Raising human rights issues as part of the Helsinki Accords was applauded by many in the West as another way to bring pressure to bear on the Soviet Union and its allies for political and economic reform. Saddam Hussein's human rights record became an issue in the relations between Washington and Baghdad only after the Iraqi dictator invaded Kuwait in August 1991. His human rights violations later became one of several reasons given by President George W. Bush to remove Hussein from power in the Iraq War of 2003. Raising human rights concerns and demanding policy change in other states can be goals in themselves, but they may also be instruments in larger political and economic struggles.

Third, states are more likely to act when the gap between the principle of sovereignty and international human rights law can be bridged. Central to the concept of sovereignty is the principle of nonintervention, which is often jealously protected by precisely those states most likely to be sanctioned by the international community for their violations of human rights law. States are, therefore, reluctant to criticize one another, except when the principle of nonintervention can be reconciled with other principles. The anti-apartheid movement was broadly supported, for instance, because it was framed not as foreign intervention but as an anticolonial struggle; thus, it fell under the right to national self-determination guaranteed in the twin covenants. Although this is changing slightly as various regional organizations, like the African Union, move toward support for their own versions of the responsibility to protect (see Chapter 11), the postcolonial states remain among the states most committed to the principle of nonintervention. Under many circumstances, they would have been reluctant to intervene in the affairs of South Africa for fear of legitimating external intervention in their own domestic politics. A key move in the anti-apartheid struggle was defining it as an anticolonial struggle against one of the last White-minority regimes on the continent.[34] So conceived,

---

34. On the construction of a norm of self-determination, see Neta C. Crawford, *Argument and Change in World Politics: Ethics, Decolonization, and Humanitarian Intervention* (New York: Cambridge University Press, 2002). On the norm of racial equality in mobilizing support for the anti-apartheid movement, see Klotz, *Norms in International Relations*.

Black-majority-rule states not only could join the sanctions against South Africa but also could actively press Western states to join in the liberation struggle.

Countries do promote international human rights and punish violators, even if only in a weaker or more episodic way than some advocates desire. When faced with strong domestic pressures and lower costs, states do act to further human rights abroad. Yet states are often inconsistent in their human rights policies. Human rights are seldom the only motivation behind a state's foreign policy. The inconsistency of enforcement may make international human rights law comparatively ineffective and, thus, may explain why international human rights treaties appear to have mostly a contingent effect on human rights practices.

Will Protection of Human Rights Improve in the Future?

As with all international cooperation, efforts to promote more effective collaboration between and among states involve building better international institutions. There are at least four ongoing innovations in international human rights institutions that may have important implications for the future.

Transitional Justice New forms of transitional justice are important innovations in international human rights practice. Following World War II, the focus of international human rights law was the criminal prosecution and punishment of individuals found to have engaged in human rights abuses. Starting in the 1980s and 1990s, however, emphasis has shifted to noncriminal and nonjudicial forms of reconciliation, which are believed to provide a better and more solid long-term foundation for rebuilding societies after major civil conflicts involving human rights abuses. These new forms include truth and reconciliation commissions that aim to document and publicize past human rights abuses; reparations to repair the suffering of human rights victims; memorials that seek to preserve evidence and commemorate victims of abuse; and institutional reforms, especially strengthening civilian control of the police and military. *Lustration* is also common and refers to government policies of limiting members of the previous regime from serving in political, bureaucratic, or sometimes even civil positions.

Advocates of transitional justice argue that it is better for the society to acknowledge and publicize past human rights abuses than focus on criminal prosecutions. Criminal proceedings are adversarial, pitting prosecutors who may not have strong evidence of abuses that the previous government intentionally hid from public view against defendants who have no incentive to admit past wrongdoing or provide information. Criminal prosecutions may also create incentives for human rights abusers to fight longer and harder to stay in power, lest they be accused in court and likely punished.[35] To ease the transition to democracy and the rule of law, advocates suggest, revealing past abuse can heal a

---

35. For a contrary view, see Kathryn Sikkink, *The Justice Cascade: How Human Rights Prosecutions Are Changing World Politics* (New York: Norton, 2011).

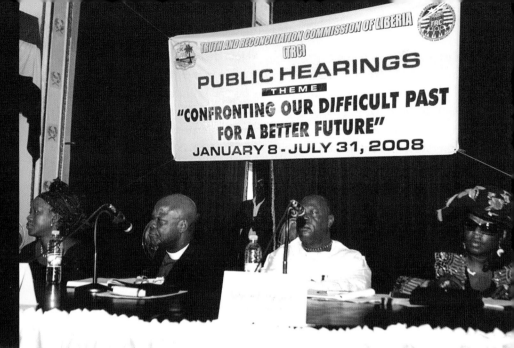

The Truth and Reconciliation Commission of Liberia collected approximately 16,800 statements in 2008, five years after the end of a ruinous civil war in which some 250,000 people were killed. The Commission analyzed the statements to identify responsibility for human rights violations.

society and allow it to move forward rather than remaining mired in the conflicts of the past.

The most difficult issue in transitional justice deals with amnesty, especially for the most serious crimes against humanity. Amnesties pardon individuals who committed rights abuses or other political crimes, typically as part of an effort to move on by putting past conflicts to rest. Amnesty was common in Latin American countries undergoing transitions to democracy in the 1980s. Conditional amnesties grant forgiveness to individuals in return for their full and truthful accountings of their role and knowledge of past abuses. One of the most successful conditional amnesties was the South African Truth and Reconciliation Commission, which ran from 1995 to 2002, following the end of apartheid. Its goals were laid out in the 1993 Interim Constitution, which stated that "there is a need for understanding but not for vengeance, a need for reparation but not retaliation, a need for *ubuntu* [the essence of being human] but not for victimization."[36] Conditional amnesties are also frequently combined with lustrations. All amnesties, however, conflict with laws against crimes against humanity, which can be prosecuted internationally, and with the new ICC, which defers to national courts only when a criminal investigation has been carried out in full (see below). The tension between the desire of countries to move beyond the past through transitional justice and international human rights law has not been resolved.

individual petition

A right that permits individuals to petition appropriate international legal bodies directly if they believe a state has violated their rights.

Individual Petition   One of the most important developments in international human rights law is the right of **individual petition** to a supranational court, found

36. Quoted in Simon Chesterman, *You, the People: The United Nations, Transitional Administration, and State-Building* (New York: Oxford University Press, 2004), 158.

most prominently in the European Convention on Human Rights and Fundamental Freedoms (ECHR) adopted in 1950 by the Council of Europe and its now 47 member states.[37] Preceding it by 26 years, the ECHR recognizes many of the same rights ultimately in the ICCPR. It does not incorporate economic, social, or cultural rights into the corpus of rights it protects. Its most innovative features are the European Court of Human Rights and its right of individual petition.[38] The court currently consists of 47 judges from the member states of the Council of Europe. It hears cases, offers decisions that are binding on members, and awards damages. Although there is no formal mechanism for ensuring compliance, responsibility for enforcing the decisions of the court rests with the Council of Ministers of the Council of Europe. Enforcement is informally overseen by the European Union.

Since 1998, individuals in all member states have possessed the right to petition the court for redress. Prior to this date, an optional protocol allowed individuals to petition the European Commission of Human Rights, which could then launch cases in the court on their behalf. By adopting Protocol 11, all members are now required to allow individuals to petition the court directly if they believe a state has violated their rights as specified in the ECHR. This provision is nearly unique in international law, in which states—not individuals—are normally the subjects. In the court, individuals can now bring suit against their own governments for violations of internationally recognized human rights. In the year before the new provisions took effect, 5,891 petitions were filed with the commission—already a large number. In 2001, the first full year under the new rules, 13,845 petitions were filed, representing an increase of approximately 138 percent. In 2014, the most recent year for which data are available, 56,250 applications were filed, of which 2,388 were ultimately decided by the court.[39] Today, nearly all petitions before the court are from private individuals and the success rate is over 50 percent, indicating that petitioners quite often win their cases against their own states. The ECHR is clearly having a profound effect on human rights practices in Europe, and especially in the relatively new democracies of eastern Europe.

Without the right of individual petition, states act as gatekeepers, blocking international courts from hearing cases that they might lose. Some human rights activists advocate expanding the right of individual petition to other supranational courts as a check against human rights abuses. This move would open channels to

---

37. Rights of individual standing are also found in the Optional Protocols to the ICCPR and the Convention on the Elimination of All Forms of Discrimination against Women (see Table 12.1) and in Article 14 of the ICERD and Article 22 of the CAT. In all cases, however, states must actively declare their willingness to allow the appropriate UN review committee to accept petitions from individuals. On the dynamics of state acceptance of the right of individual petition, see Heather Smith, "Explaining Ratification of Global Human Rights Instruments: Empirical Evidence of Regional Dynamics" (paper presented at the annual meeting of the American Political Science Association, Philadelphia, August 31–September 1, 2006).

38. On the court, see www.echr.coe.int/Pages/home.aspx?p=home (accessed 09/20/14).

39. On the court's caseload, see www.echr.coe.int/Documents/Stats_analysis_2014_ENG.pdf (accessed 06/10/15). Although the courts themselves have different rules, procedures, and roles for comparison, the U.S. Supreme Court for the 2013 term (most recent for which data are available) received 7,376 case filings, of which 77 were decided. See the annual report of the Supreme Court at www.supremecourt.gov /publicinfo/year-end/2014year-endreport.pdf (accessed 06/10/15).

international courts now blocked by states and would likely lead to greater attention to, if not better enforcement of, human rights violations.

The right of individual petition is now found in several optional protocols to international human rights treaties, such as the ICCPR (see Table 12.1 on p. 498). Ratified by fewer states than the main agreements, these optional protocols are a significant step forward.

International Criminal Court (ICC)

A court of last resort for human rights cases that possesses jurisdiction only if the accused is a national of a state party, the crime took place on the territory of a state party, or the UN Security Council has referred the case to the prosecutor.

The International Criminal Court The **International Criminal Court (ICC)** was established in 1998 and came into force in July 2002 after receiving the necessary 60 ratifications of its founding treaty. Today, more than 122 states have accepted the jurisdiction of the ICC and thus have become "state parties." The ICC possesses jurisdiction only if the accused is a national of a state party, the crime took place on the territory of a state party, or the UN Security Council has referred the case to the prosecutor. Moreover, the ICC is a court of last resort, meaning that it cannot act if a national judicial authority has genuinely investigated or prosecuted a case—regardless of the outcome of that investigation or prosecution. The ICC can act only when a state cannot or will not act itself. As of 2015, 22 cases in 8 countries have been brought before the ICC for investigation or trial.[40]

The ICC remains highly controversial. As it begins to investigate and prosecute possible crimes against humanity, critics point out that all the cases are from Africa, yet severe human rights violations are found elsewhere as well.[41] This pattern of prosecutorial conduct, they charge, reflects either blatant racism or, perhaps less insidiously, a willingness by the court to proceed only in regions where the major states do not have significant interests. Either way, the ICC risks becoming a political entity rather than a true court of last resort.

The United States remains highly critical of the court. The treaty establishing the ICC was signed by President Bill Clinton shortly before he left office, which permitted the United States to participate in further negotiations on the court's rules of procedure. Almost immediately on taking office, however, President George W. Bush "unsigned" the treaty, a largely symbolic act. The U.S. government raises many objections to the ICC.[42] Foremost is the fear of frivolous and politically motivated prosecutions against political leaders or American military personnel for actions taken to protect the security of the United States or on peacekeeping or peacemaking missions abroad. Given what is often seen as the special role of the United States in maintaining international peace and security, and real anti-Americanism in many countries, some skeptics of the ICC fear a string of political prosecutions in which leaders are tried not for violations of law

---

40. For the most recent updates, see www.icc-cpi.int/en_menus/icc/situations%20and%20cases/pages/situations%20and%20cases.aspx (accessed 06/10/15).

41. David Bosco, "Why Is the International Criminal Court Picking Only on Africa?" *Washington Post*, March 29, 2013, www.washingtonpost.com/opinions/why-is-the-international-criminal-court-picking-only-on-africa/2013/03/29/cb9bf5da-96f7-11e2-97cd-3d8c1afe4f0f_story.html (accessed 11/23/14).

42. See the statement by John R. Bolton, then undersecretary for Arms Control and International Security, Department of State, and later U.S. ambassador to the United Nations, http://2001-2009.state.gov/r/pa/prs/ps/2002/9968.htm (accessed 09/20/14). For a review, see the Congressional Research Service's report, www.fas.org/sgp/crs/misc/RL31495.pdf (accessed 09/20/14).

but merely for "show" or because others disagree with their policies. There is also concern that leaders would be constrained by fears of future politically motivated prosecutions. Although the United States could negate prosecution by the ICC by undertaking a genuine investigation or prosecution under its national laws, the statute is sufficiently ambiguous on what constitutes an adequate national-level inquiry that politically motivated prosecutions might still be possible.

In March 2012, Thomas Lubanga Dylio (seated, back right) became the first person to be convicted by the ICC. He was sentenced to 14 years in prison for the crime of forcibly recruiting child soldiers in the Democratic Republic of the Congo. Dylio appealed his conviction.

The U.S. government also claims the ICC is insufficiently accountable and lacks oversight mechanisms for both the judges and prosecutors. In the dimensions of international law discussed in Chapter 11, critics fear that the ICC has been delegated too much power to interpret still-imprecise laws. Without the ability to remove activist judges, opponents are concerned that personnel at the ICC may escape political control and develop too much independence. In addition, international human rights case law and precedent are thin. Without adequate guidance from state parties on the intent of international law, the court might not just interpret but essentially make international law itself. Finally, given its prosecutorial and judicial independence, critics claim that the ICC might clash with the more political and problem-solving approach of the UN Security Council. Where diplomacy must be flexible and aware of context, judicial proceedings that stress precedent, statutory interpretation, and equity across similar cases may conflict with the UN Security Council's charge to maintain peace and security.

After the ICC entered into force in 2002, the administration of President George W. Bush worked aggressively to exempt American nationals from its jurisdiction. Most important were the Article 98 agreements that were urged—some might say forced—on other countries. Article 98 of the ICC exempts a country from handing over a foreign national to the court if it is prohibited from doing so by a bilateral agreement with the national's country of origin. Under President Bush, over 100 countries signed bilateral agreements with the United States under threat of losing all foreign and military aid or the withdrawal of American peacekeeping forces. Despite sometimes significant aid cutoffs, other countries, including Barbados, Brazil, Costa Rica, Peru, Venezuela, Ecuador, St. Vincent and the Grenadines, and South Africa, refused to sign these agreements. This attitude changed somewhat under the administration of President Barak Obama, with Secretary of State Hillary Clinton expressing regret in 2009 that the United States was not yet a member and U.S ambassador to the United Nations Susan Rice declaring U.S. support for the investigation in Sudan. Yet, although the Obama administration softened its stance toward the ICC, it did not move toward becoming a state party and accepting the court's jurisdiction.

Harnessing Material Interests　A final source for optimism is the proliferation of RTAs with human rights provisions. As we saw in Chapter 7, nearly every country in the world now belongs to at least one RTA, and nearly all RTAs contain some provisions on human rights. Some agreements are soft, or merely declarative, and appear to have no effect on behavior. Increasingly, though, RTAs are starting to contain obligatory and precise human rights provisions that bind states to international standards of behavior and threaten to withdraw trade and financial benefits if periodic reviews find substantial abuses of human rights. These hard provisions link concrete, material benefits of market access to a state's human rights practices. Unlike human rights agreements in general, and even soft RTAs, these hard provisions do have a significant, if small, effect on the level and extent of human rights violations.[43] Ironically, those protectionist groups looking to insulate themselves from import competition by including human rights provisions in free-trade agreements may have devised effective weapons to protect human rights abroad—and their self-interest in seeing benefits revoked may make threats to use these weapons credible. Human rights advocates would do well to find other ways by which to harness often instrumental, material interests to the cause of promoting better human rights practices.

Conclusion: Why Protect Human Rights?

The puzzle of why states seek to protect the human rights of people outside their own borders is primarily explained by the interests of states. Whether because of concern for the well-being of others, an understanding of common humanity and the need to preserve democracy, or purely instrumental goals, individuals, groups, and thus states do have interests in promoting human rights abroad. TANs have been critical to the spread of international human rights norms in recent decades and in activating citizens to press their governments to act more forcefully to protect human rights. The fact that human rights are an issue today in international relations and that states concern themselves with human rights abroad is testament to the activities of the human rights TANs.

International human rights law is itself an institution. The likely positive but still-limited effectiveness of this institution in constraining abuses, in turn, follows from strategic interaction—or perhaps more precisely from the lack of real and consistent enforcement. While states have interests and are willing to pay some cost to protect human rights within other countries, rarely are they willing to make human rights a priority. As a result, states may publicly condemn abuse but impose few penalties on those who violate human rights. Knowing this, states abuse their

---

43. Hafner-Burton, "Trading Human Rights."

citizens with little fear that they will be sanctioned. The fact that the human rights clauses of RTAs do improve practice, however, suggests that institutions that link behavior to real consequences can have important effects. Current issues in international human rights law focus largely on the breadth and depth of the law itself—individual petitions, the ICC, and inclusion of obligatory human rights provisions in trade and other treaties. Given the modest effect of international human rights law on practice, perhaps human rights advocates would do better by focusing on designing more effective enforcement institutions.

Study Tool Kit

Interests, Interactions, and Institutions in Context

- International human rights law is an institution created by and largely reflecting the political norms of Western, liberal democracies. The norms embodied in these laws remain controversial, are not shared equally by all countries, and have not yet been internalized in many societies and governments. Nonetheless, there is new evidence that international human rights law is improving practice in some specific contexts.

- Individuals and states have an interest in international human rights, and thus they undertake costly acts to punish states that violate the rights of their citizens. These interests are rarely strong enough to compel states to pay high costs to protect vulnerable individuals and groups outside their own borders. Human rights practices, in turn, may be more affected by TANs that change how both individuals and states conceive of their interests.

- States that violate human rights reason that in their interactions with other states they will probably not face serious consequences for their behavior and, therefore, can freely abuse individuals and groups. Unfortunately, these states are most likely correct. Although international human rights law does appear to promote improved practices, it remains of only limited effectiveness in altering the actions of states. Despite increasing support for human rights, international law by itself is not a panacea.

Key Terms

human rights, p. 493

Universal Declaration of Human Rights (UDHR), p. 493

International Covenant on Civil and Political Rights (ICCPR), p. 496

International Covenant on Economic, Social, and Cultural Rights (ICESCR), p. 496

International Bill of Rights, p. 497

nonderogable rights, p. 500

prisoners of conscience (POCs), p. 501

individual petition, p. 524

International Criminal Court (ICC), p. 526

For Further Reading

Brysk, Alison. *Speaking Rights to Power: Constructing Political Will.* **New York: Oxford University Press, 2013.** Surveys the conditions for successful human rights campaigns by NGOs.

Donnelly, Jack. *Universal Human Rights in Theory and Practice.* **2nd ed. Ithaca, NY: Cornell University Press, 2003.** Presents a general overview of the philosophy and practice of international human rights law.

Forsythe, David. *Human Rights in International Relations.* **New York: Columbia University Press, 2000.** Offers an introduction to international human rights, with detailed analyses of international courts, regional human rights agreements, and other issues.

Hafner-Burton, Emilie. *Making Human Rights a Reality.* **Princeton, NJ: Princeton University Press, 2013.** Argues against the current universalistic and legalistic approach to human rights and for an alternative model based on human rights "stewards" who focus their efforts on issues and places where progress is possible.

Hopgood, Stephen. *The Endtimes of Human Rights.* **Ithaca, NY: Cornell University Press, 2013.** A critique of the assumption that human rights are universal and of current practices of human rights promotion.

Ishay, Micheline R. *The History of Human Rights: From Ancient Times to the Globalization Era.* **Berkeley: University of California Press, 2004.** Provides a comprehensive analysis of human rights philosophy and practice from ancient Greece to the present.

Sikkink, Kathryn. *The Justice Cascade: How Human Rights Prosecutions Are Changing World Politics.* **New York: Norton, 2011.** Examines the origins and consequences of international human rights prosecutions.

Simmons, Beth A. *Mobilizing for Human Right: International Law in Domestic Politics.* **New York: Cambridge University Press, 2009.** Examines the critical role of domestic institutions in promoting effective human rights practices.

Wong, Wendy. *Internal Affairs: How the Structure of NGOs Transforms Human Rights.* **Ithaca, NY: Cornell University Press, 2012.** Demonstrates how the organizational structures and incentives of human rights NGOs shaped the transnational advocacy movement and its effectiveness.

13

The Global Environment

THE PUZZLE *Nearly everyone wants a cleaner and healthier environment. Why, then, is it so hard to cooperate internationally to protect the environment?*

Above: Pollution in China is becoming an increasing public health hazard. Under international pressure to reduce its greenhouse gas emissions, the government is also facing increasing demands from its citizens to reduce pollution.

In the early morning of December 14, 2014, after more than 36 hours of continuous negotiations, officials from nearly every country in the world finally agreed to the first-ever global deal to reduce fossil fuel emissions that contribute to global warming. The Lima Accord, named for the capital of Peru where the conference was held, was made possible by a landmark announcement just weeks earlier by U.S. president Barack Obama and Chinese president Xi Jinping committing the world's two largest carbon polluters to significant cuts in their emissions. In the Lima Accord, countries agreed to submit, within the next three months, national plans to reduce carbon dioxide emissions after 2020, although only about 45 countries met this deadline. The plans for every country, called "Intended Nationally Determined Contributions," would form the basis for a sweeping new deal to be signed in Paris in December 2015.

Scientists warn that to avoid global temperature increases of more than 3.6 degrees Fahrenheit, a threshold seen by many as the difference between a merely unpleasant world and an uninhabitable one, global emissions must peak by 2025 and fall by half by midcentury. By asking countries to put forward plans based on their own economic and domestic political situations, rather than adopting a top-down mandate, the Lima Accord helped secure agreement by every state to some level of carbon reduction. Yet, without requiring the significant cuts scientists say are necessary to prevent catastrophic climate change, countries could submit plans with only minimal changes in current policies and practices. Written as "soft law" that relies only on "naming and shaming" (see Chapter 11), the Lima Accord lacks any mechanism for enforcement. The plans submitted as of summer 2015 would not be enough to stave off significant global warming.[1]

Even as global climate change remain a key environmental challenge for decades, other environmental problems continue to grow. For example, within the last generation, 20 percent of the world's tropical rain forest has been cleared for agriculture or logged for commercial uses. Human-induced change is causing by current estimates between 1,000 and 50,000 species to become extinct each year, greatly reducing biodiversity.

1. Coral Davenport, "Global Climate Pact Gains Momentum as China, U.S. and Brazil Detail Plans," *New York Times*, July 1, 2015, A12.

A warming planet, along with these other mounting problems, suggests a bleak future.

The news is not entirely bad, however. One environmental success is that ozone depletion caused by the release of chlorofluorocarbons (CFCs) into the atmosphere has been brought under control. The ozone layer is found in the lower stratosphere, approximately 6 to 30 miles above the earth and is essential to life on earth because it blocks harmful ultraviolet (UV) radiation from reaching the planet's surface. Within years of discovering that CFCs were harming the ozone layer, and within months of the discovery of an ozone "hole" over Antarctica, countries worldwide united to approve the Vienna Convention for the Protection of the Ozone Layer (1985) and, subsequently, the Montreal Protocol (1989), virtually eliminating the release of CFCs into the atmosphere. There are other equally notable examples of progress, especially international agreements to reduce acid rain. These cases of success suggest the possibilities of greater international environmental cooperation.

Why is such cooperation so difficult to achieve? Equally, why does it sometimes succeed despite these difficulties? One popular explanation for the relative lack of international environmental cooperation is ignorance. If populations and national leaders would only recognize or understand the problems, some observers believe, greater progress in improving the environment could occur. Transnational advocacy networks (TANs; see Chapter 11), that act on behalf of environmental issues have sought to make all of us more environmentally aware and have deepened our understanding of environmental problems. Much has been accomplished. Few people in developed countries now lack information about impending environmental degradation, and a majority of Americans believe protecting the environment should be prioritized over economic growth.[2] Yet recognizing the magnitude of the environmental problems we face is not enough to produce effective solutions.

A second common explanation for the lack of progress points to the influential role of special interests in blocking environmental regulations. There are certainly groups that would lose from policies designed to improve the environment. Such groups are important actors in the analysis we develop in this chapter. But as the case of ozone depletion indicates, progress is sometimes possible despite the presence of highly motivated special interests.

Thinking Analytically about the Global Environment

Focusing mainly on the contrasting cases of ozone depletion and global climate change, this chapter aims to explain the sources and impediments to international environmental cooperation. First, we will see that despite widely shared interests in the quality of the environment, the interactions of individuals as well as countries suffer from problems of collective action. Although each person and country has an interest in a world without climate change, for instance, they also prefer to free-ride on the efforts of others, saving themselves the cost of reducing emissions while enjoying the cutbacks of others. In the absence of any international authority that can mandate improved performance, the result is less overall environmental cooperation than individuals and even countries themselves collectively desire. Individuals, groups, and countries also have conflicting interests over who bears the costs of mitigating harmful environmental practices, with rich countries typically demanding universal cuts and poorer countries claiming they should be largely exempt from restrictions until their incomes have risen. How environmental policies distribute these costs affects how likely actors are to cooperate successfully on issues relating to the environment.

Cooperation on issues relating to the international environment is most likely when confined to small groups of actors, one of which is substantially larger than the others, and possibly forming a privileged group as defined in Chapter 2. In the absence of such groups, international institutions can also facilitate environmental cooperation, primarily by enhancing information and verifying compliance. TANs and other nongovernmental organizations (NGOs) now play an essential role in monitoring compliance with environmental agreements. The clearer and more easily verified the standard, the more likely states are to cooperate successfully.

---

2. Based on Gallup Polls conducted since 1985. See www.gallup.com/poll/1615/environment.aspx (accessed 02/02/15).

Why Are Good Intentions Not Good Enough?

Despite broad-based interests in environmental quality, cooperation is thwarted by interactions in which it is difficult to coordinate large numbers of individuals or, at the international level, moderately large numbers of states. We might personally care about the environment and want to improve the quality of the world we inhabit—that is, we have an interest in environmental cooperation—but our individual actions have little effect on the local or global ecosystem. For example, if everyone else is keeping their house warm at 70 degrees during the winter, your decision to lower your thermostat to 65 degrees will have a negligible effect on total energy usage and carbon emissions. You make a personal sacrifice to reduce pollution by keeping your house colder, while the benefits of your efforts, however small they may be, are not recouped by you alone but are broadly shared by others. Conversely, if everyone else is polluting less by setting their thermostats lower, your decision to keep your home at 70 degrees will also have negligible effects. Although you might use more energy and produce more emissions than others, your overconsumption also diffuses and imposes a very small cost on everyone. You may reap a personal benefit by staying warmer, but everyone bears the cost of your greater emissions.

Since we often benefit from others' efforts to preserve the environment while having only a marginal effect ourselves, we typically avoid changing our personal behaviors or incurring costs to reduce pollution. In short, even though we prefer a cleaner environment, we nonetheless seek to free-ride on the efforts of others. Since everyone makes the same calculation, we interact within a Prisoner's Dilemma in which we individually defect and collectively produce a suboptimal outcome for society as a whole (also known as a Pareto suboptimal or inferior outcome; see Chapter 2 "Special Topic" appendix). Thus, even though we may all have a shared interest in protecting the environment, our incentives to free-ride usually win out and, through our interactions, we collectively degrade the ecosystem. Rather than sacrificing by living in cooler homes in the winter, we keep the thermostats turned up high—and hope for the best.

The same logic applies at the international level, except—as we shall see—for especially large countries. Most countries' efforts to conserve resources or limit pollution have only a small effect on the global environment. Since the costs of their pollution fall on others as well as themselves, they do not bear the full consequences of their decision to pollute. Similarly, if they sacrifice income by imposing tighter environmental controls on themselves, they create benefits for other countries that have not paid a similarly high price. Thus, countries seek to free-ride on other countries, and the global environment suffers. Despite being the world's largest source of carbon emissions, even the United States has been unwilling to constrain significantly its own pollution in the absence of controls on all other

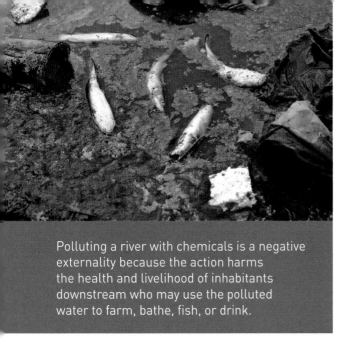

Polluting a river with chemicals is a negative externality because the action harms the health and livelihood of inhabitants downstream who may use the polluted water to farm, bathe, fish, or drink.

countries, which is why the Lima Accord is so important. As former U.S. Secretary of Energy Samuel Bodman stated in rejecting unilateral limits on emissions, "We are a small contributor to the overall [problem], when you look at the rest of the world, so it's really got to be a global solution."[3] The Prisoner's Dilemma that exists at the individual level is reproduced at the international level with the same consequences. The paradoxes of collective action are every bit as important for countries as for individuals.

Collective Action and the Environment

The problem of collective action and our incentives to free-ride on the environmental efforts of others arise because our choices produce **externalities**. An externality is created whenever a decision creates costs or benefits for stakeholders other than the actor making the decision. In other words, in an externality the decision maker does not bear all the costs or reap all the gains from its action. If a firm decides to dump waste into a river, others bear the costs of either using contaminated water or purifying it themselves. In this case, the firm has imposed a cost, or negative externality, on others. If a school club cleans a stretch of beach, not only do its members benefit from a litter-free and safer swimming area, but so do all others who might use the same spot. In this instance, the club has provided benefits, or created a positive externality, for others.

Externalities create a divergence between the individual costs or benefits of action and the broader costs or benefits to society as a whole. Individuals are typically motivated to act only by their private costs and benefits, and they do not take into account the costs and benefits imposed on others. As a result, from the point of view of society at large, people individually decide to dump too much waste or fail to clean up enough beaches. When externalities exist, the independent decisions of individual actors lead to suboptimal results. Through some form of cooperation, everyone's welfare can be improved and each individual, in principle, can be made better off.

Many environmental issues take the form of a more specific type of externality known as a *public good*. For the purpose of analysis here, a "good" is not necessarily a positive benefit or product but refers to any policy or outcome that is consumed by individuals or countries, whether this be an unwanted good like carbon emissions or a desired good like clean air. Public goods possess two characteristics that we encountered briefly in Chapter 2 when discussing problems of collaboration.

externalities

Costs or benefits for stakeholders other than the actor undertaking an action. When an externality exists, the decision maker does not bear all the costs or reap all the gains from his or her action.

---

3. Elisabeth Rosenthal and Andrew C. Revkin, "Science Panel Says Global Warming Is 'Unequivocal,'" *New York Times*, February 3, 2007, A1.

First, once a public good is available for one person, others cannot be excluded from either suffering the cost or enjoying the benefit of that good. Technically, the good is **nonexcludable**. For example, **chlorofluorocarbons (CFCs)** emitted into the atmosphere destroy ozone molecules in the stratosphere, thinning the life-protecting **ozone layer** around the entire globe. No one can be excluded from the damage, and everyone suffers from higher levels of UV radiation reaching the earth's surface (see the "Special Topic" appendix on p. 568). Conversely, now that CFC production is greatly reduced and the ozone layer is beginning to repair itself, no one can be excluded from enjoying the benefits. Carbon emissions have a similar effect in **global climate change**. Greater emissions harm everyone by raising global surface temperatures. Lower emissions, if they occur, will benefit everyone by eventually stopping or perhaps reversing the rise in temperatures.

Second, the use or consumption of a public good by one person does not diminish the quantity of the good available for use by others. Thus, the good is technically said to be **nonrival in consumption**. In the case of ozone depletion, the greater UV radiation that reaches one person, and that increases his or her risk of skin cancer, does not diminish the greater quantity of UV radiation that might also harm a second person—or the billionth person. Similarly, the increase in temperature for one country from global warming does not reduce the temperature for other countries. All suffer from the warmer atmosphere and its consequences, including rising sea levels from melting glaciers. Conversely, one individual's enjoyment of lower UV levels or cooler temperatures does not diminish others' ability to enjoy the same environmental improvements. We all suffer, or not, together. It is these qualities of nonexcludability and nonrivalry that make ozone depletion and climate change—along with many other environmental issues—global problems.

Public goods arise partly from nature. Given the existence of a single atmosphere, we all suffer from a thinner ozone layer and a warmer climate. But the public aspect of goods is also partly a function of technology and, in turn, how much we are willing to pay to exclude ourselves from harm or others from benefits. By wearing UV-protected clothing or applying sunscreen, we can significantly reduce the effects of ozone depletion and the risk of contracting skin cancer. But these personal benefits are costly and do not protect others.

Public goods are also produced by social practice and law. For centuries, villages in Europe had a commons that was open to all the villagers' animals for grazing, typically large enough that it did not suffer unduly from rivalry and congestion. One of the great social transformations of the late feudal period in Europe was the enclosure movement through which the commons was divided into private plots, most of which ended up in the hands of the already rich landowners. While perhaps unfair, this led to more efficient use of the resource. Similarly, the **Kyoto Protocol**, adopted in 1997 and entered into force in 2005, creates a carbon trading system that, in essence, privatizes the public good that previously existed. Before Kyoto, the environment was treated as a global commons, free for anyone to use even when that use produces emissions of harmful chemicals and other pollutants. Local or national governments could regulate the amount of toxic emissions allowed, but any actor meeting the national regulatory requirements essentially gained a

nonexcludable

Characteristic of a public good: if the good is available to one actor to consume, then other actors cannot be prevented from consuming it as well.

chlorofluorocarbons (CFCs)

Chemical compounds used in aerosols, insulating materials, refrigerator and air-conditioner coolants, and other products. CFCs are widely banned today due to their damaging effect on the ozone layer.

ozone layer

Part of the lower stratosphere, approximately 6 to 30 miles above the earth, with relatively high concentrations of ozone, which blocks harmful UV radiation.

global climate change

Human-induced change in the environment, especially from the emissions of greenhouse gases, leading to higher temperatures around the globe.

nonrival in consumption

Characteristic of a public good: one actor's consumption of the good does not diminish the quantity available for others to consume as well.

Kyoto Protocol

An amendment to the UN Framework Convention on Climate Change, adopted in 1997 and entered into force in 2005, that establishes specific targets for reducing emissions of carbon and five other greenhouse gases.

right to pollute. Some countries simply chose not to regulate emissions—a right that remains for any state that has not joined the Protocol. Under the provisions of the Kyoto Protocol, however, this right is overturned and the ability to pollute is restricted, at least for those countries bound by the agreement.

Since 2005, Europe has used an Emissions Trading Scheme (ETS) that covers its five "dirtiest" industries and 13,000 factories and plants rated as particularly dirty. The ETS is what is known as a **cap-and-trade** system. Each firm initially received tradable "credits" for greenhouse gases up to the level of its existing emissions. Firms wanting to exceed those levels had to purchase credits from other European firms or from developing countries with projects certified by the United Nations (UN). Buying credits from another European firm simply shifts emissions from one company to another, with little effect on overall output. Purchasing credits from developing countries actually reduces total emissions. In its first year, through this mechanism, consumers in developed countries invested $2.7 billion to cut developing-country greenhouse gases by the equivalent of 347 million tons of carbon.[4] By design, the system creates incentives for businesses to reduce emissions by selling the credits they have not used themselves, thereby privatizing the otherwise public good of the atmosphere in a way that benefits the global commons. Harnessing the profit motive to reduced emissions is key for reducing incentives to free-ride. It is also expected to lead to more efficient allocations of resources as those industries or countries that face relatively high costs in reducing their emissions can instead buy carbon credits from others for whom reducing emissions is less costly. In phase 1 of its operation (2005–7), widely regarded as a learning period, emissions allowances were set too high, driving the price of carbon credits to zero in 2007. Phase 2 (2008–12) cut the emissions caps by 7 percent below 2005 emissions levels. Phase 3, which began in 2013, aims to reduce emissions by 21 percent by 2020 simply by limiting the number of credits issued, though the credits continue to trade at prices lower than intended indicating that too many have been permitted. The effectiveness of the ETS remains hotly contested. Although emissions are lower than they would have been had the ETS not been implemented, it remains unclear whether allocation levels have been set sufficiently low to facilitate cost-effective reductions in emissions.[5] The key point, however, is that the global commons is now restricted and emissions can be bought and sold. The rules are designed to create a market in pollution credits that will correct previous incentives to free-ride on others.

In addition to public goods, other types of externalities can create collective action problems. Many environmental issues, such as those related to open ocean fisheries, wildlife, and natural resources involve common-pool resources. **Common-pool resources** are nonexcludable but rival in consumption: it is difficult

cap-and-trade

A cap-and-trade system sets limits on emissions, which are then lowered over time to reduce pollutants released into the atmosphere. Firms can sell "credits" when they emit less than their allocation or must buy from others when they emit more than their allocation.

common-pool resources

Goods that are available to everyone, such as open ocean fisheries; it is difficult to exclude anyone from using the common pool, but one user's consumption reduces the amount available for others.

---

4. "The Heat Is On: A Survey of Climate Change," *Economist* (September 9, 2006): 17–19. These figures should be treated skeptically. At least some environmental improvements in developing countries would have occurred even in the absence of the ETS and therefore should perhaps not be credited to this mechanism.

5. See Stefano Clò, "The Effectiveness of the EU Emissions Trading Scheme," *Climate Policy* 9, no. 3 (2009): 227–41.

to exclude anyone from using the common pool, but one user's consumption reduces the amount available for others. In the case of common-pool resources, the collective action problem that arises is **overexploitation**. Instead of failing to contribute, as in the case of public goods, actors are likely to overuse the resource.

Whaling provides a particularly clear example of overexploitation of a common-pool resource.[6] It is difficult to exclude whalers from the open ocean or to effectively monitor their activities on the high seas. Nonetheless, any whale that is killed reduces the population of whales available for others to catch. Indeed, if too many whales are caught and the population becomes too small or geographically dispersed, there may be insufficient opportunities to reproduce and a whale species may "crash" or even become extinct. One whaler's decision to stop or, conversely, resume hunting will have only a small effect on the total whale population. As a result, his incentive is to catch as many whales as he can find. But if every whaler follows the same logic, the sum of their actions will deplete the whale population too rapidly.

To address this issue, the whaling industry created the International Whaling Commission (IWC) in 1946. In an attempt to limit annual catches to sustainable yields, each country was assigned an annual quota by the governing council. With the governing council composed almost entirely of representatives of whaling states, and with each member country lobbying to set its quota as high as possible, the IWC set the aggregate quota far above that which would allow the whale population to regenerate itself. As a result, the number of whales plummeted. Starting in the early 1960s, annual catches fell from approximately 15,000 to under 5,000 whales per year—not as a result of strict quotas but owing to declining whale populations. Even though the industry recognized that its long-term health required lower quotas and rates of exploitation, the member states were unable to resist their incentives to catch as many whales as quickly as they could. Under pressure from environmentalists, the IWC finally enacted a complete ban on whaling in 1982, and it took effect in 1985 (see "What Shaped Our World?" on p. 540).

In sum, externalities create a disjuncture between individual interests and collective welfare. The interactions of large numbers of individuals or countries can produce outcomes that are undesirable for society as a whole. Even though we all value the environment, our individual actions have a marginal impact and we free-ride on the efforts of others. Problems of collective action apply among individuals and states. Choices that are reasonable for a single actor sometimes create collectively tragic results.

overexploitation
Consumption of a good at a rate that is collectively undesirable, even if it is efficient from the view of any single actor.

Common-pool resources like fish in the ocean or water in a lake are frequently exploited to the point of devastation because everyone benefits from using the resource but no one actor bears specific responsibility for ensuring its survival.

---

6. M. J. Peterson, "Whalers, Cetologists, Environmentalists, and the International Management of Whaling," *International Organization* 46, no. 1 (Winter 1992): 147–86.

The Campaign to Save the Whales

Since 1982, the International Whaling Commission (IWC) has banned the killing of whales for commercial purposes. Understanding the interests, institutions, and interactions that culminated in a successful ban on whaling provides lessons for other efforts trying to alter states' behavior on environmental issues.

Interactions As explained in the text, whaling is a classic example of a common-pool resource. Each whaler's kill has a marginal effect on the population of whales in the ocean, but the cumulative effect of all whalers' actions depletes the population. Voluntary efforts to restrict whaling failed, leading to the establishment of the IWC in 1946 with the goal of limiting catches to sustainable levels so as to maintain the viability of this historic industry.

Interests Despite its clear intent to preserve the whaling industry, the IWC initially failed. Because its members were all states with interests in the whaling industry, the member states voted to set each country's whaling quota as high as possible, which continued to overexploit the whale populations. Concerned about the sharp decline in the oceans' whale populations and motivated by ethical concerns about killing any marine mammals, environmentalists began to urge a complete ban on whaling. Naturally, the whaling states on the IWC vigorously opposed the ban, arguing instead that they should be permitted to continue to hunt at lower, but sustainable, rates.

Institutions After years of being thwarted by the pro-whaling states, environmentalists finally exploited a loophole in the voting rules of the IWC. These rules give each member country one vote and allow any state that pays dues to join. The membership of the IWC was intentionally left open to gain the participation of not only the current whaling states but also any state that might develop a whaling industry in the future. Environmentalists shrewdly used this rule to stack the membership of the IWC by encouraging anti-whaling states to join. For instance, in joining the IWC in 1980, Switzerland became the first landlocked country to become a member of an international fishery organization. Environmental organizations also paid the membership dues for small, poor countries that previously did not belong. By 1982, the year the ban was adopted, environmentalists had succeeded in shifting the majority membership of the IWC from those states backing the commercial exploitation of whales to those supporting a moratorium. In short, environmentalists exploited existing institutional rules to bring about a policy change. Today, only two countries, Norway and Iceland, hunt whales on a commercial basis in violation of the IWC's ban.

Interstate negotiations over whaling did not end with the IWC's ban, and both pro- and anti-whaling coalitions continue to pursue actions within the institution to impose their will on the other side. For instance, Japan is tying its growing foreign aid to smaller states to support for its efforts to overturn restrictions on commercial whaling. An attempt in June 2005 to overturn the ban was defeated by just a handful of votes. In 2010, a compromise plan was proposed that would authorize very limited commercial whaling in exchange for creating a South Atlantic Whale Sanctuary (SAWS), but no agreement was reached. In 2011, a vote on the SAWS alone was blocked when pro-whaling states left the meeting early, denying other states the necessary quorum. To date, the ban is still in effect, although its hold is tenuous and depends on the continuing membership of the IWC.

Happily for everyone, the whale populations have begun to recover. Why was the ban effective? In part, the ban was enforceable because it created a clearly observable standard: no whaling was permitted. This presumed any whale product to result from illegal activities. Equally important was the U.S. domestic law. All nations have the right to regulate fishing in their exclusive economic zone (EEZ), which in most cases extends 200 nautical miles from their coastline. The U.S. government sells rights to fish in its EEZ to foreign countries. Environmentalists pushed legislation through the U.S. Congress, requiring that fishing rights be denied to any country not in compliance with the IWC's ban on whaling. The whaling ban proves that halting the killing of endangered animals is possible, and other organizations are emulating the whaling movement and seeking complete bans on hunting or trading in the products of endangered animals.

Solving Collective Action Problems

Although they make environmental cooperation difficult, collective action problems need not thwart cooperation entirely. And although they create similar incentives for everyone to defect from cooperation, they may nonetheless vary in severity and ease of solution.

First, the magnitude of collective action problems varies by group size.[7] The larger the group of actors affected by an externality, the more likely they are to free-ride on one another, as the contribution of each will be a proportionately smaller percentage of the total. The smaller the group, the more likely actors are to contribute to solving the problem. This helps explain why acid rain, a problem in the 1970s, was relatively easy to address. Acid rain is produced when sulfur dioxide and nitrogen oxide are emitted into the atmosphere, are subsequently absorbed by water droplets, creating a mild solution of sulfuric and nitric acid, and then eventually fall to earth as precipitation. The highly acidic rain affects the chemical balance of soil, lakes, and streams. Indeed, acid rain killed many forests and both plant and aquatic life in lakes before being brought under control. Acid rain is primarily a localized phenomenon, however, falling mostly downwind of large coal-burning industrial centers. Thus, emissions from the United States fell mostly on itself and Canada; British emissions, on Scandinavia; western European emissions, on eastern Europe; and so forth. Although restricted to countries downwind of large polluters, the same problem occurs in many different regions. The limited number of countries in each acid rain region was a key factor in facilitating negotiations for the Convention on Long-Range Transboundary Air Pollution (LRTAP) and its optional protocol, completed in 1979 and now possessing 51 members from across several acid rain regions. Together, the member states have reduced sulfur emissions by more than 60 percent below 1980 levels.[8] Small numbers do not guarantee success, however. In China alone, acid rain caused by burning high-sulfur coal remains an acute problem affecting over one-third of its territory.

Since they affect the largest possible population, global environmental problems such as ozone depletion and climate change are more difficult to solve. Nonetheless, the relatively smaller number of countries involved was one of the factors that contributed to more effective collective action on ozone than on global climate change. In the case of ozone depletion, CFC production and usage was relatively concentrated in a few countries. In the late 1980s, the United States (22 percent), Japan (16 percent), and Russia (11 percent) accounted for just under half of the world's total emissions of CFCs. Just 12 countries accounted for 78 percent of all emissions. The benefits of reduced emissions would also be greatest in temperate countries, where the ozone holes would be most serious. In the case of climate change, the producers and consumers of fossil fuels that account for the majority

---

7. Mancur Olson, *The Logic of Collective Action: Public Goods and the Theory of Groups* (Cambridge, MA: Harvard University Press, 1965).

8. Keith Bull, M. Johansson, and M. Krzyzanowski, "Impacts of the Convention on Long-Range Transboundary Air Pollution on Air Quality in Europe," *Journal of Toxicology and Environmental Health*, pt. A; *Current Issues* 71, no. 1 (2008): 51–55.

FIGURE 13.1 *National Interests and Carbon Emissions, 2013*

"Enthusiastic" countries (in green) are willing to spend their own resources to control emissions. "Reluctant" countries (in blue) are usually willing to control emissions only when this coincides with other national goals. Most other countries are small emitters (in yellow) who will have relatively little effect on carbon levels, or net carbon exporters (in red) who have little interest in restricting carbon usage.

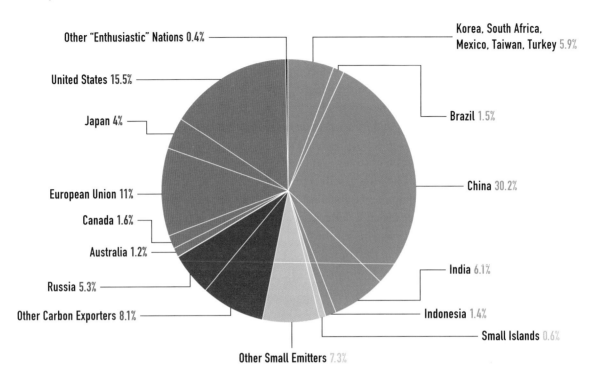

Figure source: David G. Victor, *Global Warming Gridlock: Creating More Effective Strategies for Protecting the Planet* (New York: Cambridge University Press, 2011), 10. Figure based on the 2013 data provided by David G. Victor.

of carbon emissions are very broadly dispersed (Figure 13.1). Fossil fuels are deeply integrated into the heart of nearly all industrialized and industrializing economies and are the primary sources of energy for most of the world today. Altering the usage of oil and coal will have profound effects extending throughout the economy of every nation. With the large number of countries involved in climate change, the problem of collective action is relatively more severe. Critics of global environmental treaties believe they have been and will continue to be ineffective for this reason, the Lima Accord being no exception. They propose as an alternative strategy in which smaller clubs of countries willing to make meaningful reciprocal concessions move forward in reducing emissions. If these clubs succeed, the benefits of access to clean technologies and other trade incentives will, hopefully, recruit more countries into the clubs.[9] Even within global environmental issues, group size matters.

Second, as we saw in Chapter 2, groups that interact repeatedly (iteration) or frequently on other issues (linkage) will be able to induce greater contributions from one another through strategies of reciprocal punishment in which

---

9. David G. Victor, *Global Warming Gridlock: Creating More Effective Strategies for Protecting the Planet* (New York: Cambridge University Press, 2011).

Groups that interact repeatedly and frequently are more likely to cooperate. Rice farmers, for example, are typically linked into a tight community and must cooperate along many dimensions, including managing irrigation systems that form a common-pool resource.

contributors sanction noncontributors by withholding future cooperation. Tightly linked and enduring communities with very large numbers of actors have been found to cooperate successfully over long periods. Throughout Southeast Asia, for instance, irrigation networks—a common-pool resource shared among hundreds of farmers—have endured for centuries because of the farmers' mutual dependence on each other.[10] Similarly, the resolution of the acid rain problem in North America and Europe was facilitated because the neighboring states interacted frequently on many dimensions (Canada and the United States are among each other's largest trading partners, for instance) and expected to interact intensely into the foreseeable future. Downwind states whose lakes were slowly dying from acid rain thus expected to have plenty of opportunities to punish their upwind neighbors if the latter did not live up to the terms of the LRTAP convention. Conversely, the diverse array of countries with widely varying patterns of interactions involved in global issues, including both ozone depletion and climate change, make cooperation more difficult.

Third, when public goods come bundled with private goods for which actors are willing to pay, cooperation is also facilitated. These are called joint products.[11] Rain forests absorb significant amounts of carbon and thus help reduce the problem of global climate change, and they are home to many different species, thereby enhancing biodiversity. Saving acres in a rain forest to preserve a global carbon sink and promote biodiversity also provides erosion control to local landowners

---

10. Elinor Ostrom, *Governing the Commons: The Evolution of Institutions for Collective Action* (New York: Cambridge University Press, 1990).

11. Also called selective incentives. See Todd Sandler, *Global Challenges: An Approach to Environmental, Political, and Economic Problems* (New York: Cambridge University Press, 1997), 45–46.

and opportunities for ecotourism; those landowners may pursue such measures for those private benefits. Similarly, the DuPont company saw an opportunity for increased profits as the pressure to ban CFCs began to increase in the 1980s. DuPont was a leading producer of CFCs, accounting for nearly 50 percent of all production in the United States and 25 percent of global production. But as the leading innovator of alternatives for CFCs as well, DuPont was also well positioned to gain from a ban.[12] In this case, the positive externality of eliminating the production of CFCs also provided a private profit for DuPont. A similar transition may occur for large energy companies as they diversify into alternative fuels, but none appear to have reached the critical point where the gains from wind, solar, or other energy sources appear sufficiently promising for them to strongly advocate greener technologies. For all joint products, the public good is provided as a by-product of efforts to obtain the private good. The larger the private benefits relative to the public good, the less free riding we will observe.

Finally, when actors vary in size (as states do) or in the intensity of their preferences for public goods, a privileged group may emerge (see Chapter 2). A privileged group comprises one or a small number of actors who receive sufficient benefits themselves from the public good that they are willing to bear the cost of providing that good for all. The benefits of reducing ozone depletion were sufficiently large to the United States, for example, that it was willing to bear the costs of banning CFCs unilaterally and leading the international fight against their use. The United States produced 30 percent of the world's CFCs, and the savings to it alone from reduced instances of skin cancer were sufficient to justify a major effort to limit CFC emissions. After some initial reluctance, the United States took a leadership position in the negotiations that produced the effective Vienna Convention and Montreal Protocol.

Conversely, one of the major problems in global climate change has been the relatively smaller benefits and higher costs to the United States from controlling emissions of greenhouse gases and its corresponding unwillingness to take a vanguard role in this area. Even though the United States accounts for a large percentage of carbon emissions, similar to its CFC production, it is unlikely to be affected by global warming as much as some other countries (other than in New Orleans, parts of Florida, or other low-lying coastal areas). Until recently, the United States has been a laggard rather than a leader in controlling carbon emissions. It opposed the Kyoto Protocol largely because the amendment exempts most developing countries and, in the eyes of some critics, puts an unfair burden on American producers and consumers. This position may be changing with the Lima Accord that satisfies this demand for universal participation, though significant reductions in carbon emissions in the United States will still require action by Congress where opposition to cuts remains strong.

---

12. Karen Litfin, *Ozone Discourses: Science and Politics in Global Environmental Cooperation* (New York: Columbia University Press, 1994), 123–27.

Small island nations like the Seychelles stand to suffer greatly from rising sea levels, even though they contribute very small amounts of carbon emissions.

Collective action problems are not constant across environmental issues. In all public goods, some free riding will occur. Countries will always be tempted to over-exploit a common-pool resource. Because no actor bears the full costs or benefits of its decisions, externalities will always be produced. Yet, as the contrasting outcomes in ozone depletion and global climate change suggest, some collective action problems can be solved.

Why Do Polluters Usually Win?

Political struggles over the environment often involve bargaining problems as well as collective action problems. These bargaining problems typically pit a majority favoring tighter regulations against a minority of special interests that, if not actually advocating environmental degradation, aim to block costly new regulations or to shift the costs of policy change onto others. Even though most may share an interest in the environment, any policy to improve environmental practices will create losers, who will have to give up activities or practices that were previously permitted, and winners, who will enjoy the benefits of a greener world. This situation creates a problem of bargaining or redistribution in which one side's gains come as a result of another side's losses. Why do those who stand to lose from tighter environmental restrictions often win? Why do those special interests that oppose environmental regulations tend to succeed in blocking greater controls? To answer these questions, we must examine two sets of winners and losers in international environmental policy.

Domestic Winners and Losers

Almost by definition, "dirty" industries that impose negative externalities on others enhance their profits by not paying the full costs of production, which include not only their immediate costs of production but also the harm they impose on others. Industries that emit pollutants into the air or water benefit from lax environmental policies that do not require them to pay to clean up their production processes but rather leave it to others to do so or live with dirty air or water. Similarly, clear-cutting of forests is usually cheaper than selectively harvesting trees in a way that limits deforestation and helps preserve biodiversity. The losses from deforestation, including greater erosion, possible flooding, and reduced biodiversity are costs that others continue to incur long after the lumber companies have moved on to new areas.

Even though they may extract or manufacture their products in ways that do not directly degrade the environment, industries that produce goods that harm the environment also have interests in looser environmental laws. The oil industry, which frequently promotes its clean production methods in glossy magazine ads, has fought attempts to require cleaner-burning fuels like ethanol that would, were they widely available, reduce the value of their reserves and force them to invest in new capacity to develop and distribute these alternatives. Likewise, the auto industry has opposed efforts to improve gasoline mileage or reduce emissions because the new technologies would raise the price of cars and, at least at the margin, reduce demand.

Competition at home and abroad constrains firms to reduce their costs of production as much as possible. The process of economic globalization heightens this constraint by bringing domestic firms into competition with foreign manufacturers, which may not face the same pressures for increased environmental regulations in their bases of production. By opposing new environmental regulations—and at an extreme, by lobbying to remove existing regulations as competition increases—firms lower their costs of production at the expense of the environment.[13] This competition for regulatory laxity is feared to produce a "race to the bottom" in environmental policy as countries seek to undercut one another in offering business friendly policies to internationally mobile companies. To date, there is relatively little evidence for such a race. By producing at lower cost, however, not only do the firms benefit, but so do consumers, who gain from cheaper prices for goods. Indeed, lax environmental regulations lower the cost of products and thus give consumers an incentive to ignore environmental degradation as well.

Nearly every alternative policy for protecting the global environment creates losers and winners who press their governments to change policy in their preferred direction. Nonetheless, the balance of political power typically favors entrenched or vested interests. The industries and groups that would lose from tighter environmental regulations are relatively few, in comparison with the majority that gains

---

13. Firms may also use disputes over differing international environmental regulations to attempt to restrict international trade and competition. In such cases, concern over the environment can be a form of hidden protectionism. It is no coincidence that environmentalists and labor unions have joined forces against globalization in most developed countries.

Those who stand to gain from actions with environmental costs, like drilling for oil, may find it easier to mobilize because the benefits to them—in jobs, for instance—are immediate and concentrated.

from a greener environment, and they suffer direct and immediate costs. In this way, polluters are similar to protectionist industries (discussed in Chapter 7) that gain concentrated benefits from import restrictions and are more motivated to enter the political arena as a result. Oil markets are dominated by just a few major firms, for which the costs of environmental regulations are also highly concentrated. Automobile manufacturers claim that increased mileage standards will require costly new research and development and raise the price of cars, thereby reducing demand. These concentrated costs give the potential losers a stronger incentive to attempt to influence government policy. As an exception that tests the rule, CFC producers—especially DuPont, the industry leader—dug in their heels on reducing emissions until it became clear that new chemical alternatives would soon be available and might even increase profits. When the costs of change are not large, even politically powerful industries may yield to demands for tighter environmental regulations. Once regulated, moreover, firms may then lobby hard to create international agreements that level the playing field by regulating foreign firms as well.[14]

Conversely, the benefits of a cleaner environment are diffuse and the beneficiaries, as a result, suffer from collective action problems. Because the benefits are spread across many individuals or groups, few have strong interests in lobbying their governments to alter current practices. The intensity of the losers' interests in opposing stiffer regulations typically compensates for their smaller numbers relative to the majority.

Moreover, these industries and groups have employees and stockholders who are citizens and voters. Industries can mobilize those workers and stockholders to press their case on elected politicians. Oil companies, for example, have political influence because many voters depend on that industry—or related industries that rely on inexpensive fossil fuels—for their livelihoods. Alternative industries, such as wind or solar power firms, lack the same resources. Their future growth, and the workers and stockholders who might benefit directly from their growth, are mostly promises rather than real-life voters who can reward or punish politicians for the legislation they adopt today. Even though the industries may grow in the future, the number of companies, employees, and communities that depend on electricity generated from wind or solar power remains very small. Consequently, these industries exert comparatively little influence on current policy. There are, of course, exceptions. For example, American farmers have been a driving force behind efforts to add ethanol to traditional petroleum-based gasoline products as a way of creating a

14. On domestic business interests, see Elizabeth R. DeSombre, *Domestic Sources of International Environmental Policy: Industry, Environmentalists, and U.S. Power* (Cambridge, MA: MIT Press, 2000).

new market for corn and increasing its price.[15] But in general, prospective "greener" industries do not have political clout today. This situation creates an important bias toward the status quo and against policies aimed at improving the environment. With concentrated costs and a political system biased toward existing rather than future industries, domestic groups that would lose from tighter environmental regulations tend to have more political power and to win policy contests even in the face of majorities who prefer a cleaner environment.

International Winners and Losers

Environmental issues also divide developed and developing countries. Historically, the largest polluters have been rich states in Europe and North America. Since 1950, nearly 70 percent of cumulative carbon emissions have been released by these countries. Even today, the United States uses far more energy and emits far more pollutants per capita than any other country. With 4.5 percent of the world's population, the United States emits almost 15 percent of the world's carbon. Worldwide, the average individual produces 5 metric tons of carbon each year. The average American emits 16.4 tons per year, more than in any other country other than Australia (Japan, a state at a comparable level of economic development, averages 10.4 metric tons per person per year).[16] The developed countries have by far the largest cumulative and ongoing impact on the environment.

The greatest source of new pollutants in the future will be the developing countries. As China industrializes, its carbon emissions—which now constitute about 29 percent of the world's total—will continue to rise. Although China emits only about 7.2 metric tons of carbon per person per year, about 50 percent of the level in the United States, its absolute level of emissions could exceed that of the United States, the European Union, and India combined by 2019.[17] Heavily dependent on coal for energy, China already leads the world in sulfur oxide and nitrogen oxide emissions.[18] Aerial particulates from burning coal, overgrazing, and soil erosion already blow from China to Korea, Japan, the Pacific Islands, and within a week to

---

15. Even here, however, the logic of winners and losers comes into play. Corn's net energy balance—the amount of energy it yields relative to the amount of energy required to produce it—is lower than sugar-based alternatives. Nonetheless, corn farmers have successfully lobbied for subsidies to promote corn-based ethanol. In turn, the United States is comparatively disadvantaged in producing sugar. High tariffs on imported sugar raise the price so that it is not cost-effective to use it for ethanol. The concentrated benefits of tariffs for American sugar producers and subsidies for corn growers are leading the United States toward an ethanol policy that will cost consumers more in the long run. But at pennies per gallon more for ethanol, few consumers will feel motivated to fight the more highly motivated interests in the sugar and corn lobbies.

16. C. Le Quéré et al., "Global Carbon Budget 2014," *Earth System Science Data Discussions*, doi: 10.5194/essdd-7-521-2014, www.globalcarbonproject.org/carbonbudget/14/contributions.htm (accessed 09/21/14); and Jos G. J. Olivier, Greet Janssens-Maenhout, Marilena Muntean, and Jeroen A. H. W. Peters, "Trends in Global CO$_2$ Emissions: 2013 Report" (The Hague, Netherlands: PBL Netherlands Environmental Assessment Agency, 2013).

17. C. Le Quéré et al., "Global Carbon Budget 2014."

18. Li Li, Jianhua Xu, Jianxin Hu, and Jiarui Han, "Reducing Nitrous Oxide Emissions to Mitigate Climate Change and Protect the Ozone Layer," *Environmental Science & Technology* 48, no. 9 (2014): 5290–97. The authors find that if current trends continue, China will emit five times as much nitrous oxide as the United States by 2020.

the United States. As China industrializes further, its emissions of these chemicals and particulates will increase dramatically.[19] Although China's large population and growing economy put its environmental practices on the front pages of the world's newspapers, the same story could be told for virtually every other developing country. Development has always been a dirty business—and it still is.

In addition, some of the easiest steps to prevent further environmental degradation could be taken in the developing world. It is much less expensive to reduce emissions and pollutants in developing than developed countries. As a direct result of the environmental movement and government legislation, many of the sources of pollution that are easiest to correct have already been addressed in developed countries, whereas developing countries are just beginning the process of installing cleaner technologies (Map 13.1). To reduce an extra ton of emissions from an already relatively clean European steel mill, for instance, is far more costly than to cut an equivalent ton from an Indian or Indonesian steel mill that has never used smokestack scrubbers. This is a key rationale behind the ETS adopted by the European Union that allows allows its firms, facing high costs to reduce further their emissions, to buy carbon credits from developing countries, where the costs of reducing an equivalent amount of carbon are much lower. Similarly, it is cheaper to maintain the earth's tropical rain forests in developing countries than it is to reforest areas in North America; and it is more effective to maintain biodiversity in these forests than to wait for nature to reproduce the variety that once existed in replanted North American forests.

There are strong ethical concerns created by the tension between development and the need to preserve the environment. Research indicates that environmental quality falls with economic growth and industrialization and then begins to improve once national income per capita rises above approximately $17,500 per year[20] (see "How Do We Know?" on p. 552). Below that level of income, most citizens in most countries seem to be more concerned with improving their quality of daily life—educating their children, getting electricity to rural villages to power appliances, finding cheap modes of transportation to expand markets and job opportunities—than with improving the quality of the environment per se. As China's income rises, estimated to be $12,900 in 2014, environmental movements are already forming, but for countries like India, with per capita annual income of only $5,800, the day when indigenous environmental movements are likely to arise and demand change from their governments is decades in the future. Until then, pressure to maintain environmental quality in most developing countries will continue to come from foreign environmental TANs and governments in developed countries.

Even recognizing that they have a disproportionate responsibility for cleaning up the environment, because of both their past practices and their relatively greater

---

19. On China and the environment, see Jianguo Liu and Jared Diamond, "China's Environment in a Globalizing World," *Nature* 435 (June 30, 2005): 1179–86.

20. Gene N. Grossman and Alan B. Krueger, "Economic Growth and the Environment," *Quarterly Journal of Economics* 110, no. 2 (1995): 353–77. Their figure of $8,000 (in 1985 dollars) is converted to current dollars in the text.

MAP 13.1 *Environmental Performance Index, 2014*

The EPI is an overall measure of environmental protection and is explained in more detail in "How Do We Know?" on page 552. A higher score indicates a better performance on environmental issues. The map shows countries on the EPI by quintiles. As a region, Europe is the "greenest," with most countries there scoring in the top fifth. The lowest performers, shown in red, are in Africa. The United States and China rank 33rd and 118th respectively.

Overall EPI Score by Country Quintile

- 66.6–87.7
- 53.5–66.5
- 45.2–53.4
- 36.1–45.1
- 15.5–36.0
- NO DATA

Map source: http://epi.yale.edu/downloads (accessed 09/20/14).

Arctic Ocean

RUSSIA

NORWAY

SWEDEN

FINLAND

UNITED KINGDOM

GERMANY

BELARUS

IRELAND

FRANCE

UKRAINE

KAZAKHSTAN

MONGOLIA

N. KOREA

S. KOREA

GEORGIA

ITALY

SPAIN

GREECE

TURKEY

UZBEKISTAN

KYRGYZSTAN

TAJIKISTAN

CHINA

JAPAN

Pacific Ocean

MOROCCO

ISRAEL

LEB.

SYRIA

IRAQ

IRAN

NEPAL

BHUTAN

HONG KONG

JORDAN

KUWAIT

TURKMENISTAN

TAIWAN

ALGERIA

LIBYA

EGYPT

SAUDI ARABIA

UAE

MYANMAR (BURMA)

MAURITANIA

GAL

MALI

NIGER

CHAD

SUDAN

ERITREA

YEMEN

OMAN

PAKISTAN

INDIA

VIETNAM

PHILIPPINES

GUINEA

NIGERIA

AFGHANISTAN

THAILAND

LAOS

CEN. AFR. REP.

S. SUDAN

ETHIOPIA

BANGLADESH

CAMBODIA

CAMEROON

GHANA

UGANDA

KENYA

SOMALIA

SRI LANKA

MALAYSIA

IVORY COAST

D.R. CONGO

PAPUA NEW GUINEA

TANZANIA

INDONESIA

Indian Ocean

ANGOLA

MALAWI

SOLOMON ISLANDS

ZAMBIA

NAMIBIA

MADAGASCAR

MOZAMBIQUE

ZIMBABWE

AUSTRALIA

SOUTH AFRICA

BOTSWANA

NEW ZEALAND

Patterns of Environmental Performance

Environmental protections vary widely across countries, regions, and income levels. The Center for Environmental Law and Policy at Yale University and the Center for International Earth Science Information Network at Columbia University have developed a composite environmental performance index (EPI) for 178 countries. It provides a common way to measure countries' performance on a range of important environmental issues (see Map 13.1). The index was created from 25 indicators of environmental health and ecosystem vitality and ranges, in principle, from 0 to 100 and, in practice, from 15 (Somalia) to 88 (Switzerland) in 2014.

Environmental performance typically rises with income. On average, richer countries perform better and poorer countries usually perform worse. Figure A compares GDP per capita (in 2013) with the EPI index for the countries around the world.

Fitting a line that reflects the relationship between income and the EPI index immediately reveals three key insights. First, the relationship between per capita income and environmental performance is mostly positive. Over much of the range, the curve is positively sloped. This means that as countries become wealthier, on average, their environmental performance increases. Some of the most wealthy states per capita, however, are themselves oil producers, especially Norway and Qatar, and have relatively low levels of environmental performance, which pulls the curve down.

Second, countries above the line perform better on the environmental index than other countries with the same level of per capita income. Countries below the line perform worse relative to their peers. Among poor countries, Zimbabwe and Egypt stand out as high performers, whereas Angola compares unfavorably with this same group. Among richer countries, the

Czech Republic, Spain, and Switzerland are exceptionally high performers, and the United States and Canada are well below the line and underperform relative to other high-income countries.

Third, there is much greater dispersion of environmental performance among the upper-income countries. This implies that some countries that could afford to protect their environment better choose not to do so. Very poor countries, clustered more tightly around the line at the left side of the graph, have little discretion. Most of their citizens are struggling to feed their families and rise above a subsistence level of living. At the highest level of income, however, countries do have a choice whether to invest in environmental protection. They reach different decisions based on the interests of politically important constituencies and the national political institutions that translate interests into environmental policy in different ways.

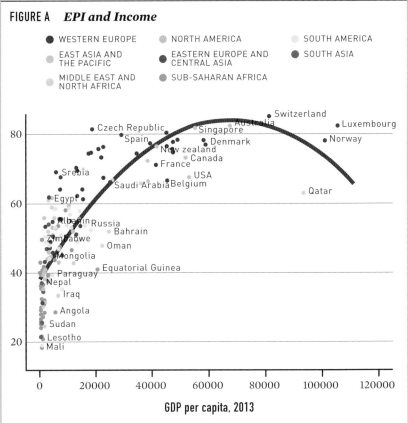

FIGURE A *EPI and Income*

- WESTERN EUROPE
- EAST ASIA AND THE PACIFIC
- MIDDLE EAST AND NORTH AFRICA
- NORTH AMERICA
- EASTERN EUROPE AND CENTRAL ASIA
- SUB-SAHARAN AFRICA
- SOUTH AMERICA
- SOUTH ASIA

GDP per capita, 2013

Source: http://epi.yale.edu/downloads (accessed 09/20/14).

present wealth, some developed countries still want to link their efforts to greater contributions by developing countries (see "Controversy" on p. 554). Opponents criticized the Kyoto Protocol for placing an unreasonable burden on the United States while exempting developing countries, especially China, from reducing their emissions. Overcoming this divide between developed and developing countries, in turn, was central to the success of the Lima Accord. Even if the national plans to be submitted under that agreement do not themselves contain significant cutbacks in carbon emissions by developing countries, the principle that all countries share in the responsibility for reducing emissions has been squarely established.

Bargaining over the Future Environment

Alternative policy solutions create gains and losses for different groups. Industries prefer that consumers or taxpayers pay to clean up their environmental waste, and developing countries prefer that developed countries restrict their pollutants more severely so that they (the developing countries) can industrialize at lower cost. Even though everyone may gain from cooperation, each actor prefers a different policy outcome. As shown in Figure 2.3 in Chapter 2 (p. 57), cooperation creates net gains through a movement toward the Pareto frontier, but actors will still bargain over where on the frontier a policy will settle. Cooperation and bargaining occur simultaneously. The political fight is not about the need for protecting the environment but about who bears the costs of a cleaner environment.

Often, the political battle results in compromise. In the European ETS discussed previously, economists argued that the most efficient system would be to auction emissions credits equal to total output, thereby allocating the credits to those firms that needed them the most and generating income for the governments involved. Instead, at the insistence of firms, the credits were initially given free to existing companies based on current emissions levels. This move allowed the firms to pass higher costs along to consumers while at the same time selling their credits in the ETS. Great Britain's power-generation sector pocketed a net profit on emissions trading alone of $1.5 billion in 2005, the first year of operation. Other industries, initially excluded from the ETS but desiring the higher profits, are now clamoring for a similar trading system—and even firms in the United States are warming to the idea of a cap-and-trade system based on the same principles—though there has been no real action on this front.[21] In the European case, although firms were capped on their emissions and had to buy credits to offset any excess, the net effect was to pay producers a hefty subsidy to reduce emissions in developing countries. Environmentalists got what they wanted—lower global emissions—but at a substantial cost to consumers in European countries.

Sometimes, however, the fight is sufficiently intense that it has blocked movements toward greater cooperation. Paradoxically, the more we care about the future and about the future environment, the more that is at stake and the more intense

---

21. "The Heat Is On," 17–20.

Who Should Bear the Costs of Addressing Global Climate Change?

Nepal's Sagarmatha National Park features an expanse of snowy ranges, ancient glaciers, deep gorges, and the ancient villages of the Sherpa people. It is also home to the rare snow leopard, musk deer, and red panda. Recently, however, Nepal has been experiencing a warming trend. In a development that scientists believe to be human-induced climate change, the average air temperature has risen by double the global average in the Himalayan region over the past 40 years, and in the past decade two-thirds of the range's glaciers have retreated.[a] Global warming will eventually affect everyone, but it affects some far more than others, and the disparity is already being felt. If these trends continue, the regions surrounding Nepal will be devastated first by floods as glaciers melt more rapidly and then by water shortages affecting a full third of the world's population. Homes, livelihoods, and cultures will be destroyed; famine, disease, and conflict will rage; some plants and animals will become extinct.

Everyone agrees that such outcomes would be tragic, affecting not just Nepal but also the rest of the world. Indeed, Nepal is a relatively "green" country compared to others at its level of per capita income (see "How Do We Know?" on p. 552), but it is affected by the emissions of others over which it has almost no influence. Halting global climate change constitutes a global public good. Yet there is also intense bargaining over which countries ought to bear the burdens of mitigating change. What sort of bargain would be fair? Who should bear the costs of change?

A Nepalese might reason as follows. Developed countries have made by far the largest contributions to current greenhouse gas concentrations. Carbon remains in the atmosphere for up to a century. Most of the carbon now warming the atmosphere was emitted by the developed countries in their own race to industrialize. Rich countries also have a much higher standard of living than Nepal and its neighbors do, meaning that those countries are both better able to protect their populations from the effects of climate change and better able to absorb the costs of environmental preservation without imposing unbearable sacrifices on their citizens. Together, these twin facts—responsibility and capacity—suggest that the developed world ought to bear the costs of reducing future carbon emissions.

An American might object that it is unfair for the United States to reduce its future emissions when developing countries—including some very large carbon emitters—are not being asked to make similar sacrifices. Nepal and especially its neighbors China and India would be free riding on U.S. efforts. The American might admit that the United States has been a major contributor historically but would likely point out that future emissions from developing countries will be many times greater than the cutbacks envisioned in any current international negotiations. Even if the rich countries substantially alter their policies, the effects will be swamped in the future by even greater emissions by developing countries. Substantial progress on reducing emissions requires the participation of all countries. The American might also emphasize that much of the country's past emissions occurred at a time when no one knew of the environmental dangers. Today's developing countries cannot use ignorance as an excuse. Finally, she might add, the same U.S. economic activity that has contributed to the melting of the Himalayan glaciers has also resulted in important benefits for the Nepalese by contributing to the worldwide dispersion of a range of products and technologies.

A Nepalese might reply that the ability to buy a TV, say, is not of much use when one's house has been swept away by floods. He could also point out that asking Nepal or other developing countries to reduce their future emissions would increase their production costs, thereby stalling their progress toward the level of economic development

a. J. Thomas and S. Rai, "An Overview of Glaciers, Glacier Retreat, and Subsequent Impacts in Nepal, India and China" (Kathmandu, Nepal: WWF Nepal Program, 2005), http://assets.panda.org/downloads/himalayaglaciersreport2005.pdf (accessed 01/16/09).

that industrialized countries have enjoyed for decades. Here the American might claim that at least the large polluters China and India ought to take up some of the burden, especially since a cleanup of their "dirty" industries would provide a more efficient means of reducing emissions than would additional efforts by the already cleaner industries of the developed world. But does country size carry unequal burdens? Does a Chinese have less of a right to increase his income than does a Nepalese just because the former lives in a large rather than a small country?

Some observers suggest that the simplest and most politically acceptable option would be to wipe the slate clean and assign each person an equal right to a fixed amount of future emissions.[b] If these rights were tradable, they would both benefit developing countries with initially low emissions and create incentives for reductions to occur where they could be achieved most inexpensively. Any such plan, however, would inevitably raise the costs of energy in the developed countries, where per capita emissions are already high, and transfer benefits to the developing countries, where per capita emissions are generally lower. This would likely run afoul of the same political cleavages described above. Could this proposal serve as a fair and workable basis for future international collaboration?

With continued resistance in many countries to significant cutbacks in carbon emissions, fairness is unlikely to be the principal criterion for success. As with other disputes, agreements reflect the bargaining power of the countries on either side of the issue. The emerging plan, embodied in the Lima Accord, is to establish the principle of universal participation in halting climate change while allowing countries to establish their own programs for reducing carbon emissions. Yet, while we continue to argue and begin the planned cutbacks only in 2025, snow and ice will continue to melt in the Himalayas.

b. Peter Singer, *One World: The Ethics of Globalization* (New Haven, CT: Yale University Press, 2002), 35, 43–44.

this political fight will be. For the winners from environmental protection, a higher value on the future environment mobilizes supporters into the political arena to change policy. Because they care more about the future, they are willing to exert greater effort today in promoting policies to protect that environment. The longer into the future the winners look, the more likely they are to forgo agreement today in hopes of getting a better agreement that guarantees their preferred policies for a longer period. Each day that passes without significant political progress means that more carbon is accumulating in the atmosphere. But even though the immediate environment might suffer from a lack of cooperation, a better bargain over a longer period might make such a delay worthwhile.

For the losers from tighter environmental regulations, a higher value on the future may also mobilize them into the political arena to try to protect the favorable policies they now enjoy. Policies that greatly reduce carbon emissions, for instance, will reduce profits in industries that depend on fossil fuels not only today but also in the years ahead. Burning less fossil fuel will not only reduce profits for oil companies but also reduce the value of the oil reserves they own. Higher costs of production not only lower incomes in developing countries in the present but reduce growth and income in the future too. The greater the value we place on the future, the more important the environment is to the winners—but the more important the costs of complying with greater regulations are to the losers as well.

When industries and environmentalists or rich and poor countries bargain, they struggle over the division of gains today and over the division of gains in the future as well. Thus, the greater the value we place on the future, the larger are the consequences of a bad bargain for either side. The result can be a political stalemate. Such a deadlock arose over global climate change, though it may be cracking with the Lima Accord. The future of the global environment is at stake, but so is the future of those industries and countries that depend on fossil fuels. The stakes are high not just because of the present but also because any agreement is likely to impact both the environment and the affected industries and countries far into the future.

Coupled with the problem of bargaining over the future is the equally difficult problem of representing future generations in current decision making. After all, no political system possesses a mechanism that represents the interests of future citizens to the present generation. Given the notoriously short attention spans of politicians, who are often driven only by the next election, who in any political system represents the interests of future citizens and voters? We know little about the interests of future generations. Although we can extrapolate from our current preferences, many factors can intervene. We do not know what the future rate of technological change will be, which may make various environmental problems easier or harder to solve than we expect. Assuming that wealth and incomes continue to rise, we do not know how future citizens may evaluate yet more consumption of physical goods, like cars, relative to consumption of intangible goods, like the scenic beauty of an unspoiled coastline or old-growth forest.

Even if we could estimate future interests, there is no one at present to advocate for those future generations in any systematic way. In bargaining between actors at a single moment in time, the winners and losers can choose to be actively involved, or not, in the political process. In bargaining between domestic groups, the winners and losers of alternative policies can fight for themselves, if they so choose. But there is no realistic way of representing future generations in present political decisions. Environmental TANs often claim that they are representing future generations, but their political clout is still limited. Future generations neither vote now nor pay membership dues to TANs that can, in turn, press governments to change policy. TANs can make normative arguments on behalf of future generations, but this is at best an indirect and significantly weaker form of representation than if the future citizens' votes and voices could be heard today. As a consequence, we are bargaining with ourselves on behalf of future generations—and it is perhaps not surprising that we usually let ourselves win.

How Can Institutions Promote International Environmental Cooperation?

Within countries, governments play an important role in mitigating externalities. Producing public goods and regulating the use of common-pool resources are fundamental roles for any government. States can command citizens to contribute to public goods and limit their exploitation of common-pool resources, or they can impose legal penalties. Historically, and even in some developing countries today, governments demand that their citizens contribute a number of days of labor per year to build and repair roads, irrigation systems, and other public works. In all but the so-called failed states, governments tax citizens and use the revenue to provide a variety of public goods, including national defense, police and fire protection, public infrastructure, public health, education, and, of course, environmental protection. Governments also impose restrictions on automobile emissions, the dumping of toxic waste, oil drilling, and so on that aim to improve environmental quality and use scarce resources more efficiently. Government is not a perfect solution (as continuing environmental problems within countries demonstrate only too clearly), but its ability to allocate resources authoritatively helps mitigate collective action problems that would otherwise make environmental cooperation even more difficult.

National laws and policies are the primary means for implementing international environmental cooperation. Even if states create international institutions, most of their provisions are enforced authoritatively through national legislation and policy. For instance, the LRTAP convention and its eight subsequent protocols, all designed to reduce acid rain, required participating states to reduce sulfur emissions by at least 30 percent, based on 1980 levels, and to reduce nitrogen oxide emissions to their 1987 levels. The treaty did not mandate how states would achieve these cuts. Instead, individual states implemented these targets through changes in national laws and regulations. Similarly, the Lima Accord will ultimately depend on national plans to reduce carbon emissions. Transnational environmental problems and solutions still require strong, effective national governments to transform aspirations into practice.

In international relations, there is no higher authority that can compel states to cooperate in mitigating externalities. On global environmental issues, states are limited to voluntary cooperation implemented by laws passed at the national level. Relative to externalities regulated by authoritative governments, international cooperation between sovereign states will always be more difficult and tenuous. States free-ride on one another's efforts and overexploit their shared resources. Institutions are not a panacea. In the absence of interests in environmental cooperation and effective bargains between countries, international institutions cannot by themselves create success. Institutions can only be as strong as the interests in cooperation. Nonetheless, as we saw in Chapter 2, international institutions facilitate cooperation among states committed to a cleaner environment by setting standards and verifying compliance, with lesser roles for reducing decision-making costs and resolving disputes.

Setting Standards and Verifying Compliance

International environmental institutions support cooperation by establishing clear standards of behavior to which states can be held accountable. Although each issue area and agreement has unique features and histories, countries often negotiate framework conventions that establish general principles to which all states can agree. The Convention on Biological Diversity, for instance, states that diversity is "a common concern of humankind" that all countries have a duty to protect; the document includes additional principles for the development and use of genetic resources. The Lima Accord aimed at reducing carbon emissions has a similar structure. After establishing such frameworks, states proceed in some issue areas to negotiate more stringent environmental safeguards specifying limits on emissions, banning certain practices, or otherwise defining unacceptable behavior. The series of protocols and amendments subsequently attached to the **Vienna Convention** for the Protection of the Ozone Layer (enacted in 1985) illustrate this common trajectory. Beginning with a general framework, additional agreements—including the **Montreal Protocol** (in force in 1989)—specified progressively deeper cuts in emissions and increased the range of restricted chemicals and practices.[22]

Vienna Convention

A framework convention adopted in 1985 to regulate activities, especially emissions of CFCs, that damage the ozone layer.

Montreal Protocol

An international treaty, signed in 1989, that is designed to protect the ozone layer by phasing out the production of a number of CFCs and other chemical compounds.

---

22. A second pattern of negotiations and agreements is simply to establish a procedural regime with a commission that makes annual decisions about regulatory rules. The IWC is an example of this type of organization. On patterns of agreement formation, see Oran R. Young, *International Governance: Protecting the Environment in a Stateless Society* (Ithaca, NY: Cornell University Press, 1994), esp. chap. 4.

Restrictions on the intentional discharge of crude oil at sea demonstrate how the clarity and transparency of the standard matter in supporting cooperation.[23] After a tanker delivers its cargo of crude oil, an average of 300 tons remains onboard, stuck to the cargo tank walls. Before regulations were put into effect, ships would clean their tanks on the return voyage by pumping seawater into the tanks and discharging the slop back into the ocean. With many ships making multiple trips each year, oil tankers were intentionally discharging approximately 1 million tons of oil into the ocean annually. In the International Convention for the Prevention of Pollution of the Seas by Oil, adopted in 1954, countries first set standards that permitted tankers to continue cleaning tanks with seawater but mandated that discharges be no more than 100 parts oil per million parts seawater. The standard was subsequently tightened in 1969. Nonetheless, both the looser and the tighter standards were widely ignored. Oil company surveys from the 1970s show that tankers owned by the oil companies themselves averaged discharges of 3 times the legal limit and that independently owned tankers averaged discharges of 30 times the legal limit.

In 1978, countries adopted new standards that required all tankers to use new but more expensive technologies that minimized discharges by preventing the oil and seawater from coming into contact or by using crude oil itself to wash the tanks. These new technologies were required for all tankers built after 1982, and all existing tankers had to be retrofitted by 1985. Despite the greater cost, compliance rates rose over to over 98 percent by 1991.

What explains the difference? Since cleaning the tanks with seawater usually took place on the open ocean, far from other observers, ship captains could act with impunity and ignore mandated discharge limits—and it appears that they usually did. The new technologies, in contrast, required the installation of clearly observable equipment on every ship. On entering port, it could easily be verified whether the tanker met with the new standard. The ease of verification forced tanker captains to alter their behavior, virtually ending the intentional discharge of crude oil into the ocean.

For similar reasons, complete bans are easier to verify than restrictions on emissions; this fact helps to account for the success of the Vienna Convention and subsequent amendments outlawing CFCs. With CFCs, as with the ban on whaling or endangered wildlife, any possession or trade in prohibited substances is

The effectiveness of environmental regulations may depend on how easy it is to verify compliance. A change in the rules related to dumping oil at sea made it much easier to check whether ship captains were adhering to the standard, and increased compliance rates to over 98 percent.

23. This case is drawn from Ronald B. Mitchell, "Regime Design Matters: Intentional Oil Pollution and Treaty Compliance," *International Organization* 48, no. 3 (Summer 1994): 425–58.

sufficient evidence of noncompliance. Enforcement efforts can then focus on tracking down any sales of CFCs (or elephant ivory, rhinoceros horns, and other banned goods). Soon after the major cuts in CFCs went into effect, for instance, the black market grew to about 20 percent of prior consumption. In 1995, the illegal trade in CFCs in the Port of Miami and along the U.S.-Mexican border was second in value only to trade in illegal drugs, prompting a unilateral effort by the United States to block the smuggling. The important point is that the clear rules banning CFCs allowed this crackdown to occur. Restrictions on carbon emissions, in turn, are harder to enforce, especially when many independent agents, such as firms, are potentially contributing to the problem. Evidence of some carbon in the atmosphere is not evidence of cheating. Only consistent monitoring of emissions over long periods can demonstrate that a country is failing to live up to its commitments on global warming—a much more daunting task.

In addition to official monitoring and reporting, environmental TANs have been central in verifying compliance with international environmental accords. Most environmental agreements depend on self-reporting of emissions. As we noted in Chapter 2, self-reporting is effective only when reports are subject to external verification. TANs often play the role of fire alarm, sounding the alert when governments violate agreements or fail to report accurately. By calling attention to failures to live up to the letter and, sometimes, the spirit of the agreements, TANs assist member states in identifying and bringing pressure on noncomplying governments. The by now dense network of committed environmental activists relieves governments of much of the responsibility for monitoring one another's performance, thereby facilitating and enhancing the prospects for successful cooperation.

As one example of TAN monitoring, as we saw earlier in the chapter, the IWC instituted a complete ban on whaling in 1982. After phasing out its commercial operations, Japan continued to engage in scientific whaling, which aims to demonstrate that whale populations are robust enough to permit some commercial whaling. Much of the whale meat nonetheless ends up for sale in Japanese fish markets. Prior to the International Court of Justice's (ICJ's) declaration that its scientific whaling program was illegal, Japan caught approximately 800 whales per year for self-declared scientific purposes, about the same as Norway's commercial catch (along with Iceland, the only country to defy the ban completely) and all aboriginal whaling catches combined (which are exempt from the ban). Japan has declared that it intends to continue this program even after the ICJ's ruling. Although it is impossible to police the entire ocean, the limited scope of scientific whaling allows NGOs to track the whaling fleets, observe their operations, often film the killing, and catalog each whale caught. Each season, ships from Greenpeace, an international environmental action group, have shadowed the Japanese fleet, sometimes attempting to disrupt its operations by harassing the factory ships and placing themselves between the hunters and their prey. Countries report their scientific whaling activities to the IWC every year, and as a result of these efforts by the NGOs, relatively accurate independent verification of these self-reports is possible.

Facilitating Decision Making

Even though international environmental institutions do not, for the most part, have highly developed governing bodies or rules, they do facilitate decision making between states. As the Vienna Convention has been modified and its provisions strengthened, it has developed a clear administrative structure. There are now rules for adjustments in controlled substances that do not require further national ratifications, and there is a supermajority requirement of two-thirds of the participating states for substantive changes to the agreement. The **Framework Convention on Climate Change (FCCC)** is perhaps more typical of other environmental agreements. Although it includes a Conference of the Parties (COP) for elaborating rules, it is primarily a forum for ongoing negotiations rather than a body with established procedures for reaching decisions.[24] Agreements frequently proceed by consensus decision making and often contain clauses allowing countries to opt in or opt out of specific obligations. Yet even framework agreements that are limited to unanimity can be important in setting a direction for future negotiations and creating a forum for continuing diplomacy. As suggested by the history of agreements on ozone-depleting substances, initial frameworks outlining the goals of environmental cooperation often generate substantive agreements and protocols. The initial agreement, in other words, provides a forum that channels progress within the issue area.

Environmental TANs also provide important policy input for international agreements, creating a nearly unique international public-private partnership on the environment that facilitates cooperation. At the UN Conference on Environment and Development in 1992—the so-called Earth Summit—that produced both the Convention on Biological Diversity and the FCCC, over 10,000 NGOs were accredited to participate. In a parallel conference, these organizations helped set the agenda, provided policy input, and brought pressure to bear on the negotiations. This role is now institutionalized in the FCCC, which allows any qualified organization to be admitted to meetings and negotiations unless at least one-third of the member states present object.[25] Many observers credit the success of the summit to the important role played by the TANs.

Resolving Disputes

International environmental agreements generally lack dispute resolution mechanisms. Few such agreements contain autonomous or independent procedures for resolving disputes; rather, most treaties depend on the good faith of countries themselves to work out disagreements within a multilateral setting. The Montreal

Framework Convention on Climate Change (FCCC)

An international agreement enacted in 1992, and entered into force in 1994, that provided an overall framework for intergovernmental efforts on climate change.

---

24. Indeed, the COP's rules remain a source of contention, with disagreement over whether the conference can proceed with a two-thirds supermajority vote or whether all decisions must be unanimous. See Daniel Bodansky, "International Law and the Design of a Climate Change Regime," in *International Relations and Global Climate Change*, ed. Urs Luterbacher and Detlef F. Sprinz, 212–13 (Cambridge, MA: MIT Press, 2001).

25. Kal Raustiala, "Nonstate Actors in the Global Climate Regime," in Luterbacher and Sprinz, *International Relations and Global Climate Change*, 96, 99.

Protocol to the Vienna Convention, however, was the first global environmental agreement to develop and use a noncompliance response system, located in its Implementation Committee. This mechanism remains focused on facilitating, not enforcing, compliance. During the 1990s, it became clear that several countries from the former Soviet Union (including Belarus, Russia, and Ukraine), as well as some developing countries, were not in full compliance with their emissions obligations. This led the Implementation Committee to urge and finally approve new phaseout plans, with additional financial resources from other industrialized countries, the Global Environmental Facility, and the World Bank facilitating compliance. In the Kyoto Protocol, often described as a model for dispute resolution for future environmental compacts, a Compliance Committee comprises a facilitative branch and an enforcement branch.[26] As its name suggests, the facilitative branch provides advice to the member states on how to implement the protocol. The enforcement branch can find a state to be in violation of the agreement, but its sole sanction is to request the member state to make up the difference between its targeted and actual emissions, plus an additional 30 percent, in a future period or to suspend its participation in the carbon trading plan. Most environmental agreements simply refer the disputing parties to mediation or the ICJ, options to which the states are entitled under international law anyway. Some environmental provisions are attached to regional trade agreements and can be adjudicated under the specialized dispute settlement procedures they contain. This is an area for future progress in international environmental institutions.

Conclusion: Can Global Environmental Cooperation Succeed?

We began this chapter asking why international environmental cooperation is so hard to achieve. To answer that puzzle and tie the threads of our analysis together, we can compare the relative success of international environmental cooperation on ozone depletion and the much slower progress of states on global climate change. Both ozone depletion and global climate change became issues at around the same time. The first convention on ozone depletion was negotiated in 1985, the first on global climate change in 1992. What accounts for the difference in the two outcomes? How can the analytic tools of interests, interactions, and institutions help us understand why we find successful international cooperation in the first case, and only limited cooperation to date in the second?

---

26. See http://unfccc.int/kyoto_protocol/compliance/introduction/items/3024.php (accessed 09/20/14).

Large-scale protests swept New York City in September 2014, demanding action on climate change. The largest environmental protests in decades called attention to global warming but failed to put forward a well-defined strategy for change.

At its root, the answer to our puzzle is quite simple. People's daily actions create significant externalities for the environment and one another. These externalities, in turn, produce severe problems of collective action. Individuals and countries would like to benefit from a cleaner environment but would also like others to bear the costs of protecting environmental quality. Both the stratospheric ozone layer and the quantity of greenhouse gases in the atmosphere are global public goods. Although everyone benefits from a thicker ozone layer and fewer greenhouse gases, and everyone is harmed by CFC and carbon emissions, this may be precisely the problem. Since we all share the benefits of a healthy atmosphere and we all face private costs in changing our behavior, we all attempt to free-ride on one another, hoping to reap the benefits of a greener environment without having to give up our current lifestyles.

In the case of ozone depletion, the gains from a ban far exceeded the costs of change. Although the cost of transitioning to new chemical alternatives was estimated to be $27 billion by 2075, the Environmental Protection Agency calculated that the reduced skin cancers for Americans alone would save $6.5 trillion in medical costs over the same period.[27] In the case of climate change, however, there are large immediate and continuing costs for reducing carbon emissions, and only long-term benefits, the magnitude of which depend on the exact rise in global temperatures—which no one can predict accurately. Reflecting again the central role of fossil fuels in the modern economy, reducing carbon emissions by 50 percent—the level necessary to stabilize concentrations at current levels—will cost between 2 and 8 percent of world product (the sum of economic

27. Litfin, *Ozone Discourses*, 128.

activity or gross domestic product [GDP] in all countries) in perpetuity. Failing to curb greenhouse gases, in contrast, will cost the United States, by one estimate, only about 0.25 percent of its annual GDP in the future. Other countries will bear higher costs, particularly those nearer the equator or with low-lying territories. Yet in most economic estimates, the total costs of a warmer climate are typically less than 2 percent of global product. Pointing this out is not to advocate doing nothing. There may be advantages to a less polluted environment that are not captured in models of future economic income. These estimates, in turn, do not consider the worst-case scenarios posited by some scientists. But given the balance between large immediate and continuing costs and only long-term benefits, it is not surprising that few politicians want to push hard for reducing the emission of greenhouse gases.

Although both issues involve collective action problems, cooperation in ozone depletion was easier to achieve due to the highly concentrated nature of the CFC industry—both in a relatively small number of firms and within a relatively small number of countries, with most production and usage occurring in just a handful of developed states. The smaller number of firms and countries involved lowered the costs of collective action and made effective cooperation possible. The United States enjoyed a preeminent position in the industry as both the largest producer and consumer of CFCs. Its leadership on the issue was decisive.

Second, the problem of collective action is compounded by the distributional consequences of alternative policy solutions, especially in the case of global climate change. Every policy creates winners and losers, but the benefits of eliminating CFCs were clear. In the case of climate change, in contrast, hydrocarbon fuels are the lifeblood of modern economies, and the interests that would lose from any significant change in policy are large and politically powerful. To date, these vested interests have played upon the basic incentive of all actors to free-ride to block any policy change—and postpone the day of final reckoning.

Finally, international institutions have played a role in facilitating and codifying cooperation in both ozone depletion and global climate change. Negotiations have occurred within meetings of global leaders, and the agreements reached at these meetings have been institutionalized into conventions and subsequently amended in various protocols. Both began with conventions outlining broad principles of cooperation and then moved on to substantive cuts in subsequent agreements. Greater cooperation on ozone depletion has been helped by relatively clear rules reducing and, later, banning specific chemicals. The rules governing reductions in carbon and other greenhouse gases, in contrast, are less well articulated, perhaps because the underlying issues remain highly contested.

Success and failure are, of course, relative terms. The damage to the ozone layer from past emissions of CFCs will continue for another century. We may be witnessing the first signs of global warming in more severe storms and other more subtle changes in ecology, but its effects are almost certain to grow in the future. Many factors contributed to the relative success of the Vienna Convention and its subsequent amendments, which helped bring about the restrictions on CFC production. The case stands out for its clear lesson that countries can cooperate quickly and effectively when the prospective harm to the environment is sufficiently large, the costs of alternative practices are sufficiently small, and it is possible to design clear and verifiable standards. Although we continue to live with the consequences of our past emissions, the ability of countries to rally together to halt harmful practices and begin to reverse the damage to the ozone layer gives reason for cautious optimism for the future of our shared planet.

Study Tool Kit

Interests, Interactions, and Institutions in Context

- Despite widely shared interests in the quality of the environment, the interactions of individuals as well as countries suffer from problems of collective action. In the absence of any international authority that can mandate improved performance, the net result is less overall environmental cooperation than individuals and even countries themselves collectively desire.

- Small groups of actors, one of whom is substantially larger than the others and all of whom interact frequently on multiple issues, are most likely to cooperate effectively on issues relating to the international environment.

- Individuals, groups, and countries have conflicting interests over who bears the costs of mitigating harmful environmental practices. How environmental policies distribute these costs affects how likely actors are to cooperate successfully on issues relating to the environment.

- International institutions facilitate environmental cooperation primarily by enhancing information and verifying compliance. TANs and other NGOs now play an essential role in monitoring compliance with environmental agreements. The clearer and more easily verified the standard, the more likely states are to cooperate successfully.

Key Terms

externalities, p. 536

nonexcludable, p. 537

chlorofluorocarbons (CFCs), p. 537

ozone layer, p. 537

global climate change, p. 537

nonrival in consumption, p. 537

Kyoto Protocol, p. 537

cap-and-trade, p. 538

common-pool resources, p. 538

overexploitation, p. 539

Vienna Convention, p. 558

Montreal Protocol, p. 558

Framework Convention on Climate Change (FCCC), p. 561

For Further Reading

Gampfer, R., T. Bernauer, and A. Kachi. "Obtaining Public Support for North–South Climate Funding: Evidence from Conjoint Experiments in Donor Countries." *Global Environmental Change* 29 (2014): 118–26. Examines public opinion on financing schemes to resolve North-South conflict on the environment.

Gore, Albert. *An Inconvenient Truth: The Planetary Emergency of Global Warming and What We Can Do about It*. Emmaus, PA: Rodale Press, 2006. Highlights the dangers of global warming and calls for urgent action.

Klein, Naomi. *This Changes Everything: Capitalism vs. The Climate*. New York: Simon and Schuster, 2014. Roots the problem of climate change deep in capitalism as an economic system.

Luterbacher, Urs, and Detlef F. Sprinz, eds. *International Relations and Global Climate Change*. Cambridge, MA: MIT Press, 2001. Offers a theoretical survey of several different international environmental regimes and institutions.

Peterson, M. J. "Whalers, Cetologists, Environmentalists, and the International Management of Whaling." *International Organization* 46, no. 1 (Winter 1992): 147–86. Examines the origins of the "Save the Whales" campaign and the politics behind the ban on commercial whaling, with a focus on scientific expertise.

Raustiala, Kal. "States, NGOs, and International Environmental Institutions." *International Studies Quarterly* 41, no. 4 (December 1997): 719–40. Focuses on the role of global civil society in the negotiation and monitoring of international environmental agreements.

Sandler, Todd. *Global Challenges: An Approach to Environmental, Political, and Economic Problems*. New York: Cambridge University Press, 1997. Reviews many global environmental problems, with an emphasis on problems of collective action.

Sprinz, Detlef, and Tapani Vaahtoranta. "The Interest-Based Explanation of International Environmental Policy." *International Organization* 48, no. 1 (Winter 1994): 77–105. Focuses on domestic winners and losers from alternative international environmental institutions.

Victor, David G. *Global Warming Gridlock: Creating More Effective Strategies for Protecting the Planet*. New York: Cambridge University Press, 2011. Critiques current international environmental strategies and agreements and offers a radical proposal for progress within smaller clubs of like-minded countries.

The Science of Ozone Depletion and Global Climate Change

Ozone depletion and climate change are global environmental problems because of the complex chemical and physical processes that occur in the upper atmosphere. The effects of chlorofluorocarbon (CFC), or carbon emissions, are not confined to the countries or even regions of origin. In fact, they spread rapidly, if somewhat unevenly, through the upper atmosphere and thus over the entire earth. As background to the political choices that are the subject of this chapter, this appendix briefly explains these chemical and physical processes.

Ozone Depletion

Ozone is a highly toxic and naturally occurring form of oxygen. Scattered throughout the stratosphere, it soaks up dangerous ultraviolet (UV) radiation from the sun. Without this shield, UV radiation would kill virtually all life on the planet. The small amount of UV radiation that does get through to ground level is a primary cause of eye disease (cataracts) and also causes about 12,000 fatal skin cancers every year. It also harms phytoplankton, a microscopic plant that drifts on the surface of the ocean, which is the base of the food chain and collectively absorbs about half of the world's carbon emissions.

FIGURE A.1 *The Chemistry of Ozone Depletion*

Ultraviolet radiatiom strikes a CFC molecule...

...and causes a chlorine atom to break away

The chlorine atom collides with an ozone molecule...

...and steals an oxygen atom to form chrlorine mon oxide and leave a molecule of ordinary oxygen.

When a free atom of oxygen collides with the chlorine monoxide...

...the two oxygen atoms form a molecule of oxygen. The chlorine atom is released and free to destroy more ozone.

Developed in the 1930s, CFCs were used widely as propellants in aerosols, insulating materials, coolants in refrigerators and air conditioners, and artificial plastic foams for packing materials. But as early as 1974, scientists began to suspect that CFCs could migrate to the stratosphere (which can take up to eight years) and break down under sunlight—a process that was later confirmed. Halocarbons, known as halons, and bromide-based substances like methyl bromide were later recognized to have similar effects.

Once in the atmosphere, CFCs break down into chlorine (see Figure A.1), which forms stable reservoirs (pockets of condensed gas) over the poles during the long, cold winters; and in spring, as the atmosphere warms, the now free chlorine begins to disperse more widely. When a chlorine atom collides with an ozone molecule, which has three oxygen atoms—unlike the familiar oxygen compound we breathe that contains two oxygen atoms—it steals an oxygen atom to form chlorine monoxide and leaves a molecule of ordinary oxygen (with two oxygen atoms). Although these chemicals are not harmful in themselves, the ozone is destroyed in the process. When a naturally-occurring free (single) atom of oxygen subsequently collides with the chlorine monoxide, the two oxygen atoms form a molecule of ordinary oxygen, releasing the chlorine atom once again. This single chlorine atom is then free to collide with and destroy more ozone. Through this iterative process, one CFC molecule can destroy up to 100,000 molecules of ozone.[a]

In 1984, scientists first confirmed that an ozone hole was opening over the Antarctic. This is now an annual occurrence. The notion of a "hole" is something of a misnomer; rather, as the spreading chlorine moves through the atmosphere each spring, it reduces the amount of ozone in the atmosphere by about 60 percent in an area roughly the size of North America. This hole then drifts northward during the summer, reaching its maximum extent usually in October (see Figure A.2). As colder weather starts to reconcentrate chlorine over the poles, the remaining ozone disperses and "fills in" the hole, resulting in a thinning of the overall ozone layer. In 1990, scientists discovered a similar hole over the North Pole, but it is not as large because of warmer temperatures in the Artic.

Since the 1960s, when CFCs were first widely used, the ozone layer has thinned by about 6 percent. Every 1 percent loss of ozone lets in about 2 percent more UV radiation, suggesting that UV exposure at ground level is now about 12 percent higher than in the 1960s. Also, CFCs can last up to 100 years, so even if their release ended today, their full effect would not be felt for up to a century. Atmospheric chlorine levels peaked in 1996 and have been slowly but steadily

FIGURE A.2
Ozone Hole on September 24, 2006.

This image depicts the largest ozone hole ever observed: 11.4 million square miles. This severe hole resulted from high levels of ozone-depleting substances combined with record cold conditions in the Antarctic stratosphere. Satellite instruments measure the amount of ozone in the stratosphere, and the data are used to illustrate the size of the hole. The purple and blue areas are where there is the least amount of ozone; the green and yellow areas are where there is more ozone.

Figure source: www.nasa.gov/images/content/160657main_OZONE_large.jpg (accessed 07/02/07).

---

a. A good website for the basics of ozone depletion is www.nasa.gov/vision/earth/environment/ozone_hole101.html (accessed 03/18/15). The animation is particularly good.

FIGURE A.3 *Atmospheric Chlorine and Ozone Hole*

Atmospheric chlorine levels peaked in the late 1990s, but the size and shape of the ozone hole continues to vary depending on the weather. Scientists estimate that full recovery of the ozone layer will not occur until sometime between 2058 and 2090, depending on the chemical breakdown and transport of ozone-depleting gases.

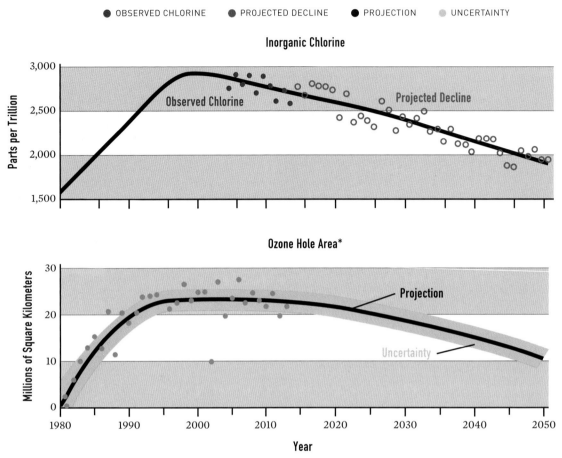

● OBSERVED CHLORINE   ● PROJECTED DECLINE   ● PROJECTION   ● UNCERTAINTY

Inorganic Chlorine

Ozone Hole Area*

*The black line represents estimates of the ozone hole area after 2014, and the blue shading represents the uncertainty of that estimate.
Source: http://earthobservatory.nasa.gov/IOTD/view.php?id=82596 (accessed 02/09/14).

decreasing since (see Figure A.3). Nearly two decades later, scientists have begun to detect signs that atmospheric ozone is gradually increasing. However, as Figure A.2 suggests, the ozone hole remains a very serious problem, and a complete restoration to 1980s levels will not be achieved until approximately 2075.[b]

Global Climate Change

The earth's atmosphere, composed of naturally occurring gases, acts as a blanket insulating the planet and, in turn, retains heat. Solar radiation, emitted from the

b. Gail Sullivan, "Earth's Ozone Layer Is Recovering," *The Washington Post*, September 11, 2014, www.washingtonpost.com/news/morning-mix/wp/2014/09/11/try-to-keep-up-earths-ozone-layer-is-recovering-but-that-is-making-global-warming-worse/ (accessed 09/12/14).

FIGURE A.4 *The Greenhouse Effect*

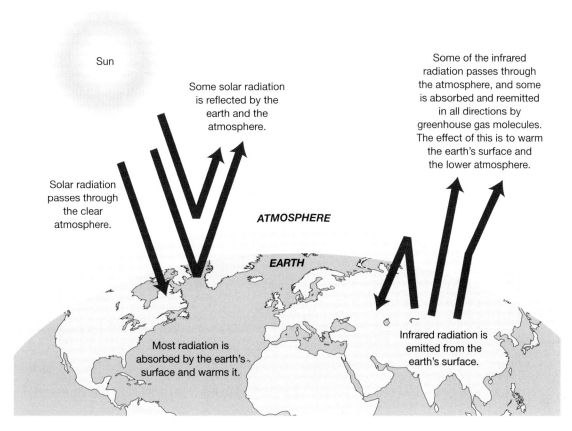

Sun

Solar radiation passes through the clear atmosphere.

Some solar radiation is reflected by the earth and the atmosphere.

Some of the infrared radiation passes through the atmosphere, and some is absorbed and reemitted in all directions by greenhouse gas molecules. The effect of this is to warm the earth's surface and the lower atmosphere.

ATMOSPHERE

EARTH

Most radiation is absorbed by the earth's surface and warms it.

Infrared radiation is emitted from the earth's surface.

Source: www.seai.ie/images_upload/Schools/Secondary_Schools/Subjects/CSPE/Lesson_Plans_for_CSPE/Climate_Change_facts/greenhouse%20effect.jpg (accessed 09/20/14).

sun, passes through our atmosphere and is either absorbed by the earth's surface, warming it and the lower atmosphere, or reflected back into space by the atmosphere and the earth itself (see Figure A.4). Infrared radiation, the portion of the solar radiation that we cannot see but feel as heat, is also captured and reflected by the earth's surface. A portion of the infrared radiation that reaches earth bounces back through the atmosphere into space, while a portion is absorbed and diffused in all directions by the so-called greenhouse gases. By capturing infrared radiation, this greenhouse effect warms the earth's surface and the lower atmosphere and prevents the earth from freezing. The bulk of the atmosphere is naturally occurring oxygen and nitrogen, which do not trap infrared radiation. The greenhouse gases that contribute to global warming are primarily carbon, as well as water vapor, CFCs (see above), methane, nitrous oxide, and 25 others. As carbon

FIGURE A.5 *Global Land and Ocean Temperature Deviations, 1880–2014*

The temperature deviation of a given year is the difference in temperature in that year from the average temperature over the period 1981–2010. So, the deviation of 0.77 in 2014 means that the global temperature was 0.77 degrees higher in 2014 than earth's average temperature across the 30-year period from 1981 to 2010.

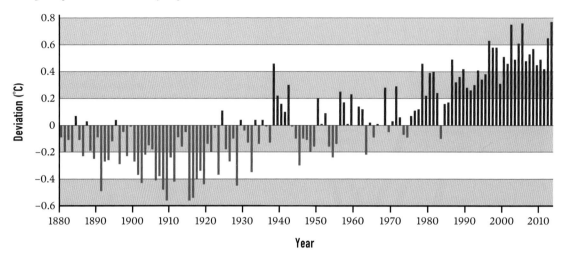

Source: www.ncdc.noaa.gov/cag/time-series/global (accessed 02/09/14).

FIGURE A.6 *Levels of Atmospheric Carbon*

These measurements were made at Mauna Loa Observatory, Hawaii. The red line is the carbon data; the black line represents seasonally adjusted data.

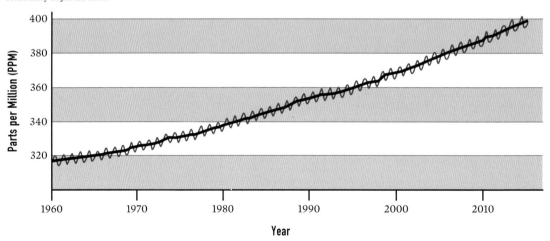

Source: www.esrl.noaa.gov/gmd/ccgg/trends/ (accessed 02/09/14).

and other greenhouse gases are added to the atmosphere, the greenhouse effect increases and earth's surface temperatures rise (see Figure A.5).

Prior to the industrial revolution in the late eighteenth century, the earth was naturally balanced between processes that added and withdrew carbon from the atmosphere. For 10,000 years, the amount of carbon changed relatively little, but it is now growing rapidly (see Figure A.6). From a pre-industrial average

FIGURE A.7 *Greenhouse Gas Emissions by Economic Sectors, 2010*

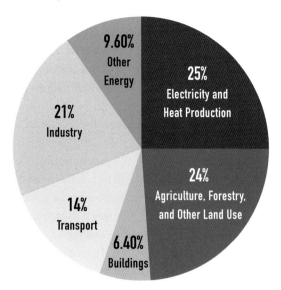

Source: Compiled from data in IPCC. *Climate Change 2014: Mitigation of Climate Change.* Contribution of Working Group III to the Fifth Assessment Report of the Intergovernmental Panel on Climate Change, ed. Edenhofer, O., R. Pichs-Madruga, Y. Sokona, E. Farahani, S. Kadner, K. Seyboth, A. Adler, I. Baum, S. Brunner, P. Eickemeier, B. Kriemann, J. Savolainen, S. Schlömer, C. von Stechow, T. Zwickel, and J. C. Minx (New York: Cambridge University Press, 2014), Executive Summary, p. 9.

of about 280 parts per million (ppm), global carbon concentrations had risen to nearly 400 ppm by 2014. At the current rate of growth in emissions, carbon concentrations in the atmosphere will double over the next century to approximately 800 ppm.[c] (Scientists widely believe 550 ppm to be an extremely dangerous threshold to cross.) Since carbon emissions remain in the atmosphere for as long as 200 years, it will take a very long time for concentrations to decline, even after new restrictions are put in place.

Greenhouse gases are emitted from various sources (see Figure A.7). The single largest source of emissions is electricity and heat, largely from burning coal and natural gas. Transportation, which has received significant attention and prompted some drivers to switch to more fuel-efficient cars, accounts for only 14 percent of all emissions worldwide (but 27.4 percent in the United States).

Global warming is sometimes described as controversial, or lacking scientific consensus. Although there is some uncertainty, there are many more points of agreement. The Intergovernmental Panel on Climate Change (IPCC), in its fourth report issued in early 2007, declared for the first time that global warming is "unequivocal" and that human activity is the main driver "very likely" causing

c. "The Heat Is On: A Survey of Climate Change," *Economist*, September 9, 2006, 23.

most of the recent rise in global temperatures.[d] Since then, this view has only gained greater support among scientists.

There is no doubt in the scientific community that human activity has increased the quantity of greenhouse gases, especially carbon, in the atmosphere. About 80 percent of this increased quantity of carbon comes from burning coal, oil, and natural gas, with the rest coming from a variety of other sources, including tropical deforestation. Only about 55 percent of the carbon we release into the atmosphere is absorbed by the oceans and plant life, and the rest is added into the atmosphere.

There is also no doubt that these increased greenhouse gases will alter the global climate. At a general level, as explained above, the mechanics of the atmosphere are very well understood. The greater the concentration of greenhouse gases, the more of the infrared radiation that will be retained and the larger the warming effect. Thus, human-made increases in greenhouse gases will increase global temperatures—producing what is widely known as global warming.

Finally, there is no doubt about the likely effects of global warming: It will cause a significant melting of the polar ice caps and a rise in sea levels. It will cause changes in weather, with more severe storms in some areas and, with less rain, increasing desertification in countries close to the equator. Along with these changes in temperature and rainfall, global warming will also cause a significant shift in ecology, creating new patterns of agriculture and new paths of disease dissemination, with previously "tropical" diseases spreading outward from equatorial regions. Despite what is often represented as a lack of scientific consensus, there is no doubt that the climate will warm and have noticeable effects on our daily lives.

What remains controversial and often debated is how large an effect this increased concentrations of greenhouse gases will have on the climate over the long run. The IPCC currently estimates that global mean temperatures will rise between 3.6 and 8.1 degrees Fahrenheit by year 2100. This is a broad range. The consequences of global warming will be determined by where in this range we will actually end up. If the actual increase is toward the low end of the range, the effect will be significant but probably not catastrophic. However, if the increase is closer to the high end, the consequences will be quite severe. Current climate models also could prove to be way off in either direction. Climate "skeptics" believe that temperature increases will be at or perhaps even below these projections where the effects on the climate will be small to nil, and "doomsayers" believe that the current estimates are too low and catastrophe awaits.

Scientists are uncertain about the magnitude of climate change for many reasons. After all, the earth's climate is an extremely complex system. There are four main sources of uncertainty. First, the earth is an evolving ecosystem that warms and cools itself over very long periods. Ice ages had come and gone of their own accord long before humans inhabited the planet. Second, although we are rapidly developing new sources of information and accumulating more data from indirect

---

d. Elisabeth Rosenthal and Andrew C. Revkin, "Science Panel Says Global Warming Is 'Unequivocal,'" *New York Times*, February 3, 2007, A1.

measures of temperature over longer periods, we lack the full history of the earth's temperature cycles and how they relate to past levels of greenhouse gases. To predict the future, it helps to understand the past.

Third, the global climate is what scientists sometimes call a "massively interactive" system. In fact, different processes can interact in unexpected ways. The IPCC's first estimates of global warming were off by a significant amount because it did not factor into the climate model the role of sulfate particles—some from burning fossil fuels—that reflect sunlight back into space and have a cooling effect. Increased carbon may also stimulate other, naturally occurring absorptive processes, such as greater plant growth. On the other hand, as the earth warms, more water evaporates, and the resulting water vapor traps more heat. The polar ice caps reflect much of the sunlight back into space, so as the ice caps shrink, more of the sun's energy will be retained within the atmosphere. The ocean absorbs carbon, with colder seas trapping more than warmer ones. As the ocean's temperature rises, less carbon will be absorbed and, in a potentially catastrophic turn, the ocean may even release large quantities of carbon back into the atmosphere. Understanding these complex interactions precisely will take time.

Fourth, as a massively interactive system, the global climate may be quite sensitive to small changes, forming what scientists call a nonlinear or "chaotic" system. For instance, forests recycle huge amounts of carbon, extracting it from the atmosphere and locking it away in plants and trees. Yet, if trees and plants cannot adapt quickly enough to the higher carbon levels in the atmosphere and die, for instance, they might release their stored carbon back into the atmosphere and greatly exacerbate the original problem that caused their demise. Another example is even moderate climate change might produce changes in the ocean currents, perhaps resulting in a more southerly course for the Gulf Stream. This would likely have a profound influence on the climate of western Europe, produce a possible reduction of upper-level ocean cycling in the Southern Ocean, and possibly lead to rapid disintegration of part of the Antarctic ice sheet, with dramatic consequences for the global sea level. In these examples, small changes in climate might have massively disproportionate effects.

Given such a complicated system, our ability to predict the global climate 100 years in the future is imperfect, and this scientific uncertainty—not about the basic phenomenon of global warming, but about exactly how hot it's going to get—is used by interest groups to shape the political debate and policy choices in their favor. Environmental groups are sometimes prone to catastrophic doomsday scenarios, emphasizing extreme predictions at the high end of the possible range of global warming and playing on our fears. Conversely, business groups sometimes exploit the uncertainty surrounding the magnitude of global warming to minimize its impact and advocate delaying policy changes while scientists do more research. It is important to separate what we know from what we don't, and avoid either worst-case or best-case thinking. Human-induced climate change is real. It is coming. And its effects will be noticeable and possibly significant in some areas. Only the question of how dramatic the changes will be remains uncertain.

14

The Future of International Politics

THE PUZZLE *In the coming decades, the international system may experience the spread of weapons of mass destruction, the rise of a new superpower in Asia, clashes over economic globalization, and demands for greater global governance. Can political science tell us what the future will hold?*

Above: As China grows economically and becomes more powerful on the world stage, its government may confront greater demands for democracy by activists aided by new technologies. Pro-democracy demonstrators in Hong Kong held cell phones aloft to signal their solidarity.

On September 19, 1898, British forces battling the Sudanese on their way up the Nile River arrived at the village of Fashoda in what is today South Sudan and found it unexpectedly occupied by 120 French soldiers. The meeting was the culmination of a "race" to the Upper Nile Valley, which was coveted by both countries. The French expeditionary force had left the French Congo, on the western coast of Africa, a year and a half earlier and had arrived in Fashoda in July; the British had traveled a shorter distance but had met greater resistance along the way. The meeting between the British commander, General Herbert Kitchener, and the French commander, Major Jean-Baptiste Marchand, was courteous, but neither would cede his country's claim to the region. Hoping to avoid a clash, the two decided to refer the matter to their respective governments and await orders.

This was not as simple as it might sound.[1] The French expedition had no direct means of communication with Paris. A message would have to be sent over land to the

Atlantic coast, about 1,500 miles away, and then by boat to France—a trip that could take nine months or more. The British were in a better position, having invested a great deal in stringing telegraph cables all over the world, as well as under its oceans. Kitchener had access to a military telegraph 400 miles down the Nile at the Sudanese town of Omdurman. A message could be sent by boat, tapped out in Morse code, and then speed along wires that ran north along a railway line to Egypt and from there to London via undersea cables. Marchand asked for permission to use the British telegraph at Omdurman, but Kitchener would only allow him access to the telegraph in Cairo, Egypt, another 1,000 miles north down the Nile. As a result, while Marchand won the race to Fashoda, Kitchener won the race to alert the world about their meeting: his telegram got to London in five days, on September 24, while Marchand's report to Paris did not arrive until a month later, on October 22. In the end, Britain's superior naval strength as well as its numerical advantage on the ground at Fashoda convinced the French to give way, and war was avoided.

Today, of course, it is much easier and faster to learn of events all over the world. The price of communication has dropped precipitously, and the coverage of high-speed

1. Daniel R. Headrick, *The Invisible Weapon: Telecommunications and International Politics, 1851–1945* (New York: Oxford University Press, 1991), 84–85.

phone and Internet networks has broadened dramatically. Given today's technology, Marchand could have used any number of ways to communicate instantaneously with Paris, including asking for assistance from one of the estimated 2.9 million South Sudanese with a cellular phone.[2] The ubiquity of these technologies was on display in 2011, when uprisings broke out throughout the Middle East and northern Africa. All across this region, protesters used cell phones and social media sites to shares news, opinions, and videos with other protesters and the outside world.

We live in a period that is witnessing extraordinary changes in the way people and countries communicate and interact, developments that present both promise and peril. Advances in technology have made the world smaller, increasing flows of information, goods, services, and people across the globe; at the same time, technology has greatly increased the ability to kill large numbers of people in horrific ways. The globalization of economic exchanges has enriched many people and turned some previously poor countries, such as China, India, and Brazil, into economic powerhouses; at the same time, these processes have created inequality, insecurity, and resistance from those who worry about being left behind.

The purpose of this concluding chapter is to use the tools developed in this book to think through the future implications of these trends. Going forward, what developments are likely to have a major impact on international politics? What might their impact be, and why? How might different policy choices influence the way events unfold?

Trying to answer these questions also gives us an opportunity to look back at history. Surveying the last several centuries of international politics, it is striking how much can change over time. There have been periods in which violent conflict was quite common and other periods in which the world was relatively peaceful. There also have been dramatic changes over time in the level of international cooperation and the depth of economic interdependence. We have to understand this variation in order to predict how current trends and developments will play out. In this chapter, we use our framework to consider four issues that are high on the agenda of world politics today and will continue to be so in the coming decades: the spread of weapons of mass destruction (WMD), the rising economic and military power of China, economic globalization, and the demand for new types of

governance in the international system. In thinking about the future of these and other international issues, theory and history are our best guides.

Thinking Analytically about the Future of World Politics

As we have done throughout this book, we approach the topic of change over time by thinking in terms of interests, interactions, and institutions. Actors' interests change when the costs and benefits associated with different strategies and outcomes change. For example, advances in technology can lower the costs of certain activities—whether trading goods across oceans, or acquiring weapons capable of killing millions in the blink of eye, or networking with activists on opposite sides of the globe. In some cases, these changes will generate common interests, as actors find new opportunities for mutual gain and/or new shared challenges. In other cases, change will benefit some actors at the expense of others, leading to conflicts between winners and losers. As interests change, so does the relative frequency of different interactions. When common goals or common threats arise, the need for cooperation grows. When changes benefit some actors and hurt others, the potential for conflict increases, as the winners seek to exploit their gains and the losers fight back. Technological change and economic growth can also shift the relative bargaining power of actors. Those that adopt new technologies or benefit from rapid development grow stronger, and they may seek to rewrite previous bargains in their favor. Finally, changes in interests and interactions can create demand for new and different institutions. Actors may seek new rules to further cooperation or to contain violent conflict, and new ideas about politics can lead to the promotion of new forms of governance.

In the four issues analyzed in this chapter, we consider how changes in underlying conditions like technology, economic resources, and ideas are driving a convergence or divergence in the interests of the relevant actors, how their interactions reflect these changes, and what role institutions might play in governing these interactions going forward.

2. This figure is a 2013 estimate from the World Bank, http://data .worldbank.org/indicator/IT.CEL.SETS.P2 (accessed 02/11/15).

Can the Spread of WMD Be Stopped?

Throughout history, changes in military technologies have had dramatic effects on international politics. Key innovations such as the stirrup, the longbow, gunpowder, automatic firing mechanisms, the airplane, the tank, the aircraft carrier, the intercontinental ballistic missile, the nuclear bomb—all profoundly influenced the nature and costs of warfare. Moreover, the emergence and diffusion of these technologies have been a major factor in changing the distribution of military power worldwide. States that innovate and adopt new technologies often gain an edge in international competition; however, as technology and knowledge spread to others, that initial advantage can diminish.

In the contemporary world, the spread of nuclear, chemical, and biological weapons—collectively known as WMD—has been a particularly pressing issue. At the time of this writing, nine states are known to possess nuclear weapons (the United States, Russia, Great Britain, France, China, India, Pakistan, Israel, and North Korea). Iran has a uranium enrichment program, which has raised strong suspicions that it is seeking a nuclear capability. In addition, about 20 states possess the technology and knowledge to produce nuclear weapons in a very short time frame if they chose to do so. Fewer states are known to have chemical and/or biological weapons—whose production and use are outlawed by international treaties—but a handful of states are suspected of having illicit stocks or programs under way to develop them.[3] Syria's chemical weapons capabilities sparked an international crisis in August 2013, when the government attacked an opposition-held town with sarin gas, killing hundreds of people. In addition to the possibility that more states will acquire such weapons, there is a looming danger of their acquisition by terrorist groups, a development that would greatly increase the damage that these nonstate actors could inflict.

Given this risk, the proliferation of WMD is likely to be high on the agenda of world politics for decades to come. Advances in technology and the diffusion of scientific knowledge have made it easier to acquire these destructive devices. Some states and nonstate actors will increasingly see the possession of WMD as an inexpensive and effective way to advance their interests. As a result, the prospect of proliferation will likely generate conflictual interactions between those who want these weapons and those who want to stop their spread. What implications would the spread of such weapons have? What, if anything, can be done to stop their proliferation to states and nonstate actors such as terrorists?

What Do Theory and History Tell Us?

Given the horrendous killing power of WMD, it may seem obvious that their spread is undesirable; however, the lessons of theory and history actually suggest

---

3. See, for example, Arms Control Association, "Chemical and Biological Weapons Status at a Glance," February 4, 2014, www.armscontrol.org/factsheets/cbwprolif (accessed 02/03/15).

otherwise. Particularly in the case of nuclear weapons, one can make a strong argument that their overwhelming destructive power has made them a force for peace. This argument hinges on the idea that nuclear war jeopardizes the overriding interest of most actors: survival. Whatever other interests states or individuals may have, those goals are meaningless if attaining them will lead to the actor's destruction.[4] Thus, a war involving nuclear weapons threatens to impose costs that far exceed the value of whatever good might be at stake in a dispute. The massive costs of nuclear war mean that the bargaining range of deals that both sides prefer to war generally includes any possible division of the good; a state should prefer any deal, even one in which it gets nothing, to starting a nuclear war, in which the risk of its complete destruction is high. At the very least, the enormous destructive potential of any war between states with nuclear weapons should induce caution and greater willingness to compromise. In short, possession of highly destructive weapons should create a condition of mutual deterrence in which neither side would contemplate an attack on the other, forcing them to resolve their disputes in other ways. During the Cold War, this condition was referred to as one of "mutually assured destruction," with the colorful acronym MAD.

To work, mutual nuclear deterrence has very few requirements.[5] The first is that each side must possess a survivable second-strike force—that is, each state must possess enough weapons so that its arsenal could survive a first strike by the other state and still be formidable enough to cause unacceptable levels of damage for the initiator. Why is this necessary? If one state's nuclear arsenal is relatively easy to destroy with a crippling first strike, then a commitment problem arises that could generate incentives on both sides to initiate preemptive war. In the event of a crisis, the stronger state would be tempted to deliver a knockout blow that would deprive the other state of any ability to retaliate. In the absence of a credible commitment by the stronger state not to strike first, the vulnerable state would face a temptation to "use them or lose them"—to launch its weapons first in order to ensure that they are not destroyed on the ground. Only when both states have enough weapons to ride out a first strike and still deliver a crippling blow of their own would neither state have a destabilizing temptation to launch preemptively. In practice, this means each side must have not only a large number of weapons but also a means of protecting them, such as by hardening missile sites against attack or by making them mobile (on vehicles, airplanes, or submarines) so that they are hard to eliminate.

The second requirement for mutual deterrence to work is that the leaders be rational, at least in the very limited sense that they care about their survival. The deterrent effect of nuclear weapons depends on their inducing caution by making the costs of war loom large relative to the potential benefits. For this to happen, those whose fingers are on the trigger must value their own survival and

---

4. Obviously, individuals who engage in suicide terrorism may have different priorities, as we saw in Chapter 6.

5. See Scott D. Sagan and Kenneth N. Waltz, *The Spread of Nuclear Weapons: A Debate Renewed*, 2nd ed. (New York: Norton, 2003), chap. 1.

the survival of their nation enough to consider war unacceptably costly. Also, the weapons must not be easily subject to accidental launch. Finally, mutual deterrence assumes that in the event of an attack, each side can reliably verify where that attack originated. Deterrence hinges on the expectation that anyone who initiates an attack will face a devastating counterattack. Hence, it must be the case that the initiator expects the target to be able to identify it. If it were impossible to know where the attack originated, then a potential initiator might think it could escape retaliation.

What does the evidence suggest? Although the logic of mutual deterrence may seem overly optimistic, the historical track record is encouraging. There has never been a nuclear war. Indeed, the only actual use of nuclear weapons—the bombings of Hiroshima and Nagasaki, Japan, by the United States in 1945—occurred when a nuclear country attacked a nonnuclear one. This observation suggests that what is dangerous about nuclear weapons is not their spread per se but their *uneven* spread, which leaves haves and have-nots. Even conventional war between states possessing nuclear weapons is extremely rare; the only such case is the 1999 Kargil War between India and Pakistan (see Chapter 4 "What Shaped Our World?" on p. 157). This effect is most prominently evident in a phenomenon known as the Long Peace, a term that refers to the absence of war between the United States and the Soviet Union from 1945 to 1990.[6] It may seem odd to use this term to describe the Cold War, which was anything but peaceful to people in much of the world. Nonetheless, despite the deep ideological hostility between the two states and the fact that they supported one another's enemies around the globe, it is remarkable that the superpower rivals never fought each other directly. Although several factors contribute to this observation (including the role of the Cold War alliance system discussed in Chapter 5), the fact that both states had enormous nuclear arsenals that gave them second-strike capability induced a level of caution and pragmatism in their relationship that allowed them to avoid direct warfare and to make compromises when necessary.

If the logic and historical track record of nuclear deterrence is so solid, why are so many people worried about the proliferation of nuclear weapons and other WMD? Why might some states have an interest in preventing the spread of these weapons? There are three main reasons. First, even if nuclear weapons may reduce the danger of war in some circumstances, they nonetheless influence the distribution of power among states. A state whose power increases—such as by acquiring a potent new weapon—may seek to revise the status quo in its favor. This development could harm the interests of other states, even if it never leads to war. For example, if Iran were to acquire nuclear weapons, its power and influence in the Middle East would increase, probably to the detriment of the United States, Israel, Saudi Arabia, and any other country that has disputes with Iran. Hence, states may have an interest in stopping the spread of WMD in order to protect other interests that would be jeopardized by the emergence of an enemy with such capabilities.

---

6. See John Lewis Gaddis, "The Long Peace: Elements of Stability in the Postwar International System," *International Security* 10 (Spring 1986): 99–142.

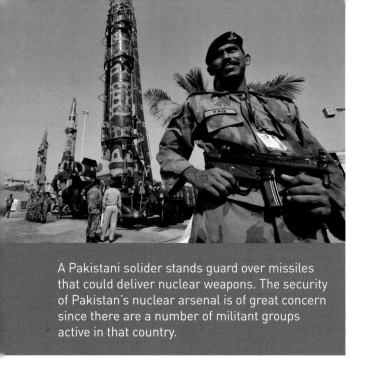

A Pakistani solider stands guard over missiles that could deliver nuclear weapons. The security of Pakistan's nuclear arsenal is of great concern since there are a number of militant groups active in that country.

Second, the states that have recently obtained, or may soon obtain, these weapons may be unable to meet all the requirements set out above. Unlike the United States and the Soviet Union during the Cold War, many of these states are relatively poor and domestically unstable. They may not have the resources to build and protect an adequate second-strike force, and they may not have the technology or resources to safeguard their weapons against theft or accidental launch. The case of Pakistan, which acquired nuclear weapons in the late 1980s, illustrates some of these concerns.[7] As we saw in Chapter 4, Pakistan's military has considerable independence from the civilian leadership, and evidence suggests that the military has handled its nuclear weapons in a risky manner during several crises with India, thereby raising the danger of unintentional use. Also, influential elements of the regime, particularly the intelligence services, have close ties to militant groups in the region, thereby raising concerns about a transfer of nuclear technology to extremists. Moreover, Pakistan seems to have exercised loose control over its nuclear scientists. A. Q. Khan, the "father" of Pakistan's bomb, is suspected of running a network that sold key technologies to Iran, Libya, and North Korea.[8] If new proliferators resemble Pakistan rather than a more stable state such as, say, Great Britain, then there is reason for concern.

The third concern, and one that has come to the fore since the 9/11 terrorist attacks, is that the spread of WMD may make it more likely that these weapons will fall into the hands of terrorist organizations. This could happen intentionally (such as if a hostile state were to give or sell a weapon to a terrorist) or unintentionally (through theft or the complicity of extremist elements within the state). There is reason to doubt whether the logic of deterrence could prevent the use of WMD by terrorist organizations in the same way it does with states. While terrorists may act in rational ways (as we discussed in Chapter 6), at least some have demonstrated their willingness to commit suicide for their cause, which suggests that the threat of retaliation may not dissuade them. Moreover, unlike states, terrorist networks do not constitute a geographically defined target, so it can be especially hard to identify the perpetrators and their base. For example, after the attack on a U.S. warship, the

---

7. For a discussion of these concerns, see Sagan and Waltz, *The Spread of Nuclear Weapons*, chap. 3; and Scott D. Sagan, "How to Keep the Bomb from Iran," *Foreign Affairs* 85 (September–October 2006): 45–59.

8. The status of these allegations is contested. Although the Pakistani government admitted Khan's involvement—and pardoned him after he confessed—Khan later retracted his confession.

USS *Cole,* in October 2000, it took months for investigators to say with confidence that the attack was the work of Al Qaeda and had been orchestrated by its leaders in Afghanistan—a delay that prevented any response to the attack.[9] And even if the responsible organization can be found, it can be difficult to carry out retaliatory strikes without also killing innocent people, since terrorists embed themselves within civilian populations that may or may not share their goals. While it might have been credible during the Cold War for the United States to threaten the Soviet Union with massive retaliation in the event its leaders ordered a nuclear strike, it is harder to make the same threat today against, say, Pakistan for the activities of a small number of terrorists operating within its borders. Hence, a terrorist organization may expect to be able to escape retaliation, and/or it may consider the risks of retaliation acceptable given terrorists' extreme preferences.

Preventing the Spread of WMD

How can the proliferation of WMD be prevented? The answer depends in part on whether one is trying to prevent the spread of these weapons to states or to nonstate actors, such as terrorists. In general, there are two ways to prevent an actor from acquiring WMD: one, by altering the actor's incentives so that abstention becomes a better course of action; or two, by preventing the actor from getting the necessary technology and material, such as the fissile material required to fuel a nuclear explosion. These strategies are not mutually exclusive, but they are likely to meet different levels of success depending on the actor in question.

As we saw in Chapter 6, terrorists have extreme interests that make them particularly willing to kill and be killed for their cause. Efforts to alter a cost-benefit analysis are less likely to succeed with such actors. It is unclear what promises or threats would induce them to alter their behavior voluntarily. As a result, preventing terrorists from acquiring a WMD capability requires a focus on the denial of technology—that is, ensuring that they do not get their hands on highly enriched uranium or plutonium for nuclear weapons, or on chemical or biological agents that can be weaponized. Since nuclear and chemical facilities are large and obvious, most clandestine terrorist organizations cannot pursue this route to developing weapons; they are more likely to buy or steal the components that they need. The task of denial therefore primarily entails securing nuclear and laboratory facilities against theft and policing efforts to buy or sell these materials on the black market. Most states share an interest in preventing nuclear fuel from falling into the wrong hands, so there is a strong basis for international cooperation to secure stockpiles of uranium and plutonium and to police theft and smuggling. Indeed, the United States and Russia, the two largest and most experienced nuclear powers, have

---

9. *The 9/11 Commission Report: Final Report of the National Commission on Terrorist Attacks upon the United States* (New York: Norton, 2004), 195, 200–201.

cooperated extensively in this area. Although these efforts have been successful, rising tensions over Russian support for separatists in the Ukraine led in early 2015 to a suspension of nuclear security cooperation. Thus, despite states' strong shared interest in preventing nuclear terrorism, joint efforts in this area can fall prey to conflicts over other issues.

Preventing the spread of WMD to states may also entail denial of nuclear, biological, and chemical ingredients; but given the current diffusion of scientific knowledge and technology, most reasonably advanced states already have the resources to develop a WMD program. As a result, efforts to slow proliferation among states focus primarily on shaping their interests. States that contemplate developing or acquiring WMD do so because they believe there will be some benefit to having them: enhanced security from an outside threat, or greater prestige and influence regionally or globally. Strategies for preventing the spread of WMD must alter these incentives, either by increasing the costs of proliferation or by increasing the benefits of abstinence.

The main strategies that have been used to this end coincide with the three core concepts of our framework: finding alternative ways to address the security interests of potential proliferators, cooperating through international institutions to establish and enforce rules against proliferation, or engaging in a coercive interaction designed to forcibly disarm hostile states.

Guaranteeing the Security Interests of Potential Proliferators One approach to preventing the spread of nuclear weapons is to address the underlying reason why a state may want such technology in the first place. The most common motive is fear of attack by another nuclear-armed state.[10] This is evident from the historical pattern of proliferation. The United States developed nuclear weapons during World War II amid a fear that Nazi Germany would acquire them first. With the onset of the Cold War, the Soviet Union responded with a nuclear program of its own, achieving a nuclear capability in 1949. This development sparked concerns in Great Britain and France, which then sought their own nuclear deterrent. In the early 1960s, a growing rift between the Soviet Union and China led the latter to seek its own nuclear arsenal, which it achieved in the mid-1960s. The Chinese bomb induced fear in neighboring India, which had already had several clashes with China over their disputed border. The Indian nuclear program produced a usable weapon in the 1980s, with the result that India's longtime enemy, Pakistan, embarked on a program of its own. Hence, the spread of nuclear weapons has been driven largely by security concerns, with each new proliferator sparking fears in its rivals and leading them to seek a bomb of their own.

It follows that proliferation can be halted by finding ways to address the security interests that lead states to proliferate. Indeed, the historical record suggests

---

10. For a discussion of the motives behind nuclear proliferation, see Scott D. Sagan, "Why Do States Build Nuclear Weapons? Three Models in Search of a Bomb," *International Security* 21, no. 3 (Winter 1996–97): 54–86.

a number of cases in which this strategy has worked—cases in which states that faced stronger and/or nuclear-armed rivals, and had the technological and scientific ability to develop nuclear weapons, nonetheless abstained from doing so. For example, why did China's acquisition of nuclear weapons lead India to respond in kind, while other states in the region that also had reason to fear China (particularly Japan, Taiwan, and South Korea) did not? The answer lies in the fact that these states found other ways to redress their insecurity. In particular, all three had defensive alliances with the United States, which meant that even though they did not have a nuclear deterrent of their own, they were protected by the "nuclear umbrella" of the United States. There is evidence that the Soviet Union induced similar restraint in its ally Syria, which was tempted to develop nuclear weapons in response to Israel.[11] By extending security guarantees to friendly states, the superpowers helped to dampen those states' incentives to seek their own arsenals. Such guarantees do not always work—as the British and French nuclear programs attest—since they must be sufficiently credible that potential attackers are deterred. It may be that the Cold War was a unique period because the intense competition between the superpowers generated particularly strong incentives for them to defend their allies. Nonetheless, the general point remains: incentives to proliferate can be lessened if states find credible alternative ways to address their security interests.

International Institutions: The Nuclear Non-Proliferation Treaty

An alternative mechanism for preventing proliferation relies on an international institution to foster cooperation among states with a shared interest in this goal. The primary institutional mechanism for this purpose is embodied in the Nuclear Non-Proliferation Treaty (NPT), the origins and main provisions of which are described in "What Shaped Our World?" on page 586. This treaty prohibits all but five states—the United States, the Soviet Union, Great Britain, France, and China—from possessing nuclear weapons and thus provides the legal framework for preventing their further spread.

As with many international institutions, the strength of the NPT lies in setting out standards of acceptable behavior and providing mechanisms for monitoring compliance through the International Atomic Energy Agency (IAEA); it is weaker when it comes to enforcement, which is left to the states themselves. IAEA inspections uncovered evidence of plutonium diversion by North Korea in the early 1990s, and they documented numerous instances of noncompliance by Iran going back several decades. But once cheating is discovered, the IAEA has no authority to impose sanctions. Instead, it must submit charges of noncompliance to the United Nations Security Council, which has the ability to authorize economic or military sanctions. As we saw in Chapter 5, however, the Security Council is not a neutral body; rather, it is dominated by five permanent members (the P5), each of which can veto any enforcement action it does not like. In the cases of both North Korea

---

11. Benjamin Frankel, "The Brooding Shadow: Systemic Incentives and Nuclear Weapons Proliferation," *Security Studies* 2 (Spring–Summer 1993): 47–51.

The Nuclear Non-Proliferation Treaty

In 1963, U.S. president John F. Kennedy predicted that by 1975 some 20 to 25 countries might possess nuclear weapons, a prospect that he considered "the greatest possible danger" facing humanity.[a] At the time, only the United States, the Soviet Union, Great Britain, and France had developed a nuclear bomb. China was on the verge, and a number of other countries were exploring the possibility. Yet Kennedy's prediction was far off the mark. By 1975, only two new nuclear states had joined the original five: Israel and India. The next forty years saw only two more: Pakistan and North Korea. Four states—South Africa, Ukraine, Kazakhstan, and Belarus—possessed nuclear weapons but gave them up, and others have the technology to produce a bomb but have chosen not to.[b]

The fact that nuclear weapons have not spread as widely as originally feared has a number of causes. Some of the credit goes to the Nuclear Non-Proliferation Treaty (NPT). Concluded in 1968, the treaty has gone from 61 signatories in 1970 to 189 today. How did the NPT come about, and what does it do?

Interests Underlying the NPT was the concern that a world of many nuclear states would be a dangerous place for everyone. In addition to the risk of nuclear war, radioactive fallout from such an event would harm even those not directly involved. Still, this common interest alone was not enough to guarantee a deal. For the states that already had nuclear weapons, their primary interest was to prevent other countries from eroding their nuclear monopoly. Most non-nuclear states had two interests at stake. In addition to their security interest in limiting non-nuclear rivals' access to these weapons, they wanted to protect their ability to develop civilian nuclear energy programs. The fissile material that makes nuclear weapons go bang—plutonium and enriched uranium—is part of the fuel cycle of a nuclear reactor. Restrictions on the ability to possess or produce these fuels could hamper these countries' ability to harness this source of energy. Finally, there were some states that did not yet have nuclear weapons but wanted to hold open the option of getting them; these states had no interest in any treaty.

Interactions The NPT reflects a bargain between the five countries that had tested a bomb by the time the treaty was concluded and everybody else. The former, recognized as nuclear-weapons states, promise not to transfer their weapons to non-nuclear states, to make good-faith efforts to reduce and eventually eliminate their own nuclear stockpiles, and to assist the non-nuclear states in the development of peaceful nuclear energy programs. In return, the other states promise not to try to develop nuclear weapons, either by purchasing them or diverting nuclear material from their reactors. As we saw in Chapter 2, however, efforts to control arms can give rise to a Prisoners' Dilemma, in which each state fears that its own restraint will be exploited by others. The solution to this problem required not just a deal, but an institution.

Institutions In addition to laying out standards of acceptable behavior, the NPT provided a mechanism for monitoring compliance, in the form of the International Atomic Energy Agency (IAEA).[c] In exchange for assistance, states must sign "safeguard agreements" with the IAEA that impose restrictions on their activities and provide for inspections to ensure that no material is diverted. In the event that a violation of the treaty is detected, enforcement is left to the UN Security Council, which can impose sanctions, as it has recently done in the case of Iran.

Instances of cheating by NPT members are rare, but this observation obscures some weaknesses of the institution. Most of the states that developed nuclear weapons after 1968—India, Pakistan, and Israel—never signed the agreement; South Africa signed in 1991 only after it decided to give them up. Moreover, the treaty permits states to withdraw with only six months' notice. This is what North Korea did in 2003 after being confronted with evidence that it had been illicitly enriching uranium. There is also no mechanism for enforcing the provision that nuclear states work toward dismantling their arsenals, a task that they have been slow to fulfill.

---

a. "Text of President Kennedy's News Conference on Foreign and Domestic Affairs," *New York Times*, March 22, 1963.

b. See Scott D. Sagan, "The Causes of Nuclear Weapons Proliferation," *Annual Review of Political Science* 14 (2011): 225–44.

c. The IAEA in fact predates the NPT, having been created in 1957.

and Iran, harsh sanctions have at times been blocked by veto threats from China and Russia, though more recently they have gone along with sanctions against those countries. Hence, enforcement of the NPT requires consensus in the Security Council—something that may not obtain if the noncompliant state has backers within that body.

Although Iran signed the NPT, there are concerns that it may develop nuclear weapons. IAEA inspectors (shown above) have criticized Iran for not fully disclosing all aspects of its nuclear program, as required by the treaty.

How well has the NPT fared in preventing the spread of nuclear weapons? The track record is mixed. From one perspective, the NPT regime has seen some notable successes. Several countries that previously refused to sign and had active nuclear pro-grams, such as South Africa, Brazil, and Argentina, have abandoned their nuclear ambitions and signed the treaty. In the cases of Brazil and Argentina, the NPT played a role in helping these two former rivals shed their nuclear programs in a transparent man-ner. The NPT regime also played a productive role in defusing a potential crisis caused by the breakup of the Soviet Union. With the dissolution of that coun-try into 15 new states, a number of the new states were "born nuclear" due to the presence of Soviet-era weapons on their territory. Although there was general agreement that Russia, the largest of these states, would inherit the former Soviet Union's designation as a nuclear-weapon state, the other three states—Ukraine, Belarus, and Kazakhstan—all came under pressure to give up their weapons and sign the NPT as non-nuclear weapons states. Because of long-standing fears of Russia, some policy makers in Ukraine thought that the arsenal they had inher-ited would serve as a useful deterrent against their larger, nuclear-armed neighbor. However, the other nuclear powers insisted that Ukraine could only join the NPT as a non-nuclear-weapon state and that the alternative was to be ostracized by the international community, threatening the new state's standing and access to eco-nomic aid.[12] Ukraine signed the NPT as a non-nuclear power in 1994; Belarus and Kazakhstan followed suit. In this example, the international institution performed exactly as one would hope: by setting a clear standard for acceptable behavior and raising the expected costs of noncompliance.

The NPT regime has also had notable weaknesses, however. Since the treaty recognizes the right of non-nuclear states to develop civilian nuclear energy pro-grams, there is danger that proliferators will use these programs to conceal illicit activity and evade punishment. Iran, for example, is openly enriching uranium and argues, correctly, that it has the right to generate fuel for nuclear reactors. The concern is that the same enrichment process can also be used to make highly enriched uranium for a nuclear weapon. While IAEA inspections seek to prevent this kind of diversion, several states have managed to cheat on their obligations and

12. Sagan, "Why Do States Build Nuclear Weapons?" 80–82.

escape detection for some time. North Korea, Iraq, Libya, and Iran were all NPT signatories, and all managed to have active or nascent nuclear programs at some point after signing. There is also no mechanism to force states to sign or to prevent them from backing out after they have signed. Hence, the NPT does not provide foolproof protection against determined proliferators.

Coercive Disarmament What, then, can be done about states like North Korea, Iran, or Iraq under Saddam Hussein—states that have actively sought or, in the case of North Korea, actually acquired nuclear weapons? These states' actions show that they do not fear the international disapproval and possible economic sanctions that come with being in noncompliance with the NPT. Nor do these states have strong protectors who can cover them with a nuclear umbrella. Moreover, these states' interests in nuclear weapons may be rooted in more than just insecurity that can be assuaged through security guarantees. For example, Iran has aspirations for regional influence, and nuclear weapons would be useful to this end.

The ultimate tool for stopping or reversing nuclear proliferation is coercive disarmament: the threat or use of military force. A state can issue a compellent threat against a would-be proliferator to dismantle its program or face attack. The United States issued veiled threats to this effect against North Korea during a 1994 crisis over that country's nuclear program, and it made such threats explicit during the crisis that led to the invasion of Iraq in 2003 (though it was later determined that Iraq had already halted its WMD programs). If threats alone are not enough to induce disarmament, the final option is to use military force to eliminate a foe's nuclear program altogether. A classic example of this strategy is Israel's attack on an Iraqi nuclear reactor in 1981. Without warning, Israeli planes entered Iraqi airspace and bombed a reactor at Osirak that had been part of Iraq's nascent nuclear program. Widely criticized at the time, the attack succeeded in setting back Iraq's program for at least a decade. In September 2007, Israeli planes launched a similar attack on an alleged nuclear site in Syria. Although there is uncertainty about exactly what the Israelis destroyed—and Syria denied that the site was part of a nuclear program—subsequent investigations by the IAEA found evidence consistent with undeclared nuclear activities.[13] More recently, Israel has hinted that it might strike Iran's nuclear facilities.

There are several major obstacles to the success of coercive disarmament. First, the threat of force alone is unlikely to work because disarmament generates a potentially dramatic power shift: the state that gives up its weapons makes itself weaker and, thus, vulnerable to further demands. To frame this point in the language of Chapter 3, coercive disarmament generates a commitment problem: the threatening state must credibly commit that if the target gives in to its demands

---

13. Director General, International Atomic Energy Agency, *Implementation of the NPT Safeguards Agreement in the Syrian Arab Republic*, November 19, 2008, www.isis online.org/publications/syria/ IAEA_Report_Syria_19Nov2008.pdf (accessed 12/10/08).

and disarms, it will not exploit the target's weakness by making further demands. If such a commitment cannot be made credibly, then the target has good reason to resist the threat.

In actual cases that the United States has confronted, a credible commitment along these lines may be hard to achieve because of the underlying conflict of interests. As we noted in Chapter 3, the United States' conflicts with North Korea and Iran were not caused by those countries' nuclear programs. In fact, the causal arrow ran in the opposite direction: the United States had long-standing conflicts with those countries, and the conflicts contributed to those countries' desire to acquire nuclear weapons. Thus, it would not be unreasonable for Iran and North Korea to fear that if they gave in to U.S. demands to dismantle their weapons programs, they would essentially be making themselves more vulnerable to further demands. Indeed, one lesson these states may have drawn from the Iraq War is that a nuclear arsenal is useful for keeping the United States at bay. After all, it was Iraq, with no nuclear weapons, that was invaded; North Korea, with a small arsenal of such weapons, was not. To enhance the chances that threats of force will succeed, they have to be matched with some effort to reassure the target that its newfound weakness will not be exploited. Given the United States' underlying conflicts with these countries, it is not always obvious how to make such a commitment believable.

If threats alone do not work, then force may be the last resort, as in the case of the Israeli attack on the Osirak reactor and the American-led war on Iraq. A central difficulty with replicating the Israeli approach, besides the costs associated with using force, is that states have learned from this example. Proliferators have taken steps to harden and disperse their nuclear sites so that they are less vulnerable to attack. North Korea, for example, makes extensive use of tunnels and underground bunkers to hide and protect key elements of its nuclear program. As a result, it is hard to ensure that air attacks will succeed. The alternative approach of invading and occupying a country, as in the case of Iraq, increases the chances of verifiably eliminating a program, but the costs associated with such a venture are much higher.

What policy makers are left with in these tough cases is making a decision from among several alternatives, each of which has drawbacks. Military force is costly and of questionable effectiveness, particularly in the long term. Economic sanctions, to be effective, require viable international cooperation, which in many cases is lacking. The international community could, of course, let the state acquire nuclear weapons and rely on deterrence to render those weapons harmless. Deterrence has a good track record historically, but one cost of this approach is that each case of proliferation generates incentives for neighboring states to follow suit. The probable chain reaction increases the risks of accidents or of weapons falling into the wrong hands.

Alternatively, the United States and its allies may need to consider bargaining with states such as North Korea and Iran to address some of the underlying conflicts that led them to seek nuclear weapons in the first place. Such a deal would require these states to relinquish their weapons in exchange for economic aid, an end to diplomatic isolation, some kind of security guarantees, and probably substantive compromises on some of the regional issues that are the source of hostility. As we saw in Chapter 3, efforts to reach such a deal with North Korea have been frustrating and so far unsuccessful at getting that country to give up its weapons. In July 2015, negotiators unveiled a deal with Iran that sought to restrict that country's nuclear program for at least 10 years in exchange for an easing of economic sanctions. At the time of this writing, many of the details were yet to be worked out, and it faced opposition both in the United States and in Iran. Whether this deal will hold and lead to further progress on areas of disagreement or whether continued conflict and the threat of war are the only possible recourse remains an ongoing question.

Will China and the United States Fight for Global Leadership?

The proliferation of WMD is a relatively recent and small part of a much older and larger phenomenon in world politics: the ever-changing distribution of military power. If this book had been written in the sixteenth century, it would have focused on the foreign policy of the Habsburg Empire, an empire ruled from Spain that reaped enormous wealth from its overseas possessions in the New World. If this book had been written in the eighteenth century, many of its pages would have been devoted to France, which built an impressive empire in the first half of the century under Louis XIV and then plunged the entire European continent into war at the end of the century under Napoleon. A nineteenth-century version would have marveled at Great Britain's emergence as a world leader, as that country took advantage of its early industrialization to build an unparalleled navy and amass a global empire on which "the sun never set." An early twentieth-century edition would have focused on the rising power and ambition of Germany, which propelled the world into the two costliest wars it has ever experienced. And had this book been written in 1985, it would have focused on the Cold War between the United States and the Soviet Union, a conflict that seemed like it would go on indefinitely—but which, we now know, ended five years later with the collapse of the Soviet Union.

The cast of major actors on the world stage is always in flux as states and empires rise and fall. The underlying mechanism usually revolves around technology and economic growth.[14] States that discover and adopt new technologies and economic models tend to experience rapid growth in resources and power, thereby extending their influence in world politics. As other states catch up or make their own innovations, previous leaders can be challenged and even usurped,

---

14. See, for example, Paul Kennedy, *The Rise and Fall of the Great Powers* (New York: Random House, 1987); and Robert Gilpin, *War and Change in World Politics* (New York: Cambridge University Press, 1981).

The Chinese economy has grown rapidly in recent decades, thanks in part to the export of manufactured goods like the McDonald's toys produced in this factory.

allowing a new set of players to take center stage. This process not only changes the identity of the main actors in international politics but also creates dynamics that are themselves important. In some cases, a shift in the distribution of power can cause massive upheaval and war, as in the rise of Germany; in other cases, like the Cold War, challenges end with a whimper rather than a bang.

As we look to the future, the potential for changes at the top is very real. While long-term economic growth projections are fraught with uncertainty, most forecasters predict a significant reshuffling of the largest economies in the coming decades. Figure 14.1 shows the ten largest economies in 2013 and compares them to projected rankings for 2050. In this figure, the size of the U.S. economy in 2013 is fixed at 100, so every other country's economy is measured as a percentage of the United States' current GDP. As the figure shows, China is expected to overtake the United States as the number one economy sometime in the next several decades. The center of economic power will also shift from the west and north to the east and south, as India and Brazil join China in the upper ranks.

Of all these changes, the remarkable growth of China has attracted the greatest attention. The country's development has not only led to increased wealth but has also translated into increased military power. Although figures on China's military spending are uncertain and controversial, it is estimated that the country's defense budget has grown at an annual rate of about 10 percent per year since the mid-1990s.[15] China has long possessed the largest army in terms

15. U.S. Department of Defense, *Annual Report to Congress: Military and Security Developments Involving the People's Republic of China 2013*, 45, www.defense.gov/pubs/2013_china_report_final.pdf (accessed 02/12/15); see also previous issues of this annual report.

FIGURE 14.1 *The Ten Largest Economies, 2013 versus 2050*

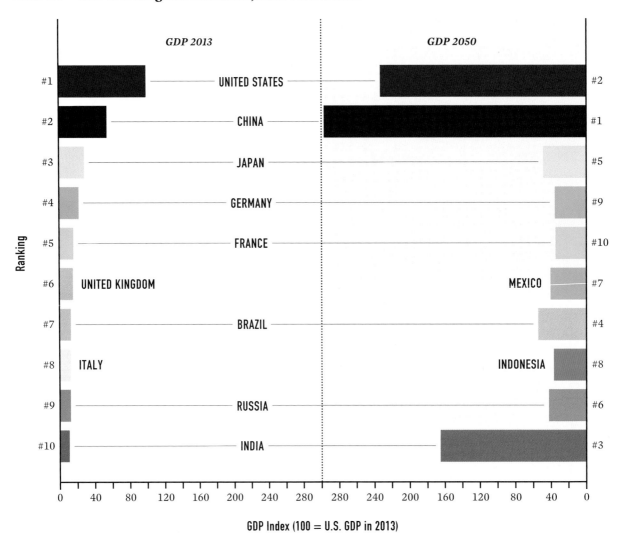

GDP Index (100 = U.S. GDP in 2013)

Figure sources: Rankings for 2013 are from the World Bank, http://data.worldbank.org/data-catalog/GDP-ranking-table (accessed 02/11/15); and projections for 2050 are from PwC Economics, "The World in 2050: The BRICS and Beyond," January 2013, www.pwc.com/gx/en/world-2050/assets/pwc-world-in-2050-report-january-2013.pdf (accessed 02/11/15).

Note: GDP is compared using market exchange rates.

of personnel, but its increases in military spending have helped modernize the Chinese military with advanced technology. In the process, China has enhanced its power projection capabilities—that is, its ability to project military force beyond its borders—through investments in aircraft carriers and midair refueling technologies. Moreover, China also possesses a modest arsenal of nuclear weapons: around 200 warheads, with 50 to 75 intercontinental ballistic missiles capable of hitting Europe or the United States.[16] To be sure, the United States will continue to be the world's dominant military power for some time. In recent years, U.S. defense spending has accounted for about 40 percent of the world's

16. U.S. Department of Defense, *Annual Report to Congress*, 31.

TABLE 14.1 *Comparing the Military Capabilities of China and the United States*

CAPABILITY	UNITED STATES	CHINA
Total military spending	$581 billion	$129 billion
Percent of world military spending	36%	8%
Active military personnel	1,433,150	2,333,000
Nuclear warheads	7,300	250
Intercontinental ballistic missiles	450	66
Nuclear submarines	14	4
Aircraft carriers	10	1
Bombers	155	136
Fighter aircraft	3,345	1,835
Main battle tanks	2,785	6,540
Artillery pieces	7,429	13,380

Note: All figures are 2014 estimates.

Sources: International Institute for Strategic Studies, *The Military Balance 2015* (London: Routledge, 2015), chapter 2. Nuclear warhead data from the Stockholm International Peace Research Institute, www.sipri.org /research/armaments/nuclear-forces (accessed 4/5/2015).

total. The United States also enjoys a large technological lead, and its nuclear arsenal dwarfs China's many times over (Table 14.1). Nonetheless, it seems likely that the gap between these countries in relative military power will shrink in the coming decades.

What are the implications of China's rise? To answer this question, we need to identify how rising power affects the interests of the rising state and its interaction with the current world leader, the United States. We also need to examine the role that institutions, both international and domestic, might play in containing potential conflict between the two.

What Do Theory and History Tell Us?

Both theory and history tell us that the rise of a new major power is potentially dangerous because of its effect on states' interests and the bargaining interaction between them. We saw in Chapter 3 that a large shift in the relative military power of two states has several effects. As a state becomes more powerful, it expects to do better in the event of a war. As a result, it will be more willing to threaten force to change the status quo. Bargains that were acceptable when the state was relatively weak will no longer be satisfactory. Hence, a rising state has an interest in using its newfound power to renegotiate preexisting arrangements. Of course, this development alone does not make war inevitable, since the costs of war ensure that a bargaining range exists. It is possible that the demands of the rising state can be defused peacefully through negotiated changes that reflect the new power distribution. Nonetheless, opportunities for crises will increase, along with the attendant danger of war due to the information and commitment problems.

One such problem is particularly dangerous in this context: because the rising state cannot commit *not* to revise deals in the future, the declining state may have an incentive to wage preventive war. As we saw in Chapter 3, the declining state may decide that war now is preferable to some future bargain that favors the rising state. An anticipated decline creates a temporary window of opportunity to try to secure one's military advantage by fighting and defeating the rising challenger. Theory tells us, then, that a change in relative power influences both interests and interactions in a way that makes conflict more likely: the rising state acquires an interest in revising the status quo, and the declining state faces a strategic environment that encourages preventive war.

Does the historical record confirm this fear? The argument that rising power increases the danger of war can be traced to one of the earliest known scholars of war, the Greek historian Thucydides. Writing in the third century B.C.E., Thucydides sought to explain the Peloponnesian Wars between two Greek city-states, Athens and Sparta. In his view, the wars arose because Sparta, which had once dominated the region, sought to contain the growing power and ambition of Athens, which was increasingly challenging Sparta's predominance. His often-quoted conclusion: "What made war inevitable was the growth of Athenian power and the fear which this caused in Sparta."[17] More recently, scholars have seen echoes of this logic in the wars that accompanied the rise of Germany in the early twentieth century.[18] As we discussed in Chapter 5, a key dynamic underlying both world wars was the growing ambition of Germany following its unification and rapid industrial and population growth in the late nineteenth century. Before World War I, this assertiveness manifested itself in a drive to acquire more territory, expand its colonial holdings, and wield influence in world politics commensurate with its power. The settlement that followed World War I—which stripped Germany of territory, colonies, and influence—only exacerbated the mismatch between what Germany possessed and what it believed it could possess, given its resources. Although Germany's fanatical, genocidal goals in World War II were due largely to Hitler's extreme ideology, this mismatch ensured that Germany would seek to revise the restrictive terms of the

17. Thucydides, *History of the Peloponnesian War*, trans. Rex Warner (London: Penguin Books, 1954), 49.
18. For an argument that Thucydides's logic is central to understanding major wars in the modern era, see Robert Gilpin, "The Theory of Hegemonic War," *Journal of Interdisciplinary History* 18 (Spring 1988): 591–613.

postwar settlement at some point.[19] Hence, the connection between rising power and an assertive foreign policy is borne out in the German case.

It is crucial, however, not to overgeneralize from this case, notwithstanding its obvious importance. There are also cases in which rising power did not lead to war. For example, the United States overtook Great Britain by most measures of power around the dawn of the twentieth century. The transition took place relatively peacefully, with Britain acquiescing to U.S. dominance in the Western Hemisphere in a series of crises over Venezuela and the Alaskan boundary with Canada. The handover of world leadership from Britain to the United States proceeded over the next several decades, aided by their common effort against Germany. By the 1950s, Britain was clearly a junior partner of its former colony. At that point, the United States faced a strong challenge from the Soviet Union, which built a massive conventional force and attained nuclear parity with the United States by the 1970s. Although the Cold War was a tense and dangerous time, this rivalry also ended without direct warfare between the two superpowers. The combination of American alliances (see Chapter 5) and nuclear weapons helped contain and deter the Soviet threat, and the Soviet Union eventually collapsed due to economic exhaustion. Finally, as the Cold War waned, there were concerns about an emerging struggle for power between the United States and either Germany, a powerhouse economy at the center of Europe, or Japan, whose dynamic economic growth in the 1980s led to warnings of a "coming war with Japan."[20] Neither of these predictions came true. Although the United States has in some ways accommodated the rising influence of these states, the process was peaceful and never escalated to threats of military conflict.

Why does the interaction between a rising power and the current leader sometimes end peacefully? A large part of the answer lies in the states' interests: how severely their interests conflict and how costly it is to use military power to force change. Consider Figure 14.2, which revisits the simple bargaining framework introduced in Chapter 3. As before, the horizontal bar represents all possible divisions of the good in dispute, and the relative military power of the states involved is captured by the line labeled *War Outcome* that divides the bar into shares that each state expects to obtain in the event of a war. Both the upper and the lower parts of this figure illustrate a power shift in favor of State A. Initially, State B is the stronger state, and the expected war outcome is close to its ideal point (the left end of the bar). We then assume that after a period of relative growth State A will be stronger, so that the war outcome after this power shift will be closer to State A's ideal point (the right end of the bar). The difference between the upper and the lower scenarios is the costs of war for each side. In the upper part, the costs of war are small relative to the shift in power, whereas in the lower part, the costs of war are relatively large.

The situation in the upper scenario is obviously quite dangerous, as we saw in Chapter 3. The declining State B expects to get more through war in the initial period (the portion of the bar to the right of the blue dotted line) than it expects to

---

19. This case is famously made by A. J. P. Taylor, *The Origins of the Second World War* (New York: Atheneum, 1961), esp. 24.

20. See, for example, George Friedman and Meredith Lebard, *The Coming War with Japan* (New York: St. Martin's Press, 1991).

FIGURE 14.2 *When Are Power Shifts Dangerous?*

Initially, State B is the stronger state, but as power shifts in favor of State A, the expected outcome of war shifts to the right, reducing the value of war for State B. Here, the costs of war are low compared to the size of the power shift, and the best possible deal that State B can get in the future is worse than its value for war now. Hence, the declining State B may have an incentive to wage preventive war.

However, if the costs of war are large enough, then a deal may be found that both states prefer to war now and after the power shift. Here, the possible deal gives both states more than their current and future values for war.

get from any deal that is in the bargaining range after the power shift—that is, any feasible bargain in the second period is farther from State B's ideal point than what it can achieve by fighting now. Hence, the danger of preventive war is quite real. This is not the case in the lower scenario, however. In this case, the bargaining range that will hold after the power shift includes deals that the declining State B prefers to fighting a war now. If the states were to reach a deal at, say, the line labeled *Possible Deal,* then State A could credibly commit not to use force to revise the deal in the future: such a deal gives State A more than it can expect to get through war even after it has grown stronger. As a result, State B has no incentive to wage a preventive war in the initial period. The danger of war is much lower in this second scenario because the costs of war loom large relative to the shift in power. These costs make it harder for the rising State A to take advantage of its newfound capabilities.

Recall that the costs of war in this model are measured relative to the value of whatever good is in dispute. Hence, the interaction between a rising and a declining state is more likely to look like the lower part if either the material costs of war are very high or the value of the good in dispute is low. In short, a power shift is not particularly dangerous if war is too costly to contemplate or if the conflict of interests in the relationship is so small that there is little worth fighting over.

This logic helps explain the relatively peaceful power shifts mentioned above. The Cold War challenge by the Soviet Union coincided with an enormous increase in the costs of war due to the advent of nuclear weapons. As we just saw, war was avoided in large part because of the threat of mutually assured destruction in the event of a nuclear exchange. In the case of Germany and Japan in the late twentieth century, there was little threat of a military confrontation with the United States because of the common interests that bound them together—common interests stemming from a shared strategic threat during the Cold War, strong commercial and financial ties, shared democratic values, and a history of beneficial cooperation.

A Coming Showdown or Peaceful Engagement?

We have then three kinds of historical precedents for thinking about the implication of China's rise: (1) the rise of Germany in the first half of the twentieth century witnessed a series of major wars, (2) the Soviet challenge during the Cold War was contained until the country collapsed, and (3) the rise of Germany and Japan in the last decades of the twentieth century was peacefully accommodated. How, then, is the rise of China in the twenty-first century likely to play out?

The pessimistic view is that China's rise is inherently dangerous because there are large conflicts of interest between that Communist nation and the United States.[21] In this view, China, unlike Japan, cannot be accommodated in an American-led international order that values capitalism and democracy, and it will instead seek to overturn that order and institute its own. Just as Germany sought mastery of Europe in the first half of the twentieth century, China will use its new

---

21. See, for example, Aaron Friedberg, "The Struggle for Mastery in Asia," *Commentary* 110 (November 2000): 17–26.

China's growing wealth has translated into increased military power that may eventually match that of the United States. As part of its effort to modernize its military capabilities, China has built submarines capable of launching nuclear missiles.

power to seek mastery in Asia, pushing out American influence. If so, the United States will have to react with alarm, since it has strong economic interests in the region that would be jeopardized. In this view, the dangers of Chinese assertiveness and the preventive incentives of the United States loom large.

Supporters of this view argue that the best way to respond to this prospect is to contain China in the same way that the West contained the Soviet Union during the Cold War.[22] Such a policy would be designed to slow down China's rise and to deter war by increasing the costs. The containment strategy would have two main prongs. The first would be an effort to slow down China's amazing economic growth by denying it access to the large U.S. market. Since a good deal of China's growth is based on exports to the West, advocates of containment argue that allowing these exports to have free access to Western markets serves only to strengthen an inevitable adversary. The second prong of the containment strategy would be to strengthen and build alliances with China's neighbors in order to provide an effective counterweight to its growing power. This would mean maintaining U.S. military bases in the region, particularly in Japan, South Korea, and the Philippines, and building ties with other states that have reason to fear China's growing might, such as India and Vietnam. By adding the power of these countries to that of the United States, such alliances would blunt the impact of China's growth on the balance of military capabilities (that is, lower p_2) and increase the costs of war (that is, increase a). In short, the containment strategy would seek to prevent China from becoming more aggressive by slowing the rise of its power and making war less attractive.

Against this pessimistic view is a more optimistic one that places faith in the role of institutions, both international and domestic, to mitigate the risk of war.[23] This argument holds that China's participation in international institutions, combined with a reform of its domestic institutions, could transform that country's interests so that it becomes a supporter, rather than a challenger, of the status quo. If so, then war can be avoided by eliminating conflicts worth fighting over. Supporters of this view advocate a strategy of engagement that seeks to encourage positive institutional changes.

At the international level, the engagement strategy would involve promoting Chinese membership in a web of institutions dealing with security, trade, and finance. For example, supporters of engagement successfully pushed for China to be admitted into the World Trade Organization (WTO); for China to play a larger role in the Association of Southeast Asian Nations (ASEAN), which deals with regional

22. See, for example, Gideon Rachman, "Containing China," *Washington Quarterly* 19 (Winter 1996): 1291–40.

23. See, for example, James Shinn, ed., *Weaving the Net: Conditional Engagement with China* (New York: Council on Foreign Relations, 1996); Audrey Cronin and Patrick Cronin, "The Realistic Engagement of China," *Washington Quarterly* 19 (Winter 1996): 141–70; and Kenneth Lieberthal, "A New China Strategy," *Foreign Affairs* 74 (November–December 1995): 35–49.

security issues; and for China to have a larger say in the decisions of the International Monetary Fund (IMF) and World Bank. Such efforts seek to increase the benefits that China derives from the existing set of international institutions and thereby diminish its incentives to upend that order. These reforms not only move the status quo in China's favor but also increase the costs of war relative to the benefits that can be won. The hope is that by enmeshing China in a web of existing institutions, that country's leaders will find a belligerent foreign policy—and the threat of exclusion from those institutions—to be too costly.[24]

At the same time, advocates of engagement hope that economic growth will, over time, lead to change in China's domestic institutions toward greater political freedom and democracy. The underlying idea is that wealth and trade will give rise to a potent middle class of businesspeople and merchants who will demand greater political liberalization. A vibrant and politically active middle class is generally seen as a key ingredient in the emergence of democracy in western Europe. If prosperity leads to political liberalization, then China's growing power can be rendered harmless through democracy, which will weaken the influence of the Chinese military and sensitize its leaders to the costs of military conflict. In this case, the rise of China could be as benign as the rise of the United States in the late nineteenth century or of western Europe and Japan in the late twentieth century.

What Will the United States Do?

U.S. policy in the last decade has combined aspects of both strategies, although the engagement approach has been emphasized. The United States has maintained its bases in East Asia while pursuing closer relations with India and Vietnam. To date, however, there has been no effort to pursue defensive alliances equivalent to an East Asian NATO, and there is no serious talk of preventive war. At the same time, the United States has pushed for Chinese admission into the WTO, guaranteeing favorable treatment of Chinese exports, and has promoted China's active participation in a variety of regional and global organizations.

The adoption, so far, of an engagement policy reflects a number of international realities. Many East Asian countries profit from trade ties with China, and they are reluctant to jeopardize those ties by taking a more confrontational approach. Moreover, the enormous potential costs of a military conflict with China make preventive war an extremely unattractive, and hence unlikely, option. Although China's nuclear arsenal is currently rather small and vulnerable, it is developing more survivable capabilities, including submarine-launched ballistic missiles, which would give it a second-strike force. Thus, nuclear deterrence may play a role in U.S.-China relations similar to the role it played during the Cold War.

In addition to these international considerations, policy toward China is heavily influenced by the interaction of domestic interests within the United States. The impressive economic development of China has not only led to concerns about its military power; it has also led businesses in the United States and around the world

---

24. For an argument that membership in security institutions can change the way China's foreign policy makers see their security interests, see Alastair Iain Johnston, *Social States: China in International Institutions, 1980–2000* (Princeton, NJ: Princeton University Press, 2008).

to eagerly contemplate the prospects of selling into that enormous market. Imagine over 1 billion Chinese consumers wealthy enough to buy cellular phones or cars. The potential profits are enormous. As a result, American businesses have lobbied hard to improve relations between the two countries. For example, President Bill Clinton threatened in 1993 to revoke China's most-favored-nation trading status unless it made concrete improvements in its human rights record. When China refused to comply, American business interests pressured the Clinton administration to drop its threat.[25] The same interests weighed in strongly in 1999 to push successfully for China's admission into the WTO. Hence, export-oriented businesses interested in the potential of the Chinese market have influenced policy makers' calculations on how much to confront or accommodate this rising power.

We should note that the word *potential* is an important qualifier here, since, to date, China has played a much larger role as an exporter of its own products (primarily low-cost clothes and toys) than as an importer of U.S. products. Indeed, the United States has consistently run an enormous trade deficit with China, more than $300 billion in 2014. One study estimated that the dramatic increase in American imports from China since 1990 was responsible for about one-quarter of the decline in American manufacturing employment in this period.[26] Thus, it is Chinese workers, not Chinese consumers, who are driving that country's economic relations with the United States. As a result, trade unions representing American workers who compete with Chinese imports have been vocal in protesting that country's human rights record and its trading practices. Although these groups have not called for anything like a preventive war to restrain China's growth, they have opposed more accommodating policies, such as China's admission into the WTO, and they have found common cause with so-called China hawks in the U.S. government and military who advocate a tougher line, including military containment. While export-oriented businesses have so far been more influential, an increase in the power of these more hawkish groups would make it harder for the United States to peacefully accommodate China's rise. It is clear that U.S. policy toward China will be driven as much by the push and pull of domestic interests as by strategic considerations at the international level.

If the coalition supporting engagement continues to hold in the United States, then we will learn whether or not the adherents of this view are right. Growing membership in international institutions and/or liberalization of political institutions at home may turn China into a partner, rather than a rival, of the United States. It is also possible, of course, that domestic political reforms may never materialize and that China will find its newfound power too tempting not to wield aggressively in international bargaining. It is also possible that the interests in the United States supporting a harder line against China will become stronger in the face of economic and military competition. If so, increased conflict will be hard to avoid. In short, the implications of China's rise will depend a great deal on the interests that come to prevail in both countries.

---

25. See David M. Lampton, "America's China Policy in the Age of the Finance Minister: Clinton Ends Linkage," *China Quarterly* 139 (September 1994): 597–621.

26. David H. Autor, David Corn, and Gordon H. Hanson, "The China Syndrome: Local Labor Market Effects of Import Competition in the United States," *American Economic Review* 103 (October 2013): 2121–68.

Will Economic Globalization Continue?

China's impressive economic growth over the past few decades is part of a much larger process that has important consequences throughout the world: economic globalization. The term *globalization* refers to the spread of activities and ideas across the globe. As applied to economics, globalization involves increasing integration of national economies through the movement of goods, services, and money across borders. This process, in its most recent manifestation, took off in the last decades of the twentieth century owing to improvements in technology, particularly transportation, communication, and information technologies. The development of containerized shipping in the 1950s—with goods placed on ships in standardized containers that can be directly transferred to trucks or train cars—dramatically lowered the costs of international trade. Advances in telecommunications and computing, and particularly the advent of the Internet in the 1990s, have reduced the effects of distance, making it possible to transmit information anywhere in the world instantaneously.

Globalization has also occurred alongside changes in ideas about the proper relationship between the state and the economy. In the eighteenth century, the ideology of mercantilism saw economics as subordinate to state interests and led states to intervene extensively in economic relations with the goal of building and protecting their wealth. The twentieth century saw the rise of an extreme form of economic intervention known as central planning. The Soviet Union and other Communist states sought to govern economic exchanges from the center, with production levels and prices determined not by supply and demand but rather by the dictates of a government bureaucracy. These systems outlawed private ownership of the means of production, making them the property of the state. Both ideologies have given way to a liberal economic view that the state should respect private property and that economic exchanges should be determined by the choices of private actors—in short, that markets, rather than governments, should be the primary driver of economic outcomes. While this view has been influential since the eighteenth century, the end of the Cold War, and the collapse of the Soviet model, ushered in a period in which the liberal economic view has been ascendant.

In concert with these changes, governments worldwide have lowered many of the barriers to trade and financial flows, as we saw in Chapters 7 and 8. This process has been aided by a series of global and regional trade agreements such as the WTO, the North American Free Trade Agreement (NAFTA), and the European Union. The result has been an explosion of world trade over the last 50 years and a dramatic increase in the flow of capital across borders. Figure 14.3 shows how the volume of world exports has grown dramatically since 1950, faster than the overall world GDP. Even the global economic downturn in 2009 registers as a onetime blip in this trend.

Although the steady upward slope of the lines in this figure suggests an inexorable trend, there are also strong forces pushing in the opposite direction. As we saw in Chapters 7 through 10, freer trade and capital flows create losers as well as winners, and the former have interests in slowing or reversing the process of globalization. The existence of an antiglobalization backlash was dramatically illustrated

FIGURE 14.3 *The Expanding Volume of World Trade, 1950–2015*

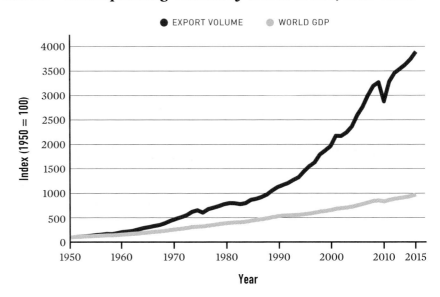

● EXPORT VOLUME   ● WORLD GDP

Figure source: World Trade Organization, *International Trade Statistics 2014* (Geneva: WTO, 2014), Table A1a. Updated with projections to 2015 using information from the WTO.

Note: The figure compares the growth of world trade and GDP by setting the values of both in 1950 equal to 100 and measuring subsequent years relative to that baseline. An index value of, say, 500 indicates that the quantity of interest is five times larger than it was in 1950.

in November 1999, when delegates to a conference of the WTO met in Seattle to jump-start a new round of global trade talks. The delegates were greeted by throngs of demonstrators protesting the WTO and the process of globalization for which it stood. Protesters blocked streets and clashed with police in an effort to disrupt the meeting and have their voices heard. Inside the WTO meeting hall, the conflicts that arose among the delegates were more diplomatic and restrained, but no less severe. The meeting adjourned without an agreement on the important issues facing the world trade system. The so-called Battle of Seattle was the first of what are now routine public demonstrations that greet meetings of the WTO and other institutions associated with globalization, such as the World Bank and the IMF.

Will globalization continue, pushed forward by the incessant march of technology? Or will the turbulence associated with these changes engender a political backlash that causes the process of globalization to grind to a halt? Thinking through these questions requires that we understand the interests generated by globalization, how the interaction between the winners and losers will play out, and whether existing institutions can survive this conflict.

What Do Theory and History Tell Us?

Changes in technology influence the way economic actors pursue their interests, particularly their interest in maximizing income. Declining transportation and communication costs create strong incentives to overcome boundaries and increase the scope of markets so that they are global, rather than national or regional. When goods are costly to transport, it makes sense for production facilities to be located close to where the goods will be sold. As transportation costs decline, proximity to the consumer becomes less important. A company trying to decide where to build a production facility can use different criteria, such as labor costs and tax or regulatory policies. Improved transportation technologies thus allow companies to look around the world to find a location that will allow them to maximize profits.

This is true whether the company produces a physical good, such as a toy or an article of clothing, or a service, such as accounting or insurance. Indeed, the decline of communication costs brought about by the Internet has allowed companies to move offshore many services that have traditionally been done domestically. For example, when you call customer support for your new computer, it is quite likely that you will be connected to someone in the Philippines. Some hospitals in the United States have even sent patients' X-rays to India to be read by radiologists there—radiologists who demand a much lower wage than do their American counterparts.[27] The ability to create a flawless digital scan of an X-ray and send it to the other side of the world instantaneously—unthinkable only a decade ago—makes this possible.

Meetings of the WTO and IMF are now routinely accompanied by demonstrations against the perceived injustices of economic globalization. Globalization has created winners and losers, and their conflicting interests raise questions about the future of the world economy.

The economic interests created by these advancements make themselves heard in the political realm as well. As companies find it profitable to increase the scope of markets, they pressure governments to lower barriers to the movement of goods, services, and money across borders. A company that wants to locate in China but sell its wares to the United States will lobby the United States to allow free entrance of Chinese-made products. Otherwise, trade barriers may nullify the advantages of making the goods in China. Multinational companies also have an interest in ensuring that they can move their capital around the globe freely, so profits made in one country can be moved to another or so they can make direct investment decisions without having to worry about barriers. Furthermore, these companies have an interest in strong protections for their property rights, so they can open facilities in any country they like without having to fear that their property or profits will be seized. As we have seen, there are a number of reasons why these multinational companies wield substantial influence on government policy and, hence, why they are a potent force in pushing globalization forward.

History also tells us, however, that globalization is neither inevitable nor irreversible. People living in 1913 could look back at similarly impressive trends. In the preceding century, trade had grown from 2 percent of world income to 18 percent. International capital flows were also increasing impressively. Foreign-held assets grew from about 7 percent of world GDP in 1870 to 17.5 percent in 1913. And the movement of people was at a scale that dwarfs migration rates of today: between 1870 and 1910, about 10 percent of the world's population relocated permanently from one country to another; the comparable figure for the past three decades is no

---

27. Frank Levy and Kyoung-Hee Yu, "Offshoring Radiology Services to India," Working Paper MIT-IPC-06-005, Industrial Performance Center, Massachusetts Institute of Technology, Cambridge, September 2006.

more than 2 percent.[28] World War I and the economic dislocations that followed brought this period of globalization crashing to a halt, and the period between the world wars saw the erection of new national barriers against the flow of goods and money. Although economic integration is today much wider and deeper than in 1913, this case offers a stark reminder that political conflict can slow or even reverse seemingly inevitable economic processes.

Indeed, globalization in its contemporary form has generated no shortage of conflicts, both among and within states. Globalization generates conflict because it creates losers as well as winners. Among the winners are those economic actors that can take advantage of increased opportunities to move money and goods throughout the world—particularly, multinational companies and investors. Increased efficiency has also benefited consumers in the form of lower prices on imported goods. Who are the economic losers?

Recall from Chapter 7 that there are two different theories for thinking about who wins and who loses from trade liberalization. The Ricardo-Viner, or specific factors, model holds that trade interests are determined by the sector one works in: those in sectors that compete with imports want protection, while those in sectors that rely on exports want liberalization. The alternative theory, Stolper-Samuelson, holds that trade interests are determined by the factor of production—capital, labor, or land—that provides one's income. In this view, free trade benefits those factors that are relatively abundant in a country at the expense of those factors that are relatively scarce. In the developed world, where capital is relatively abundant and labor is scarce (particularly, unskilled labor), capital wins from free trade, while unskilled labor loses. In the developing world, where unskilled labor is abundant, holders of capital lose from free trade, while labor benefits. It is generally thought that while the predictions of Ricardo-Viner hold in the short term, long-run patterns of conflict follow the predictions of Stolper-Samuelson.[29] In other words, as globalization persists and deepens, conflicts will increasingly crystallize along class lines: capital versus labor, with the positions of each being determined by whether they are in the developing or developed world.

Resistance to Globalization in the Developed World

In developed countries, the group most negatively affected by globalization is workers—particularly, unskilled workers. As rich countries become more closely integrated with developing countries, workers in the former face increasing competition from unskilled workers in the latter. A company that makes toys or clothing can find workers willing to accept much lower wages in China or Vietnam than in the United States. As a result, production of labor-intensive goods has moved away from developed countries to the developing world, causing job losses in the

---

28. These figures are from David Dollar and Aart Kraay, "Spreading the Wealth," *Foreign Affairs* 8, no. 1 (January–February 2002): 122–23; and Nicholas Crafts, "Globalisation and Economic Growth: A Historical Perspective," *World Economy* 27, no. 1 (January 2004): 46.

29. Michael Mussa, "Tariffs and the Distribution of Income: The Importance of Factor Specificity, Substitutability, and Intensity in the Short and Long Run," *Journal of Political Economy* 82 (November–December 1974): 1191–203.

former. For example, from 1970 to 2000, the textiles and clothing industries in the five richest developed countries shed more than 4 million jobs, over 62 percent of their labor force.[30] Workers in affected sectors who have not lost their jobs have experienced stagnant or falling wages and have suffered from job insecurity.

Given this situation, it is not surprising that labor unions in rich countries have been at the forefront of a backlash against globalization. What may be surprising is how broadly based the opposition to globalization among labor unions has been. Consider, for example, what happened in 1999, when the United States approved a treaty admitting China into the WTO—thereby giving China permanent most-favored-nation trading status. Unions representing textile and clothing workers were in full-throated opposition to the pact, which would increase international competition for this beleaguered sector. They were joined by some apparently strange bedfellows.[31] For example, the Teamsters Union, which represents truckers, lobbied against the treaty. This stance was curious because at the same time one of the Teamsters' largest employers, United Parcel Service, was lobbying for a coveted new air route for landing cargo planes in China. One U.S. official summed up the contradiction: "It seems that the Teamsters want us to have more cargo flights to China, but no cargo." Even stranger was the opposition of the United Auto Workers. Until China's admission into the WTO, virtually no U.S.-made cars could be sold in China; after the treaty passed, U.S. automakers would have freer access to the Chinese market. Why would American autoworkers not be in favor of this? Stranger yet was the opposition of a major dockworkers' union, the International Longshore and Warehouse Union. These workers make their living loading and unloading ships that are engaged in international trade. One would think that expanding trade with China should be in their interests. And yet opposition to the pact came not only from workers in sectors that directly compete with Chinese imports but also from workers in sectors that thrive on exports and might, therefore, have been expected to support the deal.

This kind of class-based, rather than sector-based, opposition is exactly what the Stolper-Samuelson theorem predicts. The insecurities that globalization has created for workers in sectors that compete with imports is rippling outward and affecting the attitudes of workers in other sectors as well, generating political cleavages along class lines. Their fears are based on a number of concerns that include, but also go beyond, issues of job losses. One fear is that globalization is exacerbating inequality, with workers increasingly left behind. Indeed, there is evidence of increasing income inequality in many countries, although economists debate how much of this trend is due to international trade. After all, other developments over the last several decades, including the weakening of labor unions and the increasing importance of technology, account for some of the gap. Regardless of the actual role of trade in exacerbating inequality, the perception of a strong effect is widespread and politically potent. (For more on this issue, see "How Do We Know?" on p. 606.)

30. Organisation for Economic Co-operation and Development, "A New World Map in Textiles and Clothing: Adjusting to Change," Table 3.1, www.oecd.org/dataoecd/29/53/34042484.pdf (accessed 09/21/06).

31. The following is based on Thomas L. Friedman, "America's Labor Pains" *New York Times*, May 9, 2000, A25.

Is Globalization Increasing Inequality?

To what extent has increased integration of the global economy contributed to inequality? We know that income inequality within countries has generally increased at the same time that globalization has increased. The amount of inequality within a country is often measured by using a number called a Gini coefficient, named after the Italian statistician Corrado Gini. The Gini coefficient ranges from 0 to 100, with a value of 0 indicating that everyone has the same income (that is, perfect equality) and a value of 100 indicating that all the income is earned by one individual (that is, maximum inequality). Using this measure, the World Bank estimates that average income inequality within countries has increased in almost every region of the world over the last two decades, with the exception of the states of the former Soviet Union and in sub-Saharan Africa. Figure A here shows changes in the Gini coefficients for selected countries from 1985 to 2012. Although inequality has gone down in a few cases, the general pattern is in the other direction.

It might be tempting to conclude that because increased globalization has gone hand in hand with increased inequality, then globalization must cause inequality. The story is more complex than that, however, because other factors drive income inequality as well. Foremost is the growing importance of technology in the global economy. The dramatic advances in information and communications technology (ICT) that helped make globalization possible have also transformed the way people work and the skills they need to be productive. As these technologies have spread around the globe, they have boosted the productivity of people with the knowledge to use them and the capital to invest in them. As a result, the demand for low-skilled labor has decreased. Hence, the growing use of ICT is a likely factor in the widening of the income gap.

How much of growing income inequality is due to trade and financial integration, and how much is due to technology? Economists at the IMF analyzed the data on income equality in order to tease out the different effects.[a]

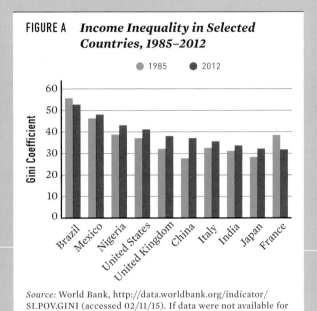

FIGURE A *Income Inequality in Selected Countries, 1985–2012*

● 1985   ● 2012

Source: World Bank, http://data.worldbank.org/indicator/SI.POV.GINI (accessed 02/11/15). If data were not available for 1985 or 2012, the closest available year was used.

They examined how income inequality changes over time in response to (1) how closely a country is integrated into global markets through trade and financial flows and (2) how much of the country's capital stock consists of ICT.

The results show that the relative contributions of globalization and technology to income inequality depend on the country's level of development. Among developed countries, both increasing economic globalization and the rising use of ICT have benefited skilled workers and owners of capital; in contrast, both factors have hurt unskilled workers who face increasing job and wage competition from computers at home and from unskilled workers abroad. In developing countries, however, trade and financial integration were estimated to cause a slight *decrease* in income inequality as unskilled workers benefited from their ability to export labor-intensive goods to the developed world. This effect was offset, however, by increasing income inequality due to the spread of ICT. Overall, then, the income gap in the developing world has increased—not because of economic globalization but because of the increasing importance of the technologies that have made globalization possible.

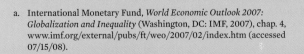

a. International Monetary Fund, *World Economic Outlook 2007: Globalization and Inequality* (Washington, DC: IMF, 2007), chap. 4, www.imf.org/external/pubs/ft/weo/2007/02/index.htm (accessed 07/15/08).

In addition, there is a growing asymmetry between labor and investment capital that derives from the fact that capital can move around the globe in search of higher profits much more easily than workers can move around looking for jobs and better wages. Companies can threaten to close up shop and move, and this threat gives managers (who represent capital) bargaining leverage over workers to lower wage and benefit demands. It also leads to increased job insecurity. Unions have also expressed concerns about a "race to the bottom" in labor standards. In the developed world, unions fought hard for a number of protections that most people now take for granted: minimum wage laws, prohibitions on child labor, limits on the length of the work week, and worker safety regulations. These protections either do not exist or are much weaker in developing countries. Unions fear that the increased mobility of investment capital means that companies can move around the world looking for places with fewer worker protections. If countries compete for capital by weakening or resisting demands for these protections, hard-fought gains in labor standards could wither away.

Opposition to globalization does not come solely from its economic losers, however. Labor unions have been joined by an ally motivated by a noneconomic interest: groups concerned about protecting the environment.[32] The environmental case against globalization is driven by several concerns. The first is that the rapid growth of economic activity will hasten the degradation of the environment. Increasing industrial production in countries like China, Brazil, India, and Mexico threatens all manner of environmental harms, including increased pollution and greenhouse gas emissions and a hastening of deforestation and biodiversity loss. These concerns are particularly pronounced because of a second concern: developing countries often lack environmental regulations that limit destructive activities. Indeed, just as workers express fears of a race to the bottom in labor standards, environmentalists worry that the globalization of production will lead to a race to the bottom in environmental regulations. Finally, these groups fear that efforts to protect the environment will be sacrificed on the altar of free trade. This concern arose in the early 1990s when a body of the General Agreement on Tariffs and Trade (GATT; see Chapter 7) ruled against an American ban on imports of tuna caught in nets that kill dolphins. While environmentalists saw this ban as a reasonable way to protect dolphins, Mexico argued successfully that the ban violated GATT rules. The GATT's successor, the WTO, similarly ruled against U.S. clean-gas standards that affected imports from Brazil and Venezuela. These rulings galvanized the environmental movement to oppose unrestricted trade liberalization.

Resistance to Globalization in the Developing World

People in poorer countries have also experienced insecurity as a result of globalization. The Stolper-Samuelson theorem predicts that in the long run, trade liberalization will raise the incomes of unskilled workers in developing countries. And,

---

32. See, for example, Daniel C. Esty, *Greening the GATT: Trade, Environment, and the Future* (Washington, DC: Institute for International Economics, 1994).

indeed, despite the lamentable conditions for workers in much of the developing world, the opportunities created by access to rich markets have improved the lot of many, as we saw in Chapter 10. Nonetheless, there are several reasons why people in poor countries face globalization with fear and resistance.

One reason has to do with the relatively weak social safety nets that exist in developing countries. In the developed world, growing exposure to international trade after World War II coincided with the expansion of government assistance designed to protect workers from economic hard times. Unemployment benefits, poverty alleviation programs, government-subsidized health insurance, job retraining programs, minimum guaranteed pensions—all these policies had the effect of cushioning workers from the hard edges of international competition. People who lose their jobs owing to foreign trade receive some assistance in making ends meet and in getting a new job. In poorer countries, however, these safety nets are generally not as strong, so workers face economic dislocations with greater insecurity.

Workers in the developing world may also have less access to institutions that give them clout in political and economic decision making. Representative democracy, for example, is still more common in rich countries than in poor ones. As a result, workers in the latter have a harder time translating their numbers into political power to demand greater redistribution. Similarly, the right to form labor unions is not as strong in many developing states as it is in the developed world. These institutions enable workers to pool their efforts and resources and to act collectively in pursuit of wage and benefit demands from employers. Even if globalization creates a larger pie of profits, weak or nonexistent unions make it harder for workers to get a larger slice of that pie.

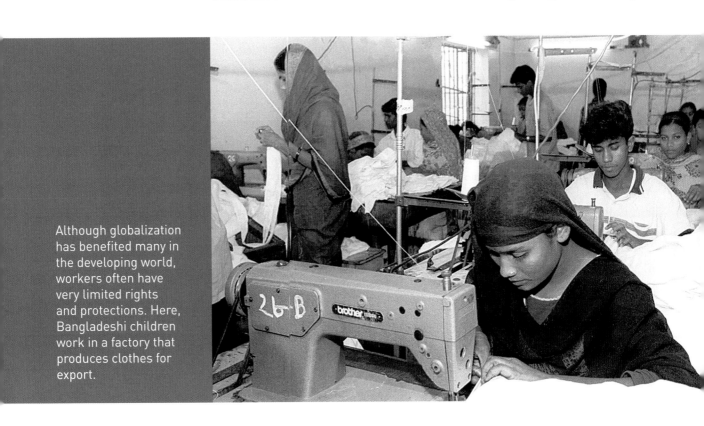

Although globalization has benefited many in the developing world, workers often have very limited rights and protections. Here, Bangladeshi children work in a factory that produces clothes for export.

Finally, increasing capital mobility has increased the volatility of poor economies, as large sums of foreign money can enter or leave at a moment's notice. As we saw in Chapters 8 and 10, countries that lose the faith of international capital markets can suffer a devastating punishment. In a very short time, capital flight can cause inflation and unemployment to spike. And while international institutions like the IMF may come to a country's rescue, their assistance often requires that governments cut back spending and subsidies that benefit the poor. Given all this, it is easy to see why many people in the developing world do not perceive what economic theory tells us is their long-term interest in globalization.

Backlash and the International Trading System

Actors who see their interests as being harmed by globalization are at the forefront of a political backlash that has the potential to create conflict both within and among states. Just as those who stand to gain from globalization have pushed governments to lower barriers to trade and money flows, those who stand to lose have sought to influence policy in the other direction. The economic losers have an incentive to seek protection from foreign competition in the form of trade barriers or restrictions on capital flows. In addition, the increased insecurity caused by globalization generates a greater demand for social welfare programs designed to cushion workers from the shocks of competition. Workers and their representatives have demanded more government spending to provide unemployment insurance, health insurance, and job retraining programs. Such redistribution would naturally come at the expense of the winners, who may or may not accommodate those demands.

Demands by those who stand to lose from globalization can also spill over into international tensions and jeopardize the institutions that govern world trade. To the extent that threatened groups are successful in raising trade barriers against foreign competition, they invite retaliation by other countries. For example, the United States frequently imposes trade restrictions on countries for allegedly dumping goods in the United States at artificially low costs. To consumers of those goods, these low costs are a boon. But to producers who have to compete with cheap imports, they are a threat. Producers who suspect they have been hurt by dumping can appeal to the U.S. government for sanctions against the alleged offender. The widespread use of antidumping measures by the United States has prompted other countries to cry foul. Since dumping is sometimes hard to prove, targets of antidumping sanctions claim that these measures are simply a guise for protectionism. As a result, the proper use and regulation of these sanctions has been an important, and divisive, issue in world trade talks.

Indeed, efforts to move forward on a new round of global trade talks have been thwarted ever since the 1999 Battle of Seattle mentioned earlier. The deadlock at the Seattle meeting presaged a series of similar failures, and even though the WTO launched the Doha Round of talks in 2001, negotiations have since broken down. Conflict between the rich and poor countries has been central to the talks' collapse.

Among the key issues of contention have been the use of antidumping and related mechanisms (which rich states favor and poor states oppose) and whether trade rules should take into account labor or environmental standards (which environmentalists and labor unions in the developed world want and developing country governments have resisted).

Most significantly, however, rich and poor countries have also come into conflict over the pace and scope of trade liberalization. Since World War II, the most dramatic liberalization has taken place in the realm of manufactured goods, the primary producers of which are located in developed countries. Rich countries have also pushed hard to liberalize trade in services, such as banking, accounting, and communications—sectors in which their companies are very competitive. Poor countries, in contrast, have sought greater liberalization of the agricultural sector, since farming constitutes a significant portion of their economies. Liberalizing trade in agriculture would require rich countries to reduce or eliminate the very generous agricultural subsidies that they pay to their farmers. These subsidies account for about 20 percent of total farm receipts in developed countries, and over 50 percent in some countries, including Japan, South Korea, and Norway.[33] These government payments support farmers' incomes, allowing them to keep the prices of agricultural products artificially low. In the process, they deprive farmers in the developing world of much-needed income. Recent trade talks have stalled owing to conflict between rich country governments, which are reluctant to alienate a politically powerful constituency, and poor country governments, which represent most of the world's farmers.

As we look forward, then, globalization generates two interrelated phenomena that have to be reconciled. On the one hand, increasing integration among national economies can produce enormous wealth. This is certainly true for the producers who can take advantage of their mobility to locate themselves in an efficient manner. There is also some evidence that it is true of countries as a whole: a study by the World Bank showed that countries that are most closely integrated in the global economy have on average grown faster than those that are less well integrated.[34] On the other hand, globalization has had negative impacts on the jobs, livelihoods, and economic security of many people. These people have understandably organized to slow the process of economic integration and to seek protection from the harms that global competition can cause.

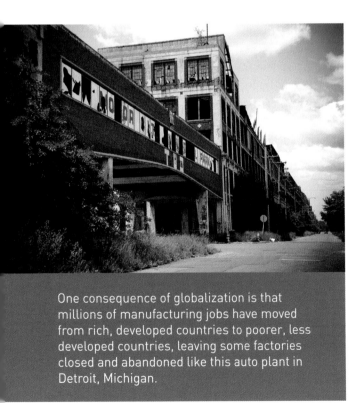

One consequence of globalization is that millions of manufacturing jobs have moved from rich, developed countries to poorer, less developed countries, leaving some factories closed and abandoned like this auto plant in Detroit, Michigan.

33. Organisation for Economic Co-operation and Development, *Agricultural Policy Monitoring and Evaluation 2014: OECD Countries* (Paris: OECD Publishing, 2014).

34. Dollar and Kraay, "Spreading the Wealth."

The global economic downturn that started in 2008 gave additional impetus to such forces, as shrinking economies and rising unemployment heightened concerns about the effects of international competition. Although there was no widespread resort to protectionism, there has been a resurgence of skepticism about trade liberalization in both developed and developing countries. One of the more ambitious trade initiatives of recent years has been an attempt by the United States and the European Union to negotiate a wide-ranging trade agreement called the Transatlantic Trade and Investment Partnership (TTIP). While governments on both sides of the Atlantic support the initiative, there is powerful opposition both in the United States and in Europe. Similar efforts to negotiate a Trans-Pacific Partnership, designed to increase trade and investment in the Asia-Pacific region, have run up against determined opposition from organized labor, environmentalists, and a variety of advocacy groups.

Although there are reasons to be concerned about how these tensions will play out, economic theory tells us that conflict is not inevitable. As we noted in Chapter 7, while trade liberalization creates winners and losers, the overall benefits generally exceed the economic value of the jobs that may be put in jeopardy. Given this observation, globalization can, in theory, make everyone better off but only if some of the gains to the winners are redistributed to compensate those who stand to lose.[35]

A central challenge is that while markets respect national boundaries less and less, the legal reach of governments still ends at their borders. Although states can try to influence one another's policies through threats and promises, the ability to impose taxes, regulate companies, manipulate the supply of money, or dole out welfare benefits to needy people is limited by their territorial reach. But globalization creates demands for redistribution and regulation on a global scale. The increasing scope of markets from national to global raises the question of whether government will need to expand in scope as well, with national governments giving way to some form of global governance. It is to this prospect that we now turn.

Will a Shrinking Globe Lead to Global Government?

On December 17, 2010, Mohamed Bouazizi, a street vendor in Tunisia, doused himself in gasoline and set himself on fire in front of a local government office. According to his family and friends, Bouazizi's act was a response to repeated harassment by police, who confiscated his wares earlier that day, and the unwillingness of local authorities to hear his grievances. Bouazizi died 18 days later, but his act of self-immolation ignited a fire that quickly spread across not only Tunisia but also

---

35. See, for example, Kenneth Scheve and Matthew Slaughter, "A New Deal for Globalization," *Foreign Affairs* 86, no. 4 (July–August 2007): 34–47.

most of northern Africa and the Middle East. As the Tunisian police tried to quell protests, and government-run news stations refused to cover the event, news of Bouazizi's act and the heavy-handed police response quickly spread through social media platforms, such as YouTube, Twitter, and Facebook. Tunisians disgruntled with their corrupt and unresponsive government mobilized rapidly, and ten days after Bouazizi's death, the country's president of 23 years fled the country. Over the next few weeks and months, similar protest movements sprang up across the region, leading to the downfall of leaders in Egypt, Libya, and Yemen; political reforms in a variety of other countries; and a raging civil war in Syria. Although the protests were fueled by long-simmering dissatisfaction with governments in the region, the spread of news, information, and ideas over the Internet and mobile phones not only inspired the demonstrators but also allowed them to coordinate their activities, communicate with one another within and across countries, and evade government efforts to clamp down on dissent.[36] That these events unfolded in the same region where Kitchener and Marchand struggled in 1898 to reach the outside world underscores how much the nature of communications has changed since that time.

The spread of unrest during the Arab Spring reminds us that many of the same developments that have increased the flow of money and goods between countries have made the world smaller and borders more permeable in other ways as well. Advances in information and communications technology (ICT) mean that events in one place can inspire people around the globe—or enrage them. In 2012, atrocities committed in Central Africa by a rebel group known as Lord's Resistance Army (LRA), led by Joseph Kony, became the subject of a "viral video" that had over 100 million views on YouTube. The abduction of over 200 Nigerian schoolgirls by the group Boko Haram in April 2014 led to the emergence of a Twitter hashtag, #BringBackOurGirls, that has been retweeted over 4 million times from dozens of countries around the world. The power of these campaigns should not be overstated: as of this writing, Kony and the LRA were still active, and the Nigerian girls had not been rescued. Still, both campaigns brought widespread attention to atrocities that, in an earlier time, might have passed unnoticed by the outside world; in both cases, the United States sent military advisers to assist with problems that it might otherwise have ignored. The ease with which we can now learn about such events intersects with and reinforces some of the developments we saw in Chapters 11 and 12: stronger norms and laws regarding human rights and growing activity by transnational advocacy networks (TANs) to promote those norms and to publicize their violations. At the same time, people have become increasingly aware of other harms that flow across borders, such human smuggling, illegal drugs, and pollution. As we saw in Chapter 13, growing threats to the global environment have propelled a search for new agreements and institutions to promote international cooperation

---

36. For an interesting examination of the role of social media in the revolts in Tunisia and Egypt, see Philip N. Howard, Aiden Duffy, Deen Freelon, Muzammil Hussain, et al., "Opening Closed Regimes: What Was the Role of Social Media during the Arab Spring?" Working Paper no. 2011.1, Project on Information Technology and Political Islam, University of Washington, Seattle, http://pitpi.org/wp-content/uploads/2013/02/2011_Howard-Duffy-Freelon-Hussain-Mari-Mazaid_pITPI.pdf (accessed 02/09/15).

in this area. As problems spill over national borders and become global in scope, the demand for global institutions increases as well.

This demand intersects with what appears to be another implication of technological innovation: the diffusion of power away from states and their governments. Emerging norms about human rights challenge the principle of sovereignty—the idea that what governments do within their own boundaries is nobody else's business. At the same time, widespread access to the Internet and mobile phones has given citizens new ways to circumvent government censorship and find alternative sources of information. The World Bank estimates that three-quarters of the world's population had access to a mobile phone in 2013. This figure is considerably higher than the percentage of people who use the Internet (40 percent) and even exceeds the percentage who have access to a toilet or latrine (64 percent) (Map 14.1).

The use of social media can also help protesters solve a fundamental challenge in confronting repressive governments. If you are the only person to show up at a protest, you are likely to end up in jail, or worse; if a million people show up, it is less likely that the government will crack down, and there is a better chance that your demands will be met (it is much harder for a government to put a million people in jail than a single person). Put another way, people who share an interest in ousting a repressive regime face a coordination problem: any individual is only willing to turn out to a demonstration if she is confident that enough other people will do so as well. Social media and texting can help solve this problem, allowing like-minded activists to coordinate their actions in real time. The use of these technologies helped mobilize large demonstrations that ousted long-serving dictators in Tunisia and Egypt in 2011. New technologies have also facilitated the global reach of transnational terrorists. Groups like Al Qaeda and the Islamic State in Iraq and Syria use the Internet and social media platforms to distribute writings and videos touting their accomplishments and atrocities. This outreach helps them attract recruits from around the world and inspire lone wolf attacks, complicating the ability of any one state to address this threat (see Chapter 6). Of course, technological developments have also created new avenues for government censorship and surveillance—as recent revelations about U.S. government collection of email and phone records attest.[37] Nevertheless, the importance of ICT to modern economies means that government efforts to interfere with communications come with a cost. For example, an Internet blackout imposed by the Egyptian government for five days in 2011 was estimated to have cost the country's economy around $100 million, or 3 to 4 percent of its GDP.[38]

Thus, globalization is not only an economic phenomenon; it also has political and social dimensions fostered by the spread of ideas and the growing ease with which individuals and groups with shared interests can communicate with one another. Will these developments render obsolete the current international system,

---

37. For a fascinating study of how China censors social media, see Gary King, Jennifer Pan, and Margaret E. Roberts, "How Censorship Allows Government Criticism but Silences Collective Expression," *American Political Science Review* 107 (May 2013): 1–18.

38. Parmy Olson, "Egypt's Internet Blackout Cost More than OECD Estimates," *Forbes*, February 3, 2011, www.forbes.com/sites/parmyolson/2011/02/03/how-much-did-five-days-of-no-internet-cost-egypt/ (accessed 02/11/15).

MAP 14.1 *Mobile Phone Use around the World*

This map shows the number of mobile phone subscriptions per 100 inhabitants for each country in 2013. Note that this number can exceed 100 because some people have more than one phone. Interestingly, cell phone use is very prevalent in a number of countries that are otherwise relatively poor, such as Cambodia, Guatemala, and Mali—all of which have mobile phone usage rates higher than that of the United States.

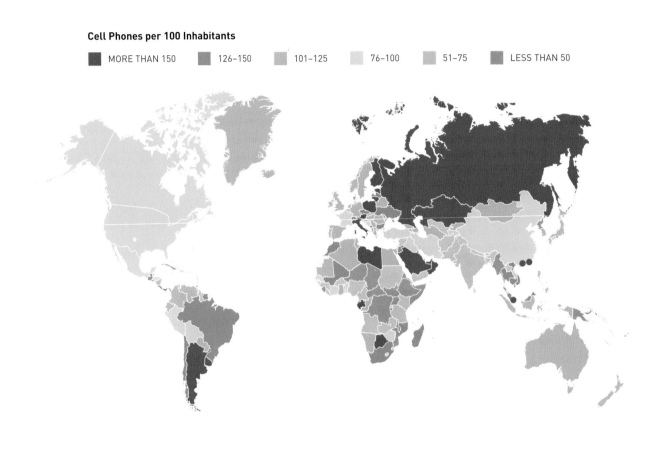

Cell Phones per 100 Inhabitants

| MORE THAN 150 | 126–150 | 101–125 | 76–100 | 51–75 | LESS THAN 50 |

Map source: World Bank, "Mobile Cellular Subscriptions (per 100 People)," http://data .worldbank.org/indicator/ IT.CEL.SETS.P2 (accessed 02/12/15).

in which territorially defined sovereign states operate without an overarching political authority? Will we witness a transition from anarchy to global government? In considering these questions, we need to think about how the interests generated by globalization influence the demand for new institutions of governance. Who will want new rules, and what kinds of rules will they want? As we will see, globalization generates demands on all sides for new institutions, but it also generates disagreement about the form and content of those institutions.

What Do Theory and History Tell Us?

We have seen throughout this book that institutions set out rules of acceptable behavior, create mechanisms for joint decision making, and provide ways to monitor and enforce compliance with the rules. Institutions are particularly valuable when actors have common interests but face collective action problems because there are incentives to cheat or free-ride, when the number of participants is so large that the procedures for making joint decisions (for example, voting rules) have to be regularized, and when the actors interact so frequently that it makes sense to have standing rules rather than to renegotiate the rules every time. This theory tells us that as the potential benefits from cooperation grow, as the number of participants in an interaction grows, and as the frequency of interaction grows, so too grows the demand for institutions.

The most dramatic example of integration driving an expansion of governance is the case of the European Union. The emergence of the European Union reflects the remarkable transformation of European relations during the twentieth century, from unprecedented violence to unprecedented cooperation. Wracked by warfare during the first half of the century, Europe is today a peaceful and prosperous continent, where former enemies like France and Germany have close political and economic relations. And the European Union is a supranational governance structure unlike any the world has seen before.

We have already encountered the European Union several times in this book. In Chapter 7, we saw how the community started in 1951 as a modest effort to cooperate in the production of coal and steel, heavy industries that were strategically important in the emerging Cold War with the Soviet bloc (see Chapter 7 "What Shaped Our World?" on p. 315). Economically, this project was intended to promote economic growth and improve living standards; politically, it would cement the alliance among countries that only six years before had been deadly enemies. In 1957, growing economic and political ties led to the creation of a customs union—that is, a union of states with low internal tariffs and a common external tariff when trading with the rest of the world. In 1992, this gave way to the European Union, which created a single market among its members, eliminating all barriers to trade. As a result of this process, Europe is the most economically integrated region in the world. About three-quarters of European countries' merchandise exports are bought by other European countries; by comparison, about half of North American or Asian exports stay within their respective regions.[39] In the process, the number of members has grown from the original 6 to 28 in 2015, with more in the process of applying for membership.

We then saw in Chapter 9 how trade integration led to efforts to stabilize exchange rates. In the 1970s, European countries experimented with an exchange rate mechanism to limit the fluctuation of currencies. When this mechanism broke down in the face of several crises, the demand for stable exchange rates led some EU members to the next logical step: eliminating national currencies altogether and issuing a common European currency, the euro. In 1999, 11 EU members adopted the euro and phased out their own currencies; by 2015, eight additional countries had followed suit. Thus, a century that began with Germany and France fighting two major wars ended with those countries using the same money.

---

39. World Trade Organization, *World Trade Report 2010* (Geneva: WTO, 2010), Table I.4.

Institutional development in Europe has not been limited to the economic realm, as the European Union has also created supranational governance structures. It has an executive branch, the European Commission, made up of representatives appointed by each member, and there is a European Parliament elected by voters throughout the region. By treaty, laws made by the European Union supersede those made by national governments. As we saw in Chapter 11, there is a European Court of Justice (ECJ), which adjudicates disputes arising from EU laws, and a European Court of Human Rights, which can rule on the human rights practices of member states (see Chapter 11 "What Shaped Our World?" on p. 462). EU institutions also oversee several policies that redistribute wealth among countries. About one-third of the EU budget, which is funded by member states, is given to needy areas to support economic and social development. Another 45 percent of the EU budget funds a system of agricultural subsidies that support farm income. Hence, the European Union does many things that used to fall under the purview of national governments.

The case of the European Union exemplifies how expanding economic ties and expanding governance can go hand in hand. As trade flows increased, the governments saw an interest not only in rules to govern trade but also rules to govern other areas, like currencies and migration. The creation of these rules spurred further integration and also created a demand for governance structures to formulate and enforce the rules. The creation of these institutions led to new supranational actors who have, as in the case of the ECJ, sought to expand the scope of their authority. Scholars debate to what extent we should see this process as one carefully managed by governments or as the product of unintended "spillovers" from one area to the next.[40] What is clear, however, is that economic interactions, interests in deeper cooperation, and institutions were mutually reinforcing, leading to the emergence of a unique new governance structure on the world stage.

At the same time, the European story invites caution about too readily assuming that changes in technology and communications will inevitably transform global politics. When it comes to the flow of information, Europe has been "shrinking" for centuries, long before the emergence and development of political union. Indeed, Europe experienced its own version of the Arab Spring over 160 years ago.[41] In February 1848, the French king was forced to abdicate after days of protests in Paris. Within days, unrest spread to neighboring German states, with protests erupting in Berlin, Vienna, and Munich. Within weeks, the tide of revolution had spread to Belgium, Denmark, Hungary, and territories that are today part of Poland, Ukraine, and Romania. By April, the wave had crossed the Atlantic, fueling a long-simmering rebellion in Brazil and encouraging reform movements from Chile to the United States. These events, sometimes referred to as the "Springtime of the People," long

---

40. This is a voluminous literature. A core statement of the "intergovernmentalist" view is Andrew Moravcsik, *The Choice for Europe* (Ithaca, NY: Cornell University Press, 1998). The foundation for the "spillover" argument is Ernst B. Haas, *The Uniting of Europe* (Stanford, CA: Stanford University Press, 1958).

41. See, for example, Kurt Weyland, "The Arab Spring: Why the Surprising Similarities with the Revolutionary Wave of 1848?" *Perspectives on Politics* 10 (December 2012): 917–34.

preceded the invention of the Internet or even the telephone. In 1848, news and ideas spread via the mail, railroad networks, and an invention that was just starting to come into use: the telegraph. Reaching even farther back in time, the spread of the Protestant Reformation in early-sixteenth-century Europe owed a good deal to the invention of the printing press a few decades earlier. These observations suggest two lessons. First, it is important not to overstate how transformative or unprecedented recent developments are; the Internet, social media platforms, and mobile phones are remarkable advances, but they are part of a long history of remarkable advances. Second, improved communications and more frequent interactions do not automatically or seamlessly give rise to supranational institutions. European institutions formed in the 1950s not simply because of growing interconnectedness, but in response to particular political and economic interests brought about by the end of World War II and the onset of the Cold War.[42]

Coming Conflicts over Global Governance

If economic integration within Europe could bring about such robust regional institutions, it is natural to ask whether globalization could have the same effect on a larger scale. In fact, we have already seen an impressive growth in the number and scale of international organizations over the past 50 years. Figure 14.4 shows estimates for the number of intergovernmental organizations—defined as organizations that have representation of at least three member states—in existence from 1815 to 2014. The explosive growth of these organizations between the end of World War II and the mid-1990s is particularly pronounced.

That said, it does not immediately follow that the experience of the European Union at the regional level can be replicated at the global level. European countries have cultural, political, and economic similarities that make close integration among them practical. It is not clear that this model could be scaled up to include a much more heterogeneous set of states. At a more fundamental level, the effort to create global governance will inevitably generate conflict. Recall that while institutions facilitate mutually beneficial cooperation, they are rarely neutral in their distributional effects. The rules inevitably advantage some set of interests over others or empower certain actors over others. Hence, even if everyone agrees that the world needs more and bigger governance structures, they may disagree strongly about the form and content of those institutions.

Indeed, even in Europe, despite all the shared interests and common qualities, the process of building institutions has seen conflicts and reversals.[43] Interstate bargaining over the terms of governance has at times been intense, and despite the enormous benefits of closer economic integration, several states have opted out of some parts of the project. For example, Danish voters rejected joining the monetary

---

42. For an interesting analysis of how deepening interconnectedness between Germany and Austria failed to bring about close political integration of these states, see Peter J. Katzenstein, *Disjoined Partners: Austria and Germany since 1815* (Berkeley, CA: University of California Press, 1976).

43. For an analysis of interstate bargaining over European integration, see Moravcsik, *The Choice for Europe*.

FIGURE 14.4 *Number of Intergovernmental Organizations, 1815–2014*

Figure sources: Jon C. Pevehouse, Timothy Nordstrom, and Kevin Warnke, "The COW-2 International Organizations Dataset Version 2.0," *Conflict Management and Peace Science* 21, no. 2 (2004): 101–19. Updated to 2014 from data provided by Pevehouse.

union, electing to preserve their national currency in spite of Denmark's strong trade ties with the rest of the Continent. Other EU members, such as Britain and Sweden, have likewise chosen not to adopt the euro. Moreover, recent economic events have put serious strain on the European Union, leaving its future direction in doubt. Debt crises in a number of countries, including Greece and Portugal, revealed serious problems within the union. Although these countries share a common currency, they still retain their own fiscal policies—that is, decisions about government spending, taxation, and borrowing—and their own forms of financial regulation. Countries whose citizens borrowed too heavily, or whose financial institutions lent unwisely, threatened the stability of the entire system. Faced with the risk that reckless borrowing and lending might bring down banking systems in the lending countries, such as Germany, EU member states were forced to intervene to bail out the troubled borrowers and their creditors. This crisis suggested that European integration had to go either further forward, by exerting more central control over states' spending, borrowing, and lending; or in reverse, with some states leaving the common currency. The member states did decide on greater centralization of financial regulation, but there has been little progress on reforming budgetary and debt policies. Moving in either direction—forward or backward—would impose significant costs, leaving the future of European integration uncertain and contentious.

Any effort to strengthen governance on the global level will similarly be rife with conflict. This is most clearly evident when thinking about institutions to govern economic globalization. The winners and losers of globalization have very different interests when it comes to defining the rules. Those actors that benefit from trade and finance have a strong interest in international rules that prevent national governments from erecting obstacles to cross-border flows. Exporters favor institutions that will lead to the elimination of trade barriers. They want rules, such as those enshrined in the WTO, that facilitate liberalization and delegitimize or even punish protectionism. International traders generally also prefer monetary rules that ensure the convertibility of currencies and lead to stable exchange rates between currencies. Likewise, actors that benefit from foreign investment want rules that lower or eliminate barriers to capital flows, so money can move freely across borders in search of higher returns. They want institutions, like the IMF, that encourage countries to dismantle capital controls that make it harder for money to flow in and out at a moment's notice. Multinational companies want rules that protect their property rights, so they can build factories wherever it makes the most economic sense without fear of having those assets seized by foreign governments. Hence, they want to extend the property protections that they enjoy in rich countries to cover poorer countries as well. These companies would also like to see international rules protecting rights to intellectual property. After all, U.S. copyright laws may protect a Hollywood film company from having its films pirated in the United States, but these do little good if the same laws do not extend to China, where large industries have grown up copying and selling Western media and software. In short, the winners of economic globalization have an interest in international institutions that will spread market-friendly policies around the world and limit the ability of national governments to slow this process.

Those actors that stand to lose from globalization also have an interest in greater global governance, but they want these institutions to enforce a very

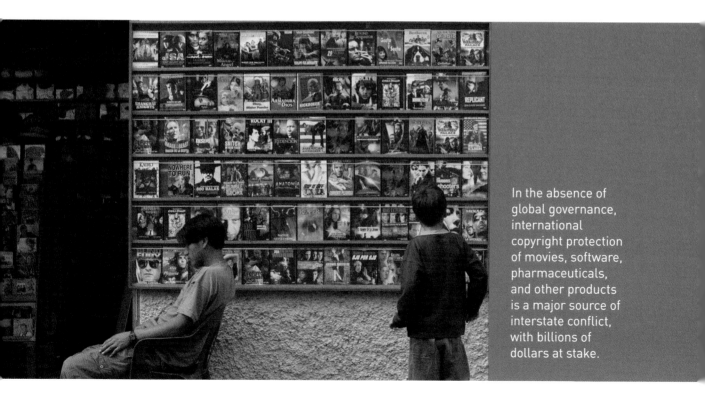

In the absence of global governance, international copyright protection of movies, software, pharmaceuticals, and other products is a major source of interstate conflict, with billions of dollars at stake.

different set of rules. In place of a single-minded push for liberalization, they want rules that permit more opportunities for countries to impose trade barriers or capital controls in order to protect their economies during hard times. Those that worry about a race to the bottom in labor or environmental regulations want these standards harmonized—at a high level—around the world. The race-to-the-bottom logic rests on the fact that each government sets its own rules, so governments can be compelled to lower their standards in the competition to attract investment. If, however, there were worldwide standards, this kind of competition could not take place. To this end, labor unions and environmental groups have sought to change the rules of the WTO to permit trade restrictions against countries that do not meet certain standards. Finally, those actors that worry about the distributional effects of globalization would prefer to see global governance structures, like those in the European Union, that can engage in redistribution: taxing the rich to give to the poor. Such an institution could create rules about how much foreign aid rich states should give and could oversee the distribution of that aid to needy regions and people.

Who Will Set the Rules?

In addition to conflict over the content of the rules, the extension of global governance can also generate conflicts over the decision-making procedures: that is, who has the ultimate say in making decisions? Which actors and interests have a seat at the table? As we have seen throughout this book, such decisions matter a great deal for the kinds of outcomes that institutions produce.

Most existing international organizations have two features that greatly limit the ability of some actors to influence decision making. First, representation is at the level of the state—each member state government appoints a representative, generally with the expectation that this person will act on that government's behalf.[44] As a result, how well any given actor is represented in an international body depends on that actor's influence with its home government. Groups or individuals who have little power domestically will similarly have little voice within international institutions, unless some other actor is willing to take up their cause. For example, as antiglobalization groups often point out, weak labor unions and nondemocratic institutions in developing countries mean that those countries' governments do not necessarily represent the interests of their workers. In this view, developing countries resist the inclusion of labor standards in WTO rules because their governments are insensitive to workers' needs. When seats at the table are reserved for states, inequalities of political influence at the domestic level will be replicated at the international level.

Second, many important international organizations have decision rules that favor some countries over others. We have already seen this several times: the permanent member veto in the UN Security Council, and the weighted voting rules of

---

44. In some institutions, such as international courts, national representatives are not supposed to advance the agenda of the government that appointed them but rather adhere to some organizational norms. It is not clear how often this ideal works in practice.

the IMF and the World Bank. As a result, countries that are wealthy or militarily powerful tend to have disproportionate influence in these bodies.

It is not by sheer chance that existing economic institutions push policies that more closely resemble the wish list of the actors that benefit from globalization than the wish list of those that oppose it. As we have seen, the main beneficiaries of globalization have been exporting and financial interests in developed countries—groups that wield considerable political influence. These actors have had a large role in creating institutions whose rules encourage further liberalization and whose decision-making procedures enshrine their influence.

Future battles over global governance will no doubt involve challenges to these procedures. Indeed, it is now common to hear the criticism that existing international institutions suffer from a democratic deficit: their voting rules are undemocratic, and they represent governments, many of them undemocratic, rather than people. This deficit is particularly striking given the overall trend toward greater democracy within countries (see Chapter 4). Not only do a majority of states have democratic institutions, but the ideal of democracy has widespread appeal, consistent with growing concerns about human rights discussed in Chapter 12.

Arguments to reform international institutions in a more democratic direction play off this normative ideal, but at the same time they serve a particular set of interests. Those actors that feel threatened by globalization see greater democracy at the international level as a way to bring a new set of actors to the table. One proposal along these lines is to expand the number of permanent member states on the UN Security Council, with seats (and perhaps vetoes) for India, Brazil, and other large developing countries. This move would bring a new set of voices into discussions of global security matters.

More expansively, some actors advocate for more truly democratic forms and processes of representation. For example, imagine what would happen if voting rules in institutions such as the IMF weighted countries by population rather than by wealth. Figure 14.5 explores this scenario. The panel on the left shows the shares of voting power held in the IMF under the institution's current rules. To save space, only the top 10 states by voting power are shown. The ranking closely matches the ranking of these countries' GDPs, with the United States possessing by far the largest bloc of votes. The panel on the right shows what would happen if the rules were changed such that voting shares were determined by each country's share of world population. Under this hypothetical scenario, the world's developing countries would have a much larger say in the operations of the IMF. Such a reform would dramatically change the kinds of policies the IMF pursues, presumably leading to greater redistribution. Of course, the current voting rules reflect the fact that the developed countries provide the bulk of the money that the IMF relies on to stabilize financial markets. If the rules were changed in a way that diminished the developed countries' influence too much, they would keep their money and leave the institution impoverished. Any reform in the direction of greater democratization would have to be modest in order to give wealthy states an interest in participating.

FIGURE 14.5 *What if Voting Rules in the IMF Counted People Rather than Wealth?*

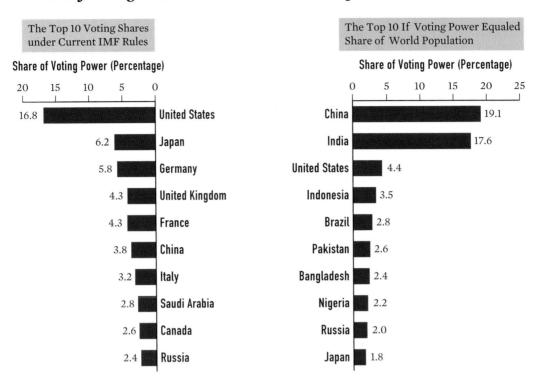

The Top 10 Voting Shares under Current IMF Rules

Share of Voting Power (Percentage)

Country	Share
United States	16.8
Japan	6.2
Germany	5.8
United Kingdom	4.3
France	4.3
China	3.8
Italy	3.2
Saudi Arabia	2.8
Canada	2.6
Russia	2.4

The Top 10 If Voting Power Equaled Share of World Population

Share of Voting Power (Percentage)

Country	Share
China	19.1
India	17.6
United States	4.4
Indonesia	3.5
Brazil	2.8
Pakistan	2.6
Bangladesh	2.4
Nigeria	2.2
Russia	2.0
Japan	1.8

Figure sources: IMF voting power from www.imf.org /external/np/sec/memdir /members.aspx (accessed 02/11/15). The 2013 population figures are from the World Bank, http://data.worldbank .org/indicator/SP.POP.TOTL (accessed 02/11/15).

Dealing with the problem of nondemocratic governments is another challenge. An international parliament elected by people throughout the world is probably impractical and undesirable. The U.S. House of Representatives, one of the larger legislatures in the world, has 435 members, each representing a district with about 650,000 people. To keep the ratio of representatives to constituents about the same, an international parliament would need about 10,000 representatives. Moreover, supervising the elections, particularly in countries without democratic institutions, would be challenging if not impossible. A more modest reform would be to institutionalize a role for nongovernmental organizations (NGOs) that speak for the interests of unrepresented groups. In recent years, NGOs have been invited to attend international meetings, though as yet they do not have formal voting rights in international organizations.

Given the obstacles of altering international institutions built around states, it is not surprising that some recent reform efforts have sought to bypass these institutions altogether and develop new forms of governance. In recent years, TANs have pressured industries into adopting codes of conduct that regulate companies' environmental, labor, and social policies.[45] Rather than relying on

---

45. For a review of this development, see Virginia Haufler, "Globalization and Industry Self-Regulation," in *Governance in a Global Economy: Political Authority in Transition*, ed. Miles Kahler and David A. Lake, 226–56. (Princeton, NJ: Princeton University Press, 2003).

governments to enact such regulations, TANs have lobbied industries to regulate themselves. Lacking the same coercive or regulatory power of a government, these groups instead try to use publicity and the threat of consumer boycotts to encourage this process. For example, when international negotiations aimed at preserving rain forests failed in the early 1990s, two environmental groups, the World Wildlife Fund and Greenpeace, joined together to bargain directly with the timber industry and wood products manufacturers. The result was the Forest Stewardship Council (FSC), which brought together industries, NGOs, and indigenous peoples to establish strict guidelines aimed at ensuring that forests are managed in a sustainable manner. The FSC certifies those products that have been harvested according to the guidelines, and stores are encouraged to sell—and consumers are encouraged to buy—certified goods. Under pressure from environmentalists, major wood-products retailers like Home Depot and IKEA participate in the program.[46] The result is a transnational institution that articulates standards of behavior, provides mechanisms for monitoring compliance, and establishes rules for joint decision making—but which does not have a single state in its membership. Similar codes of conduct now regulate a wide range of corporate behaviors.

As encouraging as such developments are, advocates of reforming global governance face an uphill battle. Current institutions and policies are the way they are because there were powerful actors who wanted them that way. It is hard to see why these actors would consent to a change in decision-making procedures that would dilute their influence. Institutions will change only if there is a change in interests of powerful actors and/or a change in the power of actors that alters the bargaining interaction between them. If those actors that benefit from globalization realize that their interests require some redistribution to the losers, then change may come from within. Alternatively, if the losers from globalization become better organized and politically powerful, they may be able to strike a better deal and create institutions more to their liking.

The danger, of course, is that this interaction will not play out peacefully. Those actors that feel they are losing out may decide to pursue their grievances through violence. In January 1994, there was a rebellion in the Mexican state of Chiapas by a group known as the Zapatista National Liberation Army. Although there were long-standing grievances about the treatment and welfare of the local population, the violence coincided with the signing of NAFTA, which added economic insecurity to the mix. There are also those who see terrorism by militant Islamists as part of a "jihad vs. McWorld"—that is, a reaction against the globalization of Western capitalism and consumerism.[47] Growing connectedness can amplify differences just as readily as it can create commonalities. It is worth recalling that some of the longest and deadliest wars in recent decades have

---

46. Haufler, "Globalization and Industry Self-Regulation," 246–47.
47. Benjamin Barber, *Jihad vs. McWorld: How Globalism and Tribalism Are Reshaping the World* (New York: Ballantine Books, 1996).

occurred not between states but within them—that is, over issues of governance. Although international anarchy needs to be tamed by institutions to promote cooperation and contain conflict, a transition toward stronger global governance will not necessarily be peaceful—or successful.

Conclusion: Can Our Common Interests Prevail?

Every case considered in this chapter points toward a similar conclusion. Changes in technology, the distribution of resources, and ideas have the potential to create winners and losers. Economic growth and the acquisition of deadly military technologies can make some states and actors more powerful and hence more threatening to others. The globalization of economic activity, driven by advances in transportation, communications, and information technology, has generated enormous wealth for some and insecurity for others. And the push for greater global governance will inevitably advantage some actors over others. The resulting clash of interests will color future interactions, leading to political, economic, and possibly military conflict. Those actors that stand to lose may lash out in the hopes of stopping the underlying changes, whether through preventive war or through efforts to disrupt global economic activity. Those actors that stand to win may try to exploit their gains through force and/or by cementing their political power in domestic and international institutions.

Set against this gloomy possibility is the recognition that change also generates common interests. The destructive potential of today's weapons means that the common interest in peace looms large relative to whatever gains could be won through war. As a result, states have an incentive to manage the rise of new powers and the spread of weapons of mass destruction in a peaceful manner. The wealth that can be created by globalization means that everyone can potentially gain, as long as the process is governed in a way that redistributes some of the gain to those actors that stand to lose. The enormous power of today's information and communications technology facilitate cooperation in pursuit of common goals, but it can also highlight differences and amplify voices of hatred. In short, the challenges posed by a changing world can be met if the winners recognize and act on a farsighted interest in spreading the benefits.

Will this happen? The history of international relations warns us not to be overly optimistic. There are real hatreds in the world, and people do not always act on the basis of an enlightened self-interest. World politics will never be free of conflicting interests and hostile interactions, and institutions will never entirely eliminate these conflicts through rules and redistribution. And yet we have also seen unmistakable signs of progress. Interstate war is not obsolete, but it is less frequent today than in the past. Although many people around the world still live in poverty, there have been tremendous advances in wealth and living standards. Democracy, considered a pernicious and destabilizing political form only two centuries ago, has spread to every continent, giving individuals greater say in the decisions that affect their lives. International cooperation to stop civil conflict and genocide, to protect human rights, and to safeguard the global environment has advanced significantly, even if these efforts fall short of the ideal.

We opened this book with the story of how a lone man prevented war between Arabs and Jews in 1921 by appealing to their shared interest in peace and prosperity. Although the peace of that day did not last forever, his efforts were still worthwhile. Progress is possible, even if perfection is not. Though conflicts will always remain, we have not yet exhausted all the opportunities to recognize and act on humanity's common interests.

Study Tool Kit

Interests, Interactions, and Institutions in Context

- The growing ease of producing nuclear, biological, and chemical weapons makes acquiring these weapons an inexpensive and effective way for some states and nonstate actors to pursue their interests. As a result, there will be growing conflict between actors who want WMD and those who would be harmed by proliferation. Whether the spread of WMD can be slowed depends on whether the latter actors can find a way—through cooperation, coercion, or institutions—to alter the interests of potential proliferators.

- The rise of China as a global power may lead to increased conflict between that country and the current world leader, the United States. Whether this dynamic will lead to war depends on the interests that prevail in both countries and on whether international and domestic institutions can make China a partner, rather than a rival, of the United States.

- Economic globalization creates winners and losers and increases the potential for political conflict within and among countries. Whether this conflict will disrupt the process of globalization depends on the winners' willingness and ability to compensate the losers so that all actors see some benefits.

- As it becomes easier for money, goods, information, and ideas to cross borders, there is a growing demand for institutions to broaden their scope from the national to the global level. Although there are common interests that make stronger global governance desirable, there will be conflicts over the rules and decision-making procedures of any such institutions.

For Further Reading

Avant, Deborah, Martha Finnemore, and Susan K. Sell, eds. *Who Governs the Globe?* Cambridge: Cambridge University Press, 2010. Examines global governance in a variety of issue areas with a focus on which actors exercise authority and why.

Frieden, Jeffry A. *Global Capitalism: Its Fall and Rise in the Twentieth Century.* New York: Norton, 2006. Explains the development of the global economy over the last century.

Gilpin, Robert. *War and Change in World Politics.* **Cambridge: Cambridge University Press, 1981.** Develops a general theory of the rise and fall of global leaders and argues that this theory explains major wars over the last several centuries.

Johnston, Alastair Iain. *Social States: China in International Institutions, 1980–2000.* **Princeton, NJ: Princeton University Press, 2008.** Argues that China's increasing engagement with international institutions can change its foreign policy outlook in a way that leads to greater cooperation.

Kahler, Miles, and David A. Lake, eds. *Governance in a Global Economy: Political Authority in Transition.* **Princeton, NJ: Princeton University Press, 2003.** Surveys the main developments in global governance that are taking place in response to globalization.

Milanović, Branko, ed. *Globalization and Inequality.* **Cheltenham: Edward Elgar, 2012.** Explores with a collection of scholarship how globalization, past and present, affects inequality among and within countries.

Moravcsik, Andrew. *The Choice for Europe: Social Purpose and State Power from Messina to Maastricht.* **Ithaca, NY: Cornell University Press, 1998.** Examines the interests and bargaining interactions that brought about the institutions of the European Union.

Sagan, Scott D. "Why Do States Build Nuclear Weapons? Three Models in Search of a Bomb." *International Security* **21, no. 3 (Winter 1996–97): 54–86.** Argues that security needs, domestic politics, and concerns about international status explain why some states try to acquire nuclear weapons while others do not.

Sagan, Scott D., and Kenneth N. Waltz. *The Spread of Nuclear Weapons: An Enduring Debate.* **3rd ed. New York: Norton, 2012.** Presents a debate between two scholars over whether the spread of nuclear weapons is good or bad for the world.

Scheve, Kenneth, and Matthew Slaughter. "A New Deal for Globalization." *Foreign Affairs* **86, no. 4 (July–August 2007): 34–47.** Argues that globalization can be made sustainable only if some of the income gains to the winners are redistributed to the economic losers.

Shirk, Susan. *China: Fragile Superpower.* **New York: Oxford University Press, 2007.** Examines how domestic politics within China will determine whether its rise as a global power takes place peacefully.

Zakaria, Fareed. *The Post-American World.* **New York: Norton, 2009.** Considers the rising economic and political influence of states like China, India, and Brazil and what these developments mean for the United States and the future of world politics.

Glossary

absolute advantage The ability of a country or firm to produce more of a particular good or service than other countries or firms using the same amount of effort and resources.

accountability The ability to punish or reward leaders for the decisions they make, as when frequent fair elections enable voters to hold elected officials responsible for their actions by granting or withholding access to political office.

actors The basic unit for the analysis of international politics; can be individuals or groups of people with common interests.

adjustable peg A monetary system of fixed but adjustable rates. Governments are expected to keep their currencies fixed for extensive periods but are permitted to adjust the exchange rate from time to time as economic conditions change.

agenda-setting power A "first mover" advantage that helps an actor to secure a more favorable bargain.

alliances Institutions that help their members cooperate militarily in the event of a war.

anarchy The absence of a central authority with the ability to make and enforce laws that bind all actors.

appreciate In terms of a currency, to increase in value in terms of other currencies.

asymmetric warfare Armed conflict between actors with highly unequal military capabilities, such as when rebel groups or terrorists fight strong states.

audience costs Negative repercussions for failing to follow through on a threat or to honor a commitment.

austerity The application of policies to reduce consumption, typically by cutting government spending, raising taxes, and restricting wages.

autocracy A political system in which an individual or a small group exercises power with few constraints and no meaningful competition or participation by the general public.

balance of power A situation in which the military capabilities of two states or groups of states are roughly equal.

bandwagoning A strategy in which states join forces with the stronger side in a conflict.

Bank for International Settlements One of the oldest international financial organizations, created in 1930; its members include the world's principal central banks, and under its auspices they attempt to cooperate in the financial realm.

bargaining An interaction in which actors must choose outcomes that make one better off at the expense of another. Bargaining is redistributive: it involves allocating a fixed sum of value between different actors.

bargaining range The set of deals that both parties in a bargaining interaction prefer to the reversion outcome. When the reversion outcome is war, the bargaining range is the set of deals that both sides prefer to war.

bilateral investment treaty An agreement between two countries about the conditions for private investment across borders. Most of these treaties include provisions to protect an investment from government discrimination or expropriation without compensation, as well as establishing mechanisms to resolve disputes.

boomerang model A process through which NGOs in one state are able to activate transnational linkages to bring pressure from other states on their own governments.

Bretton Woods monetary system The monetary order negotiated among the World War II allies in 1944, which lasted until the 1970s and which was based on a U.S. dollar tied to gold. Other currencies were fixed to the dollar but were permitted to adjust their exchange rates.

Bretton Woods System The economic order negotiated among allied nations at Bretton Woods, New Hampshire, in 1944, which led to a series of cooperative arrangements involving a commitment to relatively low barriers to international trade and investment.

brinksmanship A strategy in which adversaries take actions that increase the risk of accidental war, with the hope that the other will "blink," or lose its nerve, first and make concessions.

bureaucracy The collection of organizations—including the military, the diplomatic corps, and the intelligence agencies—that carry out most tasks of governance within the state.

cap-and-trade A system that sets limits on emissions, which are then lowered over time to reduce pollutants released into the atmosphere. Firms can sell "credits" when they emit less than their allocation or must buy from others when they emit more than their allocation.

central bank The institution that regulates monetary conditions in an economy, typically by affecting interest rates and the quantity of money in circulation.

chlorofluorocarbons (CFCs) Chemical compounds used in aerosols, insulating materials, refrigerator and air-conditioner coolants, and other products. CFCs are widely banned today due to their damaging effect on the ozone layer.

civil war A war in which the main participants are within the same state, such as the government and a rebel group.

coercion A strategy of imposing or threatening to impose costs on other actors in order to induce a change in their behavior.

coercive diplomacy The use of threats to influence the outcome of a bargaining interaction.

collaboration A type of cooperative interaction in which actors gain from working together but nonetheless have incentives to not comply with any agreement.

collective action problems Obstacles to cooperation that occur when actors have incentives to collaborate but each acts in anticipation that others will pay the costs of cooperation.

collective security organizations Broad-based institutions that promote peace and security among their members. Examples include the League of Nations and the UN.

commodity cartels Associations of producers of commodities (raw materials and agricultural products) that restrict world supply and thereby cause the price of the goods to rise.

common-pool resources Goods that are available to everyone, such as open ocean fisheries; it is difficult to exclude anyone from using the common pool, but one user's consumption reduces the amount available for others.

comparative advantage The ability of a country or firm to produce a particular good or service more efficiently than other goods or services such that its resources are most efficiently employed in this activity. The comparison is to the efficiency of other economic activities the actor might undertake, not to the efficiency of other countries or firms.

compellence An effort to change the status quo through the threat of force.

cooperation An interaction in which two or more actors adopt policies that make at least one actor better off relative to the status quo without making others worse off.

coordination A type of cooperative interaction in which actors benefit from all making the same choices and subsequently have no incentive to not comply.

credibility Believability. A credible threat is a threat that the recipient believes will be carried out. A credible commitment is a commitment or promise that the recipient believes will be honored.

crisis bargaining A bargaining interaction in which at least one actor threatens to use force in the event that its demands are not met.

customary international law International law that usually develops slowly, over time, as states recognize practices as appropriate and correct.

decolonization The process of shedding colonial possessions, especially the rapid end of the European empires in Africa, Asia, and the Caribbean between the 1940s and the 1960s.

default To fail to make payments on a debt.

delegation The degree to which third parties, such as courts, arbitrators, or mediators, are given authority to implement, interpret, and apply international legal rules to resolve disputes over the rules or to make additional rules.

democracy A political system in which candidates compete for political office through frequent, fair elections in which a sizable portion of the adult population can vote.

democratic peace The observation that there are few, if any, clear cases of war between mature democratic states.

depreciate In terms of a currency, to decrease in value in terms of other currencies.

depression A severe downturn in the business cycle, typically associated with a major decline in economic activity, production, and investment; a severe contraction of credit; and sustained high unemployment.

deterrence An effort to preserve the status quo through the threat of force.

devalue To reduce the value of one currency in terms of other currencies.

diversionary incentive The incentive that state leaders have to start international crises in order to rally public support at home.

exchange rate The price at which one currency is exchanged for another.

export-oriented industrialization (EOI) A set of policies, originally pursued starting in the late 1960s by several East Asian countries, to spur manufacturing for export, often through subsidies and incentives for export production.

externalities Costs or benefits for stakeholders other than the actor undertaking an action. When an externality exists, the decision maker does not bear all the costs or reap all the gains from his or her action.

extremists Actors whose interests are not widely shared by others; individuals or groups that are politically weak relative to the demands they make.

first-strike advantage The situation that arises when military technology, military strategies, and/or geography give a significant advantage to whichever state attacks first in a war.

fixed exchange rate An exchange rate policy under which a government commits itself to keep its currency at or around a specific value in terms of another currency or a commodity, such as gold.

floating exchange rate An exchange rate policy under which a government permits its currency to be traded on the open market without direct government control or intervention.

foreign direct investment (FDI) Investment in a foreign country via the acquisition of a local facility or the establishment of a new facility. Direct investors maintain managerial control of the foreign operation.

Framework Convention on Climate Change (FCCC) An international agreement enacted in 1992, and entered into force in 1994, that provided an overall framework for intergovernmental efforts on climate change.

free ride To fail to contribute to a public good while benefiting from the contributions of others.

General Agreement on Tariffs and Trade (GATT) An international institution created in 1947 in which member countries committed to reduce barriers to trade and to provide similar trading conditions to all other members. In 1995, the GATT was replaced by the WTO.

genocide Intentional and systematic killing aimed at eliminating an identifiable group of people, such as an ethnic or religious group.

global climate change Human-induced change in the environment, especially from the emissions of greenhouse gases, leading to higher temperatures around the globe.

gold standard The monetary system that prevailed between about 1870 and 1914, in which countries tied their currencies to gold at a legally fixed price.

Group of 77 A coalition of developing countries in the UN, formed in 1964 with 77 members; it has grown to over 130 members but maintains the original name.

Heckscher-Ohlin trade theory The theory that a country will export goods that make intensive use of the factors of production in which it is well endowed. Thus, a labor-rich country will export goods that make intensive use of labor.

hegemony The predominance of one nation-state over others.

humanitarian interventions Interventions designed to relieve humanitarian crises stemming from civil conflicts or large-scale human rights abuses, including genocide.

human rights The rights possessed by all individuals by virtue of being human, regardless of their status as citizens of particular states or members of a group or organization.

import-substituting industrialization (ISI) A set of policies, pursued by most developing countries from the 1930s through the 1980s, to reduce imports and encourage domestic manufacturing, often through trade barriers, subsidies to manufacturing, and state ownership of basic industries.

incomplete information A situation in which actors in a strategic interaction lack information about other actors' interests and/or capabilities.

individual petition A right that permits individuals to petition appropriate international legal bodies directly if they believe a state has violated their rights.

indivisible good A good that cannot be divided without diminishing its value.

infrastructure Basic structures necessary for social activity, such as transportation and telecommunications networks, and power and water supply.

institution A set of rules (known and shared by the community) that structure interactions in specific ways.

insurgency A military strategy in which small, often lightly armed units engage in hit-and-run attacks against military, government, and civilian targets.

interactions The ways in which the choices of two or more actors combine to produce political outcomes.

interest groups Groups of individuals with common interests that organize to influence public policy in a manner that benefits their members.

interests What actors want to achieve through political action; their preferences over the outcomes that might result from their political choices.

International Bill of Rights Refers collectively to the UDHR, the ICCPR, and the ICESCR. Together, these three agreements form the core of the international human rights regime.

International Covenant on Civil and Political Rights (ICCPR) The agreement completed in 1966 and in force from 1976 that details the basic civil and political rights of individuals and nations.

International Covenant on Economic, Social, and Cultural Rights (ICESCR) The agreement completed in 1966 and in force from 1976 that specifies the basic economic, social, and cultural rights of individuals and nations.

International Criminal Court (ICC) A court of last resort for human rights cases that possesses jurisdiction only if the accused is a national of a state party, the crime took place on the territory of a state party, or the UN Security Council has referred the case to the prosecutor.

international law A body of rules that binds states and other agents in world politics and is considered to have the status of law.

International Monetary Fund (IMF) A major international economic institution that was established in 1944 to manage international monetary relations and that has gradually reoriented itself to focus on the international financial system, especially debt and currency crises.

international monetary regime A formal or informal arrangement among governments to govern relations among their currencies; the agreement is shared by most countries in the world economy.

interstate war A war in which the main participants are states.

irredentist An actor that seeks to detach a region from one country and attach it to another, usually because of shared ethnic or religious ties.

iteration Repeated interactions with the same partners.

Kyoto Protocol An amendment to the UN Framework Convention on Climate Change, adopted in 1997 and entered into force in 2005, that establishes specific targets for reducing emissions of carbon and five other greenhouse gases.

League of Nations A collective security organization founded in 1919 after World War I. The League ended in 1946 and was replaced by the UN.

less developed countries (LDCs) Countries at a relatively low level of economic development.

linkage The linking of cooperation on one issue to interactions on a second issue.

mercantilism An economic doctrine based on a belief that military power and economic influence complemented each other; applied especially to colonial empires in the sixteenth through eighteenth centuries. Mercantilist policies favored the mother country over its colonies and over its competitors.

military-industrial complex An alliance between military leaders and the industries that benefit from international conflict, such as arms manufacturers.

monetary policy An important tool of national governments to influence broad macroeconomic conditions such as unemployment, inflation, and economic growth. Typically, governments alter their monetary policies by changing national interest rates or exchange rates.

Montreal Protocol An international treaty, signed in 1989, that is designed to protect the ozone layer by phasing out the production of a number of CFCs and other chemical compounds.

most-favored-nation (MFN) status A status established by most modern trade agreements guaranteeing that the signatories will extend to each other any favorable trading terms offered in agreements with third parties.

multinational corporation (MNC) An enterprise that operates in a number of countries, with production or service facilities outside its country of origin.

national interests Interests attributed to the state itself, usually security and power.

nonderogable rights Rights that cannot be suspended for any reason, including at times of public emergency.

nonexcludable Characteristic of a public good; if the good is available to one actor to consume, then other actors cannot be prevented from consuming it as well.

nonrival in consumption Characteristic of a public good; one actor's consumption of the good does not diminish the quantity available for others to consume as well.

nontariff barriers to trade Obstacles to imports other than tariffs (trade taxes). Examples include restrictions on the number of products that can be imported (quantitative restrictions, or quotas); regulations that favor domestic over imported products; and other measures that discriminate against foreign goods or services.

norms Standards of behavior for actors with a given identity; norms define what actions are "right" or appropriate under particular circumstances.

norms entrepreneurs Individuals and groups who seek to advance principled standards of behavior for states and other actors.

norms life cycle A three-stage model of how norms diffuse within a population and achieve a "taken for granted" status.

North Atlantic Treaty Organization (NATO) An alliance formed in 1949 among the United States, Canada, and most of the states of Western Europe in response to the threat posed by the Soviet Union. The alliance requires the members to consider an attack on any one of them as an attack on all.

obligation The degree to which states are legally bound by an international rule. High-obligation rules must be performed in good faith and, if breached, require reparations to the injured party.

oligopoly A situation in which a market or industry is dominated by a few firms.

outbidding A strategy of terrorist attacks designed to demonstrate superior capability and commitment relative to other groups devoted to the same cause.

outside options The alternatives to bargaining with a specific actor.

overexploitation Consumption of a good at a rate that is collectively undesirable, even if it is efficient from the view of any single actor.

ozone layer Part of the lower stratosphere, approximately 6 to 30 miles above the earth, with relatively high concentrations of ozone, which blocks harmful UV radiation.

Pax Britannica "British Peace," a century-long period beginning with Napoleon's defeat at Waterloo in 1815 and ending with the outbreak of World War I in 1914 during which Britain's economic and diplomatic influence contributed to economic openness and relative peace.

peace-enforcement operation A military operation in which force is used to make and/or enforce peace among warring parties that have not agreed to end their fighting.

peacekeeping operation An operation in which troops and observers are deployed to monitor a cease-fire or peace agreement.

Peace of Westphalia The settlement that ended the Thirty Years' War in 1648; often said to have created the modern state system because it included a general recognition of the principles of sovereignty and nonintervention.

permanent five (P5) The five permanent members of the UN Security Council: the United States, Great Britain, France, the Soviet Union (now Russia), and China.

portfolio investment Investment in a foreign country via the purchase of stocks (equities), bonds, or other financial instruments. Portfolio investors do not exercise managerial control of the foreign operation.

power The ability of Actor A to get Actor B to do something that B would otherwise not do; the ability to get the other side to make concessions and to avoid having to make concessions oneself.

precision The degree to which international legal obligations are fully specified. More precise rules narrow the scope for reasonable interpretation.

preemptive war A war fought with the anticipation that an attack by the other side is imminent.

preventive war A war fought with the intention of preventing an adversary from becoming stronger in the future. Preventive wars arise because states whose power is increasing cannot commit not to exploit that power in future bargaining interactions.

primary products Raw materials and agricultural products, typically unprocessed or only slightly processed. The primary sectors are distinguished from secondary sectors (industry) and tertiary sectors (services).

prisoners of conscience (POCs) A label coined and used by the human rights organization Amnesty International to refer to individuals imprisoned solely because of the peaceful expression of their beliefs.

protectionism The imposition of barriers to restrict imports.

provocation A strategy of terrorist attacks intended to provoke the target government into making a disproportionate response that alienates moderates in the terrorists' home society or in other sympathetic audiences.

proxy wars Conflicts in which two opposing states "fight" by supporting opposite sides in war, such as the government and rebels in a third state.

public goods Products that are nonexcludable and nonrival in consumption, such as national defense.

quantitative restriction (quota) Limit placed on the amount of a particular good that is allowed to be imported.

rally effect The tendency for people to become more supportive of their country's government in response to dramatic international events, such as crises or wars.

recession A sharp slowdown in the rate of economic growth and economic activity.

reciprocity In international trade relations, a mutual agreement to lower tariffs and other barriers to trade. Reciprocity involves an implicit or explicit arrangement for one government to exchange trade-policy concessions with another.

regional trade agreements (RTAs) Agreements among three or more countries in a region to reduce barriers to trade among themselves.

resolve The willingness of an actor to endure costs in order to acquire some good.

Ricardo-Viner (specific-factors) model A model of trade relations that emphasizes the sector in which factors of production are employed rather than the nature of the factor itself. This differentiates it from the Heckscher-Ohlin approach, for which the nature of the factor—labor, land, capital—is the principal consideration.

risk-return trade-off In crisis bargaining, the trade-off between trying to get a better deal and trying to avoid a war.

Security Council (UNSC) The main governing body of the UN, which has the authority to identify threats to international peace and security and to prescribe the organization's response, including military and/or economic sanctions.

security dilemma A dilemma that arises when efforts that states make to defend themselves cause other states to feel less secure. This dilemma can lead to arms races and war due to fear of being attacked.

separatist An actor that seeks to create an independent state on territory carved from an existing state.

sovereign lending Loans from private financial institutions in one country to sovereign governments in other countries.

sovereignty The expectation that states have legal and political supremacy—or ultimate authority—within their territorial boundaries.

spoiling A strategy of terrorist attacks intended to sabotage a prospective peace between the target and moderate leadership from the terrorists' home society.

state A central authority with the ability to make and enforce laws, rules, and decisions within a specified territory.

Stolper-Samuelson theorem The theorem that protection benefits the scarce factor of production. This view flows from the Heckscher–Ohlin approach: if a country imports goods that make intensive use of its scarce factor, then limiting imports will help that factor. So in a labor-scarce country, labor benefits from protection and loses from trade liberalization.

tariff A tax imposed on imports; this raises the domestic price of the imported good and may be applied for the purpose of protecting domestic producers from foreign competition.

terms of trade The relationship between a country's export prices and its import prices.

terrorism The use or threatened use of violence against noncombatant targets by individuals or nonstate groups for political ends.

theory A logically consistent set of statements that explains a phenomenon of interest.

trade barriers Government limitations on the international exchange of goods. Examples include tariffs, quantitative restrictions (quotas), import licenses, requirements that governments only buy domestically produced goods, and health and safety standards that discriminate against foreign goods.

transnational advocacy network (TAN) A set of individuals and nongovernmental organizations acting in pursuit of a normative objective.

Treaty of Versailles The peace treaty between the Allies and Germany that formally ended World War I on June 28, 1919.

United Nations (UN) A collective security organization founded in 1945 after World War II. With over 190 members, the UN includes all recognized states.

Universal Declaration of Human Rights (UDHR) Adopted by the UN General Assembly in 1948, this declaration defines a "common standard of achievement for all peoples" and forms the foundation of modern human rights law.

veto power The ability to prevent the passage of a measure through a unilateral act, such as a single negative vote.

Vienna Convention A framework convention adopted in 1985 to regulate activities, especially emissions of CFCs, that damage the ozone layer.

war An event involving the organized use of military force by at least two parties that reaches a minimum threshold of severity.

Warsaw Pact A military alliance formed in 1955 to bring together the Soviet Union and its Cold War allies in Eastern Europe and elsewhere; it dissolved on March 31, 1991, as the Cold War ended.

Washington Consensus An array of policy recommendations generally advocated by developed-country economists and policymakers starting in the 1980s, including trade liberalization, privatization, openness to foreign investment, and restrictive monetary and fiscal policies.

World Bank An important international institution that provides loans at below-market interest rates to developing countries, typically to enable them to carry out development projects.

World Trade Organization (WTO) An institution created in 1995 to succeed the GATT and to govern international trade relations. The WTO encourages and polices the multilateral reduction of barriers to trade, and it oversees the resolution of trade disputes.

Credits

Index

Page numbers in *italics* refer to illustrations.

cancer, ozone depletion and, 563, 568
Cancún, 326
cannibalism, 471–72
cap and trade system, 538, 553
capital flow, 345–48, 609
capitalism, 297, 623
capital-receiving nations, 347
capital-sending nations, 347
Caracazo, El (Caracas smash), 358
carbon dioxide, *532*, 533, 535, *542*, 542–44, 548, 549, 553, 556, 568, 571–75
    atmospheric levels, *572*
    emissions by country, *542*
    trading system for, 538
Cardoso, Eliana, 361*n*
Caribbean island nations, 392, 405, 437, 442
Carter, Jimmy, 140, 497
Carter Doctrine, 140
Cassin, René, 493
Castro, Fidel, 27, 159
Castro, Raúl, 159
casualties, *See* civil war; terrorism; *specific conflicts*
CAT (Convention against Torture and Other Cruel, Inhuman or Degrading Treatment or Punishment), 517
Caterpillar Tractors, 391
Catholic Church, 48, 242, 472; *See also* Christians
Caves, Richard, 366*n*
Cederman, Lars-Erik, 243*n*, 249*n*, 263*n*
cell phones, *See* mobile phones, globalization and
Center for Environmental Law and Policy, Yale University, 552
Center for International Earth Science Information Network, Columbia University, 552
Central African Republic, *207*
central bank, definition of, 385
Central Intelligence Agency (CIA), 137, 155, 162
Central Powers, 18
CFCs, *See* chlorofluorocarbons
Chamber of Deputies, Argentine, 381
Chávez, Hugo, 358, 451

Chayes, Abram, 76*n*, 465, 465*n*
Chayes, Antonia Handler, 76*n*, 465, 465*n*
Chechnya, 242, *242*, 244, 257
chemical weapons, 43, 44, *95*, 120, 579, 583, 584
Cheney, Richard, 158
Chesterman, Simon, 524*n*
Chiapas rebellion (1994), 623
Chicken, game of, 84–85, *85*
child labor, 473, 478–79, *479, 608*
Child Labor Deterrence Act, 478
children, in civil war, 248
Chile, 27, 158, 501
    anti-Allende coup in, 371
    human rights abuses in, 520
    "Springtime of the People," 616
    U.S. sponsored coup, 179
China, Imperial, *2*, 15
China, Nationalist, *See* Taiwan
China, People's Republic of, 5, 24, 25, 28, 29, 30, 38, *65*, 75, 103, 225, 304, 326, 329, 374, 430, 437, 553
    acid rain and, 541, 548–49
    as autocracy, 168
    carbon dioxide emissions of, *532*, 548–49
    competition with U.S. for global leadership, 590–600
    currency devaluation in, 393, *393*
    Darfur genocide and, *212*
    East China Sea dispute, 118–19, *119*
    economic growth of, 422, 445, *451, 591*, 591–92, 597–99
    globalization and, 605
    gold standard and, 397
    Great Leap Forward of, 513–14
    influence on international politics, 120
    intellectual property rights and, 619
    Iraq War opposed by, 43, 228
    Korean conflict and, 112–13, 115, 185, 193
    as manufacturing center, 603
    MFN status and, 605
    military capabilities, *593*

NPT and, 585, 586
nuclear program of, 584–85
Ottawa Convention and, 474
in Permanent 5, 211, 215
pro-democracy demonstrations in, *576*
proxy wars, 251
renminbi currency of, 393
Security Council seat of, 75
submarines and, *598*
territorial disputes, 36
Tibet and, 185, 186, 212, 244
trade specialization and, 297
U.S.-Taiwan relationship and, 197
world trade and, 314
China, Republic of, 22, 156
Chiozza, Giacomo, 149*n*
chlorine, ozone and, 568–70, *570*
chlorofluorocarbons (CFCs), 534, 537, 541, 544, 547, 559–60, 563–65, 568–70
Christensen, Thomas, 199*n*, 200*n*
Christianity, 9
Christians, 244
CIA, *See* Central Intelligence Agency
Cingranelli, David L., 513*n*, 514*n*, 515*n*
civil war, 214, 227, 234–64, *237, 240–41*, 286
    in Afghanistan, 95
    as bargaining failure, 253–57
    cluster tendency of, 252, *252*
    in Congo (DRC), *239*
    costs of, 253
    country-level factors in, 248–49
    definition of, 91, 237
    drugs and, 248
    factors inciting, 243–53
    group-level factors in, 246–48
    human rights violations in, 505, 510, 512
    from indivisibilities, 256–57
    international factors in, 250–51, 253
    Iraq, 95
    irredentism in, 242
    numbers of, *237*
    peacekeeping missions and, 209
    in Rwanda, 238–39
    separatism as cause of, 239, 242
    strategies, 258–62
    wealth and, *252*

in Great Depression, 412
interest rates and, 409–10
international repercussions of, 407, 409–12
international traders and, 414–15
Mexican, 410, 412
speculators and, 414
customary international law, 460–61
customs union, 315, 615
Cyprus, 244
Czechoslovakia, 27, 28, 200, 201, 230
Czech Republic, 244, 366, 408, 552

D

Dahl, Robert A., 63
Dalai Lama, 185
Darfur, 206, *212*, 223, 231, 256, *257*, 512
Davenport, Christian, 506*n*
Davis, David R., 151*n*, 518*n*
Dayton peace conference (1995), 222
deadweight loss, 338
death penalty, 468–69, 492, 496, *497*
debt, 350–53
bargaining and, 354–55
eurozone, 341–42, 382
foreign investment and, 348–49
restructuring, 355
war caused by, 355
debt crisis, Greek, 341–42
debt crisis of 1982, 347, 361
Declaration of Independence, 493
decolonization, 28–29, 442
default, 351, 353, 354
Defense Department, U.S., 155
defensive alliances, 187–88, 195*n*
deforestation, 574, 607
Delahunty, Robert, 469*n*
de la Rúa, Fernando, 381
delegation, 464
demand, 336–37, 384
democide (term), 513
democracy, 204, 452, 608, 625; *See also* democratic peace
bargaining interaction and, 174–76
civil war and, 263–64

definition of, 168–69
demonstrations in China, *576*
development and, 424, 442
election monitoring and, 71
global governance and, 620, 622
hostile to US interests, 178–79
human rights agreements and, 507–8
Kant's view of, 169, 172
lack of wars between, 166–77
protectionism and, 310, 609
spread of, 180–81, *181*
Democratic Party, U.S., 310, 398
democratic peace, 157, 167, 177, 510
Denmark, 405, 616–18
depreciation, of currency, 383; *See also* devaluation, currency
depression; *See also* Great Depression
definition of, 350
Latin America and, 361
DeSombre, Elizabeth R., 547*n*
détente, 30
deterrence, 589
definition of, 105
of terrorists, 280–81
U.S. nuclear umbrella and, 585
U.S.-China rivalry and, 599
war and, 101, 104–5
Detroit, Michigan, *610*
Deutsche mark, German, *22*, 382, 403, 409
devaluation, currency, 383, 408, 414–15
developing countries, *346*
development, 420–55
colonialism and, *435*, 435–37
country comparisons and, 424
domestic factors and, 425–27, 430, 452
domestic institutions and, 430–31, 434
early history and, 432–33
export-oriented industrialization and, 443–44, *444*
foreign aid and, 447–50
free trade and, 330
geographic location and, 423, 425
globalization and, 444–45, 450–51
import substituting industrialization and, 441–43

international economy's bias against, 438
international factors, 451–52
international institutions' bias against, 438–41, 446–47
policies/politics and, 441–47, 450–51
third world poverty and, 421–22
Diamond, Jared, 423*n*, 549*n*
Diaoyu Islands, 118–19, *119*
Dickson, Eric S., 276*n*
dictators
friendly to US interests, 178–79
human rights abuses by, 517–18
dictatorships, 179
diffuse reciprocity, 471
diplomatic immunity, 460–61, *461*
direct investment; *See also* foreign direct investment
bilateral investment treaties and, 371
host country's perception of, 368–69
international institutions and, 371
multinationals and, *See* multinational corporations
outsourcing and, 367
resource location and, 366
Dirty War, 505–6, *506*
Disney company, 343
Dispute Settlement Body (WTO), 321
diversionary incentive, 147–51
Dobbins, James, 229*n*
Dobbs, Michael, 27*n*
Doha Round, 321, 609
dollar
Canadian, 383
Eastern Caribbean, 405
Dollar, David, 604*n*, 610*n*
dollar, U.S., 25, 381, 383–84, 386–87, 390, 391, 394, 397, 399, 400, 406, 407, *407*, 409
currencies pegged to, 405
fluctuations of, 402
value of, 384, *384*
Dome of the Rock, 128, *128*

McGinn, John G., 229n
McGrew, Anthony G., 486n
McKinley, William, 302–3, 398, 399
McLaughlin Mitchell, Sara, 188n
Mead, Walter Russell, 159n
Mearsheimer, John J., 159n, 204n
Mehlum, Halvor, 431n
Meissner, Christopher M., 387n
Mellinger, Andrew, 423n
mercantilism, 5–8, 12–13, 300, 301, 601
Mercosur (Southern Common Market), 292, 317, 318, 324
Merkel, Angela, 354
Mexico, 9, 32, 69, 297, 324, 330, 372, 374, 392, 412, 450, 511, 607
  bailout of, 351–52
  Chiapas rebellion in, 623
  debt crisis of 1982 in, 351–52, 360, 361
  financial crisis of 1994 in, 360, 410
  foreign investment in, 345
  ISI in, 443
MFN, See most favored nation status
MI6, 155
Michigan, 310
middle class, 19, 599
Middle East, 43–45, 46, 78, 90, 128, 140–41, 160, 163, 246, 252, 276–78, 327; See also specific countries
  Arab Spring uprisings and, 612
  Carter Doctrine and, 140
  common currency in, 416
  oil and U.S. foreign policy in, 140–41, 163
  terrorism in, 267–68
  turmoil in early 2000s, 35–36
Midlarski, Manus, 145n
migration, 372–76, 373, 603–4
  anti-immigrant sentiment and, 374, 376
  benefits of, 373–74
  as cultural threat, 376
  domestic effects of, 374
  economic impact of, 374
  globalization and, 372, 376
  Heckscher-Ohlin theory and, 373–74
  labor and, 372–74, 376
  from Latin America, 372
  political economy and, 376

restrictions on, 374
  social programs and, 376
Miguel, Edward, 255n
Milanovic, Branko, 422n
Milesi-Ferretti, Gian Maria, 342n
military
  bureaucratic politics and, 155–56, 158
  foreign policy and, 160–61
military dictatorships, 179
military-industrial complex, 138, 154, 162
military tribunals, 462
Milner, Helen V., 49n, 310n, 330, 391n, 484n
Milošević, Slobodan, 224, 225
Mishler, William, 145n
misperceptions, war caused by, 92
misrepresentation, war and, 109–11
Mississippi, 353
Mitchell, Ronald B., 559n
Mitra, Devashish, 311n
MNCs, See multinational corporations
mobile phones, globalization and, 613, 614
Moene, Karl, 431n
Mohammed, Prophet of Islam, 128
Moldova, 244
Molotov-Ribbentrop Pact (1939), 187, 194
monarchies, 142
monetary policy, definition of, 385
monetary relations, 380–419; See also Bretton Woods System; currency; euro
  absence of international system and, 394, 402, 416
  collaboration and, 396
  commodity standard and, 397
  conflicts of interest and, 392–95
  cooperation and conflict in, 395–96, 413, 416–17
  exchange rates and, See exchange rates
  global nature of, 386
  gold standard and, 397–98
  international monetary regimes and, 396–97
  international order of, 394
  national order of, 395
  national paper currency standard and, 397
  Prisoner's Dilemma and, 396

monopolies, 6
Montreal Protocol (1989), 534, 544, 558, 561–62
Morales, Evo, 451
Moravcsik, Andrew, 463n, 507, 616n
Morocco, 18, 373
Morrow, James D., 174n, 194n, 467, 467n, 505n
Morsi, Mohamed, 178, 178, 179
Morton, David, 477n
most favored nation status (MFN), 320–21, 600, 605
Mozambique, 226
Mubarak, Hosni, and administration, 178, 179, 511
Mueller, John, 248n
multilateralism, 471
multinational corporations (MNCs), 365–71, 377, 439–40, 619
  access to local markets and, 366
  conflicts and, 368–69
  criticism of, 367
  debt crises and, 371
  definition of, 366
  environment and, 367
  expertise and, 368
  globalization and, 603
  host countries' interactions with, 369–71
  host countries' interests in, 367–69
  human rights and, 367
  labor unions and, 367
  local politics and, 370
  motivation of, 366–67
  national sovereignty and, 371
  outsourcing and, 367
  political considerations and, 370
  resource location and, 366
  restrictions on, 370–71
Mundell-Fleming conditions, 391n
Muntean, Marilena, 548n
Murdie, Amanda N., 518n
Murray, Williamson, 51n
Musharraf, Pervez, 157
Muslim Brotherhood, 179
Muslims, 35, 36, 94, 128, 221, 228, 244, 257, 276, 277; See also Islam
Mussa, Michael, 604n

Abby Card
714-342-733